SRA® MATH

Explorations and Applications

Make thinking a basic skill on the road of life.

Solve the persistent problems of teaching elementary mathematics by teaching children how to *think* mathematically.

REPORT CARD

Subjects	1	2	3	4
Math	✓	✓	✓	✓
Knows and uses basic facts		✓	✓	✓
Demonstrates understanding of the math concepts using manipulatives and abstract thinking		✓	✓	✓
Solves word problems	✓	✓		
Uses problem-solving strategies to solve real-world problems				
Language Arts				

Visit our website
www.SRA-4KIDS.com

Introducing

SRA® MATH
Explorations and Applications

Take the right path to teaching mathematics.

This comprehensive, research-based program challenges students to think every day, on every page, at every juncture. It's the answer that teachers need to make math instruction effective and math learning enjoyable.

Level K   Level 1   Level 2   Level 3

MATEMÁTICAS
Exploraciones y aplicaciones
Complete program available in Spanish

Level 4

Level 5

Level 6

Also Available

- ◆ **Professional Development Handbook**
- ◆ **Program Guide**
- ◆ **Test Preparation Practice Workbook**
- ◆ **Lesson Plans**
- ◆ *Minds on Math*
- ◆ *Math CrossSections*
- ◆ *Science, Math & YOU*
- ◆ *Cooperate 1, 2, and 3*
- ◆ *Junior Thinklab™*
- ◆ *Thinklab™*
- ◆ *Scoring High in Math*

Take along the essentials for the journey.

Core Materials

◆ Student Editions (K–2) in consumable format that introduce, integrate, and practice concepts and skills
◆ Student Editions (3–6) in hardbound format filled with lessons that integrate concept development, practice, and problem solving
◆ Thinking Story Books (Levels 1–3) for teachers to read to the class
◆ Teacher's Guides that provide the road map along with practice, reteaching, and enrichment support
◆ Basic Manipulative Kits needed for Cube Games and Mental Math Activities

Lesson Support Materials

◆ Practice Activities in Workbook and Blackline Master formats
◆ Enrichment Activities in Workbook and Blackline Master formats
◆ Reteaching Activities in Workbook and Blackline Master formats
◆ Assessment Masters
◆ Home Connections Masters
◆ Literature Library (K–3)

Manipulative Support Materials

◆ Game Mat Packages (K–6) for skill practice and problem solving
◆ Primary Manipulative Kit (K–2) to introduce basic concepts
◆ Primary Overhead Manipulative Kit (K–2)
◆ Intermediate Manipulative Kit (3–6) for variety in concept presentation
◆ Intermediate Overhead Manipulative Kit (3–6)
◆ Teacher Manipulative Kit for classroom demonstrations

Technology Support Materials

◆ *Math Explorations and Applications* Software (1–6) provides extra skill practice for every lesson.
◆ *The Cruncher* (4–6) offers a student-friendly spreadsheet application for appropriate lessons.
◆ *My Silly CD of Counting* CD-ROM (K) helps build the concept of counting.
◆ TI-108™ Calculator Package (K–3)
◆ Math Explorer™ Calculator Package (4–6)
◆ Primary Overhead Calculator (K–3)
◆ Intermediate Overhead Calculator (4–6)

Professional Development

◆ Professional Development Handbook

It's mathematics, taken off the beaten path.

Math Explorations and Applications helps students learn the real basics: traditional arithmetic skills, computation, and problem solving.

◆ **Concept Integration.** The program's organization, scope, and sequence allow integration and thorough study of math concepts.

◆ **In-Depth Study.** Lessons devote the number of pages needed to teach a concept, not artificially dividing every topic into the same lesson length. Sometimes it takes more than two pages to effectively cover the important points in a lesson.

◆ **Concepts in Context.** Skills and concepts are taught and retaught in different contexts—never in isolation.

◆ **Variety of Presentations.** Explore, Practice, Problem Solving, and Projects address a variety of learning styles so that students stay interested and motivated as they learn to think.

◆ **Cumulative Review of Content.** Once a skill has been introduced, it is integrated, practiced, and reviewed in mixed practice and in context throughout the grade level. Lesson by lesson, students accumulate the skills they need to master more complicated math concepts, as they continually review previously introduced skills.

◆ **Life-Long Learning.** As they see mathematics used to solve realistic problems, students begin to view strong math skills as useful, lifelong tools they can use both inside and outside the classroom.

◆ **Focus on Computation *and* Problem Solving.** *Math Explorations and Applications* develops and provides practice of traditional skills in problem-solving settings such as games. This makes efficient use of teacher and student time and effort.

Developing concepts in context paves the road to understanding.

Math Explorations and Applications introduces and integrates concepts so that students make connections and build on what they already know.

◆ **Early Introduction of Concepts.**
An early age-appropriate introduction to concepts such as algebra, geometry, multiplication, and division builds understanding and connections from the very beginning. Because most students actually begin to use the principles of more advanced math concepts like algebra long before the eighth grade, *Math Explorations and Applications* helps students feel comfortable with these concepts from the very start.

◆ **Core Concept Development at Every Level.** Operations, thinking skills, problem solving, mental math, estimation, data organization, geometry, probability, and statistics are emphasized at all grade levels.

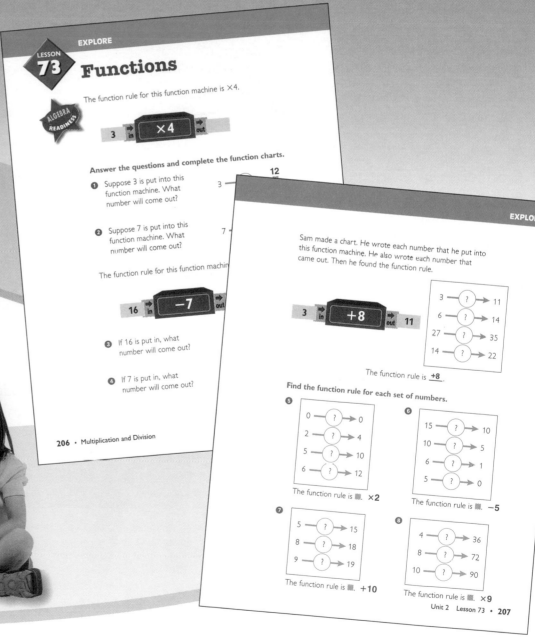

Level 3

◆ **Concepts in Context.** Concepts are developed in different contexts to help students recognize their natural connections. For example, the concept of fractions is developed in relation to time, money, and measurement.

◆ **Intelligent Use of Manipulatives.** Intelligent use of hands-on activities and manipulatives establishes concepts in the concrete, showing students a variety of ways to solve a problem. Students are encouraged to use these tools where appropriate, then to move beyond these tools as quickly as possible toward the goal of abstract thinking.

◆ **Realistic Problem-Solving Models.** Exciting **Act It Out** lessons model problem-solving strategies by having students physically work through new concepts.

◆ **Emphasizing Natural Concept Relationships** By drawing on the natural relationships that exist among concepts, students learn to make connections between concepts so that they can understand them more effectively.

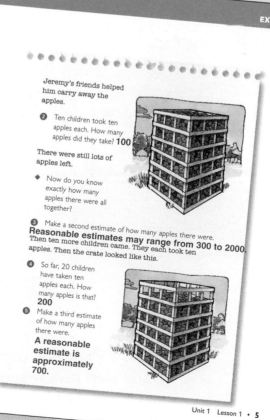

Practice—Skill Development

Step by step, students learn the basics by heart and mind.

Computational skills are essential for efficient mathematical thinking. But skill practice can be enjoyable and is one more opportunity to challenge students to think mathematically.

◆ **Practice** pages often have hidden patterns that help students understand number relationships and encourage mathematical thinking on every problem on every page.

PRACTICE

Remember, to find the area of a rectangle, multiply the length by the width.

What is the area of the rectangle?
Area = 3 × 5 square centimeters

5 cm

3 cm   3 cm

5 cm

Let's turn the rectangle on its side.
Area = 5 × 3 square centimeters

3 cm

5 cm   5 cm

3 cm

◆ Did the area of the rectangle change? **no**
◆ Does 3 × 5 = 5 × 3? **yes**
◆ What is 3 × 5? **15**
◆ What is 5 × 3? **15**

Rule: The order in which two numbers are multiplied makes no difference to the answer.

Multiply. Compare the problems in each pair.

6. 2 × 5 = n **10**
   5 × 2 = n

7. 1 × 8 = n **8**
   8 × 1 = n

8. 10 × 4 = n **40**
   4 × 10 = n

9. 5 × 5 = n **25**
   5 × 5 =

10. 9 × 0 = n **0**
   0 × 9 = n

11. 3 × 4 = n **12**
   4 × 3 = n

12. 3 × 9 = n **27**
   9 × 3 = n

13. 5 × 8 =
   8 × 5 =

14. 6 × 9 = n **54**
   9 × 6 = n

15. 7 × 9 = n **63**
   9 × 7 = n

16. 6 × 4 = n **24**
   4 × 6 = n

17. 4 × 8
   8 × 4

18. 2 × 4 = n **8**
   4 × 2 = n

19. 3 × 5 = n **15**
   5 × 3 = n

20. 9 × 1 = n **9**
   1 × 9 = n

21. 4 ×
   2 ×

Unit 2 Lesson

Level 4

◆ **Mixed Practice** pages throughout each grade level review concepts from all lessons and encourage students to think about what they're doing and how they do it.

MIXED PRACTICE

ALGEBRA READINESS

Multiply. Solve for n.

7. 6 × 5 = n **30**
8. 8 × 6 = n **48**
9. 4 × 7 = n **28**
10. 3 × 2 = n **6**
11. 7 × 3 = n **21**
12. 6 × 6 = n **36**
13. 4 × 10 = n **40**
14. 3 × 7 = n **21**
15. 2 × 5 = n **10**
16. 7 × 5 = n **35**
17. 2 × 6 = n **12**
18. 4 × 4 = n **16**

PROBLEM SOLVING

Solve.

Carolyn has seven nickels. She wants to buy a fan that costs 95¢.

19. How much money does Carolyn have in cents? **35¢**

20. How much more does she need to buy the fan? **60¢**

Solve these problems. Use shortcuts when you can. Watch the signs.

21. 324 + 479 = **803**
22. 821 − 731 = **90**
23. 601 + 399 = **1000**
24. 900 − 500 = **400**
25. 456 − 251 = **205**
26. 273 + 438 = **711**
27. 564 + 286 = **850**
28. 700 − 299 = **401**

Use the Cumulative Review on page 459 after this lesson.

Unit 2 Lesson 48 • 145

Level 3

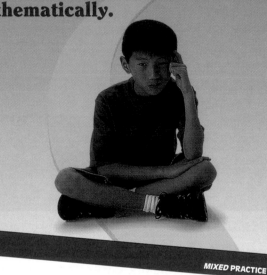

Multiplication Table Game

Math Focus:
- Practicing basic facts–multiplying two factors of 5 or less
- Using a multiplication table

Object of the Game: To have more counters at the end of the game

Players: Two

MATERIALS

Two cubes

36 counters or pennies

SET UP

▶ Every circle on the mat must be covered with a counter.
▶ Players roll the 0–5 number cube. The person who rolls the higher number goes first.

HOW TO PLAY

1. Players take turns rolling both cubes and making multiplication sentences out of the numbers. For example, if a 4 and a 2 are rolled, the player could say either "4 times 2 equals 8" or "2 times 4 equals 8."
2. After giving the multiplication sentence, players check their answers by looking under the appropriate counter. If correct, the player keeps the counter; if incorrect, the player replaces the counter.
3. Once the counter on a circle has been won, the circle remains empty. A player who cannot make a multiplication sentence that applies to a covered circle cannot win a counter that turn.
4. The player with more counters at the end of the game wins.

✗	0	1	2	3	4	5
0	0	0	0	0	0	0
1	0	1	2	3	4	5
2	0	2	4	6	8	10
3	0	3	6	9	12	15
4	0	4	8			
5	0	5	10			

Copyright © SRA/M...

GAME

PRACTICE

◆ LESSON 47 Estimating Products

COOPERATIVE LEARNING

Mul-Tack-Toe Game

Players:	Two
Materials:	Two Mul-Tack-Toe cards (like those below), two 0–5 cubes (red), eight counters or coins for each player
Object:	To cover three boxes in a line
Math Focus:	Multiplication facts

RULES

1. Each player chooses one of the two Mul-Tack-Toe cards.
2. Players take turns rolling the two 0–5 cubes.
3. Both players calculate the product of the two numbers rolled. If the product is on a player's card, he or she puts a counter on that box.
4. The first player to cover three boxes in a line (horizontally, diagonally, or vertically) wins the round.

15	16	6
25	4	5
10	0	2

Card 1

12	1	10
0	4	20
8	9	15

Card 2

Level 3

◆ **Games** are not just for fun. Throughout the program, games provide extensive, serious practice with traditional arithmetic. They also offer opportunities to identify and solve interesting problems. Students don't even realize how much math they're practicing!

MENTAL MATH

Interactive **Mental Math** activities in every lesson in the Teacher's Guide help students develop the ability to manipulate numbers in their minds, easily and with common sense.

Problem Solving—Applications

Children learn to solve problems by solving problems.

Problem-solving strategies are integrated throughout *SRA Math Explorations and Applications*, never taught in isolation. Instead of memorizing rote strategies, students learn to:

- recognize a problem,
- select an appropriate strategy,
- solve the problem, and
- reflect on their reasoning.

◆ **Thinking Stories** model mathematical thinking and problem-solving strategies. They demonstrate that real-life "problems" can appear in unexpected places.

INTEGRATED **PROBLEM SOLVING**

◆ **LESSON 150 Counting to One Million**

In the last lesson your teacher read the first part of this story to you. Now read this part yourself.

THINKING STORY

Mr. Muddle's Time Machine

Part 2

The next day Mr. Muddle bought two hands for his clock. They were both the same length and looked exactly alike. He put the hands on carefully. "There," he said, "this clock looks better than most. There's something uneven about most clocks."

INTEGRATED **PROBLEM SOLVING**

One afternoon Mark and Manolita stopped by to see how Mr. Muddle's time machine was working. "The clock works just fine," said Mr. Muddle. "Listen to it tick. But sometimes I can't tell what time it is. Look at it now."

One hand was pointing at 11. The other hand was pointing at 4. "It could be almost any time," said Mr. Muddle. "I can't tell."

"It's not that bad," said Mark. "There are only two different times it could be."

"And I think I know which is the right time," said Manolita.

Work in groups. Discuss your answers and how you figured them out. Then compare your answers with those of other groups.

❶ Why is it hard to tell what time it is with Mr. Muddle's clock? **Because the hands are the same length.**

❷ Look at the clock in the picture. What are the two times that it could be? **11:20 or 3:55**

❸ Which of these is the right time? Look for a clue in the story. **3:55; the story takes place in the afternoon**

426 • Geometry

Unit 4 Lesson 150 • **427**

Level 3

◆ **Word Problems** throughout the student books are carefully crafted to involve multiple operations, cumulative content, and sometimes, insufficient information so that students always have to think.

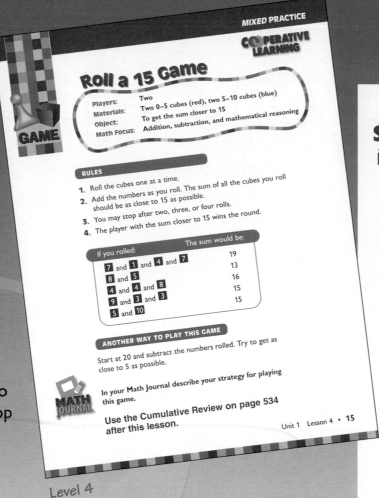

MIXED PRACTICE

COOPERATIVE LEARNING

Roll a 15 Game

Players: Two
Materials: Two 0–5 cubes (red), two 5–10 cubes (blue)
Object: To get the sum closer to 15
Math Focus: Addition, subtraction, and mathematical reasoning

RULES

1. Roll the cubes one at a time.
2. Add the numbers as you roll. The sum of all the cubes you roll should be as close to 15 as possible.
3. You may stop after two, three, or four rolls.
4. The player with the sum closer to 15 wins the round.

If you rolled:	The sum would be:
7 and 1 and 4 and 7	19
8 and 5	13
4 and 4 and 8	16
9 and 3 and 3	15
5 and 10	15

ANOTHER WAY TO PLAY THIS GAME

Start at 20 and subtract the numbers rolled. Try to get as close to 5 as possible.

 MATH JOURNAL

In your Math Journal describe your strategy for playing this game.

Use the Cumulative Review on page 534 after this lesson.

Unit 1 Lesson 4 • 15

Level 4

◆ **Games** provide lots of opportunities for students to identify problems and develop strategies for their solution.

◆ **Projects** at the end of each unit allow students to solve complex problems, many of which require outside research and data analysis.

Problem-Solving Strategies and Methods integrated throughout the program

◆ Act it out
◆ Check reasonableness
◆ Choose a strategy
◆ Choose the appropriate operation
◆ Choose the method
◆ Conduct an experiment
◆ Eliminate possibilities
◆ Identify extra information
◆ Identify needed information
◆ Interpret data
◆ Interpret the quotient and remainder
◆ Make an organized list
◆ Solve a simpler/similar problem
◆ Solve multistep problems
◆ Use a formula
◆ Use estimation
◆ Use guess and check/test
◆ Use logical reasoning
◆ Use manipulatives
◆ Use/draw a picture or diagram
◆ Use/find a pattern
◆ Use/make a model
◆ Use/make a table
◆ Work backwards
◆ Write a number sentence
◆ Write an equation

UNIT 2 WRAP-UP   PROJECT

COOPERATIVE LEARNING

NUMBER TRICKS

Put your hands in front of you. Stretch out your fingers. Think of your fingers as being numbers from 1 through 10, as shown. Now, bend down finger number 3. You have two fingers up on the left and seven fingers up on the right. What is 9 × 3? Do you see any connection?

27; The number of fingers to the left of the finger you put down is the tens digit, and the number of fingers to the right of the finger you put down is the ones digit.

Bend down finger number 4. Do you see a connection between your fingers and 4 × 9? What happens when you bend down finger number 8? **see above**

Does this work for 10 × 9? How about for 0 × 9? **yes; no**

Why does this work? If you multiply 7 by 10, you get seven tens. So put up seven fingers. Now, if you subtract 7, you have one fewer ten (so put down finger number 7). But you need three more ones (because 10 − 7 = 3, so put up three fingers.

 In your Math Journal write about how this trick can help you remember the multiples of 9.

Try this number trick on your friends. Start with a two-digit number that has two different digits. Reverse the digits. Subtract the lesser number from the greater number.

Then, reverse the digits of this last number and add. The sum will be 99.

For example, if you start with 48, the reversed number is 84.

$$84 - 48 = 36$$

Reverse the digits, and add: 36 + 63 = 99.

If you started with a three-digit number, what would the final number be? **1089**

Unit 2 Wrap-Up • 225

224 • Multiplication and Division

Level 3

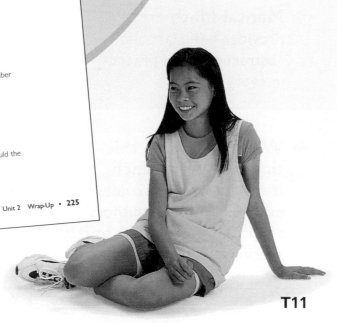

To reach your destination,

Math Explorations and Applications **gives teachers the support they need to challenge students to think mathematically, not to just complete exercises.**

◆ **Lesson Planner** offers a quick overview of the lesson objectives, materials, and resources.

◆ **Context of the Lesson** explains how this lesson fits into sequence with others.

◆ A clear, three-step lesson plan lays out how to **Warm-Up, Teach,** and **Wrap-Up** each lesson.

◆ **Problem of the Day** presents an interesting problem for students to ponder in every lesson.

◆ **Mental Math** provides basic fact and abstract-thinking practice in every lesson.

◆ **Why teach it at this time?** or **Why teach it in this way?** provides an explanation of the authors' philosophy as it relates to this specific lesson.

LESSON 106

Student Edition pages 298–299

Practicing Basic Operations

LESSON PLANNER

Objectives

✓ to assess mastery of students' ability to add and subtract decimals (with up to two decimal places)

▶ to provide practice in adding and subtracting decimals

Context of the Lesson This is the 15th of 15 lessons on decimals. This lesson also contains the 22nd of 24 Mastery Checkpoints.

Materials
graph paper (optional)
play money (optional)

Program Resources
Thinking Story Book, pages 88–89
Practice Master 106
Enrichment Master 106
Assessment Master
For extra practice:
CD-ROM* Lesson 106

❶ Warm-Up ⏱ 5 MINUTES

Problem of the Day Present this problem: Fay called her friend Samir and asked him to meet her at the library. Fay lives 3.4 kilometers away from the library, while Samir lives 1.62 kilometers away. Who must travel farthest to the library? (Fay: 3.4 > 1.62) How much farther? (1.78 km: 3.40 − 1.62 = 1.78)

MENTAL MATH Review addition and subtraction of decimals. On the chalkboard write: 4.2 − 1.14 = _____. Show that the problem can be done by changing 4.2 to the equivalent 4.20 and then subtracting. Then have students respond quickly by writing their answers on paper as you read the following problems aloud.

a. 3.57 − 2.4 = (1.17)
b. 15.63 − 4.7 = (10.93)
c. 5.3 − 2.02 = (3.28)
d. 9.1 + 6.04 = (15.14)
e. 8.35 + 3.2 = (11.55)
f. 7.06 − 1.3 = (5.76)

MIXED PRACTICE

LESSON 106

Practicing Basic Operations

Solve these problems. Watch the signs.

❶ 5.3 − 2.1 = **3.2**   ❷ 5.47 − 3.6 = **1.87**   ❸ 2.4 − 1.87 = **0.53**

❹ 4.71 + 5.62 = **10.33**   ❺ 5.62 + 4.71 = **10.33**   ❻ 5.62 − 4.71 = **0.91**

❼ 3.8 + 1.2 = **5.0**   ❽ 4.07 − 3.7 = **0.37**   ❾ 12.13 − 8.6 = **3.53**

❿ 5.81 − 3.28 = ■ **2.53**   ⓫ 9.03 + 9.3 = ■ **18.33**

⓬ 2.66 − 1.7 = ■ **0.96**   ⓭ 7.56 + 9.33 = ■ **16.89**

⓮ 4.2 − 1.75 = ■ **2.45**   ⓯ 3.44 − 2.07 = ■ **1.37**

⓰ 5.4 + 8.17 = ■ **13.57**   ⓱ 12.1 + 4.79 = ■ **16.89**

Number correct ■

RETEACHING

Students who fall short of the mastery objective should be checked to determine the nature of the difficulty. If the trouble lies with multidigit addition and subtraction of whole numbers, reteach the appropriate algorithms using concrete materials. If the difficulty is adding and subtracting decimals, have students solve problems both with and without concrete objects such as play money*. Use graph paper if students have difficulty lining up the decimal points and columns.

PRACTICE p. 106

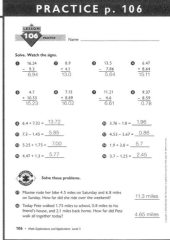

LESSON 106 PRACTICE Name _____

Solve. Watch the signs.

❶ 16.24 − 9.3 = **6.94**   ❷ 8.9 + 4.1 = **13.0**   ❸ 13.5 − 7.86 = **5.64**   ❹ 6.47 + 8.64 = **15.11**

❺ 4.7 + 10.53 = **15.23**   ❻ 7.13 + 8.89 = **16.02**   ❼ 11.21 − 4.6 = **6.61**   ❽ 9.37 − 8.59 = **0.78**

❾ 6.4 + 7.32 = **13.72**   ❿ 3.76 − 1.8 = **1.96**
⓫ 7.3 − 1.45 = **5.85**   ⓬ 4.53 − 3.67 = **0.86**
⓭ 5.25 + 1.75 = **7.00**   ⓮ 1.9 + 3.8 = **5.7**
⓯ 4.47 + 1.3 = **5.77**   ⓰ 3.7 − 1.25 = **2.45**

Solve these problems.

⓱ Maxine rode her bike 4.5 miles on Saturday and 6.8 miles on Sunday. How far did she ride over the weekend? **11.3 miles**

⓲ Today Pete walked 1.75 miles to school, 0.8 miles to his friend's house, and 2.1 miles back home. How far did Pete walk all together today? **4.65 miles**

106 • *Math Explorations and Applications Level 3*

*available separately

you need a clear road map.

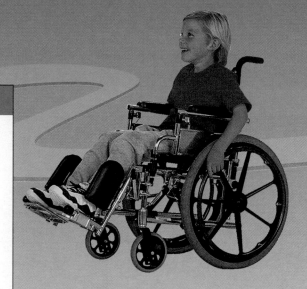

Solve.

18 Each time Amy adds a book to her bookshelf, she records how much room is left on the shelf. All her books are the same thickness. Copy and complete Amy's table.

Space on Amy's Bookshelf

Number of Books	5	6	7	8	9	10	11	12	13
Space Used	1.03	0.99	0.95	0.91	0.87	0.83	0.79 ■	0.75 ■	0.71 ■

Make up five problems using the map below and solve them. Write your problems in your Math Journal and explain how to solve them.

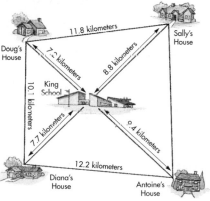

Doug's House — 11.8 kilometers — Sally's House
7.2 kilometers · 8.8 kilometers
10.1 kilometers
King School
7.7 kilometers · 9.4 kilometers
Diana's House — 12.2 kilometers — Antoine's House

Unit 3 Lesson 106 • 299

❷ Teach

Using the Student Pages Tell students that the problems on page 298 are a test. Allow students enough time to finish. When all students have finished, have them proofread their papers as a group. Remember to focus attention on the number of correct rather than the number of incorrect answers. Then have students complete page 299.

📘 **Using the Thinking Story** Have students complete three problems from among those following "Mosquito Lake" on pages 88–89 of the Thinking Story Book.

❸ Wrap-Up ⏱ 5 MINUTES

In Closing Ask students what they must remember to do when adding or subtracting numbers with decimals. Students should say they must write more zeros as necessary so that each number in the problem has the same number of decimal places.

🏁 **Mastery Checkpoint 22**

Students should demonstrate mastery of the addition and subtraction of decimals (with up to two decimal places) by correctly answering 12 of the 17 problems on page 298. The results of this assessment may be recorded on the Mastery Checkpoint Chart. You may also wish to assign the Assessment Master on page 41 to determine mastery.

◆ **Program Resources** are referenced at point of use.

◆ **Mastery Checkpoint** provides opportunities for teachers to check for student understanding of core skills and concepts.

◆ **Practice, Enrichment,** and **Reteaching** blackline masters and strategies are included for every lesson.

◆ **Assessment Criteria** tie informal assessment to the Lesson Objectives.

◆ **Homework** ideas are always included in Levels 3–6 for added practice and reinforcement.

ENRICHMENT p. 106

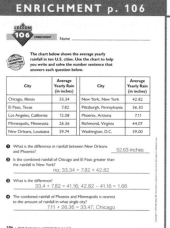

LESSON 106 ENRICHMENT   Name _____

The chart below shows the average yearly rainfall in ten U.S. cities. Use the chart to help you write and solve the number sentence that answers each question below.

City	Average Yearly Rain (in inches)	City	Average Yearly Rain (in inches)
Chicago, Illinois	33.34	New York, New York	42.82
El Paso, Texas	7.82	Pittsburgh, Pennsylvania	36.30
Los Angeles, California	12.08	Phoenix, Arizona	7.11
Minneapolis, Minnesota	26.36	Richmond, Virginia	44.07
New Orleans, Louisiana	59.74	Washington, D.C.	39.00

❶ What is the difference in rainfall between New Orleans and Phoenix? 52.63 inches

❷ Is the combined rainfall of Chicago and El Paso greater than the rainfall in New York?
no; 33.34 + 7.82 < 42.82

❸ What is the difference?
33.4 + 7.82 = 41.16; 42.82 − 41.16 = 1.66

❹ The combined rainfall of Phoenix and Minneapolis is nearest to the amount of rainfall in what single city?
7.11 + 26.36 = 33.47; Chicago

106 • Math Explorations and Applications Level 3

ASSESSMENT p. 41

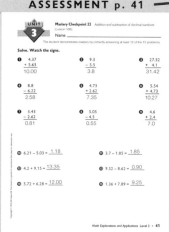

UNIT 3   **Mastery Checkpoint 22** Addition and subtraction of decimal numbers
(Lesson 106)   Name _____
The student demonstrates mastery by correctly answering at least 12 of the 15 problems

Solve. Watch the signs.

❶ 4.37 + 5.63 = 10.00   ❷ 9.3 − 5.5 = 3.8   ❸ 27.32 + 4.1 = 31.42

❹ 8.8 − 6.22 = 2.58   ❺ 4.73 + 2.62 = 7.35   ❻ 5.54 + 4.73 = 10.27

❼ 3.43 − 2.62 = 0.81   ❽ 5.05 − 4.5 = 0.55   ❾ 4.6 + 2.4 = 7.0

❿ 6.21 − 5.03 = 1.18   ⓫ 3.7 − 1.85 = 1.85

⓬ 4.2 + 9.15 = 13.35   ⓭ 9.52 − 8.62 = 0.90

⓮ 5.72 + 6.28 = 12.00   ⓯ 1.36 + 7.89 = 9.25

Math Explorations and Applications Level 3 • 41

📋 **Assessment Criteria**

Did the student . . .

✓ make up at least five word problems with solutions based on page 299?

✓ demonstrate mastery of the addition and subtraction of decimals?

Homework To reinforce the lesson concept, have students play the "Harder Rummage Sale" game with a household member.

Unit 3 Lesson 106 **299**

Level 3

Assessment tools help students stay on track.

Math Explorations and Applications aligns teaching and assessment to support learning. With a variety of options, teachers can select appropriate methods to monitor student progress.

Self-Assessment. *Are You Shiny or Rusty?* activities offer nonthreatening timed tests so that students can see how quickly and accurately they can recall the basic arithmetic facts.

Performance Assessment. Strategies in the Teacher's Guide and the Assessment Book provide opportunities for students to show what they know.

Portfolio Assessment. Suggestions throughout the Teacher's Guide give students an opportunity to demonstrate their mathematical growth.

Informal Assessment

◆ **Assessment Criteria.** In every lesson teachers are reminded what to look for as they informally assess student responses.

◆ **Varied Opportunities.** Every Game, Thinking Story, and Act It Out provides an opportunity for teachers to informally assess students' mathematical thinking.

◆ **Mental Math Exercises.** Daily interactive Mental Math activities offer opportunities for informal assessment and self-assessment.

Formal Assessment

◆ **Unit Assessment.** Mid-Unit Reviews, Unit Reviews, and Unit Tests provide ready-made formal assessment of students' comprehension.

◆ **Mastery Checkpoints.** These checkpoints and corresponding evaluations in the Assessment Books indicate times that teachers can check for mastery of specific skills and concepts.

◆ **Mastery Checkpoint Charts.** Mastery Checkpoints give teachers an easy way to keep track of students' mastery of specific skills.

◆ **Standardized-Format Tests.** Multiple-choice computation tests provide practice taking standardized tests at the same time they provide one more opportunity to assess students' math skills.

SRA MATH

Explorations and Applications

It will change the way students think about math . . . for a lifetime.

***Math Explorations and Applications* is a program
with proven results for more than 25 years.**

◆ The program was developed one grade level at a time, building on valuable field test results to ensure consistency and continuity throughout all grade levels.

◆ Successfully field-tested in urban, suburban, and rural schools, *Math Explorations and Applications* ensures effectiveness in any teaching situation.

◆ Teaching strategies throughout the program are based on substantial bodies of research indicating how children learn best.

◆ Written and updated by a team of distinguished and committed authors, *Math Explorations and Applications* reflects time-tested strategies with proven results.

◆ We have listened carefully to teachers who use the program. This edition of *Math Explorations and Applications* reflects the many valuable suggestions and comments we have received from talented teachers over the years. We look forward to receiving your comments.

Exceeds
~~Meets~~ ~~N~~CTM Standards!

Authorship

Dr. Stephen S. Willoughby
Mathematics Educator

Stephen S. Willoughby has taught mathematics at all levels, from first grade through graduate courses in schools in Massachusetts, Connecticut, Wisconsin, New York, and Arizona, including the University of Wisconsin and New York University. He is now Professor of Mathematics at the University of Arizona. He received bachelor's and master's degrees from Harvard University and a doctorate from Columbia University.

Dr. Willoughby was President of the National Council of Teachers of Mathematics from 1982 to 1984 and Chairman of the Council of Scientific Society Presidents in 1988. He was a member of the national Board of Advisors for SQUARE ONE TV, chairman of the United States Commission on Mathematics Instruction, and a member of the Education Testing Services Mathematics Advisory Committee for the successor to the National Teacher's Examination, and is now a member of the Education Advisory Panel of New American Schools Development Corporation (NASDC).

Dr. Willoughby has published more than 200 articles and books on mathematics and mathematics education and was senior author of the innovative K–8 mathematics series *Real Math™* published by Open Court.

Dr. Carl Bereiter
Cognitive Psychologist

Carl Bereiter is a professor in the Centre for Applied Cognitive Science, Ontario Institute for Studies in Education, University of Toronto. He holds a Ph.D. in educational psychology from the University of Wisconsin. He has done research and developed educational materials in such diverse areas as preschool education, thinking skills, writing, elementary school mathematics, and science understanding. He is also active in the development of advanced computer-based technology for schools. His scholarly contributions have been recognized by award of a Guggenheim Fellowship, appointments to the Center for Advanced Study in the Behavioral Sciences, election to the National Academy of Education, and an honorary Doctor of Laws from Queens University. His books include *Arithmetic and Mathematics* (1968), *Thinking Games* (1975 with Valerie Anderson), *The Psychology of Written Composition* (1987, with Marlene Scardamalia), and *Surpassing Ourselves: An Inquiry into the Nature and Implications of Expertise* (1993, also with Marlene Scardamalia) and the forthcoming *Education and Mind in the Knowledge Age*.

Dr. Peter Hilton
Mathematician

Peter Hilton is Distinguished Professor of Mathematics Emeritus at the State University of New York (Binghamton) and Distinguished Professor at the University of Central Florida. He holds M.A. and Doctorate of Philosophy degrees from Oxford University and a Ph.D. from Cambridge University. He has an honorary doctorate of humanities from Northern Michigan University, an honorary doctorate of science from the Memorial University of Newfoundland, and an honorary doctorate of science from the Autonomous University of Barcelona. In addition to his activity in research and teaching as a mathematician, he has a continuing interest in mathematics education and has served on many national and international committees and as chairman of the United States Commission on Mathematics Instruction. Dr. Hilton is the author of several important books, his most recent being *Mathematical Reflections*, jointly with Derek Holton and Jean Pedersen, and many research articles on algebraic topology, homological algebra, group theory, and category theory.

Dr. Joseph H. Rubinstein
Biologist and Educator

Joseph H. Rubinstein is Professor of Education and Chairperson of the Department of Education at Coker College, Hartsville, South Carolina. He received B.A., M.S., and Ph.D. degrees in biology from New York University, completing his studies in 1969. His interest in elementary education was kindled by his participation in the late 1960s in an experimental science curriculum development project, the Conceptually Oriented Program in Elementary Science (COPES). During that time he worked in the New York City public schools helping elementary school teachers implement science programs in their classrooms. Dr. Rubinstein served as the Director of Open Court Publishing Company's Mathematics and Science Curriculum Development Center during the development of *Real Math™*, the precursor to *SRA Math Explorations and Applications*. In 1984 he joined the faculty of Coker College, where his principal duties include training prospective teachers to teach mathematics and science.

Reviewers

Dr. Prentice Baptiste
Manhattan, KS

Debney Biggs
Shreveport, LA

Pat Dahl
Vancouver, WA

Karen Hardin
Houston, TX

Susan Humphries
BelAir, MD

Tucky Marchica
Inverness, IL

Dr. Marilyn Neil
Birmingham, AL

Bill Smith
Haddonfield, NJ

Bob Winkler
Overland Park, KS

Game Mat Testers

Grace Brethren Elementary School
Columbus, OH

Huber Ridge Elementary School
Westerville School District
Westerville, OH

St. Paul's Elementary School
Columbus Diocese
Westerville, OH

Tremont Elementary School
Upper Arlington School District
Upper Arlington, OH

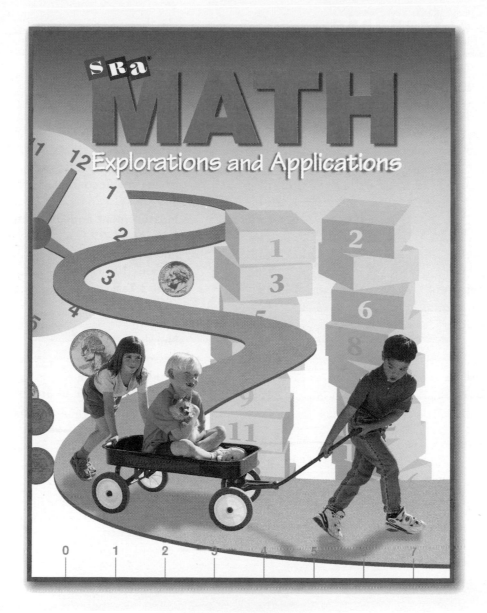

MATH
Explorations and Applications

Stephen S. Willoughby
Carl Bereiter
Peter Hilton
Joseph H. Rubinstein

SRA/McGraw-Hill

A Division of The McGraw-Hill Companies

Printed in the United States of America.

Send all inquiries to:
SRA/McGraw-Hill
250 Old Wilson Bridge Road, Suite 310
Worthington, OH 43085

ISBN 0-02-687852-6

1 2 3 4 5 6 7 8 9 VHP 02 01 00 99 98 97

TABLE OF CONTENTS

SRA/McGraw-Hill

A Division of The McGraw·Hill Companies

1999 imprint

Copyright © 1998 by SRA/McGraw-Hill. All rights reserved. Except as permitted under the United States Copyright Act, no part of this publication may be reproduced or distributed in any form or by any means, or stored in a database or retrieval system, without prior written permission from the publisher.

Printed in the United States of America.

Send all inquiries to:
SRA/McGraw-Hill
250 Old Wilson Bridge Road, Suite 310
Worthington, OH 43085

ISBN 0-02-687861-5

2 3 4 5 6 7 8 9 WEB 02 01 00 99 98

Acknowledgments

Photo Credits
p. **T1,** (l) ©Jeff Smith/Fotosmith; (r) ©Timothy Fuller; **T3,** ©Aaron Haupt; **T4,** ©Jeff Smith/Fotosmith; **T5,** ©Aaron Haupt; **T6,** ©Jeff Smith/Fotosmith; **T7,** ©Jeff Smith/Fotosmith; **T8,** (l) ©Jeff Smith/Fotosmith; (r) ©Timothy Fuller; **T9,** ©Jeff Smith/Fotosmith; **T10,** ©Jeff Smith/Fotosmith; **T11,** ©Jeff Smith/Fotosmith; **T13,** ©Jeff Smith/Fotosmith; **T14,** ©Timothy Fuller; **T15,** ©Jeff Smith/Fotosmith; **T32, T33, T184D,** ©1997/PhotoDisc; **19B,** ©Jeff Smith/Fotosmith; **119B,** ©Timothy Fuller; **274B,** ©Timothy Fuller.

Cover Credits
Front cover photo, Fotosmith; **Design and Illustration,** Morgan-Cain & Associates; **Back cover photo,** ©Timothy Fuller and Jeff Smith/Fotosmith.

Math Explorations and Applications is based upon the idea of making mathematics real for students. It builds upon what children already know when they enter school and upon what they learn from their experiences outside school. It helps children see that mathematics is useful and important in their own lives, and it makes learning mathematics enjoyable.

Math Explorations and Applications is based upon everyday teaching and learning. In the Teacher's Guide are all the activities that go together to make up the total learning experience. These activities have been tried, criticized, revised, and tried again by hundreds of teachers.

Math Explorations and Applications is based upon sound theory, research, and extensive field testing. It is a program that works.

In every grade the program emphasizes thinking skills, problem-solving strategies, real applications, mental arithmetic, estimation, approximation, measurement, organizing data, geometry, probability, statistics, and algebra. In addition, computational skills are introduced at appropriate levels and are reviewed and maintained in that level and in subsequent levels.

PROGRAM ORGANIZATION

There are three ways that *Math Explorations and Applications* has been carefully organized to introduce and reinforce concepts.

Early Introduction of Concepts

Math Explorations and Applications makes a point of exposing students to core problems and concepts from the beginning. For example, in traditional teaching, students first learn the plus sign and later are introduced to the minus sign. When signs are introduced one at a time, students learn to pay no attention to the sign because it is always the same. Students are trained in this way not to figure out the problem but to follow the pattern.

Similar confusion arises in the traditional teaching of subtraction of multidigit numbers. First, children learn to subtract with numbers that require no regrouping (65 – 32, for example). When they are later introduced to regrouping (62 – 35, for example), they are often confused because they have learned an easy and automatic way to subtract, which turns out to work only sometimes.

In *Math Explorations and Applications*, plus and minus signs are introduced at the same time in Level 1. In Level 2, multidigit subtraction problems that require regrouping, as well as those that do not, are introduced early on. Core mathematical concepts are emphasized in an age-appropriate manner at every level. The early introduction of concepts causes much less trouble and confusion later on because students don't have to unlearn patterns that they have begun to rely on. Furthermore, when students reach middle school and high school, they will already have a firm foundation in core mathematical concepts such as probability, statistics, geometry, and algebra.

Revisiting Concepts

While it is convenient to package teaching into neat, isolated units that deal with a single topic, the learning that goes on in children's minds cannot be so neatly packaged. Children learn, forget, and relearn. They catch a glimmer of an idea, lose it, catch it again, and finally get hold of it firmly enough that it becomes a solid part of understanding. In *Math Explorations and Applications*, concepts like inequalities, missing addends, and base 10 are developed and reviewed continuously over the whole year so that they become part of the child's working knowledge.

Throughout the year concepts and skills are introduced and reappear again and again in subsequent lessons and in Mixed Practice so that students never lose them. For example, basic addition, subtraction, multiplication, and division are a major focus of at least one third of the lessons in Level 3 and are practiced in virtually every Practice and Mixed Practice exercise.

Presenting Concepts in Different Contexts

In Level 4 of *Math Explorations and Applications*, multiplication is introduced and reinforced in more than 50 lessons throughout the entire year in all the following contexts:

one-digit number multiplication	conversion graphs
two-digit number multiplication	multidigit numbers
three-digit number multiplication	money
algebra readiness	multiplication facts
area	multiples of 10
commutative property (order of factors)	powers of 10
decimals	problem solving
division	repeated addition
	skip counting
	square numbers
	whole numbers

The thoughtful organization at every level of *Math Explorations and Applications* ensures that students are introduced to mathematics concepts and skills in context at appropriate age levels. They encounter these concepts and use these skills again and again throughout the year and in subsequent years in different, age-appropriate contexts.

> " There are reasons for almost everything we do in mathematics. Children should be encouraged to discover, or at least see, those reasons. Understanding the reasons will help them remember how to do the mathematics; but more important, it will help them understand that the mathematics is related to their reality and that mathematics can be used to help them understand the real world. "
>
> –Stephen S. Willoughby
> *Mathematics Education for a Changing World*

COMPONENTS CHART

A variety of resources that present math concepts in a way all students can learn!

Components	Levels						
	K	1	2	3	4	5	6
Student Edition	✓	✓	✓	✓	✓	✓	✓
Teacher's Guide	✓	✓	✓	✓	✓	✓	✓
Thinking Story Book		✓	✓	✓			
Game Mat Package	✓	✓	✓	✓	✓	✓	✓
Reteaching Masters		✓	✓	✓	✓	✓	✓
Reteaching Workbook		✓	✓	✓	✓	✓	✓
Reteaching Workbook TE		✓	✓	✓	✓	✓	✓
Practice Masters	✓	✓	✓	✓	✓	✓	✓
Practice Workbook	✓	✓	✓	✓	✓	✓	✓
Practice Workbook TE	✓	✓	✓	✓	✓	✓	✓
Enrichment Masters	✓	✓	✓	✓	✓	✓	✓
Enrichment Workbook	✓	✓	✓	✓	✓	✓	✓
Enrichment Workbook TE	✓	✓	✓	✓	✓	✓	✓
Assessment Masters	✓	✓	✓	✓	✓	✓	✓
Home Connections Masters	✓	✓	✓	✓	✓	✓	✓
Literature Library	✓	✓	✓	✓			
Primary Manipulative Kit	✓	✓	✓				
Primary Overhead Manipulative Kit	✓	✓	✓				
Intermediate Manipulative Kit				✓	✓	✓	✓
Intermediate Overhead Manipulative Kit				✓	✓	✓	✓
Teacher Manipulative Kit	✓	✓	✓	✓	✓	✓	✓
Basic Manipulative Kit	✓	✓	✓	✓	✓	✓	✓
Primary Overhead Calculator	✓	✓	✓	✓			
Intermediate Overhead Calculator					✓	✓	✓
TI-108™ Calculator Package	✓	✓	✓	✓			
Math Explorer™ Calculator Package					✓	✓	✓
Math Explorations and Applications CD-ROM Program		✓	✓	✓	✓	✓	✓
The Cruncher CD-ROM Program and Guide					✓	✓	✓
My Silly CD of Counting CD-ROM	✓						
Professional Development Handbook	✓	✓	✓	✓	✓	✓	✓

In *Math Explorations and Applications* there are a variety of resources for students and teachers to use to introduce and demonstrate concepts and to practice math skills. These carefully integrated materials each play an important and well-thought-out role in the program as a whole.

TEACHER'S GUIDE

This comprehensive manual gives specific advice for every lesson and lesson component, as well as teaching tips, explanations, and background information.

STUDENT EDITION

The Student Edition provides practice with written problems. It is also used to present games and activities. It is not, however, the main source of concept presentation or skill practice. Student Edition pages supplement the teacher's concept presentation and the practice provided by Mental Math exercises, activities, games, and Thinking Stories.

BASIC MANIPULATIVES

Basic Manipulatives—Number Cubes, Number Wheels, and Number Strips—are used throughout *Math Explorations and Applications* in Games and in Mental Math activities that appear in the Teacher's Guide. The Basic Manipulatives allow all students to participate in every Mental Math activity in a nonthreatening way. Mental Math activities provide essential, regular practice in basic math facts. Furthermore, they allow the teacher to informally assess each student's mathematical skill.

The Number Cubes used at Levels 1 and 2 allow students to make any integer from 0 through 100. The students use the cubes to form numbers in games and to show answers during Mental Math exercises. In Levels 3–6, students use Number Wheels for display. Each wheel can be dialed to show any digit from 0 to 9. The wheels allow students to make any integer from 0 through 99,999.

Most Mental Math activities are done in the following three steps. The pace should be lively enough to keep things moving yet not so fast that students have insufficient time to think.

1. **"Find."** The teacher presents the problem either orally or on the chalkboard. The students find the answer and arrange their Number Cubes or Number Wheel in a position to display it.

2. **"Hide."** The students hide the answer against their chests. The teacher waits for most of the students to have an answer. Teachers do not need to wait for every student to find and hide an answer, but long enough so that students who are making progress toward a solution have time to finish. Add a "peek-to-be-sure" step to keep all students involved while waiting for the next command.

3. **"Show."** The students hold up their Number Cubes or Number Wheel so that the teacher can see the response. The teacher quickly checks the responses, shows or tells the correct answer, and quickly moves to the next problem. Only the teacher and the students who got a wrong answer need know about it. Teachers can give these students extra teaching later on.

PRIMARY AND INTERMEDIATE MANIPULATIVE KITS

In the real world, students experience number in many different representations. If in mathematics instruction they are given only one way of representing number—whether with rods, blocks, coins, sticks, or tally marks—they are liable to become dependent upon that one method. In *Math Explorations and Applications* all these ways—and more—of representing number are used.

Whenever appropriate, manipulatives are used to show the connection between the real world and the mathematics. The use of manipulatives is discontinued after a sufficient connection has been made so that the abstract nature of mathematics is not obscured.

LESSON SUPPORT MATERIALS

A variety of extra activities is available to support lesson concepts and skills. Activities in the Practice Workbook provide extra practice in computational skills. Enrichment activities offer extensions, and Reteaching activities help those who have not yet grasped the lesson concept or skill. These activities are keyed to each lesson. Assessment masters provide the Mastery Checkpoints, Mid-Unit Reviews, and Unit Tests.

TECHNOLOGY SUPPORT MATERIALS

◆ Calculators are suggested for use in appropriate lessons.

◆ SRA Cruncher suggestions are also provided at point of use when a spreadsheet application would be appropriate or would facilitate solving a problem.

◆ The *Math Explorations and Applications* Software provides extra practice for specific skills in a motivating format.

PACING

Math Explorations and Applications is intended to be taught at a lively pace but not to be rushed through at the expense of achievement. Lessons are generally written to fill a 45-minute time period. Teachers should move quickly from activity to activity. Introductions and lesson closures should be short because these tend to be ineffective and often lose students' attention.

The efficient lesson plans in *Math Explorations and Applications* help teachers gives their students the chance to practice skills, to solve thinking problems, and to do enrichment activities. Here are some tips for using the resources efficiently.

Be prepared. Having necessary materials ready is, of course, important. To help, sections in the Lesson Plans entitled "Looking Ahead" and "Materials" will be useful. This is a good reason to read the lesson in advance.

Watch the clock. The clock can tell a teacher when he or she has concentrated on an activity too long, even before students show signs of restlessness. Teachers should keep an eye on the clock to make sure they don't spend too much time talking or shifting from one activity to another.

Extend lessons to more than one day. Teachers may occasionally find it necessary to spend an extra day on some lessons. This is expected. It is recommended that more than one day be spent on many lessons. The time gained by extending a lesson should go to more teaching and drill on related skills, to related games, or to a review of prerequisite skills.

> "*Whole-class response activities encourage practice, allow students to correct their own errors, and allow the teacher to identify difficulties that individual students are having or that are common to the entire class.*"
>
> —Stephen S. Willoughby
> *Mathematics Education for a Changing World*

If you have more than forty-five minutes a day for math. Below are some ideas for extending parts of the lessons.

◆ Lengthen game periods by five minutes each (more when new games are introduced).

◆ Repeat whole-group activities when you feel that the students will remain interested.

◆ Lengthen Mental Math exercises by up to five minutes.

◆ Lengthen demonstrations and seminars by two or three minutes at most.

◆ Use the Enrichment masters.

If you have less than forty-five minutes a day for math. Many teachers will be tempted to forgo Games or Thinking Stories in a time crunch, but these elements of *Math Explorations and Applications* arc vital for developing mathematical intelligence, without which computational skills have little value. Try these suggestions if there is little time.

◆ Present the Thinking Stories during reading or some other time outside the regular math period.

◆ Conduct games outside the regular math period. Set up game-playing sessions every Friday, for example. Be aware, however, that not all games can be transferred to special sessions, because sometimes a game provides practice that will help students complete a particular lesson.

◆ Complete Mental Math exercises during five-minute periods at the beginning or end of the day or right before or after lunch. These sessions are not always essential to a particular lesson, but they do provide regular drill with Mental Math and basic math facts.

ASSESSMENT

Math Explorations and Applications is unusually rich in opportunities to keep track of—and do something about—individual student progress.

In the Teacher's Guide

Each lesson in the Teacher's Guide provides at least two different assessment suggestions. One is Assessment Criteria, which provides questions teachers can ask themselves as they observe students completing the lesson activities. Additional suggestions include the following:

◆ Informal assessment (interviews, observation, and oral assessment)

◆ Formal assessment (Tests, Reviews, Mastery Checkpoints, and Mastery Checkpoint Masters)

◆ Self-Assessment

◆ Portfolio and Performance Assessment

In the Student Edition

A formal Mid-Unit Review as well as a Unit Review and a Unit Test are provided in the Student Edition in Levels 1–6. Self-Assessments and timed tests are included throughout the Student Editions for students to evaluate their own performances.

In the Assessment Book

In the Assessment Book, there is a master for each Mastery Checkpoint, and an additional Mid-Unit Review and two Unit Tests, one in standardized (multiple-choice) format. Each unit also provides Performance Assessment activities and Portfolio Assessment suggestions. The Assessment Book includes additional information on the various alternative assessment options that are provided in the program, as well as suggestions for using rubrics to grade these assessments.

Informal Daily Assessment

Use Mental Math, Games, Thinking Stories, and Student Edition pages for day-to-day observation and assessment of how well each student is learning the skills and grasping concepts. Because of their special nature, these activities are an effective and convenient means of monitoring. Games, for example, allow the teacher to watch students practice particular skills under conditions more natural to students than most classroom activities. Mental Math activities allow the teacher to get feedback from each student, to give immediate feedback to each student, and to keep all the students actively involved.

To follow through on daily monitoring, consider the Reteaching strategy or master in each lesson to provide immediate help to students who are having difficulty.

Mastery Checkpoints and Charts

To help teachers formally yet conveniently monitor the progress of each student, there are more than 20 skills identified at each grade level that are important for future progress. These skills are listed on the Mastery Checkpoint Chart in the Assessment Book for each grade level. Each skill is described in detail in the Mastery Checkpoint section of the Teacher's Guide lesson in which teachers can formally assess that skill. These Mastery Checkpoints are an opportunity for teachers to monitor how well students have mastered basic skills and to provide extra help to those who are having trouble. Mastery Checkpoints are placed in the lesson in which most, but not all, of the students are expected to have achieved adequate proficiency in the skill. Teachers should not hold up the class waiting for every student to demonstrate success.

Using the Mastery Checkpoint Chart

◆ Fill in the names of all the students in the class.

◆ When a Mastery Checkpoint is encountered in the Teacher's Guide, follow the suggestions for observing and assessing each student's success.

◆ ✓ Place a check mark in the appropriate column of the Mastery Checkpoint Chart beside the name of each student who demonstrates success on the objective in question.

◆ **P** Pencil in a *P* in the appropriate column for each student who grasps the concept but still needs further practice to sharpen his or her skill. Assign extra practice to students whose names you marked with a *P*.

◆ **T** Pencil in a *T* for each student who has not yet grasped the idea and needs further teaching. Give extra teaching or Reteaching to students whose names you marked with a *T*.

◆ Change Ts to Ps and Ps to check marks when students demonstrate success on the objective. Do not hold up the entire class, however, waiting for all students to demonstrate success. More teaching and practice on a particular skill is always given in a later lesson, usually the following one. At that time teachers can focus on those students who need extra help.

> " *Observation of game-playing activity resembles observation of real-life-out-of-school activities as closely as anything we are likely to see in school. Such observation will often give greater insight into a child's thought patterns than anything else the teacher can do.* "
>
> —Stephen S. Willoughby
> *Mathematics Education for a Changing World*

MANIPULATIVE KITS

Component	Game Mat Package (K-6)	Basic (K)	Basic (1-2)	Basic (3-6)	Primary (K-2)	Primary Overhead (K-2)	Intermediate (3-6)	Intermediate Overhead (3-6)	Teacher (K-6)
Angle Ruler							✓		
Attribute Blocks					✓	✓			
Base-10 Blocks				✓	✓	✓	✓		
Beakers									✓
Bills	✓*					✓		✓	
Classifying Counters					✓				
Clock Faces (demonstration or individual)					✓	✓	✓	✓	✓
Coins	✓*					✓		✓	
Counters (opaque or two-sided)	✓				✓	✓	✓	✓	
Cubes (interlocking)					✓		✓		
Decimal Set							✓		
Dual-Dial Scale									✓
Fraction Cubes							✓		
Fraction Tiles					✓	✓		✓	
Funnels							✓		
Geoboard					✓	✓			
Geometric Solids					✓				
Geometric Volume Set							✓		
Math Balance									✓
Metric Grids								✓	
Mirrors					✓		✓		
Number Cubes—0-5 and 5-10 Units	✓	✓	✓	✓					
Number Cubes—0-5 and 5-10 Tens			✓						
Number Line (walk-on)					✓				
Number Strips		✓	✓						
Number Tiles						✓		✓	
Number Wheels				✓					
Pattern Blocks					✓	✓			
Place Markers	✓								
Place Value Pad							✓		
Precision Balance									✓
Protractors							✓		
Shape Set						✓		✓	
Spinners and Dice (blank)						✓	✓	✓	
Stopwatch									✓
Tape Measure					✓		✓		
Thermometer (classroom, demonstration, or individual)					✓	✓	✓	✓	✓
Venn Diagram/Graphing Mat									✓

*not in the Kindergarten package

GAMES AND THINKING STORIES

GAMES

Games do not provide just fun or enrichment in *Math Explorations and Applications;* they are a vital, almost daily part of the program. Games give students a chance to develop their mathematical skills and understandings in situations in which those skills and understandings count. Games provide practice. They give students a means of becoming proficient in the mathematical skills to which they've been introduced. Some games give students a chance to work out important mathematical ideas and problem-solving strategies. Games also give the teacher an opportunity for informal assessment. By observing game-playing sessions, teachers can quickly assess how well individual students have learned the skill being practiced.

Each game involves the use of specific skills, but there is usually also a certain amount of luck involved, so the more able student does not always win. When a lesson plan prescribes a game, it does so because the principal skills involved in that game need attention at that time. Some lesson plans suggest that students play games of their choice. The Game Directory lists principal skills involved in each game to help the teacher select those games that will give each student an appropriate form of practice. Game Mats and Cube Games are the two types of games used in *Math Explorations and Applications*.

GAME MATS

Many of the games in *Math Explorations and Applications* are board games found in the Game Mat package for each grade level. There are five Game Mats in Kindergarten, 13 in Levels 1–3, and 14 in Levels 4–6. In each Game Mat package there are 15 copies of each Game Mat, as well as enough counters, place markers, Number Cubes, and money so that the entire class can play a game at the same time. Also included is A Guide for Using the Game Mats and an overhead transparency of each game for introducing the games to the class. Many of the Game Mats are offered in both a standard and a harder version. A copy of each game can also be found in the back of this Teacher's Guide.

CUBE GAMES

Many games don't require Game Mats. They use Number Cubes or sometimes require no materials at all. These games, presented in the Student Edition in Levels 3–6 and in the Teacher's Guide in Levels K–2, reinforce basic math skills and involve mathematical reasoning.

INTRODUCING GAMES

Here are some tips for making sure that games are played correctly.

◆ Familiarize yourself with each game by playing it before showing the students how to play it.

◆ Show, don't just tell, how a game is played. Games should be demonstrated in front of the class when they are first introduced. Overhead Game Mats are provided for this purpose. Verbalize the rules as you demonstrate.

◆ Make sure each student can see when a game is demonstrated.

◆ Supervise to see that students get off to the right start after you've introduced a game.

◆ Let students who know the game rules help those who haven't played it.

ORGANIZING SUCCESSFUL GAME SESSIONS

◆ Mixing ability levels from time to time, however, keeps some students from having an oppressive sense of their slowness.

◆ Change groupings from day to day. Students can learn different things by playing with different partners.

◆ Assign a referee to each group. The referee sees that the rules are followed, reminds players when it is their turn, settles disputes, keeps track of scores, and in some games acts as banker. Associate a sense of honor and responsibility around the role of the referee so that students will be willing to serve as referee.

◆ Encourage students to play games during free time—in school and at home—as well as during the scheduled game periods.

◆ Allow students to make up and name their own variations of the games. Whenever students regularly misinterpret a rule, there's a good chance they have discovered a new and, to them, more interesting version of the game. Be alert, however, to avoid versions that reduce the skill-practice value of the game.

◆ Encourage parents, teacher aides, or older students to participate in game-playing sessions with students.

◆ Stress enjoyment rather than competition. Emphasize sportsmanship, fair play, and giving each player a turn.

◆ Teach students to control their excitement and to speak in a low voice.

◆ Make Game Mats accessible. Store Game Mats so that students can find and return them by themselves.

THINKING STORIES

Thinking Stories are an essential part of *Math Explorations and Applications*. The stories and related thinking problems tap into the child's world of fantasy and humor. They are aimed at developing quantitative intelligence—creativity and common sense in the use of mathematics. The stories allow students to discover the power of their own mathematical common sense and of their innate capacity for reasoning. The stories and problems are filled with surprises, so students cannot apply arithmetic routinely. Instead they must apply mathematical common sense to choose which operation to use, to recognize which data are relevant to the questions asked, to determine whether an answer is absurd, and to decide when calculation isn't necessary.

THINKING STORY CHARACTERS

The various characters in the stories appear in all grade levels. The children in the stories age with each grade level so that they are about the same age as the students reading the stories. All the characters have peculiar thinking patterns that students come to know. Mr. Muddle, for example, is always forgetting things. Ferdie jumps to conclusions, and Mr. Breezy provides too much information. Students are challenged to listen carefully and to try to outthink the characters.

READING THE THINKING STORIES

The Thinking Stories are designed to be read to students. They appear in the Teacher's Guide and in separate Thinking Story books in Levels 1–3. At Levels 4–6 the Thinking Stories appear in three to five or more parts in the student book so that students have an option to read them individually or in groups, depending upon their reading abilities. As the stories unfold, students are asked questions that prompt them to think ahead of the characters—to spot what is wrong with what a character has done or said, to anticipate what is going to happen as a result, or to think of other possibilities that the character hasn't considered.

Following each story is a selection of short problems. Like the story questions, these problems generally require more thinking than computation and have a mixture of difficulty levels.

PACING

Most teachers spend about 15 minutes reading a Thinking Story and discussing the corresponding questions. In many lessons teachers may spend about five minutes on three or four of the questions that follow the story.

The Introduction to the Storybook for Levels 1–3 contains a briefing on the characters and useful hints on presenting stories and problems.

Along with problem solving and critical thinking, basic facts and computational skills help provide a solid foundation for further work in mathematics and are given serious treatment in *Math Explorations and Applications*.

TEACHING BASIC FACTS

In *Math Explorations and Applications*, special lesson sequences leading to mastery and automatic recall of the basic addition and subtraction facts are included in first and second grade, while the basic multiplication facts are covered in second and third grade. Basic fact review is continued throughout the program in a variety of traditional and non-traditional contexts. Division facts are developed along with the multiplication facts so that understanding and proficiency are achieved. For example, a student who knows that multiplication and division "undo" each other, and who also knows that 8 x 7 = 56, is but one step removed from recalling that 56 ÷ 7 = 8 and 56 ÷ 8 = 7.

There are three sequential but overlapping strategies for helping children achieve mastery of the basic facts: understanding, practice, and memorization. Each are important and each requires its own strategies and carefully developed lessons.

Understanding is developed through the intelligent use of manipulatives and other developmental activities in carefully sequenced lessons. In *Math Explorations and Applications*, a variety of manipulatives is used to represent number so that children do not become dependent on any single one. That makes it easier to move from concrete activities to those that are more abstract. Because it is important to build mathematical concepts on what children already know, fingers are one of the manipulatives used in first grade. These lessons, which illustrate how we take children from the concrete (using fingers inefficiently) towards the abstract (using fingers so efficiently that they are no longer needed) are described on page T26 of this Teacher's Guide. Understanding is also achieved by introducing addition and subtraction, and later, multiplication and division, together. By doing so, we help children see the relationships between these operations, that, for example, addition and subtraction "undo" each other.

Practice is provided through the use of carefully designed Games, Mental Math exercises, Practice Worksheets, and the *Math Explorations and Applications* CD-ROM. The unusually rich assortment of Games included in most lessons is intended as the main source of skill practice. Not only do these games provide appropriate skill practice, many of them also provide opportunities for children to solve interesting problems by developing winning strategies. Mental Math exercises are also included in every lesson to maintain recall of basic facts and for all computation, so students are not dependent upon paper and pencil or calculator when mental shortcuts are more appropriate. Practice Worksheets and the CD-ROM are provided to supplement the Games and Mental Math exercises.

Memorization of basic facts is essential for further work in mathematics. Practice alone is not an efficient or reliable method for achieving this goal. Specific procedures that involve memorization are needed and are used in *Math Explorations and Applications*. The most important procedures are the speed tests and Flash Card drills. Timed exercises are important because by decreasing the time available to think about an answer, memorization is encouraged. Another technique that we use can be found in lessons 130–135 of first grade for addition and lessons 54–62 of third grade for multiplication. In these lessons, children monitor their progress by crossing off the facts they have already memorized on an addition or multiplication table. The technique has two advantages. First, children know when they have memorized all of the facts. That is, they see an endpoint, and they can monitor their progress as they move towards that goal. Second, children do not see the facts as unrelated bits of information, but rather as a set of related facts. They learn that if they understand those relations, memorization is easier.

PLACE VALUE

Research shows that many of the difficulties students have with mathematics can be traced to a faulty understanding of place value, a problem that often develops in the early grades. *Math Explorations and Applications* takes great care to develop the concept of place value carefully and systematically.

> "*Whenever possible, addition and subtraction should be taught at about the same time so that learners can contrast the two and so that problems can be presented that are not all solved by using the same operation.*"
>
> —Stephen S. Willoughby
> *Mathematics Education for a Changing World*

> "*Often, when addition and subtraction are taught at about the same time, teachers complain that children are confused. It is true that children find it much easier to learn only one algorithm at a time, then practice that algorithm for a long time, then solve "problems" using only that algorithm, and then go on to something else. The difficulty with such a procedure is that it pretty much eliminates the need for the learner to think. When the time comes to decide which operation is appropriate, the pupil is unlikely to have given enough thought to what the operations mean to be able to make intelligent decisions.*"
>
> —Stephen S. Willoughby
> *Mathematics Education for a Changing World*

EXPANDED NOTATION

To help children visualize place value, in first grade we use a system of expanded notation and counting in which the numbers greater than ten are written with a larger tens digit and a smaller units digit. Thus, for example, the numbers are written 20, 21, 22, 23, and read 2 tens, 2 tens and 1, 2 tens and 2, 2 tens and 3, and so on. Children switch to conventional counting and notation before the end of first grade.

MANIPULATIVES

Extensive use of base-10 manipulative materials also helps children visualize place value and helps develop an understanding of why the basic multidigit algorithms work. We begin with concrete base-10 manipulatives such as craft sticks grouped with rubber bands in bunches of ten, ten bunches of ten, and so on. Later, as we move children away from the concrete and towards the abstract, we substitute play money (one, ten, and hundred dollar bills) for the craft sticks. The notion that one ten dollar bill is equivalent to ten one dollar bills is more abstract than the notion that one bunch of ten sticks is equivalent to ten single sticks.

Recent research indicates that failure to master basic facts is the most important indicator for predicting failure in mathematics. Research also shows that many of the difficulties students have with mathematics can be traced to a faulty understanding of place value. The heavy emphasis on understanding place value in the early grades pays big dividends later as the development of the multidigit multiplication and division algorithms and later work in algebra and beyond depend on that understanding. *Math Explorations and Applications* prepares students for meaningful mathematics beyond the K-6 experience.

FINGER SETS

Allowing students to use their fingers as manipulatives to count or to add and subtract is often frowned upon. Some experts fear that students will become too dependent on this method. However, the fact remains that most young students use their fingers in mathematics whether or not they are allowed to do so.

In *Math Explorations and Applications*, teachers teach students to use their fingers in a systematic way. Students learn to form "standard" finger sets, with each set representing a specific number. In this way, students will be able to recognize, for example, seven or eight fingers visually and kinesthetically without having to count individual fingers. Eventually, students will be able to abandon the use of their fingers and depend more and more upon mental operations.

The illustration below demonstrates the standard way of forming finger sets. Either hand may be used for the numbers 0 through 5. The number 1 is represented by the thumb.

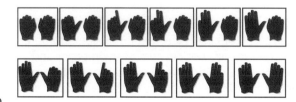

Students may enjoy learning a counting song, such as "This Old Man," "Five Little Ducks," "Over in the Meadow," or "Roll Over," as they learn to count with finger sets. Music addresses yet another intelligence and often helps young students remember what they might otherwise easily forget.

Eventually students will be able to form the finger set for each number the teacher requests and recognize each finger set by sight. This will reduce or eliminate the need to count fingers.

Children use finger sets as one of several ways to represent numbers. In addition to finger sets, students learn to use counters, number lines, number strips, tally marks, play money, and the numerals themselves. Thus they do not become overly dependent on any one method of representing numbers.

Moving from Concrete to Mental Math

As students move from concrete to Mental Math, the teacher should phase out the use of finger sets. Students should have abandoned the use of finger sets by the end of Level 1. Following are the stages in this process:

1. Students learn to form the standard finger sets for 0 through 10.

2. Students learn to recognize the standard finger sets by sight and feel without counting fingers.

3. Students learn to add or subtract with finger sets. For example, if they are adding 4 + 3, they show the finger set for 4 and count fingers to add 3. However, they recognize the answer, 7, without counting fingers.

4. Students learn to add or subtract with finger sets out of sight. They can feel the finger sets, but they cannot see them.

5. Students learn "statue" arithmetic. At this stage students only imagine themselves raising or lowering their fingers to add or subtract. For example, for 6 – 2, they show the finger set for 6, then imagine two fingers being lowered. They imagine the remaining finger set and thus get the answer, 4.

6. Students no longer need to use finger sets. They have moved from concrete to Mental Math.

Establishing a firm foundation of math skills and mathematical thinking at K–3 will enable students to enjoy and succeed in mathematics throughout their lives.

> *"If we teach children to use their fingers intelligently in the early grades, they should be more able to get along without using them later."*
>
> —Stephen S. Willoughby
> *Mathematics Education for a Changing World*

Table of Contents

▣ Calculator   **T27**

Table of Contents

UNIT 2
Addition and Subtraction

Table of Contents

UNIT 3

Measurement and Geometry

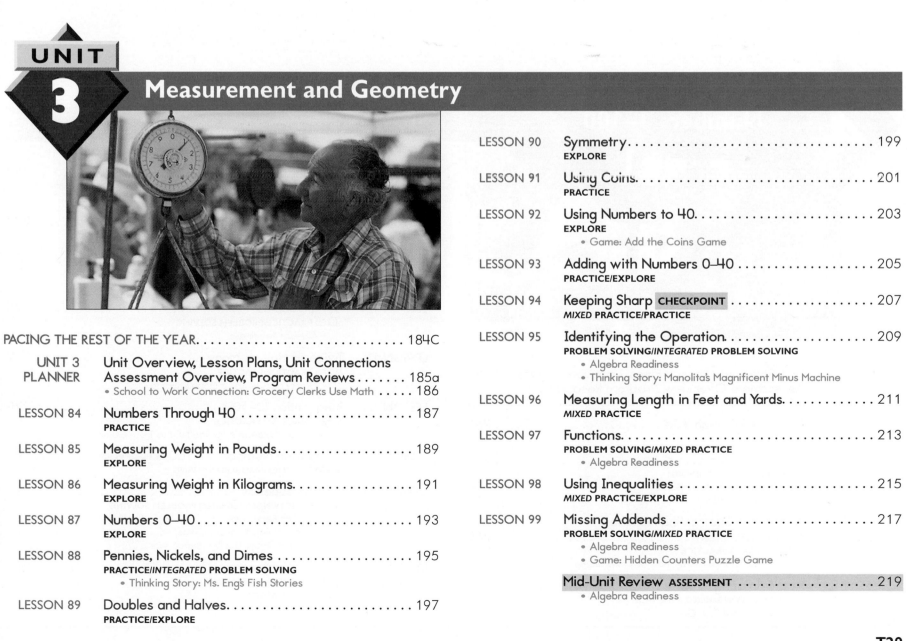

Table of Contents

UNIT 4 — Numbers 1–100

Table of Contents

HOW TO PACE THE PROGRAM

The lessons in this book are designed to be taught at a lively pace. Students should move quickly from activity to activity. In this way, they will remain alert and interested in what they are learning.

The lively pace is also important because there is much for students to learn at this grade level. Yet, 45 minutes a day is about all that most teachers can devote to mathematics. Therefore, it's important to get as much from those minutes as possible. Here are some tips to help you make the most of your time:

Tips for Making the Most of Your Time

- **Prepare items you'll need for a lesson ahead of time.** See the Lesson Planner sections titled Materials and Program Resources for a complete listing of the items you'll need. The Looking Ahead feature under the Wrap-Up alerts you to any advance preparation needed for an upcoming lesson.
- **Read the lesson plan in advance.** This will save you time and make the lesson run more smoothly.
- **Keep introductions and explanations brief.** You will lose your students' attention if you try to say too much.

HOW TO EXTEND YOUR LESSONS

You might need to spend an extra day teaching some lessons. Lessons that might take an extra day are noted in the individual Lesson Planner and in the Unit Overview Planning Chart—but only you can be the judge. When you decide to let a lesson run two days, try dividing it as follows:

Day 1

- Do all suggested activities, but not the Student Edition pages.
- Use extra time to review the skills students will need for the lesson.
- Modify the Reteaching Strategy/Master and Practice Master suggestions for use with the entire class.
- Don't greatly lengthen the demonstration period (K–3).

Day 2

- Review the Mental Math exercises from the preceding day.
- Provide additional teaching and practice on related skills.
- Devote time to a related Cube Game or Game Mat.
- Allow plenty of time for students to do the Student Edition activities.

WHEN YOU HAVE MORE THAN 45 MINUTES FOR MATH

Tips for Making the Best Use of Extra Time

- Lengthen game periods by five minutes each (more when new games are introduced).
- Repeat whole-group activities when you feel that students will remain interested.
- Lengthen Mental Math exercises by up to five minutes each.
- Lengthen demonstrations and activities by two or three minutes at most.
- Use the Reteaching, Practice, and Enrichment Masters. You might also want to use the various Cross-Curricular Connections strategies provided throughout the Teacher's Guide.

WHEN YOU HAVE FEWER THAN 45 MINUTES FOR MATH

Tips for Making the Best Use of Less Time

- Don't eliminate the games or the Thinking Stories. These help develop mathematical intelligence.
- Do the Thinking Story activities outside the regular mathematics period. There might be time the first thing in the morning, right after lunch, or when you have a read-aloud period.
- Conduct games outside the regular mathematics period—every Friday, perhaps— especially if you have another adult or older student to assist you. If a game provides practice that will help students do the Student Edition exercise, play the game during the lesson.
- Conduct Mental Math on basic facts outside the regular mathematics period.
- Reduce a few lesson components by a minute or two.
- Introduce the Problem of the Day at the start of school each morning instead of at the start of the regular mathematics period.

Numbers 1–10

NUMBER SENSE

OVERVIEW

In this unit students count and write numbers 1 through 10, exploring these numbers in many different ways, including counting objects, completing patterns, and using number lines. Students also record data and read and make graphs. In addition, they are introduced to estimating and measuring length. Students begin to work on basic facts in addition and subtraction and approach these operations in a variety of ways.

Integrated Topics in This Unit Include:

- ◆ classifying objects
- ◆ completing patterns
- ◆ counting and writing numbers through 10
- ◆ counting parts of geometric figures
- ◆ using number lines
- ◆ finding the number before and after
- ◆ using tally marks
- ◆ making graphs
- ◆ reading picture graphs
- ◆ recording and collecting data
- ◆ measuring with Number Strips
- ◆ estimating and comparing lengths
- ◆ adding and subtracting basic facts up to 10

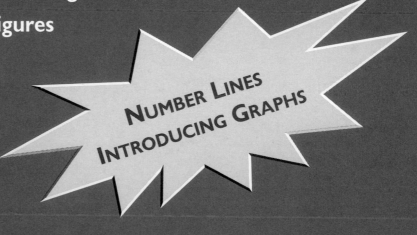

NUMBER LINES
INTRODUCING GRAPHS

> **"**_Children learn computation to solve problems; they learn to measure because measurement helps them answer questions about how much, how big, how long, and so on; and they learn to collect and organize data because doing so permits them to answer other questions. By applying mathematics, they learn to appreciate the power of mathematics._ **"**
>
> —*NCTM Curriculum and Evaluation Standards for School Mathematics*

GAMES

Motivating Mixed Practice

Games provide **basic math skills** practice in cooperative groups and develop **mathematical reasoning.**

THINKING STORY

Integrated Problem Solving

Thinking Stories provide opportunities for students to work in **cooperative groups** and develop **logical reasoning** while they integrate **reading skills** with mathematics.

Story Summaries In "How Many Piglets?" Portia and Ferdie use different methods for counting the number of piglets their Grandpa's pig has but arrive at a different answer each time.

In "Willy in the Water" Willy is never satisfied with how things are.

"Mr. Muddle's Party" focuses on using number sense to draw conclusions.

"'It's Not So Easy,' Said Mr. Breezy" emphasizes the importance of understanding what information is necessary to solve a problem.

"Mr. Muddle Goes Shopping" examines how basic addition and subtraction facts are useful when performing daily tasks.

PROJECT

Making Connections

The Unit Project makes real-world connections. Students work in **cooperative groups** to problem-solve and to communicate their findings.

The Unit Wrap-Up project asks students to make counting charts in other languages. This project can be started after Lesson 16.

NUMBERS 1–10
LESSON PLANS

LESSON	PACING	PRIMARY OBJECTIVES	FEATURE	RESOURCES	NCTM STANDARDS
1 Classifying 3–4	1 day	to provide practice classifying		Practice Master 1 Enrichment Master 1	2, 4
2 Completing Patterns 5–6	1 day	to provide opportunities to identify and complete patterns		Practice Master 2 Enrichment Master 2	3, 13
3 Identifying Patterns 7–8	1 day	to provide practice in identifying and completing more complicated patterns		Reteaching Master Practice Master 3 Enrichment Master 3	3, 13
4 Counting 9–10	1 day	to practice counting from 1–10	Thinking Story	Practice Master 4 Enrichment Master 4	6
5 Counting Objects 11–12	1 day	to provide practice for illustrating the use of orderly arrangement when counting		Reteaching Master Practice Master 5 Enrichment Master 5	1, 2, 3, 4, 6
6 Forming Finger Sets 13–14	1 day	✓ to measure individual progress toward counting objects	Game	Practice Master 6 Enrichment Master 6 Assessment Master	1, 2, 3, 4, 6
7 Tracing Numbers 15–16	1 day	to provide practice for tracing and copying the numbers 0–10		Practice Master 7 Enrichment Master 7	6
8 Reading Numbers 17–18	1 day	to provide practice for recognizing the numbers 0–4		Practice Master 8 Enrichment Master 8	1, 2, 3, 4, 6
9 Reading Numbers 19–20	1 day	to provide practice in tracing and writing numbers 0–10	Game	Reteaching Master Practice Master 9 Enrichment Master 9	6
10 Writing Numbers 21–22	1 day	to teach students to relate number names, numbers, and sets		Practice Master 10 Enrichment Master 10	6
11 Using Finger Sets 23–24	1 day	✓ to measure individual progress toward forming and recognizing finger sets for the numbers 1–10	Game	Practice Master 11 Enrichment Master 11 Assessment Master	1, 2, 3, 4, 6, 9
12 Number Lines 25–26	1 day	to teach students to move a given number of places on a 0–10 number line	Thinking Story	Reteaching Master Practice Master 12 Enrichment Master 12	2, 4, 6
13 What Comes Next? 27–28	1 day	to teach students to identify which number follows another number in the 0–10 range	Game	Practice Master 13 Enrichment Master 13	4, 6
14 Using Number Lines 29–30	1 day	✓ to assess students' ability to recognize numbers from 0–10	Game	Practice Master 14 Enrichment Master 14 Assessment Master	4, 6
15 Before and After 31–34	2 days	✓ to assess students' ability to insert the correct number in a sequence from 0–10	Game	Reteaching Master Practice Master 15 Enrichment Master 15 Assessment Master	4, 6, 7
16 Missing Numbers 35–36	1 day	✓ to assess students' ability to write recognizable numbers from 0–10		Practice Master 16 Enrichment Master 16 Assessment Master	6
17 Tally Marks 37–38	1 day	to introduce the use of tally marks for keeping an accurate count of 1–10 items		Practice Master 17 Enrichment Master 17	6, 11
18 Making Graphs 39–40	1 day	to have students make their own bar graphs with manipulatives		Practice Master 18 Enrichment Master 18	11
19 Reading Picture Graphs 41–42	1 day	to supply opportunities to collect data and report it using picture graphs		Practice Master 19 Enrichment Master 19	11
20 Recording Data 43–44	1 day	to teach students how to use tally marks to keep and report data		Practice Master 20 Enrichment Master 20	11
21 Collecting Data 45–46	1 day	to teach students to see how tally marks, numbers, and bar graphs are related		Reteaching Master Practice Master 21 Enrichment Master 21	11
Mid-Unit Review 47–48	1 day	to review numbers 1–10		Assessment Master	

	LESSON	PACING	PRIMARY OBJECTIVES	FEATURE	RESOURCES	NCTM STANDARDS
22	Number Strips 49–50	1 day	to introduce the Number Strip as a tool for representing length in units from 1 through 10	Game	Practice Master 22 Enrichment Master 22	4, 5, 10
23	Estimating Length 51–52	1 day	✓ to assess students' participation in Thinking Story Book activities	Thinking Story Game	Practice Master 23 Enrichment Master 23 Assessment Master	1, 2, 3, 4, 5, 10
24	Comparing Length 53–54	1 day	to teach students to add numbers that sum to 10 using finger sets	Game	Practice Master 24 Enrichment Master 24	7, 10
25	Measuring Length 55–56	1 day	to teach students to solve concrete addition problems in which the answers must be figured out rather than observed directly		Practice Master 25 Enrichment Master 25	1, 2, 3, 4, 7, 10
26	Addition with Hidden Counters 57–58	1 day	to provide practice for solving concrete addition problems in which a hidden addend is added to a visible one	Game	Practice Master 26 Enrichment Master 26	1, 2, 3, 4, 7
27	Adding On 59–60	1 day	✓ to assess students' ability to solve concrete addition problems with hidden addends		Reteaching Master Practice Master 27 Enrichment Master 27 Assessment Master	3, 7, 13
28	The Order Property of Addition 61–62	1 day	to introduce the commutative law of addition		Practice Master 28 Enrichment Master 28	7
29	Identifying Missing Addends 63–64	1 day	to teach students to solve simple subtraction problems with a minuend of 10 or less by using finger sets	Thinking Story Game	Practice Master 29 Enrichment Master 29	1, 2, 3, 4, 7
30	Subtraction with Hidden Counters 65–66	1 day	to teach students to solve concrete subtraction problems in which the answers must be figured out rather than observed directly		Practice Master 30 Enrichment Master 30	3, 7
31	Addition and Subtraction— Hidden Counters 67–68	1 day	✓ to assess students' ability to subtract 0, 1, 2, or 3 from numbers less than 10 in concrete subtraction problems where the remainder is hidden	Game	Reteaching Master Practice Master 31 Enrichment Master 31 Assessment Master	3, 7
32	Adding On— Counting Back 69–70	1 day	to teach students to use finger sets without looking at their fingers to solve simple addition problems		Practice Master 32 Enrichment Master 32	7, 10, 13
33	Addition and Subtraction 71–72	1 day	to teach students to use finger sets without looking at their fingers to solve simple subtraction problems	Game	Practice Master 33 Enrichment Master 33	1, 2, 3, 4, 7
34	Addition and Subtraction— Horizontal 73–74	1 day	to teach students to read and solve addition and subtraction problems in horizontal form		Practice Master 34 Enrichment Master 34	7, 10
35	Addition and Subtraction— Vertical 75–76	1 day	to teach students to read and solve addition and subtraction problems in vertical form	Thinking Story	Reteaching Master Practice Master 35 Enrichment Master 35	1, 2, 3, 4, 7, 8
36	Practicing Addition and Subtraction 77–78	1 day	to provide practice with addition and subtraction of single digit numbers		Practice Master 36 Enrichment Master 36	1, 2, 3, 4, 7, 8
37	Adding and Subtracting on a Number Line 79–80	1 day	✓ to assess student performance in solving addition and subtraction problems on a number line	Game	Practice Master 37 Enrichment Master 37 Assessment Master	7, 8
38	Adding and Subtracting with Number Strips 81–82	1 day	to introduce Number Strips as a means of representing simple addition and subtraction problems		Reteaching Master Practice Master 38 Enrichment Master 38	4, 7, 10
39	Unit 1 Review 83–86		to review numbers 1–10		Practice Master 39 Enrichment Master 39	
40	Unit 1 Test 87–90		to review numbers 1–10		Practice Master 40 Enrichment Master 40 Assessment Master	
41	Extending the Unit 91–92		to review numbers 1–10		Practice Master 41 Enrichment Master 41	
	Unit 1 Wrap-Up 92a–92b		to review numbers 1–10	Project		

UNIT CONNECTIONS

INTERVENTION STRATEGIES

In this Teacher's Guide there will be specific strategies suggested for students with individual needs—ESL, Gifted and Talented, Special Needs, Learning Styles, and At Risk. These strategies will be given at the point of use. Here are the icons to look for and the types of strategies that will accompany them:

English as a Second Language
These strategies, designed for students who do not fluently speak the English language, will suggest meaningful ways to present the lesson concepts and vocabulary.

Gifted and Talented
Strategies to enrich and extend the lesson will offer further challenges to students who have easily mastered the concepts already presented.

Special Needs
Students who are physically challenged or who have learning disabilities may require alternative ways to complete activities, record answers, use manipulatives, and so on. The strategies labeled with this icon will offer appropriate methods of teaching lesson concepts to these students.

Learning Styles
Each student has his or her individual approach to learning. The strategies labeled with this icon suggest ways to present lesson concepts so that various learning modalities—such as tactile/kinesthetic, visual, and auditory—can be addressed.

At Risk
These strategies highlight the relevancy of the skills presented, making the connection between school and real life. They are directed toward students who appear to be at risk of dropping out of school before graduation.

TECHNOLOGY CONNECTIONS

The following materials, designed to reinforce and extend lesson concepts, will be referred to throughout this Teacher's Guide. It might be helpful to order this software, or check it out of the school media center or local community library.

 Look for this **Technology Connection** *icon.*

- *Coin Critters,* from Nordic Software, Mac, IBM, for grades K–6 (software)

- *The Graph Club of Fizz and Martina,* from Tom Snyder Productions, Inc., Mac, for grades K–4 (software)

- *Graphers,* from Sunburst Communications, Mac, IBM, for grades K–4 (software)

- *Hop to It!* from Sunburst Communications, Mac, Apple, for grades K–3 (software)

- *James Discovers Math,* from Broderbund Software, Inc., Mac, IBM, for grades Pre-K–2 (software)

- *Let's Start Learning,* from the Learning Company, Mac, IBM, for grades Pre-K–1 (software)

- *Math Blaster Jr.,* from Davidson, Mac, IBM for grades Pre-K–1 (software)

- *Number Connections,* from Sunburst Communications, Mac, for grades K–3 (software)

CROSS-CURRICULAR CONNECTIONS

This Teacher's Guide offers specific suggestions on ways to connect the math concept presented in this unit with other subjects students are studying. Students can connect math concepts with topics they already know about and can find examples of math in other subjects and in real-world situations. These strategies will be given at the point of use.

Look for these icons:

 Geography

 Social Studies

 Science

 Art

Language Arts

 Health

 Music

 Math

 Physical Education

 Careers

LITERATURE CONNECTIONS

These books will be presented throughout the Teacher's Guide at the point where they could be used to introduce, reinforce, or extend specific lesson concepts. You may want to locate these books in your school or your local community library.

 Look for this **Literature Connection** *icon.*

- ♦ *Counting Sheep* by John Archambault, H. Holt, 1989
- ♦ *An Old-Fashioned 1, 2, 3 Book* by Elizabeth Allen Ashton, Viking, 1991
- ♦ *The Snow Parade* by Barbara Brenner, Crown Publishers, 1984
- ♦ *1, 2, 3, to the Zoo* by Eric Carle, Philomel Books, 1996
- ♦ *The King's Commissioners* by Aileen Friedman, Scholastic, 1994
- ♦ *Numbers* by Henry Pluckrose, Childrens Press, 1995
- ♦ *Is the Blue Whale the Biggest Thing There Is?* by Robert E. Wells, Albert Whitman & Company, 1993
- ♦ *Fish Eyes, A Book You Can Count On* by Lois Ehlert, Harcourt Brace Jovanovich, 1990
- ♦ *Ocean Parade: A Counting Book* by Patricia MacCarthy, Dial Books for Young Readers, 1990
- ♦ *Ten Little Animals* by Laura Jane Coats, Macmillan, 1990
- ♦ *Mouse Count* by Ellen S. Walsh, Harcourt Brace Jovanovich, 1991
- ♦ *A More or Less Fish Story* by Joanne and David Wylie, Childrens Press, 1984
- ♦ *Ready, Set, Hop* by Stuart J. Murphy, HarperCollins, 1996
- ♦ *Number One, Number Fun* by Kay Chorao, Holiday House, 1995

ASSESSMENT OPPORTUNITIES AT-A-GLANCE

LESSON	PORTFOLIO	PERFORMANCE	FORMAL	SELF	INFORMAL	MIXED PRACTICE	MULTIPLE CHOICE	MASTERY CHECKPOINTS	ANALYZING ANSWERS
1					✓				
2					✓				
3		✓							
4		✓				✓			
5					✓				
6			✓					✓	
7					✓				
8		✓							
9						✓			✓
10					✓				
11			✓					✓	
12		✓							
13					✓				
14			✓			✓		✓	
15			✓					✓	
16			✓					✓	
17				✓					
18	✓					✓			
19	✓								
20		✓							
21					✓				
Mid-Unit Review	✓	✓	✓						
22				✓		✓			
23		✓						✓	
24		✓							
25		✓							
26				✓					
27		✓				✓		✓	
28									✓
29		✓							
30									✓
31		✓						✓	
32		✓				✓			
33					✓				
34					✓				
35				✓					
36					✓				
37		✓				✓		✓	
38					✓				
Unit Review	✓	✓	✓						
Unit Test			✓				✓		
41					✓	✓			

ASSESSMENT OPTIONS

PORTFOLIO ASSESSMENT

Throughout this Teacher's Guide are suggested activities in which students draw pictures, make graphs, write about mathematics, and so on. Keep students' work to assess growth of understanding as the year progresses.

Lessons 18, 19, Mid-Unit Review, and Unit Review

PERFORMANCE ASSESSMENT

Performance assessment items focus on evaluating how students think and work as they solve problems. Opportunities for performance assessment can be found throughout the unit. Rubrics and guides for grading can be found in the front of the Assessment Blackline Masters.

Lessons 3, 4, 8, 12, 20, Mid-Unit Review, 24, 25, 29, 32, and Unit Review

FORMAL ASSESSMENT

A Mid-Unit Review and Unit Test help assess students' understanding of concepts, skills, and problem solving. The *Math Explorations and Applications* CD-ROM Test Generator can create additional unit tests at three ability levels. Also, Mastery Checkpoints are provided periodically throughout the unit.

Lessons 6, 11, 14, 15, 16, Mid-Unit Review, 23, 27, 31, 37, Unit Review, and Unit Test

SELF ASSESSMENT

Throughout the program students are given the opportunity to check their own math skills.

Lessons 17, 22, 26, and 35

INFORMAL ASSESSMENT

A variety of assessment suggestions is provided, including interviews, oral questions or presentations, debates, and so on. Also, each lesson includes Assessment Criteria—a list of questions about each student's progress, understanding, and participation.

Lessons 1, 2, 5, 7, 10, 13, 21, 33, 34, 36, 38, and 41

MIXED PRACTICE

Mixed Practices, covering material presented thus far in the year, are provided in the unit for use as either assessment or practice.

Lessons 4, 9, 14, 18, 22, 27, 32, 37, 41

MULTIPLE-CHOICE TESTS (STANDARDIZED FORMAT)

Each unit provides a unit test in standardized format, presenting students with an opportunity to practice taking a test in this format.

MASTERY CHECKPOINTS

Mastery Checkpoints are provided throughout the unit to assess student proficiency in specific skills. Checkpoints reference appropriate Assessment Blackline Masters and other assessment options. Results of these evaluations can be recorded on the Mastery Checkpoint Chart.

Lessons 6, 11, 14, 15, 16, 23, 27, 31, and 37

ANALYZING ANSWERS

Analyzing Answers items suggest possible sources of student error and offer teaching strategies for addressing difficulties.

Lessons 9, 28, and 30

Look for these icons:

> **"** *Assessment is the process of gathering evidence about a student's knowledge of, ability to use, and disposition toward, mathematics and of making inferences from that evidence for a variety of purposes.* **"**
>
> —*NCTM Assessment Standards*

MASTERY CHECKPOINTS

WHAT TO EXPECT FROM STUDENTS AS THEY COMPLETE THIS UNIT

❶ COUNTING OBJECTS—LESSON 6

Check to see if students can count up to ten objects by asking them to count out a given number of objects. Then show a set of objects and ask the student how many there are or you might wish to use page 2 of the Assessment Blackline Masters. Record results on the Mastery Checkpoint Chart. For more details see page 13c of this Teacher's Guide.

❷ FINGER SETS (0–10)—LESSON 11

Most students should now be able to recognize finger sets 0–10 without counting. Proficiency can be assessed by observing students during the demonstration or by assigning page 3 of the Assessment Blackline Masters. Results can be recorded on the Mastery Checkpoint Chart.

❸ NUMBER RECOGNITION—LESSON 14

At about this time you may want to formally assess students' ability to recognize numbers from 0–10. Proficiency can be demonstrated by correctly answering 80% of the questions on page 4 of the Assessment Blackline Masters. Results can be recorded on the Mastery Checkpoint Chart.

❹ NUMERICAL SEQUENCE (0–10)— LESSON 15

At about this time you may want to formally assess students' ability to insert the correct number in a sequence from 0–10. You can use pages 31 and 34 or page 5 of the Assessment Blackline Masters to assess this skill. Results can be recorded on the Mastery Checkpoint Chart.

❺ WRITING NUMBERS (0–10)—LESSON 16

At about this time you may want to formally assess students' ability to write numbers from 0–10. Proficiency can be assessed by observing students as they do the writing practice activity or by using page 6 of the Assessment Blackline Masters.

❻ THINKING STORY BOOK PARTICIPATION—LESSON 23

Proficiency for Thinking Story participation can be assessed by observing students during the Thinking Story activities or by using pages 9–10 of the Assessment Blackline Masters. Results can be recorded on the Mastery Checkpoint Chart.

❼ ADDITION WITH HIDDEN COUNTERS— LESSON 27

You may want to formally assess students' ability to solve concrete addition problems with hidden addends (adding 0, 1, 2, or 3 with sums to 10). Proficiency can be assessed by observing students' responses during the demonstration exercise or with page 11 in the Assessment Blackline Masters.

❽ SUBTRACTION WITH HIDDEN COUNTERS—LESSON 31

At about this time you may want to formally assess students' ability to solve concrete subtraction problems in which the remainders are hidden. Use page 67 or pages 12–13 of the Assessment Blackline Masters to assess proficiency.

❾ ADDITION AND SUBTRACTION ON THE NUMBER LINE—LESSON 37

By this time most students should be able to add and subtract 0–3 on a 0–10 number line. To assess proficiency use the pages in this lesson or page 14 of the Assessment Blackline Masters. Results may be recorded on the Mastery Checkpoint Chart.

PROGRAM RESOURCES

THESE ADDITIONAL COMPONENTS OF *MATH EXPLORATIONS AND APPLICATIONS* CAN BE PURCHASED SEPARATELY FROM SRA/McGRAW-HILL.

LESSON	BASIC MANIPULATIVE KIT	GAME MAT PACKAGE	TEACHER KIT	PRIMARY MANIPULATIVE KIT	OVERHEAD MANIPULATIVE KIT	MATH EXPLORATIONS AND APPLICATIONS CD-ROM	LITERATURE LIBRARY
1				attribute blocks	attribute blocks	Lesson 1	
2				pattern blocks	pattern blocks	Lesson 2	
3				pattern blocks	pattern blocks	Lesson 3	
4				counters	counters	Lesson 4	
5						Lesson 5	
6				counters	counters	Lesson 6	
7				counters	counters	Lesson 7	
8				counters	counters	Lesson 8	*Animal Orchestra*
9	Number Cubes			counters	counters	Lesson 9	
10						Lesson 10	
11	Number Cubes					Lesson 11	
12	Number Cubes	play money				Lesson 12	
13	Number Cubes			counters number line	counters	Lesson 13	
14	Number Cubes					Lesson 14	
15	Number Cubes					Lesson 15	*The Three Billy Goats Gruff*
16	Number Cubes					Lesson 16	
17						Lesson 17	
18	Number Cubes		graphing mat	counters	counters	Lesson 18	
19	Number Cubes					Lesson 19	
20		play money				Lesson 20	
21	Number Cubes					Lesson 21	
Mid-Unit Review			stopwatch				*The Apple Thief*
22	Number Cubes Number Strips			interlocking cubes		Lesson 22	
23	Number Strips					Lesson 23	
24	Number Strips					Lesson 24	
25	Number Strips			counters	counters	Lesson 25	
26	Number Cubes			counters	counters	Lesson 26	
27	Number Cubes					Lesson 27	
28				interlocking cubes		Lesson 28	
29				counters	counters	Lesson 29	
30	Number Cubes			counters	counters	Lesson 30	
31	Number Cubes			counters	counters	Lesson 31	
32						Lesson 32	
33	Number Cubes			counters	counters	Lesson 33	
34	Number Cubes			interlocking cubes		Lesson 34	
35				counters	counters	Lesson 35	
36	Number Cubes			counters	counters	Lesson 36	
37	Number Cubes	Duck Pond Game		number line		Lesson 37	
38	Number Strips					Lesson 38	
39	Number Cubes			counters number line	counters	Lesson 39	
40						Lesson 40	
41				counters		Lesson 41	
Unit Wrap-Up							*Marti and the Mango*

UNIT 1
Numbers 1–10

INTRODUCING THE UNIT

Using the Student Pages Begin your discussion of the opening unit photo by asking students if they can tell how a pattern is being formed in the picture. Then read aloud the paragraph on the student page that highlights a career in textiles. This helps make the connection between school and work and encourages students to explore how math is used in the real world.

**ACTIVITY** Have students cut out five red strips and five blue strips of paper. Ask them to lay the five red strips side by side. Then have them weave each blue strip over and under the five red strips. Challenge students to describe to a partner the pattern they have created.

FYI Explain to students that weaving was one of the first skills early people learned. From ancient China to Europe to South and North America, early humans figured out how to weave natural fibers like grass and reeds to create baskets. No one knows exactly when the weaving of cloth began, but there is evidence that by 2500 B.C. cloth was being woven in Central Europe, the Middle East, China, and Pakistan. Wall paintings in ancient Egypt show that these people had mastered weaving techniques as far back as 5000 B.C. Ancient people also learned to dye the fabrics they created in rich colors and to vary the patterns in the cloth by weaving different color strips of material in alternating bands. The invention of the loom made weaving easier and quicker. Hand looms were being used in Europe by the 1200s, and by 1795 steam-powered looms were producing finished cloth on a grand scale.

Stress to students that knowing math will help those who are interested in pursuing a career in weaving. Creating a pattern with colored threads is complicated whether it is done by hand or machine. One kind of loom created in France in 1801 used the same basic technology that would later be used in the first computers. Cards with holes punched in regular intervals reproduced the same pattern over and over again. Point out that most weaving patterns,

UNIT 1

Numbers 1–10

NUMBER SENSE

- **patterns**
- **counting**
- **writing numbers**
- **graphing**
- **number lines**

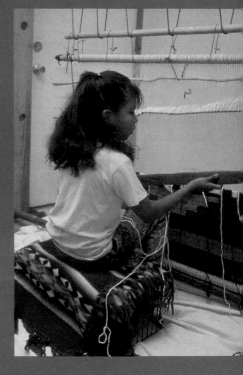

 Junior Thinklab™ 2

SRA's *Junior Thinklab™ 2** provides a series of creative and logical problem-solving opportunities for individual students. The problems are designed to appeal to different cognitive abilities.

▶ Use Activity Cards 1–5 with this unit to reinforce Ordering.

▶ Use Activity Cards 6–10 with this unit to reinforce Classifying.

▶ Use Activity Cards 11–15 with this unit to reinforce Perception and Spatial Relations.

▶ Use Activity Cards 16–20 with this unit to reinforce Reasoning and Deducing.

▶ Use Divergent Thinking Activity Sheets 1–5 with this unit to encourage creativity in art and in intellectual activity.

*available separately

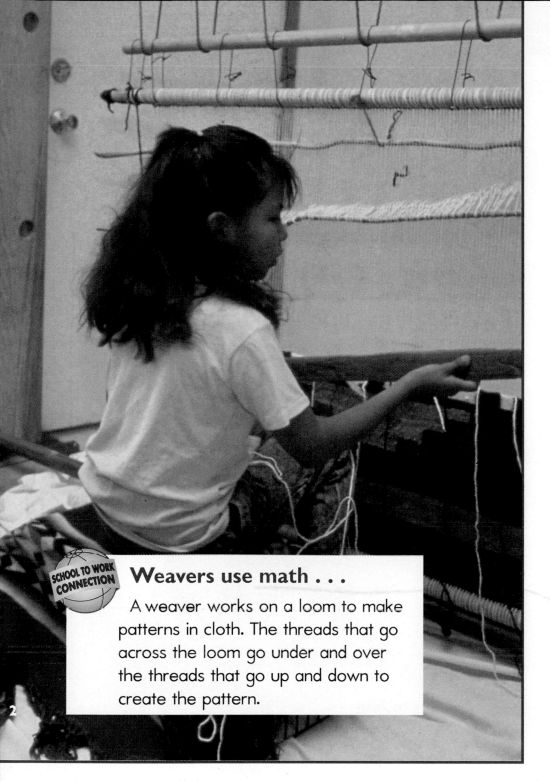

like the one in the activity, can be reduced to a set of numbers. This is true for work created by an artist working on a hand loom or by a textile designer creating patterns for everything from clothes to curtains to airplane seats. Explain that because weaving can be an art as well as a trade, art school is a good place to start such a career.

Home Connections You may want to send the letter on pages 36–37 in the Home Connections Blackline Masters to families the first week of school to introduce them to *Math Explorations and Applications*. Then use the letter on pages 38–39 of the Home Connections Blackline Masters the following week to introduce this unit.

Unit Project This would be a good time to assign the "Counting Charts" project on pages 92a–92b. Students can begin working on the project in cooperative groups in their free time as you work through the unit. The Unit Project is a good opportunity for students to apply the concepts of counting and writing numbers in real-world problem solving.

SCHOOL TO WORK CONNECTION

Weavers use math . . .

A weaver works on a loom to make patterns in cloth. The threads that go across the loom go under and over the threads that go up and down to create the pattern.

LESSON 1

Student Edition pages 3–4

Classifying

LESSON PLANNER

Objective

▶ to provide practice in classifying objects

Context of the Lesson This lesson introduces classifying to prepare students to recognize patterns, which are introduced in the next lesson.

MANIPULATIVES | **Program Resources**

attribute blocks*

clothing items (variety)

Practice Master 1

Enrichment Master 1

For extra practice: CD-ROM* Lesson 1

❶ Warm-Up

5 MINUTES

Problem of the Day Draw a triangle, a square, and a circle on the chalkboard. Ask which group each shape belongs to: shapes with sides; shapes with corners; shapes with curves. (triangle, square; triangle, square; circle)

Problem-Solving Strategies Ask students who have solved the Problem of the Day to share how they solved it and any strategies they used.

Display the following **attribute block*** shapes. Then have students explain how each two are alike and how they differ.

a. red square, red circle (same color but different shapes)

b. red triangle, blue triangle (same shape but different colors)

c. red square, blue rectangle (both have four sides but different shapes and different colors)

❷ Teach

Demonstrate Ask five students to come to the front of the room. Demonstrate how to classify them into different groups. For example, have boys stand on one side of the room and girls on the other. Then have students suggest another way they can regroup. Ask questions such as:

▶ Are students always in the same group? Why or why not?

▶ Do groups always have the same number of students? Why or why not?

3 Numbers 1–10

PRACTICE

LESSON 1

Name _____

Classifying

Listen to the story.

❶

❷

❸

 NOTE TO HOME
Students classify into groups.

Unit 1 Lesson 1 • **3**

 CULTURAL DIVERSITY With the class, make a list of students who can speak a language other than English. List their names and languages on the chalkboard. Then have students work in groups to list the information in a table, such as:

Students Who Can Speak Languages Other Than English
Spanish
Haitian
Vietnamese
Italian

RETEACHING

 Have students work in small groups with **attribute blocks.*** Give different groups different blocks. Then have students classify their blocks by instructing them as follows:

Classify your blocks into groups that have the same shape. How many groups do you have? What are they?

Classify your blocks into groups that have the same color. How many groups do you have? What are they?

Classify your blocks into groups that have the same number of sides. How many groups do you have?

*available separately

◆ LESSON 1 Classifying

Listen to the story.

④

⑤

⑥

4 · Numbers 1–10

NOTE TO HOME
Students classify into groups.

PRACTICE p. 1

LESSON
1 PRACTICE Name _____

Ring the one that is different.

Math Explorations and Applications Level 1 · 1

ENRICHMENT p. 1

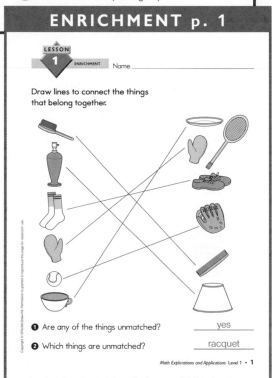

LESSON
1 ENRICHMENT Name _____

Draw lines to connect the things that belong together.

❶ Are any of the things unmatched?   yes

❷ Which things are unmatched?   racquet

Math Explorations and Applications Level 1 · 1

Hot or Cold Activity Provide a variety of clothing items such as a winter coat, swimsuit, mittens, shorts, earmuffs, sandals, winter scarf, and so on. Ask students to classify the items into two groups: clothing worn in hot weather and clothing worn in cold weather. Then encourage students to classify the clothing in a different way. For example, classify the clothing by the fasteners (buttons, zippers, or no fasteners) or classify the clothing according to where it is worn (on the feet, hands, head, or body).

Using the Student Pages Read aloud the descriptions below as students look at each picture in their books and do the exercises.

Page 3 stories:

1. These people are going to the library. Draw a ring around the one who is not a child. (teacher)
2. Marcia practiced writing letters and numbers. Draw a ring around the letters she drew. (E, A, B, C)
3. Some of these children are bringing their lunch to school. Draw a ring around those children who are not carrying a lunch box. (4th and 6th child)

Page 4 stories:

1. Draw a ring around those students who are not looking at books. (4th and 7th child)
2. This is Ms. Byers' desk. Draw a ring around those things she could not use for writing. (stapler, tape dispenser, paper clip, desk pad)
3. All the girls have long hair. Draw a ring around those girls with hair in ponytails. (1st, 3rd, 4th, and 5th)

❸ Wrap-Up ⏱ 5 MINUTES

In Closing Ask students to describe a way to classify their textbooks into at least two different groups. (Books might be classified by size, color, subject, and so on.)

ALTERNATIVE ASSESSMENT

Informal Assessment Use students' answers to the questions asked during the demonstration and on student pages 3–4 to informally assess their understanding of classifying.

Assessment Criteria

Did the student . . .

✓ provide sensible answers during the demonstration?

✓ correctly answer at least five exercises on pages 3–4?

LESSON 2

Student Edition pages 5–6

Completing Patterns

LESSON PLANNER

Objective

▶ to provide opportunities to identify and complete patterns

Context of the Lesson This lesson is the first of two lessons on patterns.

 MANIPULATIVES

Program Resources

crayons

Practice Master 2

pattern blocks* (optional)

Enrichment Master 2

index cards (optional)

For extra practice: CD-ROM* Lesson 2

① Warm-Up

 Problem of the Day Present the following problem to the class. How could you classify these foods into two groups? *milk, hot dog, pretzels, cheese* (possible answers: drinks and foods; dairy and nondairy; meat and meatless)

Problem-Solving Strategies Ask students who have solved the Problem of the Day to share how they solved it and any strategies they used.

MENTAL MATH Read aloud each set of items listed below. Have students explain what each set has in common.

a. dog, cat, hippopotamus (animals)

b. red, blue, green (colors)

c. baseball, soccer, basketball (sports)

d. telephone, computer, walkie-talkie (possible answers: can communicate with others; electronic machines)

LESSON 2

Name _____

Completing Patterns

Draw what comes next.

 Draw your own pattern in your Math Journal.

 NOTE TO HOME Students complete patterns.

Unit 1   Lesson 2 • **5**

 Art Connection Present each pair of students with ten blank white **index cards**. Have them color the cards and paste them on a sheet of paper so that they make some kind of pattern. Then have students share their pattern collages with the class.

Real-World Connection Take students on a walk around the school or the neighborhood. Have them look for patterns in their surroundings. For example, some students might notice patterns such as house, driveway, house, driveway; or each three-story building might have a pattern such as three windows, three

RETEACHING

Draw patterns with two elements, and have students identify them and tell what comes next. For example, draw red circle, blue circle, red circle, blue circle, red circle. (blue circle) After several similar patterns, divide students into pairs and give each pair a red and a blue **crayon**. Have partners create their own patterns, then exchange them with their classmates to guess what comes next in their classmates' patterns. Then have partners create patterns using **pattern blocks.***

---

*available separately

◆ **LESSON 2 Completing Patterns**

Draw the missing picture.

7

8

9

10

11

12

13

6 • Numbers 1–10

 **NOTE TO HOME**
Students complete patterns.

Copyright © SRA/McGraw-Hill

PRACTICE p. 2

LESSON 2 PRACTICE Name _____

Draw what comes next.

1

2

3

Draw the missing picture.

4

5 O X O X O X

6

7

2 • *Math Explorations and Applications Level 1*

ENRICHMENT p. 2

LESSON 2 ENRICHMENT Name _____

1 Make a color pattern. Use at least two colors. Answers will vary.

2 Make a shape pattern. Use at least two shapes.

3 Make a number pattern. Use at least two numbers.

2 • *Math Explorations and Applications Level 1*

❷ Teach

Demonstrate Without explaining why, have a girl come to the front of the room. Next have a boy stand next to her, then another girl, another boy, and finally a girl. Ask the class who should come next to continue the pattern. (a boy) Have the class add more students to the pattern. Repeat the activity with a different pattern such as alternately facing forward and backward.

Using the Student Pages Complete the first problem on each page with the class. Then have students use **crayons** to complete the rest of the patterns on their own. Have them share and compare answers when finished. Encourage students to explain how they arrived at their answers.

❸ Wrap-Up ⏱ 5 MINUTES

In Closing Ask students to come up to the chalkboard and show the pattern they drew in their Math Journals.

ALTERNATIVE ASSESSMENT **Informal Assessment** Use students' answers to the questions asked during the demonstration and on pages 5–6 to informally assess their ability to identify and complete patterns.

Assessment Criteria

Did the student . . .

✓ give sensible answers during the demonstration?

✓ correctly solve at least ten problems on pages 5–6?

Thinking is the basic skill in mathematics.

—Stephen S. Willoughby,
Teaching Mathematics: What Is Basic?

LESSON 3

Student Edition pages 7–8

Identifying Patterns

Name _____

Identifying Patterns

Draw what comes next.

LESSON PLANNER

Objective

▶ to provide practice in identifying and completing more complicated patterns

Context of the Lesson This lesson is the second of two lessons on patterns.

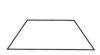 **MANIPULATIVES**

crayons

pattern blocks*
(optional)

Program Resources

Reteaching Master

Practice Master 3

Enrichment Master 3

For extra practice:
CD-ROM* Lesson 3

Copyright © SRA/McGraw-Hill

NOTE TO HOME
Students continue to practice completing patterns.

Unit 1   Lesson 3 • 7

❶ Warm-Up

Problem of the Day Draw the following figures on the chalkboard. Ask students to explain how the circle is different from these other figures. (The circle is the only figure without four sides.)

Problem-Solving Strategies Ask students who have solved the Problem of the Day to share how they solved it and any strategies they used.

 Read aloud each set of items listed below. Have students tell what each set has in common.

MENTAL MATH

a. fingers, hands, toes, legs (parts of the body)

b. book, magazine, newspaper (things you read)

c. square, circle, triangle (shapes)

d. a, e, i, o, u (vowels)

 Literature Connection Have students listen to poems from their reading books or from poetry books. Have students describe any rhyming patterns they hear.

LESSON 3 RETEACHING

Name _____

What comes next?

Draw what comes next.

Math Explorations and Applications Level 1 • 1

◆ **LESSON 3** Identifying Patterns

Draw the missing pictures.

7

8

9

10

11

12

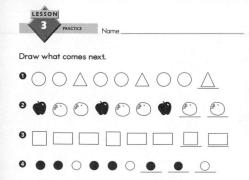 Draw your own pattern in your Math Journal.

NOTE TO HOME Students practice completing patterns.

Copyright © SRA/McGraw-Hill

PRACTICE p. 3

LESSON **3** PRACTICE   Name _____

Draw what comes next.

1 ○ ○ ○ △ ○ ○ △ ○ ○ △

2 ● ● ○ ○ ● ● ○ ○ ○ ● ○ ● ○ ○

3 ▢ ▢ ▢ ▢ ▢ ▢ ▢ ▢ ▢ ▢

4 ● ● ● ● ○ ● ● ● ● ○

Draw the missing picture.

5 ○ X X ○ X X ○ X X

6 ❀ ❀ 🌳 ❀ ❀ 🌳 ❀ ❀

7 ▢ △ △ ▢ △ △ ▢ △ △

Math Explorations and Applications Level 1 • 3

ENRICHMENT p. 3

LESSON **3** ENRICHMENT   Name _____

Use the flowers to make a pattern. Draw a line from each flower to a stem in the vase.   Answers will vary.

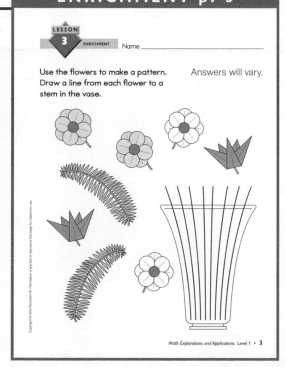

Math Explorations and Applications Level 1 • 3

available separately

❷ Teach

Demonstrate Repeat the activity you did in Lesson 2 by having students come to the front of the room and form a pattern. However, this time include three students in the pattern such as boy, boy, girl. After students have practiced identifying and completing patterns with three elements, have them practice filling in missing spaces in similar patterns. For example, have students form a pattern, but leave spaces between them such as: boy, space, girl, boy, boy, space, boy, boy, girl. Ask students how to fill in the spaces.

Using the Student Pages Complete the first problem on each page together with the class. Then have students use **crayons** to complete the rest of the patterns on their own. Have them share and compare answers when finished. Encourage students to explain how they arrived at their answers.

❸ Wrap-Up ⏱

In Closing Ask students to come up to the chalkboard and show the pattern they drew in their Math Journals.

 Performance Assessment Use students' responses during the demonstration to informally assess their understanding of patterns with three elements.

Assessment Criteria

Did the student . . .

✓ provide sensible answers during the demonstration?

✓ correctly solve at least ten problems on pages 7–8?

 Meeting Individual Needs Have auditory learners listen to different patterns you clap out. Have them repeat each pattern and add on three more claps. Have kinesthetic learners build and complete patterns using **pattern blocks.***

WHAT ARE THINKING STORIES?

Thinking Stories are short stories about common sense mathematical problems, many of which people face every day. Thinking Stories are designed to be read aloud to an entire class. Some Thinking Stories apply lesson concepts, and some introduce or pre-teach an upcoming lesson concept, but the majority of stories simply require students to use their mathematical knowledge and logical reasoning, because real life presents us with a variety of problems at the same time.

The same characters are used in all grade levels. The children in the stories are always the same age as the students at that grade level. Students become familiar with each character and how each one reacts to specific situations.

Tips for Using the Thinking Story Books (Levels 1–3)

◆ **Read the stories aloud.** Give students time to think about each question, but not so much time that they forget the point of the story.

◆ **Discuss the problems.** Ask your students how they arrived at their answers. Encourage debate. There are often many ways to solve a problem.

◆ **Encourage students to think carefully.** Speed should not be emphasized.

◆ **When possible, let students use Number Cubes.** This will encourage *all* students to respond.

◆ **Recognize sensible answers.** Even if a student gives an incorrect answer, he or she probably thought carefully about it and should be praised.

◆ **Encourage students to act out or use manipulatives to solve difficult problems.** This technique may help students organize their thinking.

Levels K–3

In Kindergarten, the Thinking Stories are found in the Teacher's Guide in each lesson. In levels 1–3, the Thinking Stories are presented in both the Teacher's Guide and in a separate book. Interspersed in each story are questions that will prompt your students to think ahead of the story characters. The questions might ask students to identify what is wrong with what a character has done or said, to anticipate what is going to happen as a result, or to think of other possibilities that the character hasn't considered. There are also many additional problems in the separate Thinking Story book (levels 1–3) that can be used at any time.

Levels 4–6

In levels 4–6, the Thinking Stories are presented in the Student Editions. After listening to the story as a class, students can reread the story, either by themselves or in small groups, and discuss the questions at the end.

WHAT ARE THE EXTRA STORY PROBLEMS IN LEVELS 1–3?

In the separate Thinking Story book, there are additional story problems that follow each story. They require students to use the same thinking skills that the story characters used. These problems can be used at any time.

WHAT MAKES THINKING STORIES AND STORY PROBLEMS UNIQUE?

The characters in the stories and problems have peculiarities that your students will come to know. Mr. Muddle, for example, easily forgets things. Ferdie jumps to conclusions without thinking. Mr. Breezy gives more information than is needed and, therefore, makes easy problems seem difficult. Ms. Eng, on the other hand, provides insufficient information to solve the questions and problems she poses. Your students will learn to recognize these peculiarities and avoid them in their own thinking. The stories and problems are filled with so many surprises that your students will be challenged as well as entertained.

WHEN SHOULD I USE THE STORIES AND PROBLEMS?

In Kindergarten, the problems are provided with each individual lesson in the Teacher's Guide. In levels 1–3, the Teacher's Guide will instruct you which of the 20 story selections to use and when to use them. In general, you will be directed to read one story about every five or six lessons. On days when no stories are read, the Teacher's Guide will suggest you read problems—usually three or four—to your students. If it has been a day or two since you read a particular story, you might want to read it again before presenting new story problems. Stories and problems become more difficult as the year progresses.

WHICH THINKING SKILLS ARE STRESSED IN THE STORIES AND PROBLEMS?

Math Skills

- Choosing which operation to use
- Recognizing relevant information
- Recognizing absurd or unreasonable answers
- Deciding when calculation isn't necessary
- Recognizing incorrect answers

Language Arts Skills

- Characterization
- Predicting what will happen in a story
- Making inferences
- Summarizing what has happened in a story
- Listening for details
- Drawing conclusions
- Evaluating information
- Recognizing cause-and-effect relationships
- Forming generalizations

Student Edition pages 9–10

Counting

Name _____

Counting

Count.

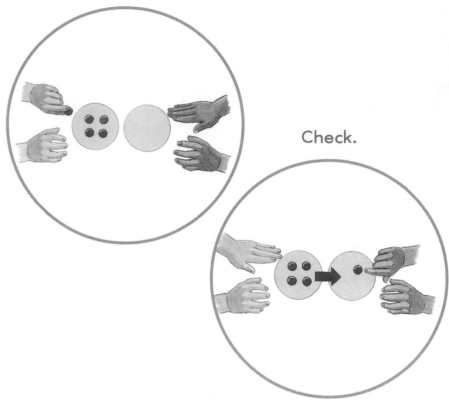

Check.

LESSON PLANNER

Objective

▶ to practice counting from 1 to 10

Context of the Lesson Counting practice is continued in the next several lessons.

 MANIPULATIVES   **Program Resources**

counters*	Thinking Story Book, pages 6–9
crayons	Practice Master 4
handkerchief or other blindfold	Enrichment Master 4

                For career connections:
                    Careers and Math*

                For extra practice:
                    CD-ROM* Lesson 4

                Mixed Practice, page 349

① Warn-Up

Problem of the Day Draw the following pattern on the chalkboard. Have students copy and draw what comes next.

○○□○○□○○□○   ○   □

Problem-Solving Strategies Ask students who have solved the Problem of the Day to share how they solved it and any strategies they used.

 Draw groups of 1–7 circles on the chalkboard. Have students count out loud and tell how many are in each set.

② Teach

Demonstrate Have students count in unison from 1 to 10, with you and then just as a class. Next, show students a handful of **crayons**. Ask them to help you count out various amounts between 1 and 10. For example, tell students: "Let's count out four crayons." Slowly put down one crayon at a time, until students say "Stop." Repeat with different numbers until students know when to say "Stop" each time.

 Talk about the Thinking Story "How Many Piglets?"

 NOTE TO HOME Students practice counting from 1–10.

Unit 1   Lesson 4 • **9**

RETEACHING

 Literature Connection To provide more practice counting, read aloud *Counting Sheep* by John Archambault, in which a child, tired of counting sheep, counts other imaginary animals in order to fall asleep.

Have students work in small groups with manipulatives such as **counters*** or **crayons** to count out different numbers of objects from 0 to 5. Encourage students to touch each object as they count aloud. Once they become proficient at these numbers, go on to numbers from 6 to 10.

*available separately

◆ **LESSON 4** Counting

Use the Mixed Practice on page 349 after this lesson.

❶ Draw one egg in the nest.

❷ Draw one fish in the bowl.

Check students' artwork.

❸ Draw one tail on the dog.

❹ Draw one mouth on each face.

COOPERATIVE LEARNING Do the "Captured!" activity.

NOTE TO HOME Students work on one-to-one correspondence.

Copyright © SRA/McGraw-Hill

10 • Numbers 1–10

Introducing the "Captured" Activity

To provide practice in counting, do the "Captured" activity. Have students spread out in an open area. Choose one student to be "It." **Blindfold** the student and have him or her capture a specific number of classmates (from 1 to 10). Repeat with different students taking turns to be "It."

Using the Student Pages

Give each pair of students about 12 **counters**.* Have one partner put a specific number of counters in the top circle on page 9. Have the other partner check by moving the counters to the bottom circle and counting aloud. Repeat for various numbers from 1 to 10. Read each problem on page 10 aloud, allowing students time to follow the directions before moving on.

Using the Thinking Story

Read aloud "How Many Piglets?" on pages 6–9 of the Thinking Story Book. Allow time for students to answer and discuss the questions in the story.

❸ Wrap-Up ⏱ 5 MINUTES

In Closing Have students take turns demonstrating how to count out a specified number of objects.

Performance Assessment Observe which students are counting correctly as they work with counters on page 9.

PRACTICE p. 4

LESSON 4 PRACTICE   Name _____

❶ Draw one tail on each cat.

❷ Draw one chimney on each house.

❸ Draw one nose on each face.

❹ Draw one hat on each child.

4 • Math Explorations and Applications Level 1

ENRICHMENT p. 4

LESSON 4 ENRICHMENT   Name _____

Draw some muffins on the plate. Have a friend count them and tell how many.

Answers will vary.

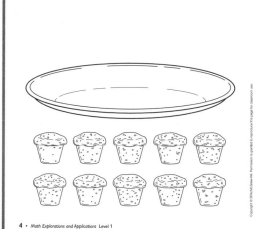

4 • Math Explorations and Applications Level 1

Assessment Criteria

Did the student . . .

✓ accurately count and check the counters, using page 9?

✓ correctly complete all of the pictures on page 10?

✓ participate in the Thinking Story discussion?

LOOKING AHEAD You will need a flannel board and an assortment of felt objects in the next lesson.

STORY 1

How Many Piglets?

1. Portia got a new coat. Before, she had only a brown coat. Now she has a green coat too.
How many coats does Portia have? two

2. Count how many things Marcus did: First he washed his hands. Then he washed his face. Then he brushed his teeth. Then he combed his hair.
How many things did Marcus do? four

3. Ms. Eng had seven rosebushes growing in her backyard. She picked one rose off each bush and gave them all to Willy.
How many roses did Willy get? seven

4. Manolita counted all the fingers on one hand, but she didn't count the thumb.
How many fingers did Manolita count? four

5. "Oh, every wheel on my tricycle is broken," moaned Ferdie.
How many wheels are broken? three

6. Mr. Breezy likes radios. He has a radio in the kitchen. He has a big radio in the living room. He has a clock radio in his bedroom. And he has a radio in his car.
How many radios is that? four

THINKING STORY

How Many Piglets?

Ferdie and Portia could hardly wait for Saturday to come. They were going out to Grandpa's farm to see Martha's babies. Martha is Grandpa's pig, and these were her first babies. Ferdie and Portia had never seen piglets before.
What do you think piglets are? baby pigs

When Saturday came, Ferdie and Portia and their mother got on the bus and rode out to Grandpa's farm. The bus driver let them out right at the gate. Ferdie and Portia ran ahead to the barnyard, where they found Grandpa standing by the pigpen. Martha was standing in the pen, eating—as usual. She didn't even look up. She is not the world's friendliest pig.
What would you have expected the world's friendliest pig to have done? look up

Would she have smiled at Ferdie and Portia? perhaps

All around Martha, running this way and that, were her piglets. Some were pink and some were black, and some were partly pink and partly black.

"Look at them run!" said Ferdie.

"How many piglets are there?" asked Portia.

"Count them yourselves," said Grandpa with a smile, "if you can."

"Of course I can count them," said Ferdie. "That's easy."

Ferdie crouched down beside the pen and counted the piglets as they ran past. He counted, "1, 2, 3, 5, . . ."

"You made a mistake," said Portia.
What mistake did Ferdie make? He skipped 4.

What should he have said? "1, 2, 3, 4, 5, . . ."

6 · How Many Piglets?

"You skipped 4," said Portia.

"All right," said Ferdie, "I'll start again."

This time he didn't skip any numbers. Every time a piglet ran past, he counted. He counted, "1, 2, 3, 4, 5, 6, 7, 8, 9, 10." Then he shouted, "Ten piglets! That's a lot!"

"H'm," said Grandpa, "I didn't think there were that many."

Could Ferdie have made a mistake? How? He may have counted some piglets more than once.

Story 1 • **7**

❼ Figure out how many horses Grandpa has: Grandpa has a horse that he rides when he wants to go horseback riding. He uses the same horse to pull a wagon when he does his farm work. That same horse, whose name is Arnold, sometimes pulls a sleigh in the winter. Grandpa takes good care of Arnold, because Arnold is the only horse he has.

How many horses does Grandpa have? one

How do you know for sure? because Arnold is his only horse

❽ Loretta the Letter Carrier was delivering the mail. Count how many letters she delivered: First she delivered a letter to Mr. Mudancia. Then she took a letter to Marcus. Then she took a letter to Ms. Eng. Then she delivered one letter to Ferdie and one to Portia.

How many letters did Loretta deliver all together? five

❾ Marcus has six jars of paint that he uses to paint model airplanes. He painted one airplane white. He painted another airplane red. And he painted another airplane yellow.

How many jars of paint does Marcus have? six

◆ **STORY 1   How Many Piglets?**

"I think you counted some piglets more than once," said Portia. "You counted every time a piglet ran past, and some of them came past more than once. Let me try."

Portia looked into the pen, where the piglets were still running around. She said, "There's a pink one. That's one. There's a black one. That's two. There's a spotted one. That's three. And, oh, there's one with a funny tail. That's four. Martha has four piglets."

"You did that wrong," said Ferdie. "You didn't count all the piglets."

How could Portia have made a mistake? She may have counted only one of each kind of piglet.

"You counted only one pink one," said Ferdie, "and there's more than one pink one. See? And there's more than one black one, too. I don't know how many piglets there are. I wish they'd stand still so we could count them."

"Just wait," said Grandpa. "Maybe they will."

In a little while Martha finished eating and lay down on her side. The piglets stopped running around. They went over to their mother and started feeding.

"Now we can count them," said Portia. "They're all in a row." She counted, "1, 2, 3, 4, 5."

How many piglets did she count? five

8 • How Many Piglets?

"Martha has five piglets!" said Portia.

"That's strange," said Grandpa. "I thought she had more. But you're right, there are only five piglets there."

Just then they heard a sound, "Eee, Eee, Eee," and another piglet that had been off by itself came running across the pen and joined the others.

How many piglets are there now? six

How do you know? There were five piglets before, and another one joined them.

. . . the end

Story 1 • **9**

Student Edition pages 11–12

LESSON 5
Counting Objects

LESSON PLANNER

Objectives

▶ to demonstrate the use of orderly arrangements when counting

▶ to demonstrate the use of markings when counting objects not arranged in order

Context of the Lesson Counting objects, introduced in Lesson 4, continues here with the teaching of strategies for counting randomly arranged objects. More counting practice is given in subsequent lessons.

 MANIPULATIVES

felt objects

flannel board

Program Resources

Thinking Story Book, pages 10–11

Reteaching Master

Practice Master 5

Enrichment Master 5

For extra practice:
  CD-ROM* Lesson 5

❶ Warm-Up

 Problem of the Day Call out a number between 1 and 10. Have students stand in groups of that size. Repeat with other numbers.

Problem-Solving Strategies Ask students who have solved the Problem of the Day to share how they solved it and any strategies they used.

MENTAL MATH Have students count in unison to different numbers between 3 and 10. Do not signal when the counting should stop. Students must keep in mind how far to count and when to stop.

Name _____

Counting Objects

How many?

❶ 8

❷ 5

❸ 6

❹ 5

 **NOTE TO HOME**
Students count from one to ten objects.

Why teach it this way?

Young students often have trouble counting randomly arranged objects. This lesson introduces strategies that students can use to help them keep an accurate count.

LITERATURE CONNECTION **Literature Connection** You may wish to read to students *An Old-Fashioned 1, 2, 3 Book* by Elizabeth Allen Ashton to provide practice in counting sets of objects.

RETEACHING p. 2

LESSON 5 RETEACHING Name _____

How many?

1 ... 2 ... 3 ... 4 ... 5 ...
6 ... 7 ... 8 ... 9

How many?

❶ ✦✦✦ ___3

❷ 🌭🌭🌭🌭🌭 ___5

❸ 🐟🐟🐟🐟🐟🐟🐟🐟 ___8

❹ 🦆🦆🦆🦆 ___4

2 • Math Explorations and Applications Level 1

*available separately

◆ **LESSON 5** **Counting Objects**

Ring the two sets that have the same number.

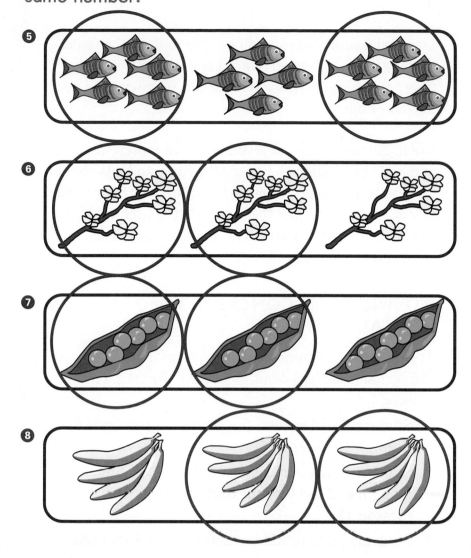

NOTE TO HOME
Students match equal numbers.

Copyright © SRA/McGraw-Hill

② Teach

Demonstrate Draw a row of six stars on the chalkboard. Have students count in unison as you point to each star. Do the same with two rows of three stars. Show that it is possible to get the same result by beginning to count at the right instead of the left, or at the bottom instead of at the top. Draw six more stars, arranged randomly. Ask students to count aloud as you show how to mark each object when it is counted.

Using the Student Pages Have students count each set of objects on page 11, marking the objects as they count them. Ask students to raise their hands when they have an answer. Compare results. Then have the class look at the first problem on page 12. Tell students to ring the two sets that have the same number of fish. Ask them to do the same on their own in the remaining problems.

Using the Thinking Story Present two problems from those following "How Many Piglets?" on pages 10–11 in the Thinking Story Book or on pages 10a–10b of this Guide.

③ Wrap-Up ⏱ 5 MINUTES

In Closing Place eight **felt objects** in a random arrangement on a **flannel board**. Ask students to count them. Discuss different ways students might mark or arrange the objects to count them.

Informal Assessment Watch students count felt objects on a flannel board. Check whether they use a strategy such as arranging objects in rows or touching each object as they count.

LESSON 5 PRACTICE Name _____

Ring the two sets that have the same number.

Math Explorations and Applications Level 1 • 5

LESSON 5 ENRICHMENT Name _____

Color some dogs red. Color some dogs yellow.   Answers will vary.

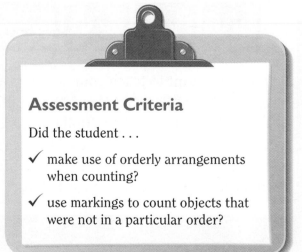

Match your picture above. Color the same number red. Color the same number yellow.

Math Explorations and Applications Level 1 • 5

Assessment Criteria

Did the student . . .

✓ make use of orderly arrangements when counting?

✓ use markings to count objects that were not in a particular order?

Allowing students to use their fingers as manipulatives to count or to add and subtract is often frowned upon. Some experts fear that students will become too dependent on this method; but the fact remains that most young students use their fingers in mathematics whether or not they are explicitly allowed to do so.

In the *Math Explorations and Applications* program, you will be teaching your students to use their fingers in a systematic way. You will be teaching them to form "standard" finger sets with each set representing a specific numeral. This way your students will be able to recognize visually and kinesthetically, for example, seven or eight fingers without having to count individual fingers. Eventually, students will be able to abandon the use of their fingers and depend more and more on mental operations.

TEACHING FINGER SETS

Use the illustration below to teach your students the standard way of forming finger sets. Either hand may be used for the numbers 0 through 5. The number 1 is represented by the thumb.

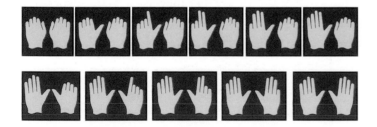

You might want to teach your students a counting song, such as "This Old Man," "Five Little Ducks," "Over in the Meadow," or "Roll Over," as they learn to count with finger sets. Music addresses yet another modality and often helps young students remember what they might otherwise easily forget.

Eventually your students will be able to form the finger set for each number you request and recognize each finger set by sight. This will reduce or eliminate the need to count fingers.

Use finger sets as one of several ways to represent numbers. In addition to finger sets, your students should learn to use counters, number lines, Number Strips, tally marks, play money, and the numerals themselves. They should not become overly dependent on any one method of representing numbers.

MOVING FROM CONCRETE TO MENTAL MATH

As students move from concrete to mental math, the use of finger sets is phased out. Below are the stages in this process:

1. Students learn to form the **standard finger sets for 0 through 10**. [Lesson 6]

2. Students learn to recognize the standard finger sets **by sight and feel without counting fingers.** [Lesson 11]

3. **Students learn to add or subtract with finger sets.** For example, if they are adding 4 + 3, they show the finger set for 4 and count fingers to add 3. However, they recognize the answer, 7, without counting fingers. [**Lesson 24, addition; Lesson 29, subtraction**]

4. Students learn "statue" arithmetic. At this stage students only imagine themselves raising or lowering their fingers to add or subtract. For example, for 6 – 2, they show the finger set for 6, then imagine two fingers being lowered. Then they imagine the remaining finger set and thus get the answer: 4. [**Lesson 48, addition; Lesson 49, subtraction**]

5. **Students no longer need to use finger sets.** They have moved from concrete to mental arithmetic.

GAMES

THE ROLE OF GAMES

Games are an important component of the *Math Explorations and Applications* program. They offer students an opportunity to practice the mathematical skills to which they've been introduced and to develop logical reasoning as they use mathematical strategies. They make learning fun. Games also offer you another way to assess how well your students have learned each skill. There are two types of games presented in this program—Game Mats and Cube Games.

Game Mats

There are five Game Mats in Kindergarten, thirteen in Levels 1–3, and fourteen in Levels 4–6. In the Game Mat package, you receive 15 copies of each Game Mat, counters, place

markers, Number Cubes, and money (not in Kindergarten). In addition, you have *A Guide for Using the Game Mats* and a color transparency for each Game Mat. Each game involves the use of several math skills including mathematical reasoning and probability. Many of the Game Mats are offered in a standard and a harder version.

Cube Games

These games, presented in the Student Edition in Levels 3–6 and in the Teacher's Guide for K–2, reinforce basic math skills and involve mathematical reasoning.

TIPS FOR TEACHING GAMES

After reading the rules for each game, which are provided in the lesson where the Cube Game is introduced or on each Game Mat, take the following steps:

- **Play the game yourself.** This will help you identify any difficulties your students might have.
- **Demonstrate how the game is played.** Making sure that everyone can see, say the rules aloud as you play another student or as two or more students play together. For the Game Mats, you may want to use the color overhead transparencies to demonstrate how each game is played.
- **Restate how the game is played.** Ask students to restate the object and rules of the game in their own words to be sure everyone understands how to play.
- **Supervise students' play.** Be sure they get off to the right start.

Tips for Organizing Successful Game Sessions

- ◆ **Stress enjoyment rather than competition.** Emphasize sportsmanship, fair play, and taking turns.
- ◆ **In general, place students of the same ability together.** This way all students have a more equal chance of winning.
- ◆ **Change groupings from day to day.** Students can learn different things by playing with different partners.
- ◆ **Be sure students are challenged by a game.** Most Game Mats have a standard and a harder version. Some Cube Games suggest variations to the game.
- ◆ **Assign one referee for the day or for each group.** Students sometimes get so absorbed in their own efforts that they do not follow the rules. A referee can monitor players' moves, keep track of scores, and in some games act as banker.
- ◆ **Make Game Mats accessible.** Store mats so that students can find and return them without your help.

✖✔ ASSESSMENT

This is the first Mastery Checkpoint at this grade level. Throughout each unit of each grade level, at benchmarks specified on the Mastery Checkpoint Chart, you are able to assess students' progress.

MASTERY CHECKPOINT CHARTS

The Mastery Checkpoint Chart contains a listing of the mastery objectives that are considered important for future progress in mathematics. These benchmarks appear on a chart in the Assessment Blackline Master Book on pages vii-viii. You can determine each student's mastery of specific objectives by his or her performance of the mastery objective in the lesson and/or by using the specific

Tips on Using the Mastery Checkpoint Chart

◆ Fill in the names of all students in your class.

◆ For each checkpoint on the Mastery Checkpoint Chart, the Teacher's Guide gives opportunities to assess either by observation or by using the Student Edition page(s). Students can also be given the Assessment Blackline Master for that specific Checkpoint.

◆ Place a check mark (✓) in the appropriate column of the Mastery Checkpoint Chart beside the name of each student who demonstrates success on the objective in question.

◆ Pencil in a *P* in the appropriate column for each student who, in your judgment, grasps the necessary idea for accomplishing the objective but needs further practice to sharpen his or her skill. Assign extra practice to identified students.

◆ Pencil in a *T* for each student who has not grasped the necessary idea and therefore needs further teaching. Give extra teaching to identified students.

◆ Replace *T*s or *P*s with check marks when students demonstrate mastery of a skill.

Mastery Checkpoint test provided in the Assessment Blackline Master Book. Those students who are having difficulty with a skill should receive extra help before continuing on in the unit. But an entire class should not be held up until all students learn the skill. Each lesson provides you with either a Reteaching Strategy or a Reteaching Master that will help you present the lesson concept in a slightly different way.

ASSESSMENT OPPORTUNITIES IN THE PROGRAM

The *Math Explorations and Applications* program offers many opportunities to assess students' skills. Activities that students engage in on a daily basis, such as Mental Math exercises, games, response exercises, Thinking Story discussions, and Student Edition exercises allow you to steadily monitor individual progress.

In the Teacher's Guide

Each lesson in the Teacher's Guide provides at least two different assessment suggestions. One is Assessment Criteria, which gives you questions to ask yourself while you observe students playing a game, completing an activity, participating in a Thinking Story discussion, or working in cooperative groups. The additional suggestions include the following types of assessment:

- informal assessment (interviews, observation, and oral)
- formal assessment (tests, reviews, and checkpoints)
- self assessment
- alternative assessment (portfolio and performance)

In the Student Editions

A formal Mid-Unit Review as well as a Unit Review and a Unit Test are provided in the Student Edition in levels 1–6. The exception is Kindergarten, which has a Mid-Book Review and a Book Test. There are also self-assessments throughout the Student Editions in which students are asked to evaluate their own performance.

In the Assessment Blackline Masters

In the Assessment Blackline Master book there is a page for each Mastery Checkpoint, an additional Mid-Unit Review, and two Unit Tests, one in standardized format. Each unit also provides Performance Assessment activities and Portfolio Assessment suggestions. There is also additional information on the various alternative assessment options that are provided in this program and suggestions for grading these assessments using rubrics.

DAILY MONITORING

The following activities will help you assess your students' progress on a daily basis:

- **Cube Games and Game Mats**
  These allow you to watch students practice specific skills under conditions natural to them.

- **Mental Math Exercises**
  These exercises, which involve Number Wheels and Number Cubes, allow you to see everyone's responses, give immediate feedback, and involve the entire class.

- **Student Edition Exercises**
  These help you determine which skills your students can use on paper and which they need to practice.

- **Thinking Story Sessions**
  These help you determine whether or not your students are able to apply their knowledge of math concepts to everyday common sense problems.

LESSON 6

Student Edition pages 13–14

Forming Finger Sets

LESSON PLANNER

Objectives

✓ to measure individual progress toward counting objects

▶ to teach the use of finger sets for representing numbers through 10

Context of the Lesson This is the first of many lessons in which students use finger sets to represent numbers through 10. Practice in forming finger sets continues in subsequent lessons. This lesson contains a Mastery Checkpoint for counting objects and is the first of 23 Mastery Checkpoints in level 1.

 MANIPULATIVES

counters*

Program Resources

Thinking Story Book, pages 10–11

Practice Master 6

Enrichment Master 6

Assessment Master

For extra practice:
CD-ROM* Lesson 6

❶ Warm-Up ⏱ 5 MINUTES

Problem of the Day Present the following problems to the class. If you use fingers to show numbers, what is the greatest number you can show with one hand? (5) with two hands? (10) What is the least number you can show with one hand? (0) with two hands? (0)

Problem-Solving Strategies Ask students who have solved the Problem of the Day to share how they solved it and any strategies they used.

 Have students draw the appropriate number of rings as you call out various numbers from 0–10.

❷ Teach

Demonstrate Show students the zero finger set. Teach the students to call that number *zero*. Then demonstrate finger sets 1 through 10, having students form them with you. Repeat several times with numbers in order from 1 to 10, then in reverse order with numbers from 10 to 1.

LESSON 6

Name _____

Forming Finger Sets

Count and show how many.

 ❶ 8

 ❷ 4

 ❸ 5

 ❹ 1

 GAME Play the "Guess How Many" game.

Copyright © SRA/McGraw-Hill

🎒 **NOTE TO HOME**
Students form finger sets for numbers 0–10.

Unit 1 Lesson 6 • **13**

RETEACHING

Some students may have physical difficulties in forming finger sets. Forming 3, 4, 8, and 9 are especially troublesome. The secret here is not to try to hold those fingers down all the way or so far that other fingers will follow involuntarily. As long as fingers have a little bend in them, the finger sets will be recognizable. Work with individual students to help them establish the proper amount of bend. You may occasionally have a student who needs to work out a nonstandard way of forming finger sets to suit his or her anatomy.

PRACTICE p. 6

LESSON 6 PRACTICE Name _____

Count and show how many. Draw a line to the correct finger set.

❶ 🪶🪶🪶🪶🪶🪶

❷ ●●●●●●●●

❸ ●●●●

❹))))))))))

❺ 🍎🍎🍎🍎🍎

❻ 🚗🚗🚗🚗🚗 🚗🚗🚗🚗🚗

6 • *Math Explorations and Applications Level 1*

13 Numbers 1–10

*available separately

◆ LESSON 6 Forming Finger Sets

Count and show how many.

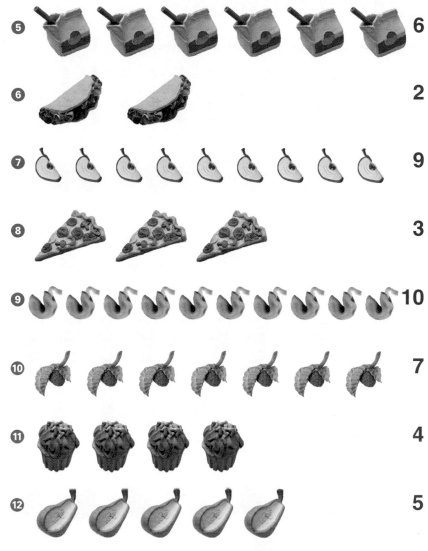

⑤ 6

⑥ 2

⑦ 9

⑧ 3

⑨ 10

⑩ 7

⑪ 4

⑫ 5

NOTE TO HOME
Students form finger sets for
numbers 0–10.

14 • Numbers 1–10

Copyright © SRA/McGraw-Hill

Introducing the "Guess How Many" Game Demonstrate and play the "Guess How Many" game to provide practice in counting and forming finger sets. Divide students into groups of three. Each group gets 10 **counters***. While other players close their eyes, the lead player hides 1–10 counters under a book. Then others try to guess how many counters are hidden, using finger sets to show their answers. The student who guesses the right number takes the next turn.

Using the Student Pages Have students silently count the objects in each row on pages 13–14, form the corresponding finger set under their desks, and hold up their hands when you say "Show."

 Using the Thinking Story Present two new problems from those following "How Many Piglets?" on pages 10–11 in the Thinking Story Book or on pages 10a–10b of this Guide.

❸ Wrap-Up

In Closing Ask students to show finger sets as you call out numbers from 0–10.

✓ Mastery Checkpoint 1

Check to see if students can count up to ten objects by asking them to count out a given number of objects. Then show a set of objects and ask the student how many there are. Or, you might wish to use page 2 of the Assessment Blackline Masters. Record results on the Mastery Checkpoint Chart. For more details see page 13c of this Teacher's Guide.

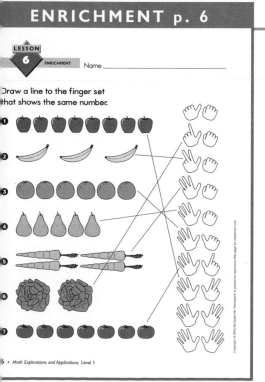
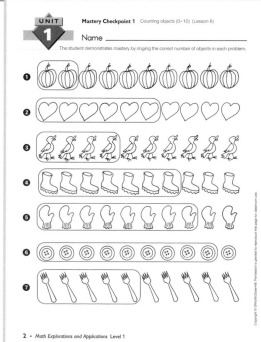

Assessment Criteria

Did the student . . .

✓ correctly form standard finger sets for numbers through 10?

✓ master counting up to ten objects quickly and accurately?

LOOKING AHEAD A large can and counters are needed for Lesson 7. An overhead projector would also be useful.

LESSON 7

Student Edition pages 15–16

Tracing Numbers

LESSON PLANNER

Objectives

▶ to provide practice for tracing and copying the numbers 0–10

▶ to provide practice in counting from one to ten objects

Context of the Lesson This is the first of a series of lessons that teach the formation of numbers.

MANIPULATIVES **Program Resources**

can (large) — Practice Master 7

counters* — Enrichment Master 7

overhead — For extra practice:
projector and — CD-ROM* Lesson 7
transparency

① Warm-Up ⏱ 5 MINUTES

Problem of the Day Draw three circles on the chalkboard. Draw three dots in the first circle, four dots in the second circle, and five dots in the third. Tell students to draw the next circle in the pattern.

Problem-Solving Strategies Ask students who have solved the Problem of the Day to share how they solved it and any strategies they used.

 Challenge students to count silently as you drop **counters*** one by one into a large **can**. Then have students form finger sets to show how many counters are in the can. Invite students to count out loud as you remove each counter to check the answer.

LESSON 7

Name _____

Tracing Numbers

Count. Trace. Then copy the number.

① ten

② nine

③ eight

④ seven

⑤ six

⑥ five

Copyright © SRA/McGraw-Hill

 **NOTE TO HOME**
Students trace and copy the numbers 0–10 and count up to 10 objects.

Unit 1   Lesson 7 • **15**

RETEACHING

Reteaching is not necessary at this point. However, you may provide students with further practice by having them repeat the Mental Math counting activity with a partner.

 Have students work in pairs. One partner sets out a group of one to ten objects. The other student counts the objects and writes the total number.

CULTURAL DIVERSITY Ask second-language learners to share their first language by saying the names of the numbers 1–10 as they show each appropriate finger set.

---

15 Numbers 1–10

*available separately

◆ **LESSON 7** Tracing Numbers

Count. Trace. Then copy the number.

7 four $\boxed{4}$

8 three $\boxed{3}$

9 two $\boxed{2}$

10 one $\boxed{1}$

11 zero $\boxed{0}$

Trace the number. Then show that many flowers.

12

 NOTE TO HOME
Students trace and copy the numbers
0–10 and count up to 10 objects.

16 • Numbers 1–10

PRACTICE p. 7

LESSON **7** PRACTICE   Name _____

Trace and write the numbers.

0	0	0	0	0	0	0	0	0	0
1	1	1	1	1	1	1	1	1	1
2	2	2	2	2	2	2	2	2	2
3	3	3	3	3	3	3	3	3	3
4	4	4	4	4	4	4	4	4	4
5	5	5	5	5	5	5	5	5	5
6	6	6	6	6	6	6	6	6	6
7	7	7	7	7	7	7	7	7	7
8	8	8	8	8	8	8	8	8	8
9	9	9	9	9	9	9	9	9	9

Math Explorations and Applications Level 1 • **7**

ENRICHMENT p. 7

LESSON **7** ENRICHMENT   Name _____

❶ Find and color 5 seals.

❷ Find and color 6 fish with spots.

❸ Find and color 2 fish with stripes.

❹ How many fish did you find? _____ 8

Math Explorations and Applications Level 1 • **7**

② Teach

Demonstrate Write the numbers 0–10 on the chalkboard or on an **overhead transparency**, saying the name of each number as you write it. Ask students to name each number as you write it again. Then have students trace the number in the air with you. Have students write each number on paper at the same time as you slowly write each number again on the transparency or the chalkboard.

Using the Student Pages Do the first exercise on page 15 together as a class. Have students count the crayons. Ask them to trace, then copy the number. Have students follow this procedure for all of the exercises on pages 15–16.

③ Wrap-Up

In Closing Ask a student to use a finger set to show the number 5. Then ask another student to write a 5 on the chalkboard. Explain that both the finger set and the 5 written on the chalkboard stand for the same thing.

 Informal Assessment Observe students as they practice tracing and copying the numbers in the Student Edition. Note those students who have difficulty forming certain numbers.

Assessment Criteria

Did the student . . .

✓ correctly trace and copy at least 8 of 11 numbers?

✓ use finger sets to keep count of numbers up to 10?

LESSON 8

Student Edition pages 17–18

Reading Numbers

LESSON PLANNER

Objective

▶ to provide practice in recognizing, tracing, and writing the numbers 0–10

Context of the Lesson This lesson covers writing and counting from 0–10, both in and out of sequence. Working with numbers continues in the next lesson.

 MANIPULATIVES

can (large)

counters*

Program Resources

*Animal Orchestra**
   from the Literature Library

Thinking Story Book, pages 10–11

Practice Master 8

Enrichment Master 8

For extra practice:
   CD-ROM* Lesson 8

❶ Warm-Up

5 MINUTES

 Problem of the Day Present these directions orally. Draw a snow person. Draw three big snowballs for the body. Draw two arms. Draw two eyes. Draw one nose and one mouth. Draw four buttons. Draw five snowballs nearby.

Problem-Solving Strategies Ask students who have solved the Problem of the Day to share how they solved it and any strategies they used.

 Place up to ten **counters*** in the **can** all at once. Write the number on the chalkboard to show how many counters are in the can. Have students show the finger set. Take the counters out of the can and drop them in again, one at a time, to count and check.

❷ Teach

Demonstrate Review with students how to trace the numbers 0–10 in the air as you write them on the chalkboard. Then challenge students to recognize the numbers out of order. Point to a number and have students show finger sets and say aloud that number. Ask volunteers to identify all the numbers in sequence.

LESSON 8

Name _____

Reading Numbers

Trace the right number.

❶
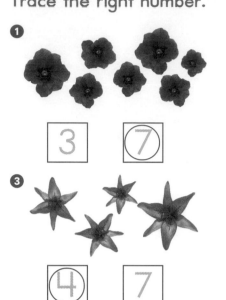

| 3 | 7 |

❷

| 2 | 1 |

❸

| 4 | 7 |

❹

| 6 | 4 |

❺

| 8 | 5 |

❻

| 9 | 8 |

Copyright © SRA/McGraw-Hill

 NOTE TO HOME
Students recognize numbers to 10.

Unit 1   Lesson 8 • **17**

 Physical Education Connection Have students stand. Using numbers between 0 and 10, direct students to jump, clap, or march in place the appropriate number of times.

Literature Connection To provide practice in counting and number recognition to 10, read *Animal Orchestra* from the Literature Library*.

RETEACHING

Provide individual practice in naming and showing finger sets corresponding to the numbers 0–10 to those children who need it. For writing practice, have students use colored chalk to trace over numbers you have drawn on the chalkboard.

*available separately

◆ LESSON 8 Reading Numbers

0 1 2 3 4 5 6 7 8 9 10

How many? Write the number.

7 `2`

8 `8`

9 `1`

10 `3`

Which number is better drawn?
Trace it.

11 3 3   **12** 6 6   **13** 9 9

14 2 2   **15** 4 4   **16** 6 6

17 8 8   **18** 5 5   **19** 7 7

18 • Numbers 1–10

NOTE TO HOME
Students practice writing numbers 0–10.

Copyright © SRA/McGraw-Hill

Using the Student Pages Do the first exercise on page 17 together. Count aloud the number of flowers. Write the number on the chalkboard. Have students trace the correct number on page 17. Tell students to follow the same process to count, identify, and trace the correct numbers as they complete page 17. Direct students to page 18. Have students count and write the correct number of objects shown in problems 7–10. Explain the directions for problems 11–19. After students select and darken the better-formed numbers, discuss what is wrong with the numbers not chosen.

Using the Thinking Story Have students solve two new problems from those following "How Many Piglets?" on pages 10–11 in the Thinking Story Book or on pages 10a–10b of this Guide.

❸ Wrap-Up ⏱ 5 MINUTES

In Closing Summarize the lesson by showing finger sets for numbers between 0 and 10. As you do so, have students identify and write the correct number on the chalkboard.

Performance Assessment Write the numbers 0–10 on the chalkboard. Point to one of the numbers and ask a student to clap his or her hands that number of times. Repeat this procedure, pointing to the numbers out of sequence, until each student has had a turn.

Assessment Criteria

Did the student . . .

✓ count the objects and trace the correct number under each student page picture?

✓ write the numbers clearly?

✓ continue to correctly form finger sets?

LOOKING AHEAD Number Cubes will be introduced in Lesson 9. It is important to be familiar with the procedure for finding, hiding, and showing them.

PRACTICE p. 8

LESSON 8 PRACTICE Name _____

Trace each number. Then write the numbers on your own.

0 1 2 3 4 5 6 7 8 9 10
0 1 2 3 4 5 6 7 8 9 10

How many? Write the number.

1 6 **2** 9 **3** 2 **4** 8 **5** 5

8 • Math Explorations and Applications Level 1

ENRICHMENT p. 8

LESSON 8 ENRICHMENT Name _____

Trace the hidden numbers. Look for 0, 1, 2, 3, and 4. How many can you find?

Students should locate and trace four 0s, 1s, 2s, 3s, and 4s.

8 • Math Explorations and Applications Level 1

Unit 1 Lesson 8 **18**

MENTAL MATH EXERCISES

Mental Math exercises offer an easy and practical technique for drilling students' math skills and assessing their performance. With these exercises students usually use either the Number Wheel (Levels 3–6) or Number Cubes (Levels K–6) to display their answers to your oral questions.

NUMBER WHEELS

Number Wheels have five wheels, each of which can be dialed to show any digit from 0 through 9. This allows students to make any integer from 0 through 99,999. To show the number 2047, for example, a student rotates the thousands wheel to show a 2, turns the hundreds wheel to show a 0, and so on. Different colors are used to identify each of the five wheels. On the back of the Number Wheels, the digits 0 through 9 are repeated with the addition of a decimal point.

NUMBER CUBES

Number Cubes allow students to make any integer from 0 through 100. In Levels 3–6, students use the 0–5 (red) and 5–10 (blue) Number Cubes. To show the number 73, for example, a student should find the 7 face on the 5–10 cube and place that next to the 3 face on the 0–5 cube.

In Levels 1 and 2, each student should be given four cubes: two units cubes—0–5 (red) and 5–10 (blue)—and two tens cubes—0–5 (yellow) and 5–10 (green). To show the number 43, for example, a student should find the 4 face on the 0–5 tens cube and place that next to the 3 face on the 0–5 units cube.

ADVANTAGES TO MENTAL MATH EXERCISES

- Provide practice in mental computation
- Provide enjoyable, active drill
- Take only 5–10 minutes
- Allow full participation of the entire class
- Provide a basis for assessment
- Offer immediate feedback to your students
- Ensure that students get their answers independently
- Protect students from embarrassment in front of their peers, because errors are not audible

MENTAL MATH EXERCISES

HOW TO USE WHEELS AND CUBES

1. Present the class with a problem (orally or on the chalkboard) and say "Find."

2. Students determine the answer and dial it on their Number Wheels or position it on their Number Cubes.

3. Say "Hide."

4. Students hide their answers by holding their Wheels or Cubes against their chests.

5. Say "Show," when you see that most students have an answer.

6. Students hold up their Wheels or Cubes so you can see their responses.

7. Check students' responses.

8. Show and/or say the correct answer.

9. Move on to the next problem.

Sometimes the problems in a Mental Math exercise will be complex enough to require paper and pencil. In these cases, have students show their answers to you as you walk around the room.

Tips for Using Number Wheels and Cubes

◆ **Add a "peek-to-be-sure" step.** This should occur between the "Hide" and "Show" steps of the procedure. It asks students who have already found answers to check them. This keeps them involved as they wait for the "Show" command.

◆ **Use good judgment to decide when to give the "Show" command.** Give students who are progressing toward a solution time enough to finish, but avoid prolonged waiting because this calls attention to slower students.

◆ **Encourage your students.** Mental Math exercises allow an active exchange between you and your students. Use this opportunity to give your students plenty of positive reinforcement.

LESSON 9

Student Edition pages 19–20

Reading Numbers

Objectives

▶ to demonstrate the use of Number Cubes

▶ to provide practice in tracing, recognizing, and writing numbers 0–10

Context of the Lesson This lesson introduces the use of Number Cubes. Students will use these cubes throughout the year to form numbers in games and to show answers to mental computation exercises.

MANIPULATIVES   **Program Resources**

counters*

posterboard (optional)

glue stick (optional)

decorating materials such as glitter, beans, etc. (optional)

Number Cubes

Reteaching Master

Practice Master 9

Enrichment Master 9

For extra practice:
  CD-ROM* Lesson 9

Mixed Practice, page 350

1 Warm-Up

  Problem of the Day As you present the following problem, write each amount on the chalkboard. Help the baker fill this order: two rolls, four muffins, one loaf of bread, three biscuits. Show each amount with **counters***.

Problem-Solving Strategies Ask students who have solved the Problem of the Day to share how they solved it and any strategies they used.

 Ask students to show finger sets to answer the following riddles: I am the number before 5. What number am I? (4) I am the number after 6. What number am I? (7) I am the number before 1. What number am I? (0) I am the number after 8. What number am I? (9)

2 Teach

Demonstrate Name and write the numbers 0–10 on the chalkboard or on a transparency. Next, ask students to say each number and show it with finger sets as you write it again. Then have students trace each number in the air. Finally, have students copy each number on a piece of paper as you write it again.

19 Numbers 1–10

LESSON 9

Name _____

Reading Numbers

0 1 2 3 4 5 6 7 8 9 10

Trace the number that is better drawn.

❶ 5 5	❷ 4 4	❸ 2 2
❹ 3 3	❺ 1 7	❻ 4 4
❼ 6 6	❽ 5 5	❾ 5 5
❿ 8 8	⓫ 9 9	⓬ 6 6
⓭ 2 2	⓮ 3 3	⓯ 8 8

NOTE TO HOME Students choose the better formed number.

Unit 1   Lesson 9 • **19**

Why teach it this way?

Number Cubes supply a basis for assessment and immediate feedback for you and the student. They allow students to be active participants in mental math practice sessions.

  Art Connection Have students trace or write the numbers 0–10 on a large piece of **posterboard**. Invite them to trace over each number with a **glue stick** and decorate it with **glitter**, **crumpled tissue paper**, **beans**, or other materials.

LESSON 9
RETEACHING   Name _____

Trace the numbers.

Write how many.

Math Explorations and Applications Level 1 • **3**

*available separately

◆ **LESSON 9** Reading Numbers

Write the number.

16 How many teddy bears?

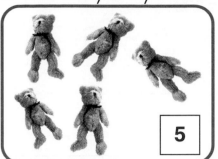

5

Use the Mixed Practice on page 350 after this lesson.

17 How many sunglasses?

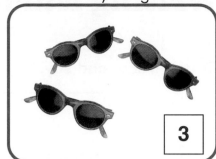

3

18 How many cats?

5

19 How many hats?

3

Play the "Find the Cube" game.

NOTE TO HOME
Students count objects and write the number.

PRACTICE p. 9

LESSON **9** PRACTICE   Name _____

Trace each number. Then write the numbers on your own.

| 0 | 1 | 2 | 3 | 4 | 5 | 6 | 7 | 8 | 9 | 10 |

| 0 | 1 | 2 | 3 | 4 | 5 | 6 | 7 | 8 | 9 | 10 |

How many? Write the number.

1 7 ⬭⬭⬭⬭⬭⬭⬭

2 9 (coins)

3 How many girls? 2

4 How many oranges? 5 (oranges and apple)

Math Explorations and Applications Level 1 • 9

ENRICHMENT p. 9

LESSON **9** ENRICHMENT   Name _____

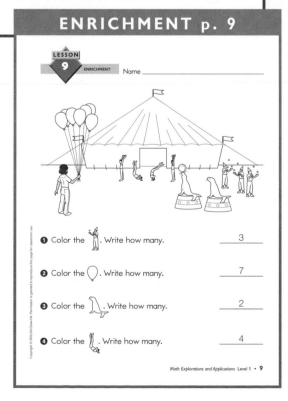

1 Color the ▢. Write how many. ___3___

2 Color the ◯. Write how many. ___7___

3 Color the (seal). Write how many. ___2___

4 Color the (hat). Write how many. ___4___

Math Explorations and Applications Level 1 • 9

Using the Number Cubes Introduce the 0–5 and 5–10 units Number Cubes following the procedures outlined on pages 19a–19b of this Teacher's Guide. Draw a *0* on the chalkboard and ask students to find it on their Number Cubes. When all students have found it, give the "Show" command and have them show their *0*s. Follow this procedure for all of the numbers from 1–10 in sequence. As students begin to understand the procedure, you can say the number and have students show the number on their cubes before you write it on the chalkboard.

Using the Student Pages Have students complete the tracing exercise on page 19, then do the counting exercises on page 20. Hold a discussion of what is wrong with the ill-formed numbers on page 19.

GAME **Introducing the "Find the Cube" Game** To provide practice for recognizing numbers and building familiarity with Number Cubes, demonstrate and then play the "Find the Cube" game. Divide students into groups of three. The lead player says a number between 0–10. Other players race to be the first to show that number on a cube. The winner becomes the lead player for the next round. A copy of this can also be found on page 6 of the Home Connections Blackline Masters.

❸ Wrap-Up

In Closing Have students show the appropriate number on their Number Cubes as you quickly call out numbers from 0–10.

ANALYZING ANSWERS Students often confuse 6 with 9 and 5 with 2. Show students that on the Number Cubes the 6 has a curved stem and the 9 has a straight one. Point out also that there are lines under the 6 and the 9 to help differentiate them. For the 5 and the 2, point out that the 5 has a flat part on the top, and the 2 has a flat part on the bottom.

Assessment Criteria

Did the student . . .

✓ use the Number Cubes properly?

✓ accurately count and write numbers from 0–10?

Student Edition pages 21–22

Writing Numbers

Name _____

Writing Numbers

0 1 2 3 4 5 6 7 8 9 10

Count, trace, and say.

LESSON PLANNER

Objectives

▶ to introduce written names for numbers 0 through 10

▶ to teach students to relate number names, numbers, and sets

Context of the Lesson
This is the first lesson in which students will read the names for numbers. Students continue to practice tracing the numbers, which they began in Lesson 7.

 MANIPULATIVES

box or cake pan (optional)

sand (optional)

Program Resources

Practice Master 10

Enrichment Master 10

For extra practice:
CD-ROM* Lesson 10

① 0
zero

② 1
one

③ 2
two

④ 3
three

⑤ 4
four

Copyright © SRA/McGraw-Hill

 NOTE TO HOME
Students practice counting and tracing numbers.

Unit 1   Lesson 10 • **21**

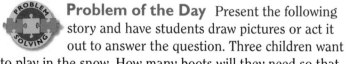

Problem of the Day Present the following story and have students draw pictures or act it out to answer the question. Three children want to play in the snow. How many boots will they need so that they are all wearing boots? (six)

Problem-Solving Strategies Ask students who have solved the Problem of the Day to share how they solved it and any strategies they used.

MENTAL MATH List the following pairs of numbers on the chalkboard. Say a number and have a volunteer come up and point to that number in each pair.

a.   5 6 (say "six")

b.   7 4 (say "seven")

c.   2 5 (say "five")

d.   0 9 (say "zero")

e.   3 8 (say "three")

f.   2 5 (say "two")

RETEACHING

Write the numbers from 0 to 10 and the names for the numbers on 20 individual index cards. Place the cards in two piles: words and numbers. Show a number word. Have a volunteer come up and find the number that goes with it. Repeat with all the words, then reverse the activity by showing the number and having students match the correct word.

*available separately

◆ **LESSON 10** Writing Numbers

 0 1 2 3 4 5 6 7 8 9 10

Count, trace, and say.

⑥ 5
five

⑦ 6
six

⑧ 7
seven

⑨ 8
eight

⑩ 9
nine

⑪ 10
ten

22 • Numbers 1–10

NOTE TO HOME
Students identify numerals and number words.

Copyright © SRA/McGraw-Hill

---

❷ Teach

Demonstrate Ask how many elephants are in the classroom. Show students how to write the word *zero* and the number *0* on the chalkboard. Next ask how many teachers are in the room. Write the word and the number for 1. Draw a symbol to show one object. Continue this process through 10.

Using the Student Pages Work with students as they trace each number on pages 21–22. Have them count aloud each object to check that the correct amount is next to each number.

❸ Wrap-Up

In Closing Write the numbers 0–10 on the chalkboard. Point to one of the numbers. Have a volunteer count out that number of objects. Repeat with other numbers and volunteers.

Informal Assessment Use pages 21–22 to informally assess students' ability to trace numbers to 10.

Assessment Criteria

Did the student . . .

✓ neatly trace the numbers on pages 21–22?

✓ accurately count from 0–10 objects?

Meeting Individual Needs
Pour about 2 inches of **sand** into a **box** or **cake pan**. Have kinesthetic learners form numbers from 0–10 in the sand. You may need to guide their hands to form the numbers at first. Then have them form the numbers on their own.

PRACTICE p. 10

LESSON 10 PRACTICE Name _____

1 one	2 two	3 three	4 four	5 five
6 six	7 seven	8 eight	9 nine	10 ten

Draw an X on the number, word, or picture that does not belong.

❶  ✗ seven

❷ ⊕⊕⊕⊕⊕ 5 four ✗

❸ 🌳🌳🌳🌳 9 nine

❹ ◇◇◇ ✗ three

❺ ⚪⚪⚪⚪⚪ 6 seven ✗

❻ ⚪⚪ ✗ two

10 • *Math Explorations and Applications Level 1*

ENRICHMENT p. 10

LESSON 10 ENRICHMENT Name _____

Each student holds a number between 1 and 10. Fill in the numbers. Put them in the right order.

Draw a line to match the number word with the correct number.

two — 6
five — 2
ten — 5
six — 10

10 • *Math Explorations and Applications Level 1*

Unit 1 Lesson 10 **22**

Student Edition pages 23–24

LESSON 11

Using Finger Sets

Objectives

✓ to measure individual progress toward forming and recognizing finger sets for the numbers 0–10

▶ to introduce geometric shapes by identifying and counting their corners

Context of the Lesson This lesson includes a Mastery Checkpoint for recognizing finger sets for the numbers 0–10. In addition, simple geometric shapes are introduced. Geometric figures will be studied again in Lesson 44 and subsequent lessons.

 MANIPULATIVES   **Program Resources**

colored pencils

flash cards

Number Cubes

Thinking Story Book, pages 10–11

Practice Master 11

Enrichment Master 11

Assessment Master

For extra practice:
CD-ROM* Lesson 11

❶ Warm-Up

Problem of the Day On the chalkboard, write all but one number from 0–10. Have students identify the missing number.

Problem-Solving Strategies Ask students who have solved the Problem of the Day to share how they solved it and any strategies they used.

 Ask students to supply the number that completes each rhyme: I'm the number before 2, and I'm lots of fun, I stand all alone because I'm the number _____. (1) Show all the fingers of one hand, then four more in a line. What is it you're showing? It's me, the number _____. (9)

❷ Teach

Demonstrate Quickly show and then hide a finger set. Challenge students to show the same finger set quickly while saying aloud the number. Hold up your fingers again to confirm the correct answer. Have students count the fingers aloud in unison. After a few more rounds, have students respond using their Number Cubes.

Name _____

Using Finger Sets

Put a ring around each corner. Then count and write how many.

❶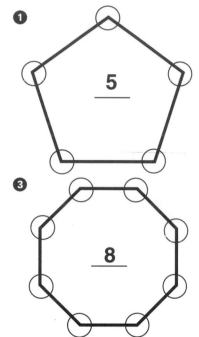

5

❷

4

❸

8

❹

3

 NOTE TO HOME
Students use finger sets and are introduced to geometric shapes.

RETEACHING

  If students have difficulty recognizing finger sets, have them practice with partners. You could also make **flash cards** with finger set illustrations such as those on student page 23. One side of the card shows the finger set, and the corresponding number is written on the other side of the card.

PRACTICE p. 11

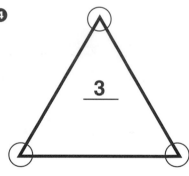

LESSON 11 PRACTICE   Name _____

Trace.

0 1 2 3 4 5 6 7 8 9 10

0 1 2 3 4 5 6 7 8 9 10

Trace.

0 1 2 3 4 5 6 7 8 9 10

0 1 2 3 4 5 6 7 8 9 10

Write.

0 1 2 3 4 5 6 7 8 9 10

0 1 2 3 4 5 6 7 8 9 10

*available separately

GAME

◆ **LESSON 11** Using Finger Sets

Take-Home Activity

Tracing and Writing Numbers

Players: **Two or more**
Materials: **Use one 0–5 Number Cube and one 5–10 Number Cube.**

RULES

Take turns. Each turn roll one cube. Then trace or write that number with a colored pencil. Each player uses a different color. When all of the numbers in a row have been written, count the numbers in each color. The player with the most numbers is the winner.

Game 1 Trace

| 0 | 1 | 2 | 3 | 4 | 5 | 6 | 7 | 8 | 9 | 10 |

Game 2 Trace

| 0 | 1 | 2 | 3 | 4 | 5 | 6 | 7 | 8 | 9 | 10 |

Game 3 Write

| | | | | | | | | | | |

Using the Student Pages Draw students' attention to the geometric figures on page 23. Point out that the place on each shape where two lines meet is called a corner. Have students draw a ring on the corner of each shape. Then have them count the number of corners on each figure and write that number on the answer line inside the shape.

Introducing the "Tracing and Writing Numbers" Game This game provides practice in recognizing, tracing, and writing numbers and in counting and probability. There are three game levels: tracing with arrows, tracing without arrows, and writing. Assign this page as a Take-Home Activity. Or in class have students work in pairs, using one Student Edition. A copy of this game can also be found on page 7 of the Home Connections Blackline Masters.

Using the Thinking Story Present three new problems from those following "How Many Piglets?" on pages 10–11 in the Thinking Story Book or page 85 of this Guide.

③ Wrap-Up

In Closing Have students name and count classroom objects with corners.

Mastery Checkpoint 2

Most students should now be able to recognize finger sets 0–10 without counting. Proficiency can be assessed by observing students during the demonstration or by assigning page 3 in the Assessment Blackline Masters. Results can be recorded on the Mastery Checkpoint Chart.

ENRICHMENT p. 11

LESSON 11 ENRICHMENT Name _____

Count the stripes on each flag.
Write how many.

❶ ___5___ stripes

❷ ___8___ stripes

❸ Draw your own flag. How many stripes does it have?
Art and answers will vary.

ASSESSMENT p. 3

UNIT 1 **Mastery Checkpoint 2** Recognizing finger sets without counting. (Lesson 11)

Name _____
The student demonstrates mastery by correctly identifying each finger set.

Tell the student that you are going to show finger sets. Explain that you will not allow enough time to count the fingers in the set.

Hold up a finger set.

Say: What number did I show?

		Identified
❶	2	_____
❷	5	_____
❸	4	_____
❹	7	_____
❺	3	_____
❻	10	_____
❼	9	_____
❽	1	_____
❾	8	_____
❿	6	_____

Assessment Criteria

Did the student . . .

✓ show mastery in recognizing finger sets 0–10 without counting?

✓ progress from tracing to writing the numbers 0–10?

✓ identify the correct number of corners in geometric shapes?

LOOKING AHEAD Each student will need a desk number line in the next lesson.

LESSON 12 ◆ Number Lines

Student Edition pages 25–26

LESSON PLANNER

Objectives

▶ to teach students to move a given number of places on a 0–10 number line

▶ to teach students to identify unnumbered places on the number line

▶ to provide practice in counting up to ten objects

Context of the Lesson This lesson introduces the number line, which is used in subsequent lessons throughout the book.

 MANIPULATIVES

can (optional)

coins* (optional)

desk number lines

Program Resources

Number Cubes

Thinking Story Book, pages 12–15

Reteaching Master

Practice Master 12

Enrichment Master 12

For career connections:
  Careers and Math*

For extra practice:
  CD-ROM* Lesson 12

① Warm-Up ⏱ 5 MINUTES

Problem of the Day Present the following problem and have students match each name with the number *2, 3,* or *4.* Rico has more cards than Jan. Jan has more cards than Brian. Brian has two cards. (Rico–4; Jan–3; Brian–2)

Problem-Solving Strategies Ask students who have solved the Problem of the Day to share how they solved it and any strategies they used.

MENTAL MATH Demonstrate the following numbers with finger sets and have students show the same number with their Number Cubes.

a. 0	b. 10	c. 2
d. 9	e. 3	f. 5

② Teach

Demonstrate Distribute **desk number lines**. Show students how to take a given number of steps from 0 by

---

LESSON 12

Name _____

Number Lines

0 1 2 3 4 5 6 7 8 9 10

Write how many.

❶ 5

❷ 3

❸ 2

❹ 0

❺ 9

❻ 8

❼ 7

❽ 6

❾ 4

❿ 1

Talk about the Thinking Story "Willy in the Water."

🎒 **NOTE TO HOME** Students use a number line.

Copyright © SRA/McGraw-Hill

Unit 1 Lesson 12 • **25**

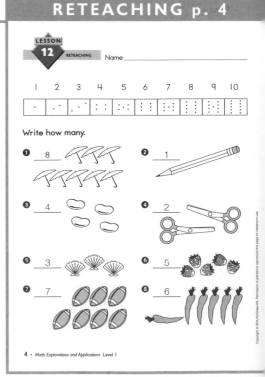

RETEACHING p. 4

LESSON 12 RETEACHING   Name _____

1 2 3 4 5 6 7 8 9 10

Write how many.

❶ 8

❷ 1

❸ 4

❹ 2

❺ 3

❻ 5

❼ 7

❽ 6

4 • *Math Explorations and Applications Level 1*

⭐ **LEARNING STYLES** ✋ **MANIPULATIVES**

Meeting Individual Needs Provide auditory learners with practice in counting by having them close their eyes and count silently as you slowly drop various numbers of **coins*** or metal objects (0–10) into a **can**. Then have students say and write the number of coins they counted. Finally, have them count aloud the coins to check their answers.

*available separately

◆ LESSON 12 Number Lines

Ring the right number.

⑪  (6)   2   5

⑫  6   (8)   9

⑬  (4)   3   5

⑭  5   (2)   3

⑮  8   6   (9)

26 • Numbers 1–10

NOTE TO HOME
Students match numerals with the correct number of objects.

Copyright © SRA/McGraw-Hill

"walking" with the index and middle fingers and counting each time a step is taken. For example, say, "Start at 0. Go up five steps. [Count with the students.] 1, 2, 3, 4, 5. What number did you stop on?" Then draw a number line on the chalkboard with only the 0 labeled. Demonstrate how to find out what number a given step is by counting the steps up from 0. Have volunteers identify various points on the number line.

Using the Number Cubes Point to a step on the chalkboard number line. Have students use their desk number lines to identify the number, then show the answer with Number Cubes.

Using the Student Pages Do the first problem on each page with the class. Then have students use the number line to help them complete the rest of each page on their own.

Using the Thinking Story Read aloud and discuss the story "Willy in the Water" on pages 12–15 of the Thinking Story Book.

Have students write about some other things Willy might have found on the beach.

❸ Wrap-Up 5 MINUTES

In Closing Have students show each answer on the chalkboard number line as you correct together pages 25–26.

Performance Assessment Observe which students can correctly identify places from 0 to 10 on the chalkboard number line.

PRACTICE p. 12

LESSON **12** PRACTICE Name _____

0 1 2 3 4 5 6 7 8 9 10

Write how many.

➊ ○○○○○ ○○○○○ [10]   **➋** 🖐 [4]

➌ ◇◇◇◇◇◇◇◇ [8]   **➍** 🖐 [3]

➎ 🎀🎀🎀🎀🎀 [5]   **➏** 👟👟 [2]

Ring the right number.

➐ 🖐🖐 **➑** 🍎🍎🍎🍎 **➒** ●●●●● ●●●●●

7 8 (9)   (6) 5 4   7 8 (10)

12 • Math Explorations and Applications Level 1

ENRICHMENT p. 12

LESSON **12** ENRICHMENT Name _____

Count. Then write how many.

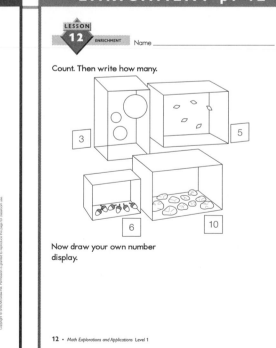

[3]   [5]   [6]   [10]

Now draw your own number display.

12 • Math Explorations and Applications Level 1

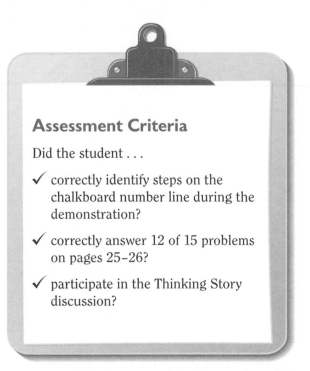

Assessment Criteria

Did the student . . .

✓ correctly identify steps on the chalkboard number line during the demonstration?

✓ correctly answer 12 of 15 problems on pages 25–26?

✓ participate in the Thinking Story discussion?

Willy in the Water

❶ Willy's uncle gave him a dog. After a while the dog had three puppies.
How many dogs did Willy have then? four

❷ "I'm six years old," said Willy. "When I have my next birthday, I'll be five."
What's wrong with what Willy said? He counted backward instead of forward.

❸ Yesterday Ferdie counted six ducks in the pond. Today there are eight ducks.
What could have happened? More ducks arrived; two eggs hatched.

❹ Portia had three nickels. She spent two for a pencil.
How many nickels does she have left? one

THINKING STORY

Willy in the Water

Willy the Wisher is always wishing that things were different, but he doesn't know what to do to make them different. One time he was on vacation at the seashore. Willy had great fun collecting things along the beach and wading in the water, but he kept wishing things were a little different.

Willy had three seashells that he had picked up along the shore. "I love these pearly shells," he said, "but I wish I had four of them instead of three."

What could Willy do to have four shells instead of three? find another shell

12 • Willy in the Water

Just then Willy happened to notice another shell on the sand. He picked it up. Then he counted his shells again.
How many shells does he have now? four
How do you know? 3 + 1 = 4

"My wish came true," said Willy. "I have four shells now." He also had four shiny white stones that he had found. But that was not how many stones he wanted.

"I wish I had two shiny stones instead of four," said Willy.

What could Willy do to have two stones instead of four? put down two or give away two

Willy couldn't think of any way to have two instead of four, so he kept those four heavy stones with him until they made a hole in his pocket and two of them fell out.

How many stones did Willy have then? two

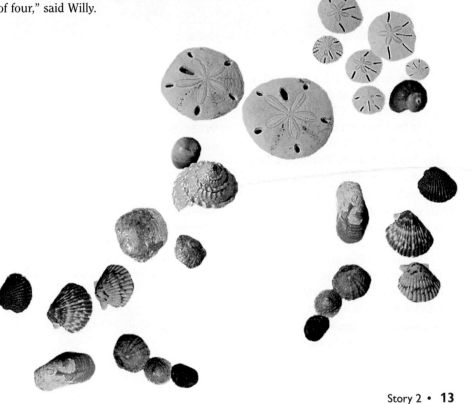

Story 2 • **13**

⑤ Marcus's mother gave him five grapes. He lost one and ate the rest.
How many grapes did he lose? one

⑥ Marcus went shopping with his mother and they bought two pairs of shoes. They put the package into the trunk of the car. One shoe slipped out of the box before they got home, but they didn't see it fall.
How many new shoes did they have when they went into the house? three

⑦ Portia had one pretzel. Mr. Muddle gave her two more, but she gave one of them to Ferdie.
How many pretzels did she have then? two

⑧ Manolita bought five notebooks at the store. Then she found out that she needed only two, so she took the others back.
How many notebooks did she take back? three

◆ **STORY 2** **Willy in the Water**

"My wish came true again," said Willy. "I have two shiny white stones now, just the way I wanted." But his wish didn't stay true for long because the other two stones fell out through the hole in his pocket too, and then he didn't have any.

Willy had also found five crab claws, but he wished he had seven.

What could Willy do to have seven crab claws instead of five? find two more

Willy was standing in the water near shore, wishing he had seven crab claws. Then he noticed that the water was about 8 inches deep where he was standing.

How deep is that? Show with your hands. [Demonstrate the correct depth.]

"The water feels good on my ankles," said Willy. "But I wish it were 10 inches deep instead of 8."

What could Willy do about it? wade in deeper

Willy didn't think about wading in deeper. He just stood there in the water, wishing. The tide was going out, so the water kept getting lower and lower. Soon the water wasn't 8 inches deep anymore, but 4 inches, then 2 inches, then 1 inch deep, and finally there wasn't any water around Willy's feet at all.

"Sometimes my wishes come true and sometimes they don't," said Willy.

. . . the end

14 • Willy in the Water

Story 2 • **15**

LESSON 13

Student Edition pages 27–28

What Comes Next?

LESSON PLANNER

Objectives

▶ to teach students to identify which number follows another number in the 0–10 range

▶ to provide practice in counting objects and writing numbers up to 10

Context of the Lesson Counting objects and writing numbers continue from previous lessons. Work on number sequence continues in the next lesson.

 MANIPULATIVES

counters*

desk number lines

Step-by-Step Number Line*

Program Resources

Number Cubes

Thinking Story Book, pages 16–17

Practice Master 13

Enrichment Master 13

For extra practice: CD-ROM* Lesson 13

1 Warm-Up

Problem of the Day Read the following problem to the class and write the number names on the chalkboard as you say them: Marvin's teacher told him to draw *four* circles at the top of his paper, *eight* circles in the middle, and *five* circles at the bottom. What should Marvin's paper look like?

Problem-Solving Strategies Ask students who have solved the Problem of the Day to share how they solved it and any strategies they used.

MENTAL MATH Point to the following steps on a number line marked with only 0. Have students count corresponding steps on their **desk number lines** and show the number with finger sets.

a. 6	b. 7	c. 4
d. 3	e. 8	f. 5

2 Teach

Demonstrate Call out specific numbers from 0–9 and have students tell what number comes next. Then count aloud to a specific number. Ask, "What number comes next?" Have students use Number Cubes to show their answers.

27 Numbers 1–10

LESSON 13

Name _____

What Comes Next?

Ring the next number.
Answers will depend on the questions asked.

① 0 1 2 3 4 5 6 7 8 9 10

② 0 1 2 3 4 5 6 7 8 9 10

③ 0 1 2 3 4 5 6 7 8 9 10

④ 0 1 2 3 4 5 6 7 8 9 10

⑤ 0 1 2 3 4 5 6 7 8 9 10

⑥ 0 1 2 3 4 5 6 7 8 9 10

⑦ 0 1 2 3 4 5 6 7 8 9 10

 GAME Play the "Which Has More?" game.

Copyright © SRA/McGraw-Hill

 NOTE TO HOME Students ring the number that comes after the number they hear.

Unit 1 Lesson 13 • **27**

 Literature Connection Students can predict what number, animal, or person comes next as you read aloud *The Snow Parade* by Barbara Brenner.

Real-World Connection List the daily schedule on the chalkboard and number each item. For example: 1. Reading; 2. Math; 3. Art; 4. Lunch, and so on. As you end an activity during the day, ask students what number comes next and what the subject is. At the end of the day, ask questions such as: "What did we do after activity number 3?"

RETEACHING

MANIPULATIVES Place the **Step-by-Step Number Line*** on the floor. Have students walk up and back along the number line to locate numbers from 0–10.

*available separately

◆ LESSON 13   What Comes Next?

Draw one more.
Then write how many.

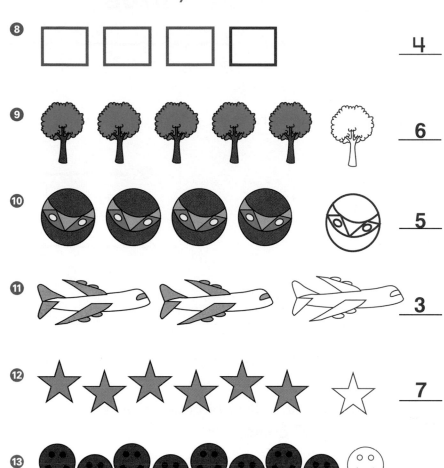

8 _4_

9 _6_

10 _5_

11 _3_

12 _7_

13 _9_

NOTE TO HOME
Students add one more.

PRACTICE p. 13

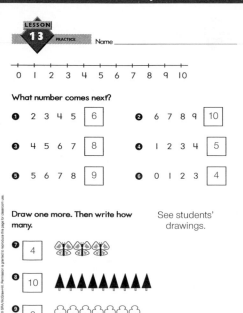

LESSON **13** PRACTICE   Name _____

```
0  1  2  3  4  5  6  7  8  9  10
```

What number comes next?

❶ 2 3 4 5 [6]   ❷ 6 7 8 9 [10]

❸ 4 5 6 7 [8]   ❹ 1 2 3 4 [5]

❺ 5 6 7 8 [9]   ❻ 0 1 2 3 [4]

Draw one more. Then write how many.   See students' drawings.

❼ [4] 🌸🌸🌸🌸

❽ [10] ▲▲▲▲▲▲▲▲▲▲

❾ [8] ☘☘☘☘☘☘☘☘

Math Explorations and Applications Level 1 • 13

ENRICHMENT p. 13

LESSON **13** ENRICHMENT   Name _____

Start at 1. Count up. Draw lines to connect the numbers.

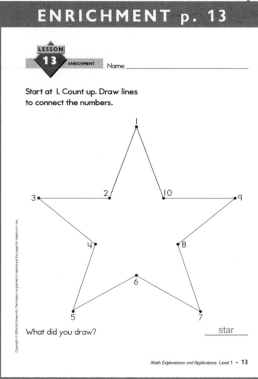

What did you draw?   ___star___

Math Explorations and Applications Level 1 • 13

Introducing the "Which Has More?" Game This game provides practice in estimating quantity and one-to-one correspondence. Have students play in pairs. Place about 40 **counters*** into a central pile. Player 1 divides all the counters into two roughly equal piles without counting. Player 2 chooses the pile he or she thinks has more counters. To find out which pile has more, players place one counter at a time from their respective piles into the center until one of them runs out of counters. The player with counters remaining keeps them. Players switch roles and repeat. The first player to get six counters wins. A copy of this game can also be found on page 8 of the Home Connections Blackline Masters.

Using the Student Pages Have students complete page 27 as you give instructions such as: "Put your finger by problem 1. Darken the number that comes after 7." For each problem, provide a different number from 0–10. Then go over the first problem on page 28 with students and have them complete the rest of the page on their own.

Using the Thinking Story Present and discuss three problems from those following "Willy in the Water" on pages 16–17 of the Thinking Story Book or on pages 26a–26b of this Guide.

❸ Wrap-Up 🕐 5 MINUTES

In Closing Have students explain how they know which number comes next.

Informal Assessment Check students' answers on pages 27–28 to informally assess their ability to tell what number comes next.

Assessment Criteria

Did the student . . .

✓ actively participate in solving Thinking Story problems?

✓ correctly answer 10 of 13 problems on pages 27–28?

LOOKING AHEAD You will need a small bouncing ball, such as a table tennis or rubber ball, for the next lesson.

LESSON 14

Student Edition pages 29–30

Using Number Lines

Name _____

Using Number Lines

```
0  1  2  3  4  5  6  7  8  9  10
```

Fill in the next number.

1   5   6   **7**

2   7   8   **9**

3   1   2   **3**

4   4   5   **6**

5   3   4   **5**

6   0   1   **2**

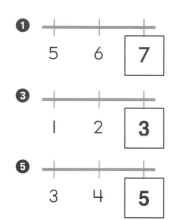 Play the "What Number Comes Next?" game.

 Do the "Counting Bounces" activity.

 NOTE TO HOME
Students indicate what number comes next on the number line.

Unit 1   Lesson 14   •   29

LESSON PLANNER

Objectives

▶ to provide practice in identifying number sequence in the 0–10 range

✓ to assess students' ability to recognize numbers from 0–10

Context of the Lesson This lesson includes Mastery Checkpoint 3 for assessing students' ability to recognize numbers from 0–10.

 MANIPULATIVES   **Program Resources**

ball that bounces	Number Cubes
desk number lines	Thinking Story Book, pages 16–17
index cards	Practice Master 14
	Enrichment Master 14
	Assessment Master

For extra practice:
CD-ROM* Lesson 14
Mixed Practice, page 351

① Warm-Up ⏱ 5 MINUTES

 Problem of the Day Read aloud the following to the class. Every day Ali exercises one minute longer than the day before. Today she exercised for eight minutes. How many minutes will she exercise the day after tomorrow? (ten)

Problem-Solving Strategies Ask students who have solved the Problem of the Day to share how they solved it and any strategies they used.

 Call out specific numbers from 0–9. Have students use finger sets to indicate the next number.

② Teach

Introducing the "What Number Comes Next?" Game This game provides practice in number sequence. Divide students into groups of three. Each player needs a set of Number Cubes and a **desk number line**. Begin by having one player point to a number from 0–9 on the number line. Both other players roll one of their cubes as quickly and often as they can until one of them rolls the next number. The first player to roll and say the right number wins the round and becomes the lead player for the next round. A copy of this game can also be found on page 9 of the Home Connections Blackline Masters.

29   Numbers 1–10

RETEACHING

Write numbers from 0–10 on the chalkboard. Then hold up a number (written on **index cards**) from 0–9. Have students take turns coming to the chalkboard and identifying the number that comes next.

PRACTICE p. 14

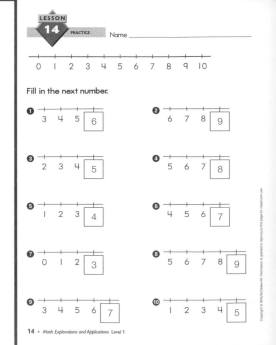

LESSON 14 PRACTICE   Name _____

```
0  1  2  3  4  5  6  7  8  9  10
```

Fill in the next number.

1 3 4 5 **6**   **2** 6 7 8 **9**

3 2 3 4 **5**   **4** 5 6 7 **8**

5 1 2 3 **4**   **6** 4 5 6 **7**

7 0 1 2 **3**   **8** 5 6 7 8 **9**

9 3 4 5 6 **7**   **10** 1 2 3 4 **5**

14 • *Math Explorations and Applications Level 1*

*available separately

◆ LESSON 14 Using Number Lines

Draw one more. Then write how many.

Use the Mixed Practice on page 351 after this lesson.

7 4

8 5

9 3

10 7

11 2

12 9

13 8

14 6

 NOTE TO HOME
Students add one more.

Copyright © SRA/McGraw-Hill

ENRICHMENT p. 14

LESSON 14 ENRICHMENT Name _____

Help the mail carrier. Fill in the missing numbers.

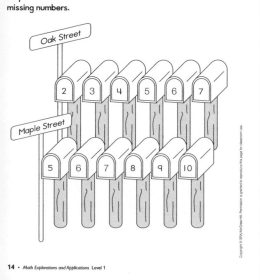

Oak Street
2 3 4 5 6 7

Maple Street
5 6 7 8 9 10

14 • Math Explorations and Applications Level 1

ASSESSMENT p. 4

UNIT 1 Mastery Checkpoint 3 Number recognition (Lesson 14)

Name _____

The student demonstrates mastery by correctly identifying all of the numbers.

9
2   10
     6
3
         7
    4
8
  5   0

1

Students say the name of each number.

4 • Math Explorations and Applications Level 1

Introducing the "Counting Bounces" Activity

This activity gives students practice in counting when counting is not done at a fixed rate. Bounce a small **ball**, such as a table tennis ball, onto a flat surface. Have students count the bounces before the ball stops or bounces off the surface. Experiment with dropping the ball from different heights and on different surfaces to see how to get the most bounces. Students may discover that bounces occur more frequently as they grow shorter.

Using the Student Pages After students complete pages 29–30 on their own, correct the pages together.

Using the Thinking Story Present and discuss three problems from those following "Willy in the Water" on pages 16–17 of the Thinking Story Book or on pages 26a–26b of this Guide.

❸ Wrap-Up 🕐 5 MINUTES

In Closing Ask students which way to step on a number line to show which number comes next. (to the right)

✓ Mastery Checkpoint 3

At about this time you may want to formally assess students' ability to recognize numbers from 0–10. Proficiency can be demonstrated by correctly answering 80% of the questions on page 4 of the Assessment Blackline Masters. Results can be recorded on the Mastery Checkpoint Chart.

Assessment Criteria

Did the student . . .

✓ demonstrate proficiency on Mastery Checkpoint 3?

✓ correctly complete 11 of 14 problems on pages 29–30?

LEARNING STYLES Meeting Individual Needs
Although this lesson focuses on written numbers, allow auditory learners to say aloud the numbers as they complete pages 29–30.

LESSON 15

Student Edition pages 31–34

Before and After

Name _____

Before and After

| 0 | 1 | 2 | 3 | 4 | 5 | 6 | 7 | 8 | 9 | 10 |

Fill in the missing numbers.

1 1   2   3   **4**   5   6   7

2 3   4   5   6   7   **8**   9

3 2   **3**   4   5   6   7   8

4 0   1   **2**   3   4   **5**   6

5 1   2   3   **4**   5   **6**   7

6 3   4   5   6   **7**   **8**   9

LESSON PLANNER

Objectives

▶ to teach students to count backward or forward from a given number in the 0–10 range

✓ to assess students' ability to insert the correct number in a sequence from 0–10

Context of the Lesson Practice in counting forward and backward from given numbers is provided throughout the year. This lesson includes Mastery Checkpoint 4 for assessing students' ability to insert the correct number in a sequence.

 MANIPULATIVES   **Program Resources**

desk number lines

The Three Billy Goats Gruff*
   from the Literature Library

Number Cubes

Thinking Story Book, pages 16–17

Reteaching Master

Practice Master 15

Enrichment Master 15

Assessment Master

For extra practice:
   CD-ROM* Lesson 15

 GAME Play the "What Number Comes Before?" Game.

 NOTE TO HOME Students count backward and forward from a given number.

Unit 1   Lesson 15 • 31

1 Warm-Up

5 MINUTES

 Problem of the Day Write the number 4 on the chalkboard. Ask volunteers to name numbers that come after 4; ask others to name numbers that come before.

Problem-Solving Strategies Ask students who have solved the Problem of the Day to share how they solved it and any strategies they used.

MENTAL MATH Write the following numbers on the chalkboard, and have students show with finger sets what comes next.

a. 7 (8)   **b.** 4 (5)

c. 2 (3)   **d.** 0 (1)

e. 1 (2)   **f.** 8 (9)

g. 6 (7)   **h.** 3 (4)

 LITERATURE CONNECTION **Literature Connection** Read *1, 2, 3 to the Zoo* by Eric Carle. After looking at this picture book of a train of circus animals illustrating numbers through 10, ask students to respond with the numbers that come before and after.

*available separately

◆ LESSON 15 Before and After

Cross out one. Then write how many are left. The first one has been done for you.

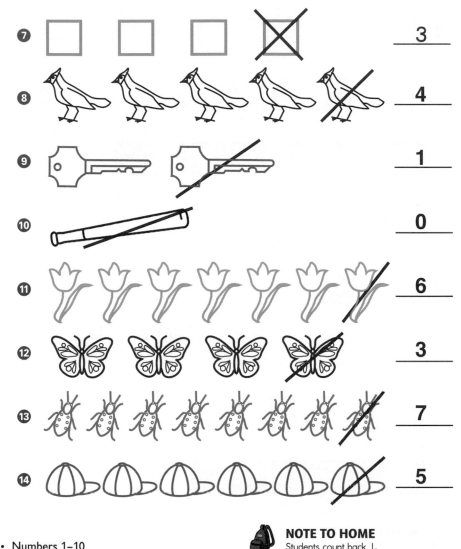

⑦ ☐ ☐ ☐ ☒   3

⑧   4

⑨   1

⑩   0

⑪   6

⑫   3

⑬   7

⑭   5

NOTE TO HOME
Students count back 1.

32 • Numbers 1–10

Copyright © SRA/McGraw-Hill

② Teach

Demonstrate Review Lessons 12 and 13 by having students say what number comes after 8, 7, and so on. Then ask: "When you count, what comes before 6?" Have students check the answer by seeing what finger set they made just before 6.

 Using the Number Cubes Write numbers from 0–10 on the chalkboard. Give students mixed practice in using their Number Cubes to show what number comes before and after.

Using the Student Pages Work the first problems on pages 31–32 as a class. Then have students complete these pages on their own.

 Introducing the "What Number Comes Before?" Game To provide practice using a number line to determine the next lower number in the 0–10 range, demonstrate the "What Number Comes Before?" game. Separate students into groups of three. Each student will need Number Cubes and a **desk number line**. Begin by having one player point to a number on a 0–10 number line. The other players each roll one of their cubes as quickly and often as they can until one of them rolls the number preceding the one selected. The player who rolls and says the right number first wins the round and becomes the lead player for the next round. A copy of this game can also be found on page 10 of the Home Connections Blackline Masters.

Technology Connection You may want to have your students use the software program *James Discovers Math* from Broderbund Software, Inc. (Mac, IBM, for grades K–2). It presents various games, including some that reinforce counting, problem solving, and numbers from 1–10.

Literature Connection Use the big book *The Three Billy Goats Gruff* from the Literature Library* to develop the concept of sequence.

> *Mathematics is not a solitary activity. It should be done and learned with others. Games, activities, projects, proofs, problem-formulation activities, and so on are all activities that should be carried on in groups. Where possible, those groups should involve children of different abilities, different interests, and different backgrounds; and each member of the group should be expected to make substantial contributions and derive substantial satisfaction.*
>
> —Stephen S. Willoughby,
> *Mathematics Education for a Changing World*

◆ LESSON 15 Before and After

Teach

Using the Student Pages Have students complete pages 33–34 on their own.

 **Using the Thinking Story** Present and discuss two problems from those following "Willy in the Water" on pages 16–17 of the Thinking Story Book or on pages 26a–26b of this Guide.

◆ LESSON 15 Before and After

Name _____

Cross out one. Then write how many are left.

15    6

16    4

17    7

18   0

19    1

20    8

21    2

22    5

Copyright © SRA/McGraw-Hill

🎒 **NOTE TO HOME**
Students count back by 1.

Unit 1 Lesson 15 • **33**

RETEACHING p. 5

LESSON 15 RETEACHING Name _____

0 1 2 3 4 5 6 7 8 9 10

1 2 3 ____ 5

1...2...3...4!

Fill in the missing numbers.

❶ 1 _2_ 3 4 5 6 7

❷ _0_ 1 2 3 4 5 6

❸ 4 5 6 _7_ 8 9 10

❹ 3 4 5 6 7 8 _9_

❺ 2 3 4 _5_ 6 7 8

Math Explorations and Applications Level 1 • **5**

PRACTICE p. 15

LESSON 15 PRACTICE Name _____

0 1 2 3 4 5 6 7 8 9 10

Fill in the missing numbers.

❶ [4] 5 6   ❷ 3 4 [5]

❸ [1] 2 3   ❹ 7 8 [9]

❺ 7 8 9   ❻ 5 6 [7]

❼ [5] 6 7   ❽ 1 2 [3]

❾ [0] 1 2   ❿ 4 5 [6]

⓫ [6] 7 8   ⓬ 2 3 [4]

⓭ [2] 3 4   ⓮ 6 7 [8]

⓯ [3] 4 5   ⓰ 0 1 [2]

Math Explorations and Applications Level 1 • **15**

33 Numbers 1–10

◆ **LESSON 15** Before and After

```
+---+---+---+---+---+---+---+---+---+---+
0   1   2   3   4   5   6   7   8   9   10
```

Write the missing number.

㉓ 3 [4] 5

㉔ 5 [6] 7

㉕ 7 [8] 9

㉖ [4] 5 6

㉗ 8 [9] 10

㉘ 0 1 [2]

㉙ 2 [3] 4

㉚ 2 3 [4]

㉛ 4 [5] 6

㉜ 3 4 [5]

㉝ 8 [9] 10

㉞ 7 8 [9]

34 • Numbers 1–10

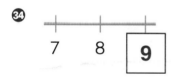

NOTE TO HOME
Students use a number line to complete
number patterns.

Copyright © SRA/McGraw-Hill

---

③ Wrap-Up ⏱ 5 MINUTES

In Closing Have students share and compare their
answers for pages 31–34.

 Mastery Checkpoint 4

At about this time you may want to formally assess
students' ability to insert the correct number in a
sequence from 0–10. You can use pages 31 and 34 in the
Student Edition or page 5 in the Assessment Blackline
Masters to assess this skill. The results of this
assessment may be recorded on the Mastery
Checkpoint Chart.

Assessment Criteria

Did the student . . .

✓ demonstrate proficiency on Mastery
Checkpoint 4?

✓ correctly answer 28 of 34 problems
on pages 31–34?

✓ recognize which number comes
before when playing the "What
Number Comes Before?" game?

Missing Numbers

LESSON PLANNER

Objectives

▶ to provide students with practice in locating a given number on the Number Cubes

 to assess students' ability to write recognizable numbers from 0–10

Context of the Lesson
This lesson provides practice in both writing numbers and finding specific numbers on the Number Cubes. This lesson includes Mastery Checkpoint 5 for assessing students' ability to write recognizable numbers from 0–10.

 **MANIPULATIVES**

paper (unruled or wide-ruled)

Program Resources

Number Cubes

Practice Master 16

Enrichment Master 16

Assessment Master

For extra practice: CD-ROM* Lesson 16

① Warb-Up ⏱ 5 MINUTES

 Problem of the Day Read the following riddle to the class. "I am a number that comes before 7, but after 4. What numbers could I be?" (5, 6)

Problem-Solving Strategies Ask students who have solved the Problem of the Day to share how they solved it and any strategies they used.

MENTAL MATH Have students use finger sets to show the next number that comes:

a. after 6 (7)	**b.** after 9 (10)
c. before 2 (1)	**d.** after 0 (1)
e. before 7 (6)	**f.** before 1 (0)
g. after 5 (6)	**h.** before 8 (7)
i. after 8 (9)	**j.** before 10 (9)

Name _____

Missing Numbers

① Which cube has a 9 on it? Draw a ring around it.

Fill in the missing numbers.

②　3　4　5　**6**　7

③　1　**2**　3　4

④　5　**6**　7　8　9

⑤　6　**7**　8　9　10

⑥　3　**4**　**5**　6　7

⑦　**0**　1　2　3

 NOTE TO HOME
Students gain experience writing numbers 0–10.

Unit 1　Lesson 16　•　35

RETEACHING

Have volunteers come to the chalkboard and write any number they choose from 0–10. Have the rest of the class show the Number Cube that the number is on. Repeat until all numbers from 0–10 have been written on the chalkboard and shown on Number Cubes.

PRACTICE p. 16

LESSON 16 PRACTICE Name _____

Fill in the missing numbers.

① 2　3　4　**5** 　　**②** 7　8　**9**　10

③ **0**　1　2　3 　　**④** 3　4　5　**6**

⑤ 6　7　**8**　9 　　**⑥** 0　**1**　2　3

Draw an X on the number, word, or picture that does not belong.

⑦ ◆◆◆◆◆◆◆◆◆　9　eight

⑧ 🎩🎩🎩　3̶　three

⑨ 〰〰〰〰〰〰　6　six

⑩ ⚽⚽⚽⚽　4̶　four

16 • *Math Explorations and Applications Level 1*

◆ **LESSON 16** Missing Numbers

Ring the number, word, or picture
that does not belong.
The first one is done for you.

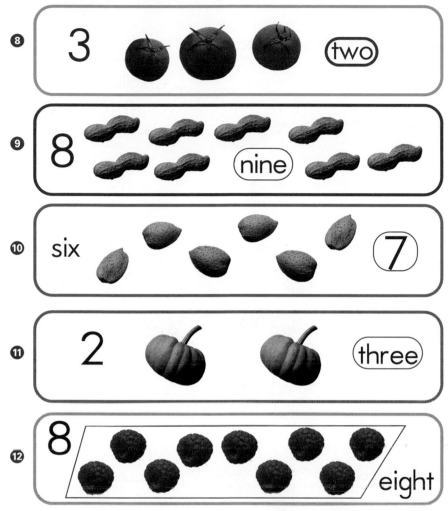

❽ 3 (two)

❾ 8 (nine)

❿ six 7

⓫ 2 (three)

⓬ 8 eight

 NOTE TO HOME
Students practice counting and number
recognition.

36 • Numbers 1–10

Copyright © SRA/McGraw-Hill

❷ Teach

Demonstrate Explore the Number Cubes
together with students. Ask them to read the
numbers on each and notice which one has the
greater numbers and which has the lesser. Point out that
there is a 5 on both cubes. Then call out a number. Have
students hold up the cube where the number is found.

Review number formation for 0–10. Have some students
stand at the chalkboard to write numbers that you call out.
Have the rest of the class write the same numbers on **paper**.
Have students proofread their own work, circling any
incorrect numbers and writing the correct one above it. Be
sure everyone has a turn at the chalkboard.

Using the Student Pages Have students complete
pages 35–36 on their own and then correct them together.

❸ Wrap-Up

In Closing Have students explain how they know which
Number Cubes the numbers 3 and 7 are on.

Mastery Checkpoint 5

At about this time you may want to formally assess
students' ability to write numbers from 0–10.
Proficiency can be **assessed** by observing students as
they do the writing practice activity or by using page 6
in the Assessment Blackline Masters. The results of this
assessment may be recorded on the Mastery
Checkpoint Chart.

ENRICHMENT p. 16

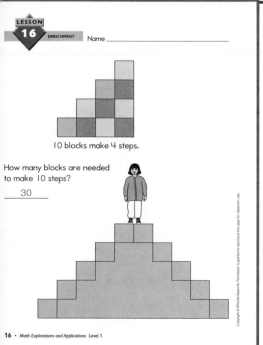
ASSESSMENT p. 6

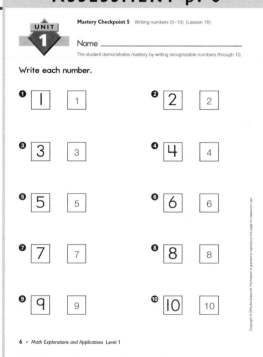
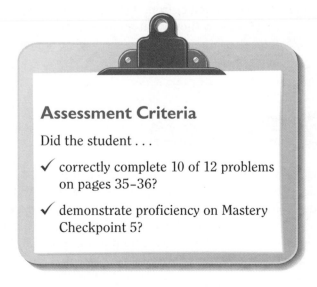

Assessment Criteria

Did the student . . .

✓ correctly complete 10 of 12 problems
on pages 35–36?

✓ demonstrate proficiency on Mastery
Checkpoint 5?

LESSON 17

Student Edition pages 37–38

Tally Marks

LESSON PLANNER

Objectives

▶ to introduce the use of tally marks for keeping an accurate count of 1–10 items

▶ to provide practice in writing sequential numbers

Context of the Lesson This is the first of a series of lessons on using tally marks to keep accurate counts.

 MANIPULATIVES

chalkboard
eraser

sponges
(optional)

Program Resources

Thinking Story Book, pages 16–17

Practice Master 17

Enrichment Master 17

For extra practice:
CD-ROM* Lesson 17

---

① Warm-Up

5 MINUTES

Problem of the Day Present the following problem to the class. Alex has six daisies. Caitlin has four tulips. How many different ways can you show how many flowers each child has? (Possible answers include Number Cubes, finger sets, numerals, illustrations, counters, or other manipulatives.)

Problem-Solving Strategies Ask students who have solved the Problem of the Day to share how they solved it and any strategies they used.

MENTAL MATH Call out a number from 0–10. Have students use finger sets to show what number comes next. Repeat, asking students to show what number comes before.

② Teach

Demonstrate Clap your hands a series of times as students form finger sets to keep count. Clap faster so that students cannot keep up. Ask students to clap quickly as you demonstrate how to use tally marks to keep count. It is not necessary to spend time introducing the conventional system of tallying groups of five here.

LESSON 17

Answers will depend on the questions asked.

Name _____

Tally Marks

Keep count.

How many times did your teacher

	Tallies	Total
❶ open a book? 	‖‖	4
❷ touch ear? 	‖‖	3
❸ touch nose?	‖‖‖	6
❹ catch an eraser?	**And so on.**	
❺ clap hands? 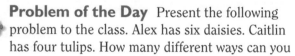		
❻ close the door?		

 NOTE TO HOME
Students use tally marks to keep accurate count of events.

Copyright © SRA/McGraw-Hill

Why **teach it at this time?**

Students are learning that there are many ways to represent numbers. Tally marks are one more way to represent numbers and are especially useful for tracking frequency.

Literature Connection You may wish to read to students *The King's Commissioners* by Aileen Friedman to reinforce lesson concepts.

RETEACHING

Students who are having difficulty forming numbers will benefit from individual help while they are in the process of writing. Encourage practice by having students write with wipe-off markers on a white board or with damp **sponges** or chalk on the chalkboard.

---

*available separately

◆ LESSON 17 Tally Marks

Fill in the missing numbers.

⑦ 4   5   6   **7**   8   9   **10**

⑧ 3   4   **5**   6   7   8   **9**

⑨ 0   **1**   2   3   4   **5**   6

⑩ 0   **1**   2   3   4   5   6

⑪ 7   6   5   **4**   3   2   1

⑫ 10   **9**   8   7   6   5   4

⑬ 3   4   5   **6**   **7**   8   9

⑭ 6   5   4   **3**   2   **1**   0

NOTE TO HOME
Students practice writing numbers in sequence.

Copyright © SRA/McGraw-Hill

Using the Student Pages Have students make tally marks on page 37 as you perform the indicated actions from 1–10 times. Then have them count the tally marks and enter the total. Compare results. Confirm each total by repeating the actions more slowly while students count aloud. As students become familiar with the use of tally marks, introduce irrelevant actions that should not be counted. Then have students keep track of two actions at once by making tally marks in two different boxes. Students can complete page 38 on their own.

Using the Thinking Story Present one or two problems from those following "Willy in the Water" on pages 16–17 in the Thinking Story Book or on pages 26a–26b of this Guide.

③ Wrap-Up ⏱ 5 MINUTES

In Closing Summarize the lesson together by brainstorming different ways to keep count, such as finger sets, tally marks, and Number Cubes. Have students discuss which method they prefer, and why.

SELF ASSESSMENT

Review the answers to page 38 with the class. Have students proofread their work by circling every incorrect number and inserting the correct answer next to it.

Assessment Criteria

Did the student . . .

✓ use tally marks correctly?

✓ demonstrate accuracy in writing numbers in sequence?

✓ form the numbers correctly?

PRACTICE p. 17

LESSON 17 PRACTICE Name _____

Fill in the missing numbers.

❶ 3 4 **5**   **❷** 8 **9** 10

❸ **4** 5 6   **❹** **3** 4 5

❺ **8** 9 10   **❻** 7 8 **9**

❼ 2 **3** 4   **❽** 0 **1** 2

❾ **5** 6 7   **❿** 0 1 **2** 3

⓫ 4 5 6 **7**   **⓬** **6** 7 8 9

⓭ 2 **3** 4 5   **⓮** 0 **1** 2 3

Copyright © SRA/McGraw-Hill. Permission is granted to reproduce this page for classroom use.

Math Explorations and Applications Level 1 • 17

ENRICHMENT p. 17

LESSON 17 ENRICHMENT Name _____

Ask friends to choose their favorite color. Keep count. Write the numbers.
Answers will vary. Check that students totaled the tally marks correctly.

	Tallies	Total
Blue	_____	____
Red	_____	____
Green	_____	____
Purple	_____	____
Brown	_____	____
Yellow	_____	____
White	_____	____
Black	_____	____

Copyright © SRA/McGraw-Hill. Permission is granted to reproduce this page for classroom use.

Math Explorations and Applications Level 1 • 17

LESSON
18

Student Edition pages 39–40

Making Graphs

LESSON PLANNER

Objectives

▶ to introduce bar graphs

▶ to have students make their own bar graphs with manipulatives

Context of the Lesson This is the first lesson on making graphs. Graphs are continued through Lesson 21.

 MANIPULATIVES

construction paper (blue, red, and yellow)

counters* (blue, red, and yellow)

graphing mat*

grid paper (optional)

Program Resources

Number Cubes

Practice Master 18

Enrichment Master 18

For extra practice:
CD-ROM* Lesson 18
Mixed Practice, page 352

❶ Warm-Up ⏱ 5 MINUTES

Problem of the Day Have students copy and complete the following pattern from the chalkboard. triangle, triangle, circle; triangle, triangle, circle; triangle _____, _____; triangle. (triangle, circle)

Problem-Solving Strategies Ask students who have solved the Problem of the Day to share how they solved it and any strategies they used.

MENTAL MATH Call out the following numbers and have students quickly hold up the Number Cube on which they think the number appears.

a. 0 (0–5)	**b.** 10 (5–10)
c. 9 (5–10)	**d.** 5 (either)
e. 4 (0–5)	**f.** 8 (5–10)

GIFTED & TALENTED **Meeting Individual Needs**
Challenge pairs of students to create a graph that shows the favorite books, movies, or television shows of classmates. Give students several days to survey their classmates and complete the graphs; then they can present them to the class.

LESSON
18

Name _____

Making Graphs

Place your counters in the right boxes. Then tell how many of each. Color your graph when you are finished.

Answers will depend on how many counters of each color the children receive.

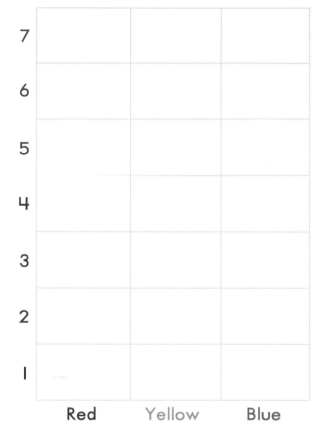

| | Red | Yellow | Blue |

NOTE TO HOME Students record data on a graph.

Copyright © SRA/McGraw-Hill

Unit 1   Lesson 18 • **39**

RETEACHING

CULTURAL DIVERSITY Work with the class to make a graph showing how many students in your class have visited countries outside the U.S. and what those countries were. Encourage students to describe some of the things they enjoyed on their visits.

> *. . . if we want students to be really good at a particular skill, or if we want them to really remember and understand a concept, we must arrange for them to practice.*
>
> —Stephen S. Willoughby,
> *Mathematics Education for a Changing World*

Provide a sheet of **grid paper** to each student. Have them draw a different colored square at the bottom of four columns: red, blue, yellow, green. Then take a survey by asking students to vote on their favorite color. After each vote, have students color in the appropriate boxes in each column. When students have finished, have them discuss the results and compare their graphs.

*available separately

◆ **LESSON 18 Making Graphs**

Look at the picture.

Use the Mixed Practice on page 352 after this lesson.

❶ How many apples? ___5___

❷ How many bananas? ___3___

❸ How many pears? ___4___

❹ Make a picture graph. Color in the right number.

5	🍎	🍌	🍐
4	🍎	🍌	🍐
3	🍎	🍌	🍐
2	🍎	🍌	🍐
1	🍎	🍌	🍐

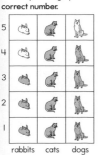 **NOTE TO HOME**
Students collect data and record it on a graph.

Copyright © SRA/McGraw-Hill

② **Teach**

Using the Student Pages Use a **graphing mat*** to teach students to read a graph. Place four small pieces of **red paper** in one column, three pieces of **yellow paper** in a second column, and five pieces of **blue paper** in a third column. Ask how many red papers, yellow papers, and blue papers are on the graphing mat. (4, 3, 5) Then provide students with 15 red, yellow, and blue **counters,*** with no more than seven counters of any one color. Have students place the counters in the appropriate columns on the graph in the book. Then have students color in the appropriate number of boxes in each column of the graph. Have students next look at the pictures at the top of page 40. Read each problem to the class. Have students answer the questions and complete the graph on their own.

③ **Wrap-Up** ⏱ 5 MINUTES

In Closing Ask students to explain how they knew the number of boxes to color for each column of the graph on page 39.

Portfolio Assessment Have students place pages 39–40 in their Math Portfolios as an assessment of their ability to make graphs.

Assessment Criteria

Did the student . . .

✓ correctly place the counters in the right columns and count them?

✓ accurately count and graph the quantity of fruit on page 40?

*available separately

LESSON 19 Reading Picture Graphs

Student Edition pages 41–42

LESSON PLANNER

Objectives

▶ to provide practice in reading picture graphs

▶ to supply opportunities to collect data and report it using picture graphs

Context of the Lesson This is the second lesson on how to read and make graphs. Practice with graphs is continued through Lesson 21.

 MANIPULATIVES

crayons (optional)

paper (optional)

Program Resources

Number Cubes

Practice Master 19

Enrichment Master 19

For extra practice:
CD-ROM* Lesson 19

1 Warm-Up ⏱ 5 MINUTES

 Problem of the Day Draw a square on the chalkboard. Ask students to make a shape that has one corner less than the square. (Students should draw a triangle.)

Problem-Solving Strategies Ask students who have solved the Problem of the Day to share how they solved it and any strategies they used.

 MENTAL MATH Call out the following numbers and have students quickly show the units Number Cube where the number appears.

a. 2 (0–5)

b. 1 (0–5)

c. 6 (5–10)

d. 7 (5–10)

e. 3 (0–5)

f. 4 (0–5)

 SPECIAL NEEDS **Meeting Individual Needs**
Have students make simple picture graphs that reflect information about themselves. For example, have them make a picture graph with two columns, one labeled "boys" and the other column labeled "girls." Then have students draw a picture of each family member in the appropriate column.

LESSON 19

Name _____

Reading Picture Graphs

REAL-WORLD CONNECTION Look at the picture graph.

How We Get to School

Number of Students			
7		🚶	
6		🚶	🚗
5	🚌	🚶	🚗
4	🚌	🚶	🚗
3	🚌	🚶	🚗
2	🚌	🚶	🚗
1	🚌	🚶	🚗

❶ How many students come to school by 🚗 ? **6**

❷ How many students take the 🚌 ? **5**

❸ How many students 🚶 ? **7**

 NOTE TO HOME Students read a picture graph to get information.

Unit 1 Lesson 19 • **41**

Copyright © SRA/McGraw-Hill

Technology Connection To help students make the transition from graphing with manipulatives to graphing in the abstract, use *The Graph Club of Fizz and Martina* from Tom Snyder Productions, Inc. (Mac).

RETEACHING

Discuss other subjects students would like to survey. List their ideas on the chalkboard. Then divide the class into small groups and assign a survey to each group. Give groups time to conduct and report their findings using picture graphs. Have groups share their results with the class.

*available separately

◆ **LESSON 19** Reading Picture Graphs

HEALTH CONNECTION

Look at the graph.

Our Favorite Lunch

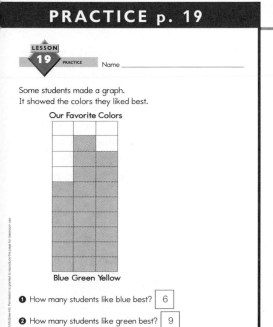

Number of Students

9 8 7 6 5 4 3 2 1

❹ How many students like sandwiches best? | 3 |

❺ How many students like pizza best? | 9 |

❻ How many students like tacos best? | 7 |

MATH JOURNAL

Make a graph in your Math Journal. Show what students in your class like for lunch.

Answers will vary.

Copyright: © SRA/McGraw-Hill

42 • Numbers 1–10

NOTE TO HOME
Students read picture graphs.

---

❷ Teach

Using the Student Pages Have students look at the picture graph on page 41. Tell them that a class made a survey of how many students get to school by bus, by walking, or by car. Ask whether the most students in that class take the bus, walk, or come in a car. (walk) Ask how many come by car. (6) Have students write this answer next to the first question and then answer the other questions on their own. Explain that the graph on page 42 shows what some students like for lunch: sandwiches, pizza, or tacos. Have students answer the questions about the graph. Then have students conduct a survey like the one on page 42 and report the results on a picture graph in their Math Journals.

❸ Wrap-Up

In Closing Ask students to share the picture graphs they made and compare them to those in the Student Edition.

Portfolio Assessment Have students save the graphs they created in their Math Portfolios as an assessment of their ability to make picture graphs.

Assessment Criteria

Did the student . . .

✓ correctly answer the first six questions on pages 41–42?

✓ participate constructively in the survey activities and accurately record the results?

PRACTICE p. 19

LESSON 19 PRACTICE Name _____

Some students made a graph. It showed the colors they liked best.

Our Favorite Colors

Blue Green Yellow

❶ How many students like blue best? | 6 |
❷ How many students like green best? | 9 |
❸ How many students like yellow best? | 8 |

Math Explorations and Applications Level 1 • 19

ENRICHMENT p. 19

LESSON 19 ENRICHMENT Name _____

Color the squares.

Blue	Red	Green	Blue	Orange
Green	Blue	Yellow	Red	Blue
Green	Yellow	Purple	Yellow	Yellow

Students should color squares to match labels.

Color the graph to show the number of squares of each color.

5 4 3 2 1

Red Yellow Green Blue Orange Purple

Math Explorations and Applications Level 1 • 19

LESSON 20

Recording Data

Student Edition pages 43–44

LESSON PLANNER

Objectives

▶ to teach students how to use tally marks to keep count and report data

▶ to explore probability

Context of the Lesson This is the third lesson involving how to read and make graphs. Practice with graphs continues in Lesson 21.

 MANIPULATIVES   **Program Resources**

coin*

Practice Master 20

Enrichment Master 20

For extra practice:
CD-ROM* Lesson 20

---

① Warm-Up

5 MINUTES

Problem of the Day Write the following number series on the chalkboard and have students complete the next four numbers in the series: 1, 2, 2, 3, 3, 3, __4__, __4__, __4__, __4__, 5, 5, 5, 5, 5. Ask students to describe the pattern. (Each number is written in order and the same number of times that the number stands for.)

Problem-Solving Strategies Ask students who have solved the Problem of the Day to share how they solved it and any strategies they used.

 MENTAL MATH Have students tell what number comes between the two numbers.

a.   4 ☐ 6 (5)   b.   1 ☐ 3 (2)

c.   0 ☐ 2 (1)   d.   7 ☐ 9 (8)

e.   3 ☐ 5 (4)   f.   2 ☐ 4 (3)

② Teach

Demonstrate Demonstrate for students how to use tally marks to keep records. Conduct a brief survey with the class. Ask each student how many siblings he or she has. On the chalkboard, record each student's response by writing a tally mark next to the appropriate number of siblings. It is not necessary to use the diagonal tally mark for every fifth tally mark, but you may if you wish. Discuss the results of your survey by asking questions such as: "How many students in the class do not have any brothers or sisters?"

LESSON 20

Name _____

Recording Data

 **MATH CONNECTION** Do the Coin Toss Activity.

Answers will vary. Check that students count tally marks accurately.

Use tally marks to keep track.

	Tally Marks	Number
(penny)		
(penny)		

Try it again.

	Tally Marks	Number
(penny)		
(penny)		

 NOTE TO HOME
Students explore probability and use tally marks to record the results of a coin-toss activity.

Real-World Connection Divide students into pairs and distribute copies of the class list. Have partners work together to use tally marks to keep count of how many last names begin with the various letters of the alphabet. When partners are finished, have them share and compare the results. Ask: "Should all of our counts be the same? Why or why not?" (Yes, because they all used the same data.)

RETEACHING

Have students use tally marks to keep track of the frequency of words. For example, read aloud a paragraph from a story. Reread the same paragraph. Each time, have students use tally marks to keep track of the number of times they hear a specific word such as *the* or *is*. Discuss and compare students' results.

◆ LESSON 20 Recording Data

Look at the picture. How many of each?

Make tally marks to record how many.

	Tally Marks	Number
One-tailed dogs	||||||	6
Two-tailed dogs	|||||	5
Three-tailed dogs	||||	4

44 • Number 1–10

NOTE TO HOME
Students gather data from a picture and record it on a table.

PRACTICE p. 20

LESSON 20 PRACTICE Name _____

Look at the picture. How many of each toy? Put a mark through each toy as you count it.

Make tally marks to record how many. Then write how many.

1. Balls ____||||____ 4
2. Cars ____|||____ 3
3. Bears ____|||____ 3
4. Tops ____||____ 2
5. Whistles ____|||____ 3

20 • Math Explorations and Applications Level 1

ENRICHMENT p. 20

LESSON 20 ENRICHMENT Name _____

Alice kept count of the colors of cars that drove past her house.

Her paper looked like this.

Blue |||
Red ||||||/|
Green ||||
Yellow |

Color the graph to match Alice's count.

20 • Math Explorations and Applications Level 1

Using the Student Pages Do the Coin Toss Activity below and have students complete the chart on page 43. Then have students count the number of one-, two-, and three-tailed dogs shown in the picture on page 44. You may wish to have students work in pairs so that one partner can cross off each dog as the other records a tally mark for it. Have students count tally marks and write the number on the chart.

Introducing the Coin Toss Activity To provide practice in using tally marks to keep count and also to explore probability, do the coin toss activity. Have students watch as you flip a **coin***. Announce whether it lands on heads or tails. Have students make tally marks on the first chart on page 43 to record the toss. Continue until you have flipped the coin fifteen times. Have students count tallies and record the number. Discuss the results. Ask students if the coin will always flip to either heads or tails. (It will always land on one or the other.) Ask if the coin could ever flip to anything other than heads or tails. (no) Then have students predict the outcome of a second coin toss activity. (Each toss has a 50-50 chance of being heads. Theoretically, if you repeat enough tosses, you should end up with half heads and half tails.) Then repeat the activity with another 15 tosses, having students record tallies on the second chart on page 43.

❸ Wrap-Up

In Closing Ask students to explain when using tally marks might help them keep count. Discuss situations in which using tally marks would not necessarily make keeping count easier.

Performance Assessment Observe partners as they work to see if they are accurately recording the data from the student pages.

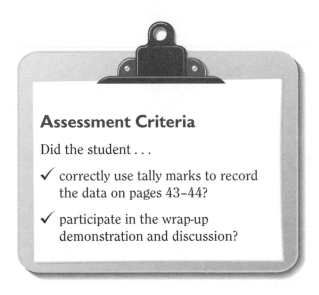

Assessment Criteria

Did the student . . .

✓ correctly use tally marks to record the data on pages 43–44?

✓ participate in the wrap-up demonstration and discussion?

*available separately

LESSON 21

Collecting Data

Student Edition pages 45–46

LESSON PLANNER

Objectives

▶ to teach students how tally marks, numbers, and bar graphs are related

▶ to teach the use of bar graphs to record data from an exploration of probability

Context of the Lesson This is the last lesson involving how to read and make graphs.

 MANIPULATIVES

Program Resources

Number Cubes

Reteaching Master

Practice Master 21

Enrichment Master 21

For extra practice:
CD-ROM* Lesson 21

① Warm-Up 🕐 ⁵MINUTES

 Problem of the Day Draw the figure below on the chalkboard. Ask students how many triangles are contained in the figure: (6)

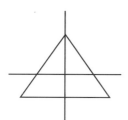

Problem-Solving Strategies Ask students who have solved the Problem of the Day to share how they solved it and any strategies they used.

MENTAL MATH Have students fill in the blocks with the number that comes before:

a. ☐, 6 (5)   b. ☐, 1 (0)   c. ☐, 10 (9)

d. ☐, 4 (3)   e. ☐, 2 (1)   f. ☐, 9 (8)

45 Numbers 1–10

LESSON 21

Name _____

Collecting Data

Listen to the story.

	Tally Marks	Number
🐕	|||||	6
🐈	|||||||	8
🐇	|||	3

Color the graph to match the story.

Dogs									
Cats									
Rabbits									
	1	2	3	4	5	6	7	8	9

How many dogs? __6__   How many cats? __8__

How many rabbits? __3__

 NOTE TO HOME
Students collect data and record it on a graph.

Unit 1   Lesson 21 • **45**

Science Connection
Have students keep track of the weather for a month. Have them make a graph showing how many days it rained each week. Have students share their graphs with the class at the end of the month.

RETEACHING p. 6

LESSON 21 RETEACHING   Name _____

Look at the graph.

Count.
Write how many.
🍐 4   🍓 6   🍎 3

Look at the graph.

Count.
Write how many.
🥕 4   🧄 2   🍄 6

*available separately

◆ LESSON 21 Collecting Data

  Roll the and build your graph.

Which number will get to the top first?

Answers will vary.

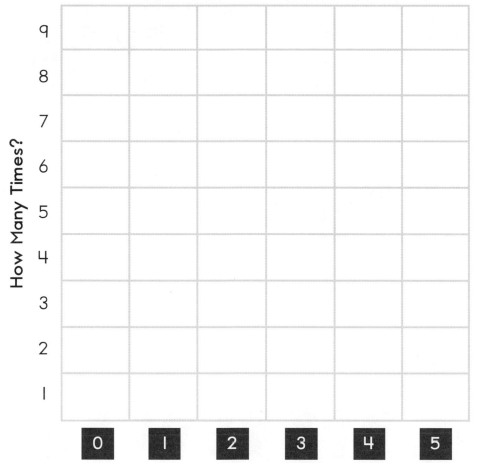

How Many Times?

9 8 7 6 5 4 3 2 1

0 1 2 3 4 5

Number on Cube

Copyright © SRA/McGraw-Hill

46 • Numbers 1–10

NOTE TO HOME
Students collect data and record it on a chart, while exploring probability.

---

② Teach

Using the Student Pages Have students look at the chart and graph on page 45. Explain that a class of first-grade students did a survey to find out who preferred dogs, cats, or rabbits as pets. Look at the results. Have students count tally marks to find how many students preferred a dog. Then have students write that number in the chart. Finish the page together. Discuss the results with the class. Guide students to see how the "Tally Marks" and "Number" columns are related on the chart and then how this number is translated onto the graph below it. Have students complete the graph and answer the questions.

COOPERATIVE LEARNING To complete page 46, have students work in pairs. As one student rolls the 0–5 units Number Cube and says the number, the other shades in a box over that number. Have partners switch roles after every five rolls of the cube. When one number makes it to the top of the graph, that number is the winner for the pair. Discuss the results with the class, focusing on the idea that although some numbers came up more often than others, all numbers had an equal chance. Point out also that it was certain that the Number Cube would roll to one number from 0–5 but impossible for the 0–5 cube to roll a number greater than 5.

③ Wrap-Up 5 MINUTES

In Closing Ask partners which number won for them and keep a record on the chalkboard using tally marks. Discuss the results. What you should find is that different numbers won for different groups, with no one number coming up substantially more often than the others.

ALTERNATIVE ASSESSMENT **Informal Assessment** Use students' responses on pages 45–46 to informally assess their ability to accurately collect, record, and present data on a graph.

Assessment Criteria

Did the student . . .

✓ correctly color the bar graph and record the numbers on page 45?

✓ work cooperatively to complete the Number Cube activity on page 46?

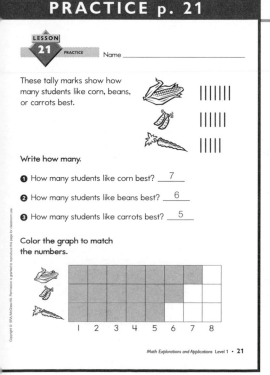

PRACTICE p. 21

LESSON 21 PRACTICE Name_____

These tally marks show how many students like corn, beans, or carrots best.

Write how many.

❶ How many students like corn best? __7__

❷ How many students like beans best? __6__

❸ How many students like carrots best? __5__

Color the graph to match the numbers.

1 2 3 4 5 6 7 8

Math Explorations and Applications Level 1 • 21

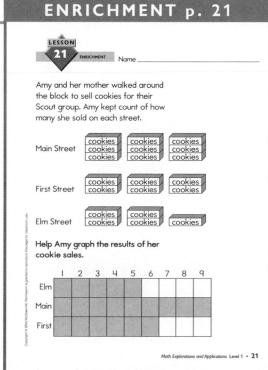

ENRICHMENT p. 21

LESSON 21 ENRICHMENT Name_____

Amy and her mother walked around the block to sell cookies for their Scout group. Amy kept count of how many she sold on each street.

Main Street — cookies
First Street — cookies
Elm Street — cookies

Help Amy graph the results of her cookie sales.

1 2 3 4 5 6 7 8 9
Elm
Main
First

Math Explorations and Applications Level 1 • 21

Mid-Unit Review

The Mid-Unit Review pinpoints troublesome skill areas for students, allowing plenty of time for additional practice and reteaching before the unit ends. If students did not do well on the Mid-Unit Review and have completed additional practice, you may want to use the Mid-Unit Review provided on pages 7–8 in the Assessment Blackline Masters.

Using the Student Pages Have students complete problems 1–10 on pages 47 and 48 on their own. You might treat this review as a formal assessment of students' skills, and have students complete this review as a timed test. See suggestions on page 48.

Name _____

Mid-Unit Review

Trace the right number.

❶ 7   ⑤   ❷ ④   6

❸ ③   5   ❹ 8   ⑦

Cross out one. Then write how many.

❺ 8

NOTE TO HOME
Students review unit skills and concepts.

Unit 1   Mid-Unit Review • **47**

Copyright © SRA/McGraw-Hill

---

47 Numbers 1–10

◆ UNIT 1 Mid-Unit Review

Fill in the missing numbers.

6 4   5   [6]   **7** 6   7   [8]

Look at the graph.

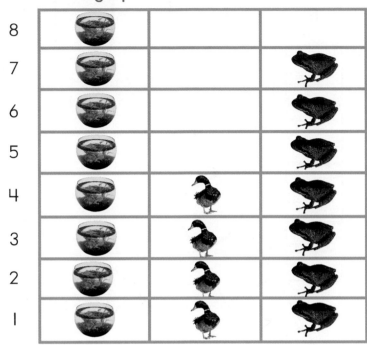

8 How many fish? ___8___

9 How many ducks? ___4___

10 How many frogs? ___7___

48 • Numbers 1–10

Copyright © SRA/McGraw-Hill

NOTE TO HOME
Students review unit skills and concepts.

ASSESSMENT p. 7

UNIT **1**   Mid-Unit Review   (Use after Lesson 21.)   Page 1 of 2

Name _____

The student demonstrates mastery by correctly answering 8 of the 10 problems.

Draw one more. Write how many.

1 ☆ ☆ ☆ ☆   4

2 🌼 🌼 🌼 🌼 🌼 🌼 🌼   8

3 ♡ ♡ ♡ ♡ ♡   6

Cross one out. Write how many are left.

4   5

5   8

6   3

Go on . . . ▸

Math Explorations and Applications Level 1 • 7

Timed Test Throughout the Teacher's Guide there are suggestions for sets of exercises to be completed as a "timed test." This usually occurs on pages of basic facts where the focus is on speedy recall. It gives each student a chance to improve as the year goes on. Invite students to keep their scores on the pages in their Math Journals or keep the actual pages in their Math Portfolios so that they can track their improvement. Use a **stopwatch*** or clock with a second hand.

Here are some suggestions for giving timed tests:

▶ Have all students start at the same time.

▶ Write 0 on the chalkboard as you tell them to start; after one minute erase the 0 and write 1; after two minutes write 2; and so on. Have students write that number at the tops of their papers when they finish the test so that they know how long they took to complete the test.

▶ Grade the papers yourself or have students correct their own papers as you call out the answers. Encourage the students to brainstorm ways to improve their times on future tests.

 Literature Connection To provide practice in counting from 1–10, read the clever mouse mystery *The Apple Thief* from the Literature Library*.

Home Connections You may want to send home the letter on pages 40–41 in the Home Connections Blackline Masters, which provides additional activities families can complete together. These activities apply the skills being presented in this unit.

 Performance Assessment Performance Assessment Tasks 1–7 provided on pages 63–64 of the Assessment Blackline Masters can be used at this time to evaluate students' ability to count and write numbers to 10. You may want to administer this assessment with individual students or in small groups.

Portfolio Assessment If you have not already completed the Portfolio Assessment task provided on page 76 of the Assessment Blackline Masters, it can be used to evaluate students' skills in writing and recognizing numbers to 10.

LOOKING AHEAD Number Strips will be introduced in the next lesson. You may want to familiarize yourself with them beforehand.

Unit Project This would be a good time to assign the "Counting Charts" project on pages 92a–92b. Students can begin working on the project in cooperative groups in their free time as you work through the unit. The Unit Project is a good opportunity for students to apply the concepts of counting and writing numbers in real-world problem solving.

*available separately

LESSON 22

Student Edition pages 49–50

Number Strips

LESSON PLANNER

Objectives

▶ to introduce the Number Strip as a tool for representing length in units from 1–10

▶ to introduce estimation of Number Strip length and ordering strips by length

Context of the Lesson The use of Number Strips is introduced in this lesson. They will be used throughout the program to measure and to represent numbers.

 **MANIPULATIVES**

interlocking cubes*

Program Resources

Number Cubes

Number Strips

Thinking Story Book, pages 16–17

Practice Master 22

Enrichment Master 22

For extra practice:
CD-ROM* Lesson 22
Mixed practice, page 353

① Warm-Up

5 MINUTES

Problem of the Day Challenge students to use interlocking cubes to make a tower five blocks high. Then ask them to make other towers that are one block shorter, one block taller, and the same size.

Problem-Solving Strategies Ask students who have solved the Problem of the Day to share how they solved it and any strategies they used.

Have students work in pairs. One student should make a train from 0–10 **interlocking cubes***. The other student should try to make the same size train.

② Teach

Demonstrate Hold up and name the 1-strip, 2-strip, and 3-strip. Show students that the 2-strip is as long as two 1-strips and that the 3-strip is as long as three 1-strips and so on. Have students lay out their strips blank side up. Ask them to find the 1-strip, the 2-strip, and so on. Finally, ask students to place their strips in order by length.

49 Numbers 1–10

LESSON 22

Name _____

Number Strips

Fill in the right number on each strip.

Copyright © SRA/McGraw-Hill

 NOTE TO HOME
Students use Number Strips to find the length of pictured Number Strips.

Unit 1   Lesson 22 • **49**

 Literature Connection You may wish to read aloud the book *Numbers* by Henry Pluckrose to direct student attention to the use of numbers in our lives.

AT RISK **Meeting Individual Needs** Divide students into groups. Challenge each group to come up with a list of five situations in which estimating length might be important.

RETEACHING

Extensive reteaching is not considered essential at this time because work with nonstandard measurement continues in subsequent lessons.

*available separately

◆ **LESSON 22** Number Strips **Use the Mixed Practice on page 353 after this lesson.**

Fill in the right number on each strip.

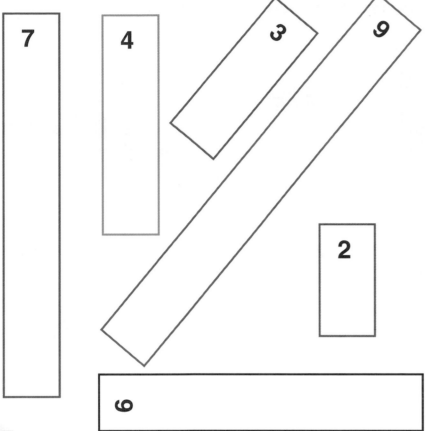

 GAME

Play the "Number Strip" game.

🎒 **NOTE TO HOME**
Students identify Number Strips by length.

50 • Numbers 1–10

Copyright © SRA/McGraw-Hill

GAME **Introducing the "Number Strip" Game**
To provide practice in estimating length and using feedback, have students play the "Number Strip" game. Divide students into pairs. Provide each pair with a set of Number Strips and units Number Cubes. To begin, place the Number Strips in the center of the playing area, blank sides up. The first player rolls either Number Cube until a number other than 0 comes up. He or she then tries to pick a Number Strip that matches the number on the cube. If correct, the player keeps the strip. If not, the strip is returned to the pile. The game continues until all the Number Strips are correctly matched. The player with the most strips wins.

MANIPULATIVES **Using the Student Pages** Have students use their Number Strips to complete pages 49–50 on their own.

Using the Thinking Story Present two problems from those following "Willy in the Water" on pages 16–17 in the Thinking Story Book or on pages 26a–26b of this Guide.

❸ Wrap-Up ⏱ 5 MINUTES

In Closing Ask students to find the 5-strip and then all the strips that are longer than the 5-strip.

SELF ASSESSMENT Have students write down which Number Strips they consistently identified correctly and those that they may have gotten wrong in the "Number Strip" game. Encourage them to think of strategies to help them remember the Number Strips they got wrong.

PRACTICE p. 22

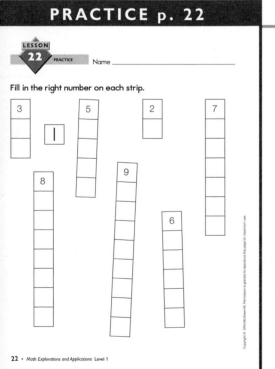

LESSON 22 PRACTICE Name _____

Fill in the right number on each strip.

ENRICHMENT p. 22

LESSON 22 ENRICHMENT Name _____

How high? Use your Number Strips to measure.

22 • Math Explorations and Applications Level 1

Assessment Criteria

Did the student . . .

✓ identify Number Strips by number with 80% accuracy?

✓ accurately complete pages 49–50?

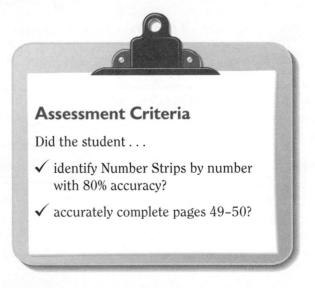 **LOOKING AHEAD** A collection of objects of specific lengths is needed for Lesson 23.

LESSON 23

Student Edition pages 51–52

Estimating Length

LESSON PLANNER

Objectives

▶ to teach students to estimate length

▶ to teach students to measure with Number Strips

✓ to assess students' participation in Thinking Story Book activities

Context of the Lesson This lesson includes a Mastery Checkpoint for assessing student participation in Thinking Story Book activities. The use of Number Strips is continued from the last lesson.

 MANIPULATIVES

pencils or crayons (red and blue)

a collection of objects to be measured with Number Strips

Program Resources

Number Strips

Thinking Story Book, pages 18–21

Practice Master 23

Enrichment Master 23

Assessment Master

For career connections:
Careers and Math*

For extra practice:
CD-ROM* Lesson 23

① Warm-Up

5 MINUTES

 Problem of the Day Present the following problem. Sally has a 10-strip, a 4-strip, and a 6-strip. Which strip is the shortest? (The 4-strip.)

Problem-Solving Strategies Ask students who have solved the Problem of the Day to share how they solved it and any strategies they used.

 Hold up a piece of chalk. Have students show the Number Strip they think corresponds to its length. Repeat with other objects. Help students understand that items can be described as "a little longer than the 4-strip," "a little shorter than the 4-strip," "about the same as the 4-strip," and so on.

LESSON 23

Name _____

Estimating Length

How long? Use your Number Strips.

🎒 **NOTE TO HOME**
Students use Number Strips to measure.

Unit 1   Lesson 23 • **51**

RETEACHING

Extra teaching is not considered essential at this time because work with nonstandard units of measurement is continued in subsequent lessons.

PRACTICE p. 23

LESSON 23 PRACTICE

Name _____

How long? Use your Number Strips.

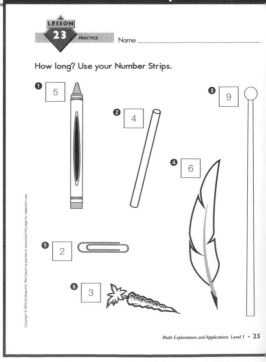

❶ 5
❷ 4
❸ 9
❹ 6
❺ 2
❻ 3

*available separately

◆ **LESSON 23** Estimating Length

Which is longest? Which is shortest?

Play the "How Long Is It?" game.

Talk about the Thinking Story "Mr. Muddle's Party."

NOTE TO HOME
Students use their Number Strips
to measure.

Copyright © SRA/McGraw-Hill

❷ Teach

 Using the Student Pages Make one or two of the measurements on page 51 with the class, then have students complete the rest on their own. Do page 52 as a class. Have students use their Number Strips. Tell them to color the flag on the longest flagpole **red** and the flag on the shortest flagpole **blue**.

 Introducing the "How Long Is It?" Game This game provides practice in estimating length and using feedback. Pairs take turns presenting **objects** and guessing which Number Strip is the same length. If the guesser is correct, he or she captures the object. If an object is longer than the 10-strip, a player wins by simply saying it is longer.

 Using the Thinking Story. Read aloud and discuss "Mr. Muddle's Party" on pages 18–21 of the Thinking Story Book.

 Ask students to draw a funny hat they would want to wear at Mr. Muddle's party. Invite them to write a sentence describing their hats.

❸ Wrap-Up ⏱ 5 MINUTES

In Closing Have students estimate the length of one of their fingers. Have them give the length in Number Strips.

 Mastery Checkpoint 6
Proficiency for Thinking Story participation can be assessed by observing students during the Thinking Story activities or by using pages 9–10 of the Assessment Blackline Masters. Results can be recorded on the Mastery Checkpoint Chart.

Assessment Criteria

Did the student . . .

✓ make reasonable estimates for the lengths of objects?

✓ demonstrate active participation in Thinking Story activities?

ENRICHMENT p. 23

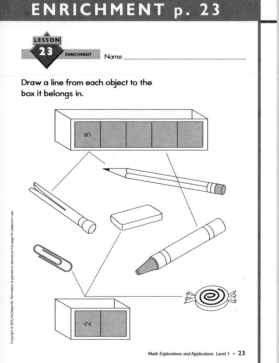

LESSON **23** ENRICHMENT   Name _____

Draw a line from each object to the box it belongs in.

Math Explorations and Applications Level 1 • 23

ASSESSMENT p. 9

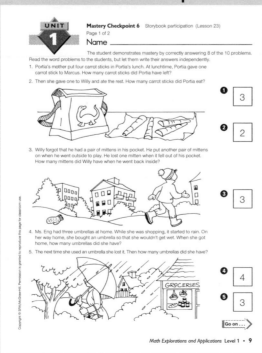

UNIT **1**   Mastery Checkpoint 6   Storybook participation (Lesson 23)
Page 1 of 2
Name _____

The student demonstrates mastery by correctly answering 8 of the 10 problems.
Read the word problems to the students, but let them write their answers independently.

1. Portia's mother put four carrot sticks in Portia's lunch. At lunchtime, Portia gave one carrot stick to Marcus. How many carrot sticks did Portia have left?

2. Then she gave one to Willy and ate the rest. How many carrot sticks did Portia eat?

❶ 3
❷ 2

3. Willy forgot that he had a pair of mittens in his pocket. He put another pair of mittens on when he went outside to play. He lost one mitten when it fell out of his pocket. How many mittens did Willy have when he went back inside?

❸ 3

4. Ms. Eng had three umbrellas at home. While she was shopping, it started to rain. On her way home, she bought an umbrella so that she wouldn't get wet. When she got home, how many umbrellas did she have?

5. The next time she used an umbrella she lost it. Then how many umbrellas did she have?

❹ 4
❺ 3

Go on . . . ➤

Math Explorations and Applications Level 1 • 9

Mr. Muddle's Party

❶ Loretta the Letter Carrier and her husband, Roger, have a baby and a dog. Loretta's mother lives with them.
How many people live in their home? four

❷ Portia gave a party. She invited two girls and two boys. They all came.
How many girls were at the party all together? three

❸ "I had six carrots this morning," said Mr. Muddle. "Then I ate one or two of them—I can't remember which."
How many carrots does he have left? four or five—can't tell
What do you need to know to be sure? how many he ate

❹ Marcus had five apples. Then he ate two apples, only they were someone else's apples, not his own.
How many apples did Marcus have left? five

Mr. Muddle's Party

Portia and Ferdie stopped by to visit Mr. Muddle. "Mrs. Muddle and I are getting ready to have a party," he said. "You can help me by setting out these funny hats for people to wear."

Portia and Ferdie counted the funny hats. There were four little hats and four big hats. Ferdie said, "I'll bet I can figure out what kind of people will be at your party: four people with little heads and four people with big heads!"

"That's good thinking," said Mr. Muddle. "You almost have it figured out."

"I have an idea," said Portia. "Are you inviting some children and some grown-ups?"

"Yes, I am," said Mr. Muddle.

Can you figure out how many children and how many grown-ups are invited to the party? four children; two or four grown-ups, depending upon whether you count Mr. and Mrs. Muddle

Are you sure? You can't tell for sure how many people are invited just by the number of hats.

18 • Mr. Muddle's Party

"I know! I know!" shouted Ferdie, who always liked to be first with an answer. "Four children and four grown-ups. Who are they?"

"Let me try to remember," said Mr. Muddle. "The grown-ups are Loretta the Letter Carrier, Mr. Mudancia and Mrs. Mudancia, and Mrs. Muddle."

Portia counted the four big hats again. "Mr. Muddle," she said, "there's going to be one grown-up at your party who isn't going to have a funny hat to wear."

Who is that? Mr. Muddle

What did Mr. Muddle forget? to count himself

Mr. Muddle said, "Yes, I forgot about myself. I had an invitation all ready to send myself, but I forgot to mail it."

"Who are the children you're inviting?" Ferdie asked.

"There are Willy and Manolita and some other children," said Mr. Muddle. "I can't remember their names right now."

How many other children should there be? two

How do you know? There are four small hats and Mr. Muddle named only two children.

Story 3 • **19**

⑤ Manolita walked two blocks to the store. Then she walked a block to Marcus's house. After they played for a while, she walked a block to get to her own house.
How far did she walk all together? four blocks

⑥ Portia planted four beans, but three of them didn't grow.
How many bean plants grew? one

⑦ Mr. Mudancia wanted to send his brother the smallest letter in the world. He made an envelope just the size of a postage stamp.
How big is that? Show with your fingers
[Demonstrate the correct size.]
He wrote his brother's address on the front of the envelope. Then he pasted a stamp on the front of the envelope and mailed it. His brother never got the letter.
Why not? The stamp covered the address.

⑧ Willy's father gave him five peanuts. Willy lost one and ate the rest.
How many peanuts did he eat? four

⑨ When Mr. Muddle got back from a trip, there were seven old newspapers on his porch. He picked up two of them.
How many old newspapers did he leave on his porch? five

◆ **STORY 3   Mr. Muddle's Party**

"There should be two other children," Ferdie said. "I can tell because there are four small hats, and Manolita and Willy and two more make four."

"Are the other two children by any chance a brother and a sister?" Portia asked.

"Yes, I believe they are," said Mr. Muddle.

"And are their names Ferdie and Portia?" asked Ferdie.

"That's right," said Mr. Muddle. "What clever children you are!"

"Oh, good!" said Portia. "We're invited to the party! When is your party, by the way?"

"It's right now," said Mr. Muddle. "I'm sorry. I must have forgotten to send out your invitation. Oh look! I see some guests coming up the sidewalk. You children can help me by standing at the door and handing out funny hats to all the people when they come in."

Do you remember how many funny hats there are? eight

How many big ones? four

How many little ones? four

First Mrs. Mudancia walked in. They gave her a funny clown's hat. Then Mr. Mudancia came in. They gave him a funny hat with a feather in it. He changed it a little by tying the feather in a knot

and said, "Thank you very much." Portia handed Mrs. Muddle a hat too.

How many big hats are left? one

"There's one big hat left," said Portia. "Oh, I know what to do with it. Here, Mr. Muddle." She put the last big funny hat on Mr. Muddle's head, and he went dancing around the room.

Next they heard a child's voice outside, saying, "I wish the door were open so I could come in."

Can you guess who that might be? Willy the Wisher

20 • Mr. Muddle's Party

"That must be Willy the Wisher," said Ferdie. "Come in, Willy." They gave him one of the little hats.

Before long they heard someone walking toward the door singing.

"That sounds like Manolita," said Portia. Sure enough, there was their friend Manolita, standing at the door. They let her in and gave her a little hat.

How many little hats are left? two

Ferdie and Portia waited, but no more children came to the door. "I guess some children that you invited aren't coming," said Ferdie.

Was he right? no

What had he forgotten? to count himself and Portia

"You forgot to count yourselves," said Mr. Muddle. He put the last two funny hats on Ferdie's and Portia's heads, and they all danced around the room.

Suddenly there was a knock at the door. It was Loretta the Letter Carrier. "I hope I'm not too late for the party," she said. "I just finished delivering the mail."

"You're not too late," said Portia, "but something is wrong. There are no hats left. There's no funny hat for you to wear."

Why not? Can anyone remember why there aren't enough hats? Portia put the last hat on Mr. Muddle's head.

"It's all right," said Loretta. "I have my letter carrier's cap, and it will do."

"It will do if we change it a little," said Mr. Mudancia. He turned Loretta's hat around and put the feather from his own hat in it.

"Now we all have funny hats," said Portia, and the party began.

. . . the end

Story 3 • **21**

LESSON 24

Student Edition pages 53–54

Comparing Length

Name _____

Comparing Length

Put an **X** on the longest side.

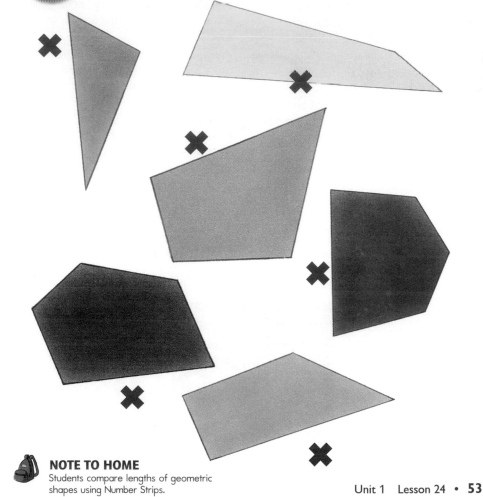

LESSON PLANNER

Objectives

▶ to teach students to use finger sets to add numbers that sum to 10

▶ to provide practice comparing lengths using Number Strips

Context of the Lesson This is the first in a series of lessons on addition. Work with nonstandard measurement continues from Lesson 23.

 MANIPULATIVES

craft sticks

Program Resources

Number Strips

Thinking Story Book, pages 22–23

Practice Master 24

Enrichment Master 24

For extra practice:
CD-ROM* Lesson 24

➊ Warm-Up ⏱ 5 MINUTES

Problem of the Day Present the following problem to students. Matt is taller than Jack. Jack is not taller than Bill. Bill is not taller than Matt. List the boys' names in order from shortest to tallest. (Jack, Bill, Matt)

Problem-Solving Strategies Ask students who have solved the Problem of the Day to share how they solved it and any strategies they used.

MENTAL MATH Have students tell what number comes after each of the following numbers:

a. 7 (8)	**b.** 0 (1)
c. 9 (10)	**d.** 5 (6)
e. 2 (3)	**f.** 4 (5)

 NOTE TO HOME
Students compare lengths of geometric shapes using Number Strips.

Unit 1 Lesson 24 • **53**

RETEACHING

Some students may need help using finger sets to add because they still count fingers one by one for each set. Give students practice in holding up different finger sets without counting. Do not have them practice adding until they have mastered this skill. Then give more practice in adding sums by holding up the first set without counting and then counting on for the second set.

 Literature Connection To illustrate the concept of big, bigger, and biggest, read aloud *Is the Blue Whale the Biggest Thing There Is?* by Robert E. Wells.

Real-World Connection Have students work in groups. Have each group go on a timed scavenger hunt to identify as many objects as they can that are the same length as each Number Strip. At the end of the time, have groups share and compare their findings.

53 Numbers 1–10

*available separately

◆ LESSON 24 Comparing Length

Color the tallest red. Color the shortest blue. Color the others any color. Use Number Strips if you need to.

①  R   R   B

② 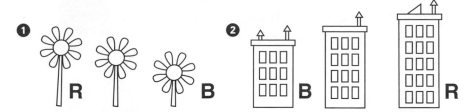 B   B   R

③    R   B

④  B   R

⑤ 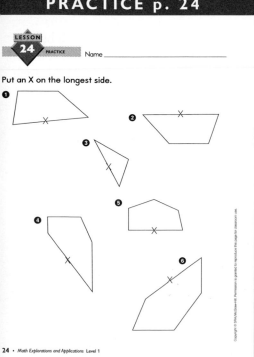 R   B

54 • Numbers 1–10

NOTE TO HOME
Students use Number Strips to measure.

PRACTICE p. 24

LESSON **24** PRACTICE   Name _____

Put an X on the longest side.

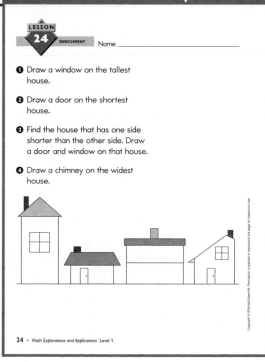

24 • Math Explorations and Applications Level 1

ENRICHMENT p. 24

LESSON **24** ENRICHMENT   Name _____

❶ Draw a window on the tallest house.

❷ Draw a door on the shortest house.

❸ Find the house that has one side shorter than the other side. Draw a door and window on that house.

❹ Draw a chimney on the widest house.

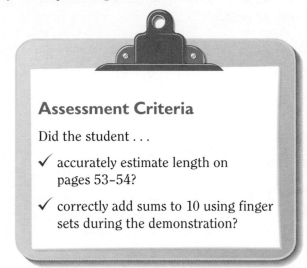

24 • Math Explorations and Applications Level 1

② Teach

Demonstrate Have a volunteer hold up five **craft sticks** while you show five fingers. Then have the volunteer pick up three more sticks while you count aloud and raise three more fingers. Show the complete finger set. Then ask: "How many fingers do I have up?" (8); "How many sticks does [student's name] have?" (8) Repeat with other examples. Next, do problems in which you hold up the sticks. Have students add with their fingers, hold up their completed finger sets, and say the numbers in unison.

Using the Student Pages Have students try to solve the problems on these pages by looking at the figures. If they cannot tell which is longest or tallest, have them use their Number Strips to measure. When finished, students can share and compare answers.

Using the "How Long Is It?" Game To provide additional practice with measurement, have students play the "How Long Is It?" game introduced in Lesson 23.

Using the Thinking Story Present two new problems from those following "Mr. Muddle's Party" on pages 22–23 of the Thinking Story Book or on pages 52a–52b of this Guide.

③ Wrap-Up ⏱ 5 MINUTES

In Closing Have volunteers model adding two numbers using finger sets as others try to identify the numbers and sum being modeled.

Performance Assessment Use students' responses during the demonstration to see which students were able to use finger sets to add. Observe how students decide which are the longest and tallest sides and figures on pages 53–54 to assess their ability to compare lengths.

Assessment Criteria

Did the student . . .

✓ accurately estimate length on pages 53-54?

✓ correctly add sums to 10 using finger sets during the demonstration?

LESSON 25
Student Edition pages 55–56
Measuring Length

LESSON PLANNER

Objectives

▶ to teach students to solve concrete addition problems in which answers must be computed rather than observed directly

▶ to provide practice measuring length

Context of the Lesson In this lesson students will practice measuring length and will continue to practice it throughout the year.

 MANIPULATIVES

MANIPULATIVES	Program Resources
can	Number Strips
counters*	Thinking Story Book, pages 22–23
craft sticks	Practice Master 25
scissors	Enrichment Master 25
string	For extra practice: CD-ROM* Lesson 25

❶ Warm-Up

 Problem of the Day Present the following problem to the class. Eric is sixth in line. Maria is behind Eric. Kim is behind Maria. What position is Kim in the line? (eighth)

Problem-Solving Strategies Ask students who have solved the Problem of the Day to share how they solved it and any strategies they used.

MENTAL MATH / **MANIPULATIVES** Display **craft sticks** in the amounts shown, and have students add and then show with finger sets how many items there are "all together."

a. 2 sticks and 1 stick (3)	**b.** 6 sticks and 0 sticks (6)
c. 5 sticks and 3 sticks (8)	**d.** 3 sticks and 2 sticks (5)
e. 4 sticks and 3 sticks (7)	**f.** 9 sticks and 1 stick (10)

❷ Teach

 Demonstrate Have a student put four **counters*** into a **can** as you raise four fingers. Have this student then add three more, one at a

55 Numbers 1–10

LESSON 25

Name _____

Measuring Length

Draw a straight line from the bee to the nearest flower. Use your Number Strips to measure.

 MATH CONNECTION Do the "Cutting Strings to Fit" activity.

 NOTE TO HOME Students use Number Strips to measure.

Unit 1   Lesson 25   •   **55**

Copyright © SRA/McGraw-Hill

 Literature Connection To reinforce measurement skills, read aloud *Fish Eyes: A Book You Can Count On* by Lois Ehlert.

ESL **Meeting Individual Needs** At this point you may wish to review the vocabulary students will use to work addition problems with hidden counters. Have ESL students read and say the number names for numbers 0–10.

RETEACHING

Because teaching addition with hidden counters is continued in the next lesson, reteaching is not suggested at this time.

*available separately

◆ LESSON 25 Measuring Length

①

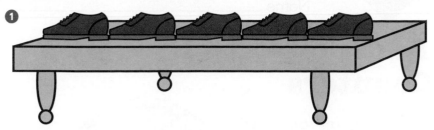

About how many shoe units long? __5__

②

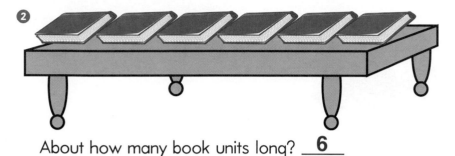

About how many book units long? __6__

Find out how long. Use , 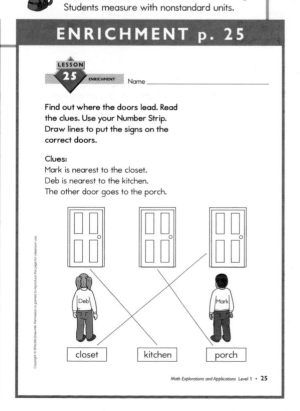 or something else.

Answers should indicate an object for measuring.

③ Which unit will you use? _____

④ About how many units long? _____ **Answers will vary.**

56 • Numbers 1–10

🎒 **NOTE TO HOME**
Students measure with nonstandard units.

---

time, as you raise and count fingers saying: "1, 2, 3." Then ask: "How many counters are in the can: 4 and 1, 2, 3 more make how many?" (7) Confirm the answer by counting the counters. Repeat as students do finger addition along with you for several similar problems.

✋ **Introducing the "Cutting String to Fit" Activity** This activity provides practice in estimating length. Have students try to cut lengths of **string** that will fit just around their waists. If they cut too little, have them try again. If they cut too much, have them trim to fit.

✋ **Using the Student Pages** Have students draw lines as directed on page 55. Then have students measure with Number Strips and share their answers. Students may use language such as "almost as long as a 6-strip" to describe lengths. Complete page 56 as a class. Discuss which unit might be used to solve the last problem and why.

📖 **Using the Thinking Story** Present two new problems from those following "Mr. Muddle's Party" on pages 22–23 of the Thinking Story Book or on pages 52a–52b of this Guide.

❸ Wrap-Up ⏱

In Closing Have volunteers model addition with counters and finger sets as the others try to find the sum.

🏁 **Performance Assessment** Observe the accuracy of students' measurements in the activity to assess their ability to estimate lengths.

Assessment Criteria

Did the student . . .

✓ use informal language to describe the distances shown on page 55?

✓ make sensible estimates of length in the measurement activity?

LESSON 26

Student Edition pages 57–58

Addition with Hidden Counters

LESSON PLANNER

Objective

▶ to provide practice for solving concrete addition problems in which a hidden addend is added to a visible one

Context of the Lesson This is one of several lessons on addition with hidden addends.

 MANIPULATIVES

Program Resources

MANIPULATIVES	Program Resources
can	Number Cubes
cardboard	Thinking Story Book, pages 22–23
counters*	Practice Master 26
	Enrichment Master 26

For extra practice:
CD-ROM* Lesson 26

① Warm-Up 5 MINUTES

 Problem of the Day Present the following problem to the class. Sarah has more than one penny. She has fewer than four. She does not have three. How many pennies does she have? (2)

Problem-Solving Strategies Ask students who have solved the Problem of the Day to share how they solved it and any strategies they used.

MENTAL MATH / **MANIPULATIVES** Place one to nine **counters*** in a **can**. Tell students how many. Then, one at a time, drop in one to three more counters as students use finger sets to add. Have students show how many with Number Cubes. Confirm answers by counting the counters. Repeat with other numbers, always adding on one to three counters.

② Teach

MANIPULATIVES **Demonstrate** Draw five circles on the chalkboard and quickly cover them with a large piece of **cardboard**. Draw two more circles that are not hidden. Ask students if they can tell how many circles are on the board. After they acknowledge that they cannot tell for sure, tell them that there are five hidden circles, and write a large number 5 on the cardboard covering them. Then ask students how many circles there are all together. (7)

57 Numbers 1–10

 LESSON 26

Name _____

Addition with Hidden Counters

How many all together?

①  5

②  6   ③ 5 7

④  4   ⑤ 4 7

 GAME   Play the "Add the Counters" game.

 NOTE TO HOME Students solve addition problems with counters, some of which are hidden.

Unit 1 Lesson 26 • **57**

 LITERATURE CONNECTION **Literature Connection** You may wish to share *Ocean Parade: A Counting Book* by Patricia MacCarthy to reinforce lesson concepts.

RETEACHING

Some students may need special instruction on how to use finger sets to solve problems. First they should form a finger set for the number of counters they do not see, then add fingers for the counters they do see.

*available separately

◆ **LESSON 26 Addition with Hidden Counters**

How many all together?

 6 **3**

 7 **6**

 8 **9**

 9 **7**

 10 **9**

 11 **5**

 12 **5**

 13 **10**

 14 **7**

 15 **8**

 16 **3**

 17 **9**

58 • Numbers 1–10

🎒 **NOTE TO HOME**
Students solve addition problems with
counters, some of which are hidden.

Challenge them to explain how they figured it out. Remove
the cardboard, and have students count the total number of
circles.

Using the Number Cubes Repeat the
demonstration with hidden addends 1–10 and
observable addends 0–3 that sum to 10 and
under. Have students show answers with Number Cubes.

🎮 **Introducing the "Add the Counters"
Game** To provide practice in adding without
counting to get the answer, have students play the
"Add the Counters" game. Divide students into pairs, with
ten **counters*** per pair. The lead player counts aloud as he
or she sets out some counters. Then the lead player covers
these counters with a Student Edition, silently puts more
counters on top of the Student Edition, and asks how many
in total. If the other player correctly answers, he or she wins
the round. Players then reverse roles. Have students keep
track of wins using tally marks. A copy of this game can also
be found on page 14 of the Home Connections Blackline
Masters.

Using the Student Pages Have students complete
pages 57–58 on their own. Remind them to use finger sets.
They start with a finger set corresponding to the number of
counters under the dish, and then raise one finger for each
counter that shows.

📖 **Using the Thinking Story** Present two
new problems from those following "Mr.
Muddle's Party" on pages 22–23 of the
Thinking Story Book or on pages 52a–52b of this Guide.

③ Wrap-Up 🕐 5 MINUTES

In Closing Invite volunteers to tell how they solved one of
the problems in the lesson.

✅ **SELF ASSESSMENT** Have students work with partners to give each
other five hidden counter problems. Students
who get fewer than three problems right may
need more practice or further explanations.

Assessment Criteria

Did the student . . .

✓ understand that the visible counters
should be added to the hidden ones?

✓ correctly answer 13 of 17 problems
on pages 57–58?

PRACTICE p. 26

How many all together?

❶ 4 🎾🎱 **7**   ❷ 2 🎾🎱 **5**

❸ 8 🎱🎾 **10**   ❹ 3 🎾🎱 **5**

❺ 7 🎾 **8**   ❻ 5 **5**

❼ 2 🎾 **4**   ❽ 🎾🎱 1 **4**

❾ 9 **9**   ❿ 6 🎾 **7**

26 • Math Explorations and Applications Level 1

ENRICHMENT p. 26

How many hats in each picture?

❶ 6 ___ **8**   ❷ 6 ___ **9**

How many ties in each picture?

❸ 4 ___ **7**   ❹ 4 ___ **6**

❺ 5 ___ **7**   ❻ 5 ___ **8**

26 • Math Explorations and Applications Level 1

*available separately

LESSON
27

Student Edition pages 59–60

Adding On

LESSON
27

Name _____

Adding On

How many in all?

 ❶ 5   7   ❷ 6   7

 ❸ 2   4   ❹ 4   5

 ❺ 7   8   ❻ 7   9

 ❼ 5   8   ❽ 5   6

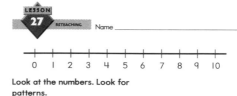 ❾ 4   7   ❿ 3   5

LESSON PLANNER

Objectives

▶ to provide practice in identifying and completing patterns

✓ to assess students' ability to solve concrete addition problems with hidden addends

Context of the Lesson This lesson includes Mastery Checkpoint 7 for assessing students' ability to solve concrete addition problems with hidden addends.

MANIPULATIVES   **Program Resources**

cardboard

craft sticks

Number Cubes

Reteaching Master

Practice Master 27

Enrichment Master 27

Assessment Master

For extra practice:
   CD-ROM* Lesson 27
   Mixed Practice, page 354

Copyright © SRA/McGraw-Hill

 NOTE TO HOME
Students solve addition problems with counters, some of which are hidden.

Unit 1   Lesson 27 • **59**

❶ Warm-Up ⏱ 5 MINUTES

 Problem of the Day Present the following problem to the class. Taro has less than ten minutes, but more than five minutes before bedtime. He wants to watch the last four minutes of a TV show. Can he watch the rest of the program before bedtime? Why or why not? (Yes; he has more than 5 minutes left, and there are only 4 minutes left to the show.)

Problem-Solving Strategies Ask students who have solved the Problem of the Day to share how they solved it and any strategies they used.

MENTAL MATH **MANIPULATIVES** Display **craft sticks** in the amounts shown, and have students add and then show with finger sets how many items there are "all together."

a.   8 sticks and 2 sticks (10)

b.   7 sticks and 3 sticks (10)

c.   1 stick and 2 sticks (3)

d.   5 sticks and 1 stick (6)

e.   10 sticks and 0 sticks (10)

f.   6 sticks and 3 sticks (9)

59   Numbers 1–10

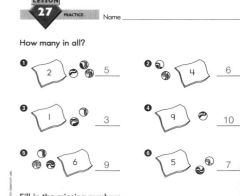

RETEACHING p. 7

LESSON **27** RETEACHING   Name _____

0 1 2 3 4 5 6 7 8 9 10

Look at the numbers. Look for patterns.

❶ 1 [2] 3 4 5 6

❷ 1 2 3 1 2 [3]

❸ 5 6 7 8 [9] 10

❹ 4 4 [4] 4 4 4

Fill in the missing numbers. Look for patterns.

❺ 0 [1] 2 3 4 5

❻ 1 2 [3] [4] 5 6

❼ 3 [4] 5 6 [7] 8

❽ 1 [2] 1 2 1 2

Math Explorations and Applications Level 1 • **7**

PRACTICE p. 27

LESSON **27** PRACTICE   Name _____

How many in all?

❶ 2   5   ❷ 4   6

❸ 1   3   ❹ 9   10

❺ 6   9   ❻ 5   7

Fill in the missing numbers. Look for patterns.

❼ 3 4 5 [6] [7] 8 9

❽ 5 6 5 6 [5] [6] 5 6

❾ 9 9 9 [9] 9 9 9

Math Explorations and Applications Level 1 • **27**

*available separately

◆ **LESSON 27** Adding On

Fill in the missing numbers.
Look for patterns.

Use the Mixed Practice on page 354 after this lesson.

⑪ 1   2   3   **4** **5** 6   7   8

⑫ 7   6   5   4   **3** 2   1   0

⑬ 1   2   1   2   **1** 2   **1** 2

⑭ 2   1   2   1   2   **1** **2** 1

⑮ 1   2   3   1   2   **3** 1   2

⑯ 4   5   6   **7** **8** 9   10 11

⑰ 3   3   **3** **3** 3   3   3   3

⑱ 4   3   2   **1** 4   **3** 2   1

60 • Numbers 1–10

 NOTE TO HOME
Students practice completing number patterns.

Copyright © SRA/McGraw-Hill

---

 ② Teach

Demonstrate At the chalkboard, present problems involving figures hidden under **cardboard**, as in Lesson 26. Have students who have shown a mastery of this kind of problem present problems to the class to solve. Have other students use their Number Cubes to show answers.

Using the Student Pages Work the first problem on page 59 together. Then have students complete pages 59 and 60 on their own. When students have finished, correct both pages with the class.

Using the "Add the Counters" Game Provide more practice in adding without counting with the "Add the Counters" game from Lesson 26. A copy of this game can also be found on page 14 of the Home Connections Blackline Masters.

③ Wrap-Up ⏱ 5 MINUTES

In Closing Have students work in groups of three. One student makes up a hidden addend, another shows counters for the second addend, and a third adds the sum. Have students switch roles and repeat the activity.

Mastery Checkpoint 7
You may want to formally assess students' ability to solve concrete addition problems with hidden addends (adding 0, 1, 2, or 3 with sums to 10). Proficiency can be assessed by observing students' responses during the demonstration or with page 11 in the Assessment Blackline Masters. The results of this assessment can be recorded on the Mastery Checkpoint Chart.

ENRICHMENT p. 27

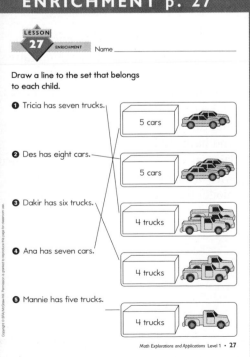

ASSESSMENT p. 11

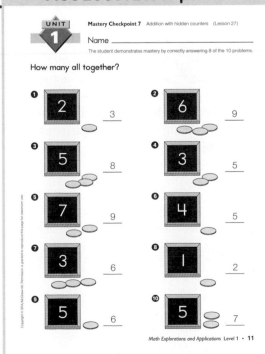

Assessment Criteria

Did the student . . .

✓ demonstrate proficiency on Mastery Checkpoint 7?

✓ correctly answer 14 of 18 problems on pages 59–60?

LESSON
28

Student Edition pages 61–62

The Order Property of Addition

LESSON PLANNER

Objectives

▶ to reinforce students' ability to solve concrete addition problems in which the answers must be computed rather than observed directly

▶ to introduce the commutative law of addition

Context of the Lesson This is the last lesson on addition with hidden counters. The next lesson begins subtraction.

MANIPULATIVES **Program Resources**

interlocking cubes* (optional)
cardboard

Thinking Story Book, pages 22–23
Practice Master 28
Enrichment Master 28
For extra practice:
CD-ROM* Lesson 28

❶ Warm-Up

Problem of the Day Present the following problem to the class. Manuel has six gerbils. Four of his gerbils are male. How many are female? (2)

Problem-Solving Strategies Ask students who have solved the Problem of the Day to share how they solved it and any strategies they used.

 Have students use finger sets to add the following:

a.	2, 3 (5)	**b.**	3, 2 (5)
c.	4, 1 (5)	**d.**	7, 3 (10)
e.	4, 2 (6)	**f.**	8, 1 (9)

LESSON
28

Name _____

The Order Property of Addition

How many all together?

①  7   ⑦  6

②  7   ⑧  6

③  7   ⑨  9

④  7   ⑩  9

⑤  4   ⑪  9

⑥ 3   ⑫  8

🎒 **NOTE TO HOME**
Students practice addition with hidden counters to discover the order property.

Language Arts Connection Invite students to write a mystery story involving hidden numbers. Encourage them to plan their story by first coming up with a hidden-number problem.

RETEACHING

 Use **interlocking cubes*** to demonstrate the commutative law of addition. For example, link three red cubes and five blue cubes, and have students find the sum. Then link three blue cubes and five red cubes, and have students find the sum again. Discuss why the sum is the same. Repeat with other examples by having students model them with their own interlocking cubes.

*available separately

◆ LESSON 28 The Order Property of Addition

ALGEBRA READINESS

The number tells how many fish are behind the rock. Write how many fish there are all together.

⑬
4

⑰
5

⑭
5

⑱
7

⑮
6

⑲
5

⑯
6

⑳
5

62 • Numbers 1–10

NOTE TO HOME
Students identify missing addends and work with related addition facts.

Copyright © SRA/McGraw-Hill

❷ Teach

Demonstrate Present hidden-counter problems similar to those you demonstrated in Lessons 26 and 27. This time give related problems such as 4 + 2 and 2 + 4. Remove the **cardboard** to reveal the circles and have students count to check equivalence. Then go on to the student pages.

Using the Student Pages Work together with students to solve the first problem on each page. Remind them that the numbers indicate how many are hidden and to use a finger set for that number and then proceed to count on. Explain that there are patterns in these problems that should help them solve the problems more easily.

Using the Thinking Story Present three new problems from among those following "Mr. Muddle's Party" on pages 22–23 of the Thinking Story Book or on pages 52a–52b of this Guide.

❸ Wrap-Up ⏱ 5 MINUTES

In Closing Have a student explain what patterns helped to solve the problems. Guide students to see that the order of the addends does not change the sum. Point out how this may help them remember math facts.

ANALYZING ANSWERS

Use students' answers for the problems on pages 61 and 62 to determine whether they need reteaching. Students who consistently answer commutative addition problems incorrectly should have the concept explained further to them.

Assessment Criteria

Did the student . . .

✓ correctly solve 16 of 20 problems on pages 61–62?

✓ understand and use the commutative law of addition?

PRACTICE p. 28

LESSON 28 PRACTICE Name _____

How many all together?

❶ 3 5
❷ 5 7
❸ 4 5
❹ 4 7
❺ 3 4
❻ 5 8
❼ 8 9
❽ 6 8

28 • Math Explorations and Applications Level 1

ENRICHMENT p. 28

LESSON 28 ENRICHMENT Name _____

Write how many things are in the bags.

❶ Cam bought six apples. How many apples are in the bag? 4

❷ Elly bought eight boxes of juice. How many are in the bag? 7

❸ Jeanne bought five carrots. How many carrots are in the bag? 5

❹ Tad bought nine boxes of raisins. How many are in the bag? 5

❺ Sheri bought three pears. How many are in the bag? 0

❻ How many things were left in Elly's bag and Sheri's bag all together? 7

28 • Math Explorations and Applications Level 1

LESSON 29
Identifying Missing Addends

Student Edition pages 63–64

Identifying Missing Addends

LESSON PLANNER

Objective
▶ to teach students to solve simple subtraction problems with a minuend of 10 or less by using finger sets

Context of the Lesson
This is the first in a series of lessons teaching the concept of subtraction.

 MANIPULATIVES
counters*

Program Resources
Thinking Story Book, pages 24–27
Practice Master 29
Enrichment Master 29
For career connections:
Careers and Math*
For extra practice:
CD-ROM* Lesson 29

❶ Warm-Up

 Problem of the Day Write the following pattern on the chalkboard and have students describe the pattern: 10, 9, 8, 7, 6, 5, 4, 3, 2, 1. (The pattern is counting back by ones.)

Problem-Solving Strategies Ask students who have solved the Problem of the Day to share how they solved it and any strategies they used.

 MENTAL MATH Have students use finger sets to add:

a. 1 + 1 (2)	b. 3 + 3 (6)
c. 5 + 3 (8)	d. 8 + 2 (10)
e. 6 + 1 (7)	f. 4 + 3 (7)

SPECIAL NEEDS **Meeting Individual Needs**
Some students may have trouble turning down their fingers one at a time. Demonstrate that they do not need to turn their fingers down so far that others come along involuntarily. Point out that if this happens they will have an inaccurate finger set showing. Have students practice showing different finger sets.

Name _____

Identifying Missing Addends

 ALGEBRA READINESS

Write how many are covered.

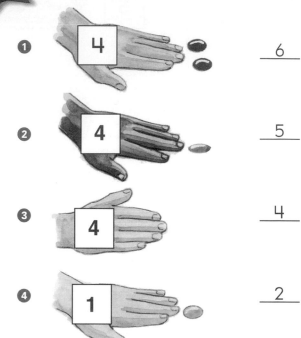

① 4 ____ 6

② 4 ____ 5

③ 4 ____ 4

④ 1 ____ 2

 THINKING STORY
Talk about the Thinking Story "'It's Not So Easy,' Said Mr. Breezy."

🎒 **NOTE TO HOME**
Students solve subtraction problems with counters, some of which are hidden.

Unit 1   Lesson 29 • **63**

 REAL-WORLD CONNECTION At the beginning of the week, have students show how many days of school they have left in the week by using finger sets. For each day, have them turn down one more finger to show how many days are left.

RETEACHING

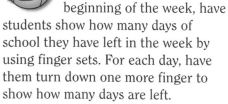 Have students work in groups. Give each group ten **counters.** Have them work together using counters to solve the problems on page 63. Make another practice page similar to these problems and have students use counters to solve them also.

GAME

Don't Take Them All

Players: Two or more
Materials: 10 counters or pennies

RULES

Place ten counters or pennies in a pile. Take turns. Each turn take one or two counters from the pile. Continue playing until all the counters are taken. The player who takes the last counter loses.

I played the game with

_____

Copyright © SRA/McGraw-Hill

64 • Numbers 1–10

② Teach

Demonstrate Have a student show a set of nine **counters*** while you make a finger set of nine. Then have this student put two away. As he or she does this, turn down two fingers to demonstrate a finger set of seven. Have students count the remaining objects to see that there are seven. Demonstrate several more problems. Then, present concrete subtraction problems, and have students calculate with fingers, saying the results in unison. Count the objects to confirm the answers.

Using the Student Pages Demonstrate the first problem on page 63 with the class. Then have students complete the rest of the page independently.

Introducing the "Don't Take Them All" Game To provide practice in subtracting concrete objects and mathematical reasoning, demonstrate the "Don't Take Them All" game shown on page 64. You may want to have students play the game at home. A copy of this game can also be found on page 12 of the Home Connections Blackline Masters.

Using the Thinking Story Read and discuss the Thinking Story "'It's Not So Easy,' Said Mr. Breezy" on pages 24–27 of the Thinking Story Book.

③ Wrap-Up ⏱ 5 MINUTES

In Closing Have students make up problems like those on page 63 and demonstrate the solutions to the class.

Performance Assessment Observe students during the demonstration to determine whether they are able to find the solutions without counting each finger.

Assessment Criteria

Did the student . . .

✓ correctly solve the problems on page 63?

✓ play the "Don't Take Them All" game?

✓ contribute to the Thinking Story Discussion?

PRACTICE p. 29

LESSON **29** PRACTICE   Name_____

Write how many are covered.

❶ 6 • • 8

❷ 1 • • • 3

❸ 4 • • 6

❹ 5 • • • 8

❺ 3 • 4

❻ 3 • • 5

❼ 4 ___ 4

❽ 0 • • 2

Math Explorations and Applications Level 1 • 29

ENRICHMENT p. 29

LESSON **29** ENRICHMENT   Name_____

Emma has nine teddy bears. She has more brown bears than black bears. She has more black bears than yellow bears. She has twice as many brown bears as yellow bears.

❶ How many teddy bears are brown? ___ 4

❷ How many teddy bears are black? ___ 3

❸ How many teddy bears are yellow? ___ 2

Color the bears to match the story.

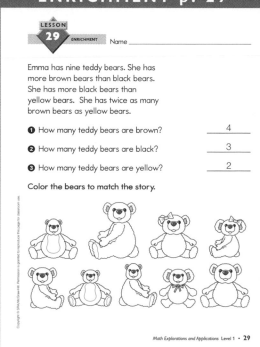

Math Explorations and Applications Level 1 • 29

"It's Not So Easy," said Mr. Breezy

❶ Mr. Breezy said, "Our cat, Abigail, had two kittens last year. This year she had three kittens. How many feet does Abigail have all together?"
How many? four, like any other cat

❷ Marcus got up early to mail a letter. Three people saw him while he walked to the mailbox. Nobody saw him while he walked home.
How many people all together saw him walking? three

❸ Ferdie was doing dishes. He had ten plates left to wash. He washed three spoons.
How many plates did he have left to wash? ten

❹ Manolita had three sheets of paper, and she made each sheet into a paper airplane. Two of the planes didn't fly right, so she threw them away. Another one got wet, so she threw it away, too.
How many places did she have left? zero

"It's Not So Easy," Said Mr. Breezy

Mr. Breezy runs a training school for dogs where he teaches them to obey commands and do tricks. People in the community who don't have the time or patience to train their dogs take them to Mr. Breezy. After school and on the weekends, Mr. Breezy's son Marcus helps out at the dog-training school.

"Any jobs for me today?" Marcus asked one Saturday.

"I have some work that needs to be done, but it's not so easy," said Mr. Breezy. "The first job is to figure out how many cans of dog food we have left."

"I'll go to the storeroom and start counting," said Marcus.

"It's not that easy," said Mr. Breezy. "You'll find there are ten cans of dog food there all together. But six of the cans are right-side up. And three cans are upside down. Oh, one can is on its side. Do you think you can handle all those numbers?"

"I don't need to," said Marcus. "I think I know the answer already."

How can Marcus know the answer without going to the storeroom? Mr. Breezy has told him there are ten cans in the storeroom.

How many cans of dog food are there all together? ten

What about the six cans that are right-side up and the three that are upside down and the one that is on its side? It doesn't matter what position they are in.

"There are just ten cans," said Marcus. "I don't have to go to the storeroom because you told me how many at the beginning. It doesn't matter how many are right-side up and upside down and on their sides."

"You're pretty good with numbers," said Mr. Breezy. "I'm proud of you. But here's a problem that's not so easy. You know the chains we use to lead the dogs with when we're teaching them to follow us? Well, I'm trying to figure out how long the chains should be."

"Maybe we can find a book on dog training that will help," said Marcus.

"I've already looked it up in a book," said Mr. Breezy, "but the book gives so many different numbers that there's no way to know which number is best."

Mr. Breezy started to read from the book: "A good chain should weigh about 1 kilogram, should be made of wire $\frac{1}{2}$ centimeter thick, should be 5 meters long, should have about 25 links to the meter, and should be shiny."

"I told you this wouldn't be easy," said Mr. Breezy.

"I think I have the answer already," said Marcus.

How long should each chain be? five meters

What about all the other numbers? They don't matter.

Story 4 • **25**

5 Ferdie doesn't always pay attention to what people tell him. His mother asked him to get six forks from the kitchen, but he got only five. His mother sent him back for more.
How many more forks did Ferdie have to get? one

6 Mr. Breezy said, "I earned three dollars, then I caught two fish, then I caught a cold, then I lost all my money, then I ate two walnuts. How many dollars do I have left?"
How many? zero

7 Willy lives with his father, his grandmother, his sister, and his brother. Willy and his grandmother were sick on Tuesday, but everyone else felt all right.
How many felt all right on Tuesday? three

8 The teacher said, "Now open your books to page 8." Marcus opened his to page 10.
Should Marcus turn toward the beginning or toward the end of the book? the beginning

◆ **STORY 4** "It's Not So Easy," Said Mr. Breezy

"The book says the chains should be 5 meters long," said Marcus. "The rest of those numbers don't tell how long they should be. They tell you other things about them."

"Spoken like a true Breezy," said Mr. Breezy. "Since you're so good with numbers, maybe you can help with a really tough problem. We need to buy more pens because we can keep only one dog in each pen. We have so many dogs here now that there aren't enough pens for all of them. What is not so easy is to figure out exactly how many new pens we need."

"How many pens do we have now?" Marcus asked.

"I don't know," said Mr. Breezy, "but they're all full."

"Then how many dogs do we have here?" Marcus asked.

"Let me think," said Mr. Breezy. "We have six dogs in the pens out back, four dogs in the pens downstairs, four dogs in the pens upstairs, and three dogs in no pens at all."

"And you want to know how many more pens we need?" Marcus asked.

26 • "It's Not So Easy," Said Mr. Breezy

"I knew you wouldn't think this one is easy," said Mr. Breezy. "So how will we get the answer?"

"But I already have the answer!" said Marcus.

How many more pens do they need? three

How can you tell? Three dogs aren't in any pens.

"We need three more pens," Marcus told his dad, "for the three dogs that aren't in any pens now."

"You make it all sound easy!" exclaimed Mr. Breezy. "What's your secret?"

"My secret," said Marcus, "is to pay attention only to the numbers that matter."

How can you tell what numbers matter? Listen carefully.

. . . the end

Story 4 • **27**

LESSON 30

Student Edition pages 65–66

Subtraction with Hidden Counters

LESSON PLANNER

Objective

▶ to teach students to solve concrete subtraction problems in which the answers must be computed rather than observed directly

Context of the Lesson Subtraction with hidden counters was introduced in Lesson 29. It continues in this lesson and the next.

 MANIPULATIVES
can
counters*

Program Resources
Number Cubes
Thinking Story Book, pages 28–29
Practice Master 30
Enrichment Master 30
For extra practice:
  CD-ROM* Lesson 30

① Warm-Up

 Problem of the Day Present the following problem to the class. Jamie is one year older than Ben. Amy is one year younger than Jamie. Ben is six years old. Who is the same age as Ben? (Amy)

Problem-Solving Strategies Ask students who have solved the Problem of the Day to share how they solved it and any strategies they used.

 Have students use finger sets to add:

a. 8 + 2 (10)	**b.** 4 + 3 (7)
c. 3 + 1 (4)	**d.** 8 + 0 (8)
e. 6 + 1 (7)	**f.** 3 + 1 (4)

② Teach

 Demonstrate Have a student put nine **counters*** into the **can** and then take out three, one at a time, as you demonstrate the corresponding finger operations. Repeat with similar problems and other student volunteers.

65 Numbers 1–10

LESSON 30

Name _____

Subtraction with Hidden Counters

 How many now?

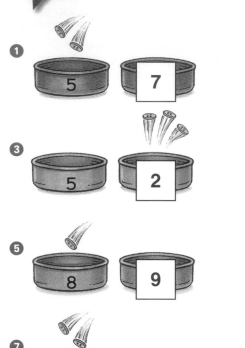

1. 5 | 7
2. 2 | 4
3. 5 | 2
4. 4 | 6
5. 8 | 9
6. 9 | 7
7. 6 | 8
8. 8 | 6

 NOTE TO HOME
Students solve addition and subtraction problems with counters, some of which are hidden.

Copyright © SRA/McGraw-Hill

Unit 1 Lesson 30 • **65**

 Why teach it this way?

Mixed addition and subtraction problems are included in this and subsequent lessons in order to encourage students to think about what they must do to solve a problem rather than to automatically add or subtract two numbers.

 **Literature Connection** Read *Ten Little Animals* by Laura Jane Coats, a counting book in which ten animals fall off the bed one by one, to illustrate the concept of subtracting ones.

RETEACHING

Because subtracting with hidden counters is reinforced in the next lesson, reteaching is not suggested at this time.

*available separately

◆ LESSON 30 Subtraction with Hidden Counters

How many now?

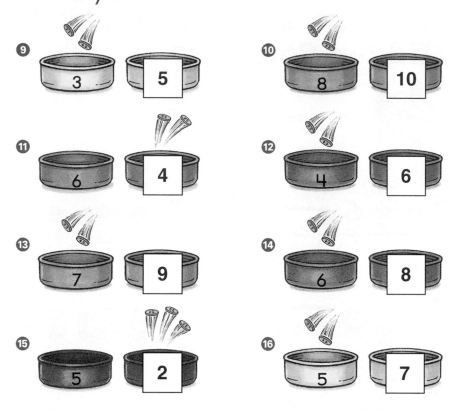

⑨ 3 | 5

⑩ 8 | 10

⑪ 6 | 4

⑫ 4 | 6

⑬ 7 | 9

⑭ 6 | 8

⑮ 5 | 2

⑯ 5 | 7

FANTASTIC FACT

Over 5 billion people live on Earth. At the present rate, world population doubles every 41 years.

66 • Numbers 1–10

NOTE TO HOME
Students solve addition and subtraction problems with hidden counters.

Using the Number Cubes Present more subtraction problems like those in the demonstration, but do not model the finger operations. Instead, have students calculate with their fingers and then show the answers with Number Cubes. Include addition problems as well. Confirm each answer by counting the counters in the can.

Using the Student Pages Explain how to interpret the pictures in the first two problems on page 65. The first picture shows five counters in the can because "five" is written on the can. As two more counters are being added, ask how many counters are now in the can. (7) Problem 3 shows five counters in the can and then three of them being taken out. Ask how many are left. (2) Have students work in pairs to complete pages 65–66. When finished, have partners explain how they arrived at each answer.

Using the Thinking Story Present two new problems from those following "'It's Not So Easy,' Said Mr. Breezy" on pages 28–29 of the Thinking Story Book or on pages 64a–64b of this Guide.

❸ Wrap-Up 🕐 5 MINUTES

In Closing Have students use counters and a can to present problems like those on pages 65–66 for other students to solve.

ANALYZING ANSWERS Use students' answers and explanations of their answers to pages 65–66 to determine whether they understand the concepts behind concrete subtraction problems.

Assessment Criteria

Did the student . . .

✓ correctly solve 13 of 16 problems on pages 65–66?

✓ use finger sets to correctly solve problems during the demonstration?

PRACTICE p. 30

LESSON 30 PRACTICE Name_____

How many now?

❶ 4 | 3 ? | ❷ 2 | 0 ?

❸ 7 | 5 ? | ❹ 6 | 4 ?

❺ 3 | 2 ? | ❻ 5 | 2 ?

❼ 8 | 5 ? | ❽ 1 | 0 ?

ENRICHMENT p. 30

LESSON 30 ENRICHMENT Name_____

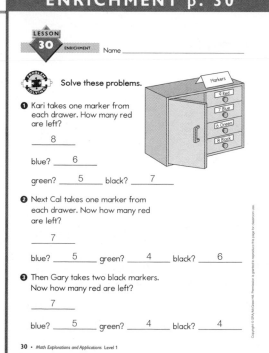

Solve these problems.

Markers
4 Red
7 Blue
5 Green
8 Black

❶ Kari takes one marker from each drawer. How many red are left?

_____8_____

blue? ___6___

green? ___5___ black? ___7___

❷ Next Cal takes one marker from each drawer. Now how many red are left?

_____7_____

blue? ___5___ green? ___4___ black? ___6___

❸ Then Gary takes two black markers. Now how many red are left?

_____7_____

blue? ___5___ green? ___4___ black? ___4___

LESSON 31

Student Edition pages 67–68

Addition and Subtraction— Hidden Counters

LESSON PLANNER

Objective

✓ to assess students' ability to subtract 0, 1, 2, or 3 from numbers less than 10 in concrete subtraction problems with hidden remainders

Context of the Lesson This lesson includes Mastery Checkpoint 8 for assessing students' ability to solve concrete subtraction problems.

👋 **MANIPULATIVES**   **Program Resources**

cardboard
counters*

Number Cubes
Thinking Story Book, pages 28–29
Reteaching Master
Practice Master 31
Enrichment Master 31
Assessment Master
For extra practice:
 CD-ROM* Lesson 31

❶ Warm-Up ⏱ 5 MINUTES

Problem of the Day Ask students to name all the pairs of numbers that make a sum of 8. (1, 7; 6, 2; 3, 5; 4, 4; 8, 0)

Problem-Solving Strategies Ask students who have solved the Problem of the Day to share how they solved it and any strategies they used.

 Present addition problems with one addend of 0, 1, or 2. Have students show answers with Number Cubes.

❷ Teach

Demonstrate Draw six figures on the chalkboard, then count them and cover them with **cardboard**. Ask how many figures are covered. (6) Next, reveal two of the figures. Ask how many are still covered. (4) Have students explain how they know this. Check students' answers. Repeat with similar problems.

67 Numbers 1–10

LESSON 31

Name _____

Addition and Subtraction— Hidden Counters

How many now?

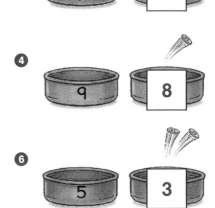

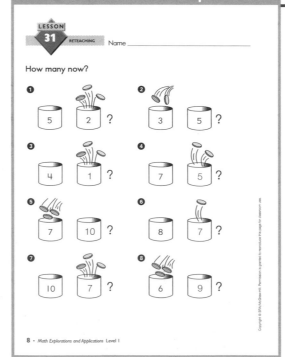

GAME Play the "Take Away the Counters" game.

🎒 **NOTE TO HOME**
Students solve concrete addition and subtraction problems in which one number is hidden.

Copyright © SRA/McGraw-Hill

Unit 1   Lesson 31 • **67**

RETEACHING p. 8

LESSON **31** RETEACHING   Name _____

How many now?

❶ 5 2 ?   ❷ 3 5 ?
❸ 4 1 ?   ❹ 7 5 ?
❺ 7 10 ?   ❻ 8 7 ?
❼ 10 7 ?   ❽ 6 9 ?

8 • Math Explorations and Applications Level 1

PRACTICE p. 31

LESSON **31** PRACTICE   Name _____

How many now?

❶ 4 7 ?   ❷ 6 7 ?
❸ 7 4 ?   ❹ 9 6 ?
❺ 5 3 ?   ❻ 4 6 ?
❼ 8 7 ?   ❽ 3 6 ?

Math Explorations and Applications Level 1 • **31**

*available separately

◆ **LESSON 31** Addition and Subtraction—Hidden Counters

Listen to the problems.

7 Brady caught four fish. Then he put them back in the lake. How many fish does Brady have now?

`0`

8 Sara collected four sports cards. Then Stephanie gave her three more. Now how many sports cards does she have?

`7`

9 Rodney had some marbles. Then he lost one. Now how many does he have?

not enough information

☐

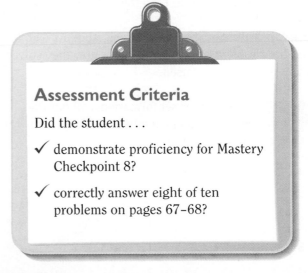

10 The Blue Sox played a baseball game against the Green Sox. Draw a ring around the highest score. By how many runs are they winning?

BLUE SOX 6
GREEN SOX 3

`3`

68 • Numbers 1–10

🎒 **NOTE TO HOME** Students solve word problems.

Copyright © SRA/McGraw-Hill

GAME **Introducing the "Take Away the Counters" Game** To provide practice in subtracting with concrete objects, demonstrate and play the "Take Away the Counters" game. Students work in pairs. Player 1 counts aloud as he or she takes up to ten **counters*** from a central pile. Player 1 then covers these counters with a book and removes some of them so that Player 2 can see how many have been removed. Player 2 then states how many counters are left under the book. If correct, he or she wins the round. Players switch roles and repeat. A copy of this game can also be found on page 14 of the Home Connections Blackline Masters.

Using the Student Pages Have students complete page 67 on their own. When students finish, check this page as a class. Then do the problems on page 68 as a class.

📖 **Using the Thinking Story** Present two new problems from among those following "'It's Not So Easy,' Said Mr. Breezy" on pages 28–29 of the Thinking Story Book or on pages 64a–64b of this Guide.

❸ Wrap-Up ⏱ 5 MINUTES

In Closing Have students make up story problems to share with the class. Have the other students solve them.

✅ **Mastery Checkpoint 8**

At about this time you may want to formally assess students' ability to solve concrete subtraction problems. Use student page 67 or pages 12–13 of the Assessment Blackline Masters. The results of this assessment may be recorded on the Mastery Checkpoint Chart.

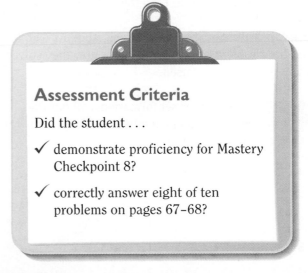

Assessment Criteria

Did the student . . .

✓ demonstrate proficiency for Mastery Checkpoint 8?

✓ correctly answer eight of ten problems on pages 67–68?

LOOKING AHEAD You will need a piece of string and a washer for the next lesson.

ENRICHMENT p. 31

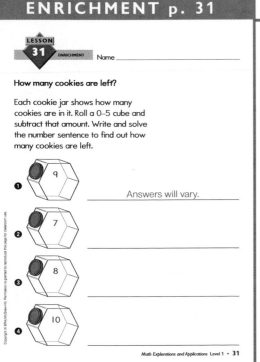

LESSON **31** ENRICHMENT Name _____

How many cookies are left?

Each cookie jar shows how many cookies are in it. Roll a 0–5 cube and subtract that amount. Write and solve the number sentence to find out how many cookies are left.

1 9

_____ Answers will vary.

2 7 _____

3 8 _____

4 10 _____

Math Explorations and Applications Level 1 • **31**

ASSESSMENT p. 12

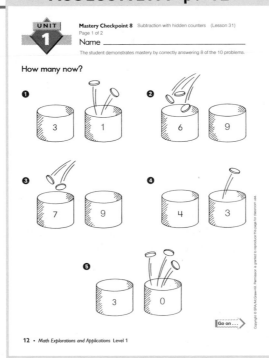

UNIT **1** **Mastery Checkpoint 8** Subtraction with hidden counters (Lesson 31)
Page 1 of 2
Name _____

The student demonstrates mastery by correctly answering 8 of the 10 problems.

How many now?

1 3 1   **2** 6 9

3 7 9   **4** 4 3

5 3 0

Go on ▶

12 • *Math Explorations and Applications Level 1*

---

*available separately

LESSON
32
Student Edition pages 69–70
Adding On—
Counting Back

LESSON PLANNER

Objectives

▶ to teach students to use finger sets without looking at their fingers to solve simple addition problems

▶ to provide experience in estimating time intervals by counting pendulum swings

▶ to provide practice in recognizing and completing number patterns

Context of the Lesson Subtraction with fingers out of sight will be introduced in the next lesson. More work with a pendulum will be done in Lesson 34.

 MANIPULATIVES
string

washer or other small weight

Program Resources
Thinking Story Book, pages 28–29

Practice Master 32

Enrichment Master 32

For extra practice:
CD-ROM* Lesson 32

Mixed Practice, page 355

① Warp-Up ⏱

Problem of the Day Present the following problem. Maria can read a page in seven minutes. Jesse can read it one minute faster than Maria. Hector can read it two minutes faster than Jesse. How long does it take Hector to read the page? (4 minutes)

Problem-Solving Strategies Ask students who have solved the Problem of the Day to share how they solved it and any strategies they used.

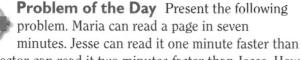 To review finger set formation, call out the following numbers and have students show the corresponding finger sets.

a.	10	b.	5
c.	3	d.	2
e.	9	f.	7
g.	8	h.	1
i.	4	j.	6

LESSON
32

Name _____

Adding On—Counting Back

 How many now?

①  5 | 2

②  3 | 5

③  6 | 3

④  6 | 4

⑤  5 | 8

⑥  8 | 7

 Do the "Be Your Own Stopwatch" activity.

 NOTE TO HOME
Students solve addition and subtraction problems with counters, some of which are hidden.

Unit 1 Lesson 32 • **69**

Why teach it this way?

Teaching students to add by using finger sets without looking at their fingers represents a further step toward making addition a mental rather than a mechanical process.

 **Literature Connection** To provide counting practice, read *Mouse Count* by Ellen S. Walsh.

RETEACHING

Because subtraction without looking at finger sets is taught in the next lesson, reteaching of both addition and subtraction can be postponed until the end of Lesson 33.

*available separately

◆ **LESSON 32** Adding On—Counting Back

Use the Mixed Practice on page 355 after this lesson.

Fill in the missing numbers.

7 1 2 **3** 4 5 6 7

8 2 3 4 **5** 6 7 8

9 2 3 4 5 6 **7** 8

10 6 5 4 **3** 2 1 0

11 6 5 4 3 2 **1** 0

12 6 5 4 3 **2** 1 0

13 1 2 1 **2** 1 2 1

14 2 1 2 **1** 2 1 2

15 1 2 1 2 **1** **2** 1

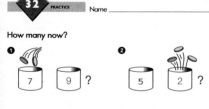

In your Math Journal describe one of the patterns.

70 • Numbers 1–10

 NOTE TO HOME
Students practice completing number patterns.

PRACTICE p. 32

LESSON **32** PRACTICE   Name_____

How many now?

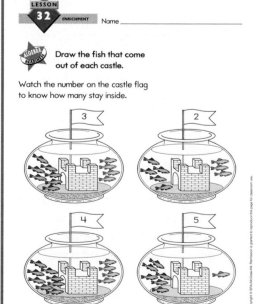

1 7 9 ?
2 5 2 ?
3 9 6 ?
4 3 6 ?
5 6 8 ?
6 5 6 ?
7 8 6 ?
8 2 5 ?

32 • Math Explorations and Applications Level 1

ENRICHMENT p. 32

LESSON **32** ENRICHMENT   Name_____

Draw the fish that come out of each castle.

Watch the number on the castle flag to know how many stay inside.

3   2

4   5

32 • Math Explorations and Applications Level 1

---

② Teach

Demonstrate Demonstrate how to use finger sets without looking at your fingers to solve simple addition problems. Then, have students perform a problem while keeping their eyes turned toward the ceiling, before they check their fingers to see the result.

 Introducing the "Be Your Own Stopwatch" Activity To provide practice in rhythmic counting, do the "Be Your Own Stopwatch" activity. Make a pendulum by tying a **weight** to a $2\frac{1}{2}$-foot-long **string**. Start the pendulum. Have students count each cycle as the weight swings and returns. Invite students to start counting, then to close their eyes while counting, and then to open their eyes to see if they are still in the right rhythm. Next, have them close their eyes from the beginning. Count the first two cycles aloud and then have students keep counting silently until you call "Stop."

Using the Student Pages Have students work with partners to complete student pages 69–70.

 Using the Thinking Story Present two new problems from among those following "'It's Not So Easy,' Said Mr. Breezy" on pages 28–29 of the Thinking Story Book or on pages 64a–64b of this Guide.

③ Wrap-Up

In Closing Have students demonstrate how they used finger sets without looking to solve problems on page 69.

 **Performance Assessment** Observe which students use finger sets without looking to solve problems during the demonstration.

Assessment Criteria

Did the student . . .

✓ correctly solve 7 of 9 problems on pages 69–70?

✓ actively participate in the "Be Your Own Stopwatch" activity?

Unit 1 Lesson 32 **70**

LESSON 33

Student Edition pages 71–72

Addition and Subtraction

LESSON PLANNER

Objectives

▶ to teach students to use finger sets without looking at their fingers to solve simple subtraction problems

▶ to provide practice with word problems

Context of the Lesson The procedure for subtraction in this lesson is similar to that for addition in Lesson 32.

 MANIPULATIVES

counters*

Program Resources

Number Cubes

Thinking Story Book, pages 28–29

Practice Master 33

Enrichment Master 33

For extra practice:
CD-ROM* Lesson 33

① Warm-Up ⏱ 5 MINUTES

Problem of the Day Draw the following shapes on the chalkboard and have students draw the missing shape in the pattern:

Problem-Solving Strategies Ask students who have solved the Problem of the Day to share how they solved it and any strategies they used.

MENTAL MATH Present addition problems with one addend of 0, 1, 2, or 3. Have students show answers with Number Cubes.

② Teach

 Demonstrate Use the same procedure as taught in Lesson 32. Demonstrate subtraction with finger sets without looking at fingers. Have students keep their fingers under their desks and then show their response with Number Cubes. Provide practice with both addition and subtraction problems.

71 Numbers 1–10

LESSON 33

Name _____

Addition and Subtraction

How many now?

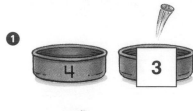

① 4 | 3

② 7 | 4

③ 5 | 6

④ 2 | 1

⑤ 2 | 4

⑥ 3 | 6

⑦ 8 | 5

⑧ 9 | 6

Copyright © SRA/McGraw-Hill

GAME Play the "Add or Take Away the Counters" game.

 NOTE TO HOME Students solve concrete addition and subtraction problems with one number hidden.

Unit 1   Lesson 33 • **71**

 Literature Connection To reinforce math concepts, read *A More or Less Fish Story* by Joanne and David Wylie.

GIFTED & TALENTED Meeting Individual Needs Allow these students to help others who are still having difficulty adding and subtracting without looking at finger sets during the demonstration and when completing pages 71 and 72.

RETEACHING

Have students practice holding specific finger sets behind their backs without adding or subtracting. For example, have students make a finger set of seven while their hands are behind their backs. Then have them hold up their fingers to check if they are correct. Repeat this until students are confident in how to make finger sets without looking. Then review finger-set addition and subtraction without looking.

*available separately

◆ LESSON 33 Addition and Subtraction

Listen to the problems.

9 Some students looked at books. Some students weighed blocks. Draw a ring around the photo with more students.

How many more students?

3

How many students are there all together?

7

10 Mr. Jones had five dogs. He gave all but three to a friend. How many dogs did he give away?

2

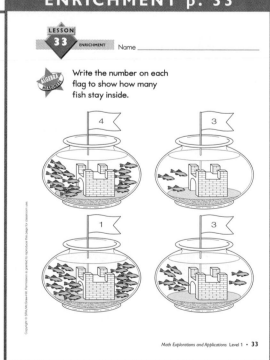

Copyright © SRA/McGraw-Hill

72 • Numbers 1–10

NOTE TO HOME
Students solve word problems.

PRACTICE p. 33

LESSON **33** PRACTICE Name _____

How many now?

1 7 6 ?   **2** 5 7 ?

3 4 2 ?   **4** 8 5 ?

5 3 6 ?   **6** 6 9 ?

7 4 7 ?   **8** 9 8 ?

Math Explorations and Applications Level 1 • 33

ENRICHMENT p. 33

LESSON **33** ENRICHMENT Name _____

Write the number on each flag to show how many fish stay inside.

4   3

1   3

Math Explorations and Applications Level 1 • 33

GAME Introducing the "Add or Take Away the Counters" Game Play this game to provide practice in addition and subtraction without counting. Each pair of students gets ten **counters*** to place in a "bank." Player 1 counts aloud as he or she takes up to ten counters from the bank and then covers the counters with a book. The same player then either sets out more counters from the bank or removes some from under the book and places them in full view of Player 2. Player 2 must then guess how many counters there are either all together or under the book. If correct, Player 2 wins the round. Players switch roles and repeat. A copy of this game can also be found on page 14 of the Home Connections Blackline Masters.

Using the Student Pages Have students complete page 71 on their own. Emphasize that they must pay attention to whether counters are being put in or taken out. Then do the word problems on page 72 as a class. Point out that the puppies shown in problem 10 are those Mr. Jones kept.

Using the Thinking Story Present two new problems from among those following "'It's Not So Easy,' Said Mr. Breezy" on pages 28–29 of the Thinking Story Book or on pages 64a–64b of this Guide.

❸ Wrap-Up ⏱ 5 MINUTES

In Closing Have students demonstrate how they used finger sets to solve some of the problems on page 71.

ALTERNATIVE ASSESSMENT **Informal Assessment** Use student pages 71–72 to informally assess ability to add and subtract numbers.

Assessment Criteria

Did the student . . .

✓ correctly solve eight of ten problems on pages 71–72?

✓ refrain from looking at his or her finger sets during the demonstration?

LOOKING AHEAD The pendulum used in Lesson 32 will be needed again in Lesson 34.

---

*available separately

LESSON 34

Student Edition pages 73–74

Addition and Subtraction (Horizontal)

LESSON PLANNER

Objectives

▶ to teach students to read and solve addition and subtraction problems in horizontal form

▶ to provide students with experience in estimating time

Context of the Lesson Addition and subtraction in vertical form will be introduced in Lesson 35. This is the second lesson in which a pendulum is used to estimate time.

MANIPULATIVES

interlocking cubes* (optional)

pendulum (used in Lesson 32)

Program Resources

Number Cubes

Practice Master 34

Enrichment Master 34

For extra practice:
  CD-ROM* Lesson 34

1 Warm-Up

5 MINUTES

Problem of the Day Draw or display a number line. Then write the following on the chalkboard and ask students what rule was followed on the number line to go from "Start" to "Finish" each time. (Move up one place.)

| Start | 2 | 6 | 1 | 9 |
| Finish | 3 | 7 | 2 | 10 |

Problem-Solving Strategies Ask students who have solved the Problem of the Day to share how they solved it and any strategies they used.

MENTAL MATH Present the following subtraction problems. Have students show their answers with Number Cubes.

a. 6 – 2 = (4) b. 5 – 1 = (4)

c. 7 – 2 = (5) d. 8 – 3 = (5)

e. 9 – 3 = (6) f. 8 – 2 = (6)

g. 9 – 2 = (7) h. 8 – 1 = (7)

LESSON 34

Name _____

Addition and Subtraction (Horizontal)

Solve these problems.
Watch the signs.

❶ 4 + 1 = __5__   ❷ 1 + 5 = __6__

❸ 4 – 1 = __3__   ❹ 1 + 3 = __4__

❺ 6 + 1 = __7__   ❻ 8 + 1 = __9__

❼ 7 + 1 = __8__   ❽ 9 – 1 = __8__

❾ 5 – 1 = __4__   ❿ 3 + 1 = __4__

Do the "Race Against Time" activity.

NOTE TO HOME
Students solve addition and subtraction problems.

Unit 1 Lesson 34 • **73**

Why teach it this way?

This lesson requires students to pay attention to the **+** and **–** signs before they can solve problems. Presenting all addition or all subtraction problems allows students to solve problems without paying attention to the sign. When both signs are taught together, students must stop to think about what they must do.

Literature Connection To reinforce the concept of number sentences, have students read aloud *Ready, Set, Hop* by Stuart J. Murphy.

RETEACHING

Have students use **interlocking cubes*** to model horizontal number sentences like those on pages 73–74. Students can work in pairs as they model each problem.

---

*available separately

◆ LESSON 34 Addition and Subtraction (Horizontal)

Solve these problems.
Watch the signs.

⑪ 3 + 0 = __3__   ⑲ 0 + 3 = __3__

⑫ 3 − 0 = __3__   ⑳ 0 + 4 = __4__

⑬ 5 − 0 = __5__   ㉑ 0 + 5 = __5__

⑭ 5 − 1 = __4__   ㉒ 6 + 1 = __7__

⑮ 5 − 2 = __3__   ㉓ 6 + 2 = __8__

⑯ 5 − 3 = __2__   ㉔ 6 + 3 = __9__

⑰ 2 + 2 = __4__   ㉕ 0 − 0 = __0__

⑱ 1 − 1 = __0__   ㉖ 0 + 0 = __0__

NOTE TO HOME
Students solve addition and
subtraction problems.

74 • Numbers 1–10

PRACTICE p. 34

PRACTICE Name _____

Solve these problems. Watch the
signs.

❶ 2 − 1 = __1__   ❷ 7 + 0 = __7__

❸ 1 + 1 = __2__   ❹ 1 + 6 = __7__

❺ 5 + 1 = __6__   ❻ 4 − 0 = __4__

❼ 8 − 1 = __7__   ❽ 0 + 1 = __1__

❾ 3 + 0 = __3__   ❿ 6 − 1 = __5__

⓫ 9 − 1 = __8__   ⓬ 7 − 0 = __7__

⓭ 1 + 2 = __3__   ⓮ 1 + 4 = __5__

⓯ 3 − 1 = __2__   ⓰ 2 + 1 = __3__

⓱ 1 + 7 = __8__   ⓲ 4 + 4 = __8__

34 • Math Explorations and Applications Level 1

ENRICHMENT p. 34

ENRICHMENT Name _____

Help the clown color his balloons.

❶ Color red the
balloons that make 4.

❷ Color blue the balloons that make 5.

❸ Color green the balloons that
make 6.

❹ Color orange the balloons that
make 7.

❺ Color yellow the balloons that
make 8.

❻ Color purple the balloons that
make 9.

34 • Math Explorations and Applications Level 1

---

② Teach

Demonstrate Ask students: "How much is 4 and 1?"
Explain and demonstrate how to write the problem 4 + 1 = 5
in horizontal form on the chalkboard. Repeat with subtraction
sentences such as 4 − 1 = 3. Provide practice in recognizing
and reading the plus, minus, and equal signs. Then
introduce false or incomplete number sentences. Have
students correct or complete them. For example, write:
3 + 1 = 8. Have students read the sentence, explain what is
wrong, and correct it. Then write incomplete addition and
subtraction sentences such as 6 + 1 = ___ and 6 − 1 = ___.
Have students explain what they must do to complete each,
and show their answers with their Number Cubes.

**Introducing the "Race Against Time"
Activity** This activity provides practice in
estimating duration of time. Have students predict
how long it will take to complete certain tasks, such as
finding a given page in a book, tying their shoes, or printing
their names. Set the pendulum swinging, give the order to
start, and then count the cycles aloud. Have students record
the time it takes for each task. Then have them compare the
time for the three activities and put them in order from
shortest to longest or vice versa.

Using the Student Pages Complete the first problem
on both of these pages as a class. Remind students to focus
first on whether they need to add or subtract. Have students
complete the rest of the problems on their own.

③ Wrap-Up 5 MINUTES

In Closing Have students make up problems that have
plus signs or minus signs, then solve each other's problems.

Informal Assessment Use students'
answers to pages 73 and 74 to informally
assess their ability to solve horizontal addition
and subtraction problems.

Assessment Criteria

Did the student . . .

✓ correctly solve 22 of 26 problems on
pages 73–74?

✓ make reasonable estimates during
the pendulum activity?

Addition and Subtraction (Vertical)

LESSON PLANNER

Objective
▶ to teach students to read and solve addition and subtraction problems in vertical form

Context of the Lesson This lesson introduces vertical-form addition and subtraction. Horizontal- and vertical-form practice will be continued in subsequent lessons.

 MANIPULATIVES   **Program Resources**

can
counters*

Number Cubes
Thinking Story Book, pages 30–33
Reteaching Master
Practice Master 35
Enrichment Master 35
For career connections:
   Careers and Math*
For extra practice:
   CD-ROM* Lesson 35

① Warm-Up

 Problem of the Day Present the following problem to the class: Meg has more pennies than Joe, but fewer than Gary. Match the names with the correct number of pennies: three pennies, five pennies, seven pennies. (Joe–3; Meg–5; Gary–7)

Problem-Solving Strategies Ask students who have solved the Problem of the Day to share how they solved it and any strategies they used.

 Present counters-in-the-can problems. Start with the first number of **counters*** in a **can**. Add the second number of counters. Have students show answers with Number Cubes.

a. 3, 2 (5)   b. 5, 0 (5)   c. 6, 3 (9)
d. 9, 1 (10)   e. 3, 1 (4)   f. 7, 2 (9)

② Teach

Demonstrate Review reading and solving horizontal addition and subtraction sentences. Introduce the vertical

---

Name _____

Addition and Subtraction (Vertical)

Solve these problems.
Watch the signs.

①   6
   + 1
   7

②   8
   − 1
   7

③   1
   + 5
   6

④   6
   − 1
   5

⑤   2
   + 0
   2

⑥   2
   + 1
   3

⑦   2
   + 2
   4

⑧   2
   − 1
   1

⑨   1
   + 0
   1

⑩   1
   + 7
   8

⑪   3
   + 1
   4

⑫   1
   − 0
   1

 Talk about the Thinking Story "Mr. Muddle Goes Shopping."

 NOTE TO HOME
Students solve addition and subtraction problems.

Unit 1   Lesson 35   •   **75**

 Literature Connection Students will enjoy adding and subtracting numbers of pigs, chickens, and other farm animals as you read aloud *Number One, Number Fun* by Kay Chorao.

RETEACHING p. 9

LESSON
35   RETEACHING   Name _____

Add when you see +.

     4 + 1 = 5

Subtract when you see −.

     4 − 1 = 3

Solve these problems. Watch the signs.

① 2 + 2 = _4_   ② 5 − 3 = _2_

③ 6 + 3 = _9_   ④ 1 + 5 = _6_

⑤   2
   + 3
   _5_

⑥   4
   − 2
   _2_

⑦   1
   + 6
   _7_

⑧   2
   − 1
   _1_

⑨   6
   − 2
   _4_

⑩   4
   + 1
   _5_

⑪   8
   − 3
   _5_

⑫   7
   + 1
   _8_

Math Explorations and Applications Level 1 • 9

*available separately

◆ LESSON 35 Addition and Subtraction (Vertical)

Solve these problems.
Watch the signs.

⑬
$$\begin{array}{r} 5 \\ + 0 \\ \hline 5 \end{array}$$

⑭
$$\begin{array}{r} 4 \\ + 0 \\ \hline 4 \end{array}$$

⑮
$$\begin{array}{r} 3 \\ + 2 \\ \hline 5 \end{array}$$

⑯
$$\begin{array}{r} 3 \\ + 1 \\ \hline 4 \end{array}$$

⑰
$$\begin{array}{r} 3 \\ - 1 \\ \hline 2 \end{array}$$

⑱
$$\begin{array}{r} 2 \\ - 1 \\ \hline 1 \end{array}$$

⑲
$$\begin{array}{r} 8 \\ + 1 \\ \hline 9 \end{array}$$

⑳
$$\begin{array}{r} 8 \\ + 2 \\ \hline 10 \end{array}$$

㉑
$$\begin{array}{r} 8 \\ - 1 \\ \hline 7 \end{array}$$

㉒
$$\begin{array}{r} 8 \\ - 2 \\ \hline 6 \end{array}$$

㉓
$$\begin{array}{r} 9 \\ + 0 \\ \hline 9 \end{array}$$

㉔
$$\begin{array}{r} 9 \\ + 1 \\ \hline 10 \end{array}$$

㉕
$$\begin{array}{r} 9 \\ - 1 \\ \hline 8 \end{array}$$

㉖
$$\begin{array}{r} 9 \\ - 2 \\ \hline 7 \end{array}$$

㉗
$$\begin{array}{r} 7 \\ - 1 \\ \hline 6 \end{array}$$

㉘
$$\begin{array}{r} 7 \\ + 2 \\ \hline 9 \end{array}$$

76 • Numbers 1–10

NOTE TO HOME
Students solve addition and
subtraction problems.

form by writing, reading, and solving problems in pairs: Tell
students that 7 is another way of showing 7 – 1 = 6.
$$\begin{array}{r} - 1 \\ \hline 6 \end{array}$$

Provide students with oral practice in reading vertical
problems. Then say aloud problems such as "add 7 and 3"
and have volunteers write the problems on the chalkboard
in vertical form while the rest of the class solves them.

Using the Student Pages Complete the first two
problems on page 75 with students. Remind students to watch
the signs as they work the vertical problems on their own.

 Using the Thinking Story Read aloud and
discuss the story "Mr. Muddle Goes Shopping"
on Thinking Story Book pages 30–33.

❸ Wrap-Up

In Closing Have students explain how the following
problems are alike and different: 3 + 1 = 4 and
$$\begin{array}{r} 3 \\ + 1 \\ \hline 4 \end{array}$$

 When correcting pages 75–76, have students
write the number of answers they got correct
on each page. Then have them correct any
incorrect answers.

Assessment Criteria

Did the student . . .

✓ correctly solve 22 of 28 problems on
pages 75–76?

✓ participate in the Thinking Story
discussion?

LOOKING AHEAD Students will need calculators for the
next lesson.

 Meeting Individual Needs
Pair auditory and visual learners. Provide
mixed addition and subtraction problems in both
vertical and horizontal forms. Have auditory learners
read aloud the problems as visual learners point to the
problems and then solve them. Reverse the procedure
by having visual learners point to the problems for
auditory learners to read aloud and solve.

PRACTICE p. 35

LESSON 35 PRACTICE Name _____

Solve these problems. Watch the
signs.

❶
$$\begin{array}{r} 4 \\ + 1 \\ \hline 5 \end{array}$$
❷
$$\begin{array}{r} 0 \\ + 6 \\ \hline 6 \end{array}$$
❸
$$\begin{array}{r} 7 \\ - 1 \\ \hline 6 \end{array}$$
❹
$$\begin{array}{r} 1 \\ + 6 \\ \hline 7 \end{array}$$

❺
$$\begin{array}{r} 1 \\ - 0 \\ \hline 1 \end{array}$$
❻
$$\begin{array}{r} 8 \\ + 1 \\ \hline 9 \end{array}$$
❼
$$\begin{array}{r} 4 \\ - 1 \\ \hline 3 \end{array}$$
❽
$$\begin{array}{r} 5 \\ + 1 \\ \hline 6 \end{array}$$

❾
$$\begin{array}{r} 7 \\ + 1 \\ \hline 8 \end{array}$$
❿
$$\begin{array}{r} 1 \\ - 1 \\ \hline 0 \end{array}$$
⓫
$$\begin{array}{r} 0 \\ - 0 \\ \hline 0 \end{array}$$
⓬
$$\begin{array}{r} 2 \\ - 0 \\ \hline 2 \end{array}$$

⓭
$$\begin{array}{r} 0 \\ + 8 \\ \hline 8 \end{array}$$
⓮
$$\begin{array}{r} 9 \\ - 0 \\ \hline 9 \end{array}$$
⓯
$$\begin{array}{r} 2 \\ - 1 \\ \hline 1 \end{array}$$
⓰
$$\begin{array}{r} 2 \\ + 1 \\ \hline 3 \end{array}$$

Math Explorations and Applications Level 1 • **35**

ENRICHMENT p. 35

LESSON 35 ENRICHMENT Name _____

 Help finish the page. Fill in
the missing signs.

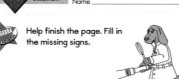

❶
$$\begin{array}{r} 9 \\ - 5 \\ \hline 4 \end{array}$$
❷
$$\begin{array}{r} 8 \\ - 2 \\ \hline 6 \end{array}$$
❸
$$\begin{array}{r} 6 \\ + 1 \\ \hline 7 \end{array}$$
❹
$$\begin{array}{r} 3 \\ + 2 \\ \hline 5 \end{array}$$

❺
$$\begin{array}{r} 7 \\ - 7 \\ \hline 0 \end{array}$$
❻
$$\begin{array}{r} 4 \\ - 3 \\ \hline 1 \end{array}$$
❼
$$\begin{array}{r} 5 \\ + 1 \\ \hline 6 \end{array}$$
❽
$$\begin{array}{r} 8 \\ - 4 \\ \hline 4 \end{array}$$

❾
$$\begin{array}{r} 2 \\ + 1 \\ \hline 3 \end{array}$$
❿
$$\begin{array}{r} 9 \\ - 6 \\ \hline 3 \end{array}$$
⓫
$$\begin{array}{r} 6 \\ - 4 \\ \hline 2 \end{array}$$
⓬
$$\begin{array}{r} 3 \\ - 2 \\ \hline 1 \end{array}$$

⓭
$$\begin{array}{r} 8 \\ - 7 \\ \hline 1 \end{array}$$
⓮
$$\begin{array}{r} 5 \\ - 3 \\ \hline 2 \end{array}$$
⓯
$$\begin{array}{r} 4 \\ + 2 \\ \hline 6 \end{array}$$
⓰
$$\begin{array}{r} 1 \\ + 7 \\ \hline 8 \end{array}$$

Math Explorations and Applications Level 1 • **35**

Mr. Muddle Goes Shopping

❶ Somebody asked Mr. Muddle, "How many children do you have?" "Well, I'll tell you this," said Mr. Muddle, "it's one fewer than the number of noses I have."
How many children does Mr. Muddle have? zero
How did you figure it out? He has one nose, and $1 - 1 = 0$

❷ "How old are you?" somebody asked Portia. Portia pointed to her ears, her eyes, her nose, and her mouth. "Count them all up," she said. "That's how old I am."
How old is she? six

❸ Yesterday Ferdie borrowed three pennies from Manolita. Today he gave back two pennies.
Does he still owe Manolita any money? yes
How much? 1¢

❹ The Engs' dog, Muffin, buried two bones, then three cans, then one potato, then two bones, and then three old newspapers.
How many bones did Muffin bury all together? four

❺ "We've had bad weather for five days," said Loretta the Letter Carrier. "It rained for two days and snowed the rest of the time."
How many days did it snow? three

Mr. Muddle Goes Shopping

Mr. Muddle invited some friends to his house for lunch. Then he looked in his refrigerator and saw that he didn't have enough food, so he figured out just what he needed to buy and made a list. Then Mr. Muddle left the list on the kitchen table and went to the store.

"Good morning, Mr. Muddle," said Mrs. Frazier, who owns the grocery store. "What do you need today?"

"Well," said Mr. Muddle, "I need eggs, apples, oranges, and tomatoes."

"How many eggs?" asked Mrs. Frazier.

"I don't know for sure," said Mr. Muddle.

Why isn't Mr. Muddle sure how many eggs he needs? He forgot his list.

"Oh, I see you forgot your list again," said Mrs. Frazier. "Can you remember *about* how many eggs you need?"

"All I can remember," said Mr. Muddle, "is that it is one more than five."

30 • Mr. Muddle Goes Shopping

Can you figure out how many eggs Mr. Muddle needs? six

"I believe you need six eggs," said Mrs. Frazier. She gave Mr. Muddle a half-carton of eggs with six eggs in it.

"Now," said Mrs. Frazier, "how many apples do you need?"

"I can't remember that either," said Mr. Muddle, "but I know it is less than ten."

Can Mrs. Frazier be sure exactly how many apples Mr. Muddle needs? Why not? No; Mr. Muddle hasn't told her enough.

"You haven't told me enough, Mr. Muddle," said Mrs. Frazier. "There are lots of numbers that are less than 10. Is it eight apples you need?"

"No," said Mr. Muddle. "It is one less than eight."

Now can Mrs. Frazier be sure? yes

How many apples does Mr. Muddle need? seven

Story 5 • **31**

❻ Willy has a rabbit that is worth one dollar. His brother has two rabbits just like it.
How much are his brother's rabbits worth all together? $2

❼ Portia ate two apples and an orange after lunch. Later she ate another apple.
How many oranges did she eat all together? one

❽ The puddle in Willy's backyard is 4 feet wide. It used to be 5 feet wide.
What could have happened? It might have dried up or drained.

❾ Ferdie and Portia each have a pillow stuffed with feathers. Portia thinks her pillow has more feathers in it, and Ferdie thinks his does. "I know how we can find out," said Portia. "Let's open up our pillows and count all the feathers."
Is that a good idea? Why not? too many feathers to count; they'd blow all over and the pillows would be ruined
Can you think of a better way for them to tell without counting? by weighing the pillows or measuring their thicknesses, for instance

◆ STORY 5   Mr. Muddle Goes Shopping

"You need seven apples," said Mrs. Frazier. "Here they are. Now, how many oranges do you need?"

"I don't know," said Mr. Muddle, "but it's the same as the number of fingers I have on one hand."

How many oranges does Mr. Muddle need? five

How do you know? Five is the same as the number of fingers on one hand.

"That was easy," said Mrs. Frazier. "Here are your five oranges, one for each finger. Now all we need to know is how many tomatoes you need."

"I really can't remember that," said Mr. Muddle. "All I know is that I'm going to use eight tomatoes for lunch, and I don't have that many tomatoes in my refrigerator."

Can Mrs. Frazier be sure how many tomatoes Mr. Muddle needs to buy? no

What else does she need to know? how many tomatoes are in his refrigerator

32 • Mr. Muddle Goes Shopping

"I can't be sure how many you need," said Mrs. Frazier. "If you have a lot of tomatoes in your refrigerator already, then you won't need to buy very many. I know you want to have eight tomatoes all together. It would help if I knew how many tomatoes you have in your refrigerator right now."

"Oh, I can tell you that," said Mr. Muddle. "I don't have any tomatoes at home."

Now can you figure out how many tomatoes Mr. Muddle needs to buy? Yes. He needs to buy eight tomatoes.

"I think I can figure that one out," said Mrs. Frazier. "You need eight tomatoes and you don't have any, so you need to buy all eight tomatoes. Well, here they are. I hope we didn't forget anything."

"I don't think we did," said Mr. Muddle. "I can't remember anything we forgot."

. . . the end

Story 5 • **33**

LESSON 36

Practicing Addition and Subtraction

Student Edition pages 77–78

LESSON PLANNER

Objectives

▶ to provide practice in recognizing steps 5 through 10 on an unlabeled number line

▶ to introduce use of the calculator

▶ to provide practice with addition and subtraction of single-digit numbers

Context of the Lesson Number lines were first introduced in Lesson 12. This is the first of numerous lessons on the calculator.

 MANIPULATIVES   **Program Resources**

calculators*	Number Cubes
counters* (optional)	Thinking Story Book, pages 34–35
cardboard	Practice Master 36
	Enrichment Master 36

For extra practice:
  CD-ROM* Lesson 36

1 Warp-Up

Problem of the Day Present the following problem to the class. Natasha has five shells. She wants to keep some on her desk and some on her dresser. Explain the different ways she could place the shells. (four on dresser, one on desk; four on desk, one on dresser; three on desk, two on dresser; two on desk, three on dresser)

Problem-Solving Strategies Ask students who have solved the Problem of the Day to share how they solved it and any strategies they used.

MENTAL MATH Call out addition problems that involve adding 1 or 2, for example: 5 + 1, 6 + 2, and so on. Have students use Number Cubes to show answers.

2 Teach

Demonstrate Draw a large 0–10 number line on the chalkboard. Label only the zero but make the marks for the 5 and 10 steps larger than the rest. Count the steps on the number line. Next, cover some of the steps below 5 with a

---

LESSON 36

Name _____

Practicing Addition and Subtraction

Solve these problems.
Watch the signs.

1 $\begin{array}{r} 8 \\ +2 \\ \hline 10 \end{array}$ **2** $\begin{array}{r} 6 \\ -1 \\ \hline 5 \end{array}$ **3** $\begin{array}{r} 1 \\ +3 \\ \hline 4 \end{array}$ **4** $\begin{array}{r} 3 \\ +1 \\ \hline 4 \end{array}$

5 $\begin{array}{r} 0 \\ +8 \\ \hline 8 \end{array}$ **6** $\begin{array}{r} 6 \\ -0 \\ \hline 6 \end{array}$ **7** $\begin{array}{r} 2 \\ +4 \\ \hline 6 \end{array}$ **8** $\begin{array}{r} 7 \\ -2 \\ \hline 5 \end{array}$

9 $7 + 2 = \underline{9}$ **10** $7 - 1 = \underline{6}$

11 $7 + 0 = \underline{7}$ **12** $9 - 2 = \underline{7}$

13 $6 + 2 = \underline{8}$ **14** $6 + 1 = \underline{7}$

15 $4 - 0 = \underline{4}$ **16** $4 - 1 = \underline{3}$

17 $9 - 0 = \underline{9}$ **18** $9 - 1 = \underline{8}$

 NOTE TO HOME
Students solve addition and subtraction problems.

Unit 1   Lesson 36 • **77**

 Music Connection
Make a musical number line. Mark off ten keys on a piano keyboard or a xylophone. Invite a volunteer to start at the lowest note and play three notes up. Have the rest of the class count as the notes are played. Repeat this procedure using other numbers of notes, having students play notes up and down the scale. You may also wish to mark the fifth and tenth keys and have the students count up and down from these keys.

RETEACHING

MANIPULATIVES Work with students who have difficulty solving addition and subtraction problems. Orally provide some number sentences. Have them act out each problem with **counters.***

*available separately

◆ **LESSON 36** Practicing Addition and Subtraction

First write your answer.
Then see if the calculator
shows the same answer.

⑲ (2) (**+**) (3) (**=**)

⎡ 5 . ⎤ My answer

⎡ 5 . ⎤ Calculator answer

⑳ (8) (**−**) (5) (**=**)

⎡ 3 . ⎤ My answer

⎡ 3 . ⎤ Calculator answer

㉑ (I) (**+**) (I) (**+**) (I) (**+**) (I) (**=**)

⎡ 4 . ⎤ My answer

⎡ 4 . ⎤ Calculator answer

78 • Numbers 1–10

NOTE TO HOME
Students become familiar with a calculator.

---

piece of **cardboard**. Point to step 6 and ask students to identify it and explain how they knew. Repeat with other steps, leading students to discover that they can use 5 as the starting point and count up from there. Use a similar procedure to show students how they can count down from 10.

Using the Student Pages Have students do the exercises on page 77. Then pass out **calculators.*** Tell students that calculator buttons are called *keys* and that the place where the numbers appear is called the *display*. Guide students through the use of the *clear*, numeral, *plus*, *minus*, and *equals* keys. Let them practice simple addition and subtraction problems on the calculator along with you before doing page 78 on their own.

Using the Thinking Story Present two or more problems from those following "Mr. Muddle Goes Shopping" on pages 34–35 of the Thinking Story Book or on pages 76a–76b of this Guide.

❸ Wrap-Up ⏱ 5 MINUTES

In Closing Invite students to tell ways that people use calculators.

Informal Assessment Observe students during the lesson to identify who is having difficulty using the number line or the calculator. Proficiency with both methods is important because they will be used frequently.

Assessment Criteria

Did the student . . .

✓ use strategies to count up and back on a number line?

✓ correctly solve 17 of 21 problems on pages 77–78?

PRACTICE p. 36

LESSON 36 PRACTICE   Name _____

Solve these problems. Watch the signs.

❶ 9 – 1 = __8__   ❷ 2 + 5 = __7__

❸ 1 + 4 = __5__   ❹ 8 – 2 = __6__

❺ 5 – 0 = __5__   ❻ 3 + 2 = __5__

❼ 6 – 1 = __5__   ❽ 4 + 2 = __6__

❾ 8 + 1 = __9__   ❿ 0 + 7 = __7__

⓫   6   ⓬   9   ⓭   2   ⓮   6
   – 2   – 0   + 7   + 1
   ___   ___   ___   ___
    4   9   9   7

⓯   4   ⓰   7   ⓱   3   ⓲   0
   + 0   – 1   – 2   + 8
   ___   ___   ___   ___
    4   6   1   8

36 • Math Explorations and Applications Level 1

ENRICHMENT p. 36

LESSON 36 ENRICHMENT   Name _____

Solve the problems. Crack the code.

| 7+2 | 2 + 4 | 5 – 1 |
| 9 – 1 | 8 – 7 | |

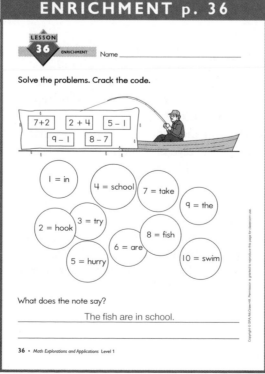

1 = in   4 = school   7 = take   9 = the
2 = hook   3 = try   8 = fish
5 = hurry   6 = are   10 = swim

What does the note say?

_____The fish are in school._____

36 • Math Explorations and Applications Level 1

*available separately

LESSON 37

Adding and Subtracting on a Number Line

Student Edition pages 79–80

LESSON PLANNER

Objectives

▶ to introduce the 0–10 number line as a means of solving addition and subtraction problems

✓ to assess student performance in solving addition and subtraction problems on a number line

Context of the Lesson This lesson includes a Mastery Checkpoint for addition and subtraction on the number line.

 MANIPULATIVES

Step-By-Step Number Line* (optional)

Program Resources

"Duck Pond" Game Mat

Number Cubes

Thinking Story Book, pages 34–35

Practice Master 37

Enrichment Master 37

Assessment Master

For additional math integration:
Math Throughout the Day*

For extra practice:
CD-ROM* Lesson 37
Mixed Practice, page 356

① Warm-Up ⏱ 5 MINUTES

 Problem of the Day Write *1, 2, 3, 4* on the chalkboard. Have students write addition and subtraction sentences, using any three of these numbers. (1 + 3 = 4; 3 + 1 = 4; 4 − 3 = 1; 4 − 1 = 3; 1 + 2 = 3; 2 + 1 = 3; 3 − 2 = 1; 3 − 1 = 2)

Problem-Solving Strategies Ask students who have solved the Problem of the Day to share how they solved it and any strategies they used.

MENTAL MATH Challenge students to perform these exercises:

a. Show the finger set for 4; put up 1 more (5)

b. Show the finger set for 6; put up 1 more (7)

c. Show the finger set for 5; put up 2 more (7)

d. Show the finger set for 6; put down 2 (4)

e. Show the finger set for 9; put down 4 (5)

f. Show the finger set for 3; put up 5 more (8)

79 Numbers 1–10

LESSON 37

Name _____

Adding and Subtracting on a Number Line

```
0  1  2  3  4  5  6  7  8  9  10
```

Solve these problems.
Use the number line.

❶ 4 + 2 = __6__   ❷ 7 + 1 = __8__

❸ 5 − 1 = __4__   ❹ 8 − 3 = __5__

❺ 3 + 2 = __5__   ❻ 3 + 3 = __6__

❼ 2 + 3 = __5__   ❽ 6 − 3 = __3__

❾ 8 − 2 = __6__   ❿ 9 − 2 = __7__

 Play the "Duck Pond" game.

 NOTE TO HOME
Students use a number line to help them solve addition and subtraction problems.

Unit 1   Lesson 37 • **79**

RETEACHING

MANIPULATIVES Make a large number line on the floor using masking tape for lines and taped-down cards for numbers, or use the **Step-By-Step Number Line***. Give students simple addition and subtraction problems that they can solve by walking through the problem on the number line.

Watch for students whose answers to addition problems are one too small and whose answers to subtraction problems are one too large. It is likely they are counting the numbers they touch instead of the number of steps they take.

PRACTICE p. 37

LESSON 37 PRACTICE

Name _____

```
0  1  2  3  4  5  6  7  8  9  10
```

Solve these problems. Use the number line.

❶ 6 + 1 = __7__   ❷ 2 + 5 = __7__

❸ 4 − 3 = __1__   ❹ 8 − 2 = __6__

❺ 5 + 3 = __8__   ❻ 3 + 0 = __3__

❼ 6 − 2 = __4__   ❽ 4 + 2 = __6__

❾ 9 − 1 = __8__   ❿ 0 + 7 = __7__

⓫ 6 + 3 = __9__   ⓬ 8 − 3 = __5__

⓭ 3 − 1 = __2__   ⓮ 2 + 2 = __4__

Math Explorations and Applications Level 1 • **37**

*available separately

◆ **LESSON 37** Adding and Subtracting on a Number Line

```
0   1   2   3   4   5   6   7   8   9   10
```

Solve these problems.
Use the number line.

Use the Mixed Practice on page 356 after this lesson.

⑪ 3 − 1 = __2__

⑫ 1 + 2 = __3__

⑬ 7 + 2 = __9__

⑭ 6 − 1 = __5__

⑮ 6 + 2 = __8__

⑯ 8 + 1 = __9__

⑰ 1 + 3 = __4__

⑱ 6 − 2 = __4__

⑲ 5 + 2 = __7__

⑳ 8 − 2 = __6__

㉑ 8 − 3 = __5__

Copyright © SRA/McGraw-Hill

 NOTE TO HOME
Students solve addition and subtraction
problems using a number line.

80 • Numbers 1–10

ENRICHMENT p. 37

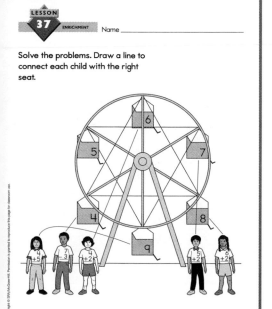

LESSON **37** ENRICHMENT   Name _____

Solve the problems. Draw a line to
connect each child with the right
seat.

Math Explorations and Applications Level 1 • 37

ASSESSMENT p. 14

UNIT **1**   **Mastery Checkpoint 9** Addition and subtraction on the number line
(Lesson 37)
Name _____

The student demonstrates mastery by correctly answering 8 of the 10 problems.

```
0   1   2   3   4   5   6   7   8   9   10
```

Solve these problems.
Use the number line.

❶ 5 + 3 = __8__   ❷ 5 − 3 = __2__

❸ 7 − 1 = __6__   ❹ 5 + 1 = __6__

❺ 5 + 2 = __7__   ❻ 6 + 2 = __8__

❼ 8 − 0 = __8__   ❽ 9 + 0 = __9__

❾ 4 + 2 = __6__   ❿ 1 + 2 = __3__

14 • *Math Explorations and Applications Level 1*

② Teach

Demonstrate Draw a number line on the chalkboard to
show, for example, how 4 + 2 means start on 4 and go two
steps ahead to land on 6. Emphasize that the number they
start on is not counted as one of the steps.

Using the Number Cubes Orally present
addition and subtraction problems using 0, 1, and
2. Have students solve the problems on the
number line and respond using Number Cubes.

Using the Student Pages Have students use number
lines to solve the problems on pages 79 and 80.

Using the Thinking Story Present two
new problems from those following "Mr.
Muddle Goes Shopping" on pages 34–35 of
the Thinking Story Book or on pages 76a–76b of this Guide.

GAME **Introducing the "Duck Pond" Game Mat**
Use the Game Mat transparency to demonstrate
and play a round of this game, which provides
addition practice with sums of 10 or less. Complete
directions are on the Duck Pond Game Mat. A copy can also
be found of page 397 of this Teacher's Guide.

③ Wrap-Up 5 MINUTES

In Closing Have students show a simple addition problem
using Number Strips. Then have them solve the same
problem on the number line.

✓ **Mastery Checkpoint 9**

By this time most students should be able to add and
subtract 0–3 on a 0–10 number line. To assess
proficiency, use the pages in this lesson or use page 14
of the Assessment Blackline Masters. Results may be
recorded on the Mastery Checkpoint Chart.

Assessment Criterion

Did the student . . .

✓ demonstrate mastery in solving
addition and subtraction problems
on a 0–10 number line?

LESSON 38

Student Edition pages 81–82

Adding and Subtracting with Number Strips

LESSON PLANNER

Objective

▶ to introduce Number Strips as a means of solving addition and subtraction problems

Context of the Lesson Students were first introduced to Number Strips in Lesson 22.

✋ **MANIPULATIVES** **Program Resources**

desk number lines

Number Strips

Thinking Story Book, pages 34–35

Reteaching Master

Practice Master 38

Enrichment Master 38

For extra practice:
CD-ROM* Lesson 38

① Warm-Up ⏱ 5 MINUTES

Problem of the Day Present the following problem to the class. Monica writes 5 + 3 = 8. She lays out a 5-strip, a 3-strip, and an 8-strip. What other Number Strips could she use to write a number sentence that sums to 8? (7-strip, 1-strip; 6-strip, 2-strip; 4-strip, 4-strip)

Problem-Solving Strategies Ask students who have solved the Problem of the Day to share how they solved it and any strategies they used.

MENTAL MATH Have students use their **desk number lines** to solve each of the following problems:

a. 6 + 2 = (8)	b. 4 + 2 = (6)
c. 5 + 2 = (7)	d. 8 + 1 = (9)
e. 5 + 4 = (9)	f. 6 + 4 = (10)
g. 5 + 3 = (8)	h. 2 + 1 = (3)
i. 1 + 4 = (5)	j. 3 + 2 = (5)

81 Numbers 1–10

LESSON 38

Name _____

Adding and Subtracting with Number Strips

Fill in the correct numbers on these Number Strips.

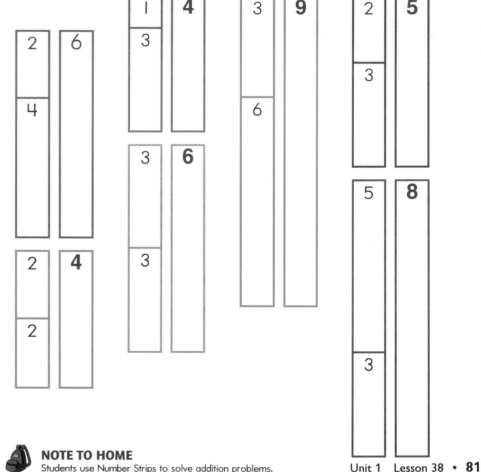

Copyright © SRA/McGraw-Hill

🎒 **NOTE TO HOME**
Students use Number Strips to solve addition problems.

Unit 1   Lesson 38 • **81**

🌐 **LANGUAGE ARTS CONNECTION**

Language Arts Connection Challenge students to make up stories involving simple addition facts. For example, "Dana and Luke went to the zoo. They saw four female gorillas in one cage and three male gorillas in another. To feed all the gorillas, they bought seven bananas . . ." Encourage them to write about fanciful trips to outer space, to the circus, and under the sea. Students may want to share their stories with the class.

RETEACHING p. 10

LESSON 38 RETEACHING   Name _____

Fill in the correct numbers on the Number Strips.

10 • Math Explorations and Applications Level I

*available separately

◆ **LESSON 38** Adding and Subtracting with **Number Strips**

Fill in the correct numbers on
the Number Strips.

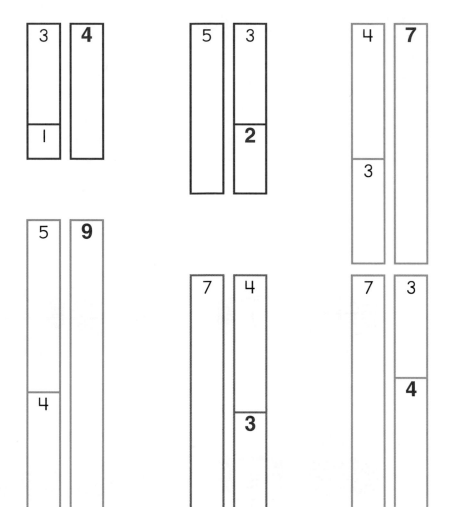

NOTE TO HOME
Students use Number Strips to solve
addition and subtraction problems.

Copyright © SRA/McGraw-Hill

PRACTICE p. 38

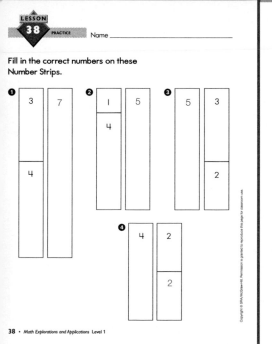

LESSON
38 PRACTICE Name _____

Fill in the correct numbers on these
Number Strips.

38 • Math Explorations and Applications Level 1

ENRICHMENT p. 38

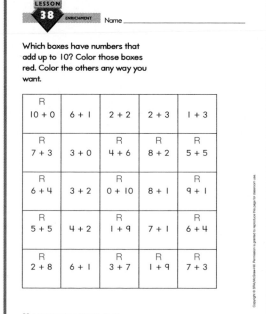

LESSON
38 ENRICHMENT Name _____

Which boxes have numbers that
add up to 10? Color those boxes
red. Color the others any way you
want.

R 10 + 0	6 + 1	2 + 2	2 + 3	1 + 3
R 7 + 3	3 + 0	4 + 6	R 8 + 2	R 5 + 5
R 6 + 4	3 + 2	R 0 + 10	8 + 1	R 9 + 1
5 + 5	4 + 2	R 1 + 9	R 7 + 1	6 + 4
2 + 8	6 + 1	R 3 + 7	R 1 + 9	R 7 + 3

38 • Math Explorations and Applications Level 1

❷ Teach

Demonstrate Show two Number Strips totaling 10 or less, holding them end to end. Challenge students to estimate the total length. Then hold a strip of the estimated length against the two combined strips to verify their estimate. Write the result on the chalkboard as a number sentence, for example: 4 + 2 = 6. Repeat with similar problems. Follow the same procedures for subtraction, but hold the two Number Strips side by side. Challenge students to find a third strip that corresponds to the difference between the two strips you are holding.

Using the Student Pages Have students work in pairs to do pages 81–82. Tell students to think of themselves as detectives. If they lay out Number Strips like those on the page, they can figure out what the missing numbers are. Students who finish early can use the "Duck Pond" Game Mat to practice addition facts.

Using the Thinking Story Present two new problems from those following "Mr. Muddle Goes Shopping" on pages 34–35 of the Thinking Story Book or on pages 76a–76b of this Guide.

❸ Wrap-Up ⏱ 5 MINUTES

In Closing Present number sentences such as 3 + 3 = 6 or 7 – 4 = 3 on the chalkboard. Invite volunteers to come up to the front and represent these problems using Number Strips.

Informal Assessment Based on your observations during the demonstration, record which students seem to be struggling to understand the use of Number Strips. Record also any observations you made while students completed the student pages.

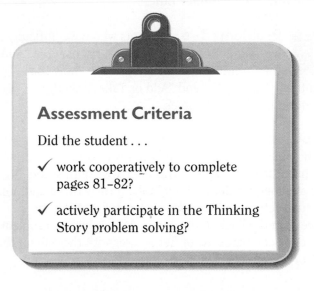

Assessment Criteria

Did the student . . .

✓ work cooperatively to complete pages 81–82?

✓ actively participate in the Thinking Story problem solving?

LESSON 39

Student Edition pages 83–86

Unit 1 Review

Using the Student Pages Use this Unit Review as a preliminary unit test to indicate areas in which each student is having difficulty or in which the entire class may need help. If students do well on the Unit Review, you may wish to skip directly to the next unit. If not, you may spend a day or so helping students overcome their individual difficulties before they take the Unit Test.

Next to each instruction line is a list of the lessons in the unit covered in that set of problems. Students can refer to the specific lesson for additional instruction if they need help. You can also use this information to make additional assignments based on the previous lesson concepts.

If students have difficulty understanding how to solve the counters-in-the-can problems on page 83, act out the situation for them with **counters***, coins, buttons, or other appropriate materials.

Have students fill in the missing numbers on page 85. Have students answer the questions on page 86 using the picture graph.

Problems 1–26 Students who need help writing numbers can play the Tracing and Writing Numbers game (Lesson 11).

  Problems 1–2 Students who have difficulty with numerical sequence can practice oral counting and play the "What Number Comes Next?" game (Lesson 14) and the "What Number Comes Before?" game (Lesson 15). Or have students practice counting up and back as they walk along the **Step-by-Step Number Line.***

Problems 3–6 Students who have difficulty with hidden-counter problems can play the "Add the Counters" (Lesson 26), "Take Away the Counters" (Lesson 31), and "Add or Take Away the Counters" (Lesson 33) games.

Problems 7–19 Have students who have difficulty with addition and subtraction signs work with other students who have stronger skills in this area. Give both students slips of paper. Students should take turns writing addition and subtraction problems for each other, putting the answers on the back of the paper. After solving a problem, each child compares his or her answer with the one on the back of the paper.

83 Numbers 1–10

LESSON 39

Name _____

Unit 1 Review

Fill in the missing numbers.

Lessons 14, 15, 32

❶ 0　1　[2]　3　[4]　5　6

❷ 4　5　6　[7]　8　[9]　10

How many all together?

Lessons 26, 27, 28

❸ 5　7

❹ 2　5

How many now?

Lessons 30, 31, 33

❺ 5　8

❻ 7　6

🎒 **NOTE TO HOME**
Students review unit skills and concepts.

Unit 1　Review • **83**

*available separately

◆ **LESSON 39 Unit 1 Review**

0 1 2 3 4 5 6 7 8 9 10

Lesson 34, 35, 36, 37

Solve these problems.

Use the number line.

7
$$\begin{array}{r} 8 \\ + 2 \\ \hline \mathbf{10} \end{array}$$

8
$$\begin{array}{r} 6 \\ - 2 \\ \hline \mathbf{4} \end{array}$$

9
$$\begin{array}{r} 3 \\ + 3 \\ \hline \mathbf{6} \end{array}$$

10 $1 + 5 = \underline{\mathbf{6}}$

11 $1 + 1 = \underline{\mathbf{2}}$

12 $8 - 3 = \underline{\mathbf{5}}$

13 $3 + 6 = \underline{\mathbf{9}}$

14 $5 - 0 = \underline{\mathbf{5}}$

15 $7 - 3 = \underline{\mathbf{4}}$

16 $7 + 2 = \underline{\mathbf{9}}$

17 $6 + 1 = \underline{\mathbf{7}}$

18 $2 + 2 = \underline{\mathbf{4}}$

19 $4 + 3 = \underline{\mathbf{7}}$

 NOTE TO HOME
Students review skills presented in the unit.

 Performance Assessment The Performance Assessment Tasks 8–10 provided on page 65 of the Assessment Blackline Masters can be used at this time to evaluate addition, subtraction, and counting skills. You may want to administer this assessment with individual students or in small groups.

 Portfolio Assessment If you have not already completed the Portfolio Assessment task provided on page 77 of the Assessment Blackline Masters, it can be used at this time to evaluate addition skills with sums to 10.

Unit Project If you have not already assigned the "Counting Charts" project on pages 92a–92b, you may want to do so at this time. The Unit Project is a good opportunity for students to apply the concepts of counting and writing numbers in real-world problem solving.

◆ **LESSON 39 Unit 1 Review**

Name _____

Lesson   Fill in the missing numbers.
27, 32   Look for patterns.

20 1   2   3   **4**   5   6   7

21 2   3   **4**   5   6   7   8

22 9   8   7   **6**   5   4   3

23 3   4   **5**   6   7   8   9

24 4   **5**   6   7   8   9   10

25 10   9   8   **7**   6   5   4

26 7   6   5   4   3   **2**   1

27 8   7   6   **5**   4   3   2

28 3   4   5   **6**   7   **8**   9

Copyright © SRA/McGraw-Hill

NOTE TO HOME
Students review unit skills and concepts.

Unit 1   Review • **85**

RETEACHING

Students who have difficulty with this Unit Review should have further opportunity to review and to practice the skills before they proceed on with the next unit. For each set of problems there are specific suggestions for reteaching. These suggestions can be found in the margins.

◆ **LESSON 39   Unit 1 Review**

Lesson
18, 19

Look at the picture graph.

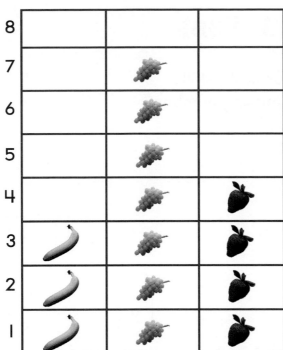

8			
7		🍇	
6		🍇	
5		🍇	
4		🍇	🍓
3	🍌	🍇	🍓
2	🍌	🍇	🍓
1	🍌	🍇	🍓

㉙ How many bananas? **3**

㉚ How many grapes? **7**

㉛ How many strawberries? **4**

NOTE TO HOME
Students review unit skills and concepts.

86 • Numbers 1–10

PRACTICE p. 39

LESSON **39** PRACTICE   Name _____

Fill in the missing numbers.

❶ 3 4 5 6 7 8 9

How many all together?

❷ [4] • •   6
❸ • [7]   8
❹ • • • [3]   6
❺ • • [6]   9

Solve these problems.
Watch the signs.

❻ 3 + 4 = _7_   ❼ 2 + 2 = _4_

❽ 7 – 1 = _6_   ❾ 8 – 2 = _6_

❿ 4 + 0 = _4_   ⓫ 9 – 1 = _8_

Math Explorations and Applications Level 1 • 39

ENRICHMENT p. 39

LESSON **39** ENRICHMENT   Name _____

Fill in the missing numbers.

7 + [3] = 10
– 6

4 + 4 = 8
– 6
2

9 – 6 = [3]
– 8
[1] + 1 = 2

9
– 2
+ 1
[3] + 4 = [7]

Math Explorations and Applications Level 1 • 39

LESSON 40

Student Edition pages 87–90

Unit 1 Test

Using the Student Pages The Unit Test on Student Edition pages 87–90 provides an opportunity to formally evaluate your students' proficiency with concepts developed in this unit. It is similar in content and format to the Unit Review. Students who did well on the Unit Review may not need to take this test. Students who did not do well on the Unit Review should be provided with additional practice opportunities before taking the Unit Test. For further evaluation, you may wish to have these students take the Unit Test in standardized format, provided on pages 86–95 in the Assessment Blackline Masters, or the Unit Test, provided on pages 15–18 in the Assessment Blackline Masters.

LESSON 40

Name _____

Unit 1 Test

Check your math skills.
Fill in the missing numbers.

❶ 2   3   4   5   6 | 7 | 8

❷ 4   5   6   7 | 8 | | 9 | 10

❸ 0   1   2 | 3 | 4   5   6

How many all together?

❹ | 3 | ⬤⬤⬤ _6_   ❺ | 7 | ⬤⬤ _9_

NOTE TO HOME
This test checks unit skills and concepts.

Unit 1 Test • **87**

◆ **LESSON 40   Unit 1 Test**

How many now?

 **6**   3   5

 **7**   4   1

 **8**   8   5

 **9**   5   8

Solve these problems.
Watch the signs.

10 $4 + 2 = \underline{\textbf{6}}$ **11** $5 - 2 = \underline{\textbf{3}}$

12 $8 - 1 = \underline{\textbf{7}}$ **13** $3 + 3 = \underline{\textbf{6}}$

14
$$\begin{array}{r} 9 \\ -\ 2 \\ \hline \textbf{7} \end{array}$$

15
$$\begin{array}{r} 5 \\ +\ 1 \\ \hline \textbf{6} \end{array}$$

16
$$\begin{array}{r} 3 \\ -\ 3 \\ \hline \textbf{0} \end{array}$$

NOTE TO HOME
This test checks unit skills and concepts.

◆ **LESSON 40   Unit 1 Test**

Name _____

```
┼───┼───┼───┼───┼───┼───┼───┼───┼───┼───┼
0   1   2   3   4   5   6   7   8   9   10
```

Solve these problems.
Use the number line.

17 6 + 2 = __8__

18 6 − 2 = __4__

19 8 − 1 = __7__

20 2 + 4 = __6__

21 4 + 3 = __7__

22 5 + 3 = __8__

23 3 − 3 = __0__

24 5 − 3 = __2__

25 7 + 2 = __9__

26 7 + 0 = __7__

27 8 − 3 = __5__

28 6 + 1 = __7__

Copyright © SRA/McGraw-Hill

NOTE TO HOME
This test checks unit skills and concepts.

Unit 1   Test • 89

RETEACHING

Students who have difficulty with this Unit Test should have further opportunity to review and to practice the skills before they proceed on with the next unit. After students have reviewed the skills you may want to use the Unit Test on pages 15–18 in the Assessment Blackline Masters which covers the Unit 1 concepts.

PRACTICE p. 40

LESSON **40** PRACTICE   Name _____

Fill in the missing numbers.

1 | 3 | 4 | 5 | 6 | 7 | 8 | 9 |

How many all together?

2 [5]  __7__

3 [7] __7__

4 [5] __8__

5 [8]  __10__

Solve these problems.
Watch the signs.

6 8 − 1 = __7__

7 6 − 3 = __3__

8 4 − 1 = __3__

9 3 + 2 = __5__

10 1 + 5 = __6__

11 9 − 2 = __7__

40 • Math Explorations and Applications Level 1

◆ **LESSON 40 Unit 1 Test**

Draw the missing picture.

29

30

○ ○ [blue] ○ ○ ■

Fill in the missing numbers. Look
for patterns.

31 3   4   5   **6** **7**   8   9   10

32 9   8   7   **6**   5   4   3   2

33 2   3   4   5   **6**   7   **8**   9

34 1   2   3   **4**   5   6   **7**   8

35 7   6   **5**   4   3   2   1   0

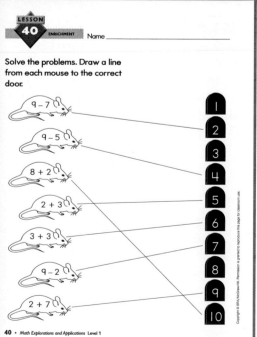

NOTE TO HOME
This test checks unit skills and concepts.

Copyright © SRA/McGraw-Hill

ENRICHMENT p. 40

LESSON **40** ENRICHMENT Name _____

Solve the problems. Draw a line
from each mouse to the correct
door.

9 – 7 |1|
9 – 5 |2|
8 + 2 |3|
2 + 3 |4|
3 + 3 |5|
9 – 2 |6|
2 + 7 |7|
        |8|
        |9|
        |10|

40 • Math Explorations and Applications Level 1

ASSESSMENT p. 15

UNIT **1**   Unit 1 Test (Use after Lesson 39.)   Page 1 of 4

Name _____

The student demonstrates mastery by correctly answering 32 of the 40 problems.

Check your math skills.
Fill in the missing numbers.

1 1   2 |3| 4   5 |6|

2 5   6   7 |8| 9   10

3 0 |1| 2   3   4 |5|

How many all together?

4  _2_   **5**  _4_

6  _6_   **7**  _5_

Go on ...

Math Explorations and Applications Level 1 • 15

LESSON 41

Student Edition pages 91–92

Extending the Unit

LESSON PLANNER

Objectives

▶ to provide practice problems in hidden-counter addition for remediation and enrichment

▶ to provide practice counting to and from 10

Context of the Lesson This is the first of four "Extending the Unit" lessons in this book.

 MANIPULATIVES **Program Resources**

cardboard   Number Cubes

counters*   Practice Master 41

                  Enrichment Master 41

                  For extra practice:
                  CD-ROM* Lesson 41
                  Mixed Practice, page 357

❶ Warm-Up

 Problem of the Day Present the following problem to the class. Juan is not younger than Kelly. Max is younger than Kelly. Match the age with each child: 10 years old; 5 years old; and 3 years old. (Max is 3, Kelly is 5, and Juan is 10.)

Problem-Solving Strategies Ask students who have solved the Problem of the Day to share how they solved it and any strategies they used.

 Have students mentally add and then show answers with Number Cubes.

a. 3 + 1 = (4)   **b.** 5 + 2 = (7)   **c.** 3 + 3 = (6)

d. 2 + 6 = (8)   **e.** 4 + 5 = (9)   **f.** 7 + 2 = (9)

❷ Teach

 Demonstrate Review hidden-counter addition with the class by doing several problems similar to the following:

Display for students five **counters***. Write 5 on a piece of **cardboard** and cover the counters. Display three more counters, one at a time, and put each under the cardboard. Have students indicate how many counters are under the cardboard in all. (eight) Lift up the cardboard and count counters to confirm.

91 Numbers 1–10

LESSON 41

Name _____

Extending the Unit

❶ Connect the dots. Start at 0 and count up.

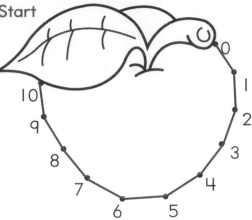

❷ Connect the dots. Start at 10 and count down.

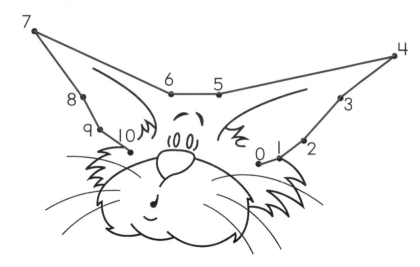

 **NOTE TO HOME** Students count up and down from 0–10.

Unit 1 Lesson 41 • **91**

 Technology Connection You might want students to use the software *Hop To It!* from Sunburst Communications (Mac, Apple) to provide practice with addition and subtraction, number line skills, and counting.

COOPERATIVE LEARNING **Meeting Individual Needs** Pair students who need remediation in hidden-counter addition with those who have mastered the skill. Present problems as in the demonstration. Before answering, have the partners discuss the process; a student who understands the skill explains to his or her partner how to find each answer.

RETEACHING

 GAME To reteach skills in this unit, demonstrate and then have students play the "Add or Take Away the Counters" game. This game was first introduced on page 58. It can also be found on page 14 of the Home Connections Blackline Masters.

*available separately

◆ **LESSON 41** **Extending the Unit**

Use the Mixed Practice on page 357 after this lesson.

How many all together?

3  3 ___6___

4  2 ___5___

5  5 ___8___

6 1 ___4___

7 3 ___6___

8 3 ___5___

How many all together?

9  4 ___6___

10  5 ___7___

11  6 ___9___

12  7 ___9___

92 • Numbers 1–10

NOTE TO HOME
Students solve addition and subtraction problems with counters, some of which are hidden.

Copyright © SRA/McGraw-Hill

Using the Student Pages Have students who understand hidden-counter addition do the dot-to-dot pictures on page 91. Work with students who need remediation on the hidden-counter addition problems on page 92. Model the first few problems using the cardboard and counters as you did in the demonstration. Then work with students to complete several more problems using only the pictures on the page. Finally, have students complete the rest of the problems on their own. When they finish, have them share their answers and explain how they arrived at each.

❸ Wrap-Up ⏱ 5 MINUTES

In Closing Have students who did the dot-to-dot indicate what pictures they drew. Ask what the second picture would have looked like if they had started at 0 and counted up.

Informal Assessment Observe students' responses during the demonstration to informally assess who can do the dot-to-dot activities and who needs to complete page 92 for hidden-counter addition remediation.

Assessment Criteria

Did the student . . .

✓ correctly respond to the problems during the demonstration?

✓ correctly complete the dot-to-dot pictures on page 91?

✓ correctly solve 80% of the remaining problems on page 92 after working with the teacher?

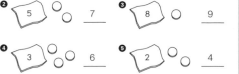

UNIT 1 Wrap-Up

Student Edition pages 92a–92b

PRESENTING THE PROJECT

Project Objectives

▶ to introduce students to the methods of completing a long-term project

▶ to introduce students to number names from other cultures

▶ to provide practice in counting to 10 and recognizing numbers to 10

 **MANIPULATIVES**

chart paper or posterboard

markers or crayons

Program Resources

*Marti and the Mango**
    from the Literature Library

SRA's *Minds on Math**

In this project, students make counting charts in two or more languages. To begin, write on the chalkboard the numbers and number words for the digits 1–10. Have students count from 1–10 in unison as you point to each number. Then write the Spanish words for 1–10 on the chalkboard next to the English. Have students count with you in Spanish as you say the name for each number from 1–10. Ask volunteers, from your class or another, who speak other languages to count from 1–10 in their language.

Invite students to make their own counting charts in English and Spanish. Have them write the numbers 1–10 and the number words in English and Spanish. Then have them illustrate each number with the appropriate number of objects. Students can draw them or use cut-outs from magazines or other sources. If desired, provide students with the number words for additional languages so that they can add these to their number charts.

To extend the activity, invite parents, teachers, or older students who speak other languages to visit your class to share counting words and information about the language and culture. Then have students work in small groups to prepare counting charts for one of the languages presented. Encourage students to decorate their posters with a flag or cultural icons suggested by those who speak the language.

What Is a Math Project? Math projects in *Math Explorations and Applications* are real-world, problem-solving activities in which students use many different mathematics skills. These mathematics projects are not word problems that focus on one skill area. Rather, students must draw from all that they already know about mathematics to complete them. They offer students freedom to problem-solve on their own or ask teachers and classmates to help them with the necessary mathematics skills.

Why Use Projects in Mathematics? Projects give students a reason to learn mathematics. They provide students a direct route to mathematics literacy and are a powerful way for students to apply math concepts in real-world applications. As with the problems and projects people face in their daily lives, the problem solver has to make decisions as to which skills to use to complete the project. These projects are suggestions only; you and your students may wish to generate and implement your own ideas where different math skills are explored and used.

Creating a Project Environment Projects invite students to explore and experiment. When students begin a project, you may want to arrange the classroom furniture to be more conducive to group work. Students will be better able to focus on the project if resources are readily available in the classroom, so you may wish to gather materials ahead of time.

The Teacher's Role During a project, the teacher's role is to serve as a "guide on the side" rather than a "sage on the stage" by helping students find information, asking questions that encourage students to think about the problem and use their problem solving skills, and encouraging students to generate more questions to explore in the project. For these projects, you are not expected to know all the answers or be able to solve all the problems but rather to model good problem-solving and investigative behaviors. Treat every student question as an opportunity to demonstrate how to approach a problem and pursue the answer.

Grouping Projects can be completed by individual students, but students often learn more by working together. Ideally, cooperative group projects mix students of different ability levels so that all students learn from each other and have a chance to succeed.

Successful group work does not just happen. Groups need to establish expectations of the roles and responsibilities of every member of the group. Encourage group members to take specific roles that ensure that everyone makes an overall contribution to the project by inviting students to assign a specific role to each group member.

*available separately

When to Assess the Project Assessment should occur throughout all stages of a project.

▶ **Before a project,** assess to find out what students already know and what their needs, interests, and experiences are.

▶ **During a project,** assess to check progress, provide assistance, or modify activities, if necessary.

▶ **After a project,** assess to find out what students learned, evaluate the quality of the learning, and gauge the effectiveness of the project approach.

What to Assess In the project approach to mathematics students have the opportunity to demonstrate a variety of competencies. Teachers can choose to evaluate students on any or all of the following.

▶ **Basic skills** include reading, writing, arithmetic and mathematics, speaking, and listening.

▶ **Thinking skills** include thinking creatively, making decisions, solving problems, thinking visually, knowing how to learn, and reasoning.

▶ **Interpersonal skills** include individual responsibility, self-esteem, ability to work in a group, self-management, and integrity.

How to Assess Record and use information in ways that you determine will be helpful to you and your students. Below are some ideas for routine forms of assessment that can provide regular feedback.

▶ **Observations** can take the form of watching, listening, discussing, questioning, challenging, or answering students' questions.

▶ **Checklists** can help you focus on specific aspects of your students' learning and behavior.

▶ **Interviews** of individuals, pairs, or small groups can provide valuable insights into students' thoughts about a project and the project approach, as well as how students view themselves and others.

▶ **Group assessment** can focus on how well all members of the group fulfill their roles, enabling the group to function successfully.

▶ **Student self-assessment** provides an opportunity to understand your students' perception of their own strengths, problems, and work habits, as well as their perception of the value of the project.

▶ **Portfolio assessment** can be accomplished by collecting samples of students' work on this project and throughout the unit.

English	Spanish	Vietnamese	Turkish
one	uno	môt	bir
two	dos	hai	iki
three	tres	ba	úç
four	cuatro	bôn	dört
five	cinco	nám	bes
six	seis	chang	alti
seven	siete	máy	yedi
eight	ocho	tám	sekiz
nine	nueve	chin	dokuz
ten	diez	múoi mot	on

Wrapping Up the Project Have students count in unison in Spanish. Then challenge students to compare differences and similarities in the number names for English and Spanish.

COOPERATIVE LEARNING **Minds on Math** SRA's *Minds on Math* is a series of units covering Problem Solving, Data Collection, Number Sense, Measurement, Money, and Geometry and Spatial Relations. Each unit provides a series of open-ended projects for individuals or small groups. These projects develop problem-solving and critical-thinking skills, utilize real-world materials, emphasize language, and integrate cross-curricular connections. Use projects from *Number* to help develop number sense and an awareness of the different uses of numbers around us.

 **Assessing the Project** Observe as students make their counting charts. Do they understand that the same number has different names in other languages? Do they recognize the word names for numbers?

LITERATURE CONNECTION **Literature Connection** You may want to read to your class *Count Your Way Through China* by Jim Haskins to introduce the countries and languages of China, Japan, Germany, India, Israel, Italy, and others. You may also want to use *Marti and the Mango* from the Literature Library* to demonstrate data collection and to compare the size and shape of different kinds of fruit.

*available separately

UNIT 2

Addition and Subtraction

INTRODUCING BASIC FACTS

OVERVIEW

This unit begins by using money to teach addition and subtraction facts. Students then identify plane and solid geometric figures. Students learn different strategies for finding sums and differences. They apply their skills to a variety of problems. Students use expanded numbers to increase their understanding of place value and use doubles to learn more addition facts. Students learn to use an addition table and find missing addends. They are also introduced to skip counting, comparing numbers, using maps, and counting collections of pennies, nickels, and dimes. Students also estimate and measure length in both customary and metric units.

Integrated Topics in This Unit Include:

- ◆ counting pennies and nickels
- ◆ using $1 and $5 bills to add
- ◆ identifying geometric figures
- ◆ finding tens
- ◆ using finger sets to add and subtract
- ◆ adding and subtracting mentally
- ◆ using function machines
- ◆ applying addition and subtraction
- ◆ counting from 10–20
- ◆ using expanded numbers
- ◆ using an addition table
- ◆ finding missing addends

- ◆ using number patterns
- ◆ using maps
- ◆ using doubles
- ◆ measuring length

FUNCTION MACHINES
MISSING ADDENDS

" *Understanding the fundamental operations of addition, subtraction, multiplication, and division is central to knowing mathematics. One essential component of what it means to understand an operation is recognizing conditions in real-world situations that indicate that the operation would be useful in those situations.* "

—NCTM Curriculum and Evaluation Standards for School Mathematics

GAMES

Motivating Mixed Practice

Games provide **basic math skills** practice in cooperative groups and develop **mathematical reasoning.**

THINKING STORY

Integrated Problem Solving

Thinking Stories provide opportunities for students to work in **cooperative groups** and develop **logical reasoning** while they integrate **reading skills** with mathematics.

Story Summaries In "Exactly What To Do" Mr. Breezy answers Marcus' questions with a lot of irrelevant information.

"Manolita's Amazing Number Machine" focuses on simple addition and subtraction function machines.

In "Silly Dreamer" Willy is never satisfied with how things are.

"Mr. Mudancia Builds a Better Tree" explores solving everyday problems with addition and subtraction.

"Marcus Builds a Birdhouse" focuses on estimating sizes and shapes.

"Ferdies Buys a Snack" challenges students to use their knowledge of money to solve Ferdie's problem.

PROJECT

Making Connections

The Unit Project makes real-world connections. Students work in **cooperative groups** to problem-solve and to communicate their findings.

The Unit Wrap-Up project asks students to use patterns and one-to-one correspondence.

LESSON	PACING	PRIMARY OBJECTIVES	FEATURE	RESOURCES	NCTM STANDARDS
42 Pennies and Nickels........ 95–96	1 day	to introduce the use of pennies and nickels to form amounts of money from 1¢ through 10¢	Thinking Story Game	Practice Master 42 Enrichment Master 42	1, 2, 3, 4, 6, 7, 8
43 Using $1 and $5 Bills....... 97–98	1 day	to teach students to use $1 and $5 bills to make specific amounts of money	Game	Reteaching Master Practice Master 43 Enrichment Master 43	4, 7, 8
44 Geometric Figures 99–100	1 day	to provide practice identifying and counting shapes		Practice Master 44 Enrichment Master 44	9
45 Geometric Patterns 101–102	1 day	to provide opportunities to make patterns using shapes		Practice Master 45 Enrichment Master 45	9
46 Identifying Solid Figures ... 103–104	1 day	to give examples of and practice identifying cubes, spheres, cones, and cylinders		Reteaching Master Practice Master 46 Enrichment Master 46	9
47 Adding—Finding Tens 105–106	1 day	to teach students how to find sums up to ten using concrete objects		Practice Master 47 Enrichment Master 47	1, 2, 3, 4, 7, 8
48 Statue Addition 107–108	1 day	to teach students how to add by thinking of finger sets rather than showing them		Practice Master 48 Enrichment Master 48	
49 Statue Subtraction 109–110	1 day	to teach students how to subtract by thinking of finger sets rather than showing them	Game	Practice Master 49 Enrichment Master 49	4, 7, 8
50 Mental Addition........... 111–112	1 day	to teach students how to add problems mentally in the 0–10 range when one of the addends is 0, 1, or 2		Practice Master 50 Enrichment Master 50	1, 2, 3, 4, 7, 8
51 Mental Subtraction........ 113–114	1 day	✓ to assess students' ability to mentally solve subtraction problems in the 0–10 range when the subtrahend is 0, 1, or 2	♟	Practice Master 51 Enrichment Master 51 Assessment Master	7, 8
52 Functions................. 115–116	1 day	to provide opportunities to practice addition and subtraction facts using a function machine	Thinking Story	Practice Master 52 Enrichment Master 52	3, 8, 13
53 Mental Math 117–118	1 day	to teach students to add or subtract mentally when one of the addends or subtrahends is 3		Reteaching Master Practice Master 53 Enrichment Master 53	1, 2, 3, 4, 8
54 Counting from 10–20 119–120	1 day	to practice in counting from 10–20 in expanded form		Practice Master 54 Enrichment Master 54	6
55 Writing Numbers to 20 ... 121–122	1 day	to provide practice writing the numerals for numbers from 10–20		Practice Master 55 Enrichment Master 55	6
56 Expanded Numbers 123–124	1 day	✓ to assess student proficiency in reading, writing and counting numbers through 20 in expanded form	♟	Practice Master 56 Enrichment Master 56 Assessment Master	6
57 Counting to 20............ 125–126	1 day	to teach students to count on from 10		Reteaching Master Practice Master 57 Enrichment Master 57	6
58 Adding—Doubles.......... 127–128	1 day	to teach students to memorize the doubles of numbers from 0–5	Game	Practice Master 58 Enrichment Master 58	7, 8
59 Adding Fives 129–130	1 day	to teach students a quick way to solve addition problems in which 5 is one of the addends	Thinking Story	Practice Master 59 Enrichment Master 59	6, 7, 8
60 Solving Function Problems 131–132	1 day	to show students how a calculator can be used as a function machine		Practice Master 60 Enrichment Master 60	8, 13
61 Adding—Finding Tens 133–134	1 day	to practice finding pairs of numbers whose sum is 10		Reteaching Master Practice Master 60 Enrichment Master 60	7, 8
Mid-Unit Review 135–136	1 day	to review addition and subtraction	♟	Assessment Master	
62 Addition Facts 137–138	1 day	to provide practice for memorization of the sums of numbers adding up to 10 or less		Practice Master 62 Enrichment Master 62	8

LESSON	PACING	PRIMARY OBJECTIVES	FEATURE	RESOURCES	NCTM STANDARDS
63 The Addition Table 139–140	1 day	to introduce the addition table for addends 0–5		Practice Master 63 Enrichment Master 63	7, 8, 10
64 Skip Counting by Twos 141–142	1 day	to provide practice for skip counting	Game	Practice Master 64 Enrichment Master 64	1, 2, 3, 4, 7
65 Finding Missing Addends 143–144	1 day	to provide practice for solving missing-addend and subtrahend problems by using concrete objects, if the missing number is 1 or 2	Thinking Story	Practice Master 65 Enrichment Master 65	1, 2, 3, 4, 7
66 Missing Addends 145–146	1 day	✓ to assess students' ability to solve missing addend problems by using concrete objects, if the missing number is 1 or 2		Reteaching Master Practice Master 66 Enrichment Master 66 Assessment Master	1, 2, 3, 4, 7
67 Less Than, Greater Than 147–148	1 day	to introduce inequality and quality signs (and =) to show the relationship of two numbers	Game	Practice Master 67 Enrichment Master 67	6, 8, 10
68 Comparing Amounts...... 149–150	1 day	to provide practice in the use of equality, inequality, and equal signs		Practice Master 68 Enrichment Master 68	6, 8
69 Reviewing Addition Facts 151–152	1 day	✓ to assess mastery of addition facts with sums of 10 or less	Game	Practice Master 69 Enrichment Master 69 Assessment Master	8
70 Number Patterns 153–154	1 day	to teach students to identify simple number patterns	Thinking Story Game	Practice Master 70 Enrichment Master 70	13
71 Using Number Patterns ... 155–156	1 day	to provide more practice in detecting number patterns	Game	Practice Master 71 Enrichment Master 71	9, 13
72 Solving Problems......... 157–158	1 day	to help students develop familiarity with geometric figures		Practice Master 72 Enrichment Master 72	1, 2, 3, 4, 9
73 Using Maps 159–160	1 day	to introduce the creation and use of maps and symbols		Practice Master 73 Enrichment Master 73	1, 2, 3, 4 , 9
74 Using Money 161–162	1 day	to teach the use of pennies, nickels, and dimes to form amounts from 1¢ through 20¢	Game	Reteaching Master Practice Master 74 Enrichment Master 74	4, 6, 8, 9
75 Using Doubles 163–164	1 day	to use pennies, nickels, and dimes to double given amounts of money from 0¢ through 10¢	Thinking Story Game	Practice Master 75 Enrichment Master 75	1, 2, 3, 4, 7
76 Adding and Subtracting on a Number Line 165–166	1 day	to teach students to use a 0–20 number line to add and subtract		Practice Master 76 Enrichment Master 76	7, 8, 13
77 Number Line Practice..... 167–168	1 day	to provide practice using the 0–20 number line for addition and subtraction problems	Game	Reteaching Master Practice Master 77 Enrichment Master 77	8, 9, 10
78 Measuring Length in Inches and Feet 169–170	1 day	to provide opportunities to use measurements to improve estimates		Practice Master 78 Enrichment Master 78	5, 10
79 Measuring Length in Metric Units 171–172	1 day	to teach students to estimate lengths of objects in centimeters		Reteaching Master Practice Master 79 Enrichment Master 79	5, 10
80 Adding and Subtracting Using Money 173–174	1 day	to assess students' ability to subtract in the 0–20 range		Practice Master 80 Enrichment Master 80 Assessment Master	7, 8
81 Unit 2 Review............. 175–178		to review addition and subtraction		Practice Master 81 Enrichment Master 81	
82 Unit 2 Test................ 179–182		to review addition and subtraction		Practice Master 82 Enrichment Master 82 Assessment Master	
83 Extending the Unit........ 183–184		to review addition and subtraction	Game	Practice Master 83 Enrichment Master 83	
Unit 2 Wrap-Up 184a–184b		to review addition and subtraction	Project		

UNIT CONNECTIONS

INTERVENTION STRATEGIES

In this Teacher's Guide there will be specific strategies suggested for students with individual needs—ESL, Gifted and Talented, Special Needs, Learning Styles, and At Risk. These strategies will be given at the point of use. Here are the icons to look for and the types of strategies that will accompany them:

English as a Second Language
These strategies, designed for students who do not fluently speak the English language, will suggest meaningful ways to present the lesson concepts and vocabulary.

Gifted and Talented
Strategies to enrich and extend the lesson will offer further challenges to students who have easily mastered the concepts already presented.

Special Needs
Students who are physically challenged or who have learning disabilities may require alternative ways to complete activities, record answers, use manipulatives, and so on. The strategies labeled with this icon will offer appropriate methods of teaching lesson concepts to these students.

Learning Styles
Each student has his or her individual approach to learning. The strategies labeled with this icon suggest ways to present lesson concepts so that various learning modalities—such as tactile/kinesthetic, visual, and auditory—can be addressed.

At Risk
These strategies highlight the relevancy of the skills presented, making the connection between school and real life. They are directed toward students that appear to be at risk of dropping out of school before graduation.

TECHNOLOGY CONNECTIONS

The following materials, designed to reinforce and extend lesson concepts, will be referred to throughout this Teacher's Guide. It might be helpful to order this software, or check it out of the school media center or local community library.

 Look for this **Technology Connection** *icon.*

- *Balancing Bear,* from Sunburst Communications, Mac, IBM, for grades K–4 (software)

- *Basic Math Facts,* from Orange Cherry, Mac, for grades Pre-K–3 (software)

- *Dancing Dinos,* from Micrograms, Mac, IBM, for grades 1–3 (software)

- *Kid's Math,* from Great Wave, Mac, IBM, for grades Pre-K–3 (software)

- *Math Blaster 1: In Search of Spot,* from Davidson, Mac, IBM, for grades 1–6 (software)

- *Math Keys,* from MECC, Mac, IBM, for grades K–2 (software)

- *Mathosaurus,* from Micrograms, Mac, IBM, for grade 1 (software)

- *Mighty Math Carnival Countdown,* from Edmark, Mac, IBM, for grades K–2 (software)

- *Mighty Math Zoo Zillions,* from Edmark, Mac, IBM, for grades K–2 (software)

- *Money Town,* from Davidson Co., Mac, IBM, for grades K–3 (software)

CROSS-CURRICULAR CONNECTIONS

This Teacher's Guide offers specific suggestions on ways to connect the math concepts presented in this unit with other subjects students are studying. Students can connect math concepts with topics they already know about and can find examples of math in other subjects and in real-world situations. These strategies will be given at the point of use.

Look for these icons:

 Geography

 Social Studies

 Science

 Art

 Language Arts

 Health

 Music

 Math

 Physical Education

 Careers

LITERATURE CONNECTIONS

These books will be presented throughout the Teacher's Guide at the point where they could be used to introduce, reinforce, or extend specific lesson concepts. You may want to locate these books in your school or your local community library.

 Look for this **Literature Connection** *icon.*

♦ *Polygons* by David L. Stienecker, Benchmark Books, 1997

♦ *Shapes* by Ivan Bulloch, Thomson Learning, 1994

♦ *Numbers* by John J. Reiss, Bradbury Press, 1971

♦ *12 Ways to Get to 11* by Eve Merriam, Simon & Schuster Books for Young Readers, 1993

♦ *The Balancing Act: A Counting Song* illustrated by Merle Peek, Clarion Books, 1987

♦ *Counting Wildflowers* by Bruce McMillan, Lothrop, Lee & Shepard Books, 1986

♦ *Each Orange Had 8 Slices: A Counting Book* by Paul Giganti, Greenwillow Books, 1992

♦ *A Game of Functions* by Robert Froman, Thomas Y. Crowell, 1974

♦ *Six Sleepy Sheep* by Jeffie Ross Gordon, Caroline House, 1991

♦ *Ten Sly Piranhas: A Counting Story in Reverse* by William Wise, Dial Books for Young Readers, 1993

♦ *Counting* by Henry Pluckrose, Childrens Press, 1995

♦ *Counting by Kangaroos* by Joy N. Hulme, Scientific American Books for Young Readers, 1995

♦ *Bunches and Bunches of Bunnies* by Louise Matthews, Dodd, Meade, 1978

♦ *Eating Fractions* by Bruce McMillan, Scholastic, 1991

♦ *As the Roadrunner Runs* by Gail Hartman, Bradbury Press, 1994

♦ *The One That Got Away* by Percival Everett, Clarion Books, 1992

ASSESSMENT OPPORTUNITIES AT-A-GLANCE

LESSON	PORTFOLIO	PERFORMANCE	FORMAL	SELF	INFORMAL	MIXED PRACTICE	MULTIPLE CHOICE	MASTERY CHECKPOINTS	ANALYZING ANSWERS
42	✓								
43					✓				
44	✓					✓			
45	✓								
46					✓				
47		✓				✓			
48		✓							
49		✓				✓			
50		✓							
51			✓				✓		
52									✓
53		✓							
54	✓					✓			
55		✓							
56			✓				✓		
57					✓				
58				✓					
59				✓		✓			
60		✓							
61		✓							
Mid-Unit Review	✓	✓	✓						
62				✓					
63						✓			✓
64		✓							
65					✓				
66			✓				✓		
67		✓							
68					✓	✓			
69			✓				✓		
70					✓				
71					✓				
72	✓								
73				✓					
74					✓	✓			
75		✓							
76									✓
77					✓				✓
78		✓							
79		✓							
80						✓	✓		
Unit Review	✓	✓	✓						
Unit Test			✓				✓		
83					✓	✓			

✓ ASSESSMENT OPTIONS

PORTFOLIO ASSESSMENT

Throughout this Teacher's Guide are suggested activities in which students draw pictures, make graphs, write about mathematics, and so on. Keep students' work to assess growth of understanding as the year progresses.

Lessons 42, 44, 45, 54, Mid-Unit Review, 72, and Unit Review

PERFORMANCE ASSESSMENT

Performance assessment items focus on evaluating how students think and work as they solve problems. Opportunities for performance assessment can be found throughout the unit. Rubrics and guides for grading can be found in the front of the Assessment Blackline Masters.

Lessons 47, 48, 49, 50, 53, 55, 60, 61, Mid-Unit Review, 64, 67, 75, 78, 79, and Unit Review

FORMAL ASSESSMENT

A Mid-Unit Review and Unit Test help assess students' understanding of concepts, skills, and problem solving. The *Math Explorations and Applications* CD-ROM Test Generator can create additional unit tests at three ability levels. Also, Mastery Checkpoints are provided periodically throughout the unit.

Lessons 51, 56, Mid-Unit Review, 66, 69, Unit Review, and Unit Test

SELF ASSESSMENT

Throughout the program students are given the opportunity to check their own math skills.

Lessons 58, 59, 62, and 73

INFORMAL ASSESSMENT

A variety of assessment suggestions is provided, including interviews, oral questions or presentations, debates, and so on. Also, each lesson includes Assessment Criteria — a list of questions about each student's progress, understanding, and participation.

Lessons 43, 46, 57, 65, 68, 70, 71, 74, 77, and 83

MIXED PRACTICE

Mixed Practices, covering material presented thus far in the year, are provided in the unit for use as either assessment or practice.

Lessons 44, 54, 59, 63, 68, 74, 80, 83

MULTIPLE-CHOICE TESTS (STANDARDIZED FORMAT)

Each unit provides a unit test in standardized format, presenting students with an opportunity to practice taking a test in this format.

MASTERY CHECKPOINT

Mastery Checkpoints are provided throughout the unit to assess student proficiency in specific skills. Checkpoints reference appropriate Assessment Blackline Masters and other assessment options. Results of these evaluations can be recorded on the Mastery Checkpoint Chart.

Lessons 51, 56, 66, 69, and 80

ANALYZING ANSWERS

Analyzing Answers items suggest possible sources of student error and offer teaching strategies for addressing difficulties.

Lessons 52, 63, 76, and 77

Look for these icons:

> **"***An inference about learning is a conclusion about a student's cognitive processes that cannot be observed directly. The conclusion has to be based instead on the student's performance.***"**
>
> —*NCTM Assessment Standards*

MASTERY CHECKPOINTS

WHAT TO EXPECT FROM STUDENTS AS THEY COMPLETE THIS UNIT

⑩ MENTAL ADDITION AND SUBTRACTION OF 0, 1, OR 2—LESSON 51

Most students should now be able to add or subtract 0, 1, or 2 mentally when the sums or minuends are 10 or less. Use student performance during the lesson or page 19 of the Assessment Blackline Masters to assess mastery. Record results on the Mastery Checkpoint Chart.

⑪ NUMBERS (10–20)—LESSON 56

Most students should be able to read, write, and count the numbers through 20 in expanded form. Proficiency may be assessed on the exercises on pages 123–124 or by using pages 20–21 of the Assessment Blackline Masters. Record assessment results on the Mastery Checkpoint Chart.

⑫ CONCRETE MISSING-ADDEND PROBLEMS—LESSON 66

Students should now be able to solve missing-addend problems using concrete objects when the missing addends are 1 or 2 for sums of 10 or less. You can assess students during the demonstration and as they complete pages 145–146, recording your results on the Mastery Checkpoint Chart. You may also wish to assign pages 25–26 of the Assessment Blackline Masters.

⑬ ADDITION FACTS WITH SUMS OF 10 OR LESS—LESSON 69

Most students should have memorized addition facts with sums of 10 or less. Compare the results of the time trials for pages 151–152 to those from Lesson 62, recording results on the Mastery Checkpoint Chart. Note which students have achieved mastery, which have demonstrated substantial improvement, and which are still having difficulty. You may wish to assign pages 27–28 of the Assessment Blackline Masters, or to provide additional practice in other ways, to those students who have not demonstrated mastery.

⑭ ADDING AND SUBTRACTING (0–20)— LESSON 80

At about this time students should be able to solve addition and subtraction problems in the 0–20 range using play money or a number line, providing they do not have to add or subtract more than 6. Students should be able to correctly answer 80% of the problems on pages 173–174 or pages 29–30 of the Assessment Blackline Masters. Results of this assessment may be recorded on the Mastery Checkpoint Chart.

PROGRAM RESOURCES

THESE ADDITIONAL COMPONENTS OF *MATH EXPLORATIONS AND APPLICATIONS* CAN BE PURCHASED SEPARATELY FROM **SRA/McGRAW-HILL.**

LESSON	BASIC MANIPULATIVE KIT	GAME PACKAGE	TEACHER KIT	OPTIONAL MANIPULATIVE KIT	OVERHEAD MANIPULATIVE KIT	*MATH EXPLORATIONS AND APPLICATIONS* CD-ROM	LITERATURE LIBRARY
42	Number Cubes	play money		counters	coins	Lesson 42	
43	Number Cubes	play money		counters	bills	Lesson 43	
44	Number Cubes			attribute blocks geoboards	attribute blocks geoboards	Lesson 44	
45	Number Cubes			pattern blocks	pattern blocks	Lesson 45	
46	Number Cubes			geometric solids		Lesson 46	
47	Number Cubes	play money		counters	counters, bills, coins	Lesson 47	
48	Number Cubes					Lesson 48	*Squeeze In*
49	Number Cubes	Flea Market Game				Lesson 49	
50	Number Cubes			interlocking cubes		Lesson 50	
51	Number Cubes			counters	counters, coins	Lesson 51	
52						Lesson 52	
53	Number Cubes					Lesson 53	
54	Number Cubes					Lesson 54	
55		play money				Lesson 55	
56	Number Cubes, Number Strips			counters	counters	Lesson 56	
57	Number Cubes	play money			coins	Lesson 57	
58	Number Cubes	play money		counters	counters	Lesson 58	
59	Number Cubes	play money				Lesson 59	
60						Lesson 60	
61	Number Cubes					Lesson 61	
Review							*Animal Orchestra*
62	Number Cubes		stopwatch			Lesson 62	
63	Number Strips, Number Cubes					Lesson 63	
64	Number Cubes			interlocking cubes		Lesson 64	
65	Number Strips, Number Cubes					Lesson 65	
66	Number Cubes			counters	counters	Lesson 66	
67	Number Cubes					Lesson 67	
68	Number Cubes					Lesson 68	*Marti and the Mango*
69	Number Cubes	Addition Table Game	stopwatch			Lesson 69	
70	Number Cubes	Map Game				Lesson 70	
71		Pattern Game				Lesson 71	
72						Lesson 72	
73	Number Cubes					Lesson 73	
74	Number Strips, Number Cubes	play money			coins	Lesson 74	
75	Number Cubes	play money			coins	Lesson 75	
76	Number Cubes					Lesson 76	
77						Lesson 77	
78						Lesson 78	
79	Number Cubes					Lesson 79	
80	Number Cubes	play money			coins	Lesson 80	
81	Number Cubes	play money	math balance		coins	Lesson 81	
82						Lesson 82	
83	Number Cubes					Lesson 83	
Wrap-Up							*How Do You Measure Up?*

Addition and Subtraction **93j**

UNIT 2

Addition and Subtraction

INTRODUCING THE UNIT

Using the Student Pages Begin your discussion of the opening unit photo by asking students, "How could you use addition and subtraction to save endangered animals? Why would a slight increase or decrease in the number of animals be important to a scientist?" Then read aloud the paragraph on the student page that highlights a career as a wildlife conservationist. This helps make the connection between school and work and encourages students to explore how math is used in the real world.

ACTIVITY Contact the Department of Natural Resources in your state to find out about endangered animals in your state or community. Find out how the size of the population of these animals has changed. Have students tell what operation they would use to calculate the change in population. Have students tell whether they think these population figures are estimates or precise measures.

FYI Make clear to students that the idea of wildlife conservation is not a new issue. There is some evidence that prehistoric hunters may have deliberately limited their hunting to preserve game. Later, ancient cultures created game preserves in which royalty hunted. But the first serious laws were passed in Britain's colonies in America in the 1600s, and they were largely ignored. Over the last 200 years at least 50 species of birds and 75 species of mammals have been wiped out of existence. The birds include the dodo, the great auk, the moa, and the passenger pigeon—which was hunted to extinction in this century. Some of the extinct mammals are the quagga, a kind of zebra, and Stellar's sea cow. By the late nineteenth century, however, it was becoming obvious to many people that some animals were becoming extinct. You may wish to point out that the American buffalo nearly suffered the same fate when it was hunted for sport by pioneers on the Great Plains. In 1872 the world's first national park was established at Yellowstone, Montana, in part to preserve animals like the buffalo. After the turn of the century one American managed to make a huge step in conservation. President Theodore Roosevelt loved the American wilderness and in 1903 he established the nation's first national wildlife preserve at Pelican Island. Two years later he created the National Forest Service, adding five new national parks and 150 million acres to national forest land.

UNIT 2

Addition and Subtraction

INTRODUCING BASIC FACTS

- **skip counting**
- **money**
- **number sentences**
- **algebra readiness**
- **shapes**

Junior Thinklab™ 2

SRA's *Junior Thinklab™ 2** provides a series of creative and logical problem-solving opportunities for individual students. The problems are designed to appeal to different cognitive abilities.

▶ Use Activity Cards 21–25 with this unit to reinforce Ordering.

▶ Use Activity Cards 26–30 with this unit to reinforce Classifying.

▶ Use Activity Cards 31–35 with this unit to reinforce Perception and Spatial Relations.

▶ Use Activity Cards 36–40 with this unit to reinforce Reasoning and Deducing.

▶ Use Divergent Thinking Activity Sheets 6–10 with this unit to encourage creativity in art and in intellectual activity.

*available separately

SCHOOL TO WORK CONNECTION

Scientists use math . . .

A scientist records how many animals there are in a herd. Sometimes numbered tags are put on the animals to keep track of how many there are. It is important to know if the number of animals changes.

Stress to students that math skills can be very important to wildlife conservationists. Understanding the science of ecology is essential in this career, and this involves a basic understanding of chemistry. Conservationists today also use statistics and other kinds of numbers to find out whether a given population of animals is shrinking or growing. Statistics generated by the government's Fish and Wildlife Service are used to find out if any one creature is in danger of extinction. A modern wildlife conservationist is one part scientist, one part detective. Because the culprit is sometimes not a human but an environmental problem—whether caused by industry or a weather condition—using science and math is essential to preserving wildlife.

Home Connections You may want to send the letter on Home Connections Blackline Masters pages 42–43 to families to introduce this unit.

Unit Project This would be a good time to assign the "Place Setting" project on pages 184a–184b. Students can begin working on the project in cooperative groups in their free time as you work through the unit. The Unit Project is a good opportunity for students to apply the concepts of patterns and one-to-one correspondence in real-world problem solving.

LESSON
42

Student Edition pages 95–96

Pennies and Nickels

LESSON PLANNER

Objectives

▶ to introduce the use of pennies and nickels to form amounts of money from 1¢ through 10¢

▶ to provide practice for solving addition and subtraction problems

Context of the Lesson Play money will be used in this and subsequent lessons as a way to represent numbers and as a concrete aid for addition and subtraction.

 MANIPULATIVES

play coins*

overhead coins*

overhead projector

Program Resources

Number Cubes

Thinking Story Book, pages 36–39

Practice Master 42

Enrichment Master 42

For career connections:
Careers and Math*

For extra practice:
CD-ROM* Lesson 42

➊ Warm-Up

Problem of the Day Present this problem. Jan found a penny, Josh found a penny, Bill found a penny, Emma found a penny, and Alison found a penny. How many pennies did they find in all? (5)

Problem-Solving Strategies Ask students who have solved the Problem of the Day to share how they solved it and any strategies they used.

MENTAL MATH Present these problems on the chalkboard, telling students to use finger sets to solve them before showing answers with Number Cubes.

a. 3 + 3 = (6)   b. 4 – 2 = (2)

c. 5 – 1 = (4)   d. 2 – 2 = (0)

e. 7 + 1 = (8)

f.	g.	h.	i.
9	3	6	2
−1	−3	+2	+1
(8)	(0)	(8)	(3)

➋ Teach

Demonstrate Provide each student with five pennies and two nickels in **play money***. Use an **overhead projector** and **overhead coins*** to show

95 Addition and Subtraction

Name _____

Pennies and Nickels

How many cents?

➊ _____4_____ ¢

➋ _____7_____ ¢

➌ _____9_____ ¢

Work these problems. Watch the signs.

➍ 6 + 2 = ___8___   ➎ 2 + 2 = ___4___

➏ 7 – 2 = ___5___   ➐ 7 + 2 = ___9___

 Play the "Pennies and Nickels" game.

 Talk about the Thinking Story "Exactly What to Do."

 NOTE TO HOME
Students add with nickels and pennies.

Unit 2   Lesson 42 • **95**

RETEACHING

 Invite students to play a guessing game with a partner. Have one partner hide a play penny in one hand and a play nickel in the other. The other partner picks a hand and guesses which coin is in it. If the guess is correct, he or she gets to keep that coin. Play continues until the partner who is guessing has coins totaling ten cents. Then have partners switch roles.

 CULTURAL DIVERSITY Some students may be more familiar with the currency of their country of origin than of the United States. To reinforce recognition of United States coins, challenge each of these students—or any other students who might benefit—to draw large-sized copies of pennies and nickels, both front and back.

*available separately

◆ LESSON 42 Pennies and Nickels

Use coins to help. Use nickels whenever you can. Draw the coins you used.

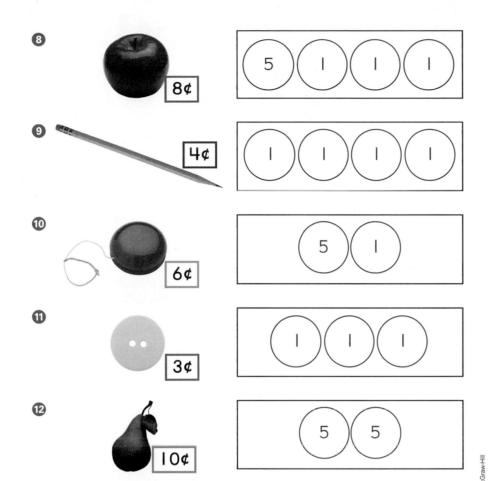

8 apple 8¢ → 5 1 1 1

9 pencil 4¢ → 1 1 1 1

10 yo-yo 6¢ → 5 1

11 button 3¢ → 1 1 1

12 pear 10¢ → 5 5

96 • Addition and Subtraction

 NOTE TO HOME
Students use coins to form amounts of money.

Copyright © SRA/McGraw-Hill

---

students how to count pennies to make 5¢. Then tell them that they can trade five pennies for a nickel and still have five cents. Challenge them to use their coins to make 6¢. Be sure they know what the *cent* sign is. Then provide practice in forming various amounts of money.

Introducing the "Pennies and Nickels" Game To provide practice with changing pennies for nickels, divide students into groups of two or three. Each group uses 20 pennies, 15 nickels, and a 0–5 Number Cube. The coins are placed in a "bank." Players take turns rolling the cube and taking the number of pennies indicated. When a player has five pennies, he or she trades them in for a nickel. The player who is first to accumulate five nickels is the winner. A copy of this game can also be found on page 20 of the Home Connections Blackline Masters.

Using the Student Pages Tell students that they may use pennies and nickels to help them complete pages 95 and 96. After they finish, ask them to count in unison to check their answers.

Using the Thinking Story Read aloud "Exactly What to Do" on pages 36–39 of the Thinking Story Book. Stop and discuss the questions asked throughout the story.

Invite students to list some chores they do at home. Ask them to think about how they can tell what is important information when someone gives them instructions.

❸ Wrap-Up ⏱ 5 MINUTES

In Closing Challenge students to make up addition and subtraction problems for the class to solve with the play coins.

Portfolio Assessment Ask students to choose one of the lesson pages to keep in their Math Portfolios.

Assessment Criteria

Did the student . . .

✓ correctly form various amounts of money?

✓ participate in the discussion of the Thinking Story?

PRACTICE p. 42

LESSON 42 PRACTICE Name _____

How many cents?

1 2 ¢
2 8 ¢
3 6 ¢
4 6 ¢
5 3 ¢
6 7 ¢

42 • Math Explorations and Applications Level 1

ENRICHMENT p. 42

LESSON 42 ENRICHMENT Name _____

Work with a partner. Use play money. Take turns buying and selling. Buy two things. Draw what you buy and the coins you used.

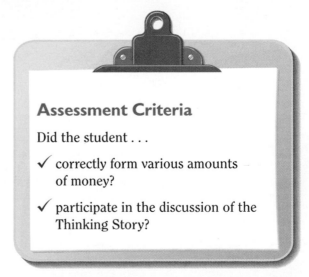

Buy This	How Much
Answers will vary.	

42 • Math Explorations and Applications Level 1

Exactly What to Do

❶ "It's not so easy," Mr. Breezy told Marcus, "but here's what you'll need to do: The first thing is to put on your shoes. The third thing is to bring in the newspaper. The fourth thing is to pet the dog."
What did Mr. Breezy forget? the second thing

❷ Yesterday it rained for two hours before lunch. Then the sun came out for a while. Then it rained for another hour.
How long did it rain all together? three hours

❸ The Tates have three children. Two have gone on a bus to visit their grandmother. One is away at college.
How many children are at home? zero

❹ Mr. Muddle has five fishbowls. Each bowl has zero fish in it.
How many fish does Mr. Muddle have all together? zero

❺ Mr. Breezy made up this riddle: "I'm thinking of a number that's less than seven and greater than two and less than four and greater than one."
Can you figure out what number it is? three
How can you be sure? It's the only number that's greater than two and less than four.

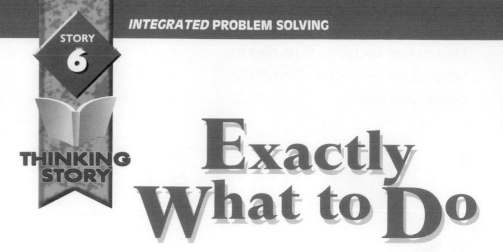

THINKING STORY

Exactly What to Do

" It's time to walk the dogs," said Mr. Breezy.

That was a job Marcus sometimes did at his dad's training school for dogs. He took the dogs to a small park that was right next to the school.

"How many times should I walk around the park with the dogs tonight?" Marcus asked.

"That's not so easy to figure out," said Mr. Breezy. "But here's exactly what you'll need to do. First pat each dog on the head two times. Then walk the dogs around the park two times. Then stop at the drinking fountain for three drinks of water. Then walk the dogs around the park one time. Then say 'Nice doggie' two times. Then put the dogs back into their pens."

36 • Exactly What to Do

"I see what you mean," said Marcus. "That's not so easy, but at least now I know how many times to walk around the park."

How many times does Marcus need to walk the dogs around the park? Three; [Repeat Mr. Breezy's instructions if necessary.]

Marcus figured out that his dad wanted him to walk the dogs around the park three times. He knew that patting the dogs on their heads and saying "Nice doggie, nice doggie" wouldn't help him figure out how far to walk.

When Marcus brought the dogs back from their walk, he remembered that one dog, Bowser, hadn't been fed yet. "How much dog food should I give Bowser?" Marcus asked.

❻ Mr. Breezy, Mr. Eng, and Mr. Mudancia were having coffee at Mr. Muddle's. "I'm going to have a piece of pie," said Mr. Muddle. "How about the rest of you?"

"Yes, thank you," said Mr. Breezy.

"Yes, thanks," said Mr. Eng.

"No, thank you," said Mr. Mudancia. "I'm on a diet."

How many pieces of pie should Mr. Muddle serve? three

❼ Mr. Mudancia had a wooden chair with four legs. Then he changed it a little. He took a broomstick and cut it in half. He put each half under the chair for an extra leg.

Picture that chair in your mind. How many legs does it have? six

❽ Marcus's mother likes rings. Marcus wants to buy her a ring for her birthday. He wants to be sure it's the right size for her finger, but he can't ask her—he wants it to be a surprise.

Think of ways that Marcus could find out what size ring to buy. Measure one of her rings; make a clay model of it; find a stick that fits into it; try it on his thumb.

❾ Mr. Breezy said, "Our cabin was full of flies. I swatted six flies with a newspaper. Then I swatted four more with a magazine. Then I got two of them with a dust cloth and three of them with a bath towel. But there were still a lot of flies left."

What worked best for swatting flies—paper or cloth? paper [Repeat the problem if necessary]

◆ **STORY 6 Exactly What to Do**

"That question's not so easy," said Mr. Breezy. "Bowser's pretty fussy about how much he eats, so you have to do everything exactly right."

Does that help Marcus to know how much food to give Bowser? no

"Okay," said Marcus. "I'll listen very carefully."

"Here's exactly what to do," said Mr. Breezy. "Take two spoons. Then put one spoon into the sink. Then take the other spoon and put two spoonfuls of dog food into the bowl. Then say 'Good old Bowser!' three times. Then put two spoonfuls of water onto the flowers on the windowsill. Then mop the floor. Then put another spoonful of dog food into the bowl, and then another one. Then watch the news on television. Then put one more spoonful of water onto the flowers."

38 • Exactly What to Do

"Now I know exactly how much food to give Bowser," said Marcus.

Do you know how much food Bowser should get? four spoonfuls

Marcus did everything exactly the way his dad had told him to. It took almost an hour until he finished feeding Bowser.

"You're quick at figuring things out," said Mr. Breezy, "but you don't seem to move very fast. How could it take you almost an hour to feed a dog four spoonfuls of dog food?"

Why did it take so long? Marcus had other things to do.

What other things did Marcus have to do? He had to put one spoon in the sink, say "Good old Bowser!" three times, put two spoonfuls of water onto the flowers on the window sill, mop the floor, watch the news on television, and put one more spoonful of water onto the flowers.

. . . the end

Story 6 • **39**

LESSON 43

Student Edition pages 97–98

Using $1 and $5 Bills

LESSON PLANNER

Objectives

▶ to teach students to use $1 and $5 bills to make specific amounts of money

▶ to teach students to calculate specific amounts of money in a variety of ways

Context of the Lesson This lesson is an introduction to common paper money denominations used in the United States.

 MANIPULATIVES

can

counters*

play money*
($1, $5, and
$10 bills)

overhead bills*

overhead
projector

Program Resources

Number Cubes

Thinking Story Book, pages 40–41

Reteaching Master

Practice Master 43

Enrichment Master 43

For extra practice:
CD-ROM* Lesson 43

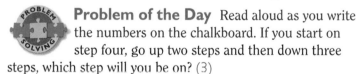

1 Warm-Up

Problem of the Day Read aloud as you write the numbers on the chalkboard. If you start on step four, go up two steps and then down three steps, which step will you be on? (3)

Problem-Solving Strategies Ask students who have solved the Problem of the Day to share how they solved it and any strategies they used.

MENTAL MATH Present counters-in-the-can problems. Start with the first number of **counters*** in a **can**. Add in the second number of counters. Have students show answers with Number Cubes.

a. 4, 4 (8)   b. 7, 2 (9)   c. 5, 2 (7)
d. 6, 4 (10)   e. 4, 2 (6)   f. 4, 3 (7)

2 Teach

Introducing the "Making Money" Activity Use an **overhead projector** and **overhead bills*** to teach students to identify $1, $5, and $10 bills. Then have students work in small groups to do this activity to provide practice forming amounts of money. Give each group ten **$1 bills**, two **$5 bills**, and one

97 Addition and Subtraction

Name _____

Using $1 and $5 Bills

Use play money to help. Draw bills to make the correct amount.
Possible answers are shown.

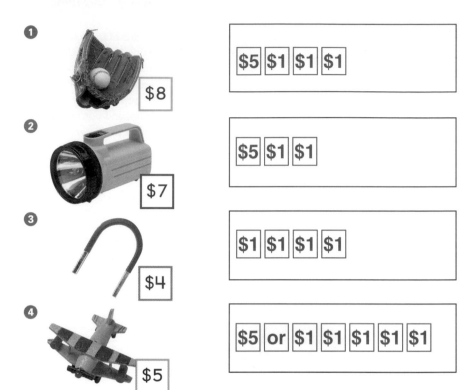

1   $8 | $5 | $1 | $1 | $1 |

2   $7 | $5 | $1 | $1 |

3   $4 | $1 | $1 | $1 | $1 |

4   $5 | $5 | or | $1 | $1 | $1 | $1 | $1 |

COOPERATIVE LEARNING   Do the "Making Money" activity.

 NOTE TO HOME
Students form amounts of money with $1 and $5 bills.

Unit 2   Lesson 43 • **97**

SPECIAL NEEDS   **MANIPULATIVES**

Meeting Individual Needs Work individually with students to calculate money amounts from $1 through $10 with only $1 bills. After they become proficient at this, demonstrate how to change five $1 bills for one $5 bill. Then have them change amounts from $6 to $10 using a $5 bill. Finally, have them play the "$1 and $5 Bills" game.

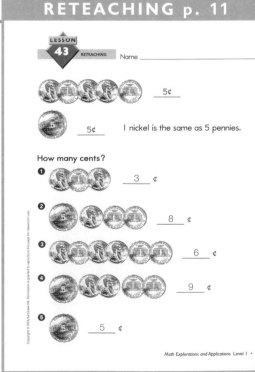

LESSON 43 RETEACHING   Name _____

_____ 5¢

_____ 5¢   I nickel is the same as 5 pennies.

How many cents?

1   _____ 3 ¢

2   _____ 8 ¢

3   _____ 6 ¢

4   _____ 9 ¢

5   _____ 5 ¢

Math Explorations and Applications Level I • **11**

*available separately

◆ LESSON 43 Using $1 and $5 Bills

Use play money to help. Make each amount two different ways.
Possible answers are shown.

⑤

$10

| $5 | $5 |

| $5 | $1 | $1 | $1 | $1 | $1 |

⑥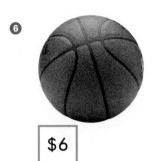

$6

| $5 | $1 |

| $1 | $1 | $1 | $1 | $1 | $1 |

 Play the "$1 and $5 Bills" game.

98 • Addition and Subtraction

NOTE TO HOME
Students form amounts of money with $1 and $5 bills.

Copyright © SRA/McGraw-Hill

$10 bill. Name a price of $10 or less, such as $8. Have groups show that amount using as few bills as they can. (one $5 and three $1 bills) Check their responses and repeat several times.

Using the Student Pages Have students work in groups to complete pages 97–98. Explain that for page 98, they should find at least two ways to solve each question and that they can use as many bills as they like.

Introducing the "$1 and $5 Bills" Game To provide practice in changing money, have students play the "$1 and $5 Bills" game. Give two or three players twenty $1 bills and fifteen $5 bills to place in a central pile. Players take turns rolling a 0–5 Number Cube and taking the amount rolled in $1 bills from the bank. Players trade $1 bills at the bank for a $5 bill whenever they can. The first player to have five $5 bills is the winner. This game is also on page 16 in the Home Connections Blackline Masters.

Using the Thinking Story Present two new problems from those following "Exactly What to Do" on pages 40–41 of the Thinking Story Book or pages 96a–96b of this Guide.

❸ Wrap-Up ⏱ 5 MINUTES

In Closing Have students work together to list all the possible ways to make $10. (one $10; two $5; one $5 and five $1; and ten $1)

Informal Assessment Use students' answers to pages 97–98 to informally assess their ability to make different money amounts with $1 and $5 bills.

PRACTICE p. 43

LESSON 43 PRACTICE Name _____

How many dollars?

❶  $ __8__

❷ $ __6__

❸ $ __9__

Draw bills to make the correct amount.

❹ | any combination that totals $7 |

❺ | $1 $ | $1 $ | $1 $ | $1 $ |

❻ | any combination that totals $6 |

❼ | any combination that totals $9 |

Math Explorations and Applications Level 1 • 43

ENRICHMENT p. 43

LESSON 43 ENRICHMENT Name _____

Look at the bills and answer the questions.

❶ Whose picture do you see on the one-dollar bill?
Washington

❷ How many times do you see the word **one** on the front of the bill? __2__

❸ How many times do you see the number 1 on the front of the bill? 4 (not counting year)

❹ How many times do you see the word **five** on the front of the bill?
__4__

❺ How many times do you see the number 5 on the front of the bill? 4 (not counting year or serial numbers)

❻ Whose picture do you see on the five-dollar bill?
Lincoln

Math Explorations and Applications Level 1 • 43

Assessment Criteria

Did the student . . .

✓ work cooperatively and show correct money amounts during the "Making Money" activity and game-playing time?

✓ correctly answer five of the problems on pages 97–98?

Observation of game-playing activity . . . will often give greater insight into a child's thought patterns than anything else the teacher can do.

—Stephen S. Willoughby,
Mathematics Education for a Changing World

LESSON
44

Student Edition pages 99–100

Geometric Figures

LESSON PLANNER

Objectives

▶ to introduce simple geometric shapes: triangle, circle, square, and rectangle

▶ to provide practice identifying and counting shapes

Context of the Lesson This is the first formal lesson on geometry.

 MANIPULATIVES

attribute blocks*
(optional)

crayons

geoboards*
(optional)

Program Resources

Number Cubes

Thinking Story Book, pages 40–41

Practice Master 44

Enrichment Master 44

For extra practice:
CD-ROM* Lesson 44

Mixed Practice, page 358

① Warm-Up

 Problem of the Day Present the following problem to the class. How many different ways can you make 10¢ using pennies and/or nickels?

(three ways: two nickels, one nickel and five pennies, ten pennies)

Problem-Solving Strategies Ask students who have solved the Problem of the Day to share how they solved it and any strategies they used.

MENTAL MATH Have students add the following numbers and respond with Number Cubes.

a. 5 + 2 = (7)   b. 6 + 1 = (7)

c. 3 + 1 = (4)   d. 2 + 1 = (3)

e. 4 − 1 = (3)   f. 7 + 2 = (9)

GIFTED & TALENTED **Meeting Individual Needs**
Challenge students to make riddles about specific shapes. Have students write the riddle on one side of an index card and draw the shape on the other. For example, write: "I have no straight lines or corners. What am I?" (a circle) Have the class use these cards as flash cards for practice in identifying shapes.

99 Addition and Subtraction

LESSON
44

Name _____

Geometric Figures

triangle   circle   square   rectangle

Color the shapes this way.

s red   s green

s yellow   s blue

Use any colors you like for the others.

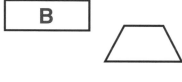

B   R   G

Y   G   Y   R   B

 Write about the shapes in your Math Journal. Tell how they are different. Tell how they are the same.

NOTE TO HOME
Students identify geometric figures.

 Literature Connection Read aloud *Polygons* by David L. Stienecker. This book uses games, activities, and puzzles to explore polygons.

 MANIPULATIVES Provide **attribute blocks*** for students to use. Discuss and identify each shape and its properties. Have students trace each shape on separate sheets of paper labeled with the figure's name.

Have students use **geoboards*** to make shapes on the grids. Discuss the different examples of each shape.

*available separately

◆ **LESSON 44** Geometric Figures

Use the Mixed Practice on page 358 after this lesson.

❶ Ring each triangle.

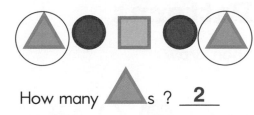

How many ▲s ? __2__

❷ Color each circle.

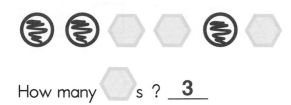

How many ⬡s ? __3__

❸ Ring each square.

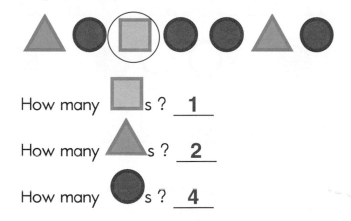

How many ◻s ? __1__

How many ▲s ? __2__

How many ⬤s ? __4__

100 • Addition and Subtraction

NOTE TO HOME
Students identify and count geometric figures.

❷ Teach

Demonstrate Have a volunteer draw a triangle on the chalkboard. Discuss the characteristics of a triangle (three straight sides, three angles, three corners). Repeat for a circle (one curved line with all points the same distance from the center), a square (four sides all the same length and four right angles), and a rectangle (four straight sides, opposite sides the same length, and four right angles).

Using the Student Pages Have **crayons** available. Read the instructions to students and then have students work independently to complete page 99. For page 100, read the instructions for each problem as students do them one at a time. Check students' work when they are finished.

Using the Thinking Story Present two new problems from those following "Exactly What to Do" on pages 40–41 of the Thinking Story Book or pages 96a–96b of this Guide.

❸ Wrap-Up ⏱ 5 MINUTES

In Closing Have students name objects they see in the classroom that have a triangle, rectangle, circle, or square on them.

Portfolio Assessment Have students draw and label an example of each shape. Have them save the drawings in their Math Portfolios.

Assessment Criteria

Did the student . . .

✓ participate in solving the Thinking Story problems?

✓ correctly answer 80% of the problems on pages 99–100?

PRACTICE p. 44

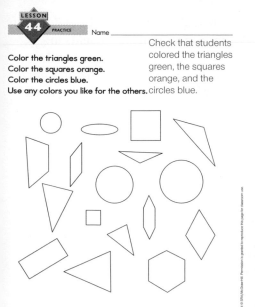

LESSON 44 PRACTICE Name _____

Color the triangles green.
Color the squares orange.
Color the circles blue.
Use any colors you like for the others.

Check that students colored the triangles green, the squares orange, and the circles blue.

44 • Math Explorations and Applications Level 1

ENRICHMENT p. 44

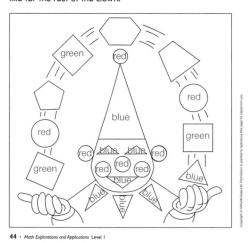

LESSON 44 ENRICHMENT Name _____

Color the circles red. Color the squares green. Color the triangles blue. Use any other colors you like for the rest of the clown.

44 • Math Explorations and Applications Level I

LESSON
45

Student Edition pages 101–102

Geometric Patterns

LESSON PLANNER

Objectives

▶ to provide practice recognizing and making patterns using geometric shapes

▶ to provide practice identifying shapes

Context of the Lesson This is the second lesson on plane geometric figures. The next lesson will introduce solid geometric figures.

 MANIPULATIVES   **Program Resources**

pattern blocks*   Number Cubes

Thinking Story Book, pages 40–41

Practice Master 45

Enrichment Master 45

For extra practice:
CD-ROM* Lesson 45

❶ Warm-Up

 Problem of the Day Present the following problem on the chalkboard: Manuel's mother gives him one $5 bill and two $1 bills for lunch each week. Rita's mother gives her three $1 bills and her father gives her three more $1 bills for her lunch each week. Who gets more money for lunch each week? How can you tell? (Manuel; $5 + $2 = $7 is more than $3 + $3 = $6)

Problem-Solving Strategies Ask students who have solved the Problem of the Day to share how they solved it and any strategies they used.

 Have students solve the following problems and respond with Number Cubes.

a.   2 − 0 = (2)   b.   2 + 2 = (4)   c.   6 − 1 = (5)

d.   1 + 1 = (2)   e.   7 − 1 = (6)   f.   2 − 2 = (0)

 **Meeting Individual Needs** Have kinesthetic learners use **pattern blocks*** to create their own patterns. Have auditory learners make clapping patterns and challenge other students to describe or imitate their sound patterns.

101 Addition and Subtraction

LESSON
45

Name _____

Geometric Patterns

Look for the pattern. Then draw the missing shape.

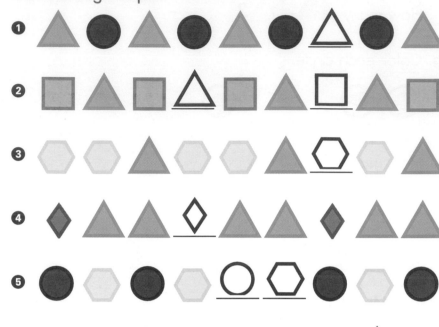

 Make your own pattern. See if a friend can figure it out.

 NOTE TO HOME
Students find and complete patterns.

Unit 2   Lesson 45 • **101**

 Music Connection Display a sheet of music for students. Have them identify any patterns they see in the notes within several measures. If a piano is available, play the sample measures and have students look at the patterns created on the keyboard.

RETEACHING

Teach students how to make and identify patterns by arranging students in different patterns in the front of the room. For example: boy, girl, boy, girl, etc.; or boy, boy, girl, boy, boy, girl, etc.

*available separately

◆ LESSON 45 Geometric Patterns

ART CONNECTION

Color the circles red.
Color the triangles green.
Color the squares orange.

O O O G O O O G

102 • Addition and Subtraction

 NOTE TO HOME
Students identify geometric figures.

Copyright © SRA/McGraw-Hill

---

❷ Teach

Demonstrate Present a simple repeating pattern on the chalkboard using squares, rectangles, circles, and/or triangles. Have students explain what the pattern is. Then draw a second pattern, leaving two shapes out. Discuss how to determine which are the missing shapes by having students say the pattern aloud from the beginning.

MANIPULATIVES **Using the Student Pages** Explain to students that they must use the same approach as in the demonstration to complete page 101. When students finish, have them make up their own patterns to trade with classmates. Before students begin page 102, use a square **pattern block*** to demonstrate how a figure can rotate to look slightly different and still be a square. Demonstrate the same property with rectangles and triangles. Afterward, have students go on to complete page 102 on their own.

Using the Thinking Story Present two new problems from those following "Exactly What to Do" on pages 40–41 of the Thinking Story Book or pages 96a–96b of this Guide.

❸ Wrap-Up

In Closing Have students share with the class any patterns they thought were especially difficult to see how many of their classmates can identify and complete them.

ALTERNATIVE ASSESSMENT **Portfolio Assessment** Have students save the patterns they created in their Math Portfolios as an informal assessment of their ability to identify, complete, and create patterns.

Assessment Criteria

Did the student . . .

✓ correctly complete four of the six patterns on page 101?

✓ create an interesting pattern of his or her own?

PRACTICE p. 45

LESSON **45** PRACTICE Name_____

Look for the pattern. Then draw the missing shape.

❶ ○ △ ○ △ ○ △ ○ △

❷ □ ○ ○ □ □ ○ □ □ ○

❸ △ △ □ □ △ □ △ △

❹ □ ○ □ ○ □ ○

❺ △ □ △ □ △ □

❻ ○ □ △ □ ○ □ △

Math Explorations and Applications Level 1 • 45

ENRICHMENT p. 45

LESSON **45** ENRICHMENT Name_____

❶ Color the triangles red, the squares blue, the rectangles yellow, and the circles orange.

❷ How many of each shape do you see?

circles __2__ rectangles __3__

squares __7__ triangles __4__

❸ The outline of a man riding his horse is made from geometric figures. Draw in the missing lines to show the shapes. What shapes are they?

triangles, squares

and a rectangle

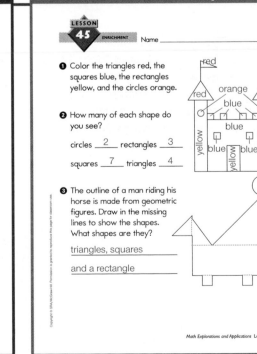

Math Explorations and Applications Level 1 • 45

*available separately

LESSON 46

Student Edition pages 103–104

Identifying Solid Figures

LESSON PLANNER

Objectives

▶ to provide examples of and practice identifying cubes, spheres, cones, and cylinders

▶ to provide practice counting shapes

Context of the Lesson This lesson provides students with an introduction to solid geometric figures.

 MANIPULATIVES

globe

ice-cream cone or paper cone

can

wooden geometric solids*

Program Resources

Number Cubes

Thinking Story Book, pages 40–41

Reteaching Master

Practice Master 46

Enrichment Master 46

For extra practice:
CD-ROM* Lesson 46

① Warm-Up ⏱ 5 MINUTES

Problem of the Day Present the following problem to the class. Kevin has more games than Aida and Noelle, but fewer than Warren. One of the children has seven games, another eight, another nine, and another ten. How many games does Kevin have? (9)

Problem-Solving Strategies Ask students who have solved the Problem of the Day to share how they solved it and any strategies they used.

MENTAL MATH Have students orally answer:

Which number comes _____ ?

a. before 2 (1) b. before 8 (7)

c. before 7 (6) d. after 0 (1)

e. before 9 (8) f. after 6 (7)

SPECIAL NEEDS **Meeting Individual Needs**
Have kinesthetic learners use wooden **geometric solids*** to match and identify the solid figures on the student pages.

LESSON 46

Name _____

Identifying Solid Figures

cube sphere cone cylinder

Ring objects with the same shape.

①

②

③

④

🎒 **NOTE TO HOME**
Students identify solid figures.

Unit 2 Lesson 46 • **103**

LITERATURE CONNECTION **Literature Connection** The book *Shapes* by Ivan Bulloch presents a look at plane and solid geometric figures with art activities that can be used to further the concepts.

RETEACHING p. 12

LESSON 46 RETEACHING Name _____

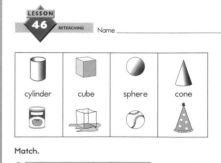

cylinder cube sphere cone

Match.

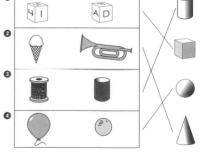

12 • *Math Explorations and Applications Level 1*

*available separately

◆ **LESSON 46** Identifying Solid Figures

Color the shapes this way.

red yellow

blue green

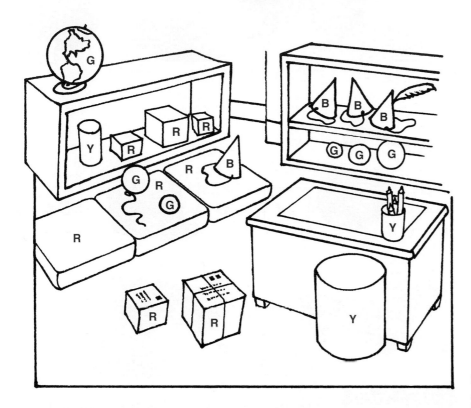

2 Teach

Demonstrate Display the wooden **geometric solid*** cube, sphere, cone, and cylinder. Then display examples of real-world materials with these shapes. Use a Number Cube for an example of a cube, a **globe** for a sphere, a **can** for a cylinder, and an **ice-cream cone** for a cone. (If cans or cones are not available, a rectangular sheet of paper rolled from end to end makes a cylinder; twisting one end to a point makes a cone.) Have students find other objects in the classroom that are like these shapes.

Using the Student Pages Go over the directions for pages 103–104 with the class. Then have students complete these pages on their own.

Using the Thinking Story Present two new problems from among those following "Exactly What to Do" on pages 40–41 of the Thinking Story Book or pages 96a–96b of this Guide.

3 Wrap-Up ⏱ 5 MINUTES

In Closing Have students name examples of objects outside the classroom that are cones, cylinders, cubes, and spheres. (Possible answers: party hat, soup can, basketball, box)

Informal Assessment Use student participation in the demonstration and closing activity as an informal assessment of their ability to recognize solid figures.

---

104 • Addition and Subtraction

🎒 **NOTE TO HOME**
Students identify solid figures.

Copyright © SRA/McGraw-Hill

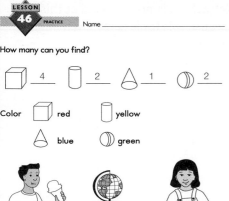

Assessment Criteria

Did the student . . .

✓ correctly answer at least 80% of the problems on pages 103–104?

✓ correctly identify the solid shapes in and outside of the classroom?

GIFTED & TALENTED **Meeting Individual Needs**
Ask students to name and count any plane geometric shapes they see on a cube (six squares), **cylinder** (two circles), and **cone** (circle).

*available separately

LESSON 47
Adding— Finding Tens

Student Edition pages 105–106

LESSON PLANNER

Objectives

▶ to teach students how to find sums up to ten using concrete objects

▶ to provide practice solving word problems involving money

Context of the Lesson This lesson provides students with an introduction to finding sums up to ten. This topic is continued in Lesson 61.

 MANIPULATIVES **Program Resources**

cardboard	**Number Cubes**
counters*	**Practice Master 47**
craft sticks	**Enrichment Master 47**
play money*	For extra practice:
	CD-ROM* Lesson 47

---

❶ Warm-Up ⏱ 5 MINUTES

 Problem of the Day Present the following problem to the class. Tomas has a nickel and four pennies. Renee has two nickels. Can either child buy a 10¢ pencil? Why or why not? (Yes, Renee can because she has 10¢. Tomas can't because he has only 9¢.)

Problem-Solving Strategies Ask students who have solved the Problem of the Day to share how they solved it and any strategies they used.

MENTAL MATH Have students use Number Cubes to show answers to the following problems.

a.	3 + 1 = (4)	**b.**	5 + 1 = (6)
c.	3 − 2 = (1)	**d.**	8 − 2 = (6)
e.	4 − 1 = (3)	**f.**	6 + 3 = (9)

❷ Teach

Using the Number Cubes Review addition and subtraction with hidden **counters*** and a piece of **cardboard**. Have students show their answers using their Number Cubes.

105 Addition and Subtraction

LESSON 47

Name _____

Adding–Finding Tens

Use coins to figure out how much each pair would cost.

❶  7¢   ❷  5¢

❸  9¢   ❹ 10¢

 COOPERATIVE LEARNING   Do the "Find Your Partner" activity.

 NOTE TO HOME Students practice addition with nickels and pennies.

Unit 2   Lesson 47 • **105**

Copyright © SRA/McGraw-Hill

 Literature Connection Read aloud *Numbers* by John J. Reiss to provide more practice with numbers.

 Technology Connection Use the software *Money Town* from Davidson Co. (Mac) for practice with making change and coin recognition.

RETEACHING

Reteaching is not essential at this time because this topic is reviewed in later lessons.

*available separately

◆ **LESSON 47** Adding—Finding Tens

Listen to the problems. Then use play money to act them out.

5 Terri had 8¢. She spent some. Now she has 5¢. How much did Terri spend? **3** ¢

6 Rodney has $5. If he earns three more dollars, how much will he have? $ **8**

7 A ball costs $8. A bat costs $2. How much for the bat and ball? $ **10**

8 Richard had $10. If he buys a puzzle for $2, how much will he have? $ **8**

9 Nadia had $9. Then she bought a plant. Now how much does she have? **not enough information** $____

106 · Addition and Subtraction

 NOTE TO HOME Students solve word problems.

PRACTICE p. 47

Use coins to figure out how much each pair would cost.

6¢ 4¢ 3¢ 2¢ 7¢

1 9¢ **2** 5¢
3 9¢ **4** 7¢
5 6¢ **6** 8¢

Math Explorations and Applications Level 1 · 47

ENRICHMENT p. 47

8, 9, 10 Three have sprouted. How many have not?

Count ten seeds. Plant the seeds. Look at them every day. Fill in this chart. Results will vary.

Day	A How many have sprouted?	B How many have not sprouted?
1		
2		
3		
4		
5		
6		
7		

Check your results. For each day, do the numbers in column A and column B add up to ten?

Math Explorations and Applications Level 1 · 47

---

*available separately

Introducing the "Find Your Partner" Activity To have students practice finding numbers that sum to ten, have them do the "Find Your Partner" activity. Provide each student with a different number of **craft sticks** (any amount between one and nine). At a signal, have students hunt for a partner who has the right number of craft sticks to make a total of ten. Vary the activity by having students hunt for partners to total nine.

Using the Student Pages Do the first problem on page 105 together with the class. Then have students work in pairs using **play money*** to find out how much the items will cost. Correct the page together with the class. Then go on to page 106, and read each story problem aloud. Have students complete a problem, then correct it as a class before going on to the next. Ask students to tell what information is needed in order to solve problem 9.

❸ Wrap-Up ⏱ 5 MINUTES

In Closing Have students name various pairs of numbers that sum to ten.

Performance Assessment Use students' responses in the closing activity to informally assess their knowledge of sums of ten.

Assessment Criteria

Did the student . . .

✓ correctly answer seven of nine problems on pages 105–106?

✓ find the right partner to make 10 during the "Find Your Partner" activity?

Meeting Individual Needs Have visual learners use graph paper and two different colors to color grids that make sums of ten. See how many different patterns they can make. For example, with red and blue crayons a student might color: 1 red, 9 blue; 2 red, 8 blue; 3 red, 7 blue, and so on.

LESSON 48 ▷ "Statue" Addition

Student Edition pages 107–108

LESSON PLANNER

Objective
▶ to teach students how to add by thinking of finger sets rather than showing them

Context of the Lesson
The corresponding procedure for subtraction is taught in the next lesson.

 MANIPULATIVES

Program Resources

Squeeze In*
  from the Literature Library
Number Cubes
Practice Master 48
Enrichment Master 48

For extra practice:
CD-ROM* Lesson 48

① Warp-Up ⏱ 5 MINUTES

Problem of the Day Present the following problem. Al, Ben, and Carlos are told to stand in line. How many different ways can they stand in line? What are the ways? (6; Al, Ben, Carlos; Al, Carlos, Ben; Ben, Al, Carlos; Ben, Carlos, Al; Carlos, Al, Ben; Carlos, Ben, Al)

Problem-Solving Strategies Ask students who have solved the Problem of the Day to share how they solved it and any strategies they used.

 Have students use finger sets to solve each problem and show each answer.

a. 3 + 1 = (4)   b. 5 + 2 = (7)   c. 6 + 3 = (9)

d. 3 + 0 = (3)   e. 9 + 1 = (10)   f. 1 + 4 = (5)

② Teach

Demonstrate Present the addition problem 7 + 2. Ask students to raise the finger set for the number 7. Then have them pretend they are statues and are not able to move their fingers anymore. Explain how to add the 2 by thinking of which fingers they would raise to make the new set. (9) Repeat with similar problems.

LESSON 48

"Statue" Addition

Name _____

Add. Use statue addition.

① + 2 = __8__   ② + 1 = __8__

③ + 1 = __6__   ④ + 2 = __6__

⑤ + 3 = __5__   ⑥ + 3 = __7__

⑦ + 2 = __5__   ⑧ + 2 = __10__

⑨ + 3 = __3__   ⑩ + 3 = __4__

COOPERATIVE LEARNING Do the "Funny Numbers" activity.

 NOTE TO HOME Students use a strategy to solve addition problems.

Unit 2   Lesson 48 • **107**

Why teach it this way?

Statue addition is an intermediate stage between finger set operations and mental math.

Literature Connection Read aloud *12 Ways to Get to 11* by Eve Merriam. This book uses ordinary experiences to present 12 combinations of numbers that add up to 11.

To provide practice adding on by two and three, read aloud *Squeeze In* from the Literature Library*.

RETEACHING

For students who are not quite ready to progress to statue addition, provide an intermediate step. For instance, to solve 7 + 2, have students raise the first set of seven fingers. Then rather than raise the next number, have them count the knuckles of the fingers they would normally raise to get the final finger set. (9) Repeat with similar examples.

107 Addition and Subtraction

*available separately

◆ LESSON 48 "Statue" Addition

Listen to the problems.

$3

$5

$2

$1

$4

How much?

⑪ pompoms and pinata? $ __5__

⑫ basketball and pompoms? $ __7__

⑬ harmonica and basketball? $ __9__

⑭ basketball and harmonica? $ __9__

⑮ basketball and piggy bank? $ __6__

Make up your own problems. Write them in your Math Journal. Share them with a friend.

MATH JOURNAL

108 · Addition and Subtraction

NOTE TO HOME
Students solve word problems.

Copyright © SRA/McGraw-Hill

PRACTICE p. 48

LESSON 48 PRACTICE   Name _____

Add. Use statue addition.

❶ 👐👌 + 3 = __6__   ❷ 👐👌 + 2 = __7__

❸ 👐✋ + 1 = __8__   ❹ 👐👐 + 1 = __9__

❺ 👌👌 + 3 = __5__   ❻ ✊👌 + 1 = __4__

❼ ✋👌 + 2 = __6__   ❽ ✊👌 + 2 = __3__

❾ 👐👌 + 3 = __8__   ❿ ✊👌 + 1 = __3__

⓫ 👐✋ + 1 = __9__   ⓬ 👐👐 + 2 = __9__

⓭ 👌👌 + 3 = __7__   ⓮ ✊👌 + 2 = __5__

48 · Math Explorations and Applications Level 1

ENRICHMENT p. 48

LESSON 48 ENRICHMENT   Name _____

SOCIAL STUDIES CONNECTION

Solve the problems. Follow the code.

Code	
7 = red	10 = black
6 = blue	9 = white
8 = green	

Thailand

| 3 + 4 = red |
| 6 + 3 = white |
| 4 + 2 = blue |
| 5 + 4 = white |
| 5 + 2 = red |

Italy

5 +3 green	7 +2 white	6 +1 red

Chile — star: white, field: blue

| 3 + 3 = ⭐ |
| 0 + 9 = white |
| 2 + 5 = red |

Sudan — triangle: green

| 7 + 0 = red |
| 6 +2 | 8 + 1 = white |
| 6 + 4 = black |

48 · Math Explorations and Applications Level 1

Using the Number Cubes Write horizontal and vertical addition problems on the chalkboard. Have students use statue addition to solve them, then show their answers with Number Cubes.

Introducing the "Funny Numbers" Activity The "Funny Numbers" activity provides practice in mental math. For example, say: "The number I'm thinking of is my feet, my arms, my nose, and my mouth. What number is it?" (6) Then have students think of similar combinations of items to add. Those who need help can whisper a number to you. Then you can suggest ways to present it, such as the number of buttons on a shirt or the number of windows in the room.

Using the Student Pages Do the first problem on page 107 with the class. Remind students that they should not raise fingers to add the second number. Students can complete the page on their own. On page 108, read the problems aloud as students complete them independently.

③ Wrap-Up 🕐 5 MINUTES

In Closing Have volunteers demonstrate how to use statue addition to solve the problem they wrote in their Math Journals.

ALTERNATIVE ASSESSMENT

Performance Assessment Observe which students use statue addition during the demonstration and Number Cube activity.

Assessment Criteria

Did the student . . .

✓ correctly answer problems using statue addition in the demonstration and Number Cube activity?

✓ correctly answer eight of ten problems on page 107 using statue addition?

✓ correctly answer four of the five word problems on page 108?

LEARNING STYLES **Meeting Individual Needs**
Allow auditory learners to count numbers aloud (quietly) when completing page 107. For example, with the first problem they would quietly whisper the finger set shown, then count up two more: "6 . . . 7, 8."

LESSON 49
Student Edition pages 109–110
"Statue" Subtraction

Name _____

"Statue" Subtraction

LESSON PLANNER

Objective
► to teach students how to subtract by thinking of finger sets rather than showing them

Context of the Lesson
The procedure corresponds to the one taught in Lesson 48 for addition.

 MANIPULATIVES
none

Program Resources
"Flea Market" Game Mat
Number Cubes
Practice Master 49
Enrichment Master 49
For additional math integration:
Math Throughout the Day*
For extra practice:
CD-ROM* Lesson 49
Mixed Practice, page 359

Subtract. Use statue subtraction.

1.  – 2 = __3__   2.  – 3 = __2__

3. – 1 = __5__   4.  – 3 = __4__

5. – 3 = __7__   6. – 2 = __6__

7. – 4 = __2__   8. – 4 = __4__

9. – 2 = __1__   10. – 3 = __6__

 GAME   Play the "Flea Market" game.

 NOTE TO HOME
Students use a strategy to solve subtraction problems.

Unit 2   Lesson 49 • **109**

① Warm-Up ⏱ 5 MINUTES

 Problem of the Day Present the following problem to the class. A line of children is standing in front of school. No matter which end you start counting, Rico is third in line. How many children are in line? (5)

Problem-Solving Strategies Ask students who have solved the Problem of the Day to share how they solved it and any strategies they used.

 Have students use finger sets to solve each problem and show each answer.

a. 7 – 2 = (5)   b. 9 – 0 = (9)
c. 1 – 1 = (0)   d. 4 – 2 = (2)
e. 5 – 3 = (2)   f. 9 – 2 = (7)

② Teach

Demonstrate Present students with a problem to solve using statue subtraction, such as 8 – 2. Have them raise the finger set for the first number (8). Then say: "Think of which fingers you would turn down to subtract 2, but don't turn them down. Try to see how many fingers would be left." (6) Repeat with similar examples.

Why teach it this way?

As with statue addition, this procedure is an intermediate stage between finger set operations and mental math for subtraction.

Whenever possible, addition and subtraction should be taught at about the same time so that learners can contrast the two and so that problems can be presented that are not all solved by using the same operation.

—Stephen S. Willoughby,
Mathematics Education for a Changing World

RETEACHING

For students not quite ready to progress to statue subtraction, provide an intermediate step. For instance, to solve 8 – 2, explain that students should raise the first set of eight fingers, and then rather than turning down two fingers, they can wiggle them to see which fingers remain. (6) Repeat with other similar examples.

109 Addition and Subtraction

*available separately

◆ **LESSON 49** "Statue" Subtraction

Use statue subtraction to help find the answer.

Use the Mixed Practice on page 359 after this lessson.

If you have this much money	and you buy this...	you will have this much left
⑪	$3	$2
⑫	$2	$2
⑬	$4	$3
⑭	$5	$5
⑮	$1	$5
⑯	$2	$6
⑰	$3	$3
⑱	$1	$2

110 • Addition and Subtraction

NOTE TO HOME
Students add and subtract with money.

PRACTICE p. 49

LESSON 49 PRACTICE Name _____

Solve these problems. Watch the signs. Use statue addition and subtraction.

❶  + 3 = __9__   ❷ + 2 = __6__

❸ − 4 = __3__   ❹ + 1 = __5__

❺ − 4 = __5__   ❻ − 1 = __2__

❼ + 2 = __6__   ❽ + 2 = __3__

❾ + 3 = __8__   ❿ − 1 = __3__

⓫ − 3 = __5__   ⓬ − 2 = __5__

Math Explorations and Applications Level 1 • **49**

ENRICHMENT p. 49

LESSON 49 ENRICHMENT Name _____

Solve the problems. Follow the code.

Code	
5 = red	3 = black
4 = blue	6 = green
2 = yellow	

star: yellow

10 − 8 =

8 − 3 = __red__

Vietnam

triangle: black

9 − 6

5 − 1 = blue
7 − 5 = yellow
9 − 5 = blue

The Bahamas

5 −2 black	8 −6 yellow	10 −5 red

Belgium

star: black

7 − 2 = red
yellow ☆ 9 − 7 =
7 − 1 = green

Ghana

Math Explorations and Applications Level 1 • **49**

Using the Number Cubes Write horizontal and vertical subtraction problems on the chalkboard. Have students solve them with statue subtraction and show their answers with Number Cubes.

Using the Student Pages Do the first problem on page 109 with the class. Remind students not to turn down any fingers. Have students complete the pages on their own.

Introducing the "Flea Market" Game Mat To provide practice in changing $1 bills for $10 bills, demonstrate, then play the "Flea Market" game. Use the "Flea Market" Game Mat transparency to explain the game. Complete rules are found on the "Flea Market" Game Mat, a copy of which can be found on page 399 of this Teacher's Guide.

❸ Wrap-Up 5 MINUTES

In Closing Have volunteers demonstrate how they used statue subtraction to solve problems on pages 109–110.

Performance Assessment Observe which students use statue subtraction during the demonstration and Number Cube activity.

Assessment Criteria

Did the student . . .

✓ correctly answer problems using statue subtraction in the demonstration and Number Cube activity?

✓ correctly answer 15 of 18 problems on pages 109–110 using statue subtraction?

Meeting Individual Needs

As you did for statue addition, allow auditory learners to count numbers aloud (quietly) when completing pages 109–110. For example, for the first problem they would quietly whisper the finger set for five, then count down two more: "5 . . . 4, 3."

LESSON 50

Student Edition pages 111–112

Mental Addition

LESSON PLANNER

Objective

▶ to teach students how to add problems mentally in the 0–10 range when one of the addends is 0, 1, or 2

Context of the Lesson Mental subtraction of 0, 1, or 2 will be introduced in Lesson 51.

 MANIPULATIVES **Program Resources**

interlocking cubes* (optional)

Number Cubes

Practice Master 50

Enrichment Master 50

For extra practice:
CD-ROM* Lesson 50

 # ❶ Warm-Up

Problem of the Day Present the following problem. Anna put her blocks in this order: a red block in front of two blue ones, a yellow one behind the two blue ones, and a green one between the two blue ones. What order were they in? (red, blue, green, blue, yellow)

Problem-Solving Strategies Ask students who have solved the Problem of the Day to share how they solved it and any strategies they used.

Have students use statue subtraction to solve the following problems before answering in unison.

a. 2 − 0 = (2)	b. 6 − 1 = (5)	c. 10 − 1 = (9)
d. 5 − 1 = (4)	e. 5 − 3 = (2)	f. 6 − 3 = (3)

❷ Teach

Demonstrate Review statue addition problems involving the addition of 0, 1, and 2. Then write an addition problem on the chalkboard that involves adding 1. Explain to students that they do not need to use fingers to add 1. They can just count up in their heads one number more. For example: 6 + 1 is 6 and 1 more, which is 7. Have students imagine finger sets as they practice solving similar examples mentally. Point out that if they always think of the greater number first, the problems are easier to solve.

111 Addition and Subtraction

LESSON 50

Name _____

Mental Addition

Solve these problems in your head. Then write the answers.

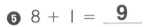

❶
5
+ 1
___
6

❷
2
+ 1
___
3

❸
5
+ 2
___
7

❹
6
+ 0
___
6

❺ 8 + 1 = **9**

❻ 4 + 2 = **6**

❼ 5 + 2 = **7**

❽ 4 + 1 = **5**

❾ 2 + 2 = **4**

❿ 1 + 2 = **3**

⓫ 3 + 2 = **5**

⓬ 3 + 1 = **4**

⓭ 8 + 2 = **10**

⓮ 7 + 2 = **9**

Copyright © SRA/McGraw-Hill

 NOTE TO HOME
Students solve addition problems in their heads.

Unit 2   Lesson 50 • **111**

 Literature Connection Read the counting book *The Balancing Act: A Counting Song,* illustrated by Merle Peek, so students can mentally count the number of elephants balanced on a circus high wire.

RETEACHING

 Have students practice counting up from different numbers. For example, say: "Count up two numbers from 4." Students should count: "4, 5, 6." Repeat with other examples by counting up zero, one, and two numbers.

Use **interlocking cubes,*** held first horizontally then vertically, to model horizontal and vertical addition.

*available separately

◆ **LESSON 50** Mental Addition

Do you have enough money?
Write yes or no.

This much money	Buy these things	Yes or no?
15	$3 $4	no
16	$3 $3	yes
17	$4 $4	no
18	$3 $2	yes
19	$2 $2	yes

Pick one problem. In your Math Journal tell how you knew if you had enough money.

112 • Addition and Subtraction

NOTE TO HOME
Students add and subtract with money.

Copyright © SRA/McGraw-Hill

PRACTICE p. 50

LESSON **50** PRACTICE   Name _____

Solve these problems in your head.
Then write the answers.

1	**2**	**3**	**4**
1 +1 2	3 +0 3	4 +1 5	6 +1 7

5	**6**	**7**	**8**
7 +0 7	2 +4 6	1 +2 3	0 +8 8

9 7 + 2 = __9__   **10** 0 + 6 = __6__

11 2 + 0 = __2__   **12** 2 + 2 = __4__

13 3 + 2 = __5__   **14** 1 + 7 = __8__

15 5 + 1 = __6__   **16** 8 + 1 = __9__

17 9 + 0 = __9__   **18** 3 + 1 = __4__

19 3 + 1 = __4__   **20** 5 + 2 = __7__

50 • Math Explorations and Applications Level 1

ENRICHMENT p. 50

LESSON **50** ENRICHMENT   Name _____

Annie forgot her phone number.

Her mother gave her some clues.

1. The first number is 2 more than 3.

2. The next number is 1 less than 6.

3. The next number is 4 more than 1.

4. The next number is 2 more than the first number.

5. The next number is 1 more than 1.

6. The next number is 2 less than 7.

7. The last number is 0 more than 6.

Write Annie's phone number.

5	5	5	–	7	2	5	6

50 • Math Explorations and Applications Level 1

GIFTED & TALENTED   **Meeting Individual Needs**
Have students work with a partner to make up simple addition word problems about animals. Present several models for them to follow. For example:

▶ Three puppies are in the front yard. Two are in the back yard. How many puppies are there all together?

▶ Four fish are in a bowl. One more is put into the bowl. How many fish are there now?

Have students write a problem on one side of an index card and the answer on the other. Have all of the class use the cards for extra practice whenever there is time.

Using the Number Cubes Write horizontal and vertical addition problems involving the addition of 0, 1, or 2 on the chalkboard. Have students use mental math to solve them and then show their answers with Number Cubes.

Using the Student Pages Do the first problem on each page together with the class. Remind students that they should not use finger sets to solve the problems. Have students complete the rest of the problems on their own. Then correct the problems together with the class.

❸ Wrap-Up

5 MINUTES

In Closing Have students explain how they would solve 5 + 2 mentally.

Performance Assessment As they work on pages 111 and 112, observe which students are able to add mentally to arrive at the correct answers.

Assessment Criteria

Did the student . . .

✓ correctly answer 20 of 25 problems on pages 111–112 using mental math?

✓ use mental math to correctly answer the problems during the Number Cube activity?

LESSON
51

Student Edition pages 113–114

Mental Subtraction

LESSON PLANNER

Objectives

✓ to assess students' ability to mentally solve subtraction problems in the 0–10 range when the subtrahend is 0, 1, or 2

▶ to provide practice in addition and subtraction using a calculator

Context of the Lesson Students practice solving subtraction problems without the use of finger sets, Number Strips, or any other aid using procedures similar to those introduced in Lesson 50 for mental addition. The use of calculators was introduced in Lesson 36. This lesson contains a Mastery Checkpoint for assessing proficiency in mental subtraction of 0, 1, or 2.

🖐 **MANIPULATIVES**

calculators*
can (optional)
coins* (optional)
counters* (optional)

Program Resources

Number Cubes
Practice Master 51
Enrichment Master 51
Assessment Master
For extra practice:
CD-ROM* Lesson 51

❶ Warm-Up

 Problem of the Day Present this problem orally. Rick had six pennies. He found one more on the way to school. He spent two pennies at the store. He gave one to his little sister. How many pennies does Rick have now? (4)

Problem-Solving Strategies Ask students who have solved the Problem of the Day to share how they solved it and any strategies they used.

MENTAL MATH Have students respond to the following problems with Number Cubes:

a. $2 - 1 = (1)$	b. $8 - 1 = (7)$
c. $7 - 0 = (7)$	d. $10 - 2 = (8)$
e. $9 - 2 = (7)$	f. $6 - 1 = (5)$
g. $3 - 1 = (2)$	h. $5 - 0 = (5)$
i. $4 - 2 = (2)$	j. $9 - 1 = (8)$

113 Addition and Subtraction

LESSON
51

Name _____

Mental Subtraction

Can you solve these problems in your head? Write the answers.

❶ $7 + 2 = \underline{9}$ ❷ $7 - 1 = \underline{6}$

❸ $4 - 1 = \underline{3}$ ❹ $4 - 2 = \underline{2}$

❺ $2 + 2 = \underline{4}$ ❻ $2 + 4 = \underline{6}$

❼ $\begin{array}{r} 9 \\ -1 \\ \hline 8 \end{array}$ ❽ $\begin{array}{r} 9 \\ -0 \\ \hline 9 \end{array}$ ❾ $\begin{array}{r} 8 \\ +1 \\ \hline 9 \end{array}$ ❿ $\begin{array}{r} 7 \\ -2 \\ \hline 5 \end{array}$

⓫ $\begin{array}{r} 6 \\ -2 \\ \hline 4 \end{array}$ ⓬ $\begin{array}{r} 8 \\ -2 \\ \hline 6 \end{array}$ ⓭ $\begin{array}{r} 7 \\ -0 \\ \hline 7 \end{array}$ ⓮ $\begin{array}{r} 5 \\ -2 \\ \hline 3 \end{array}$

 NOTE TO HOME
Students add and subtract problems to 10.

Unit 2   Lesson 51 • **113**

RETEACHING

🖐 **MANIPULATIVES** Students who have trouble with mental addition and subtraction may need more practice in counting up or down from given numbers. Say, for example, "Count down from 6." When the student says, "5, 4, 3," stop the student and ask him or her to "Count up from 3" until the student reaches 6. You might also present hidden-counter problems, using **counters*** in the **can** or **coins*** under a book, removing or adding only one or two counters.

PRACTICE p. 51

LESSON 51 PRACTICE   Name _____

Can you solve these problems in your head? Write the answers.

❶ $\begin{array}{r} 7 \\ -2 \\ \hline 5 \end{array}$ ❷ $\begin{array}{r} 5 \\ -1 \\ \hline 4 \end{array}$ ❸ $\begin{array}{r} 4 \\ -0 \\ \hline 4 \end{array}$ ❹ $\begin{array}{r} 3 \\ -2 \\ \hline 1 \end{array}$

❺ $\begin{array}{r} 2 \\ -2 \\ \hline 0 \end{array}$ ❻ $\begin{array}{r} 6 \\ -0 \\ \hline 6 \end{array}$ ❼ $\begin{array}{r} 6 \\ -1 \\ \hline 5 \end{array}$ ❽ $\begin{array}{r} 8 \\ -1 \\ \hline 7 \end{array}$

❾ $9 - 2 = \underline{7}$ ❿ $0 - 0 = \underline{0}$

⓫ $9 - 0 = \underline{9}$ ⓬ $2 - 1 = \underline{1}$

⓭ $4 - 2 = \underline{2}$ ⓮ $3 - 1 = \underline{2}$

⓯ $2 - 0 = \underline{2}$ ⓰ $6 - 2 = \underline{4}$

⓱ $9 - 1 = \underline{8}$ ⓲ $7 - 1 = \underline{6}$

⓳ $8 - 2 = \underline{6}$ ⓴ $5 - 2 = \underline{3}$

Math Explorations and Applications Level 1 • **51**

◆ **LESSON 51** Mental Subtraction

First write your answer. Then use your calculator to find its answer.

⑮ (5) (+) (2) (=)

| 7 . | My answer |

| 7 . | Calculator answer |

⑯ (6) (–) (1) (=)

| 5 . | My answer |

| 5 . | Calculator answer |

⑰ (7) (–) (2) (=)

| 5 . | My answer |

| 5 . | Calculator answer |

114 • Addition and Subtraction

 NOTE TO HOME
Students use a calculator to compare answers.

---

② Teach

 Demonstrate Challenge students to solve subtraction problems without using their fingers. Have them form their hands into fists and imagine finger movements. Present problems involving the subtraction of 0, 1, or 2. Have students respond with Number Cubes.

Using the Student Pages Have students do the problems on page 113. Then review with students how to add and subtract 0, 1, or 2 using the **calculator**.* Have students perform successive additions or subtractions, such as: $4 + 2 + 2 + 2 = 10$. On page 114, students should first solve the problems mentally, then use a calculator to find the answer.

③ Wrap-Up

In Closing Invite students to suggest times when using a calculator would be faster or easier than mental math. Discuss their reasoning.

Mastery Checkpoint 10

Most students should now be able to add or subtract 0, 1, or 2 mentally when the sums or minuends are 10 or less. Use student performance during the lesson, or the Assessment Blackline Master page 19, to assess mastery. Record results on the Mastery Checkpoint Chart.

ENRICHMENT p. 51

LESSON **51** ENRICHMENT Name _____

All these children have the same birthday. They are not the same age.

❶ How old was Bin two years ago? _5 years old_

❷ How old was Clair last year? _7 years old_

❸ How many years have passed since Paul was 2? _4_

❹ How old was Paul when Rhea was born? _1 year old_

❺ How old was Clair when Bin was born? _1 year old_

Bin is 7 · Paul is 6 · Rhea is 5 · Clair is 8

Math Explorations and Applications Level 1 • 51

ASSESSMENT p. 19

UNIT **2** **Mastery Checkpoint 10** Mental addition and subtraction of 0, 1, or 2 (Lesson 51)
Name _____

The student demonstrates mastery by correctly answering 12 of the 15 problems.

Can you solve these problems in your head? Write the answers.

❶ $6 - 2 =$ _4_   ❷ $6 + 1 =$ _7_

❸ $5 + 1 =$ _6_   ❹ $7 - 2 =$ _5_

❺ $2 + 5 =$ _7_   ❻ $9 - 1 =$ _8_

❼ $8 + 2 =$ _10_

Solve these problems.

❽ $\begin{array}{r} 8 \\ -1 \\ \hline 7 \end{array}$ ❾ $\begin{array}{r} 2 \\ +2 \\ \hline 4 \end{array}$ ❿ $\begin{array}{r} 2 \\ +7 \\ \hline 9 \end{array}$ ⓫ $\begin{array}{r} 4 \\ -2 \\ \hline 2 \end{array}$

⓬ $\begin{array}{r} 6 \\ -1 \\ \hline 5 \end{array}$ ⓭ $\begin{array}{r} 8 \\ -0 \\ \hline 8 \end{array}$ ⓮ $\begin{array}{r} 7 \\ +1 \\ \hline 8 \end{array}$ ⓯ $\begin{array}{r} 8 \\ +2 \\ \hline 10 \end{array}$

Math Explorations and Applications Level 1 • 19

Assessment Criteria

Did the student . . .

✓ demonstrate mastery of mental subtraction of 0, 1, and 2?

✓ use a calculator to solve the problems on page 114?

LOOKING AHEAD You will need a very large cardboard box for the next lesson.

*available separately

LESSON 52 Functions

Student Edition pages 115–116

LESSON PLANNER

Objectives

▶ to provide practice finding patterns using a function machine

▶ to provide opportunities to practice addition and subtraction facts using a function machine

Context of the Lesson This lesson introduces function machines and continues practice involving addition and subtraction concepts.

MANIPULATIVES **Program Resources**

large cardboard box

Thinking Story Book, pages 42–45

Practice Master 52

Enrichment Master 52

For career connections:
Careers and Math*

For extra practice:
CD-ROM* Lesson 52

❶ Warm-Up

Problem of the Day Read aloud as you write the following numbers on the chalkboard: 10, 8, 6, □, 2. What number comes next in the pattern and why? (4, because you are counting backwards by twos)

Problem-Solving Strategies Ask students who have solved the Problem of the Day to share how they solved it and any strategies they used.

MENTAL MATH Have students add the following problems mentally:

a. 5 + 2 = (7)   b. 6 + 1 = (7)

c. 4 + 0 = (4)   d. 6 + 2 = (8)

e. 9 + 1 = (10)   f. 7 + 1 = (8)

❷ Teach

Demonstrate Write the following pair of numbers on the chalkboard: 4, 3. Ask students what they would have to do to get from the first number to the second. (–1) Repeat with similar examples.

115 Addition and Subtraction

LESSON 52

Name _____

Functions

What is the number machine doing? Fill in the missing numbers.

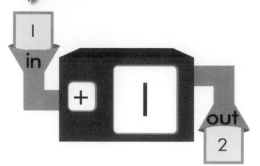

❶

In	Out
1	2
4	5
6	7
3	4

❷

In	Out
4	6
3	5
2	**4**
0	2

❸

In	Out
6	4
7	5
3	**1**
2	0

THINKING STORY

Talk about the Thinking Story "Manolita's Amazing Number Machine."

NOTE TO HOME Students solve addition and subtraction function problems.

Unit 2   Lesson 52 • **115**

Art Connection Have students design and decorate the cardboard box you used for the Amazing Number Machine. Have small groups of students take turns designing different sections of the box.

RETEACHING

Teach students that they can figure out rules by asking sensible questions. Discuss the first chart on page 115. Have students ask themselves:

Is 1 greater or less than 2? (less)

Do I add or subtract to go from 1 to 2? (add)

How much do I add to go from 1 to 2? (1)

Can I follow the same rule to go from 4 to 5? 6 to 7? and so on? (yes)

*available separately

◆ **LESSON 52** Functions

ALGEBRA READINESS

Tell the rule.

4

In	Out
3	5
4	6
5	7
6	8
7	9

Rule **+2**

5

In	Out
5	3
6	4
7	5
8	6
9	7

Rule **−2**

6

In	Out
7	8
6	7
3	4
2	3
1	2

Rule **+1**

7

In	Out
8	7
7	6
5	4
3	2
1	0

Rule **−1**

8

In	Out
5	5
4	4
3	3
6	6
7	7

Rule **+0**
or **−0**

9

In	Out
3	6
4	7
2	5
6	9
7	10

Rule **+3**

116 • Addition and Subtraction

NOTE TO HOME
Students solve addition and subtraction function problems.

Introducing the "Amazing Number Machine" Activity

MANIPULATIVES

To teach the concept of a function machine, have a volunteer go inside a **large cardboard box** to be the "Amazing Number Machine." Have other students write numbers on slips of paper and put them into the machine one at a time. The volunteer inside crosses out the number and writes a new number beneath it, according to a prearranged rule you have chosen (either + 0, + 1, or + 2). On the chalkboard write a table like the ones on page 116. Record the numbers that go in and come out of the Amazing Number Machine. Have students try to figure out the function rule and predict what number the Amazing Number Machine will give back.

Using the Student Pages Explain that the charts on pages 115–116 are the records of what the Amazing Number Machine has done. Help students find the rule to the first chart on page 115 and have them fill in the missing number. Then have them work in pairs to complete the remaining problems.

Using the Thinking Story Read aloud and then discuss "Manolita's Amazing Number Machine" on pages 42–45 of the Thinking Story Book or pages 116a–116d of this Guide.

❸ Wrap-Up

In Closing Have students explain the rule for problem 9 on page 116. Students should see that the rule could have been +0 or −0 and that different rules can sometimes produce the same results.

ANALYZING ANSWERS

Students who are not correctly solving the function machine problems should be checked to see if their difficulties are with the addition and subtraction facts or with the concept of function machines.

PRACTICE p. 52

Fill in the missing numbers. Tell the rule.

1

In	Out
1	3
2	4
3	5
4	6
5	7

Rule **+2**

2

In	Out
2	5
4	7
5	8
6	9
0	3

Rule **+3**

3

In	Out
4	1
8	5
7	4
9	6
6	3

Rule **−3**

4

In	Out
3	4
2	3
0	1
5	6
4	5

Rule **+1**

52 • *Math Explorations and Applications Level 1*

ENRICHMENT p. 52

Roll a 0–5 Number Cube. Move down the path that number of spaces. Then follow the math direction on the space where you land. Keep following the math directions until you get to the playground.

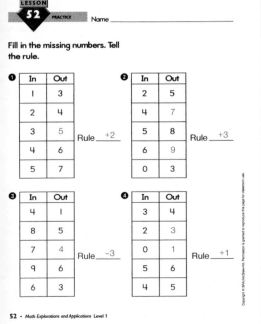

52 • *Math Explorations and Applications Level 1*

Assessment Criteria

Did the student . . .

✓ correctly answer 80% of the problems on pages 115–116?

✓ correctly predict incoming or outgoing numbers for the class's Amazing Number Machine?

Manolita's Amazing Number Machine

❶ Another night Manolita dreamed about a money-changing machine. If you put in a dime, it gave back 11 pennies. If you put in a quarter, it gave back 26 pennies. **How many pennies would it give back if you put in a nickel?** six

❷ Manolita put ten potatoes into a different kind of change machine. She got back eight potatoes. She put in five books and got back three.
What was the machine doing? subtracting two

❸ Willy had six marbles. He lost half of them.
How many marbles did he lose? three

❹ Ferdie had one dollar. He bought two bagels.
How much money did he have left? can't tell
What do you need to know before you can tell? the cost of a bagel

❺ "That tree is two years older than I am," said Mr. Burns, "and I am 40 years old."
How old is the tree? 42

❻ Portia lives on the second floor of an apartment building. Her friend Janet lives on the fourth floor.
How many floors up does Portia have to go to visit Janet? two
How many floors up does Janet have to go to visit Portia? She doesn't go up; she goes down two floors.

THINKING STORY

Manolita's Amazing Number Machine

Ever since Manolita saw the super-computer her mother works with, she often dreams about amazing machines. One night in a dream she came upon a big machine with an opening on the top and a door at the bottom. Manolita had no idea what kind of machine it was, but she thought she might find out by putting some money in it. She put a penny into the top of the machine. The machine went "Glinka-Glinka" and out popped three pennies at the bottom.

Then Manolita put in a pencil. The machine went "Glinka-Glinka" again and out popped three pencils! "This is great!" chirped Manolita. "I wonder what will happen if I put in three pencils."

What do you think will happen? Offer praise to students who say five (+2) or nine (×3) pencils will come out.

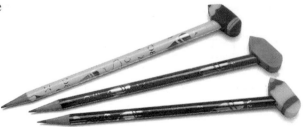

42 • Manolita's Amazing Number Machine

Manolita dropped in the three pencils. The machine went "Glinka-Glinka" and out came five pencils. Manolita had thought there might be a few more than that, but she was happy to have five pencils anyway. "I have a great idea!" she said. "I'll put all my money into the machine, and maybe it will give me back so much money that I'll be rich."

She opened her piggy bank and took out all her money. There were 30 pennies. Eagerly she put all 30 pennies into the top of the machine.

How many pennies do you think she will get back? 32

Would it have been better for Manolita to put in the pennies one at a time? yes

Story 7 • **43**

❼ Willy had a frog that could jump very high. One day it was hopping across the lawn. Suddenly it jumped 2 feet straight up. Then it fell back down to the lawn.
How far did it fall? 2 feet

❽ Marcus invited five boys to his party. They all came.
How many boys were at the party all together? six

❾ Ferdie is usually 4 inches taller than Portia, but now Portia is standing on a box that is 4 inches high. They are both standing against the wall.
Who comes up higher on the wall-Ferdie or Portia? Neither, they are the same.
How do you know? If Ferdie is taller than Portia by 4 inches, but she is standing on a box that is 4 inches high, then they are the same height.

❿ Ms. Eng counted 22 roses on her rose bush in the morning. In the afternoon, there were 18.
What could have happened? Some fell off; some were picked.

⓫ Mrs. Mudancia had a mirror with four lightbulbs on one side and four on the other. One day Mr. Mudancia changed it a little. He took out two of the lightbulbs.
How many lightbulbs does it have now? six

◆ **STORY 7** **Manolita's Amazing Number Machine**

The machine went "Glinka-Glinka" and out came 32 pennies. Manolita thought the machine might have made a mistake. She put the 32 pennies in, the machine went you-know-what again, and out came 34 pennies. Manolita tried it once more. She put in the 34 pennies, and this time the machine gave back 36 pennies. "I think I have it figured out," said Manolita as she put in the 36 pennies.

How many pennies will she get back this time? 38

The machine went "Glinka-Glinka" and out came a heap of pennies. Manolita counted them. "Just as I thought," she said. "When I put in 36 pennies, the machine gave me back 38. Every time I put some things into the machine I get more."

How many more? two

44 • Manolita's Amazing Number Machine

"I always get two more than I put in," said Manolita. "So, if I put my two turtles into the machine . . .

What will happen? She'll get four turtles.

Manolita did it; and, sure enough, the machine gave back four turtles. Then Manolita took five of her mother's silver spoons and put them into the machine.

How many silver spoons will she get back? seven

The machine gave back seven silver spoons, two more than Manolita had put in. Then Manolita had a wild idea: "What if I climb into the machine myself?"

What do you think will happen? Perhaps two more Manolitas will come out.

We'll never know for sure because Manolita woke up just as she was starting to climb into the Amazing Number Machine.

. . . the end

Story 7 • **45**

LESSON 53

Student Edition pages 117–118

Mental Math

LESSON PLANNER

Objectives

▶ to teach students to add mentally when one of the addends is 3

▶ to teach students to subtract mentally when the subtrahend is 3

Context of the Lesson This lesson extends the range of mental math to include addition and subtraction of 0, 1, 2, and 3.

 MANIPULATIVES

chalkboard or desk number line

Program Resources

Number Cubes

Thinking Story Book, pages 46–47

Reteaching Master

Practice Master 53

Enrichment Master 53

For extra practice:
CD-ROM* Lesson 53

① Warm-Up ⏱ 5 MINUTES

Problem of the Day Present the following problem to the class: How many phone calls must be made if Meg, Betty, and Carl all want to talk to each other at least once? (3)

Problem-Solving Strategies Ask students who have solved the Problem of the Day to share how they solved it and any strategies they used.

 MENTAL MATH Have students add the following problems mentally, then show their answers with Number Cubes.

a. 3 + 2 = (5)   b. 4 + 1 = (5)

c. 7 + 2 = (9)   d. 10 + 0 = (10)

e. 8 + 2 = (10)   f. 5 + 1 = (6)

117 Addition and Subtraction

LESSON 53

Name _____

Mental Math

0 1 2 3 4 5 6 7 8 9 10

Try to solve these problems in your head. Use the number line if you need to.

❶ 1 + 3 = __4__   ❷ 0 + 5 = __5__

❸ 2 + 1 = __3__   ❹ 9 − 1 = __8__

❺ 3 − 0 = __3__   ❻ 4 + 3 = __7__

❼ 3 + 0 = __3__   ❽ 8 − 3 = __5__

❾ 5 + 2 = __7__   ❿ 7 + 1 = __8__

⓫ 6 − 1 = __5__   ⓬ 9 − 3 = __6__

⓭ 7 − 3 = __4__   ⓮ 6 − 2 = __4__

🎒 **NOTE TO HOME**
Students use mental math to solve addition and subtraction problems.

Unit 2   Lesson 53 • **117**

Why teach it this way?

Allowing students to look at but not finger-step along a number line gives them help in doing mental addition and subtraction, without relying on concrete objects.

> *. . . in the early grades, we should try to teach so that most children will become very efficient at simple operations and can spend their time and thought on more advanced ideas.*
>
> —Stephen S. Willoughby,
> *Mathematics Education for a Changing World*

RETEACHING p. 13

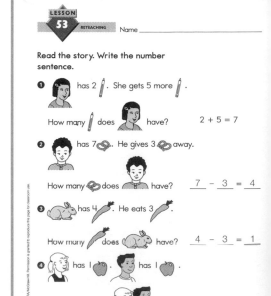

LESSON 53 RETEACHING   Name _____

Read the story. Write the number sentence.

❶ ___ has 2 ✏. She gets 5 more ✏.

How many ✏ does ___ have?   2 + 5 = 7

❷ ___ has 7 🥕. He gives 3 🥕 away.

How many 🥕 does ___ have?   7 − 3 = 4

❸ ___ has 4 🥕. He eats 3 🥕.

How many 🥕 does ___ have?   4 − 3 = 1

❹ ___ has 1 🍎 ___ has 1 🍎.

How many 🍎 do ___ have?   1 + 1 = 2

Math Explorations and Applications Level 1 • **13**

*available separately

PROBLEM SOLVING

◆ **LESSON 53** Mentol Moth

Listen to the problems. Try to solve them in your head.

⑮ Courtney has five sports cards. If she gets three more, how many will she have?   **8**

⑯ Paige needs $8. She has $4. How much more does she need? $ **4**

⑰ Crystal has two cans of red paint and one can of white paint. If she mixes them together, how much paint will she have?   **3**

What color will it be?   **pink**

⑱ Ms. Beck walked 3 miles from her home to the library. Later she walked back. How many miles did she walk?   **6** miles

118 • Addition and Subtraction

 NOTE TO HOME
Students solve word problems.

Copyright © SRA/McGraw-Hill

❷ Teach

Demonstrate Review mental addition and subtraction of 0, 1, and 2. Then give examples involving addition and subtraction of 3. Allow students to use a desk or chalkboard **number line** to help them. However, encourage them only to look at the number line without actually doing the finger stepping.

Using the Number Cubes Continue giving examples as in the demonstration. Have students mentally solve problems with addition and subtraction of 3 and show their answers with Number Cubes.

Using the Student Pages Have students complete page 117 on their own. Then read the stories on page 118 aloud, stopping to allow students to solve the problems.

Using the Thinking Story Present two new problems from among those following "Manolita's Amazing Number Machine" on pages 46–47 of the Thinking Story Book or pages 116a–116b in this Guide.

❸ Wrap-Up

In Closing Have students explain how they would use mental math to solve 6 + 3 and 7 – 3.

Performance Assessment Have students solve a series of ten problems like those in Mental Math to assess their knowledge of the facts.

Assessment Criteria

Did the student . . .

✓ use mental math to correctly answer 14 of 18 problems on pages 117–118?

✓ use mental math to find the correct answers in the Number Cube activity?

PRACTICE p. 53

LESSON **53** PRACTICE Name _____

Try to solve these problems in your head. Watch the signs. Then write the answers.

❶ 6 +2 = **8** ❷ 8 –1 = **7** ❸ 8 +1 = **9** ❹ 5 –2 = **3**

❺ 7 –1 = **6** ❻ 4 –0 = **4** ❼ 5 +0 = **5** ❽ 4 –2 = **2**

❾ 5 – 1 = **4**   ❿ 4 + 2 = **6**
⓫ 4 + 1 = **5**   ⓬ 3 + 1 = **4**
⓭ 3 – 1 = **2**   ⓮ 6 – 0 = **6**
⓯ 3 + 2 = **5**   ⓰ 7 – 2 = **5**
⓱ 9 – 2 = **7**   ⓲ 8 – 2 = **6**

Math Explorations and Applications Level 1 • 53

ENRICHMENT p. 53

LESSON **53** ENRICHMENT Name _____

Raoul and Marna made a piñata. Help them color it. Solve each problem to crack the code.

Code		
4 = red	6 = blue	7 = orange
2 = yellow	5 = black	8 = white

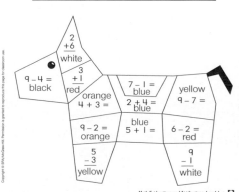

Math Explorations and Applications Level 1 • 53

Unit 2 Lesson 53 **118**

EXPANDED COUNTING

WHAT IS EXPANDED COUNTING?

Expanded counting is a practical solution to the traditional problem of teaching place value. Once students begin working with numbers above 10, they often have difficulty understanding the significance of the ones position and the tens position. As students encounter addition and subtraction with regrouping, a knowledge of place value becomes even more important. Teaching expanded counting from the beginning helps students understand the true value of a number. They recognize that the number 57, for example, is really five tens and seven. Below are some examples of oral and written forms of expanded counting that your students will be using:

Instead of counting . . . "nineteen, twenty, twenty-one, twenty-two"

Expand the counting to . . . "ten and nine, two tens, two tens and one, two tens and two"

Instead of writing . . . 19, 20, 21, 22

Make the digits in the tens place larger than the digits in the units place . . . 19, 20, 21, 22

WHY USE EXPANDED COUNTING?

1. It helps students understand the decimal structure of our number system.
   - The expanded oral form (ten and one, ten and two, and so on) helps show the relationship between 1 and 11, between 2 and 12, and so on.
   - The expanded written form (19, 20, 21, 22) helps show the difference between the role of 1 in 19 and in 91.

2. It helps students understand addition and subtraction.
   - Once place value is mastered, students better understand the concept of renaming and regrouping. Adding 57 and 4, for example, becomes almost as easy as adding 7 and 4.

Toward the end of the school year (in Lesson 141), your students will change over to the conventional way of writing and saying numbers. This transition is usually quite smooth.

LESSON 54

Counting from 10–20

Student Edition pages 119–120

LESSON PLANNER

Objectives

▶ to provide practice in counting from 10–20 in expanded form

▶ to introduce the 0–5 tens Number Cube

Context of the Lesson This lesson extends the numbers students work with to 20, teaching the numbers in expanded form. Students will make the transition to conventional ways of counting, reading, and writing numbers in Lesson 142.

 MANIPULATIVES

Program Resources

Number Cubes

Thinking Story Book, pages 46–47

Practice Master 54

Enrichment Master 54

For extra practice:
CD-ROM* Lesson 54
Mixed practice, page 360

❶ Warm-Up ⏱ 5 MINUTES

 Problem of the Day Present the following problem to the class. Kayla has seven marbles. She wants to share them with Kim. How many ways can she break them into two groups? (3 ways: 1 + 6, 2 + 5, 3 + 4)

Problem-Solving Strategies Ask students who have solved the Problem of the Day to share how they solved it and any strategies they used.

MENTAL MATH Ask students to answer the following problems using finger sets:

a. 10 + 0 = (10)   **b.** 8 + 2 = (10)

c. 6 + 4 = (10)   **d.** 7 + 3 = (10)

e. 9 + 1 = (10)   **f.** 5 + 5 = (10)

g. 4 + 6 = (10)   **h.** 1 + 9 = (10)

i. 2 + 8 = (10)   **j.** 3 + 7 = (10)

LESSON 54

Name _____

Counting from 10–20

 Use your Number Cubes.
Find. Hide. Show.

Count and show.

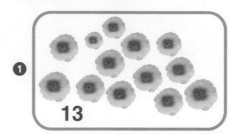
❶ 13

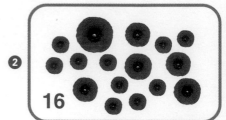
❷ 16

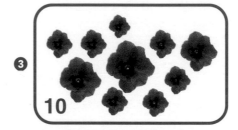
❸ 10

❹ 12

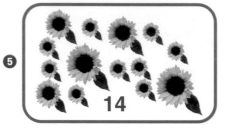
❺ 14

❻ 20

Copyright © SRA/McGraw-Hill

🎒 **NOTE TO HOME**
Students extend the range of numbers they work with to 20.

Unit 2   Lesson 54 • **119**

Why teach it this way?

The expanded form of counting helps students understand the decimal structure. It shows the relationship, for example, between 5 and 15 and 6 and 16. In expanded form the number 15 is pronounced "ten and five." Ten and five is written as 15, with the tens digit enlarged. The use of different-sized digits stresses that the number 1 plays a different role in 15 than it does in 1.

RETEACHING

COOPERATIVE LEARNING Have students who are having difficulty counting in expanded form practice with a partner who has mastered this skill.

*available separately

◆ **LESSON 54** Counting from 10–20

Use the Mixed Practice on page 360 after this lesson.

Count and show.

❼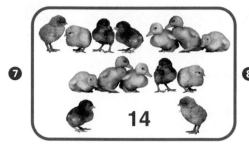
14

❽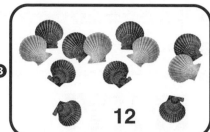
12

❾
19

❿
11

⓫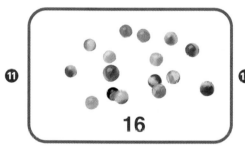
16

⓬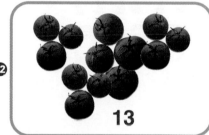
13

120 • Addition and Subtraction

 NOTE TO HOME
Students count objects to 20 and show
the number with Number Cubes.

Copyright © SRA/McGraw-Hill

---

② Teach

Demonstrate Draw figures on the chalkboard as you count aloud to 20. Then tell students that they are going to learn a special way of counting to 20 that will help them do addition and subtraction with greater numbers. Write each number in expanded form as you count the figures in expanded form ("ten and one," "ten and two," and so on). Then have the students count to 20 in unison. Note that 20 is said as "two tens."

 Using the Number Cubes Introduce the larger yellow 0–5 tens Number Cube. Show students how to hold a tens Number Cube together with a unit cube to form the numbers 10–20. Have students show the number with cubes as you call out numbers from 10–20.

Using the Student Pages Complete pages 119 and 120 as a class. Have students use their Number Cubes to "Find, Hide, and Show" their answers to the counting exercises.

Using the Thinking Story Present two problems from those following "Manolita's Amazing Number Machine" on pages 46–47 of the Thinking Story Book or pages 116a–116b of this Guide.

③ Wrap-Up ⏱ 5 MINUTES

In Closing Have students count numbers from 10–20, in unison, using expanded form.

Portfolio Assessment Have students draw sets of 10–20 objects to keep in their Math Portfolios.

Assessment Criteria

Did the student . . .

✓ use both units and tens Number Cubes to form numbers 10–20?

✓ correctly count from 10–20 using expanded form?

PRACTICE p. 54

LESSON 54 PRACTICE Name _____

Draw lines to match sets with the same number.

ENRICHMENT p. 54

LESSON 54 ENRICHMENT Name _____

❶ Color the cars red. Write how many. _____ 16

❷ Color the bikes blue. Write how many. _____ 8

❸ Color the boards on the fence brown. Write how many. _____ 18

❹ Color the trees green. Write how many. _____ 9

❺ Color the trash cans black. Write how many. _____ 7

54 • Math Explorations and Applications Level 1

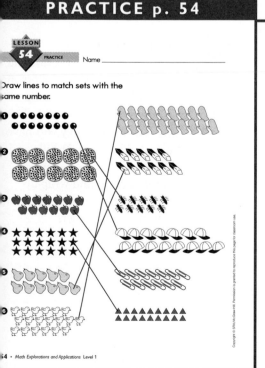

LESSON 55

Student Edition pages 121–122

Writing Numbers to 20

LESSON PLANNER

Objectives

▶ to provide practice counting groups of 10 to 20 objects

▶ to provide practice writing the numerals for numbers between 10 and 20

Context of the Lesson Recognizing groups of ten is introduced in this lesson and is a follow-up to the expanded counting learned in Lesson 54.

 MANIPULATIVES

craft sticks

play money*
(optional)

rubber bands

Program Resources

Thinking Story Book, pages 46–47

Practice Master 55

Enrichment Master 55

For extra practice:
CD-ROM* Lesson 55

➊ Warm-Up

 Problem of the Day Present the following problem to the class. Kenya has eight superhero figures. She will arrange them on two shelves. How many should she put on each shelf? Name all the different ways. (8 and 0; 7 and 1; 6 and 2; 5 and 3; 4 and 4; 3 and 5; 2 and 6; 1 and 7; or 0 and 8)

Problem-Solving Strategies Ask students who have solved the Problem of the Day to share how they solved it and any strategies they used.

MENTAL MATH Have students solve the following problems mentally:

a. $4 - 1 = (3)$ b. $2 + 1 = (3)$

c. $6 + 0 = (6)$ d. $5 - 2 = (3)$

e. $9 + 1 = (10)$ f. $10 - 3 = (7)$

LESSON 55

Name _____

Writing Numbers to 20

Count. Then write the number.

➊ ✿✿✿✿✿✿✿✿✿✿ ✿✿✿✿✿✿✿✿✿✿   **20**

➋ ★★★★★★★★★★ ★★★★★★★★★   **19**

➌ ♥♥♥♥♥♥♥♥♥♥ ♥♥♥♥♥♥♥♥   **18**

➍   **17**

➎   **16**

➏   **15**

➐   **14**

➑   **13**

➒   **12**

➓   **11**

 NOTE TO HOME Students count and write numbers to 20.

 Technology Connection For practice with number sets and numerals to 20 and addition and subtraction to 10, use the software *Mathosaurus* from Micrograms (Mac, IBM).

RETEACHING

MANIPULATIVES Use **play money*** to demonstrate how to count and write amounts and numbers from 11 to 20. Rather than displaying two bunches of ten, show two $10 bills. Ask students how much money you have. Then trade a $10 bill for ten $1 bills and take away a $1 (for 19). Proceed as you did in the demonstration and wrap-up activity, having volunteers count different amounts and write the numbers.

*available separately

◆ LESSON 55 Writing Numbers to 20

Write how many.

 **11** ⬜ 5

 **12** ⬜ 15

 **13** ⬜ 10

 **14** ⬜ 20

 **15** ⬜ 19

 **16** ⬜ 9

 **17** ⬜ 14

122 • Addition and Subtraction

NOTE TO HOME
Students count objects up to 20 and
write how many.

Copyright © SRA/McGraw-Hill

---

②Teach

Demonstrate Display two bunches of ten **craft sticks** wrapped with a **rubber band** and ask students how many they think are in each bunch. Count to confirm answers. (10) Explain that two tens can also be called 20. Demonstrate how to write the number 20 on the chalkboard in expanded form. (20) Next unwrap one bunch of ten sticks and remove one stick. Explain that you now have one ten and nine left. Ask how this number would be read and written. (one ten and nine; 19) Continue removing one stick at a time and having volunteers explain how to say and write each number for the remaining amount.

Using the Student Pages Have students complete pages 121–122 independently.

Using the Thinking Story Present two new problems from among those following "Manolita's Amazing Number Machine" on pages 46–47 of the Thinking Story Book or pages 116a–116b of this Guide.

③Wrap-Up

In Closing Display one bunch of ten sticks and one extra stick. Ask students how many sticks you have and how to write the number. one ten and one; 11) Repeat with several similar examples.

Performance Assessment Call out numbers from 10–20. Have students say and write the numbers in expanded notation.

Assessment Criteria

Did the student . . .

✓ participate in the Thinking Story and closing activities?

✓ correctly answer 14 of 17 problems on pages 121–122?

PRACTICE p. 55

LESSON **55** PRACTICE   Name _____

Write how many.

❶ ⬜ 11

❷ ⬜ 14

❸ ⬜ 16

❹ ⬜ 12

❺ ⬜ 10

❻ ⬜ 17

❼ ⬜ 13

❽ ★★★★★★★★★★★★★★★ ⬜ 15

Math Explorations and Applications Level 1 • **55**

ENRICHMENT p. 55

LESSON **55** ENRICHMENT   Name _____

Color the right amount of things to match each number.

❶ 12

❷ 17

❸ 20

❹ 14

On a sheet of paper, draw 18 leaves. Then color them any way you like.

Math Explorations and Applications Level 1 • **55**

LESSON 56

Expanded Numbers

Student Edition pages 123–124

Name _____

Expanded Numbers

How many?

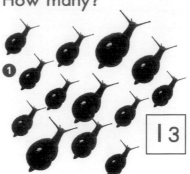

❶ 13

❷ 11

❸ 15

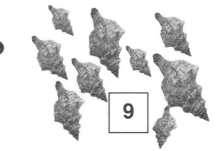

❹ 9

❺ 6

❻ 12

LESSON PLANNER

Objectives

▶ to teach students to read and write numbers 10–20 using expanded notation

✓ to assess student proficiency in reading, writing and counting numbers 10–20 in expanded form

Context of the Lesson In Lesson 54, students learned to count through 20 in expanded form. In this lesson, students read and write numbers in their expanded form. The lesson contains a Mastery Checkpoint to assess student proficiency in these skills.

 MANIPULATIVES

counters*
(optional)

paper (double-lined)

Program Resources

Number Cubes

Number Strips

Thinking Story Book, pages 46–47

Practice Master 56

Enrichment Master 56

Assessment Master

For extra practice:
CD-ROM* Lesson 56

Copyright © SRA/McGraw-Hill

NOTE TO HOME
Students count and write to 20.

Unit 2   Lesson 56 • **123**

---

❶ Warm-Up ⏱ 5 MINUTES

 Problem of the Day Present the following riddle to the class: I am more than 12. I am less than 16. What number could I be? (13, 14, or 15)

Problem-Solving Strategies Ask students who have solved the Problem of the Day to share how they solved it and any strategies they used.

 MENTAL MATH Write each number in expanded form on the chalkboard. Have students show each number with Number Cubes as they say the numbers in expanded form.

a.	11	
c.	13	
e.	15	
g.	20	

b.	14
d.	16
f.	19
h.	12

123 Addition and Subtraction

RETEACHING

 MANIPULATIVES Students who are having difficulty with number concepts often benefit from practicing with concrete materials. Have students write the numbers 1–20 on a large piece of paper. Tell them to count aloud, using expanded form where appropriate, as they place **counters*** above each number.

PRACTICE p. 56

LESSON 56 PRACTICE

Name _____

| 11 | 12 | 13 | 14 | 15 | 16 | 17 | 18 | 19 | 20 |

Trace and write the numbers.

❶ 12 12 12
❷ 13 13 13
❸ 14 14 14
❹ 15 15 15
❺ 16 16 16
❻ 17 17 17
❼ 18 18 18
❽ 19 19 19
❾ 20 20 20

56 • Math Explorations and Applications Level 1

*available separately

◆ **LESSON 56** **Expanded Numbers**

How many?

7 10

8 17

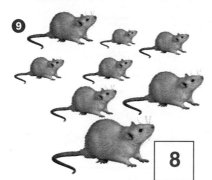

9 8

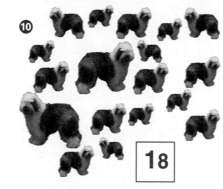

10 18

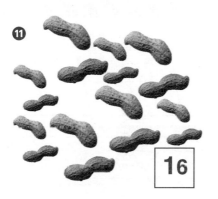

11 16

12 19

124 • Addition and Subtraction

 NOTE TO HOME Students count and write to 20.

Copyright © SRA/McGraw-Hill

---

② Teach

Demonstrate Show students how to use the expanded form notation for the numbers 10–20 by writing each number on the chalkboard. Have students count in unison using expanded form, for example, "ten and one." Then call out different numbers from 10–20 and have students write them on double-lined **paper** in this style.

| 0

Using the Student Pages Students can complete pages 123–124 independently.

Using the Thinking Story Present three problems from those following "Manolita's Amazing Number Machine" on pages 46–47 of the Thinking Story Book or pages 116a–116b of this Guide.

③ Wrap-Up ⏱ 5 MINUTES

In Closing Summarize the lesson by holding up a 10-strip and a 4-strip. Explain that this is another way of showing the number 14. Challenge each student to use his or her Number Strips to represent a number from 10–20.

✓ Mastery Checkpoint 11

Most students should be able to read, write, and count the numbers through 20 in expanded form. Proficiency may be assessed by evaluating student performance on pages 123–124 or by using Assessment Blackline Masters pages 20–21. Record assessment results on the Mastery Checkpoint Chart.

ENRICHMENT p. 56

❶ How many nests?	10
❷ How many hens?	13
❸ How many eggs?	17
❹ Are there more hens or eggs?	eggs
❺ Are there more nests or hens?	hens
❻ Are there more nests or eggs?	eggs

56 • Math Explorations and Applications Level 1

ASSESSMENT p. 20

UNIT 2 **Mastery Checkpoint 11** Writing numbers (10–20) (Lesson 56)
Page 1 of 2
Name _____
The student demonstrates mastery by correctly answering 8 of the 10 problems.

How many?

❶ 14
❷ 8
❸ 12
❹ 15
❺ 11

Go on . . . ▶

20 • Math Explorations and Applications Level 1

Assessment Criterion

Did the student . . .

✓ demonstrate mastery in reading, writing, and counting numbers 10–20 in expanded form?

LESSON 57
Counting to 20

Student Edition pages 125–126

Counting to 20

Draw a ring around a group of ten. Then count and write the correct number.

1 `14`

2 `13`

3 `18`

4 `17`

5 `15`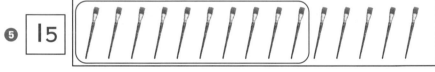

6 `10`

 NOTE TO HOME
Students count objects by making groups of ten.

LESSON PLANNER

Objectives

▶ to teach students to identify steps on an unlabeled and a labeled 0–20 number line

▶ to teach students to count on from 10

Context of the Lesson This lesson builds on students' earlier work with the 0–10 number line.

✋ MANIPULATIVES   **Program Resources**

number line	Number Cubes
paper	Reteaching Master
play money* (optional)	Practice Master 57
	Enrichment Master 57
tape	For extra practice: CD-ROM* Lesson 57

① Warm-Up ⏱ 5 MINUTES

 Problem of the Day Present the following problem to the class. How many legs would you see if there were two dogs and a bird outside your house? (10)

Problem-Solving Strategies Ask students who have solved the Problem of the Day to share how they solved it and any strategies they used.

MENTAL MATH Have students solve the following problems mentally and show their answers with Number Cubes.

a.	6 + 3 = (9)	**b.**	4 – 3 = (1)
c.	8 + 2 = (10)	**d.**	7 – 3 = (4)
e.	2 + 3 = (5)	**f.**	9 – 3 = (6)

② Teach

Demonstrate On the chalkboard draw a 20-step **number line**, with only the 0 point labeled. Have students count aloud in unison as you point to the steps in order. Next, have a volunteer point to a step and count with the class to determine what step it is. Then **tape** a sheet of **paper** to

---

 Real-World Connection Have students count **money*** amounts between 10¢ and 20¢ and $10 and $20 by counting on from ten. For example, show them a dime and four pennies. Have students show how to count the total by starting at 10¢ and then counting up four more cents.

 Literature Connection Read aloud *Counting Wildflowers* by Bruce McMillan to practice counting and one-to-one correspondence with numbers to 20.

RETEACHING p. 14

LESSON 57 RETEACHING   Name _____

0 1 2 3 4 5 6 7 8 9 10 11 12 13 14 15 16 17 18 19 20

How many marks?   `10 marks`

0 1 2 3 4 5 6 7 8 9 10

❶ How many marks?   `12`

0

❷ How many marks?   `16`

0

❸ Color the first 9 marks.

0

❹ Color the first 14 marks.

0

*available separately

◆ **LESSON 57** Counting to 20

7 How many marks? **15**

0

8 How many marks? **14**

0

9 How many marks? **16**

0

10 Darken the first 17 marks.

0

11 Darken the first 12 marks.

0

12 Darken the first 19 marks.

0

126 • Addition and Subtraction

🎒 **NOTE TO HOME**
Students count up to 20 on the number line.

cover some of the steps below 10 and have volunteers name a step between 11 and 20. Guide students to see that they can start counting from 10 or 15 and then count up to name a step.

 Using the Number Cubes Continue problems as in the demonstration, but have students show their answers with Number Cubes. Have them explain how they arrived at each answer. Then count up from 10 to confirm the answer.

Using the Student Pages Do the first problem on page 125 and page 126 together with the class. Have students complete the rest of the problems on the pages independently.

❸ Wrap-Up

In Closing Have students explain how they arrived at various answers on page 126.

 Informal Assessment Observe which students explain that they counted on from 10 to find the answers to page 126 to informally assess their understanding of the number line and numbers from 0–20.

Assessment Criteria

Did the student . . .

✓ correctly count on the number line during the demonstration and Number Cube activity?

✓ correctly answer 10 of 12 problems on pages 125–126?

PRACTICE p. 57

LESSON **57** PRACTICE Name_____

1 How many marks?
0 _____ 12

2 How many marks?
0 _____ 13

3 How many marks?
0 _____ 16

4 Darken the first 11 marks.
0

5 Darken the first 18 marks.
0

6 Darken the first 14 marks.
0

7 Darken the first 16 marks.
0

Math Explorations and Applications Level 1 • 57

ENRICHMENT p. 57

LESSON **57** ENRICHMENT Name_____

Color the first and last cars of the train red. Color the others yellow.

1 How many yellow cars? _____ 18

Color the first 12 cars blue.
Color the others red.

2 How many red cars? _____ 8

Color the first eight cars green, the next eight blue, and the others purple.

3 How many purple cars? _____ 4

Color the first 17 cars orange. Color the others brown.

4 How many brown cars? _____ 3

Math Explorations and Applications Level 1 • 57

LESSON 58

Student Edition pages 127–128

Adding— Doubles

Name _____

Adding—Doubles

The coats on the Button people have the same number of buttons in back as they do in front. How many buttons are there on each coat?

❶  | 4

❷  | 6

❸  | 2

❹  | 8

❺  | 10

❻  | 0

Copyright © SRA/McGraw-Hill

NOTE TO HOME
Students count visible buttons and double them to find the answer.

Unit 2 Lesson 58 • **127**

LESSON PLANNER

Objective

▶ to teach students to memorize the doubles of numbers from 0–5

Context of the Lesson This lesson is the first step toward memorizing addition facts.

 MANIPULATIVES **Program Resources**

counters* or pennies*

paper (optional)

paint (optional)

paintbrush (optional)

Number Cubes

Thinking Story Book, pages 46–47

Practice Master 58

Enrichment Master 58

For extra practice: CD-ROM* Lesson 58

❶ Warm-Up 5 MINUTES

 Problem of the Day Present the following problem to the class. Miko is older than Hal and Grace, but younger than Jason. Who is the oldest? Make a list to show how to tell. (From youngest to oldest, H, G, M, J or G, H, M, J both fit the clues. Jason must be oldest.)

Problem-Solving Strategies Ask students who have solved the Problem of the Day to share how they solved it and any strategies they used.

MENTAL MATH Have students solve the following problems mentally, then show their answers with Number Cubes.

a. 5 – 0 = (5)   b. 6 – 1 = (5)

c. 10 – 3 = (7)   d. 8 + 2 = (10)

e. 4 + 1 = (5)   f. 7 – 2 = (5)

❷ Teach

Demonstrate List the doubles addition facts in order from 0–5 on the chalkboard. Have students solve them one at a time and then recite them in unison. Erase one answer at a time, having students recite the whole list each time.

127 Addition and Subtraction

Why teach it at this time?

Once doubles are memorized, they provide reference points for the other addition facts that are more difficult to remember.

Knowing the addition, subtraction, multiplication, and division facts "by heart" (or by mind) is at least as important as it ever was, and many other lower-order skills are still essential so that we can concentrate on the higher-order skills.

—Stephen S. Willoughby, *Mathematics Education for a Changing World*

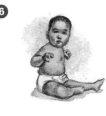 **MANIPULATIVES** Provide several sheets of **paper**, **paint**, and a **paintbrush** for each student. Have them paint one spot near the bottom of a sheet of paper, fold the paper in half from the top down, press the halves together, and then open the sheet. Ask how this can help them remember 1 + 1. (1 + 1 = 2) Do the same with two, three, four, and five spots. Have students predict the number of spots they will see before they unfold the paper each time.

*available separately

◆ LESSON 58 Adding—Doubles

Take-Home Activity

Roll a Double

Players: Two or more

Materials: One 0–5 Number Cube per person and 20 counters or pennies

RULES

Place 20 counters in a pile. Take turns. Roll all the cubes. If a double is rolled, state the sum of the cubes. If correct, take a counter from the pile. If more than one double is rolled, take one counter for each correct sum. Keep taking turns. The player with the most counters at the end of the game time is the winner.

I played the game with

_____ .

128 • Addition and Subtraction

 Using the Number Cubes Present doubles problems orally. Have students show their answers with Number Cubes.

Using the Student Pages Do the first problem on page 127 together with the class. Have students complete the rest of the problems on the page independently.

 Using the "Roll a Double" Game To provide practice in adding doubles through 5 + 5, demonstrate the "Roll a Double" game on page 128. Provide **counters*** or **pennies***. Have students take the game home to play, or have classmates play in groups of two or three. A copy of this game can be found on page 17 of the Home Connections Blackline Masters.

 Using the Thinking Story Present two of the problems following "Manolita's Amazing Number Machine" on pages 46–47 of the Thinking Story Book or pages 116a–116b of this Guide.

❸ Wrap-Up ⏱ 5 MINUTES

In Closing Have students recite as many doubles facts as they can from memory.

 Have students list on paper the doubles facts they already know and then write down those they still need help with on the other side. They can use the paper as a study sheet whenever they have time.

PRACTICE p. 58

LESSON 58 PRACTICE   Name _____

Each card has the same number of dots on the back as on the front. How many dots are on each card?

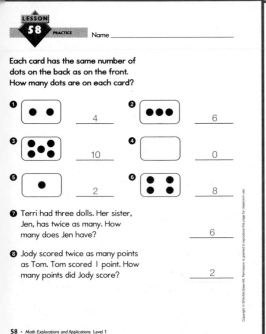

❶ [dice with 2 dots]   4

❷ [dice with 3 dots]   6

❸ [dice with 5 dots]   10

❹ [blank card]   0

❺ [dice with 1 dot]   2

❻ [dice with 4 dots]   8

❼ Terri had three dolls. Her sister, Jen, has twice as many. How many does Jen have?   6

❽ Jody scored twice as many points as Tom. Tom scored 1 point. How many points did Jody score?   2

58 • Math Explorations and Applications Level 1

ENRICHMENT p. 58

LESSON 58 ENRICHMENT   Name _____

Workers have almost finished with this tile floor. Both rooms will have the same number of tile shapes.

❶ How many circles in one room?   2

❷ How many circles all together?   4

❸ How many triangles in one room?   3

❹ How many triangles all together?   6

❺ How many squares in one room?   4

❻ How many squares all together?   8

❼ How many stars in one room?   5

❽ How many stars all together?   10

Finish drawing the tiles. Color the floor any way you like.

58 • Math Explorations and Applications Level 1

Assessment Criteria

Did the student . . .

✓ participate in the demonstration and show the correct answers during the Number Cube activity?

✓ correctly answer five of six problems on page 127?

✓ cooperatively play the "Roll a Double" game?

*available separately

LESSON 59

Student Edition pages 129–130

Adding Fives

LESSON PLANNER

Objectives

▶ to teach students a quick way to solve addition problems in which 5 is one of the addends

▶ to give students experience in visually comparing sizes of pictured objects without direct measurement

Context of the Lesson This lesson demonstrates that using finger sets with addition involving 5 is easier than other addition facts students have learned up to now.

 MANIPULATIVES

play money* (optional)

Program Resources

Number Cubes

Thinking Story Book, pages 48–51

Practice Master 59

Enrichment Master 59

For career connections:
Careers and Math*

For extra practice:
CD-ROM* Lesson 59
Mixed practice, page 361

① Warm-Up

 **Problem of the Day** Present the following problem to the class. Kendra gave a clerk a dime for a pencil. She got three coins back in change. How much did the pencil cost? (7¢ if all coins are pennies; 3¢ if the coins are one nickel and two pennies.)

Problem-Solving Strategies Ask students who have solved the Problem of the Day to share how they solved it and any strategies they used.

MENTAL MATH Have students add mentally:

a. 2 + 1 = (3)   b. 8 + 2 = (10)

c. 4 + 1 = (5)   d. 7 + 3 = (10)

e. 0 + 7 = (7)   f. 6 + 4 = (10)

g. 3 + 3 = (6)   h. 5 + 5 = (10)

i. 4 + 4 = (8)   j. 7 + 2 = (9)

LESSON 59

Name _____

Adding Fives

Write the number sentences.

❶   5 + 4 = 9

❷   5 + 2 = 7

❸   5 + 5 = 10

❹   5 + 0 = 5

❺   5 + 3 = 8

 THINKING STORY   Talk about the Thinking Story "Silly Dreamer."

 **NOTE TO HOME**
Students use finger sets to solve addition problems.

Copyright © SRA/McGraw-Hill

Unit 2   Lesson 59 • **129**

 Literature Connection To provide counting practice, read aloud *Each Orange Had 8 Slices: A Counting Book* by Paul Giganti.

RETEACHING

 MANIPULATIVES Have students use **play nickels*** and **pennies*** to practice adding sums involving 5 as an addend.

*available separately

◆ **LESSON 59** Adding Fives

Ring the larger one.

Use the Mixed Practice on page 361 after this lesson.

⑥

⑦

⑧

⑨

⑩

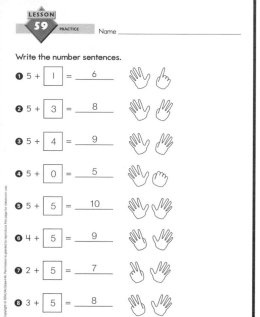

NOTE TO HOME
Students judge relative size.

130 • Addition and Subtraction

② Teach

Demonstrate Show students how to add problems with 5 as an addend by making 5 with one hand and the other addend with the other hand rather than counting one finger at a time. Give children practice in this method with examples such as: $5 + 3$; $2 + 5$; and $5 + 4$. Continue to present addition problems with fives. Have students show their answers with Number Cubes.

Using the Student Pages Do the first problem on page 129 together with the class. Have students complete the rest of the problems on this page independently. For page 130, ask students to look at each picture and ring the larger object in each set.

Introducing the Thinking Story Read aloud and discuss the story "Silly Dreamer" from pages 48–51 in the Thinking Story Book.

Have students list some other things Willy might have wished to change in his room.

③ Wrap-Up

5 MINUTES

In Closing Have volunteers explain their strategy and demonstrate how they solved problems on page 129.

Have students list the +5 facts that they know on one side of a paper and those they still need help with on another. They can use the paper as a study sheet whenever they have time.

PRACTICE p. 59

LESSON 59 PRACTICE   Name _____

Write the number sentences.

❶ $5 + \boxed{1} = \underline{6}$

❷ $5 + \boxed{3} = \underline{8}$

❸ $5 + \boxed{4} = \underline{9}$

❹ $5 + \boxed{0} = \underline{5}$

❺ $5 + \boxed{5} = \underline{10}$

❻ $4 + \boxed{5} = \underline{9}$

❼ $2 + \boxed{5} = \underline{7}$

❽ $3 + \boxed{5} = \underline{8}$

Math Explorations and Applications Level 1 • 59

ENRICHMENT p. 59

LESSON 59 ENRICHMENT   Name _____

REAL-WORLD CONNECTION   How much money does each child need?

Stars	Cats	Dogs	Hearts	Birds
5 cents	4 cents	5 cents	6 cents	3 cents

❶ Ann wants a cat and a star. How much money will she need? — 9 cents

❷ Brad wants a heart and a dog. How much money will he need? — 11 cents

❸ Leah wants a dog and a bird. How much money will she need? — 8 cents

❹ Kimble wants a heart and a cat. How much money will she need? — 10 cents

❺ Katie has 35¢. How many stars can she buy? — 7

❻ Is there money left over? — no

Math Explorations and Applications Level 1 • 59

Assessment Criteria

Did the student...

✓ participate in the demonstration to quickly solve addition problems when 5 is an addend?

✓ correctly solve eight of ten problems on pages 129–130?

Silly Dreamer

❶ "I'm thinking of a number that's less than 6 and greater than 7," said Ferdie.
What number could it be? None—but a child might suggest 6 1/2.
What's wrong with what Ferdie said? A number cannot be less than 6 but greater than 7.

❷ "This is the third time today that I've asked you to hang up your coat," said Marcus's father.
What will the next time be? fourth

❸ "How old are you?" somebody asked Ferdie. Ferdie held up a cube. "One year for each side of this cube, plus one extra year," he said.
How old is Ferdie? seven; [Allow students to use Number Cubes to solve the problem.]

❹ Ms. Eng took five friends for a ride in her new minivan. The next day she took five more friends for a ride.
How many friends did she take for a ride all together? ten

THINKING STORY

Silly Dreamer

Willy the Wisher is always wishing things were different. One day when he didn't have anything better to do, Willy sprawled out on his bed and started looking around his room. His eyes fell upon a stack of library books on his desk. He counted four books in the stack. "I wish there were twice as many books in that stack," said Willy.

How many books did Willy wish were in the stack? eight

Next Willy began staring at the ceiling where he had hung three baseball posters. "I wish I had seven more posters," said Willy, who was very fond of baseball.

How many posters did Willy wish he had? ten

Next to Willy's bed is a chair, which that particular day had four T-shirts piled on it. Willy has never been a child who likes to put away his clothes. "I wish there were four fewer shirts on that chair," said Willy.

How many shirts would there be on the chair if Willy's wish came true? zero

Willy's attention was then drawn to a large wooden bookcase, where he proudly displays his rock collection. He especially likes shiny rocks, but he has only three good ones. "I wish I had five more shiny rocks," said Willy.

How many shiny rocks did Willy wish to have? eight

Story 8 • **49**

5. Poor Ferdie dropped a nickel down the drain and couldn't reach it. A boy with long arms came along and said, "I'll get it for you if you'll pay me 10 cents."
Should Ferdie pay him? no
Why would it be a silly thing to do? It would cost more than the nickel he lost.

6. Manolita went fishing with Ms. Eng. Manolita caught one fish at two o'clock, one at three o'clock, and one at four o'clock.
How many fish did she catch all together? three

7. Portia can jump 3 feet. Ferdie can jump 6 inches farther.
How far can Portia jump? 3 feet

8. When Mrs. Mudancia stretches as far as she can, she can reach 2 yards up.
If she stands on a stepstool 1 yard high, how high can she reach? 3 yards

9. Remember, Mrs. Mudancia can reach 2 yards up if she stretches. She wants to paint a windowsill that is 4 yards high.
How high a platform will she need to stand on? 2 yards

◆ **STORY 8   Silly Dreamer**

Just for fun, Willy likes to scrunch up pieces of paper into balls and toss them into his wastepaper basket. Willy noticed there were five paper balls on the floor near his wastepaper basket. "I wish there were four fewer balls of paper on the floor," said Willy.

How many paper balls would there be on the floor if his wish came true? one

Trying to get more comfortable, Willy stretched out on his back and placed his hands behind his head. This gave him a view of his entire bedroom, which is 10 feet wide and 13 feet long. "I wish my room were 2 feet wider and 3 feet longer," said Willy.

What would be the size of Willy's room if his wishes came true? 12 feet wide and 16 feet long

Just then Willy's mother poked her head into Willy's doorway. "Hey, silly dreamer," she said. "How about dreaming up a way to get your chores done before dinner?"

"OK, Mom," said Willy, pulling himself up to a sitting position. "Now there's a wish I'd *really* like to come true," he thought to himself.

. . . the end

Story 8 • **51**

LESSON 60

Solving Function Problems

LESSON PLANNER

Objectives

▶ to provide practice identifying patterns through function machines

▶ to demonstrate how a calculator can be used as a function machine

Context of the Lesson This lesson builds on the concepts students learned about function machines in Lesson 52.

MANIPULATIVES

calculators*
with constant
feature

function
machine box
from
Lesson 57
(optional)

Program Resources

Number Cubes

Thinking Story Book, pages 52–53

Practice Master 60

Enrichment Master 60

For extra practice:
CD-ROM* Lesson 60

1 Warm-Up

5 MINUTES

 Problem of the Day Write the following pattern on the chalkboard: 1, 2, 3, 1, 2, 3, 1, 2, 3, □, □, □, 1, 2, 3. Have students complete the pattern. (1, 2, 3)

Problem-Solving Strategies Ask students who have solved the Problem of the Day to share how they solved it and any strategies they used.

 Have students add the following doubles and show their answers with Number Cubes.

a. 0 + 0 = (0) **b.** 1 + 1 = (2) **c.** 2 + 2 = (4)

d. 3 + 3 = (6) **e.** 4 + 4 = (8) **f.** 5 + 5 = (10)

GIFTED & TALENTED **Meeting Individual Needs**

Challenge students to find more difficult rules by making a calculator into a x 2 function machine. Then have students work in pairs and try to make their own "harder rule" function machines with a calculator. Have them try to guess each other's rules. Partners can switch roles and repeat several times.

131 Addition and Subtraction

Name _____

Solving Function Problems

 Tara was thinking about a +2 number machine.

If she put these in

These came out

Tara dreamed about putting these things into her number machine.

Draw what would come out.

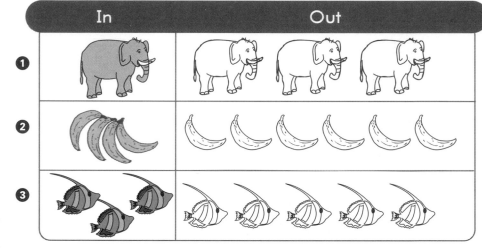

In	Out

 NOTE TO HOME
Students solve addition function problems.

Unit 2 Lesson 60 • **131**

 Literature Connection
Read *A Game of Functions* by Robert Froman. This book gives directions for a game that demonstrates the basic principles of functions and graphs.

RETEACHING

MANIPULATIVES If students have difficulty with pages 131 and 132, use the **function machine box** made in Lesson 52 and have students take turns being the function machines.

*available separately

◆ **LESSON 60** Solving Function Problems

You can make your calculator a +2 machine. Here's how.

Push these buttons. Write what the display shows.

④   2.

⑤ 5 = 7

⑥ 7 = 9

⑦ 1 = 3

⑧ 0 = 2

⑨ = 4

⑩ = 6

Keep pushing the = button.

Tell what the calculator is doing.

It is adding 2.

 Challenge: Make your calculator a +3 number machine. Make your calculator a −1 machine.

132 • Addition and Subtraction

 NOTE TO HOME
Students use a calculator as a function machine.

Copyright © SRA/McGraw-Hill

---

② Teach

Demonstrate On a **calculator*** press the clear key, then ➕ ② ＝ ③ ＝. The display should show 5. Do not press clear. Next press ② ＝. The display should show 4. Explain that you have made the calculator into a +2 function machine. Next have a student pick a number and then press the key for that number and the ＝ key. Read the display to the class. Ask what they think the calculator did. (added 2 to the number) Repeat until everyone understands that the calculator is adding 2 to each number.

Using the Student Pages Read aloud page 131 to the class. Have students answer the questions on their own. Then have them work with partners to complete the activities on page 132, including the challenge.

Using the Thinking Story Present two new problems from among those following "Silly Dreamer" on pages 52–53 of the Thinking Story Book or pages 130a–130b of this Guide.

③ Wrap-Up

In Closing Have pairs of students make their calculators into function machines and take turns guessing what rule has been entered.

Performance Assessment Observe which pairs of students seem to understand how to make their calculators into function machines as they complete the activities on page 132.

PRACTICE p. 60

Fill in the missing numbers.

❶
In	Out
4	5
6	7
10	11
16	17
19	20

❷
In	Out
20	19
17	16
15	14
9	8
1	0

❸
In	Out
6	3
10	7
13	10
18	15
20	17

❹
In	Out
5	7
7	9
10	12
15	17
18	20

60 • Math Explorations and Applications Level 1

ENRICHMENT p. 60

Roll a 0–5 Number Cube three times. Add the numbers to those below. Answers will vary with numbers students roll.

Solve the number sentences.

❶ 2 + (Roll 1) _____ = _____

❷ 4 + (Roll 2) _____ = _____

❸ 1 + (Roll 3) _____ = _____

Roll a 0–5 Number Cube three times. Subtract the numbers from those below.

Solve the number sentences.

❹ 6 − (Roll 1) _____ = _____

❺ 9 − (Roll 2) _____ = _____

❻ 5 − (Roll 3) _____ = _____

60 • Math Explorations and Applications Level 1

Assessment Criteria

Did the student . . .

✓ participate during the demonstration?

✓ correctly answer all of the questions on page 131?

✓ demonstrate understanding of the calculator activities when doing page 132?

Student Edition pages 133–134

Adding— Finding Tens

LESSON PLANNER

Objective

▶ to provide practice finding pairs of numbers whose sum is ten

Context of the Lesson This lesson builds on the concepts students learned in Lesson 47 in which they used concrete objects to find pairs of numbers whose sums were ten.

 MANIPULATIVES
index cards

Program Resources

Number Cubes

Thinking Story Book, pages 52–53

Reteaching Master

Practice Master 61

Enrichment Master 61

For extra practice:
CD-ROM* Lesson 61

❶ Warm-Up

 Problem of the Day Draw the following lines on the chalkboard.

Ask: "Which shape comes next in the pattern: a triangle, a square, or a circle? Why?" (the square because the sides are increasing by one each time)

Problem-Solving Strategies Ask students who have solved the Problem of the Day to share how they solved it and any strategies they used.

 MENTAL MATH Have students add the following doubles, then show their answers with Number Cubes.

a. $3 + 3 = (6)$ b. $1 + 1 = (2)$ c. $0 + 0 = (0)$

d. $5 + 5 = (10)$ e. $4 + 4 = (8)$ f. $2 + 2 = (4)$

❷ Teach

Demonstrate Have students show six fingers and then tell how many more are needed to make ten. Ask: "How

133 Addition and Subtraction

Name _____

Adding—Finding Tens

Draw lines to make ten. The first one is already done for you.

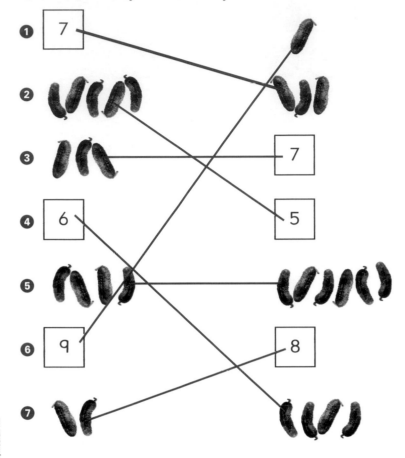

❶ 7

❷

❸

7

❹ 6

5

❺

❻ 9

8

❼

 NOTE TO HOME
Students select numbers that add up to 10.

Unit 2   Lesson 61 • **133**

Why teach it at this time?

This topic is part of a sequence leading to skills needed to solve the missing-addend problems presented in Lessons 65 and 66. It is also an important foundation for adding numbers whose sum is more than ten.

Technology Connection For practice with early math facts and computation skills, use the software *Dancing Dinos* from Micrograms (Mac, IBM).

RETEACHING p. 15

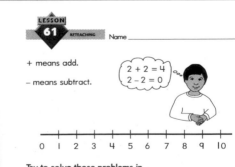

◆ **LESSON 61** Adding—Finding Tens

Solve these problems. Talk about shortcuts.

8 7 − 1 = **6**   **9** 4 + 2 = **6**

10 5 + 3 = **8**   **11** 7 + 2 = **9**

12 6 − 1 = **5**   **13** 1 + 1 = **2**

| **14** 9
− 8
1 | **15** 8
+ 2
10 | **16** 0
+ 3
3 | **17** 3
− 2
1 |

| **18** 6
+ 2
8 | **19** 5
+ 2
7 | **20** 4
+ 2
6 | **21** 4
+ 3
7 |

 **C** **OPERATIVE LEARNING** Do the "Find a Partner to Make Ten" activity.

134 • Addition and Subtraction

 **NOTE TO HOME** Students work addition and subtraction problems to 10.

Introducing the "Find a Partner to Make Ten" Activity Use this activity to provide practice in identifying missing addends in sums to ten. Assign each student a number from 0–10 and have him or her write it on an **index card**. At a signal have students get up and find a partner whose number, when added to their own, makes ten. Pairs of students then sit down. Some students may be left over. You can start a new round by collecting, shuffling, and distributing the index cards again.

Using the Student Pages Have students complete page 133 individually. Then discuss the following shortcuts: doubles; using addends that sum to 5; adding or subtracting 0, 1, or 2 mentally; or knowing the answer from memory. Then have students complete page 134 on their own.

Using the Thinking Story Present two new problems from among those following "Silly Dreamer" on pages 52–53 of the Thinking Story Book or pages 130a–130b of this Guide.

❸ Wrap-Up ⏱

In Closing Have students name all the pairs of numbers whose sums are ten as you make a list on the chalkboard.

Performance Assessment Observe which students can quickly find a partner during the "Find a Partner to Make Ten" activity.

Assessment Criteria

Did the student . . .

✓ accurately use finger sets to find numbers that sum to ten during the demonstration and activity?

✓ correctly work 16 of 21 problems on pages 133–134?

PRACTICE p. 61

LESSON 61 PRACTICE   Name _____

Solve these problems. Watch the signs.

1 8 − 2 = __6__   **2** 2 + 3 = __5__

3 4 + 2 = __6__   **4** 9 − 1 = __8__

5 5 − 3 = __2__   **6** 6 + 2 = __8__

7 5 + 1 = __6__   **8** 7 − 2 = __5__

9 8 − 3 = __5__   **10** 2 + 7 = __9__

11 4 − 1 = __3__   **12** 8 + 2 = __10__

| **13** 2
+ 2
4 | **14** 4
− 0
4 | **15** 2
+ 7
9 | **16** 1
+ 6
7 |

| **17** 3
− 3
0 | **18** 5
− 1
4 | **19** 5
+ 2
7 | **20** 2
+ 0
2 |

ENRICHMENT p. 61

LESSON 61 ENRICHMENT   Name _____

SCIENCE CONNECTION Sunlight shines on the moon. That is why the moon looks so bright at night.

Draw lines for the light rays from the sun to the moon to Earth. Complete the problems.

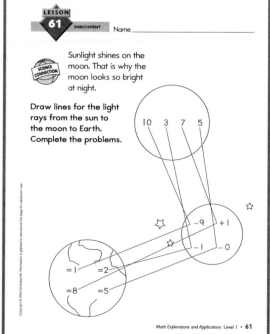

10   3   7   5

−9   +1
−1   −0

=1   =2
=8   =5

Mid-Unit Review

The Mid-Unit Review pinpoints troublesome skill areas for students, allowing plenty of time for additional practice and reteaching before the unit ends. If students did not do well on the Mid-Unit Review and have completed additional practice, you may want to use the Mid-Unit Review provided on pages 22–24 in the Assessment Blackline Masters.

Using the Student Pages Have students complete problems 1–15 on pages 135 and 136 on their own. You might treat this review as a formal assessment of students' skills and have students complete this review as a timed test. See suggestions for administering timed tests on page 48.

Name _____

Mid-Unit Review

How many cents?

1.  __11__ ¢

2.  __8__ ¢

Draw $1 and $5 bills to make the correct amount.

3. $4

| 1 | 1 | 1 | 1 |

4. $7

| 5 | 1 | 1 |

5. Color the cones red.
6. Color the spheres blue.
7. Color the cylinders yellow.

Check the students' work.

 NOTE TO HOME
Students review skills presented in this unit.

Unit 2 Mid-Unit Review • 135

◆ UNIT 2   Mid-Unit Review

8 Seth has $10. If he buys a puzzle for $3, how much will he have left? __$7__

9 A game costs $5. A ball costs $3. How much for the game and the ball? __$8__

Try to solve these problems in your head. Then write the answers.

10 1 + 7 = __8__   **11** 6 + 4 = __10__

12 9 − 4 = __5__   **13** 8 − 2 = __6__

14

In	Out
3	7
4	8
5	9
16	20

The rule is __+4__.

15 Count and write how many.   __19__ marbles

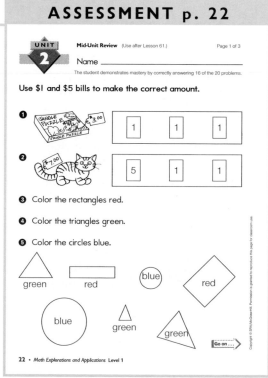

NOTE TO HOME Students review unit skills and concepts.

Copyright © SRA/McGraw-Hill

Literature Connection Use the big book *Animal Orchestra* from the Literature Library* to practice counting as students view and count the number of instruments in an animal orchestra.

Home Connections You may want to send home the letter on pages 44–45 in the Home Connections Blackline Masters, which provides additional activities families can complete together. These activities apply the skills being presented in this unit.

Performance Assessment The Performance Assessment Tasks 1–4 provided on pages 66–67 of the Assessment Blackline Masters can be used at this time to evaluate students' skills in identifying geometric figures and solving addition and subtraction problems. You may want to administer this assessment with individual students or in small groups.

Portfolio Assessment If you have not already completed the Portfolio Assessment task provided on page 78 of the Assessment Blackline Masters, it can be used to evaluate students' skills in creating patterns with geometric shapes.

Unit Project This would be a good time to assign the "Place Setting" project on pages 184a–184b. Students can begin working on the project in cooperative groups in their free time as you work through the unit. The Unit Project is a good opportunity for students to apply the concepts of patterns and one-to-one correspondence in real-world problem solving.

ASSESSMENT p. 22

UNIT 2	Mid-Unit Review (Use after Lesson 61.) Page 1 of 3

Name _____

The student demonstrates mastery by correctly answering 16 of the 20 problems.

Use $1 and $5 bills to make the correct amount.

1

| 1 | 1 | 1 |

2

| 5 | 1 | 1 |

3 Color the rectangles red.

4 Color the triangles green.

5 Color the circles blue.

green   red   (blue)   red

blue   green   green   Go on ...

22 • Math Explorations and Applications Level 1

---

*available separately

LESSON 62

Student Edition pages 137–138

Addition Facts

LESSON PLANNER

Objective

▶ to provide practice for memorization of the sums of numbers adding up to 10 or less

Context of the Lesson
This lesson reinforces the concept of relying on memory rather than counting for some addition facts.

 MANIPULATIVES

stopwatch*

Program Resources

Number Cubes

Thinking Story Book, pages 52–53

Practice Master 62

Enrichment Master 62

For extra practice:
CD-ROM* Lesson 62

① Warm-Up

 Problem of the Day Present the following problem to the class. You want to buy a pencil for 16¢. Write all the ways you could pay for it, using nickels and pennies. (3 nickels, 1 penny; 2 nickels, 6 pennies; 1 nickel, 11 pennies; 16 pennies)

Problem-Solving Strategies Ask students who have solved the Problem of the Day to share how they solved it and any strategies they used.

 Present the following problems orally, at a fairly fast pace. Have students answer in unison.

a. 2 + 2 = (4) **b.** 3 + 2 = (5) **c.** 1 + 0 = (1)

d. 5 + 5 = (10) **e.** 4 + 3 = (7) **f.** 6 + 2 = (8)

② Teach

Using the Number Cubes Tell students that they are now ready to begin to solve problems without having to count them out. Challenge them to do this with some easy problems such as doubles and plus-one problems. Have students mentally solve problems with sums of 10 or less, showing their answers with Number Cubes. Present problems at a fast pace, repeat them frequently, give reversals of problems (for example, follow

137 Addition and Subtraction

LESSON 62

Name _____

Addition Facts

Add the numbers. Write the sums.

① 5 + 2 = **7**

② 3 + 3 = **6**

③ 5 + 1 = **6**

④ 1 + 1 = **2**

⑤ 7 + 2 = **9**

⑥ 5 + 5 = **10**

⑦ 6 + 3 = **9**

⑧ 2 + 3 = **5**

⑨ 6 + 1 = **7**

⑩ 4 + 3 = **7**

⑪ 1 + 5 = **6**

⑫ 4 + 4 = **8**

⑬ 1 + 3 = **4**

⑭ 2 + 2 = **4**

⑮ 1 + 2 = **3**

⑯ 4 + 1 = **5**

⑰ 8 + 2 = **10**

⑱ 1 + 7 = **8**

⑲ 2 + 5 = **7**

⑳ 0 + 5 = **5**

My time

My time

 NOTE TO HOME
Students time themselves doing addition problems.

Copyright © SRA/McGraw-Hill

Unit 2   Lesson 62 • **137**

 Language Arts Connection Have students identify an addition fact that they are having difficulty remembering. Challenge them to compose a poem or riddle to help them remember it, such as, "If you have five and add in four, nine will open up the door."

 Literature Connection You may wish to read aloud *Six Sleepy Sheep* by Jeffie Ross Gordon to reinforce lesson concepts.

RETEACHING

Reteaching is not necessary at this time, because subsequent lessons continue practice with memorization of addition facts.

*available separately

◆ LESSON 62 Addition Facts

Add the numbers. Write the sums.

㉑ 3 + 2 = __5__

㉒ 2 + 6 = __8__

㉓ 7 + 1 = __8__

㉔ 3 + 3 = __6__

㉕ 9 + 1 = __10__

㉖ 4 + 0 = __4__

㉗ 5 + 5 = __10__

㉘ 4 + 2 = __6__

㉙ 1 + 1 = __2__

㉚ 5 + 2 = __7__

㉛ 1 + 8 = __9__

㉜ 2 + 4 = __6__

㉝ 4 + 4 = __8__

㉞ 0 + 6 = __6__

㉟ 2 + 2 = __4__

㊱ 1 + 3 = __4__

㊲ 4 + 3 = __7__

㊳ 5 + 3 = __8__

㊴ 9 + 0 = __9__

㊵ 0 + 0 = __0__

My time

My time

In your Math Journal write what you can do to improve your time.

138 • Addition and Subtraction

NOTE TO HOME Students time themselves doing addition problems.

Copyright © SRA/McGraw-Hill

PRACTICE p. 62

LESSON **62** PRACTICE   Name _____

Add the numbers. Write the sums.

❶ 5 + 1 = __6__

❷ 3 + 5 = __8__

❸ 5 + 2 = __7__

❹ 5 + 5 = __10__

❺ 0 + 5 = __5__

❻ 5 + 4 = __9__

❼ 2 + 5 = __7__

❽ 4 + 5 = __9__

❾ 1 + 5 = __6__

❿ 5 + 3 = __8__

⓫ 2 + 5 = __7__

⓬ 5 + 0 = __5__

⓭ 4 + 5 = __9__

⓮ 5 + 3 = __8__

⓯ 1 + 5 = __6__

⓰ 5 + 5 = __10__

⓱ 5 + 4 = __9__

⓲ 5 + 1 = __6__

⓳ 3 + 5 = __8__

⓴ 5 + 2 = __7__

My time

My time

62 • Math Explorations and Applications Level 1

ENRICHMENT p. 62

LESSON **62** ENRICHMENT   Name _____

Color the number that correctly matches each description.

❶ I am greater than three.
I am less than seven.
What number am I? 6

2 6 7

❷ If you add me to two,
you will get more than five.
If you add me to five,
you will get less than ten.
What number am I? 4

3 4 6

❸ If you subtract one from me,
you will get more than five.
If you add two to me,
you will get more than nine.
What number am I? 8

6 7 8

❹ If you add one to me,
you will get less than nine.
If you subtract four from me,
you will get more than two.
What number am I? 7

5 6 7

62 • Math Explorations and Applications Level 1

*available separately

---

4 + 2 = 6 with 2 + 4 = 6), and end with easy problems all students can solve quickly.

Using the Student Pages These exercises are to be done as time trials. You will need a **stopwatch*** or clock with a second hand. When you give the signal, students should do the first column of problems as fast as they can. As they work, write the elapsed time on the chalkboard, changing it every five seconds. Students should record their finish times. Tell students not to start the second column until you give the signal. Students should strive to improve their time in each subsequent column of problems.

 Using the Thinking Story Present three new problems from among those following "Silly Dreamer" on pages 52–53 in the Thinking Story Book or on pages 130a–130b of this Guide.

❸ Wrap-Up

In Closing Quickly call out addition problems with sums of 10 or less. Have students show the answers with Number Cubes. Point out how automatic students' responses have become. Remind students that even though they have memorized most or all of the addition facts, they can always use finger sets or manipulatives to check an answer.

 Have students check their work after they have completed pages 137–138. Tell students that the goal is to improve their own performance, not to be the fastest in the class. To this end, have students keep these pages in their Math Portfolios so that they can compare them with the next trials they complete.

Assessment Criteria

Did the student . . .

✓ rely on memorization to find the answers?

✓ improve his or her times from one column of exercises to the next on pages 137–138?

 The next lesson uses paper cut into strips. See the "Paper Partners" activity on page 140 of this Teacher's Guide for instructions.

Student Edition pages 139–140

The Addition Table

LESSON PLANNER

Objectives

▶ to introduce the addition table for addends 0–5

▶ to provide practice for addition facts for numbers with sums of 10 or less

▶ to provide practice for estimating and measuring length

Context of the Lesson The addition table is introduced as a handy reference for students who have not yet memorized addition facts and to show students the orderly relationships between these facts.

 MANIPULATIVES

plain paper

Program Resources

Number Cubes

Number Strips

Practice Master 63

Enrichment Master 63

For extra practice:
CD-ROM* Lesson 63
Mixed Practice, page 362

❶ Warm-Up

Problem of the Day Present this problem. Kevin is three years older than Lisa. Lisa is two years older than Marta. Marta is four years old. How old is Kevin? (9)

Problem-Solving Strategies Ask students who have solved the Problem of the Day to share how they solved it and any strategies they used.

 Quickly present the following problems. Have students answer them using Number Cubes.

a. 2 + 0 = (2)   b. 5 + 4 = (9)   c. 3 + 3 = (6)

d. 3 + 4 = (7)   e. 3 + 5 = (8)   f. 4 + 1 = (5)

❷ Teach

 Demonstrate To introduce students to the addition table, copy the number/letter code table from page 139 onto the chalkboard. Show how to find the code letter for 3, 4, moving your fingers until they come together at the *K*. Ask volunteers to find other

139 Addition and Subtraction

Name _____

The Addition Table

	1	2	3	4	5
1	A	B	C	D	E
2	B	F	G	H	I
3	C	G	J	K	L
4	D	H	K	M	N
5	E	I	L	N	O

Do the "Paper Partners" activity.

Figure out these code words.

❶ B E E
   1,2 1,5 5,1

❷ M A D E
   4,4 1,1 4,1 5,1

❸ H E
   2,4 1,5

❹ H I D E
   4,2 2,5 1,4 1,5

❺ A I M
   1,1 2,5 4,4

❻ B O N E
   1,2 5,5 5,4 5,1

❼ O L D
   5,5 5,3 1,4

❽ M E A N
   4,4 1,5 1,1 5,4

Copyright © SRA/McGraw-Hill

 **NOTE TO HOME** Students complete a puzzle which helps prepare them to use an addition table.

Unit 2   Lesson 63 • **139**

To aid memorization of addition facts, include some memory drill of oral addition facts every day. Even a minute or two of fact practice is significant when repeated daily.

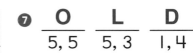

Meeting Individual Needs
Some students have great difficulty using an addition table because moving their fingers at right angles to one another is a challenge. Show them how to place their fingers on the appropriate numbers and then move the right finger down until it is even with the left finger. Then move the left finger across to meet the right, finding the correct box in the addition table. Provide further practice with finding letters and numbers using the tables on pages 139 and 140.

◆ **LESSON 63 The Addition Table**

⑨ Fill in the missing numbers.

+	0	1	2	3	4	5
0	0	1	**2**	3	4	5
1	1	2	3	4	**5**	6
2	2	**3**	4	5	6	7
3	3	4	5	**6**	7	8
4	**4**	5	**6**	7	8	9
5	5	6	**7**	**8**	9	10

Now use the table to solve these problems.

⑩ $3 + 5 =$ __8__   ⑪ $3 + 4 =$ __7__

⑫ $0 + 4 =$ __4__   ⑬ $4 + 5 =$ __9__

⑭ $2 + 5 =$ __7__   ⑮ $5 + 2 =$ __7__

⑯ $3 + 1 =$ __4__   ⑰ $4 + 4 =$ __8__

⑱ $2 + 0 =$ __2__   ⑲ $2 + 4 =$ __6__

⑳ $5 + 5 =$ __10__   ㉑ $3 + 3 =$ __6__

 **NOTE TO HOME**
Students use an addition table to solve problems.

140 • Addition and Subtraction

Copyright © SRA/McGraw-Hill

Use the Mixed Practice on page 362 after this lesson.

code letters. Present addition-table problems, challenging students to predict the answers before using the addition table.

Using the Student Pages Have students complete the pages on their own.

 Introducing the "Paper Partners" Activity Cut **paper** into strips the length of a 10-Number Strip. Then cut each of the paper strips in two at a different place. Show that when a strip is put together with its mate, the two pieces make a strip as long as the 10-Number Strip. Give one strip to each student. At a signal, students search for a partner whose strip will combine with theirs to match the length of a 10-strip.

❸ Wrap-Up

In Closing Have students tell why they might use mental math instead of the addition table.

Students who have difficulty using an addition table may be confused by looking at so many numbers. Have these students use an index card as a placeholder.

Assessment Criteria

Did the student . . .

✓ demonstrate understanding of how to use the addition table?

✓ correctly decode the message on page 139?

✓ use intuitive addition to find a partner in the "Paper Partners" activity?

PRACTICE p. 63

 LESSON **63** PRACTICE Name _____

❶ Fill in the missing numbers.

+	0	1	2	3	4	5
0	0	1	2	3	4	5
1	1	2	3	4	5	6
2	2	3	4	5	6	7
3	3	4	5	6	7	8
4	4	5	6	7	8	9
5	5	6	7	8	9	10

Now use the table to solve these problems.

❷ $2 + 4 =$ __6__   ❸ $4 + 4 =$ __8__

❹ $5 + 3 =$ __8__   ❺ $3 + 0 =$ __3__

❻ $1 + 4 =$ __5__   ❼ $3 + 3 =$ __6__

❽ $4 + 5 =$ __9__   ❾ $5 + 2 =$ __7__

❿ $3 + 4 =$ __7__   ⓫ $2 + 2 =$ __4__

Math Explorations and Applications Level 1 • 63

ENRICHMENT p. 63

 LESSON **63** ENRICHMENT Name _____

	1	2	3	4	5	6	7
1	A	B	C	D	E	F	A
2	B	G	H	I	J	K	E
3	C	H	L	M	N	O	P
4	D	I	M	Q	R	S	T
5	E	J	N	R	U	V	W
6	F	K	O	S	V	X	Y
7	A	E	P	T	W	Y	Z

Figure out these animal names.

$\underset{(3,1)}{C} \underset{(3,6)}{O} \underset{(7,5)}{W}$ $\underset{(6,4)}{S} \underset{(5,1)}{E} \underset{(7,1)}{A} \underset{(3,3)}{L}$

$\underset{(2,2)}{G} \underset{(6,3)}{O} \underset{(1,1)}{A} \underset{(7,4)}{T}$ $\underset{(7,7)}{Z} \underset{(7,2)}{E} \underset{(2,1)}{B} \underset{(4,5)}{R} \underset{(7,1)}{A}$

$\underset{(6,2)}{K} \underset{(1,7)}{A} \underset{(5,3)}{N} \underset{(2,2)}{G} \underset{(1,1)}{A} \underset{(5,4)}{R} \underset{(6,3)}{O} \underset{(3,6)}{O}$

 COOPERATIVE LEARNING Make other animal names. Share them with a friend.

Math Explorations and Applications Level 1 • 63

The goal in teaching mathematics is to get people to think quantitatively and spatially, and if possible to enjoy thinking, so that they will solve problems by thinking even when they are not required to do so in school. By incorporating games and activities into the mathematics curriculum, we can help students see the importance of thinking and discover the enjoyment and benefits that come from thinking mathematically.

–Stephen S. Willoughby,
Teaching Mathematics: What Is Basic?

LESSON

64

Student Edition pages 141–142

Skip Counting— by Twos

Name _____

Skip Counting—by Twos

Make double hops up the number line.

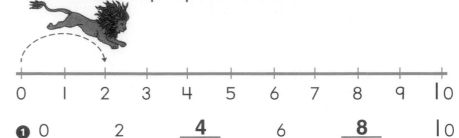

0 1 2 3 4 5 6 7 8 9 10

1 0   2   **4**   6   **8**   10

2 0   **2**   4   **6**   8   10

Can you hop back?

0 1 2 3 4 5 6 7 8 9 10

Solve these problems.
Use the number line.

3 4 + 2 = **6**   **4** 6 − 2 = **4**

5 8 + 2 = **10**   **6** 8 − 2 = **6**

NOTE TO HOME
Students use the number line to practice counting by twos.

Unit 2   Lesson 64 • 141

LESSON PLANNER

Objective

▶ to teach skip counting by twos

Context of the Lesson Counting by twos is introduced in this lesson. Skip counting up and down is practiced in subsequent lessons.

MANIPULATIVES   **Program Resources**

interlocking cubes*

Number Cubes
Thinking Story Book, pages 52–53
Practice Master 64
Enrichment Master 64
For extra practice:
CD-ROM* Lesson 64

1 Warm-Up

5 MINUTES

Problem of the Day Draw ten pairs of hands on the chalkboard. Ask: How many children are there? (ten)

Problem-Solving Strategies Ask students who have solved the Problem of the Day to share how they solved it and any strategies they used.

Have students use Number Cubes to show answers to addition fact problems with sums from 0–10.

2 Teach

Demonstrate Have five volunteers stand in front of the class. Tell students that you are going to determine the total number of feet these students have without counting each foot. Point to each of the students as you count, saying, "2, 4, 6, 8, 10." Tell students that this is called counting by twos. Invite five more volunteers to the front. Using the same procedure, challenge students to join you in counting to 20 by twos. Demonstrate how to count down by twos, challenging students to join in.

 Physical Education Connection

Tape 20 pieces of cardboard in a row on the floor, with space around each one. Write a number from 1–20 on each square. Have pairs of students take turns playing leapfrog. One student stands in front of square number 1. A second student crouches down on that square. The first student leaps over the second student onto square 2 and crouches down, the second student then leaps over the first student onto square 3, and so on. Encourage students to say the number of the square as they land on it (2, 4, 6, 8, and so on).

RETEACHING

For students who do not grasp counting by twos, teach the method of whispering the intervening numbers and saying the correct numbers aloud.

141 Addition and Subtraction

*available separately

◆ **LESSON 64 Skip Counting—by Twos**

+	0	1	2	3	4	5	6
0	0	1	2	3	4	5	6
1	1	2	3	4	5	6	7
2	2	3	4	5	6	7	8
3	3	4	5	6	7	8	9
4	4	5	6	7	8	9	10
5	5	6	7	8	9	10	11
6	6	7	8	9	10	11	12

Solve these problems. Use the table.

7 5 + 4 = 9 **8** 3 + 4 = 7 **9** 4 + 5 = 9 **10** 6 + 6 = 12

11 3 + 6 = 9 **12** 3 + 3 = 6 **13** 6 + 4 = 10 **14** 5 + 6 = 11

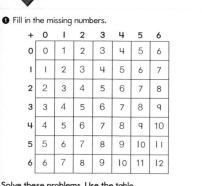

Play the "Roll and Add" game.

142 • Addition and Subtraction

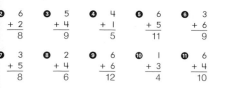 **NOTE TO HOME** Students practice using an addition table.

Copyright © SRA/McGraw-Hill

Introducing the "Roll and Add" Game
Demonstrate and play this game, which provides practice with adding sums of ten or less and probability. Each player writes a row of five numbers from 0–10. Players take turns rolling two 0–5 Number Cubes. If the sum of the two numbers rolled is in any player's row of five numbers, he or she writes the number sentence for that problem. Play continues until a player has completed sums for all five of his or her numbers. Then other players check the sums to be sure they are correct. A copy of this game can also be found on page 18 of the Home Connections Blackline Masters.

Using the Student Pages Have students complete pages 141–142 independently.

Using the Thinking Story Present two problems from those following "Silly Dreamer" found on pages 52–53 of the Thinking Story Book or pages 130a–130b of this Guide.

❸ Wrap-Up ⏱ 5 MINUTES

In Closing Have students practice counting by twos through 20 in unison.

Performance Assessment Have students join pairs of **interlocking cubes***, counting by twos up to 20.

Assessment Criteria

Did the student . . .

✓ demonstrate understanding of how to count by twos up to and down from 20?

✓ correctly answer 11 of 14 problems on pages 141–142?

LOOKING AHEAD Safety pins or tape will be needed for Lesson 65.

PRACTICE p. 64

LESSON **64** PRACTICE Name _____

1 Fill in the missing numbers.

+	0	1	2	3	4	5	6
0	0	1	2	3	4	5	6
1	1	2	3	4	5	6	7
2	2	3	4	5	6	7	8
3	3	4	5	6	7	8	9
4	4	5	6	7	8	9	10
5	5	6	7	8	9	10	11
6	6	7	8	9	10	11	12

Solve these problems. Use the table.

2 6 + 2 = 8 **3** 5 + 4 = 9 **4** 4 + 1 = 5 **5** 6 + 5 = 11 **6** 3 + 6 = 9

7 3 + 5 = 8 **8** 2 + 4 = 6 **9** 6 + 6 = 12 **10** 1 + 3 = 4 **11** 6 + 4 = 10

64 • Math Explorations and Applications Level 1

ENRICHMENT p. 64

LESSON **64** ENRICHMENT Name _____

Start with 2. Count up by twos. Connect the dots.

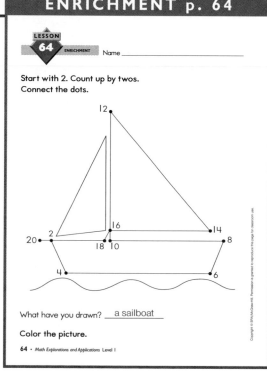

What have you drawn? __a sailboat__

Color the picture.

64 • Math Explorations and Applications Level 1

---

*available separately

Unit 2 Lesson 64 **142**

LESSON 65
Finding Missing Addends

Student Edition pages 143–144

LESSON PLANNER

Objective

▶ to teach students to solve missing-addend and missing-subtrahend problems by using concrete objects, if the missing number is 1 or 2

Context of the Lesson Although students work with missing subtrahends, proficiency is only expected for solving missing-addend problems.

 MANIPULATIVES

manila folder

safety pins or tape

Program Resources

Number Cubes

Number Strips

Thinking Story Book, pages 54–57

Practice Master 65

Enrichment Master 65

For career connections:
  Careers and Math*

For extra practice:
  CD-ROM* Lesson 65

❶ Warm-Up

 5 MINUTES

 Problem of the Day Read the problem aloud. Kathryn had eight crackers, which she planned to eat at morning and afternoon recess. How could she divide the crackers into two snacks? (7 morning, 1 afternoon; 1 morning, 7 afternoon; 6 morning, 2 afternoon; 2 morning, 6 afternoon; 5 morning, 3 afternoon; 3 afternoon, 5 morning; 4 morning, 4 afternoon)

Problem-Solving Strategies Ask students who have solved the Problem of the Day to share how they solved it and any strategies they used.

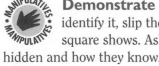 Have students use Number Cubes to show answers to addition problems with doubles up to 5.

❷ Teach

 Demonstrate Hold up a 5-strip. After students identify it, slip the strip into a **folder** so only one square shows. Ask students how many squares are hidden and how they know. Repeat with other strips, leaving one or two squares showing.

143 Addition and Subtraction

LESSON 65

Name _____

Finding Missing Addends

 ALGEBRA READINESS

Look at the Number Strips. How many squares do you have to add? Draw the squares.

5	7	8	6	4	3	9

 THINKING STORY

Talk about the Thinking Story "Mr. Mudancia Builds a Better Tree."

 NOTE TO HOME
Students use Number Strips to model missing addend problems.

RETEACHING

Literature Connection You may wish to read aloud *Ten Sly Piranhas: A Counting Story in Reverse* by William Wise to reinforce the skill of counting down from 10.

If some students do not understand the puzzle activity, play another round with them. Model the process of solving the problem by "thinking out loud."

*available separately

◆ LESSON 65 Finding Missing Addends

Correct the Number Strips. Draw the missing parts.

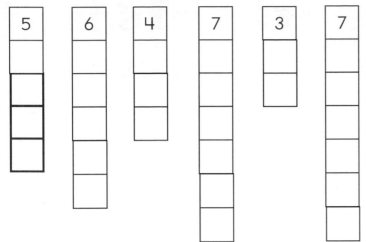

Listen to these problems.
Write the answer.

1 Sandra has $5. She needs $7 to buy a book. How much more does she need? $__2__

2 Joe has four plates. He needs six to set the table. How many more does he need? __2__

 COOPERATIVE LEARNING Do the "Missing Addend Puzzle" activity.

144 • Addition and Subtraction

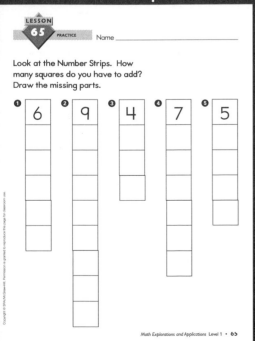 **NOTE TO HOME** Students use Number Strips to model missing addend problems.

PRACTICE p. 65

Name _____

Look at the Number Strips. How many squares do you have to add? Draw the missing parts.

1 6 **2** 9 **3** 4 **4** 7 **5** 5

Math Explorations and Applications Level 1 • **65**

ENRICHMENT p. 65

Name _____

How many cars do you need to finish the trains? Draw them.

6 cars

8 cars

5 cars

7 cars

9 cars

Math Explorations and Applications Level 1 • **65**

 Introducing the "Missing- Addend Puzzle" Activity Fasten, with **pins** or **tape** a slip of paper with a *1* or *2* written on it to the back of a volunteer. Fasten any number from 1–10 to the back of another. Ask the pair to stand facing the chalkboard. They may look at their partner's number but not at their own. Other students can call out the sum of the players' numbers. Challenge each player to figure out his or her own number based on this sum and knowledge of the other student's number. Repeat until all students get a turn. As the activity gets easier, have students call out the difference between the two numbers.

 Using the Student Pages Do the first problem on page 143 as a class. Then have students complete pages 143–144 on their own. Students may use Number Strips to act out the problems in their books.

 Using the Thinking Story Read aloud "Mr. Mudancia Builds a Better Tree" on pages 54–57 of the Thinking Story Book. Stop and discuss the questions asked throughout the story.

 Have students draw what they think the tree looked like after Mr. Mudancia changed it. Ask them to write a sentence describing their drawings.

❸ Wrap-Up

In Closing Present more problems like those of the demonstration. Have students show their answers with Number Cubes.

 Informal Assessment Observe whether students use any strategies or whether they are guessing randomly to solve missing-addend problems.

Assessment Criteria

Did the student . . .

✓ correctly solve 75% of the exercises on pages 143–144?

✓ participate during the Thinking Story discussion?

Mr. Mudancia Builds a Better Tree

① Willy had a favorite branch on the tree in his backyard. One day he counted the leaves on the branch and found there were 12. A few days later there were 15.
Which season of the year do you think it was? spring
Why? There aren't very may leaves on the tree, but the number of leaves is growing.

② "Whenever I loose a tooth," said Willy, "I find ten cents under my pillow the next morning. But today I found only nine cents and a note that said 'You'll get the rest tomorrow.'"
How much money will Willy find under his pillow tomorrow? 1¢

③ Mr. Mudancia changed his bed a little by putting new legs on it. Now, when he lies on the bed, his head is higher than his feet.
What can you figure out about the legs on the bed? The legs at the top of the bed are longer than those at the other end.

④ Mr. Muddle's house used to be 10 yards high. Now it is 9 yards high.
What could have happened? It's sinking or settling: the chimney fell off.

Mr. Mudancia Builds a Better Tree

One day Mr. Mudancia looked out at the tree in his backyard. "I've changed everything else around this house," he said, "but that tree is still the same. It's a nice tree, but I think I'll change it a little."

He measured the tree and found it was 6 yards tall. He changed it so it was 5 yards tall.
How could he do that? by cutting off the top, for example
How much would he have to cut off the top? 1 yard
What would the tree look like afterward? a little flat

Mr. Mudancia took a saw and cut off the top part of the tree so that the tree was a yard shorter. "H'm," he said, "a little flat, but at least it's different." Then he noticed that the tree had eight branches on one side and ten branches on the other side. He wanted the tree to have the same number of branches on both sides, so he changed it a little.
How could he make the tree have the same number of branches on both sides? by cutting two branches off one side

Mr. Mudancia chopped off one branch from the side of the tree that had ten branches. Then he nailed that branch to the side of the tree that had eight branches.

How many branches are on each side of the tree now? nine

Is there anything wrong with this way of changing the tree? The branch will die.

Mr. Mudancia was happy to find that there were now nine branches on one side of the tree and nine branches on the other side, although one branch looked a bit strange. Then he counted 18 apples growing on the tree. "Not bad," he said, "but I'd like it to have 20 apples."

What could he do? He will need to get more apples somewhere else.

How many more apples does he need? two

Story 9 • **55**

5 Poor Willy is carrying a heavy load. He was already carrying three books, and then Ferdie got him to carry his books too.
How many books is Willy carrying all together? can't tell
What do you need to know before you can tell? how many books Ferdie gave him

6 Willy lives three blocks from school. Ferdie lives one block farther away from school than Willy does.
How far from school does Ferdie live? four blocks

7 Portia had six pennies. She put one in her pocket, then one fell down a sewer. She noticed one penny was three years old.
How many pennies does she have left? five

8 "Last night I went to bed at nine o'clock," said Ferdie. "Tonight I have to go to bed by ten."
How much later does Ferdie get to stay up tonight? one hour

9 Karen is about 3 feet tall. Her uncle is about twice as tall.
About how many feet tall is Karen's uncle? six

10 Manolita and Portia sat on one side of the seesaw, while Virginia sat on the other. They balanced nicely.
Who is the heaviest? Virginia
How do you know? She balances the weight of the other two.

◆ STORY 9   Mr. Mudancia Builds a Better Tree

He bought two apples at the store and then tied them to the tree with string. "The tree is almost perfect now," he said. "All it needs is a flag at the top." He took a pole about 1 yard long and put it on top of the tree. Then he attached a flag with a big *M* on it.

How high was the tree before he added the flag? 5 yards

How high is the whole thing now? about 6 yards

Tell all you know about what the tree looks like. Do you think it is really better than it was before? The tree has a flat top. It is 5 yards high with a 1 yard flag pole on top. There are nine branches on each side of the tree, but one of the branches has been nailed on. There are 20 apples on the tree, two of which are tied on with string.

. . . *the end*

Story 9 • **57**

LESSON 66

Missing Addends

Student Edition pages 145–146

LESSON PLANNER

Objectives

✓ to assess students' ability to solve missing-addend problems by using concrete objects, if the missing number is 1 or 2

▶ to provide practice in solving missing-subtrahend problems by using concrete objects, if the missing number is 1 or 2

Context of the Lesson This is the second lesson on missing addends. A Mastery Checkpoint for this skill is provided in this lesson. Work with this concept will continue in Lesson 99.

 MANIPULATIVES   **Program Resources**

can   Number Cubes

counters*   Thinking Story Book, pages 58–59

paper (opaque)   Reteaching Master

                        Practice Master 66

                        Enrichment Master 66

                        Assessment Master

                        For extra practice:
                        CD-ROM* Lesson 66

① Warp-Up

 Problem of the Day Present this problem orally. The sum of two numbers is 7. One of the numbers is 2. What is the other number? (5)

Problem-Solving Strategies Ask students who have solved the Problem of the Day to share how they solved it and any strategies they used.

MENTAL MATH Write these problems on the chalkboard as you present them aloud. Have students use Number Cubes to answer. Then write the answers on the chalkboard.

a. 4 − 2 = (2)	b. 2 + 2 = (4)
c. 6 − 4 = (2)	d. 4 + 2 = (6)
e. 6 − 1 = (5)	f. 5 + 1 = (6)
g. 8 − 2 = (6)	h. 6 + 2 = (8)
i. 3 − 1 = (2)	j. 2 + 1 = (3)

LESSON 66

Missing Addends

Name _____

 Cover the red squares below.

❶ What goes with 2 to make 4? __2__

❷ What goes with 2 to make 3? __1__

❸ What goes with 2 to make 5? __3__

Uncover the squares to check.

Solve the same problems this way.

❹ 2 + [2] = 4   ❺ 2 + [1] = 3

❻ 2 + [3] = 5

 NOTE TO HOME Students use Number Strips to model missing addend problems.

Unit 2   Lesson 66 • **145**

RETEACHING p. 16

LESSON 66 RETEACHING Name _____

What goes with 2 to make 3?

☐ 2
☐+ 1
———
    3

Cover the ▨ **below.**

❶ What goes with 3 to make 5? ___2___

❷ What goes with 3 to make 4? ___1___

❸ What goes with 3 to make 6? ___3___

❹ What goes with 3 to make 3? ___0___

5	4	6	3

16 • Math Explorations and Applications Level 1

PRACTICE p. 66

LESSON 66 PRACTICE Name _____

Solve these problems.

❶ 1 + [2] = 3	❷ 9 + [0] = 9
❸ 6 + [1] = 7	❹ 5 + [1] = 6
❺ 0 + [2] = 2	❻ 4 + [2] = 6
❼ 5 + [0] = 5	❽ 3 + [2] = 5
❾ 3 + [1] = 4	❿ 1 + [1] = 2
⓫ 2 + [1] = 3	⓬ 7 + [2] = 9
⓭ 6 + [2] = 8	⓮ 2 + [2] = 4
⓯ 7 + [0] = 7	⓰ 8 + [0] = 8
⓱ 4 + [1] = 5	⓲ 3 + [0] = 3
⓳ 8 + [1] = 9	⓴ 9 + [1] = 10

66 • Math Explorations and Applications Level 1

---

*available separately

◆ **LESSON 66** Missing Addends

Cover the red squares below.

7 What goes with 4 to make 5? __1__

8 What goes with 4 to make 6? __2__

9 What goes with 2 to make 6? __4__

10 What goes with 5 to make 7? __2__

Uncover
the squares
to check.

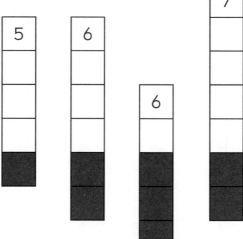

Solve the same problems this way.

11 4 + [1] = 5   **12** 2 + [4] = 6

13 4 + [2] = 6   **14** 5 + [2] = 7

146 • Addition and Subtraction

NOTE TO HOME
Students use Number Strips to
model missing addend problems.

Copyright © SRA/McGraw-Hill

---

❷ Teach

Demonstrate Have students count as you put five **counters*** in a **can.** Ask a volunteer to secretly keep track as you place additional counters in the can. Show the group that there are now six counters in the can. Challenge students to tell how many more were put in. Give similar problems in which one or two counters are added or removed. Write these problems on the chalkboard as number sentences, for example: 8 − □ = 7; 4 + □ = 6.

Using the Student Pages Have students do the activities on pages 145–146. Tell them to cover the shaded squares with thick **paper** before doing the problems at the top of each page.

Using the Thinking Story Present three problems from those following "Mr. Mudancia Builds a Better Tree" on pages 58–59 of the Thinking Story Book or pages 144a–144b of this Guide.

❸ Wrap-Up

In Closing Present more counters-in-the-can problems.

Mastery Checkpoint 12

Students should now be able to solve missing-addend problems using concrete objects when the missing addends are 1 or 2 for sums of 10 or less. You can assess students during the demonstration and as they complete pages 145–146, recording your results on the Mastery Checkpoint Chart. Or you may wish to assign Assessment Blackline Masters pages 25–26.

Assessment Criteria

Did the student . . .

✓ demonstrate mastery in solving concrete missing-addend problems?

✓ correctly answer 11 of 14 problems on pages 145–146?

*available separately

LESSON 67

Student Edition pages 147–148

Less Than, Greater Than

LESSON PLANNER

Objectives

▶ to introduce inequality and equality signs (<, >, and =) to show the relationship of two numbers

▶ to teach students to compare the sum of two numbers to a given number

▶ to increase students' awareness of unit size in measurement

Context of the Lesson This is the first of two lessons on inequalities and equalities. The topic will be reintroduced in Lesson 97.

MANIPULATIVES

plain paper

Program Resources

Number Cubes

Thinking Story Book, pages 58–59

Practice Master 67

Enrichment Master 67

For extra practice: CD-ROM* Lesson 67

❶ Warm-Up ⏱ 5 MINUTES

Problem of the Day Ask the following question. Which is more—six baskets of carrots or nine baskets of potatoes? (By basketful, there are more potatoes. In absolute numbers or weight, we don't have enough information to answer.)

Problem-Solving Strategies Ask students who have solved the Problem of the Day to share how they solved it and any strategies they used.

MENTAL MATH Skip count by twos, stopping at various points so that students can supply the missing numbers.

❷ Teach

Demonstrate Draw students' attention to the illustration on page 147. Explain that the Hungry Alligator always wants to "bite" the larger of two numbers. Then show students how they can write *5 > 2* to mean 5 is greater than 2. Similarly, tell students that they can write *3 < 10* to mean 3 is less than 10.

147 Addition and Subtraction

LESSON 67

Name _____

Less Than, Greater Than

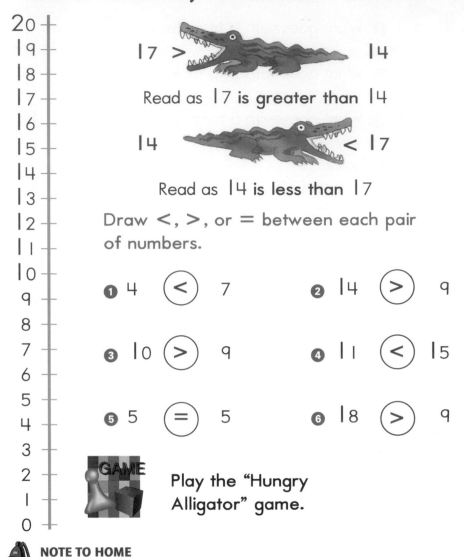

Read as **17 is greater than 14**

14 < 17

Read as **14 is less than 17**

Draw <, >, or = between each pair of numbers.

❶ 4 (<) 7   ❷ 14 (>) 9

❸ 10 (>) 9   ❹ 11 (<) 15

❺ 5 (=) 5   ❻ 18 (>) 9

Play the "Hungry Alligator" game.

NOTE TO HOME
Students learn to use relation signs.

Copyright © SRA/McGraw-Hill

Unit 2   Lesson 67 • **147**

LITERATURE CONNECTION **Literature Connection** You may wish to read aloud *Counting* by Henry Pluckrose to reinforce the lesson concepts.

RETEACHING

Some students have difficulty remembering what the inequality symbols stand for. Challenge groups of students to come up with and draw pictures to help them remember what the < and > symbols mean. Invite groups to share their pictures with the class. You may also wish to display them in the classroom so students can refer to them.

---

*available separately

◆ **LESSON 67** Less Than, Greater Than

9 Ring each number that is greater than 6.

⑦ 4 6 5 ⑨ I ⑧

10 Ring each amount that makes more than 5.

2 + 2   3 + 2   ⑤ + ②

④ + ②   I + 2   ⑧ + ②

11 Ring each number that is less than 7.

8 ⑥ ④ 7 ⑤ 9

12 Ring each amount that makes less than 6.

③ + ②   6 + 2   5 + 2

5 + 2   ② + ②   4 + 2

13 Ring each amount that makes 6.

③ + ③   ④ + ②   5 + 2

① + ⑤   6 + I   3 + 4

Do the "Giant Steps" activity.

148 · Addition and Subtraction

Copyright © SRA/McGraw-Hill

NOTE TO HOME
Students find numbers that are greater than, less than or equal to others.

PRACTICE p. 67

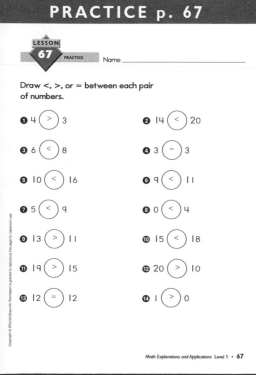

LESSON **67** PRACTICE Name _____

Draw <, >, or = between each pair of numbers.

1 4 ⟩ 3   **2** 14 ⟨ 20

3 6 ⟨ 8   **4** 3 = 3

5 10 ⟨ 16   **6** 9 ⟨ II

7 5 ⟨ 9   **8** 0 ⟨ 4

9 13 ⟩ II   **10** 15 ⟨ 18

11 19 ⟩ 15   **12** 20 ⟩ 10

13 12 = 12   **14** I ⟩ 0

Math Explorations and Applications Level 1 · 67

ENRICHMENT p. 67

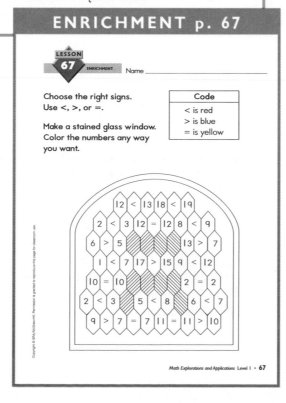

LESSON **67** ENRICHMENT Name _____

Choose the right signs.
Use <, >, or =.

Make a stained glass window.
Color the numbers any way you want.

Code
< is red
> is blue
= is yellow

Math Explorations and Applications Level 1 · 67

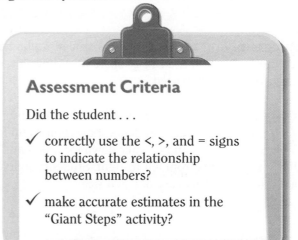

Introducing the "Hungry Alligator" Game To provide practice in identifying equalities and inequalities in the 0–10 range, using relation signs, and probability, play the "Hungry Alligator" game. Divide the group into pairs. Each pair needs two 0–5 and two 5–10 Number Cubes. While one player looks away, the lead player selects two Number Cubes, places them slightly apart from each other on a sheet of **paper**, and covers one cube with a hand. The other player draws a relation sign (<, >, =) between the two cubes. The lead player uncovers the cube and both players check to see if the right sign was drawn. Then partners switch roles. A copy of this game can also be found on page 19 in the Home Connections Blackline Masters.

Using the "Giant Steps" Activity Have students do the "Giant Steps" activity. Students estimate the number of giant steps it takes a particular student to stride from one place to another in the room. This activity should point out the importance of standard units in measurement because not all students cover the same distance in one step.

Using the Student Pages Have students complete pages 147–148 on their own.

Using the Thinking Story Present three problems from those following "Mr. Mudancia Builds a Better Tree" on pages 58–59 in the Thinking Story Book or pages 144a–144b of this Guide.

❸ Wrap-Up ⏱ 5 MINUTES

In Closing Continue to present pairs of numbers and ask students to use relation signs to indicate which is greater and which is lesser. Include several pairs that are equal.

Performance Assessment Observe students as they play the "Hungry Alligator" game. Ask each student to say the equation out loud so that you can be sure that he or she understands the meaning of the symbols.

Assessment Criteria

Did the student . . .

✓ correctly use the <, >, and = signs to indicate the relationship between numbers?

✓ make accurate estimates in the "Giant Steps" activity?

LESSON 68 Comparing Amounts

LESSON PLANNER

Objectives

▶ to provide practice in the use of equality, inequality, and equal signs

▶ to provide practice in recognizing when the sum of two numbers is larger or smaller than a given number

▶ to reinforce the use of tally marks to record and compare frequencies

Context of the Lesson Inequalities and equalities are continued from Lesson 67. In this lesson students practice using tally marks to record frequencies, a skill first taught in Lesson 17. More work with this skill is provided in Lesson 111.

 MANIPULATIVES

plain paper (optional)

Program Resources

Marti and the Mango* from the Literature Library

Number Cubes

Thinking Story Book, pages 58–59

Practice Master 68

Enrichment Master 68

For extra practice:
CD-ROM* Lesson 68

Mixed Practice, page 363

① Warm-Up

Problem of the Day Write these number sentences on the board: 8 < 10, 4 > 2. Challenge students to write other inequality number sentences using only these four numbers. (8 > 2; 8 > 4; 10 > 8; 10 > 4; 10 > 2; 4 < 10; 4 < 8; 2 < 4; 2 < 8; 2 < 10)

Problem-Solving Strategies Ask students who have solved the Problem of the Day to share how they solved it and any strategies they used.

MENTAL MATH Write the following pairs of numbers on the chalkboard. Have students show thumbs up for greater than and thumbs down for less than, reading the numbers from left to right. Students should stand up if the numbers are of equal size.

a. 12 10 (thumbs up) b. 4 0 (thumbs up)

c. 19 20 (thumbs down) d. 6 5 (thumbs up)

149 Addition and Substraction

Name _____

Comparing Amounts

14  < 17

Read as 14 **is less than** 17

17 > 14

Read as 17 **is greater than** 14

Draw <, >, or = between each pair of numbers.

① 13 (<) 15   ② 18 (>) 15

③ 19 (=) 19   ④ 17 (<) 19

⑤ 14 (>) 4   ⑥ 10 (<) 11

⑦ 8 (<) 10   ⑧ 10 (>) 0

⑨ 10 (>) 8   ⑩ 0 (<) 10

My word

 NOTE TO HOME
Students learn to use relation signs.

Tally. Then count.

Unit 2 Lesson 68 • **149**

RETEACHING

LANGUAGE ARTS CONNECTION Write on the chalkboard the words used in the tallying activity. Challenge students to write a sentence using at least two of the words. You may wish to extend this activity by inviting all or selected students to write a story that includes all of the words.

LITERATURE CONNECTION To contrast the concept of comparing amounts to that of comparing sizes, read aloud *Marti and the Mango* from the Literature Library*.

Some students have difficulty remembering what the inequality symbols stand for. Challenge groups of students to come up with and draw pictures to help them remember what the < and > symbols mean. Invite groups to share their pictures with the class. You may also wish to display them in the classroom so that students can refer to them.

*available separately

◆ **LESSON 68** Comparing Amounts

Use the Mixed Practice on page 363 after this lesson.

⑪ Ring each number that is greater than 6.

4   3   ⑧   5   ⑨

⑫ Ring each number that is less than 7.

④   ③   8   ⑤   9

⑬ Ring each amount that makes more than 6.

2 + 0

2 + 1

2 + 2

2 + 3

2 + 4

(2 + 5)

(2 + 6)

(2 + 7)

⑭ Ring each amount that makes less than 7.

(1 + 0)

(1 + 1)

(1 + 2)

(1 + 3)

(1 + 4)

(1 + 5)

1 + 6

1 + 7

NOTE TO HOME
Students find numbers that are greater or less than others.

Copyright © SRA/McGraw-Hill

150 • Addition and Subtraction

PRACTICE p. 68

LESSON **68** PRACTICE Name_____

❶ Ring each number that is greater than 3.

④ 2 ⑤ 1 ⑥

❷ Ring each number that is less than 6.

7 ④ ③ 8 ⑤

❸ Ring each amount that makes more than 7.

5 + 0

5 + 1

5 + 2

(5 + 3)

(5 + 4)

(5 + 5)

❹ Ring each amount that makes less than 5.

(2 + 0)

(2 + 1)

(2 + 2)

2 + 3

2 + 4

2 + 5

68 • Math Explorations and Applications Level 1

ENRICHMENT p. 68

LESSON **68** ENRICHMENT Name_____

SCIENCE CONNECTION

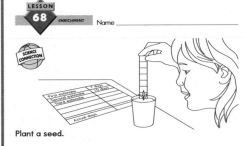

Plant a seed.

How many days do you think it will take the plant to grow to the top of the Number Strip? Use this chart to keep your records. Answers will vary.

First estimate	days
Second estimate	days
Third estimate	days
Actual days	

68 • Math Explorations and Applications Level 1

---

e. 1   11 (thumbs down)   f. 20 10 (thumbs up)

g. 5   5 (stand up)   h. 13 15 (thumbs down)

❷ Teach

COOPERATIVE LEARNING **Using the Student Pages** Students can do exercises 1–14 on pages 149–150 independently. Before beginning the tally activity on page 149, review how to use tally marks to keep count. Place students in small groups and assign a commonly used word, such as *use* or *today,* to each pair of students. Tell each group to discuss their favorite recess activities. Challenge each pair to keep track of how many times their word is used in a five-minute period or less, entering their tally marks in the space provided on page 149. Afterwards, discuss with the class which words were used more frequently and why different students got different counts for the same word.

 Present two new problems from those following "Mr. Mudancia Builds a Better Tree" on pages 58–59 of the Thinking Story Book or pages 144a–144b of this Guide.

❸ Wrap-Up

5 MINUTES

In Closing Challenge students to count groups of objects in the classroom and to keep count using tally marks. Then have them compare their counts, using <, >, and = signs. For example: 4 (pieces of chalk) > 2 (crayons).

ALTERNATIVE ASSESSMENT **Informal Assessment** Observe students as they count tallies. Do they group tallies together and count in sets? Take notes on what strategies are being used by students who seem to be struggling with current lesson material.

Assessment Criteria

Did the student . . .

✓ demonstrate understanding of how to use the three relationship signs?

✓ keep an accurate count using tally marks?

✓ correctly answer 11 of 14 problems on pages 149–150?

LESSON 69 Student Edition pages 151–152

Reviewing Addition Facts

LESSON PLANNER

Objectives
▶ to review addition facts with sums of 10 or less

✓ to assess mastery of addition facts with sums of 10 or less

Context of the Lesson This lesson reviews addition facts with sums of 10 or less. A Mastery Checkpoint for this skill is provided in this lesson.

 MANIPULATIVES **Program Resources**

stopwatch*
- "Addition Table" Game Mat
- Number Cubes
- Thinking Story Book, pages 58–59
- Practice Master 69
- Enrichment Master 69
- Assessment Master
- For additional math integration:
  Math Throughout the Day*
- For extra practice:
  CD-ROM* Lesson 69

1 Warm-Up ⏱ 5 MINUTES

Problem of the Day Ask students: How many numbers are greater than 11 and less than 19? (7) What are the numbers? (12, 13, 14, 15, 16, 17, 18)

Problem-Solving Strategies Ask students who have solved the Problem of the Day to share how they solved it and any strategies they used.

MENTAL MATH Orally present addition problems with sums to 10. Have students respond using Number Cubes.

2 Teach

Using the Student Pages Have students complete pages 151–152 as time trials. You will need a **stopwatch*** or a clock with a second hand. When you give the signal, students should do the first column of problems as fast as they can. As they work, write the elapsed time on the chalkboard, changing it every five seconds. Students should record their finish times. Tell students not to start each column until you give the signal. Remind students that the goal is to improve their own performance over time.

151 Addition and Subtraction

LESSON 69

Name _____

Reviewing Addition Facts

Solve these problems.

1. 5 + 5 = __10__
2. 4 + 1 = __5__
3. 4 + 0 = __4__
4. 1 + 3 = __4__
5. 6 + 3 = __9__
6. 8 + 2 = __10__
7. 4 + 3 = __7__
8. 2 + 3 = __5__
9. 1 + 7 = __8__
10. 4 + 2 = __6__

11. 5 + 3 = __8__
12. 6 + 1 = __7__
13. 2 + 5 = __7__
14. 1 + 1 = __2__
15. 9 + 0 = __9__
16. 3 + 4 = __7__
17. 5 + 4 = __9__
18. 0 + 5 = __5__
19. 5 + 2 = __7__
20. 0 + 0 = __0__

My time

My time

Copyright © SRA/McGraw-Hill

NOTE TO HOME
Students review addition facts to 10.

Unit 2 Lesson 69 • **151**

RETEACHING

Help students determine which addition facts they are having trouble remembering. Then have them practice those facts with a partner using any appropriate aids: finger sets for sums involving 10 or less, counting for sums involving addition of 1 or 2, recitation of doubles, and working up and down from doubles. Continue giving practice in the addition facts during the Mental Math activity.

PRACTICE p. 69

LESSON 69 PRACTICE Name _____

Solve these problems.

1. 2 + 5 = __7__
2. 4 + 1 = __5__
3. 7 + 3 = __10__
4. 8 + 2 = __10__
5. 5 + 1 = __6__
6. 1 + 2 = __3__
7. 3 + 3 = __6__
8. 0 + 2 = __2__
9. 3 + 1 = __4__
10. 4 + 2 = __6__

11. 2 + 3 = __5__
12. 1 + 3 = __4__
13. 6 + 2 = __8__
14. 3 + 5 = __8__
15. 1 + 8 = __9__
16. 0 + 7 = __7__
17. 2 + 4 = __6__
18. 3 + 4 = __7__
19. 1 + 0 = __1__
20. 6 + 3 = __9__

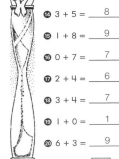

My time	

My time	

Math Explorations and Applications Level 1 • **69**

*available separately

◆ LESSON 69 Reviewing Addition Facts

Solve these problems.

㉑ 3 + 2 **5**	㉒ 1 + 9 **10**	㉛ 9 + 1 **10**	㉜ 7 + 2 **9**
㉓ 3 + 3 **6**	㉔ 2 + 2 **4**	㉝ 1 + 4 **5**	㉞ 6 + 2 **8**
㉕ 2 + 6 **8**	㉖ 7 + 3 **10**	㉟ 1 + 1 **2**	㊱ 4 + 3 **7**
㉗ 2 + 1 **3**	㉘ 5 + 2 **7**	㊲ 3 + 5 **8**	㊳ 6 + 3 **9**
㉙ 2 + 3 **5**	㉚ 4 + 2 **6**	㊴ 8 + 1 **9**	㊵ 3 + 7 **10**

My time

My time

Play the "Addition Table" game.

 NOTE TO HOME
Students review addition facts to 10.

Copyright © SRA/McGraw-Hill

 Introducing the "Addition Table" Game Mat This game provides self-checking practice with addition facts. Use the "Addition Table" Game Mat transparency to demonstrate and play a practice game. Full directions are on the "Addition Table" Game Mat, a copy of which is found on page 392 of this Teacher's Guide.

Using the Thinking Story Present two new problems from those following "Mr. Mudancia Builds a Better Tree" on pages 58–59 of the Thinking Story Book or pages 144a–144b of this Guide.

❸ Wrap-Up

In Closing Remind students of how much quicker and easier it has become for them to remember their math facts. Demonstrate this by orally presenting addition problems with sums to 10. Set a timer to see how many math problems they can solve in two minutes.

 Mastery Checkpoint 13

Most students should have memorized addition facts with sums of 10 or less. Compare the results of the time trials for pages 151–152 to those from Lesson 62, recording the results on the Mastery Checkpoint Chart. Note which students have achieved mastery, which have demonstrated substantial improvement, and which are still having difficulty. You may wish to assign Assessment Blackline Masters pages 27–28. Provide additional practice to those students who have not yet demonstrated mastery.

ENRICHMENT p. 69

LESSON 69 ENRICHMENT Name _____

⭐ Color petals on each flower to show an addition problem.

Write the number sentence that matches the flower.

Coloring on petals may vary, but distribution should match the number sentences.

❶ 1 + 4 = 5

❷ _____ = 7

❸ _____ = 9

❹ _____ = 6

❺ _____ = 8

❻ _____ = 10

Math Explorations and Applications Level 1 • 69

ASSESSMENT p. 27

UNIT 2 Mastery Checkpoint 13 Addition facts I (Lesson 69)
Page 1 of 2
Name _____

The student demonstrates mastery by correctly answering 24 of the 30 problems.

Solve these problems.

❶ 3 + 4 = __7__	⓫ 1 + 1 = __2__
❷ 6 + 1 = __7__	⓬ 4 + 6 = __10__
❸ 2 + 4 = __6__	⓭ 6 + 3 = __9__
❹ 1 + 5 = __6__	⓮ 5 + 4 = __9__
❺ 0 + 0 = __0__	⓯ 2 + 8 = __10__
❻ 6 + 2 = __8__	⓰ 7 + 1 = __8__
❼ 5 + 5 = __10__	⓱ 1 + 9 = __10__
❽ 2 + 1 = __3__	⓲ 6 + 0 = __6__
❾ 1 + 4 = __5__	⓳ 5 + 3 = __8__
❿ 2 + 7 = __9__	⓴ 8 + 1 = __9__

Go on . . .

Math Explorations and Applications Level 1 • 27

Assessment Criteria

Did the student . . .

✓ demonstrate mastery of addition facts with sums to 10?

✓ improve his or her performance on the time trials?

LESSON 70

Student Edition pages 153–154

Number Patterns

LESSON PLANNER

Objectives

▶ to teach students to identify simple number patterns

▶ to introduce the use of numbers to show magnitude and direction

Context of the Lesson The work with patterns from this lesson will continue in Lesson 71.

 MANIPULATIVES

cardboard

local road map (optional)

Program Resources

"Map" Game Mat

Number Cubes

Thinking Story Book, pages 60–63

Practice Master 70

Enrichment Master 70

For career connections:
   Careers and Math*

For additional math integration:
   Math Throughout the Day*

For extra practice:
   CD-ROM* Lesson 70

❶ Warm-Up ⏱ 5 MINUTES

 Problem of the Day Present the following problem to the class. Eli wants a game that costs $8. He has saved a $5 bill and two $1 bills so far. How much more does he need to buy the game? ($1)

Problem-Solving Strategies Ask students who have solved the Problem of the Day to share how they solved it and any strategies they used.

MENTAL MATH Have students answer the following problems orally:

a. What can be added to 5 to make 10? (5)

b. What can be added to 6 to make 10? (4)

c. Nine and how many make 10? (1)

d. Three and how many make 10? (7)

e. Two and how many make 10? (8)

LESSON 70

Name _____

Number Patterns

Solve these problems. Look for a pattern.

❶ 4 + 2 = __6__   ❾ 1 + 3 = __4__

❷ 4 + 3 = __7__   ❿ 2 + 4 = __6__

❸ 4 + 4 = __8__   ⓫ 3 + 5 = __8__

❹ 4 + 5 = __9__   ⓬ 4 + 6 = __10__

❺ 4 + 6 = __10__   ⓭ 5 + 7 = __12__

❻ 4 + 7 = __11__   ⓮ 6 + 8 = __14__

❼ 4 + 8 = __12__   ⓯ 7 + 9 = __16__

❽ 4 + 9 = __13__   ⓰ 8 + 10 = __18__

 Play the "Map" game.

 Talk about the Thinking Story "Marcus Builds a Birdhouse."

 NOTE TO HOME Students practice addition.

Unit 2   Lesson 70 • 153

RETEACHING

Reteaching number patterns is not essential at this time as it is addressed in the next lesson. You may want to assign Enrichment Master 70 at this time.

 Social Studies Connection Display a **local road map** and identify the location of your school. Have students name other locations that are north, south, east, and west of the school. Point out the scale for miles. Explain about how many miles each location is from the school, using the direction such as: "Millville is about 25 miles north."

 Literature Connection Read aloud *Counting by Kangaroos* by Joy N. Hulme to reinforce number concepts.

*available separately

◆ LESSON 70 Number Patterns

Fill in the missing numbers. Look for patterns.

⑰ 5   6   7   8   **9** **10** 11   12

⑱ 1   3   5   7   **9** 11   13   15

⑲ 2   4   **6** 8   **10** 12   14   16

⑳ 15   13   11   **9** 7   5   3   **1**

㉑ 0   2   4   **6** 8   10   12   14

㉒ 2   4   **6** 8   **10** 12   14   16

㉓ 4   6   8   **10** 12   14   16   **18**

㉔ 6   **8** 10   12   14   **16** 18   20

Pick one problem. In your Math Journal tell how you solved it.

154 • Addition and Subtraction

 **NOTE TO HOME**
Students complete number patterns.

Copyright: © SRA/McGraw-Hill

PRACTICE p. 70

 Name _____

Solve these problems.

❶ 5 + 1 = __6__   ❷ 2 + 3 = __5__

❸ 5 + 2 = __7__   ❹ 3 + 4 = __7__

❺ 5 + 3 = __8__   ❻ 4 + 5 = __9__

❼ 5 + 4 = __9__   ❽ 6 + 7 = __13__

❾ 5 + 6 = __11__   ❿ 7 + 8 = __15__

Fill in the missing numbers. Look for patterns.

⑪ 2   4   6   8   10   12

⑫ 5   7   9   11   13   15

⑬ 1   2   3   4   5   6   7

⑭ 10   12   14   16   18   20   22

70 • Math Explorations and Applications Level 1

ENRICHMENT p. 70

 Name _____

Fill in the blanks in the math stairs.

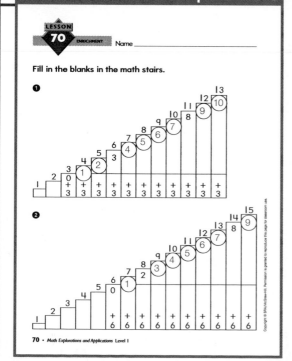

70 • Math Explorations and Applications Level 1

---

② Teach

Demonstrate Write the following array on the chalkboard:

1	2	3	4	5
3	4	5	6	7
5	6	7	8	9

Then have students look away as you cover a number with a piece of **cardboard**. Ask students what number you are covering and how they figured it out. (Possible answers: it is one more than the number to the left; two more than the number above it.) Repeat with different numbers.

Using the Student Pages Have students complete the first column on page 153. Discuss the patterns in the **addends** (The second addend in each problem increases by 1 in each subsequent problem.) and the answers. (They increase by 1 each time.) Then do the same for the second column. (Each addend increases by 1; the answers increase by 2.) Have students complete page 154 independently.

 **Introducing the "Map" Game Mat** To provide practice with compass directions, use the "Map" Game Mat transparency to demonstrate and play a round of the game. Complete instructions can be found on the Game Mat, a copy of which can be found on page 403 of this Teacher's Guide.

Using the Thinking Story Read aloud and then discuss "Marcus Builds a Birdhouse" on pages 60–63 of the Thinking Story Book.

③ Wrap-Up

In Closing Have volunteers make up number patterns. Have classmates try to guess the pattern and the next number.

Informal Assessment Use the answers to pages 153–154 to informally assess students' ability to identify patterns.

Assessment Criteria

Did the student . . .

✓ actively participate in the Thinking Story and Game Mat activities?

✓ correctly answer 20 of 24 problems on pages 153–154?

STORY 10

Marcus Builds a Birdhouse

❶ "I want to measure the inside of this box," said Marcus, "but it's too small to get the ruler inside."
Can you think of some ways to measure the inside of the box? by using string or a paper strip; by measuring the outside of the box

❷ Willy has a piggy bank with different slots for pennies and nickels. Nickels will not fit into the slot for pennies.
Do you think a penny will fit into the slot for nickels? yes
Why? A penny is smaller than a nickel.

❸ Ms. Eng likes rings, so Mr. Eng bought her a ring for every finger on each hand, including the thumbs.
How many rings did he buy her? ten

❹ Manolita had two dimes. She spent one for a red balloon.
How many dimes did she have left? one

THINKING STORY

Marcus Builds a Birdhouse

Marcus and Mr. Muddle built a big, beautiful birdhouse. They made it out of a wooden box. They put a roof on it, painted it green, and set it on a post in the backyard. Some big birds came and looked at it, but they didn't go in. "No wonder," said Marcus's mother. "You forgot something important."

What do you think Marcus forgot? to make a hole so the birds could get in

"I see what it is," said Marcus. "We forgot to make a hole in the front of the birdhouse so the birds can get in!"

Marcus went down the street to Mr. Muddle's store and told him the problem. Mr. Muddle brought a drill to Marcus's house. With it Mr. Muddle drilled a hole about 1 inch wide in the front of Marcus's birdhouse.

How wide is 1 inch? Show with your fingers. [Demonstrate the correct width.]

The next day the big birds came and looked at Marcus's birdhouse again, but they still didn't go in.

Why not? The hole is only 1 inch in diameter.

"I'm afraid that hole is too small for those big birds," said Marcus's mother. "What you need is a hole that's the same size as the birds."

Marcus went back to Mr. Muddle and told him he needed something to cut a bigger hole in his birdhouse. "Exactly how big?" asked Mrs. Muddle, who was helping out her husband that day.

"I don't know exactly," said Marcus. "It should be a sort of bird-size hole."

"Birds come in all different sizes," said Mr. Muddle. "You'll have to find out how wide the birds are before you'll know how wide a hole to make."

Marcus took a ruler and went out and tried to measure the birds.

Do you think that worked? Why not? Probably not; the birds would just fly away.

Story 10 • **61**

⑤ Portia has nine baseball cards. Willy has one more than that.
How many baseball cards does Willy have? ten

⑥ Marcus walked five blocks to school. After school he went home on the bus.
How many blocks did he walk all together? five

⑦ For dinner Mr. Muddle ate two ears of sweet corn and two sausages. He left the corncobs on his plate.
How many corncobs were on the plate? two

⑧ A mother duck had four ducklings. When she wanted to go somewhere, she quacked so the ducklings would all follow her. One day when she quacked, one duckling came out of the barn and two came out from under a bush. After a while another duckling came out of a pile of straw.
How many ducklings were still lost? zero

⑨ Ferdie lives in an apartment on the second floor. One day he looked out his window and said, "I wonder how to measure how far it is to the ground."
How could he find out? Can you think of ways to measure how far it is? Drop a string, then measure it; measure from the first floor to the ground, then double the measure; ask somebody who knows; estimate on the basis of a known height nearby.

◆ STORY 10 Marcus Builds a Birdhouse

The birds were friendly and Marcus had no trouble getting close to them; but every time he reached out to put the ruler against one, it flew away.

Marcus's friend Portia said, "I have an idea. Why don't you find a picture of that kind of bird in a book and measure the picture? The picture won't fly away."

Does that sound like a good idea? Why not? The picture might not be the same size as the bird.

Marcus looked through a bird book until he found a picture of a bird that looked just like the birds that had come to his birdhouse. He measured the picture with his ruler and found that the bird was 1 inch long. "That can't be right," Marcus said.

How did Marcus know that couldn't be the right size? If birds are wider than 1 inch, they surely must be longer.

62 • Marcus Builds a Birdhouse

Marcus took the bird book over to the Muddles' house and showed the picture to them. "Here's the kind of bird it is," said Marcus, "but I can't find out what size it is."

"Oh, I know that kind of bird," said Mrs. Muddle. "There are some birds like that building a nest in our house, up in the attic."

"How do they get into your attic?" Marcus asked.

"There's a hole in the roof just big enough for them to get through," said Mr. Muddle. "We were going to fix it someday, but now I guess we won't."

Does that give you an idea? How could you find out what size hole to make in the birdhouse? by measuring the hole in the Muddles' roof

Marcus hurried up to the Muddles' attic, stood on some sturdy boxes, and measured the hole in the roof. It was just 2 inches wide.

How wide is that? Show with your fingers. [Demonstrate.]

The Muddles didn't have a drill 2 inches wide, but they had a little saw that would do the job. Mrs. Muddle and Marcus cut a neat hole 2 inches wide in the front of Marcus's birdhouse. Before long the birds came back. This time they went inside and came out again and soon began bringing grass, string, and feathers to put inside their new home.

. . . the end

Story 10 • **63**

LESSON 71

Student Edition pages 155–156

Using Number Patterns

LESSON PLANNER

Objectives

▶ to provide more practice in detecting number patterns

▶ to provide an introduction to cross-sectional size

Context of the Lesson This lesson continues work on number patterns from Lesson 70.

 MANIPULATIVES

paper (large sheets)

scissors

Program Resources

"Pattern" Game Mat

Thinking Story Book, pages 64–65

Practice Master 71

Enrichment Master 71

For additional math integration:
  Math Throughout the Day*

For extra practice:
  CD-ROM* Lesson 71

❶ Warm-Up ⏱ 5 MINUTES

Problem of the Day Present the following problem to the class: I am thinking of two different numbers. Their sum is 6. Their difference is 2. What are the numbers? (4, 2)

Problem-Solving Strategies Ask students who have solved the Problem of the Day to share how they solved it and any strategies they used.

 Have students count up and count down by twos. Use both odd and even beginning numbers.

❷ Teach

Demonstrate Show the following number pattern:

9	☐	15	18	(12)
7	10	☐	16	(13)
5	8	11	☐	(14)
☐	6	9	12	(3)

155 Addition and Subtraction

Name _____

Using Number Patterns

Use patterns to fill in the missing numbers.

❶

+	0	1	2	3	4	5
0	0	1	2	3	**4**	5
1	1	2	3	**4**	5	6
2	2	3	**4**	5	6	7
3	3	**4**	5	6	7	8
4	**4**	5	6	7	8	9
5	5	6	7	8	9	10

 Play the "Pattern" game.

❷ 6 + **0** = 6

❸ 5 + **1** = 6

❹ 4 + **2** = 6

❺ 3 + **3** = 6

❻ 2 + **4** = 6

❼ 7 + **0** = 7

❽ 6 + **1** = 7

❾ 5 + **2** = 7

❿ 4 + **3** = 7

⓫ 3 + **4** = 7

Copyright © SRA/McGraw-Hill

 NOTE TO HOME
Students look for number patterns.

Unit 2   Lesson 71 • **155**

Physical Education Connection As a class, assign body movements for numbers 1–10. For example, 1, clap your hands; 2, reach your arms up; 3, snap your fingers; and so forth. Ask groups of students to develop patterns based on these body movements. As each group demonstrates their body movements, have the others guess the number patterns.

Literature Connection You may wish to read aloud *Bunches and Bunches of Bunnies* by Louise Matthews to reinforce the concept of number patterns.

RETEACHING

Because the skill of pattern recognition evolves slowly, reteaching is not necessary at this time.

*available separately

◆ LESSON 71 Using Number Patterns

Fill in the missing numbers.

⑫

+	0	1	2	3	4	5
0	**0**	1	2	3	4	5
1	1	**2**	3	4	5	6
2	2	3	**4**	5	6	7
3	3	4	5	**6**	7	8
4	4	5	6	7	**8**	9
5	5	6	7	8	9	**10**

 Do the "Making Openings" activity.

Solve these problems.

⑬ $10 - 0 = $ __**10**__

⑭ $10 - 1 = $ __**9**__

⑮ $10 - 2 = $ __**8**__

⑯ $10 - 3 = $ __**7**__

⑰ $10 - 4 = $ __**6**__

⑱ $10 - 3 = $ __**7**__

⑲ $9 - 3 = $ __**6**__

⑳ $8 - 3 = $ __**5**__

㉑ $7 - 3 = $ __**4**__

㉒ $6 - 3 = $ __**3**__

156 • Addition and Subtraction

 NOTE TO HOME
Students look for number patterns.

PRACTICE p. 71

LESSON **71** PRACTICE   Name _____

Use patterns to fill in the missing numbers.

❶

+	0	1	2	3	4	5
0	0	1	2	3	4	5
1	1	2	3	4	5	6
2	2	3	4	5	6	7
3	3	4	5	6	7	8
4	4	5	6	7	8	9
5	5	6	7	8	9	10

Solve these problems.

❷ $4 + \boxed{4} = 8$ ❸ $3 + \boxed{4} = 7$

❹ $5 + \boxed{3} = 8$ ❺ $4 + \boxed{3} = 7$

❻ $6 + \boxed{2} = 8$ ❼ $5 + \boxed{2} = 7$

❽ $10 - 5 = \boxed{5}$ ❾ $6 - 2 = \boxed{4}$

Math Explorations and Applications Level 1 • 71

ENRICHMENT p. 71

LESSON **71** ENRICHMENT   Name _____

When the birds land in the park, they make math problems. Write the number sentences.

❶ the big bird on the trash can $4 + 0 = 4$

❷ the tiny bird on the birdbath $1 + 7 = 8$

❸ the spotted bird on the fence $2 + 8 = 10$

❹ the blackbird on the flowers $3 + 4 = 7$

❺ the tiny bird on the bush $1 + 3 = 4$

❻ the spotted bird on the tree $2 + 6 = 8$

❼ the blackbird on the trash can $3 + 0 = 3$

Math Explorations and Applications Level 1 • 71

Invite volunteers to supply the missing numbers and explain how they knew which answers were correct. If necessary, point out the pattern: each number is two more than the number below it or three more than the number to its left.

Using the Student Pages You may wish to begin the lesson by demonstrating the "Pattern" Game Mat that students can play as they finish pages 155–156.

Have students complete pages 155–156 independently.

 Introducing the "Making Openings" Activity Hold up an object like a pencil or a book. Ask students to cut a hole that is just large enough for the object to pass through without tearing a sheet of **paper**. Repeat, using other objects. This activity gives students an introduction to cross-sectional size and helps to reinforce ideas developed in the Thinking Story "Marcus Builds a Birdhouse."

 Introducing the "Pattern" Game Mat You can use the Game Mat transparency to demonstrate how to play the game. Complete directions are on the Game Mat. *Note:* The "Harder Pattern" game will be introduced in Lesson 134. A copy of this game can also be found on page 406 of this Teacher's Guide.

 Using the Thinking Story Present three problems from those following "Marcus Builds a Birdhouse" on pages 64–65 of the Thinking Story Book or pages 154a–154b of this Guide.

❸ Wrap-Up

In Closing Skip-count aloud by threes, pausing for students to supply some of the numbers.

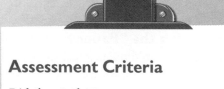 **Informal Assessment** Make up some short number patterns and informally quiz students on the patterns that they find. Ask them how they identified the patterns.

Assessment Criteria

Did the student . . .

✓ find the number patterns on pages 155–156?

✓ intuitively apply the concept of cross-sectional size?

LESSON 72

Student Edition pages 157–158

Solving Problems

LESSON PLANNER

Objectives

▶ to provide practice in solving word problems

▶ to help students develop familiarity with geometric figures

Context of the Lesson The two paper-folding operations taught in this lesson are used to distinguish squares from related shapes.

 MANIPULATIVES **Program Resources**

crayons	Thinking Story Book, pages 64–65
scissors	Practice Master 72
sheets of paper	Enrichment Master 72
	For extra practice: CD-ROM* Lesson 72

❶ Warm-Up

Problem of the Day Present the following problem. Mario has seven cents. He has at least three pennies. What coins does he have? (seven pennies; He can't have a nickel because three pennies and a nickel equals eight cents.)

Problem-Solving Strategies Ask students who have solved the Problem of the Day to share how they solved it and any strategies they used.

 Present addition doubles through 5 + 5. Have students answer in unison.

❷ Teach

 Introducing the "Paper Folding" Activity To teach paper folding as a test for squareness, demonstrate the following directions and have students follow along one step at a time.

1. Fold an $8\frac{1}{2}$" x 11" sheet of **paper** so that the bottom edge of the paper lies along one side.

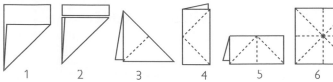

LESSON 72

Name _____

Solving Problems

Listen to the problems.

❶   2

❷   2

❸   6

 Do the "Paper Folding" activity.

 NOTE TO HOME Students listen to and solve word problems.

Unit 2   Lesson 72 • **157**

 Literature Connection Read aloud *Eating Fractions* by Bruce McMillan, to reinforce the concept of equal parts.

GIFTED & TALENTED **MANIPULATIVES**

Meeting Individual Needs Have students identify 12 or more triangles in their folded squares. Then have them identify seven or more rectangles, including squares.

RETEACHING

Because this lesson was an introduction to paper folding, reteaching is not essential at this time. Practice with word problems continues throughout the year.

*available separately

Copyright © SRA/McGraw-Hill

◆ **LESSON 72** Solving Problems

Typical answers are shown
Answers will vary.

Draw one line in each figure to make
two triangles. Color one triangle red.
What color will you make the
other triangle?

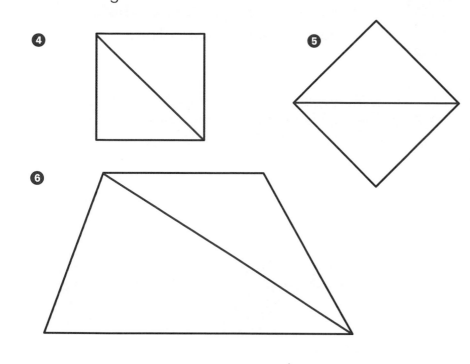

❹

❺

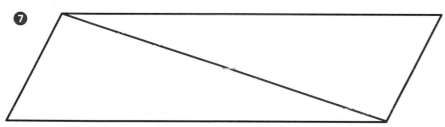

❻

❼

NOTE TO HOME
Students explore the relationship
between triangles and quadrilaterals.

Copyright © SRA/McGraw-Hill

158 • Addition and Subtraction

2. Cut off the strip at the top of the paper.

3. Open the square and fold it on the other diagonal.

4. Open the square again. Fold along the midline so that
one side is folded over to the opposite side.

5. Open the square again. Fold it so that the top and
bottom meet.

6. Open the square. Darken the creases with a **crayon**.

Using the Student Pages Read the following problems
as students look at page 157. Allow time for students to
work each problem before you read the next.

1. Mr. Stein rents bicycles to others, but he always saves one
bicycle for himself. Here are all his bicycles. The Brodys
rent four bicycles. How many bicycles can the next group
rent from Mr. Stein?

2. Six children came to Nora's house. Each one carried an
umbrella and hung it by the window. How many children
have already taken their umbrellas and gone home?

3. These crawling children are tearing holes in their pants.
One pair of pants is too worn to be repaired. Patches can
be sewn on the knees of all the others. How many patches
are needed?

Have students then complete page 158 on their own.

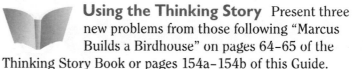

Using the Thinking Story Present three
new problems from those following "Marcus
Builds a Birdhouse" on pages 64–65 of the
Thinking Story Book or pages 154a–154b of this Guide.

❸ Wrap-Up ⏱ 5 MINUTES

In Closing Have students make up a different word
problem for one of the pictures on page 157. Then solve
these problems as a class.

Portfolio Assessment Have students save
their folded squares in their Math Portfolios as
an informal assessment of their explorations
with geometry.

ALTERNATIVE ASSESSMENT

Assessment Criteria

Did the student . . .

✓ correctly fold and mark the creases
in the square?

✓ correctly answer six of seven
problems on pages 157–158?

PRACTICE p. 72

Solve these problems.

❶ Two of the cars have a flat tire.
How many tires are not flat?

___10___

❷ Sarah ate three cookies. Alan ate
two cookies. How many cookies
were there to start?

___15___

❸ Nora rolled a 6 and a 3. Ari rolled
once and got the same sum. What
number did he roll?

___9___

❹ There are two cows in the barn.
How may cows are there all
together?

___9___

72 • Math Explorations and Applications Level 1

ENRICHMENT p. 72

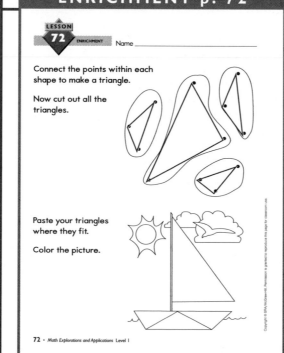

Connect the points within each
shape to make a triangle.

Now cut out all the
triangles.

Paste your triangles
where they fit.

Color the picture.

72 • Math Explorations and Applications Level 1

LESSON

73 Using Maps

Student Edition pages 159–160

LESSON

73

Name _____

Using Maps

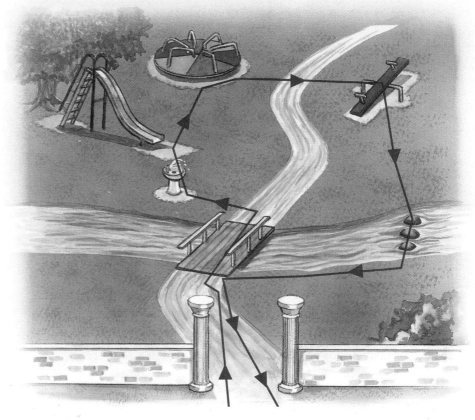

Listen to the story. Show where Roger walked. Draw a line.

LESSON PLANNER

Objectives

▶ to introduce the creation and use of maps

▶ to introduce symbols as a means to represent objects

Context of the Lesson Work on map reading will continue in the next lesson.

✋ MANIPULATIVES   **Program Resources**

paper (optional)   Number Cubes

markers (optional)   Thinking Story Book, pages 64–65

crayons (optional)   Practice Master 73

Enrichment Master 73

For extra practice: CD-ROM* Lesson 73

---

① Warm-Up

Problem of the Day Present the following problem to the class. Louis is taking his dog for a walk. He leaves his house and walks six blocks. He turns right and walks three blocks. He turns right again and walks six blocks. Then he turns right again and walks the remaining three blocks. How many blocks did Louis and his dog walk in all? (18 blocks) Where did he end up? (at the starting point)

Problem-Solving Strategies Ask students who have solved the Problem of the Day to share how they solved it and any strategies they used.

 MENTAL MATH Write the following number sequences on the chalkboard. Challenge students to show the missing numbers with their Number Cubes.

a.   1, _____, 5, 7, 9 (3)

b.   2, 5, _____, 11, 14, (8)

c.   11, _____, 13, 14, 15 (12)

d.   4, 8, 12, _____, 20 (16)

e.   11, 13, 15, _____, 19 (17)

f.   0, 5, 10, 15, _____ (20)

NOTE TO HOME
Students are introduced to a map described in a story.

Unit 2   Lesson 73   •   **159**

 Geography Connection Ask students to name places they would like to visit. Help them find their locations on a map or globe.

Literature Connection You may wish to read aloud *As the Roadrunner Runs* by Gail Hartman to reinforce lesson concepts.

RETEACHING

Extra teaching on map reading is not considered essential at this time, because the next lesson continues work on this skill. However, you might want to have students draw a map of the route they take to and from school, noting landmarks along the way. Then ask students to explain their route to the class.

*available separately

◆ **LESSON 73** Using Maps

Solve these problems.

1. $1 + 8 = \underline{9}$

2. $3 + 2 = \underline{5}$

3. $1 + 5 = \underline{6}$

4. $4 + 2 = \underline{6}$

5. $3 + 3 = \underline{6}$

6. $2 + 6 = \underline{8}$

7. $2 + 4 = \underline{6}$

8. $4 + 4 = \underline{8}$

9. $5 + 1 = \underline{6}$

10. $1 + 3 = \underline{4}$

11. $4 + 3 = \underline{7}$

12. $7 + 1 = \underline{8}$

13. $0 + 6 = \underline{6}$

14. $3 + 4 = \underline{7}$

15. $2 + 2 = \underline{4}$

16. $7 + 2 = \underline{9}$

17. $1 + 1 = \underline{2}$

18. $1 + 2 = \underline{3}$

19. $9 + 1 = \underline{10}$

20. $2 + 3 = \underline{5}$

My time

My time

 NOTE TO HOME
Students practice solving addition problems quickly.

Copyright © SRA/McGraw-Hill

160 · Addition and Subtraction

PRACTICE p. 73

LESSON **73** PRACTICE Name _____

Solve these problems.

1. $7 + 2 = \underline{9}$
2. $3 + 3 = \underline{6}$
3. $4 + 1 = \underline{5}$
4. $5 + 3 = \underline{8}$
5. $0 + 7 = \underline{7}$
6. $2 + 8 = \underline{10}$
7. $1 + 9 = \underline{10}$
8. $4 + 4 = \underline{8}$
9. $3 + 2 = \underline{5}$
10. $2 + 2 = \underline{4}$
11. $8 + 1 = \underline{9}$
12. $1 + 3 = \underline{4}$
13. $3 + 4 = \underline{7}$
14. $5 + 1 = \underline{6}$
15. $9 + 0 = \underline{9}$
16. $7 + 1 = \underline{8}$
17. $4 + 4 = \underline{8}$
18. $1 + 1 = \underline{2}$
19. $2 + 4 = \underline{6}$
20. $6 + 2 = \underline{8}$

My time ☐   My time ☐

Math Explorations and Applications Level 1 · 73

ENRICHMENT p. 73

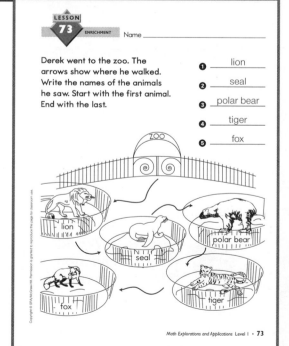

LESSON **73** ENRICHMENT Name _____

Derek went to the zoo. The arrows show where he walked. Write the names of the animals he saw. Start with the first animal. End with the last.

1. lion
2. seal
3. polar bear
4. tiger
5. fox

Math Explorations and Applications Level 1 · 73

---

❷ Teach

Demonstrate Draw a map of the classroom on the chalkboard. Include a few of the room's landmarks, such as your desk, a door, or a window. Draw an *X* on the map to represent another landmark in the classroom, and ask students to determine what the *X* represents.

Using the Student Pages Read the following story aloud, stopping after each sentence to give students time to draw the route onto page 159. "Roger came into the park through the gate that has two big posts. He walked along the path and over the bridge. Right after crossing the bridge, he turned and got a drink of water at the drinking fountain by the stream. Then he went past the slide, straight to the merry-go-round. After playing on the merry-go-round, he went across the path to play on the seesaw (teeter-totter). Then he crossed the stream where there were some rocks to walk on and went out through the gate where he had entered."

Have students complete page 160 as a time trial.

 Using the Thinking Story Present three problems from those following "Marcus Builds a Birdhouse" on pages 64–65 of the Thinking Story Book or pages 154a–154b of this Guide.

❸ Wrap-Up

In Closing Draw routes on the classroom map and invite volunteers to travel the corresponding route in the room.

 Have students compare their time trials from this lesson to those from Lesson 69. Have them write a sentence summarizing their progress.

Assessment Criteria

Did the student . . .

✓ draw the correct route on page 159?

✓ understand the use of an *X* or other symbol to designate a location?

✓ improve his or her time and/or accuracy in the time trials?

LOOKING AHEAD For Lesson 74, each student will need a copy of the classroom map.

LESSON 74 Using Money

Student Edition pages 161–162

LESSON PLANNER

Objectives

▶ to teach the use of pennies, nickels, and dimes to form amounts from 1¢ through 20¢

▶ to continue developing map-reading skills

▶ to provide practice in using a calculator

Context of the Lesson This lesson continues work with maps begun in Lesson 73. It also expands on counting coins, begun in Lesson 42.

 MANIPULATIVES

calculators*
classroom maps
play coins*
school maps (optional)
overhead primary calculator*

Program Resources

Number Cubes
Number Strips
Reteaching Master
Practice Master 74
Enrichment Master 74
For extra practice:
CD-ROM* Lesson 74
Mixed Practice, page 364

Note: This lesson may take more than one day.

① Warm-Up ⏱ 5 MINUTES

 Problem of the Day Present the following problem to the class. Donna gives Eddie 12¢. What coins might she have given him?

(12 pennies; 2 nickels, 2 pennies; 1 dime, 2 pennies; 1 nickel, 7 pennies)

Problem-Solving Strategies Ask students who have solved the Problem of the Day to share how they solved it and any strategies they used.

MENTAL MATH Ask students to tell the total number of cents in the following examples:

a. 1 dime (10)
b. 2 nickels (10)
c. 1 nickel, 3 cents (8)
d. 1 nickel, 4 cents (9)
e. 1 nickel, 5 pennies (10)
f. 1 nickel, 2 cents (7)

② Teach

 Demonstrate Give each student a set of **play coins***. Show how to make 10¢, with two nickels, one dime, or ten pennies. Have students practice making amounts through 20¢.

161 Addition and Subtraction

Name _____

Using Money

 REAL-WORLD CONNECTION Use coins to figure out how much each pair would cost.

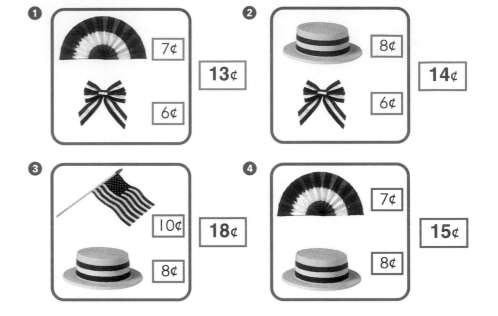

❶ 7¢ / 6¢ → 13¢   ❷ 8¢ / 6¢ → 14¢
❸ 10¢ / 8¢ → 18¢   ❹ 7¢ / 8¢ → 15¢

 **GAME** Play the "Pennies, Nickels, and Dimes" game.

Copyright © SRA/McGraw-Hill

 NOTE TO HOME Students calculate cost using pennies, nickels, and dimes.

Unit 2   Lesson 74 • **161**

 Geography Connection Show students **maps** of your school or community and help them locate different landmarks that may be familiar to them, such as a park. Challenge students to determine the most direct route from one location to another, such as from the school to the playground.

 Real-World Connection Using a calculator, have students find how old they were three years ago and how old they will be three years from now.

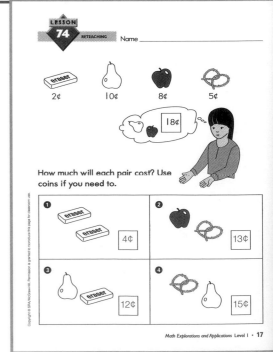

LESSON 74 RETEACHING   Name _____

eraser 2¢   10¢   apple 8¢   5¢

18¢

How much will each pair cost? Use coins if you need to.

❶ eraser eraser → 4¢   ❷ apple → 13¢
❸ pear eraser → 12¢   ❹ → 15¢

Math Explorations and Applications Level I • **17**

*available separately

◆ **LESSON 74** Using Money

Fill in the missing keys. See if the calculator agrees.

⑤ [4] **[+]** [1] **[=]** [5.]

⑥ [4] **[−]** [1] **[=]** [3.]

⑦ [3] [+] [2] **[=]** [5.]

⑧ [3] [−] [2] **[=]** [1.]

⑨ [8] [+] [1] **[=]** [9.]

⑩ [8] [−] [1] **[=]** [7.]

⑪ [5] [+] [**2**] [=] [7.]

⑫ [2] [−] [**1**] [=] [1.]

⑬ [2] [+] [**3**] [=] [5.]

⑭ [3] [−] [**3**] [=] [0.]

GEOGRAPHY CONNECTION

Do the "Treasure Map" activity.

162 • Addition and Subtraction

NOTE TO HOME
Students get more practice with their calculators.

PRACTICE p. 74

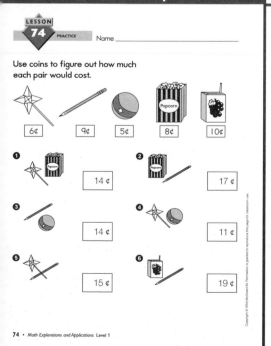

LESSON **74** PRACTICE   Name _____

Use coins to figure out how much each pair would cost.

6¢	9¢	5¢	8¢	10¢

❶ [14 ¢]   ❷ [17 ¢]

❸ [14 ¢]   ❹ [11 ¢]

❺ [15 ¢]   ❻ [19 ¢]

74 • Math Explorations and Applications Level 1

ENRICHMENT p. 74

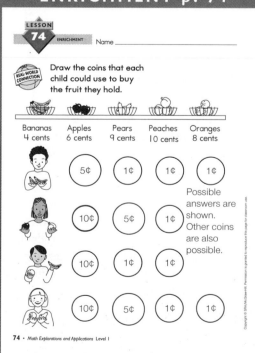

LESSON **74** ENRICHMENT   Name _____

REAL-WORLD CONNECTION
Draw the coins that each child could use to buy the fruit they hold.

Bananas 4 cents	Apples 6 cents	Pears 9 cents	Peaches 10 cents	Oranges 8 cents
5¢	1¢	1¢	1¢	
10¢	5¢	1¢		
10¢	1¢	1¢		
10¢	5¢	1¢	1¢	

Possible answers are shown. Other coins are also possible.

74 • Math Explorations and Applications Level 1

*available separately

Introducing the "Pennies, Nickels, and Dimes" Game Demonstrate and have students play the "Pennies, Nickels, and Dimes" game to reinforce the skill of changing money. Students play in groups of two or three. Each group places 25 play pennies, dimes, and nickels in a "bank." Players take turns rolling a 0–5 Number Cube, taking from the bank the number of pennies indicated. Players then trade their pennies to the bank for nickels and nickels for dimes. The first player to have five nickels and five dimes is the winner. A copy of this game can be found on page 20 of the Home Connections Blackline Masters.

Using the Student Pages Have students do page 161 on their own. Then use the **overhead primary calculator*** to show a display of the number 4. Ask what you would need to do to change the display to the number 5. (Add the 1 by pushing the following keys: **[+]**, **[1]**, **[=]**.) Have students do the exercises on page 162.

Introducing the "Treasure Map" Activity Hide five or six small objects around the classroom. Distribute copies of the **classroom map**. Give directions for finding each treasure by indicating Number Strip distances to be measured on the map. For example, say, "Go three units south from the pencil sharpener, then five units east." Have students draw this route on their maps before looking in the chosen spot. After one object has been located, give directions for the next.

❸ Wrap-Up ⏱ 5 MINUTES

In Closing Have students tell how to form different amounts of money up to 20¢.

Informal Assessment Observe students to see who might need more practice in changing money. Encourage these students to play the "Pennies, Nickels, and Dimes" game again.

Assessment Criteria

Did the student . . .

✓ make accurate change using pennies, nickels, and dimes?

✓ follow the map route during the "Treasure Map" activity?

✓ use a calculator to effectively complete page 162?

LESSON 75
Using Doubles

Student Edition pages 163–164

Name _____

Using Doubles

REAL-WORLD CONNECTION

Solve these problems. Use coins to help you.

	Number of Cents	Twice as much
①	3 ¢	6 ¢
②	6 ¢	12 ¢
③	6 ¢	12 ¢
④	8 ¢	16 ¢
⑤	10 ¢	20 ¢
⑥	10 ¢	20 ¢
⑦	7 ¢	14 ¢

Copyright © SRA/McGraw-Hill

NOTE TO HOME
Students double amounts of money from 0–20.

Unit 2   Lesson 75 • **163**

LESSON PLANNER

Objective
▶ to use pennies, nickels, and dimes to double given amounts of money from 0¢ through 10¢

Context of the Lesson This lesson expands on the work of Lesson 74. In Lesson 89, students will learn to double amounts through 40¢.

 MANIPULATIVES
play coins*

Program Resources
Number Cubes
Thinking Story Book, pages 66–69
Practice Master 75
Enrichment Master 75
For career connections:
  Careers and Math*
For extra practice:
  CD-ROM* Lesson 75

---

❶ Warm-Up ⏱ 5 MINUTES

Problem of the Day Present the following problem to the class: I have 16¢. What is the greatest number of nickels I could have? (3) What is the greatest number of dimes? (1)

Problem-Solving Strategies Ask students who have solved the Problem of the Day to share how they solved it and any strategies they used.

MENTAL MATH Present the following problems for students to solve mentally:

a. 3 + 3 = (6)   b. 0 + 0 = (0)
c. 4 + 4 = (8)   d. 6 + 6 = (12)
e. 8 + 8 = (16)   f. 10 + 10 = (20)
g. 2 + 2 = (4)   h. 5 + 5 = (10)

❷ Teach

Using the Student Pages Have students solve the problems on pages 163 and 164, using **play coins*** if needed.

163 Addition and Subtraction

LEARNING STYLES   **MANIPULATIVES**

Meeting Individual Needs
To help students who are visual learners, ask a volunteer to stand in front of the room. Ask the class to double the number of standing students by bringing another student to the front. Write the number sentence on the chalkboard: 1 + 1 = 2. Then ask students to double the number already standing, and so on. Continue this activity using different numbers.

RETEACHING

MANIPULATIVES Some students may not understand the concept of doubling. Work through easy examples until they do. For example, if they have 4¢ tell them you will give them 4¢ more. Then they will have twice as much. Ask students to use **play coins*** to figure out how many they will have in all.

*available separately

◆ **LESSON 75** Using Doubles

Solve these problems.
How much all together?

⑧ 1¢ + 1¢ = __2__ ¢

⑨ 2¢ + 2¢ = __4__ ¢

⑩ 3¢ + 3¢ = __6__ ¢

⑪ 4¢ + 4¢ = __8__ ¢

⑫ 5¢ + 5¢ = __10__ ¢

⑬ 6¢ + 6¢ = __12__ ¢

⑭ 7¢ + 7¢ = __14__ ¢

⑮ 8¢ + 8¢ = __16__ ¢

⑯ 9¢ + 9¢ = __18__ ¢

⑰ 10¢ + 10¢ = __20__ ¢

Talk about the Thinking Story
"Ferdie Buys a Snack."

164 • Addition and Subtraction

 NOTE TO HOME
Students double amounts of money.

Copyright © SRA/McGraw-Hill

 Using the Number Cubes Give each student a set of play coins and have them make 6¢. Ask them to double that amount by showing another 6¢. Challenge them to show the total amount of cents (12¢) with their Number Cubes. Ask them to double other coin amounts including 0¢, showing each result with their Number Cubes.

 Using the Thinking Story Read aloud and discuss "Ferdie Buys a Snack" on pages 66–69 of the Thinking Story Book.

Ask students what Ferdie could have done if Mr. Mudancia had not come along to help him. Have them write their response in their Math Journal.

 Using the "Pennies, Nickels, and Dimes" Game To provide extra practice working with coins, have students replay the "Pennies, Nickels, and Dimes" game, introduced in Lesson 74. A copy of this game can also be found on page 20 of the Home Connections Blackline Masters.

❸ Wrap-Up ⏱ 5 MINUTES

In Closing Ask students what a double is. (the same number added to itself) Have students give examples of addition sentences that use doubles such as 4 + 4 = 8 and 10 + 10 = 20.

Performance Assessment Observe students during the Number Cube activities and as they work on the student pages. Assess individual students who seem to be having difficulty by drawing six squares and asking students to double the amount. Repeat this with other amounts as needed.

PRACTICE p. 75

LESSON 75 PRACTICE Name _____

Solve these problems. Use coins to help you.

	Number of Cents	Twice as Much
❶	4 ¢	8 ¢
❷	10 ¢	20 ¢
❸	6 ¢	12 ¢
❹	7 ¢	14 ¢
❺	9 ¢	18 ¢

How much all together?

❻ 10¢ + 10¢ = __20__ ¢   ❼ 9¢ + 9¢ = __18__ ¢

❽ 8¢ + 8¢ = __16__ ¢   ❾ 7¢ + 7¢ = __14__ ¢

❿ 6¢ + 6¢ = __12__ ¢   ⓫ 5¢ + 5¢ = __10__ ¢

Math Explorations and Applications Level 1 • 75

ENRICHMENT p. 75

LESSON 75 ENRICHMENT Name _____

BUS FARE
Red Bus—9 cents   Blue Bus—10 cents
Green Bus—7 cents   Orange Bus—6 cents
Yellow Bus—8 cents

Use play money to help.

❶ Sean and Barb have four pennies and two nickels. Can they both take the Orange Bus? If so, how much money is left?   __yes; 2¢__

❷ Kiri and Ted have three pennies and three nickels. Can they both take the Red Bus? If so, how much money is left?   __yes; 0¢__

❸ Brian and Deb have three pennies and two nickels. Can they both take the Green Bus? If so, how much money is left?   __no__

❹ Shanika and Fran have seven pennies and two nickels. Can they both take the Yellow Bus? If so, how much money is left?   __yes; 1¢__

Math Explorations and Applications Level 1 • 75

Assessment Criteria

Did the student . . .

✓ demonstrate understanding of how to form amounts of money?

✓ correctly answer 14 of 17 problems on pages 163–164?

✓ participate in the discussion of the Thinking Story?

Ferdie Buys a Snack

➊ Manolita had a nickel. She traded it for pennies at Mr. Muddle's store.
How many pennies did she get? five

➋ Portia ate half a muffin. Ferdie ate just as much as Portia.
How many muffins did the two of them eat together? one

➌ Ferdie is one year older than Portia, his younger sister. "I'll catch up," said Portia.
Will she? Why not? Ferdie will always be one year older.
How old will Portia be when Ferdie is ten? nine

➍ "I have three coins in my purse," said Ms. Eng, "and together they make 15 cents."
Can anyone figure out what they are? three nickels

"In my coat pocket I have only two coins," said Ms. Eng, "and together they make 15 cents."
What are they? a dime and a nickel

"That's nothing," said Ferdie. "I have four coins in my pocket, and together they make eight cents. I'll bet nobody can figure out what I have!"
Can you? a nickel and three pennies

THINKING STORY

Ferdie Buys a Snack

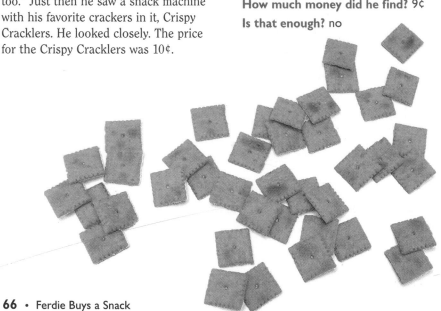

One day when Ferdie was walking down the street he got very hungry. "I guess I forgot to eat breakfast today," he said, "and lunch too." Just then he saw a snack machine with his favorite crackers in it, Crispy Cracklers. He looked closely. The price for the Crispy Cracklers was 10¢.

Ferdie looked through his pockets. He found six cents in one pocket, two cents in another pocket, and one cent in another.

How much money did he find? 9¢

Is that enough? no

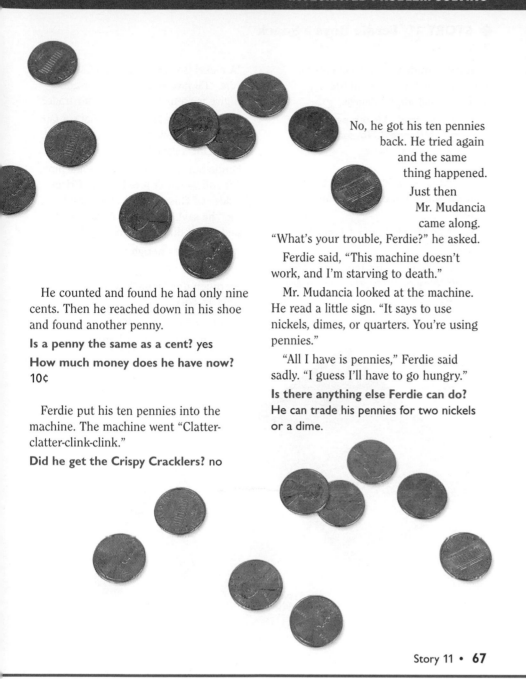

No, he got his ten pennies back. He tried again and the same thing happened.

Just then Mr. Mudancia came along. "What's your trouble, Ferdie?" he asked.

Ferdie said, "This machine doesn't work, and I'm starving to death."

Mr. Mudancia looked at the machine. He read a little sign. "It says to use nickels, dimes, or quarters. You're using pennies."

"All I have is pennies," Ferdie said sadly. "I guess I'll have to go hungry."

Is there anything else Ferdie can do? He can trade his pennies for two nickels or a dime.

He counted and found he had only nine cents. Then he reached down in his shoe and found another penny.

Is a penny the same as a cent? yes
How much money does he have now? 10¢

Ferdie put his ten pennies into the machine. The machine went "Clatter-clatter-clink-clink."

Did he get the Crispy Cracklers? no

Story 11 • **67**

❺ Mr. Mudancia had a desk with six empty drawers in it. He filled two of the drawers with dirt and is growing mushrooms in them.
What does he have now? a desk with four empty drawers, plus two drawers with mushrooms

❻ Loretta the Letter Carrier and her husband, Roger, had two dogs and a cat. Yesterday one of the dogs had three puppies.
How many dogs does she have now? five

❼ Loretta and Roger's cat had five kittens. Loretta gave one to Manolita, one to Willy, and one to Marcus. But Marcus's mother wouldn't let him keep his, so he had to give it back.
How many kittens does Loretta have now? three

❽ Portia had nine dandelions. She gave away all but two of them.
How many are left? two

❾ Mr. Muddle gets lost every time he does downtown at night. He went downtown six times last week.
How many times did he get lost? can't tell
What do you need to know before you can be sure? how many times he went downtown at night

◆ STORY 11 Ferdie Buys a Snack

"You can trade your ten pennies for something that will work in the machine," said Mr. Mudancia.

Could Ferdie trade his ten pennies for a quarter? Why not? No, ten pennies are not equal to a quarter.

"A great idea!" said Ferdie. "I believe a dime is worth ten cents. Do you have a dime?"

"No," said Mr. Mudancia. " I only have nickels."

Should Ferdie trade his ten pennies for a nickel? Why not? No, ten pennies are worth two nickels.

"A nickel is worth five cents," said Ferdie. "I'll give you five pennies and you give me a nickel. Is that a fair trade?"

"Yes," said Mr. Mudancia, "that's a fair trade." Ferdie gave him five pennies and Mr. Mudancia gave Ferdie a nickel.

Ferdie put the nickel into the machine, but it still wouldn't give him the Crispy Cracklers. "This machine still doesn't work," he said. "I put in a nickel just as it said, but it didn't give me anything."

Did Ferdie put enough money into the machine? no

How much does a pack of Crispy Cracklers cost? 10¢

How many cents is a nickel? five

How many nickels does Ferdie need? two

68 • Ferdie Buys a Snack

"A nickel is only five cents," said Mr. Mudancia. "Crispy Cracklers cost ten cents. You have to put in two nickels."

"But I have only one nickel," said Ferdie.

How could Ferdie get another nickel? trade his five pennies for one nickel

"You still have five more pennies," said Mr. Mudancia. "If you give them to me, I'll give you another nickel."

Ferdie gave Mr. Mudancia the five pennies and got another nickel. Then Ferdie looked at the two nickels in his hand, and his face grew sad. "I used to have ten pennies and now all I have are these two nickels. I think I'm losing money on this deal."

Is Ferdie losing money? Why not? No, two nickels are worth ten pennies.

How many cents are two nickels worth? ten

Ferdie put the two nickels in the machine and out dropped the Crispy Cracklers. Ferdie opened them and began eating. "What a marvelous cracker!" he said. "Why, it's worth more than two nickels. It's almost worth a dime!"

Does that make sense? Why not? No, two nickels have the same value as a dime.

. . . the end

Story 11 • **69**

LESSON 76

Student Edition pages 165–166

Adding and Subtracting on a Number Line

LESSON PLANNER

Objectives

▶ to teach students to use a 0–20 number line to add and subtract

▶ to provide experience in estimating height in nonstandard units of measurement

Context of the Lesson Adding and subtracting numbers in the 10–20 range will be continued in subsequent lessons.

 MANIPULATIVES

craft sticks

0–20 chalkboard and desk number lines

Program Resources

Number Cubes

Thinking Story Book, pages 70–71

Practice Master 76

Enrichment Master 76

For extra practice:
CD-ROM* Lesson 76

1 Warm-Up

Problem of the Day Draw the following shape on the chalkboard. Have students copy the shape and show two more ways to divide a square.

Problem-Solving Strategies Ask students who have solved the Problem of the Day to share how they solved it and any strategies they used.

 Copy the following array onto the chalkboard. Cover one number at a time and have students identify the number.

7	8	9	10	11
4	5	6	7	8
10	11	12	13	14

LESSON 76

Name _____

Adding and Subtracting on a Number Line

Solve these problems. Use the number line.

```
20
19
18
17
16
15
14
13
12
11
10
 9
 8
 7
 6
 5
 4
 3
 2
 1
 0
```

❶ 11 + 2 = __13__   ❷ 13 − 4 = __9__

❸ 9 + 3 = __12__   ❹ 11 − 3 = __8__

❺ 18 − 4 = __14__   ❻ 16 − 6 = __10__

❼ 15 + 4 = __19__   ❽ 12 + 4 = __16__

❾ 8 + 3 = __11__   ❿ 9 − 2 = __7__

⓫ 14 − 2 = __12__   ⓬ 12 − 7 = __5__

⓭ 7 + 3 = __10__   ⓮ 8 + 9 = __17__

 HEALTH CONNECTION Do the "Estimating Height" activity.

NOTE TO HOME
Students use a number line to add and subtract to 20.

Unit 2   Lesson 76   •   **165**

RETEACHING

Because work with addition and subtraction on a number line continues in the following lesson, reteaching is not required at this time.

 SPECIAL NEEDS • **MANIPULATIVES**

Meeting Individual Needs Have 21 students each hold up a number from 0–20, and stand next to each other to make a human number line. Other students can practice adding and subtracting using the human number line. For example, to add 14 + 3, have a student start with the number 14 student and count up three more people.

*available separately

◆ **LESSON 76** Adding and Subtracting on a Number Line

Solve these problems. They are easier than they look.

⑮ 2 + 8 = __10__   ㉓ 19 – 5 = __14__

⑯ 2 + 9 = __11__   ㉔ 18 – 5 = __13__

⑰ 2 + 10 = __12__   ㉕ 17 – 5 = __12__

⑱ 2 + 11 = __13__   ㉖ 16 – 5 = __11__

⑲ 3 + 11 = __14__   ㉗ 15 – 5 = __10__

⑳ 4 + 11 = __15__   ㉘ 16 – 6 = __10__

㉑ 5 + 11 = __16__   ㉙ 17 – 7 = __10__

㉒ 6 + 11 = __17__   ㉚ 18 – 8 = __10__

In your Math Journal tell why these problems are easier than they look.

166 · Addition and Subtraction

 NOTE TO HOME Students solve addition and subtraction problems up to 20.

Copyright © SRA/McGraw-Hill

---

②Teach

Demonstrate Draw a 0–20 vertical **number line** on the chalkboard. Demonstrate finger stepping on the number line. Then provide students problems to solve by finger stepping on their desk number lines. Have them show their answers with Number Cubes.

Introducing the "Estimating Height" Activity Use this activity to provide experience estimating in nonstandard units. A volunteer stands against the wall in front of the room and students estimate the student's height in **craft sticks**. Have several students come up and try to measure with craft sticks. Guide students to try methods such as having the student lie on the floor and laying sticks alongside him or her; pasting sticks to a strip of paper; or using sticks to mark off units on a strip of paper to make a ruler.

Using the Student Pages Have students use their number lines to complete pages 165–166 on their own.

Using the Thinking Story Present three new problems from those following "Ferdie Buys a Snack" on pages 70–71 of the Thinking Story Book or pages 164a–164b of this Guide.

③Wrap-Up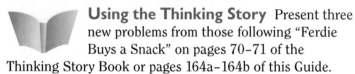

In Closing Correct pages 165–166 with the class. Have volunteers demonstrate how they solved the problems.

 Check students' answers to the problems on pages 165–166 to determine if they are having difficulty using the number line.

Assessment Criteria

Did the student . . .

✓ correctly solve 24 of 30 problems on pages 165–166?

✓ make sensible suggestions for measuring height during the activity?

PRACTICE p. 76

LESSON 76 PRACTICE Name_____

Solve these problems. Use the number line.

```
20
19
18       ❶   8      ❷   7      ❸   9      ❹  12
17          + 4        + 5        + 3        + 4
16          ----       ----       ----       ----
15           12         12         12         16
14
13       ❺  11      ❻  13      ❼   6      ❽  17
12          + 5        + 2        + 4        + 0
11          ----       ----       ----       ----
10           16         15         10         17
 9
 8       ❾ 16 + 2 = __18__     ❿ 7 + 4 = __11__
 7
 6       ⓫ 9 + 5 = __14__     ⓬ 6 + 5 = __11__
 5
 4       ⓭ 18 + 0 = __18__    ⓮ 13 + 5 = __18__
 3
 2
 1       ⓯ 11 + 4 = __15__    ⓰ 12 + 6 = __18__
 0
```

76 · Math Explorations and Applications Level 1

ENRICHMENT p. 76

LESSON 76 ENRICHMENT Name_____

Write number sentences to solve the problems.

Maria and Paul stack 20 blocks.

❶ Four blocks fall.   20 – 4 = 16

❷ Paul adds two blocks.   16 + 2 = 18

❸ Seven blocks fall.   18 – 7 = 11

❹ Maria adds three blocks.   11 + 3 = 14

❺ Paul adds one block.   14 + 1 = 15

❻ Ten blocks fall.   15 – 10 = 5

❼ Paul adds four blocks.   5 + 4 = 9

❽ Maria adds eight blocks.   9 + 8 = 17

❾ All the blocks fall.   17 – 17 = 0

76 · Math Explorations and Applications Level 1

LESSON 77

Student Edition pages 167–168

Number Line Practice

LESSON PLANNER

Objectives

▶ to provide practice using the 0–20 number line for addition and subtraction problems

▶ to teach how to test a geometric figure for squareness

▶ to provide practice in estimating heights in nonstandard units

Context of the Lesson Adding and subtracting numbers in the 0–20 range is continued in the next lesson. Geometric paper folding was first introduced as the basis for testing squareness in Lesson 72.

 MANIPULATIVES **Program Resources**

craft sticks   Thinking Story Book, pages 70–71

scissors   Reteaching Master

   Practice Master 77

   Enrichment Master 77

   For extra practice:
   CD-ROM* Lesson 77

1 Warm-Up ⏱ 5 MINUTES

Problem of the Day Present the following problem to the class. Carlos started at 5 on the number line. He moved his finger up two places. Then he moved it back three places. Where did he end? (4)

Problem-Solving Strategies Ask students who have solved the Problem of the Day to share how they solved it and any strategies they used.

MENTAL MATH Tell students to suppose that they are standing at the number 10 on a number line. Have them mentally count the number of steps they must take to arrive at the following numbers. Repeat, having students begin at the number 5. Guide students to see that they don't need a number line, because they know that 10 + 5 = 15, and so on.

a. 15 (5) (10)   b. 18 (8) (13)

c. 12 (2) (7)   d. 14 (4) (9)

2 Teach

Using the Student Pages Have students do the problems on page 167. Then work on page 168 as a class. Review the paper-folding technique used in Lesson 72. Ask students to predict whether the garden will be a square. Then have them cut out the garden and fold it to check their prediction. (a square)

167 Addition and Subtraction

LESSON 77

Name _____

Number Line Practice

Solve these problems. Use the number line.

1 $10 + 2 = \underline{12}$ **2** $8 - 5 = \underline{3}$

3 $9 + 2 = \underline{11}$ **4** $18 - 5 = \underline{13}$

5 $14 + 4 = \underline{18}$ **6** $16 + 3 = \underline{19}$

7
$$\begin{array}{r} 17 \\ +\ 2 \\ \hline 19 \end{array}$$
8
$$\begin{array}{r} 16 \\ -\ 5 \\ \hline 11 \end{array}$$
9
$$\begin{array}{r} 14 \\ -\ 5 \\ \hline 9 \end{array}$$
10
$$\begin{array}{r} 11 \\ -\ 6 \\ \hline 5 \end{array}$$

11
$$\begin{array}{r} 19 \\ +\ 0 \\ \hline 19 \end{array}$$
12
$$\begin{array}{r} 12 \\ +\ 3 \\ \hline 15 \end{array}$$
13
$$\begin{array}{r} 1 \\ +\ 8 \\ \hline 9 \end{array}$$
14
$$\begin{array}{r} 2 \\ +\ 8 \\ \hline 10 \end{array}$$

 **GAME** Play the "Count to 20 by Ones and Twos" game.

 NOTE TO HOME Students use the number line to do addition and subtraction problems to 20.

 Math Connection Challenge groups of students to look around the room and find as many square figures as they can. Invite groups to share their lists with the class.

Literature Connection You might want to read to students *The One That Got Away* by Percival Everett to reinforce lesson concepts.

RETEACHING p. 18

LESSON 77 RETEACHING

Name _____

Solve these problems. Use the number line.

1 $10 + 5 = \underline{15}$ **2** $8 - 4 = \underline{4}$

3 $9 + 3 = \underline{12}$ **4** $16 + 1 = \underline{17}$

5 $14 - 2 = \underline{12}$ **6** $13 - 3 = \underline{10}$

7 $11 - 3 = \underline{8}$ **8** $10 + 0 = \underline{10}$

9
$$\begin{array}{r} 18 \\ +\ 2 \\ \hline 20 \end{array}$$
10
$$\begin{array}{r} 12 \\ -\ 3 \\ \hline 9 \end{array}$$
11
$$\begin{array}{r} 17 \\ -\ 4 \\ \hline 13 \end{array}$$
12
$$\begin{array}{r} 10 \\ -\ 6 \\ \hline 4 \end{array}$$

18 • *Math Explorations and Applications Level 1*

*available separately

◆ LESSON 77 Number Line Practice

Look at this garden. Is it a square?

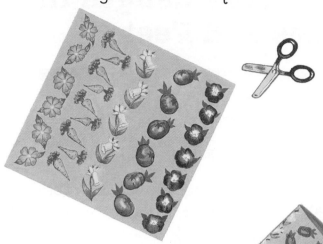

Now cut out the garden. Fold it to be sure that it is a square. First fold it down the middle like this.

Then fold it from corner to corner like this.

Does it fit both times? **yes**

What can you say about this shape?
A square can be divided into equal triangles.

168 • Addition and Subtraction

 NOTE TO HOME
Students test a geometric figure for squareness.

Copyright © SRA/McGraw-Hill

PRACTICE p. 77

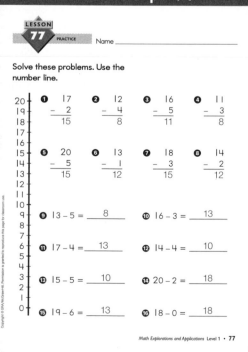

Solve these problems. Use the number line.

❶ $\begin{array}{r} 17 \\ -\ 2 \\ \hline 15 \end{array}$ ❷ $\begin{array}{r} 12 \\ -\ 4 \\ \hline 8 \end{array}$ ❸ $\begin{array}{r} 16 \\ -\ 5 \\ \hline 11 \end{array}$ ❹ $\begin{array}{r} 11 \\ -\ 3 \\ \hline 8 \end{array}$	
❺ $\begin{array}{r} 20 \\ -\ 5 \\ \hline 15 \end{array}$ ❻ $\begin{array}{r} 13 \\ -\ 1 \\ \hline 12 \end{array}$ ❼ $\begin{array}{r} 18 \\ -\ 3 \\ \hline 15 \end{array}$ ❽ $\begin{array}{r} 14 \\ -\ 2 \\ \hline 12 \end{array}$	

❾ $13 - 5 = \underline{\ 8\ }$ ❿ $16 - 3 = \underline{\ 13\ }$

⓫ $17 - 4 = \underline{\ 13\ }$ ⓬ $14 - 4 = \underline{\ 10\ }$

⓭ $15 - 5 = \underline{\ 10\ }$ ⓮ $20 - 2 = \underline{\ 18\ }$

⓯ $19 - 6 = \underline{\ 13\ }$ ⓰ $18 - 0 = \underline{\ 18\ }$

Math Explorations and Applications Level 1 • 77

ENRICHMENT p. 77

Start at ★. Follow the number path. You should end with 5.

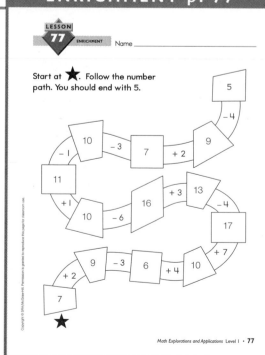

Math Explorations and Applications Level 1 • 77

 Using the "Estimating Height" Activity
Continue the activity on estimating heights from Lesson 76, giving more students a chance to be measured. Have **craft sticks** available.

Introducing the "Count to 20 by Ones or Twos" Game Demonstrate and have students play the "Count to 20 by Ones or Twos" game to reinforce the skill of counting. Each pair of students places a marker at 0 on a number line. Partners take turns moving the marker one or two steps ahead, saying each number as the marker touches it. The player who reaches 20 first is the winner. A copy of this game can also be found on page 21 of the Home Connections Blackline Masters.

Using the Thinking Story Present two problems from those following "Ferdie Buys a Snack" on pages 70–71 of the Thinking Story Book or pages 164a–164b of this Guide.

❸ Wrap-Up

In Closing Give students a problem, for example, 16 + 2. Have a volunteer show how to use the number line to find the answer. Ask students to share other strategies used to solve the problem.

ANALYZING ANSWERS The most common difficulty students experience in solving number line problems is that they count the starting number. That is, for 18 + 2, they count 18, 19. Demonstrate how to move your finger on the number line and count the spaces moved.

ALTERNATIVE ASSESSMENT **Informal Assessment** Interview students who are having difficulty to determine the specific problem involved. If students are making counting errors, provide help as in Analyzing Answers or have students play this lesson's game again. For other kinds of errors, have students play one of the games already introduced to help them practice specific skills.

Assessment Criteria

Did the student . . .

✓ understand that he or she must move one space up or down before starting to count?

✓ correctly test the garden for squareness?

✓ improve his or her accuracy in estimating heights?

LESSON 78

Measuring Length in Inches and Feet

Measuring Length in Inches and Feet

LESSON PLANNER

Objectives

▶ to provide practice in estimating and measuring lengths of objects in inches and feet

▶ to provide opportunities to use measurements to improve estimates

Context of the Lesson This lesson is a follow-up to the measurement activity in Lesson 76.

 MANIPULATIVES

MANIPULATIVES	Program Resources
chalkboard eraser	Thinking Story Book, pages 70–71
inch rulers	Practice Master 78
markers	Enrichment Master 78
staplers	For extra practice: CD-ROM* Lesson 78

❶ Warm-Up 5 MINUTES

Problem of the Day Present the following problem to the class: The police department gives out badges in order. So far their officers have badges #01, #03, and #05. What badge number will the next police officer receive? (#07)

Problem-Solving Strategies Ask students who have solved the Problem of the Day to share how they solved it and any strategies they used.

MENTAL MATH Read aloud the following problems and have students write the answers quickly on paper.

a. 3 – 2 = (1)   b. 9 – 0 = (9)   c. 5 + 2 = (7)

d. 10 – 2 = (8)   e. 7 – 2 = (5)   f. 4 + 3 = (7)

❷ Teach

Demonstrate Display and demonstrate how to use an **inch ruler** to measure inches and feet by measuring objects, such as the width of a book and the height of your desk.

169 Addition and Subtraction

Measuring Length in Inches and Feet

Measuring Length in Inches and Feet

The pencil is about 5 inches long.

 REAL-WORLD CONNECTION Measure things in your classroom. Estimate first, then use your ruler to check. **Accept all reasonable answers.**

	Estimate	Measure
		inches
		inches
		inches

 NOTE TO HOME Students estimate and measure in inches.

Copyright © SRA/McGraw-Hill

Unit 2   Lesson 78 • **169**

 PHYSICAL EDUCATION CONNECTION **Physical Education Connection**

Have students write an estimate for the distance they think they can broad-jump. Then have students work in pairs, taking turns doing a broad jump while a partner measures it. Have partners share and compare their estimates and actual measurements.

RETEACHING

 MANIPULATIVES Have students use their rulers to draw lines that are 3 inches, 4 inches, 8 inches, and 11 inches long. Then have volunteers come up to the chalkboard and use their rulers to measure and draw lines that are 1, 2, and 3 feet long.

*available separately

◆ **LESSON 78** Measuring Length in Inches and Feet

There are 12 inches in 1 foot.
Your math book is a little less
than 1 foot long.

REAL-WORLD CONNECTION

Listen to the teacher.
How many feet? Estimate first, then
use your ruler to check.

Answers will depend on objects chosen.

Object	Estimate	Measure
		feet
		feet
		feet
		feet
		feet

Copyright © SRA/McGraw-Hill

170 • Addition and Subtraction

NOTE TO HOME
Students estimate and measure in feet.

PRACTICE p. 78

LESSON 78 PRACTICE Name_____

Measure each object. Estimate first.
Then use your ruler to check. Estimates will vary.

❶ Estimate _____ Measure __3__ inches

❷ Estimate _____ Measure __5__ inches

❸ Estimate _____ Measure __2__ inches

❹ Estimate _____ Measure __4__ inches

❺ Estimate _____ Measure __1__ inches

78 • Math Explorations and Applications Level 1

ENRICHMENT p. 78

LESSON 78 ENRICHMENT Name_____

Choose the unit of measurement.
You can pick inches or feet.

How tall?

❶ 48 ____inches____

❷ 6 ____feet____

❸ 3 ____inches____

❹ 2 ____feet____

❺ 26 ____feet____

❻ 26 ____inches____

❼ 2 ____feet____
   24 ____inches____

❽ 36 ____inches____
   3 ____feet____

78 • Math Explorations and Applications Level 1

MANIPULATIVES

Using the Student Pages Explain that
students can determine that the pencil on page
169 is about 5 inches long by looking at the ruler
next to it. Then display a **chalkboard eraser**, a **stapler**, and a
marker. Have students estimate the length of each object
and write the estimate in the table before measuring the real
object and writing the actual measurement. Encourage them
to use the information from each estimate to help them make
a better estimate the next time.

For page 170, explain that there are 12 inches in a foot. Have
students use a foot **ruler** to measure their math book. Then
write the names of the following objects on the chalkboard:
teacher's bookcase; door; chalkboard; student's desk; chair.
Have students copy the names of these objects on the table
on page 170 and write their estimates (to the nearest foot)
next to the first item. Have students work in small groups to
measure the object and record their measurements (to the
nearest foot) on the chart. Have students estimate, then
measure, the second object before they estimate and measure
the third, fourth, and fifth.

Using the Thinking Story Present two
new problems from those following "Ferdie
Buys a Snack" found on pages 70–71 of the
Thinking Story Book or pages 164a–164b of this Guide.

❸ Wrap-Up

5 MINUTES

In Closing Have students estimate the height of the
classroom door in feet. Have them write their estimates on
paper before measuring and writing the actual measurement.

ALTERNATIVE ASSESSMENT
Performance Assessment Observe
students as they measure objects to see who
can accurately measure to the nearest inch and
nearest foot.

Assessment Criterion

Did the student . . .

✓ make sensible estimates and
accurate measurements for the
objects listed on pages 169–170?

LESSON 79

Student Edition pages 171–172

Measuring Length in Metric Units

LESSON PLANNER

Objectives

▶ to teach students to estimate lengths of objects in centimeters

▶ to provide practice in measuring lengths of objects in centimeters

▶ to provide practice in using measurements to improve estimates

Context of the Lesson This is the second lesson on measuring length in standard units. In Lesson 78 students measured length in customary units.

 MANIPULATIVES

centimeter rulers

crayon

Program Resources

Number Cubes

Reteaching Master

Practice Master 79

Enrichment Master 79

For extra practice:
CD-ROM* Lesson 79

❶ Warm-Up

5 MINUTES

 Problem of the Day Present the following problem to the class. Helen has nine grapes. Can she share them evenly with her sister? Why or why not? (No, because no matter how you group them, there is always one left over and individual grapes cannot be easily divided.)

Problem-Solving Strategies Ask students who have solved the Problem of the Day to share how they solved it and any strategies they used.

MENTAL MATH Read aloud the following problems and have students show their answers with Number Cubes.

a. 4 + 2 = (6)   b. 6 + 1 = (7)

c. 8 – 2 = (6)   d. 5 – 0 = (5)

e. 4 + 0 = (4)   f. 7 + 2 = (9)

LESSON 79

Name _____

Measuring Length in Metric Units

REAL-WORLD CONNECTION

The pen is 8 centimeters long.

How many centimeters? Use your ruler to find out.

 7

14

9

3

Copyright © SRA/McGraw-Hill

🎒 **NOTE TO HOME**
Students measure in centimeters.

Unit 2   Lesson 79 • **171**

 Have students draw triangles, squares, and rectangles with sides of various centimeters in length, for example, a triangle with sides of 4 centimeters; or a square with sides of 5 centimeters. Then have them exchange papers with other students and write an estimate for the length of each side. Then, have students meet with those students who drew them to compare the estimate to the actual measurement.

COOPERATIVE LEARNING

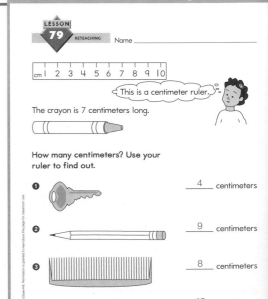

LESSON 79 RETEACHING   Name _____

This is a centimeter ruler.

The crayon is 7 centimeters long.

How many centimeters? Use your ruler to find out.

❶ _____4_____ centimeters

❷ _____9_____ centimeters

❸ _____8_____ centimeters

❹ _____10_____ centimeters

Math Explorations and Applications Level I • **19**

*available separately

◆ LESSON 79 Measuring Length in Metric Units

How many centimeters? Estimate first. Then use your ruler to check. **Accept all reasonable estimates.**

	Estimate	Measure
leaf		**6** centimeters
hot dog		**10** centimeters
pepper		**7** centimeters
pencil		**14** centimeters

Copyright © SRA/McGraw-Hill

172 • Addition and Subtraction

NOTE TO HOME
Students estimate and measure in centimeters.

❷ Teach

Demonstrate Display a **centimeter ruler**. Demonstrate how to use it to measure various objects, such as the length of a piece of chalk or a paper clip.

Using the Student Pages Show students how to use a ruler to measure the pen on page 171. Then have students complete page 171. For page 172, tell students to estimate and measure the leaf before going on to the hot dog. Remind them to use each estimate and exact measurement to help them make more accurate estimates for the next object. When finished, have students share and compare their estimates and answers.

❸ Wrap-Up 🕐 5 MINUTES

In Closing Have students estimate in centimeters the length of a **crayon**. Have them write their estimates on paper before measuring and writing the actual measurement.

Performance Assessment Observe students as they measure objects to see who can accurately measure in centimeters.

Assessment Criteria

Did the student . . .

✓ correctly measure lengths of objects in centimeters?

✓ use actual measurements to improve the accuracy of subsequent estimates of length?

✓ make sensible estimates and accurate measurements for the objects shown on pages 171–172?

PRACTICE p. 79

LESSON 79 PRACTICE Name _____

How many centimeters? Estimate first. Estimates will vary. Then use your ruler to check.

❶
Estimate _____ Measure __11__ centimeters

❷
Estimate _____ Measure __6__ centimeters

❸
Estimate _____ Measure __12__ centimeters

❹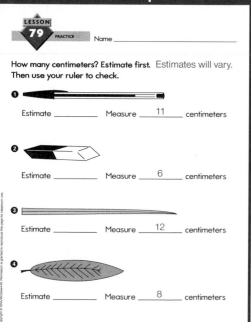
Estimate _____ Measure __8__ centimeters

Math Explorations and Applications Level 1 • **79**

ENRICHMENT p. 79

LESSON 79 ENRICHMENT Name _____

Follow the steps. Answer the questions.

❶ Start at A. Draw a straight line to B.

❷ How long is the line? ____15____ cm

❸ Draw a line from A to C.

❹ How long is the line? ____11____ cm

❺ Draw a line from C to B.

❻ How long is the line? ____9____ cm

❼ What shape did you make? ___triangle___

Math Explorations and Applications Level 1 • **79**

LESSON 80

Adding and Subtracting Using Money

Student Edition pages 173-174

Name _____

Adding and Subtracting Using Money

REAL-WORLD CONNECTION

Solve these problems. Use play money to help you.

1 10 and (pennies)   10 + 3 = __13__

2 5 and 10   5 + 10 = __15__

3 10   spend 5   11 − 5 = __6__

4 10 10 spend 5   20 − 6 = __14__

5   1 and 10   1 + 12 = __13__

6 5 and 10 1   5 + 11 = __16__

NOTE TO HOME
Students use money to practice adding and subtracting to 20.

Copyright © SRA/McGraw-Hill

Unit 2   Lesson 80 • **173**

LESSON PLANNER

Objectives

✓ to assess students' ability to add and subtract in the 0–20 range

▶ to give practice in adding and subtracting numbers through 20 using a number line and play money

Context of the Lesson This lesson is the third of three lessons on adding and subtracting numbers in the 0–20 range. It contains a Mastery Checkpoint for this skill.

 MANIPULATIVES   **Program Resources**

play money*   Number Cubes

overhead coins*   Thinking Story Book, pages 70–71

Practice Master 80

Enrichment Master 80

Assessment Master

For extra practice:
  CD-ROM* Lesson 80
  Mixed Practice, page 365

---

❶ Warm-Up ⏱ 5 MINUTES

Problem of the Day Present the following problem to the class. Oscar has one dime, one nickel, and two pennies (17¢). Kari has three nickels and one penny (16¢). Who has more? (Oscar) How much more? (1¢)

Problem-Solving Strategies Ask students who have solved the Problem of the Day to share how they solved it and any strategies they used.

 MENTAL MATH Have students solve the following using mental math. Use Number Cubes to show their answers. Present the problems orally.

a. 9¢ + 9¢ = (18¢)   **b.** 2¢ + 2¢ = (4¢)

c. 5¢ + 5¢ = (10¢)   **d.** 0¢ + 5¢ = (5¢)

e. 6¢ + 6¢ = (12¢)   **f.** 7¢ + 7¢ = (14¢)

g. 8¢ + 8¢ = (16¢)   **h.** 4¢ + 4¢ = (8¢)

i. 3¢ + 3¢ = (6¢)   **j.** 10¢ + 10¢ = (20¢)

173 Addition and Subtraction

RETEACHING

 MANIPULATIVES Encourage students who had problems with the demonstration exercise to think through the problems more extensively. For example, for 12¢ − 3¢, help them verbalize that after they subtract 2¢ they will have to change a dime for ten pennies in order to subtract 1¢ more. Have **play coins*** available.

PRACTICE p. 80

LESSON 80 PRACTICE

Name _____

Solve these problems. Use the number line.

```
20
19
18
17
16
15
14
13
12
11
10
 9
 8
 7
 6
 5
 4
 3
 2
 1
 0
```

1 14 + 2 = __16__   **2** 12 + 2 = __14__

3 18 − 3 = __15__   **4** 11 − 3 = __8__

5 7 + 4 = __11__   **6** 13 − 2 = __11__

7 16 + 2 = __18__   **8** 15 + 1 = __16__

9 14 − 6 = __8__   **10** 20 − 2 = __18__

11 9 + 2 = __11__   **12** 9 + 3 = __12__

13 19 − 3 = __16__   **14** 17 − 5 = __12__

15 14 + 3 = __17__   **16** 16 − 3 = __13__

17 15 − 2 = __13__   **18** 10 + 3 = __13__

19 12 − 0 = __12__   **20** 11 + 3 = __14__

80 • Math Explorations and Applications Level 1

*available separately

◆ LESSON 80   Adding and Subtracting Using Money

Solve these problems. Use the number line.

Use the Mixed Practice on page 365 after this lesson.

```
20
19
18
17
16
15
14
13
12
11
10
 9
 8
 7
 6
 5
 4
 3
 2
 1
 0
```

7 18
  + 0
  18

8 19
  − 5
  14

9 17
  + 2
  19

10 14
  − 5
  9

11 8
  + 4
  12

12 9
  + 4
  13

13 16 − 5 = __11__

14 7 + 4 = __11__

15 3 + 2 = __5__

16 15 − 5 = __10__

17 13 − 4 = __9__

18 9 − 3 = __6__

19 3 + 12 = __15__

20 15 − 6 = __9__

NOTE TO HOME
Students use a number line to add and subtract to 20.

174 • Addition and Subtraction

ENRICHMENT p. 80

 LESSON **80** ENRICHMENT   Name _____

Cut out the circus posters. Fold them to find out which one is a square. Trim the other one to make it a square.

This one is a square.

0 • Math Explorations and Applications Level 1

ASSESSMENT p. 29

UNIT **2**   Mastery Checkpoint 14   Adding and subtracting in the 0–20 range   (Lesson 80)
Page 1 of 2
Name _____
The student demonstrates mastery by correctly answering 12 of the 15 problems.

Solve these problems.
Use play money to help you.

1 10 and 5   10 + 5 = __15__

2 and 5   5 + 7 = __12__

3 10 1 spend 5   12 − 5 = __7__

4 10 10 spend 5   20 − 6 = __14__

5 5 and 5   6 + 7 = __13__

[Go on ... >]

Math Explorations and Applications Level 1 • **29**

---

❷ Teach

 Demonstrate Give each student **play coins***: eight pennies, four nickels, and two dimes. Have students lay out 12¢. Then ask them to find how much they will have if they add 5¢ (17¢). Present subtraction problems in the same way. Use the **overhead coins*** to model these problems.

Using the Student Pages Have students work on pages 173–174 independently.

 Using the Thinking Story Present two of the problems from those following "Ferdie Buys a Snack" on pages 70–71 in the Thinking Story Book or pages 164a–164b of this Guide.

❸ Wrap-Up  5 MINUTES

In Closing To summarize the lesson, present addition and subtraction problems involving numbers from 0–20 and have students solve them using play money or the number line.

✔ Mastery Checkpoint 14

At about this time students should be able to solve addition and subtraction problems in the 0–20 range using play money or a number line, provided they do not have to add or subtract more than 6. Students should be able to correctly answer 80% of the problems on pages 173 and 174 or on Assessment Blackline Masters pages 29–30. Results of this assessment may be recorded on the Mastery Checkpoint Chart.

Assessment Criteria

Did the student . . .

✔ correctly answer 75% of the problems on pages 173–174?

✔ demonstrate mastery of addition and subtraction problems with numbers 0–20 using play money or the number lines?

*available separately

LESSON 81

Student Edition pages 175–178

Unit 2 Review

 MANIPULATIVES

crayons

play money*

 Using the Student Pages Use this Unit Review as a preliminary unit test to indicate areas in which each student is having difficulty or in which the entire class may need help. If students do well on the Unit Review, you may wish to skip directly to the next unit. If not, you may spend a day or so helping students overcome their individual difficulties before they take the Unit Test.

Next to each instruction line is a list of the lessons in the unit covered in that set of problems. Students can refer to the specific lesson for additional instruction if they need help. You can also use this information to make additional assignments based on the previous lesson concepts.

Have students complete pages 175–176. Read the directions to the students, and explain what is being asked in each problem, if necessary.

Have students complete problem 25 on page 177, using **crayons** to color in the figures. For page 178 you may want to allow some students to use **play money*** to complete problems 27–28.

 Problems 1–2 Have students who need more help with coin values play the "Pennies, Nickels, and Dimes" game.

Problems 1–30 Have students who need more help with counting and number formation play the "Tracing and Writing Numbers" game or practice writing numbers at the chalkboard. For students who form numbers too large, it may be helpful to prepare a worksheet with boxes that start out fairly large and gradually shrink to the size of those used in the Student Edition.

Problems 13–24 Review addition and subtraction with finger sets with students who are making calculation errors. Use any of the following games to provide extra practice in addition and subtraction: "Add the Counters" (Lesson 26), "Take Away the Counters" (Lesson 33), "Don't Take Them All" (Lesson 29), "Duck Pond" (Lesson 37), "Roll and Add" (Lesson 64), or "Addition Table" (Lesson 69).

175 Addition and Subtraction

LESSON 81

Name _____

Unit 2 Review

How many cents?

Lessons 42, 75

1   __17__ ¢

2    __13__ ¢

What is the right sign?
Draw <, >, or =.

Lessons 67, 68

3 4 $<$ 8   **4** 17 $=$ 17

5 15 $>$ 12   **6** 0 $<$ 19

 Solve these problems.

Lessons 65, 66

7 6 + [2] = 8   **8** 5 + [1] = 6

9 5 + [2] = 7   **10** 3 + [1] = 4

NOTE TO HOME
Students review unit skills and concepts.

Unit 2 Review • **175**

Copyright © SRA/McGraw-Hill

*available separately

◆ LESSON 81 Unit 2 Review

Fill in the missing numbers.

Lessons 70, 71

⑪ 6　7　**8**　**9**　**10**　11

⑫ 11　12　**13**　**14**　**15**　16

Solve these problems.
Watch the signs.

Lessons 50, 51, 53, 62, 69, 76, 77, 80

⑬ 6 + 3 = **9**　　⑭ 6 + 4 = **10**

⑮ 6 − 3 = **3**　　⑯ 6 − 4 = **2**

⑰ 5
　+ 4
　9

⑱ 6
　− 2
　4

⑲ 6
　+ 2
　8

⑳ 8
　− 5
　3

㉑ 15 + 4 = **19**　　㉒ 15 − 4 = **11**

㉓ 12 − 3 = **9**　　㉔ 9 + 3 = **12**

NOTE TO HOME
Students review skills presented in the unit.

176 • Addition and Subtraction

Problems 7–10 Have students who need more help with missing-addend problems do the Missing Addend Puzzle activity from Lesson 65. Or have them use the **math balance***. For example, place a 10 on one side of the balance and a 6 on the other. Then ask the student to find the number that when added to 6 sums to 10 (4).

Problems 3–6 Have students who need help with relation signs play the "Hungry Alligator" game from Lesson 67.

Performance Assessment The Performance Assessment Tasks 5–7 provided on pages 67–68 of the Assessment Blackline Masters can be used at this time to evaluate students' abilities to add and subtract 0, 1, 2, and 3 from numbers to 10 and to count to 20. You may want to administer this assessment to individual students or in small groups.

Portfolio Assessment If you have not already completed the Portfolio Assessment task provided on page 81 of the Assessment Blackline Masters, it can be used at this time to evaluate students' skills in forming money amounts.

Unit Project If you have not already assigned the "Place Setting" project on pages 184a–184b, you may want to do so at this time. The Unit Project is a good opportunity for students to apply the concepts of counting and writing numbers in real-world problem solving.

◆ **LESSON 81   Unit 2 Review**

Name _____

Lessons
44, 45

㉕ Color the circles red.
Color the triangles yellow.
Color the squares blue.
Color the rectangles green.

Check students' answers.

Lesson
70

㉖	1	3	5	**7**	9	11	13
㉗	2	4	**6**	8	10	12	14
㉘	8	10	12	**14**	16	**18**	20
㉙	5	**7**	9	**11**	13	15	17
㉚	17	15	**13**	11	9	7	5

NOTE TO HOME
Students review unit skills and concepts.

Unit 2   Review • **177**

RETEACHING

Students who have difficulty with this Unit Review should have further opportunity to review and to practice the skills before they proceed on with the next unit. For each set of problems there are specific suggestions for reteaching. These suggestions can be found in the margins.

◆ **LESSON 81** **Unit 2 Review**

Lessons
47, 48

Listen to the problems. Use play money or finger sets to help find the answer.

㉛ Josh has $5. He buys a toy car for $2. How much will he have left?

$ __**3**__

㉜ A pen costs $1. A pad of paper costs $3. How much for the pen and the paper?

$ __**4**__

Lessons
52, 60

Fill in the missing numbers.

㉝
In	Out
2	4
3	5
4	**6**
5	**7**
6	8

㉞
In	Out
9	8
8	**7**
7	6
6	**5**
4	3

Copyright © SRA/McGraw-Hill

178 • Addition and Subtraction

PRACTICE p. 81

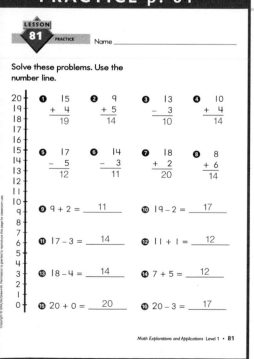

LESSON
81 PRACTICE Name _____

Solve these problems. Use the number line.

❶ 15 / + 4 / 19
❷ 9 / + 5 / 14
❸ 13 / − 3 / 10
❹ 10 / + 4 / 14

❺ 17 / − 5 / 12
❻ 14 / − 3 / 11
❼ 18 / + 2 / 20
❽ 8 / + 6 / 14

❾ 9 + 2 = __11__
❿ 19 − 2 = __17__
⓫ 17 − 3 = __14__
⓬ 11 + 1 = __12__
⓭ 18 − 4 = __14__
⓮ 7 + 5 = __12__
⓯ 20 + 0 = __20__
⓰ 20 − 3 = __17__

Math Explorations and Applications Level 1 • 81

ENRICHMENT p. 81

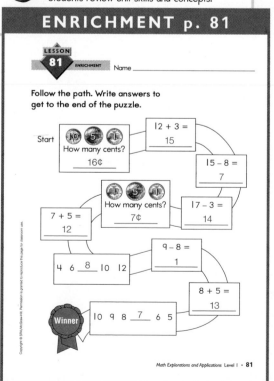

LESSON
81 ENRICHMENT Name _____

Follow the path. Write answers to get to the end of the puzzle.

Start — How many cents? __16¢__

12 + 3 = 15

15 − 8 = 7

How many cents? __7¢__

17 − 3 = 14

7 + 5 = 12

4 6 **8** 10 12

9 − 8 = 1

8 + 5 = 13

Winner — 10 9 8 **7** 6 5

Math Explorations and Applications Level 1 • 81

Student Edition pages 179–182

Unit 2 Test

Using the Student Pages This Unit Test on Student Edition pages 179–182 provides an opportunity to formally evaluate your students' proficiency with concepts developed in this unit. It is similar in content and format to the Unit Review. Students who did well on the Unit Review may not need to take this test. Students who did not do well on the Unit Review should be provided with additional practice opportunities before taking the Unit Test. For further evaluation, you may wish to have these students take the Unit Test in standardized format, provided on pages 96–103 in the Assessment Blackline Masters or the Unit Test on pages 31–34 in the Assessment Blackline Masters.

Name _____

Unit 2 Test

Check your math skills.
How many cents?

❶ _____ **3** ¢

❷ _____ **16** ¢

❸ _____ **7** ¢

❹ _____ **19** ¢

Fill in the missing numbers.

❺　9　　10　　11　　**12**　　13　　**14**　　15

❻　12　　13　　**14**　　15　　**16**　　**17**　　18

NOTE TO HOME
This test checks unit skills and concepts.

Unit 2　Test　•　**179**

◆ LESSON 82   Unit 2 Test

Solve these problems. Watch the signs.

7 5 + 3 = __8__   **8** 5 + 4 = __9__

9 8 − 2 = __6__   **10** 9 − 1 = __8__

11 4 + 4 = __8__   **12** 7 − 2 = __5__

13 4 + 0 = __4__   **14** 7 + 2 = __9__

15 6 + 2 = __8__   **16** 10 − 2 = __8__

17
```
   3
 + 2
 ———
   5
```

18
```
   4
 − 1
 ———
   3
```

19
```
   3
 + 6
 ———
   9
```

20
```
   6
 + 1
 ———
   7
```

21
```
   9
 − 2
 ———
   7
```

22
```
   4
 + 3
 ———
   7
```

NOTE TO HOME
This test checks unit skills and concepts.

◆ **LESSON 82   Unit 2 Test**

Name _____

Solve these problems.

㉓ 4 + [**1**] = 5   ㉔ 7 + [**1**] = 8

㉕ I + [**5**] = 6   ㉖ 8 + [**2**] = 10

㉗ 13 + 2 = **15**   ㉘ 17 − 3 = **14**

㉙ 12 − 3 = **9**   ㉚ 8 + 5 = **13**

What is the right sign?
Draw >, <, or =.

㉛ 9 (**<**) 10   ㉜ 4 (**=**) 4

㉝ 13 (**>**) 8   ㉞ 12 (**<**) 18

㉟ 4 (**<**) 17   ㊱ 8 (**>**) 6

NOTE TO HOME
This test checks unit skills and concepts.

Unit 2   Test • **181**

RETEACHING

Students who have difficulty with this Unit Test should have further opportunity to review and to practice the skills before they proceed on with the next unit. After students have reviewed the skills, you may want to use the Unit Test on pages 31–34 in the Assessment Blackline Masters, which cover the Unit 2 concepts.

PRACTICE p. 82

LESSON
82   PRACTICE   Name _____

Solve these problems. Watch the signs.

❶ 4 + 2 = ___6___   ❷ 6 − 3 = ___3___
❸ 6 + 3 = ___9___   ❹ 2 + 7 = ___9___

❺   5   ❻   3   ❼   6   ❽   8
  + 3   − 2   − 4   + 2
  ‾‾‾   ‾‾‾   ‾‾‾   ‾‾‾
   8   1   2   10

Solve these problems.

❾ 5 + [2] = 7   ❿ 3 + [3] = 6
⓫ 2 + [6] = 8   ⓬ 4 + [4] = 8

What is the right sign? Draw <, >, or =.

⓭ 3 (<) 5   ⓮ 11 (<) 14
⓯ 8 (=) 8   ⓰ 19 (>) 9

◆ **LESSON 82 Unit 2 Test**

37 Draw a ring around each square.

38 Draw a ring around each triangle.

Fill in the missing numbers.

39

ALGEBRA READINESS

In	Out
6	4
3	**1**
5	3
4	**2**
2	0

40

In	Out
4	7
5	**8**
3	6
6	**9**
2	5

182 • Addition and Subtraction

NOTE TO HOME
This test checks unit skills and concepts.

Copyright © SRA/McGraw-Hill

ENRICHMENT p. 82

LESSON 82 ENRICHMENT   Name _____

Answers shown are examples only.

❶ Ring 14 cents.

❷ Ring 9 cents.

❸ Ring 18 cents.

Fill in the missing numbers.

❹ 20 19 __18__ 17 16 __15__ 14 13

❺ 6 8 10 __12__ 14 16 __18__ 20

82 • Math Explorations and Applications Level 1

ASSESSMENT p. 31

UNIT 2   Unit 2 Test (Use after Lesson 81.)   Page 1 of 4

Name _____

The student demonstrates mastery by correctly answering 32 of the 40 problems.

How many cents?

❶ _____ 4 ¢

❷ _____ 17 ¢

❸ _____ 15 ¢

❹ _____ 18 ¢

Fill in the missing numbers.

❺ 8 9 10 11 12 13 14

❻ 14 15 16 17 18 19 20

Go on ...

Math Explorations and Applications Level 1 • 31

LESSON 83

Extending the Unit

Student Edition pages 183–184

LESSON PLANNER

Objectives

▶ to provide practice with addition and subtraction of 0, 1, 2, 3, and 10, and numbers to 40

▶ to provide the opportunity to find patterns produced by a function table

Context of the Lesson This is the second "Extending the Unit" lesson. The first was Lesson 41.

MANIPULATIVES **Program Resources**

calculators* Number Cubes

overhead Practice Master 83
  calculator* Enrichment Master 83

  For extra practice:
  CD-ROM* Lesson 83
  Mixed Practice, page 366

① Warm-Up ⏱ 5 MINUTES

Problem of the Day Present the following problem to the class. Eric has 12 pennies. He spends three pennies. Can he share the rest evenly between himself and his brother? Why or why not? (No, because he has 9 left; 9 cannot be divided into two equal groups.)

Problem-Solving Strategies Ask students who have solved the Problem of the Day to share how they solved it and any strategies they used.

MENTAL MATH Have students use mental math to add or subtract, then show answers with Number Cubes.

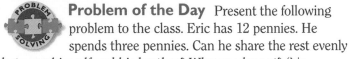

a. 32 + 1 = (33) b. 9 – 2 = (7) c. 10 – 2 = (8)
d. 15 + 2 = (17) e. 19 – 1 = (18) f. 29 + 2 = (31)

② Teach

Demonstrate Use an **overhead calculator.*** Put a function rule such as ➕ 3️⃣ 🟰 into the calculator. Then key in any number up to 40 and an 🟰 so that the display will not show the function rule. For example, if you key in 5️⃣ 🟰, *8* will be on the display. Have a volunteer pick a number, key it into the calculator, and press 🟰. Repeat this with several numbers. Have the volunteer look at the display each time and then try to guess the rule. Repeat with several different function rules.

183 Addition and Subtraction

LESSON 83

Name _____

Extending the Unit

Use your calculator to find the rule. Write it in the space.

①

In	Out
0	3
2	5

Rule **+3**

②

In	Out
12	14
7	9

Rule **+2**

③

In	Out
32	22
10	0

Rule **−10**

④

In	Out
7	17
23	33

Rule **+10**

⑤

In	Out
6	3
3	0

Rule **−3**

⑥

In	Out
6	6
38	38

Rule **+0 or −0**

 NOTE TO HOME Students use a calculator to help identify function rules.

Unit 2 Lesson 83 • **183**

 Technology Connection You might want students to use the software *Balancing Bear*, from Sunburst Communications (Mac, IBM, Apple) to provide practice with equalities and inequalities, problems with multiple solutions, and weight.

RETEACHING

Have students use Number Cubes to indicate answers to problems such as those on the student pages. For example, write a function chart on the chalkboard and ask: "If the function rule is +2, what do you get if 3 goes in?" Write 3 in the column of the chart and have students indicate the answer with their Number Cubes. (5) Then write a function table on the chalkboard and have students find the rule. They can demonstrate a + sign by crossing their arms in front of them and a minus sign by holding out an arm. Have them do this part first, agree on the sign, and then indicate the number with their Number Cubes.

*available separately

◆ **LESSON 83** **Extending the Unit**

Use your calculator to find the rule. Fill in the missing numbers.

Use the Mixed Practice on page 366 after this lesson.

❼

In	Out
3	5
7	**9**
15	**17**

Rule __+2__

❽

In	Out
6	4
5	**3**
20	**18**

Rule __−2__

Use your calculator to find the rule.

❾

In	Out
20	19
7	6

Rule __−1__

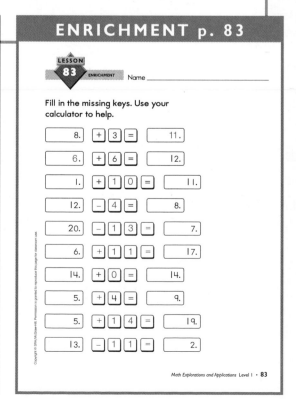

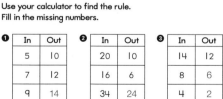

Play the "Guess the Rule" game.

 NOTE TO HOME
Students solve function problems.

Copyright © SRA/McGraw-Hill

184 • Addition and Subtraction

 **Introducing the "Guess the Rule" Game**
Demonstrate this game, then have students play it in groups. Each group needs a **calculator***. Have the lead player put in a function rule, for example, ➕ ❸ 🟰 followed by another number up to 40, such as ❼ 🟰. The function rule is limited to +0, 1, 2, 3, or 10. The lead player passes the calculator to a second player, who chooses a number, says it, and presses that number and the equal sign. The second player reads the answer on the display and passes the calculator to a third player. Repeat keying in numbers followed by an equal sign until a player guesses the rule. This player then becomes the next leader.

 Using the Student Pages For page 183, have students guess the function rules from the first pair of numbers in each table. Have them write down the rule, then check it by keying it into their calculators, then pressing each of the numbers in column one, followed by the equal sign. The display should show the numbers in column two.

Students can complete page 184 and then check their answers using their calculators in the same way.

❸ Wrap-Up ⏱

In Closing Have students explain how they figured out a function rule for a table of their choice on pages 183 or 184.

Informal Assessment Use students' answers to page 184 as an informal assessment of their ability to find patterns in function tables and use calculators to check their answers.

PRACTICE p. 83

LESSON 83 PRACTICE Name _____

Use your calculator to find the rule.
Fill in the missing numbers.

❶

In	Out
5	10
7	12
9	14
3	8

Rule __+5__

❷

In	Out
20	10
16	6
34	24
12	2

Rule __−10__

❸

In	Out
14	12
8	6
4	2
10	8

Rule __−2__

❹

In	Out
6	8
8	10
12	14
5	7

Rule __+2__

❺

In	Out
3	4
10	11
1	2
5	6

Rule __+1__

❻

In	Out
11	10
7	6
20	19
15	14

Rule __−1__

Math Explorations and Applications Level 1 • 83

ENRICHMENT p. 83

LESSON 83 ENRICHMENT Name _____

Fill in the missing keys. Use your calculator to help.

8. ➕ 3 🟰 11.

6. ➕ 6 🟰 12.

1. ➕ 10 🟰 11.

12. ➖ 4 🟰 8.

20. ➖ 13 🟰 7.

6. ➕ 11 🟰 17.

14. ➕ 0 🟰 14.

5. ➕ 4 🟰 9.

5. ➕ 14 🟰 19.

13. ➖ 11 🟰 2.

Math Explorations and Applications Level 1 • 83

Assessment Criteria

Did the student . . .

✓ correctly name the function rules during the demonstration?

✓ correctly guess the function rules on pages 183–184?

✓ understand and use a calculator to check function rules?

---

*available separately

Unit 2 Lesson 83 **184**

PRESENTING THE PROJECT

Project Objectives

▶ to provide practice in counting

▶ to provide practice in identifying patterns

▶ to provide practice in using one-to-one correspondence

 **MANIPULATIVES**

crayons or markers

white paper

 Program Resources

How Do You Measure Up?*
    from the Literature Library

SRA's *Minds on Math**

In this project, students use patterns and one-to-one correspondence to draw pictures of family members and dinner table settings. To begin, draw on the chalkboard a typical place setting with plate, fork, spoon, knife, napkin, and glass. Invite students to tell how this place setting compares to those they see at home or in restaurants. Tell students to draw a picture of a dinner table set for all the members of their household including each of the items in the chalkboard picture. Suggest that students start by drawing the face of each household member at the top of their paper to make sure they draw one place setting for each person pictured.

After students have completed their pictures talk about patterns on their drawings. Point out how each place setting is part of a pattern that goes around the dinner table. Then ask students to count how many spoons, forks, knives, dinner plates, and glasses are on the table. To extend the activity, use these counts to make a class picture graph. Discuss how the number of plates in a student's drawing relates to the number of household members.

What Is a Math Project? If this is the first time you have used math projects in your classroom you may want to refer to pages 92a–93a in this Teacher's Guide for more detailed information about effectively implementing and assessing projects.

Wrapping Up the Project Talk about other patterns students used in their drawings, such as designs on dinner plates, place mats, or tablecloths, or colors used in the drawing. Discuss also shapes and patterns created by shapes.

Minds on Math SRA's *Minds on Math** is a series of units covering Problem Solving, Data Collection, Number Sense, Measurement, Money, and Geometry and Spatial Relations. Each unit provides a series of open-ended projects for individuals or small groups. These projects develop problem-solving and critical-thinking skills, utilize real-world materials, emphasize language, and integrate cross-curricular connections. Use projects from *Problems to Solve* to emphasize that there is more than one way to look at and solve any problem.

 Assessing the Project Observe students throughout the project. Did students match objects to people using one-to-one correspondence? Did students use and identify a pattern in their drawings?

 Performance Assessment Have students draw a picture of the cafeteria tables where they sit at lunch. Discuss patterns reflected by those pictures.

 Literature Connection Use the Literature Library* lap book *How Do You Measure Up?* to look at patterns in body measurements and making size comparisons and estimations.

Technology Connection The software *Math and Me* from Davidson and Associates (Apple, IBM, for grades K–2) develops number recognition, patterns, numerical order, and addition using objects and numbers.

Perhaps you have less than 45 minutes to devote to each lesson. Perhaps you have a slower-than-average class that needs extra time on various lessons. Or, perhaps you simply feel comfortable proceeding at a more leisurely pace. Whatever the reason, a few tips will help you trim the program with the fewest consequences.

Because each unit should take up about one fourth of the school year, you can use the units somewhat as mileposts. From time to time, after each unit or halfway though each unit, do a rough calculation to see whether your pace will allow you to finish the program. If it appears that you won't finish, check the suggestions given below; but don't speed up at the expense of students' understanding. If you are moving at an appropriate pace and yet won't finish the program, that is all right. The material in Unit 4 is reviewed in depth or retaught in Level 2.

MORE THAN 90 DAYS LEFT AFTER UNIT 2

If more than 90 days remain, you'll probably be able to finish the Level 1 program, so you won't need to significantly modify the lesson plans for the rest of the year.

80–90 DAYS LEFT AFTER UNIT 2

If, after you finish Unit 2, 80–90 days remain in the school year, go though the lesson list below and decide which lessons or portions of lessons to omit. The lessons listed may be omitted without creating undue difficulty for students when they enter the second grade. Any of these lessons may be omitted, but if you can skip only a few lessons, try to choose lessons from later in the year rather than earlier. This will minimize disruption of the lesson continuity. Whenever possible, do the Mental Math exercises of the lessons you omit.

Unit 3

Lesson 102   Fractional Length
Lesson 103   Estimating Fractional Parts
Lesson 104   Estimating Length
Lesson 105   Fractional Parts

Unit 4

Lesson 140   Using Arrays and Repeated Addition
Lesson 148   Symmetry
Lesson 149   Counting by Fives
Lesson 150   Counting Nickels
Lesson 151   Amounts of Money
Lesson 152   Quarters, Dimes, and Nickels

If you omit any material from a unit, be sure to modify the Unit Review and Unit Test to take into account the deleted material.

FEWER THAN 80 DAYS LEFT AFTER UNIT 2

If, after you finish Unit 2, fewer than 80 days remain in the school year, omit the items listed below.

Unit 3

Lesson 102   Fractional Length
Lesson 103   Estimating Fractional Parts
Lesson 104   Estimating Length
Lesson 105   Fractional Parts

Unit 4

Lesson 128   Missing Addends
Lesson 139   Repeated Addition
Lesson 140   Using Arrays and Repeated Addition
Lesson 148   Symmetry
Lesson 149   Counting by Fives

Lesson 150   Counting Nickels
Lesson 151   Amounts of Money
Lesson 152   Quarters, Dimes, and Nickels

Don't omit any lessons on addition facts and traditional counting. These lessons lay a foundation for future work in mathematics.

IF YOU ADMINISTER STANDARDIZED TESTS

You might want to review the test that you will be administering to your students at this time. Note any topics that will be assessed that you have not covered in your mathematics curriculum. You might want to introduce a series of lessons earlier to accommodate your testing schedule.

UNIT 3

Measurement and Geometry

COMPARING AND DIVIDING

OVERVIEW

In the beginning of the unit students expand their understanding of numbers through 40 and measure weights in customary and metric units. They model numbers with pennies, nickels, and dimes. They also explore doubling and halving and begin to learn about fractions. Estimating length is interspersed throughout the unit and students use their ability to add and subtract to solve a variety of problems. By the end of the unit students are counting by tens and relating that activity to counting the value of a collection of dimes.

Integrated Topics in This Unit Include:

- ◆ ordering objects by weight
- ◆ estimating weight
- ◆ using pennies, nickels, and dimes to model numbers through 40
- ◆ doubles and halves
- ◆ exploring symmetry of figures
- ◆ adding 1, 2, or 3 to a number
- ◆ rotating triangles
- ◆ estimating and measuring in centimeters
- ◆ identifying the operation
- ◆ using inequality signs
- ◆ missing addends

- ◆ estimating fractional lengths
- ◆ finding fractional parts
- ◆ counting by tens
- ◆ writing money amounts

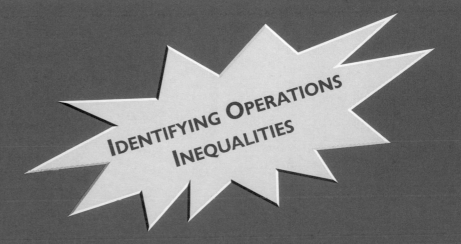

IDENTIFYING OPERATIONS
INEQUALITIES

 GAMES

Motivating Mixed Practice

Games provide **basic math skills** practice in cooperative groups and develop **mathematical reasoning.**

 THINKING STORY

Integrated Problem Solving

Thinking Stories provide opportunities for students to work in **cooperative groups** and develop **logical reasoning** while they integrate **reading skills** with mathematics.

Story Summaries "Ms. Eng's Fish Stories" focuses on how to draw conclusions from incomplete information.

In "Manolita's Magnificent Minus Machine," Manolita creates a function machine.

In "Mr. Mudancia Makes Lunch," Mr. Mudancia uses addition, subtraction, and division to make changes in the lunch he is making.

"How Ms. Eng Doubled Her Money" examines how Ms. Eng uses a function rule to help guide her in her business transactions.

PROJECT

Making Connections

The Unit Project makes real-world connections. Students work in **cooperative groups** to problem-solve and to communicate their findings.

The Unit Wrap-Up project asks students to conduct a paper-folding exercise.

UNIT 3

MEASUREMENT AND GEOMETRY
LESSON PLANS

	LESSON	PACING	PRIMARY OBJECTIVES	FEATURE	RESOURCES	NCTM STANDARDS
84	Numbers Through 40 187–188	1 day	to introduce ordering objects according to weight		Practice Master 84 Enrichment Master 84	6, 10
85	Measuring Weight in Pounds 191–192	1 day	to provide opportunities to estimate and weigh objects in pounds		Practice Master 85 Enrichment Master 85	10
86	Measuring Weight in Kilograms 191–192	1 day	to help students become aware that there are two systems of measurement used in the world today: customary and metric	**Game**	Reteaching Master Practice Master 86 Enrichment Master 86	10
87	Numbers 0–40 193–194	1 day	to teach students to recognize standard finger sets for numbers 0–40 without counting		Practice Master 87 Enrichment Master 87	6
88	Pennies, Nickels, and Dimes 195–196	1 day	to teach the use of pennies, nickels, and dimes to form given amounts from 1¢–40¢	**Thinking Story**	Practice Master 88 Enrichment Master 88	1, 2, 3, 4, 6
89	Doubles and Halves 197–198	1 day	to teach doubling given amounts of money from 0¢–40¢		Practice Master 89 Enrichment Master 89	1, 2, 3, 4, 5, 7, 12
90	Symmetry................. 199–200	1 day	to introduce the idea of symmetry		Practice Master 90 Enrichment Master 90	7, 9
91	Using Coins 201–202	1 day	to practice counting and making amounts of money through 40¢		Reteaching Master Practice Master 91 Enrichment Master 91	6
92	Using Numbers to 40 203–204	1 day	to teach students to solve addition problems with numbers through 40 using concrete objects	**Game**	Practice Master 92 Enrichment Master 92	6, 7, 8
93	Adding with Numbers 0–40 205–206	1 day	to provide practice solving addition problems with numbers through 40 by using concrete objects	**Game**	Practice Master 93 Enrichment Master 93	7, 8, 9
94	Keeping Sharp 207–208	1 day	✓ to assess students' ability to use concrete objects to solve addition and subtraction problems with numbers through 40		Reteaching Master Practice Master 94 Enrichment Master 94 Assessment Master	8, 10
95	Identifying the Operation............ 209–210	1 day	to teach students to recognize the operations of addition and subtraction	**Thinking Story**	Practice Master 95 Enrichment Master 95	3, 7, 13
96	Measuring Length in Feet and Yards 211–212	1 day	to show students how to measure in yards		Practice Master 96 Enrichment Master 96	4, 10
97	Functions................. 213–214	1 day	to practice simple addition and subtraction functions		Reteaching Master 23 Practice Master 97 Enrichment Master 97	3, 6, 8, 13
98	Using Inequalities 215–216	1 day	to provide practice using inequality and equality signs		Practice Master 98 Enrichment Master 98	1, 2, 3, 4, 5, 6, 8, 9
99	Missing Addends 217–218	1 day	to teach students to solve missing-addend problems presented in numerical form	**Game**	Reteaching Master 24 Practice Master 99 Enrichment Master 99	6, 7
	Mid-Unit Review 219–220	1 day	to review skills and concepts presented in the first half of the unit		Assessment Master	
100	Dividing Sets into Halves................ 221–222	1 day	to teach students to divide an even number of objects through ten into two sets of equal numbers	**Game**	Practice Master 100 Enrichment Master 100	6, 7, 12
101	Estimating One Half 223–224	1 day	to teach students to estimate half of a length or height		Practice Master 101 Enrichment Master 101	5, 10, 12
102	Fractional Length 225–226	1 day	to provide practice estimating one unit of length when given a length of two through six arbitrary units	**Thinking Story**	Practice Master 102 Enrichment Master 102	1, 2, 3, 4, 7, 10

LESSON	PACING	PRIMARY OBJECTIVES	FEATURE	RESOURCES	NCTM STANDARDS
103 Estimating Fractional Parts.........227–228	1 day	to introduce students to the use of fractional terms and notation	Thinking Story	Reteaching Master 25 Practice Master 103 Enrichment Master 103	1, 2, 3, 4, 5, 7, 10
104 Estimating Length........229–230	1 day	to have students estimate the length of a line of up to six units in length		Practice Master 104 Enrichment Master 104	1, 2, 3, 4, 5, 10
105 Fractional Parts..........231–232	1 day	to provide practice dividing a circle into equal parts using a paper-folding technique		Practice Master 105 Enrichment Master 105	10, 13
106 Using Doubles 233–234	1 day	to practice using doubles in the 0–5 range or halves of even numbers to solve concrete problems	Game	Practice Master 106 Enrichment Master 106	7, 8
107 Estimating Length........235–236	1 day	to have students produce lengths two to six times longer than a given unit of length		Reteaching Master Practice Master 107 Enrichment Master 107	10, 12
108 Using Prices..............237–238	1 day	to teach students the relationship between money and value and the prices of real things		Practice Master 108 Enrichment Master 108	7, 8
109 Mental Math 239–240	1 day	✓ to teach and assess students' ability to add or subtract 0, 1, or 2 mentally with numbers through 40		Practice Master 109 Enrichment Master 109 Assessment Master	7, 8, 13
110 Making Tens 241–242	1 day	to teach students to find pairs of numbers whose sum is 10 without using concrete objects	Game	Practice Master 110 Enrichment Master 110	6, 7
111 Counting by Tens 243–244	1 day	to extend the range of numbers that students work with to 100		Practice Master 111 Enrichment Master 111	6, 11
112 Tens and Ones 245–246	1 day	to teach students to count up to 100 objects by counting groups of ten and then adding the extras	Game	Practice Master 112 Enrichment Master 112	6
113 Counting with Dimes......247–248	1 day	✓ to teach and assess students' ability to form given amounts of money up to $1 using pennies, nickels, and dimes	Thinking Story Game	Reteaching Master Practice Master 113 Enrichment Master 113 Assessment Master	4, 6, 7
114 Unit 3 Review.............249–252		to review measurement and geometry		Practice Master 114 Enrichment Master 114	
115 Unit 3 Test................253–256		to review measurement and geometry		Practice Master 115 Enrichment Master 115 Assessment Master	
116 Extending the Unit........257–258		to review measurement and geometry	Game	Practice Master 116 Enrichment Master 116	
Unit 3 Wrap-Up 258a–258b		to review measurement and geometry	Project		

UNIT CONNECTIONS

INTERVENTION STRATEGIES

In this Teacher's Guide there will be specific strategies suggested for students with individual needs—ESL, Gifted and Talented, Special Needs, Learning Styles, and At Risk. These strategies will be given at the point of use. Here are the icons to look for and the types of strategies that will accompany them:

English as a Second Language
These strategies, designed for students who do not fluently speak the English language, will suggest meaningful ways to present the lesson concepts and vocabulary.

Gifted and Talented
Strategies to enrich and extend the lesson will offer further challenges to students who have easily mastered the concepts already presented.

Special Needs
Students who are physically challenged or who have learning disabilities may require alternative ways to complete activities, record answers, use manipulatives, and so on. The strategies labeled with this icon will offer appropriate methods of teaching lesson concepts to these students.

Learning Styles
Each student has his or her individual approach to learning. The strategies labeled with this icon suggest ways to present lesson concepts so that various learning modalities—such as tactile/kinesthetic, visual, and auditory—can be addressed.

At Risk
These strategies highlight the relevancy of the skills presented, making the connection between school and real life. They are directed toward students who appear to be at risk of dropping out of school before graduation.

TECHNOLOGY CONNECTIONS

The following materials, designed to reinforce and extend lesson concepts, will be referred to throughout this Teacher's Guide. It might be helpful to order this software, or check it out of the school media center or local community library.

 Look for this **Technology Connection** *icon.*

- *Countdown,* from Voyager, Mac, IBM, for grades K–6 (software)

- *Early Learning Math,* from Jostens Home Learning, Mac, for grades K–2 (software)

- *Hands-On Math Series: Volumes 1, 2, and 3,* from Ventura Educational Systems, Mac, IBM, for grades K–8 (software)

- *Junior Mega Math Playground,* from Decision Development, Mac, IBM, for grades Pre-K–4 (software)

- *Kid's Math,* from Great Wave Software, Mac, for grades K–3 (software)

- *Millie's Math House,* from Edmark, Mac, IBM, for grades PreK–2 (software)

- *Talking Addition and Subtraction,* from Orange Cherry, Mac, for grades K–3 (software)

- *Money Town,* from Davidson Co., Mac, IBM, for grades K–3 (software)

CROSS-CURRICULAR CONNECTIONS

This Teacher's Guide offers specific suggestions on ways to connect the math concepts presented in this unit with other subjects students are studying. Students can connect math concepts with topics they already know about and can find examples of math in other subjects and in real-world situations. These strategies will be given at the point of use.

Look for these icons:

 Geography

 Social Studies

 Science

 Art

 Language Arts

 Health

 Music

 Math

 Physical Education

 Careers

LITERATURE CONNECTIONS

These books will be presented throughout the Teacher's Guide at the point where they could be used to introduce, reinforce, or extend specific lesson concepts. You may want to locate these books in your school or your local community library.

 Look for this **Literature Connection** *icon.*

- ◆ *How Many Bears?* by Cooper Edens, Atheneum, 1994
- ◆ *The Five Pennies* by Barbara Brenner, Knopf, 1964
- ◆ *Arithmetic* by Carl Sandburg, Harcourt Brace Jovanovich, 1993
- ◆ *Right in Your Own Backyard: Nature Math*, Time-Life for Children, 1992
- ◆ *The Cat's Midsummer Jamboree* by David Kherdian and Nonny Hogrogian, Philomel Books, 1990
- ◆ *Moon to Sun* by Sheila Samton, Caroline House, 1991
- ◆ *Is It Larger? Is It Smaller?* by Tana Hoban, Greenwillow Books, 1985
- ◆ *I Read Symbols* by Tana Hoban, Greenwillow Books, 1994
- ◆ *Fraction Action* by Loreen Leedy, Holiday House, 1994
- ◆ *Give Me Half!* by Stuart J. Murphy, HarperCollins Publishers, 1996
- ◆ *The Line Up Book* by Marisabina Russo, Greenwillow Books, 1986
- ◆ *How Big Is a Foot?* by Rolf Myller, Dell, 1991
- ◆ *The Case of the Missing Zebra Stripes* by Time-Life, Inc., Time-Life for Children, 1992
- ◆ *Look Twice* by Duncan Birmingham, Tarquin, 1992
- ◆ *Much Bigger Than Martin* by Steven Kellogg, Dial Books for Young Readers, 1976
- ◆ *The Purse* by Kathy Caple, Houghton Mifflin, 1986
- ◆ *Richard Scarry's Best Counting Book Ever* by Richard Scarry, Random House, 1975

ASSESSMENT OPPORTUNITIES AT-A-GLANCE

LESSON	PORTFOLIO	PERFORMANCE	FORMAL	SELF	INFORMAL	MIXED PRACTICE	MULTIPLE CHOICE	MASTERY CHECKPOINTS	ANALYZING ANSWERS
84					✓				
85					✓				
86					✓				
87				✓		✓			
88					✓				
89	✓								
90	✓								
91		✓				✓			
92		✓							
93					✓				
94			✓					✓	
95					✓				
96		✓							
97					✓	✓			
98	✓								
99		✓							
Mid-Unit Review	✓	✓	✓						
100					✓				
101		✓				✓			
102				✓					
103					✓				
104		✓							
105		✓							
106					✓				
107		✓				✓			
108		✓							
109			✓					✓	
110		✓							
111					✓	✓			
112					✓				
113			✓					✓	
Unit Review	✓	✓	✓						
Unit Test			✓				✓		
116					✓	✓			

✓ ASSESSMENT OPTIONS

PORTFOLIO ASSESSMENT

Throughout this Teacher's Guide are suggested activities in which students draw pictures, make graphs, write about mathematics, and so on. Keep students' work to assess growth of understanding as the year progresses.

Lessons 89, 90, 98, Mid-Unit Review, and Unit Review

PERFORMANCE ASSESSMENT

Performance assessment items focus on evaluating how students think and work as they solve problems. Opportunities for performance assessment can be found throughout the unit. Rubrics and guides for grading can be found in the front of the Assessment Blackline Masters.

Lessons 91, 92, 96, 99, Mid-Unit Review, 101, 104, 105, 107, 108, 110, and Unit Review

FORMAL ASSESSMENT

A Mid-Unit Review and Unit Test help assess students' understanding of concepts, skills, and problem solving. The *Math Explorations and Applications CD-ROM Test Generator* can create additional unit tests at three ability levels. Also, Mastery Checkpoints are provided periodically throughout the unit.

Lesson 94, Mid-Unit Review, 109, 113, Unit Review, and Unit Test

SELF ASSESSMENT

Throughout the program students are given the opportunity to check their own math skills.

Lessons 87 and 102

INFORMAL ASSESSMENT

A variety of assessment suggestions is provided, including interviews, oral questions or presentation, debates, and so on. Also, each lesson includes Assessment Criteria—a list of questions about each student's progress, understanding, and participation.

Lessons 84, 85, 86, 88, 93, 95, 97, 100, 103, 106, 111, and 112

MIXED PRACTICE

Mixed Practices, covering material presented thus far in the year, are provided in the unit for use as either assessment or practice.

Lessons 87, 91, 97, 101, 107, 111, 116

MULTIPLE-CHOICE TESTS (STANDARDIZED FORMAT)

Each unit provides a unit test in standardized format, presenting students with an opportunity to practice taking a test in this format.

MASTERY CHECKPOINT

Mastery Checkpoints are provided throughout the unit to assess student proficiency in specific skills. Checkpoints reference appropriate Assessment Blackline Masters and other assessment options. Results of these evaluations can be recorded on the Mastery Checkpoint Chart.

Lessons 94, 109, and 113

ANALYZING ANSWERS

Analyzing Answers items suggest possible sources of student error and offer teaching strategies for addressing difficulties.

Look for these icons:

> **" Communicating with students about their performance is part of a shift toward viewing students as active participants in assessment. "**
>
> —*NCTM Assessment Standards*

MASTERY CHECKPOINTS

WHAT TO EXPECT FROM STUDENTS AS THEY COMPLETE THIS UNIT

⑮ CONCRETE ADDITION AND SUBTRACTION THROUGH 40—LESSON 94

At about this time you may want to formally assess students' ability to add and subtract with numbers through 40 using concrete objects. Proficiency can be assessed during the Number Cube activities or by checking students' answers to page 207. Or use pages 35–36 of the Assessment Blackline Masters. Results can be recorded on the Mastery Checkpoint Chart.

⑯ MENTAL ADDITION AND SUBTRACTION (0–40)—LESSON 109

At about this time, you may want to formally assess students' ability to mentally add and subtract 0, 1, and 2 with numbers through 40. Proficiency can be assessed during the Number Cube activities or by checking students' answers to page 239. Or use page 40 of the Assessment Blackline Masters. Results can be recorded on the Mastery Checkpoint Chart.

⑰ FAMILIARITY WITH MONEY (COINS)—LESSON 113

At about this time you may want to formally assess students' ability to form specific amounts of money up to $1 and their skills in trading pennies for nickels, nickels for dimes, and dimes for dollars. Proficiency can be assessed during the demonstration or by checking students' answers to page 248. Or use page 41 of the Assessment Blackline Masters. Results can be recorded on the Mastery Checkpoint Chart.

UNIT 3

PROGRAM RESOURCES

THESE ADDITIONAL COMPONENTS OF *MATH EXPLORATIONS AND APPLICATIONS* CAN BE PURCHASED SEPARATELY FROM SRA/McGRAW-HILL.

LESSON	BASIC MANIPULATIVE KIT	GAME PACKAGE	TEACHER KIT	OPTIONAL MANIPULATIVE KIT	OVERHEAD MANIPULATIVE KIT	*MATH EXPLORATIONS AND APPLICATIONS* CD-ROM	LITERATURE LIBRARY
84			scale/balance			Lesson 84	
85			scale/balance			Lesson 85	*The Seesaw*
86		Measurement Game	scale/balance, thermometer, weights		thermometer	Lesson 86	
87	Number Cubes					Lesson 87	
88	Number Cubes	play money			coins	Lesson 88	
89	Number Cubes	play money			coins	Lesson 89	
90						Lesson 90	
91		play money			coins	Lesson 91	
92	Number Cubes	play money				Lesson 92	
93	Number Cubes			counters	counters	Lesson 93	
94	Number Cubes, Number Strips					Lesson 94	
95	Number Cubes			counters	counters	Lesson 95	
96						Lesson 96	
97	Number Cubes					Lesson 97	
98	Number Cubes					Lesson 98	
99	Number Cubes			counters	counters	Lesson 99	
Mid-Unit Review				counters	counters		*Squeeze In*
100	Number Cubes					Lesson 100	*Half a Slice of Bread and Butter*
101						Lesson 101	
102				fraction tiles	fraction tiles	Lesson 102	
103	Number Cubes					Lesson 103	
104				interlocking cubes		Lesson 104	
105	Number Cubes					Lesson 105	
106	Number Cubes			counters		Lesson 106	
107	Number Cubes					Lesson 107	
108		play money			coins	Lesson 108	
109	Number Cubes	play money			coins	Lesson 109	
110	Number Cubes		scale/balance			Lesson 110	
111	Number Cubes					Lesson 111	
112	Number Cubes		stopwatch	counters	counters	Lesson 112	
113	Number Cubes	School Bookstore Game, play money			coins	Lesson 113	
114	Number Cubes	play money	math balance	counters base-10 materials	coins counters	Lesson 114	
115						Lesson 115	
116		Addition Table Game				Lesson 116	
Unit Wrap-Up							*Here Be Giants*

INTRODUCING THE UNIT

Using the Student Pages Begin your discussion of the opening unit photo by asking students, "Have you seen a scale like this at the grocery store? What does it measure?" Then read aloud the paragraph on the student page that highlights the duties of a grocery clerk. This helps make the connection between school and work and encourages students to explore how math is used in the real world.

 **ACTIVITY** Challenge students to use a scale next time they go to a grocery store. Suggest that they find out about how many apples are in a pound.

FYI Make clear to students that money was not always used for making purchases. In ancient times most transactions were made through barter. Grocery stores like the one described above did not exist. Instead, farmers brought their produce to a common marketplace where it could be traded for other goods. In the old Mayan culture of Mesoamerica, people traded crops for intricately woven blankets or elegant bird feathers, which became a kind of currency. Other ancient cultures used cocoa beans, salt, shells, or stones. The first coins did not appear until 600 B.C., in what is now Turkey, though the Chinese were using miniature bronze tools for money as early as 1100 B.C. The Chinese were also the first to use paper money, which they had issued by the time of Marco Polo in the 1300s (much to Polo's amazement). Europe did not adopt paper cash until the 1600s. In Canada during the 1700s, due to a shortage of the standard currency, playing cards signed by the governor were issued as money! Point out to students that the money they use every day is worth very little in itself but instead represents a promise that it is worth something. It is because the money is backed by banks everyone trusts that our monetary system can work.

Stress to students that good math skills are absolutely essential to any career that involves exchanges of money for goods and services. A grocery clerk today has sophisticated devices to aid in making change, but even with electronic calculators, the clerk must still be able to quickly determine correct change and know the values of each type of currency. Clerks must also be able to calculate such things as taxes and discounts. These skills are also an aid to consumers. Make the point that at the end of the day, a

UNIT 3

Measurement and Geometry

COMPARING AND DIVIDING

- **length and weight**
- **symmetry**
- **fractions**
- **inequalities**
- **algebra readiness**

185

 Junior Thinklab™

SRA's *Junior Thinklab*™* provides a series of creative and logical problem-solving opportunities for individual students. The problems are designed to appeal to different cognitive abilities.

▶ Use Activity Cards 41-45 with this unit to reinforce Ordering.

▶ Use Activity Cards 46-50 with this unit to reinforce Classifying.

▶ Use Activity Cards 51-55 with this unit to reinforce Perception and Spatial Relations.

▶ Use Activity Cards 56-60 with this unit to reinforce Reasoning and Deducing.

▶ Use Divergent Thinking Activity Sheets 11-15 with this unit to encourage creativity in art and in intellectual activity.

*available separately

clerk must be able to examine the tape from the cash register and check it against the actual cash in the drawer to find discrepancies. Calculators are useless if the individuals responsible cannot check the work they have done.

Home Connections You may want to send the letter on Home Connections Blackline Masters pages 46–47 to families to introduce this unit.

Unit Project This would be a good time to assign the "Paper Folding" project on pages 258a–258b. Students can begin working on the project in cooperative groups in their free time as you work through the unit. The Unit Project is a good opportunity for students to apply the concepts of the properties of squares and the relationship between fractions and a whole in real-world problem solving.

SCHOOL TO WORK CONNECTION

Grocery clerks use math . . .

A grocery clerk uses a scale to weigh meats, cheeses, fruits, and vegetables. These items are usually sold by weight. That means the price is greater if the weight is greater. Customers use the scale to estimate the price.

186

LESSON 84

Student Edition pages 187–188

Numbers Through 40

LESSON PLANNER

Objectives

▶ to teach the ordinal position of numbers 0–40

▶ to introduce the double-pan balance as a tool for comparing weights of objects

▶ to introduce ordering objects according to weight

Context of the Lesson Students will continue to work frequently with number tables throughout the program. By Lesson 117 students should be able to find numbers through 100.

MANIPULATIVES

assorted objects for weighing

double-pan balance*

index cards

Program Resources

Practice Master 84

Enrichment Master 84

For extra practice: CD-ROM* Lesson 84

❶ Warm-Up ⏱ 5 MINUTES

Problem of the Day Present the following problem to the class. How many different two-digit numbers can you make using these three digits: *1, 2, 3?* You can use a digit more than once. (11, 12, 13, 21, 22, 23, 31, 32, 33)

Problem-Solving Strategies Ask students who have solved the Problem of the Day to share how they solved it and any strategies they used.

MENTAL MATH Say the following numbers and have volunteers quickly point to them on a 0–20 number line: 14, 18, 6, 8, 0, 20, 9, 17, 14, 11, 3, 16.

❷ Teach

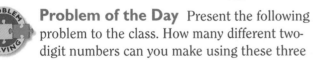

Introducing the "Which is the Lightest" Activity Show five **objects**, one of which is significantly lighter than the others. Ask students to predict which object is lightest. Then use a **double-pan balance*** to check. Test to see which object is next to the lightest and so on until all the objects have been ranked. Have pairs of students repeat the exercise with other objects.

If a balance is not available, use **index cards** numbered from 0–40, arranged in random order. Have students draw five cards and arrange them in increasing order.

187 Measurement and Geometry

LESSON 84

Name _____

Numbers Through 40

Connect the dots. Start with 1 and count up.

Copyright © SRA/McGraw-Hill

NOTE TO HOME Students practice counting to 40.

Unit 3   Lesson 84 • **187**

Literature Connection Read aloud to students *I Can Count More* by Dick Bruno to reinforce lesson concepts.

GIFTED & TALENTED

Meeting Individual Needs Write values from 1¢ – 40¢ on index cards. Arrange them in random order. Challenge students to place these cards in numerical order.

RETEACHING

MANIPULATIVES Put **index cards** with the numbers 0–40 in a bag. Have a student pick a number and give a clue such as, "This number is less than 15 but more than 12." The student who guesses correctly picks the next number.

You might also pair students who are having difficulty with students who have mastered ordering numbers from 0–40. Have the more proficient student help his or her partner practice this skill using the bulleted exercises in the Teach section.

*available separately

◆ **LESSON 84** Numbers Through 40

Fill in the missing numbers.

0	1	2	3	**4**	5	6	**7**	8	9
10	**11**	12	13	14	**15**	16	17	18	**19**
20	21	**22**	23	24	25	**26**	27	**28**	29
30	**31**	32	33	**34**	35	36	37	38	39
40									

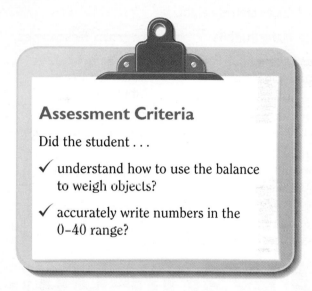

The blue whale is the heaviest animal on Earth. It weighs about as much as 2000 cars.

Do the "Which is the Lightest?" activity.

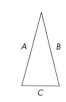

NOTE TO HOME
Students sequence numbers 0–40 by filling in the chart.

188 • Measurement and Geometry

Using the Student Pages Have students complete pages 187–188 independently. Then have students use their number tables for the following exercises:

▶ Say and write a number. Have students quickly find it.

▶ Ask students to locate "three tens and . . ." numbers. Pause after naming how many tens so that students can first find the appropriate row.

❸ Wrap-Up

In Closing Ask students to count with you in unison through the number 40.

Informal Assessment Observe students during the demonstration and student page exercises to assess their progress.

Assessment Criteria

Did the student . . .

✓ understand how to use the balance to weigh objects?

✓ accurately write numbers in the 0–40 range?

LOOKING AHEAD A pumpkin and a **double-pan balance*** or **platform (dual-dial) scale*** will be needed in Lesson 85.

PRACTICE p. 84

ENRICHMENT p. 84

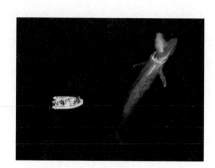
*available separately

Student Edition pages 189–190

LESSON 85

Measuring Weight in Pounds

LESSON PLANNER

Objectives

▶ to provide opportunities to estimate and weigh objects in nonstandard units

▶ to provide opportunities to estimate and weigh objects in pounds

▶ to teach students to appreciate the benefits of standard units of measure

Context of the Lesson This is the first lesson involving measurement in customary weight. Lesson 86 introduces metric weight.

 MANIPULATIVES

blocks and books of uniform weight

double-pan balance* or platform (dual-dial) scale*

pumpkin (or object weighing between 4 and 8 lbs)

Program Resources

The Seesaw * from the Literature Library

Practice Master 85

Enrichment Master 85

For extra practice: CD-ROM* Lesson 85

① Warm-Up 5 MINUTES

 Problem of the Day Have students copy and complete the following number pattern: 1, 3, 5, 7, 9, _____, 13. Then ask: "What pattern helped you complete the number series?" (11; Pattern: +2)

Problem-Solving Strategies Ask students who have solved the Problem of the Day to share how they solved it and any strategies they used.

MENTAL MATH Have students answer the following problems orally:

a. 16 + 2 = (18)   b. 10 + 2 = (12)

c. 18 − 2 = (16)   d. 12 − 3 = (9)

e. 17 + 3 = (20)   f. 14 − 3 = (11)

189 Measurement and Geometry

LESSON 85

Name _____

Measuring Weight in Pounds

 ❶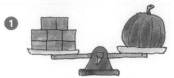

How much do you think the pumpkin weighs? Tell what you think.

Students may say 8 blocks or 5 books. Answers will vary.

Later some students measured the pumpkin in 1-pound units.

❷

How many pounds does the pumpkin weigh? _____ **5**

Tell how you know. **The scale shows that it weighs 5 pounds.**

 NOTE TO HOME Students estimate weight in pounds.

Unit 3   Lesson 85 • **189**

 COOPERATIVE LEARNING Have partners list objects in the classroom that they think weigh less than 5 pounds and more than 5 pounds. They can make a table similar to the following, weigh the objects, list the exact weight, and check their estimates.

Object	Less than 5 pounds	Exact Weight	More than 5 pounds	Exact Weight

 Literature Connection Read aloud *The Seesaw* from the Literature Library* to develop the concept of weights and balance.

RETEACHING

 MANIPULATIVES Display several objects such as a book, pencil sharpener, wastebasket, and globe. Have students try to arrange the objects in order from lightest to heaviest. Then have students weigh the objects to see if they are correct.

*available separately

◆ **LESSON 85** Measuring Weight in Pounds

5 pounds

20 pounds

1 pound

❸ Ring the objects that weigh less than 5 pounds. **Accept all reasonable answers.**

Tell how you know.

❹ Ring the objects that weigh more than 20 pounds. **Accept all reasonable answers.**

Tell how you know.

190 • Measurement and Geometry

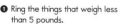 **NOTE TO HOME**
Students estimate weight in pounds.

Copyright © SRA/McGraw-Hill

② Teach

Using the Student Pages Do the activity as pictured on page 189. Divide students into three groups. Have one group weigh the **pumpkin** in **book** units. Have a second group weigh the same pumpkin in **block** units. Then ask them to report the results to the third group. Ask the third group whose pumpkin is heavier. Students should realize the pumpkin's weight has not changed but that the units of measurement are different. Point out that the number of units is related to the unit of measurement. Guide students to see why standard units of measurement are needed. Finally, have the third group use a **scale*** to measure the pumpkin in pound units. Point out that since other people also use pounds as a standard unit of measure, this measurement is more useful and understandable.

To introduce page 190, first ask students if they think you weigh more or less than five pounds. Repeat with other objects. Then have them complete the page on their own. When finished, correct the page together with the class.

③ Wrap-Up ⏱ 5 MINUTES

In Closing Have students name an advantage to using standard units to measure weight. Students should understand that without common units, they would have a more difficult time communicating the weight of objects to others.

Informal Assessment Use the answers to pages 189–190 and the closing discussion as an informal assessment of students' understanding of standard weight measurement.

PRACTICE p. 85

LESSON 85 PRACTICE Name _____

5 pounds   20 pounds   1 pound

❶ Ring the things that weigh less than 5 pounds.

❷ Ring the things that weigh more than 20 pounds.

Math Explorations and Applications Level 1 • **85**

ENRICHMENT p. 85

LESSON 85 ENRICHMENT Name _____

Cut out the bags of potatoes. Show the bags you need to make each weight. Then paste them down.

Typical answers are shown. Other answers are possible.

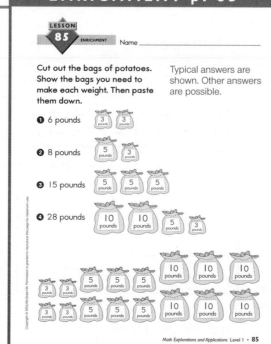

❶ 6 pounds   3 pounds / 3 pounds

❷ 8 pounds   5 pounds / 3 pounds

❸ 15 pounds   5 pounds / 5 pounds / 5 pounds

❹ 28 pounds   10 pounds / 10 pounds / 5 pounds / 3 pounds

Math Explorations and Applications Level 1 • **85**

Assessment Criteria

Did the student . . .

✓ weigh objects accurately when doing the activity on page 189?

✓ understand the advantages of using standard units of measurement?

✓ estimate the weights of objects pictured on page 190?

LOOKING AHEAD For Lesson 86 you will need a pumpkin, a **double-pan balance***, a **1–kilogram weight***, and a variety of classroom objects that can be weighed.

*available separately

LESSON 86

Student Edition pages 191–192

Measuring Weight in Kilograms

LESSON PLANNER

Objectives

▶ to provide opportunities to estimate and weigh objects in kilograms

▶ to help students develop awareness of the two systems of measurement used in the world today: customary and metric

Context of the Lesson This is the first lesson involving measurement in metric units of weight. The previous lesson dealt with customary units of weight.

 MANIPULATIVES

classroom thermometer*

double-pan balance*

five classroom objects to be weighed, such as a stapler, book, scissors, tape dispenser, and calculator

1-kilogram weights*

pumpkin

Program Resources

"Measurement" Game Mat

Reteaching Master

Practice Master 86

Enrichment Master 86

For additional math integration:
Math Throughout the Day*

For extra practice:
CD-ROM* Lesson 86

① Warm-Up ⏱ 5 MINUTES

 Problem of the Day Present the following problem to the class. Melanie's birthday is on Saturday. She will have a party three days before her birthday. On what day is her party? (Wednesday)

Problem-Solving Strategies Ask students who have solved the Problem of the Day to share how they solved it and any strategies they used.

 Have students answer the following problems orally:

a. 13 − 3 = (10)	b. 6 + 2 = (8)
c. 19 − 3 = (16)	d. 14 + 2 = (16)
e. 13 + 2 = (15)	f. 10 + 1 = (11)
g. 16 − 1 = (15)	h. 17 − 0 = (17)

191 Measurement and Geometry

LESSON 86

Name _____

Measuring Weight in Kilograms

Sometimes we measure in kilograms.

About 20 kilograms

About 1 kilogram

Much less than 1 kilogram

❶ Ring the objects that weigh less than 1 kilogram.

❷ Ring the objects that weigh more than 20 kilograms.

Copyright © SRA/McGraw-Hill

 NOTE TO HOME
Students estimate weight in kilograms.

Unit 3   Lesson 86 • **191**

COOPERATIVE LEARNING **MANIPULATIVES** As in the previous lesson, have partners work together to list objects in the classroom that they think weigh less than 3 kilograms and more than 3 kilograms. They can make a table with headings similar to the following:

Object	Less than 3 kilograms	Exact Weight	More than 3 kilograms	Exact Weight

Have students then weigh the objects, list the weight, and check their estimates.

LESSON 86 RETEACHING

Name _____

Sometimes we measure in kilograms.

 weighs much less than 1 kilogram (kg)

 weighs about 1 kilogram (kg)

 weighs much more than 1 kilogram (kg)

❶ Ring the thing that weighs less than 1 kg.

❷ Ring the thing that weighs about 1 kg.

❸ Ring the thing that weighs much more than 1 kg.

20 • Math Explorations and Applications Level 1

*available separately

◆ **LESSON 86** Measuring Weight in Kilograms

How many kilograms?
Estimate. Then measure to check.
Listen to the teacher.

Draw or write the object	Estimate	Measure
	Kilograms	

Play the "Measurement Game."

192 • Measurement and Geometry

NOTE TO HOME
Students estimate and measure objects
in kilograms.

Copyright © SRA/McGraw-Hill

PRACTICE p. 86

20 kilograms   1 kilogram   Much less than 1 kilogram

❶ Ring the things that weigh less than 1 kilogram.

❷ Ring the things that weigh more than 20 kilograms.

86 • Math Explorations and Applications Level 1

ENRICHMENT p. 86

Ms. Orta weighed the students in her class. She made a graph to show what she found.

Use the graph to answer the questions.

Weight (in kilograms)

❶ How many students weighed 27 kilograms? _____ 4

❷ What was the most common weight? _____ 26 kilograms

❸ How much more did the heaviest student weigh than the lightest student? _____ 6 kilograms

❹ How many students weighed 28 kilograms? _____ none

❺ How many students are in Ms. Orta's class? _____ 21

86 • Math Explorations and Applications Level 1

*available separately

---

② Teach

Demonstrate Explain to the class that most of the world uses the metric system, which measures weight in grams and kilograms. Pass a **kilogram weight*** around the class. Then have the class guess how much the **pumpkin** will weigh in kilograms. Then weigh the pumpkin using a **balance***. Point out that the number of units is related to the unit of measurement.

Using the Student Pages Start with page 192. Display various **classroom objects** such as a stapler, scissors, tape dispenser, and calculator. Have students draw and write the name of each object to be weighed. Have them estimate the weight of the first item, and then weigh it. Continue the process, first estimating and then weighing. Encourage students to use feedback from earlier measurements to estimate more accurately.

Introducing the "Measurement" Game Mat To provide practice with measurement and estimation, have students play the game. Since the Game Mat refers to thermometers and temperature, display a **classroom thermometer*** and tell the room temperature. Talk about the difference between very warm air temperatures and very cold ones. A copy of this game can be found on page 404 of this Teacher's Guide.

③ Wrap-Up

In Closing Have students discuss their ideas about having two systems of measurement: metric and customary.

Informal Assessment Use students' answers to pages 191–192 and the closing discussion as an informal assessment of their understanding of measurement in metric units.

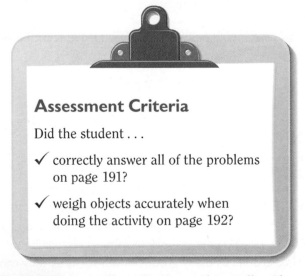

Assessment Criteria

Did the student . . .

✓ correctly answer all of the problems on page 191?

✓ weigh objects accurately when doing the activity on page 192?

LOOKING AHEAD You will need string and a small washer or weight to make a pendulum in Lesson 87.

LESSON 87

Student Edition pages 193–194

Numbers 0–40

LESSON PLANNER

Objectives

▶ to teach students to recognize standard finger sets for numbers 0–40 without counting

▶ to provide opportunities to investigate factors that affect how fast a pendulum swings

Context of the Lesson In previous lessons, students have used standard finger sets in the 0–10 range only. In previous lessons, a pendulum was used to estimate time intervals.

 MANIPULATIVES **Program Resources**

craft sticks (optional)

string

washer or other small weight

Number Cubes

Practice Master 87

Enrichment Master 87

For extra practice:
CD-ROM* Lesson 87
Mixed Practice, page 367

1 Warm-Up 5 MINUTES

 Problem of the Day Present the following problem to the class. A first-grader wrote her name in code: 452295. She said that the number 4 stood for D, and 5 stood for E. What do you think her name is? (Debbie)

Problem-Solving Strategies Ask students who have solved the Problem of the Day to share how they solved it and any strategies they used.

MENTAL MATH Quickly present the following problems and have students answer orally.

a. 14 – 7 = (7)   b. 9 – 7 = (2)   c. 16 + 3 = (19)
d. 13 + 3 = (16)   e. 11 – 3 = (8)   f. 13 – 2 = (11)

  Meeting Individual Needs
Have kinesthetic learners use **craft sticks** to count groups of numbers through 40. Place a pile of craft sticks (40 or fewer) in the center of a table. Have students work in pairs to wrap rubber bands around as many groups of ten sticks as they can. Then have them count the total number of sticks by counting by tens and then counting on.

193 Measurement and Geometry

LESSON 87

Name _____

Numbers 0–40

Count how many fingers.

❶ How many fingers? `20`

❷ How many fingers? `30`

❸ How many fingers? `36`

 SCIENCE CONNECTION Do the "Slow It Down, Speed It Up" activity.

 NOTE TO HOME
Students count finger sets for numbers 0–40.

Unit 3 Lesson 87 • **193**

Copyright © SRA/McGraw-Hill

 **Literature Connection** Read *How Many Bears?* by Cooper Edens to practice counting, addition, and subtraction skills while finding out how many bears it takes to run a bakery.

RETEACHING

Because substantial work with numbers through 40 is given in subsequent lessons, reteaching is not essential at this time.

*available separately

◆ LESSON 87 Numbers 0–40

Use the Mixed Practice on page 367 after this lesson.

Draw a ring around groups of ten.
Then write how many.

❹ How many pencils? __16__

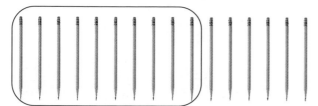

❺ How many marbles? __23__

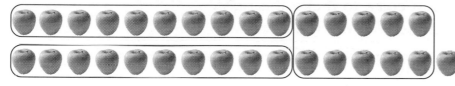

❻ How many apples? __31__

194 • Measurement and Geometry

NOTE TO HOME
Students group objects into sets of ten and count in the 0–40 range.

Copyright © SRA/McGraw-Hill

② Teach

Demonstrate Have four students kneel behind a desk and show only their hands. Have them demonstrate different numbers in finger sets wherein all but one student shows a complete finger set of 10. For example, whisper instructions to show 34 fingers. Have the first three students hold up 10 fingers and the fourth hold up 4 fingers. Guide students to count by tens each time and then count up the remaining fingers.

 Introducing the "Slow It Down, Speed It Up" Activity This activity provides practice in rhythmic counting and estimating rate. Make a pendulum from a **string** about two feet long with a **weight** tied to the end. Set the pendulum in motion and have students count how many swings the pendulum makes in 15 seconds (about 10). Ask: "What could be done to make more swings?" Try out the suggestions. (Shortening the string will increase the number of swings.)

Using the Student Pages Have students ring each group of ten fingers shown on page 193. Then have students complete pages 193–194 on their own. Check and correct their answers as a class.

③ Wrap-Up ⏱ 5 MINUTES

In Closing Have students model the process they used to complete page 194.

 Have students write the number of problems they got correct on these pages. Have brief interviews with students to assess their ability to count to 40 using finger sets.

Assessment Criteria

Did the student . . .

✓ correctly count by tens to solve problems on pages 193–194?

✓ make reasonable predictions of rate and sensible suggestions as to how to make the pendulum swing faster?

PRACTICE p. 87

LESSON 87 PRACTICE Name _____

Fill in the missing numbers.

❶ 16 17 18 ❷ 26 27 [28]
❸ 19 [20] 21 ❹ 9 10 [11]
❺ [30] 31 32 ❻ 38 [39] 40
❼ 22 23 [24] ❽ [18] 19 20
❾ 14 [15] 16 ❿ 19 [20] 21
⓫ [10] 11 12 ⓬ 23 24 [25]
⓭ [38] 39 40 ⓮ [13] 14 15
⓯ 35 [36] 37 ⓰ 8 9 [10]
⓱ 29 30 [31] ⓲ 27 [28] 29
⓳ 20 [21] 22 ⓴ [32] 33 34

Math Explorations and Applications Level 1 • 87

ENRICHMENT p. 87

LESSON 87 ENRICHMENT Name _____

❶ Leann knitted two pairs of gloves this week. She also knitted three fingers of a new glove. How many fingers has she knitted so far this week? __23__

❷ Leann made gloves for Bonnie, Eric, and Shandra. How many fingers did she knit? __30__

❸ Leann made one pair of gloves with four red fingers. The rest of the fingers were blue. How many were blue? __6__

❹ Holly has two pairs of old gloves. All but eight fingers have holes! How many fingers have holes? __12__

❺ Use four different colors for the gloves on this page. Each color should cover the same number of fingers. Check student drawings.

Math Explorations and Applications Level 1 • 87

Unit 3 Lesson 87 **194**

LESSON 88

Student Edition pages 195–196

Pennies, Nickels, and Dimes

LESSON PLANNER

Objective

▶ to teach the use of pennies, nickels, and dimes to form given amounts from 1¢ through 40¢

Context of the Lesson
In Lesson 74 students used play coins to form amounts of money through 20¢.

MANIPULATIVES

overhead coins*

play coins*
(4 dimes,
1 nickel,
4 pennies
per student)

Program Resources

Number Cubes

Thinking Story Book, pages 72–75

Practice Master 88

Enrichment Master 88

For career connections:
Careers and Math*

For extra practice:
CD-ROM* Lesson 88

① Warm-Up ⏱ 5 MINUTES

Problem of the Day Present the following problem to the class. I have four coins. I have dimes, nickels, and pennies. Only two coins are the same. What is the greatest amount of money I can have? (26¢)

Problem-Solving Strategies Ask students who have solved the Problem of the Day to share how they solved it and any strategies they used.

MENTAL MATH Have students respond to the following problems using Number Cubes:

a. 0 + 10 = (10)	**b.** 10 − 0 = (10)
c. 6 + 4 = (10)	**d.** 10 − 6 = (4)
e. 5 + 5 = (10)	**f.** 10 − 5 = (5)
g. 4 + 6 = (10)	**h.** 10 − 4 = (6)
i. 8 + 2 = (10)	**j.** 10 − 2 = (8)
k. 7 + 3 = (10)	**l.** 10 − 3 = (7)

195 Measurement and Geometry

LESSON 88

Name _____

Pennies, Nickels, and Dimes

REAL-WORLD CONNECTION

How many cents?

❶ __21__ ¢

❷ __36__ ¢

❸ __23__ ¢

❹ __35__ ¢

Use coins to make the right amount. Draw the coins.

❺ 40¢
(10)(10)(10)(10)

❻ 30¢
(10)(10)(10) **Answers may vary.**

🎒 **NOTE TO HOME**
Students use coins to form amounts to 40¢.

Unit 3 Lesson 88 • **195**

Copyright © SRA/McGraw-Hill

Literature Connection Read aloud *The Five Pennies* by Barbara Brenner to reinforce lesson concepts.

Social Studies Connection Ask students if they know the names of the presidents whose images are on the penny, the nickel, and the dime. Share with the class a few interesting facts about Washington, Lincoln, and Roosevelt.

RETEACHING

Extra teaching for students who are having trouble with money values may be postponed until Lesson 89. However, you may wish to preteach the next lesson's focus—doubling amounts of money—by giving problems like those in the Number Cube exercise found in the next lesson.

◆ LESSON 88 Pennies, Nickels, and Dimes

Use coins to make the right amount.

Draw the coins.

Possible answers are shown.

7 20¢ ⑩ ⑩

8 0¢

9 25¢ ⑩ ⑩ ⑤

10 35¢ ⑩ ⑩ ⑩ ⑤

11 31¢ ⑩ ⑩ ⑩ ①

12 17¢ ⑩ ⑤ ① ①

Talk about the Thinking Story
"Ms. Eng's Fish Stories."

196 • Measurement and Geometry

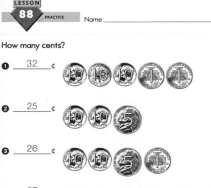

NOTE TO HOME
Students use coins to form
amounts up to 40¢.

Copyright © SRA/McGraw-Hill

---

❷ Teach

Demonstrate Give each student four **dimes**, one **nickel**, and four **pennies**. Use an overhead projector and **overhead coins,** * or hold up one, two, three, and four dimes, and ask students to identify the amounts represented. Give problems that ask for specified amounts of money through 40¢. Encourage students to first set out the required number of dimes and then use pennies to form the remaining amount.

Using the Student Pages Have students complete the exercises on pages 195–196 on their own. If needed, students should lay out coins before writing their answers.

Using the Thinking Story Read aloud and discuss "Ms. Eng's Fish Stories" from the Thinking Story Book, pages 72–75.

Invite students to draw a scene from the story in their Math Journals.

❸ Wrap-Up

In Closing To summarize the lesson, have students tell different ways to form given amounts of money through 40¢.

Informal Assessment Observe students during the demonstration and as they complete the student pages to see who is having difficulty. Interview these students to try to ascertain the nature of their difficulty.

PRACTICE p. 88

How many cents?

1 __32__ ¢

2 __25__ ¢

3 __26__ ¢

4 __37__ ¢

5 __18__ ¢

6 __24__ ¢

88 • Math Explorations and Applications Level 1

ENRICHMENT p. 88

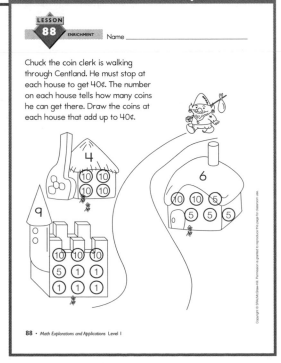

Chuck the coin clerk is walking through Centland. He must stop at each house to get 40¢. The number on each house tells how many coins he can get there. Draw the coins at each house that add up to 40¢.

88 • Math Explorations and Applications Level 1

Assessment Criteria

Did the student . . .

✓ use mental math to do related fact problems?

✓ correctly form given amounts of money through 40¢?

✓ participate in the Thinking Story discussion?

*available separately

Unit 3 Lesson 88 **196**

STORY 12
Ms. Eng's Fish Stories

❶ "I always carry five pens with me," said Ms. Eng, "but I've lost two of them. I'm on my way to buy some more."
How many pens does she have with her now? three
How many pens do you think she will buy? two

❷ Manolita is having a birthday party. She just blew out six candles on the cake. Two candles are still burning.
How old is Manolita? eight

❸ Portia weighed 40 pounds. Over summer vacation she grew 1 inch and gained 0 pounds.
How much does she weigh now? 40 pounds

❹ Ferdie had five tadpoles. Something happened to one of them.
How many tadpoles does he have now? can't tell
What do you need to know? whether that one is no longer a tadpole; [If child insists that one turned into a frog or died, ask: Do you know for sure? What if it just got bigger? How many would he have then?]

THINKING STORY

Ms. Eng's Fish Stories

Ms. Eng likes to go fishing and she likes to tell other people about it, but sometimes she doesn't tell enough. One day when she got back from a fishing trip, the children were all out in front of her house to meet her.

"How many fish did you catch?" they asked.

"Well," said Ms. Eng, "in the morning I caught four fish and in the afternoon I caught some more. So you should be able to figure out how many I caught all together."

Can you figure it out? Why not? No, she doesn't say how many she caught in the afternoon.

"Wait a minute," said Marcus. "How many fish did you catch in the afternoon?"

72 • Ms. Eng's Fish Stories

"I caught only two fish in the afternoon," said Ms. Eng. "They weren't biting as well then."

Now can you figure out how many fish she caught all together? six

"You caught six fish!" the children all shouted, except for Ferdie. Ferdie thought Ms. Eng had caught only two fish.

What did Ferdie forget about? the fish she caught in the morning

"Did you catch any big fish?" asked Willy.

"Indeed I did!" said Ms. Eng. "I caught one that is almost as big as the biggest fish I ever caught."

"How long is the fish?" Willy asked.

"You should be able to figure that out for yourself," said Ms. Eng, "when I tell you that the big fish I caught today

is only 1 centimeter shorter than the biggest fish I ever caught."

Can you figure it out? no

"I wish I knew the answer," said Willy.

"Wait a minute," said Marcus. "I have a question, Ms. Eng."

What question do you think Marcus is going to ask? How long was the biggest fish she ever caught?

Marcus asked, "How long was the biggest fish you ever caught?"

"It was 41 centimeters long," said Ms. Eng.

Now can you figure out how long the fish is that Ms. Eng caught today? yes, by subtracting one from 41

How much shorter is it than the biggest fish? 1 cm

Story 12 • **73**

5 "I'll bet my paper airplane can fly farther than yours," said Manolita. Willy threw his plane and it went 4 yards. Manolita threw hers and it went 3 yards. Then she threw it again and it went 3 more yards.
Whose airplane can fly farther? Willy's

6 Marcus is growing fast. He grew 2 inches in just nine months.
How tall is he now? can't tell
What do you need to know before you can figure it out? how tall he was

7 Ferdie's pencil broke near the middle. He wonders if he has more than half or less than half of it left.
How could he find out? by seeing which piece is longer

8 Mrs. Mudancia drove Manolita to her friend Joyce's house and then drove her home. Joyce lives 2 miles away.
How far did Manolita ride all together? 4 miles

9 Willy can wear Ferdie's shoes, but Ferdie can't get into Willy's shoes.
Who has bigger feet? Ferdie

◆ **STORY 12 Ms. Eng's Fish Stories**

"You caught a fish 40 centimeters long!" cried Portia.

How long is that? Show with your hands. [Demonstrate.]

Is that very long for a fish? for some kinds of fish, but not for the biggest fish a person has ever caught

Ms. Eng took a basket out of her car and showed the children the 40-centimeter-long fish.

"You may think this is a big fish,"

Ms. Eng said, "but it's nothing compared to the one that got away."

"How long was it?" Ferdie asked.

"I don't know how long it was," said Ms. Eng, "but it had eyes as big as my husband's pocket watch."

"Wow!" said Ferdie. "A giant fish!"

"Wait a minute," said Marcus. "I have a question."

What question do you think Marcus will ask? How big is Mr. Eng's pocket watch?

74 • Ms. Eng's Fish Stories

"How big is Mr. Eng's pocket watch?" Marcus asked.

"About a centimeter wide," said Ms. Eng.

How wide is that? Show with your fingers. [Demonstrate.]

"Yes," said Ms. Eng, "my husband has the smallest pocket watch I've ever seen. And the fish didn't have very big eyes, either. But it was heavy. I'll bet that fish weighed twice as much as my Aunt Minnie's hairbrush."

"That's not very heavy," said Manolita. "Everybody knows that a hairbrush doesn't weigh much!"

"Wait a minute," said Marcus. "I have another question."

What question do you think Marcus will ask this time? How much does Aunt Minnie's hairbrush weigh?

"How much does your Aunt Minnie's hairbrush weigh?" Marcus asked.

"It weighs 5 kilograms," said Ms. Eng. "It is a very big hairbrush. My Aunt Minnie uses it to brush her pet giraffe."

Now can you figure out how many kilograms the fish weighed? about ten kilograms

. . . the end

Story 12 • **75**

LESSON 89

Student Edition pages 197–198

Doubles and Halves

LESSON PLANNER

Objectives

▶ to teach doubling given amounts of money from 0 through 40¢

▶ to provide practice estimating half a length

Context of the Lesson Lesson 72 introduced basic paper-folding techniques. Lesson 75 introduced the doubling of given amounts of money through 20¢. In this lesson students are given more practice in doubling amounts and dividing in half.

 MANIPULATIVES

play coins*
  (4 dimes,
  2 nickels,
  8 pennies
  per student)

scissors

Program Resources

Number Cubes

Thinking Story Book, pages 76–77

Practice Master 89

Enrichment Master 89

For extra practice:
  CD-ROM* Lesson 89

① Warm-Up ⏱ 5 MINUTES

 Problem of the Day Present the following problem to the class. I have four coins. I have dimes, nickels, and pennies. Only two of them are the same. What is the least amount I can have? (17¢)

Problem-Solving Strategies Ask students who have solved the Problem of the Day to share how they solved it and any strategies they used.

MENTAL MATH Ask students to tell how much each amount is worth, saying their answers in unison:

a. one nickel (5¢)

b. two nickels (10¢)

c. one dime (10¢)

d. two dimes (20¢)

e. five pennies (5¢)

f. one nickel, two pennies (7¢)

g. one dime, two pennies (12¢)

h. one dime, one nickel (15¢)

LESSON 89

Name _____

Doubles and Halves

 REAL-WORLD CONNECTION

How many cents?

① _____ 20 _____ ¢

② _____ 40 _____ ¢

③ _____ 7 _____ ¢

④ _____ 14 _____ ¢

⑤ _____ 8 _____ ¢

⑥ _____ 16 _____ ¢

⑦ _____ 10 _____ ¢

⑧ _____ 20 _____ ¢

 NOTE TO HOME
Students count pennies, nickels, and dimes.

Unit 3   Lesson 89 • **197**

RETEACHING

 GAME Ask students who are having difficulty forming amounts of money through 40¢ to play the "Pennies, Nickels, and Dimes" game introduced in Lesson 74. Demonstrate the equivalence of five pennies to a nickel, and so on, as needed.

LITERATURE CONNECTION **Literature Connection** You may wish to read aloud *Arithmetic* by Carl Sandburg to reinforce lesson concepts.

PHYSICAL EDUCATION CONNECTION **Physical Education Connection** Ask students to think about swimming pools they have seen. Encourage them to think of reasons why lines are sometimes painted on the pool floor. (to mark lanes for swimmers and racers) Ask students how they think painters know where to put the lines. (They measure set distances from the wall or other lines.)

*available separately

◆ **LESSON 89** Doubles and Halves

Draw a line down the middle of the swimming pool, like this.

Cut out the pool and fold it along the line. Now cut the pool along the line.

Are both pieces the same size?

198 • Measurement and Geometry

NOTE TO HOME
Students estimate half a given width and explore symmetry.

Copyright © S=A/McGraw-Hill

② Teach

Using the Number Cubes Name an amount of money up to 20¢. Have students make the amount with **coins***, then double it by putting out the same coins again. Then have students show the amount with Number Cubes.

Using the Student Pages Have students do the exercises on page 197. Be sure to correct this page before assigning the paper-folding activity on page 198. Begin work on page 198 by telling students that the picture shows Ms. Eng's swimming pool from the air. Ms. Eng wants to paint a line down the middle, but she needs their help.

Using the Thinking Story Present three problems from those following "Ms. Eng's Fish Stories" on pages 76–77 of the Thinking Story Book or pages 196a–196b of this Guide.

③ Wrap-Up ⏱ 5 MINUTES

In Closing Write numbers on the chalkboard and ask students to tell what coins could make these amounts.

Portfolio Assessment Have students pick and write down five amounts between 0–20¢. Then have them draw coins that show twice that amount. Have students add these problems to their portfolios.

Assessment Criteria

Did the student . . .

✓ double amounts of money up to 40¢ with 75% accuracy?

✓ correctly estimate where the line in the pool should be drawn?

PRACTICE p. 89

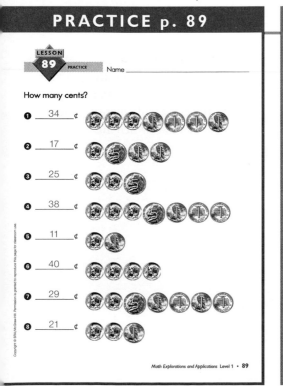

LESSON **89** PRACTICE   Name _____

How many cents?

❶ ___34___ ¢
❷ ___17___ ¢
❸ ___25___ ¢
❹ ___38___ ¢
❺ ___11___ ¢
❻ ___40___ ¢
❼ ___29___ ¢
❽ ___21___ ¢

Math Explorations and Applications Level 1 • **89**

ENRICHMENT p. 89

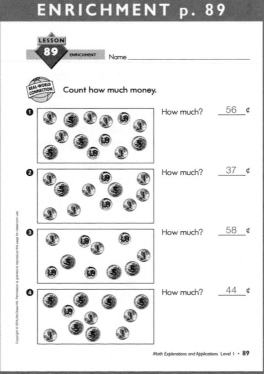

LESSON **89** ENRICHMENT   Name _____

REAL-WORLD CONNECTION   Count how much money.

❶ How much? ___56___ ¢
❷ How much? ___37___ ¢
❸ How much? ___58___ ¢
❹ How much? ___44___ ¢

Math Explorations and Applications Level 1 • **89**

*available separately

Unit 3 Lesson 89 **198**

LESSON 90
Symmetry

Student Edition pages 199–200

LESSON 90

Name _____

Symmetry

ART CONNECTION

Fold your paper.

Draw a shape.

What shape will you make? __**Answers will vary.**__

Cut it out.

Open it up.

Do both parts match? ____**yes**____

NOTE TO HOME
Students explore the concept of symmetry.

Unit 3   Lesson 90 • **199**

LESSON PLANNER

Objectives

▶ to introduce the idea of symmetry

▶ to provide practice recognizing and creating symmetrical figures

▶ to provide practice doubling numbers

Context of the Lesson   In this lesson students are introduced to symmetry and experiment with making symmetrical shapes.

 MANIPULATIVES   **Program Resources**

brushes

nonporous paper

paints or markers

Practice Master 90

Enrichment Master 90

For extra practice:
CD-ROM* Lesson 90

---

① Warm-Up

5 MINUTES

PROBLEM SOLVING

Problem of the Day   Present the following problem to the class. Four basketball teams played in the championships: Tigers, Spiders, Dunkers, and Bears. The Bears beat the Dunkers. The Dunkers beat the Spiders. The Tigers won the championship. Write the names of the teams in order from first to fourth place. (Tigers, Bears, Dunkers, Spiders)

Problem-Solving Strategies   Ask students who have solved the Problem of the Day to share how they solved it and any strategies they used.

MENTAL MATH   Whisper instructions to four students as to how many fingers they must each show to the class in order to make the following sets. Have the class count finger sets and answer orally.

a. 14   b. 35

c. 27   d. 33

e. 2   f. 20

LITERATURE CONNECTION

Literature Connection   The stories, games, activities, and poems found in *Right in Your Own Backyard: Nature Math*, from Time-Life for Children, introduce students to math in everyday life. The section "Mirror, Mirror" has activities on symmetry.

RETEACHING

Draw a variety of symmetrical and asymmetrical shapes on the chalkboard that all have "lines of symmetry" through them. Have students identify which are symmetrical and which are not.

---

199 Measurement and Geometry

*available separately

◆ LESSON 90 Symmetry

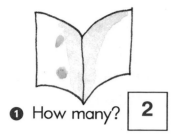

❶ How many? 2

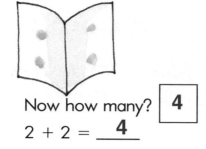

Now how many? 4

2 + 2 = 4

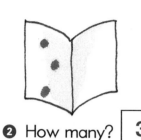

❷ How many? 3

Now how many? 6

3 + 3 = 6

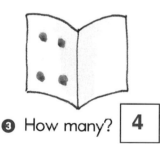

❸ How many? 4

Now how many? 8

4 + 4 = 8

200 • Measurement and Geometry

Copyright © SRA/McGraw-Hill

🎒 **NOTE TO HOME**
Students explore the relationship between symmetry and doubles.

PRACTICE p. 90

LESSON 90 PRACTICE   Name _____

Look at the shapes on both sides of the dotted line. Do they match?

Color the shape if both sides match.

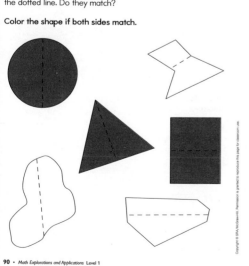

90 • *Math Explorations and Applications Level 1*

ENRICHMENT p. 90

LESSON 90 ENRICHMENT   Name _____

Draw a line through every picture to try to make two parts that look the same.

Ring the picture that is not symmetrical.

Draw two lines through each picture to try to make four parts that look the same.

Put a check by the ones with four symmetrical parts.

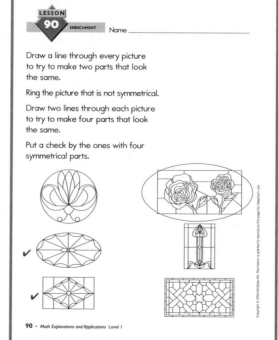

90 • *Math Explorations and Applications Level 1*

---

❷ Teach

Using the Student Pages Read the directions on page 199 to the class and help students follow the directions to make a symmetrical shape. Explain that the fold of the paper is called the line of symmetry. Then have students answer the questions on page 199.

Before beginning page 200, have students **paint** several dots on a sheet of **paper** and then, while the paint is still wet, fold the paper in half with the dots on the inside. When the paper is unfolded, students will see a symmetric array of dots. Again, explain that the fold is the line of symmetry. Then have students answer the questions on page 200.

❸ Wrap-Up ⏱ 5 MINUTES

In Closing Draw a pattern of seven dots on the chalkboard, and ask how many there are. Then say, "If these were on a sheet of paper and I folded it as you did in the second activity, how many dots would there be all together?" Challenge a volunteer to come up and draw the dots where they would be. Repeat for numbers 6, 8, 9, and 10.

Portfolio Assessment As an informal assessment of students' ability to create and identify symmetrical figures, have them place the shapes they made in their Math Portfolios.

Assessment Criteria

Did the student . . .

✓ demonstrate understanding of symmetry by making a symmetrical shape and a symmetrical pattern?

✓ correctly answer 80% of the questions on pages 199–200?

GIFTED & TALENTED **Meeting Individual Needs**
Have students draw large letters of the alphabet, fold them in half, and tell which letters have lines of symmetry. For example, they should discover that A, H, K, and E do have lines of symmetry, while N, Z, and S do not.

LESSON 91

Student Edition pages 201–202

Using Coins

LESSON PLANNER

Objective

▶ to practice counting and making amounts of money through 40¢

Context of the Lesson Students practice counting and making money in this lesson in order to learn a game using money in Lesson 92.

MANIPULATIVES

play coins*

craft sticks (optional)

Program Resources

Thinking Story Book, pages 76–77

Reteaching Master

Practice Master 91

Enrichment Master 91

For extra practice:
CD-ROM* Lesson 91
Mixed Practice, page 368

① Warm-Up ⏱ 5 MINUTES

Problem of the Day Present the following problem to the class. You want to use exact change to buy a memo pad that costs 19¢. What is the least number of coins you would need to pay for it and what are they? (6: 1 dime, 1 nickel, 4 pennies)

Problem-Solving Strategies Ask students who have solved the Problem of the Day to share how they solved it and any strategies they used.

MENTAL MATH Whisper instructions to four students as to how many fingers they must each show to the class in order to make the following sets. Have the class count finger sets and answer orally.

a. 31   b. 34   c. 23

d. 25   e. 39   f. 17

SPECIAL NEEDS **MANIPULATIVES** **Meeting Individual Needs**
Have students use **craft sticks** to complete pages 201–202. For example, 26¢ can be shown as two bundles of ten, one bundle of five, and one single stick. Then guide students to see how many craft sticks each coin stands for: one dime equals ten; one nickel equals five; one penny equals one.

201 Measurement and Geometry

LESSON 91

Name _____

Using Coins

REAL-WORLD CONNECTION

Draw coins to make the right amount.
Possible answers are shown.

❶ 21¢ ⟨ (10) (10) (1) ⟩

❷ 30¢ ⟨ (10) (10) (10) ⟩

❸ 26¢ ⟨ (10) (10) (5) (1) ⟩

❹ 22¢ ⟨ (10) (10) (1) (1) ⟩

❺ 40¢ ⟨ (10) (10) (10) (10) ⟩

❻ 37¢ ⟨ (10) (10) (10) (5) (1) (1) ⟩

COOPERATIVE LEARNING Do the "Store" activity.

NOTE TO HOME
Students use nickels, dimes, and pennies to form amounts through 40¢.

Unit 3   Lesson 91 • **201**

TECHNOLOGY CONNECTION
Technology Connection Use the software *Money Town* by Davidson Co. (Mac, IBM) for practice with coin recognition and making change.

LESSON 91 RETEACHING   Name _____

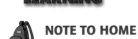

Draw coins to make the right amount.

❶ 23¢ ⟨ (10) (10) (1) (1) (1) ⟩

❷ 37¢   Answers will vary.

❸ 18¢

❹ 50¢

Math Explorations and Applications Level I • 21

*available separately

◆ **LESSON 91** Using Coins

Use the Mixed Practice on page 368 after this lesson.

Draw coins to make the right amount.

Make each amount two ways.
Possible answers are shown.

❼ 31¢
⑩ ⑩ ⑩ ①

⑩ ⑩ ⑤ ⑤ ①

❽ 20¢
⑩ ⑩

⑤ ⑤ ⑤ ⑤

❾ 35¢
⑩ ⑩ ⑩ ⑤

⑩ ⑩ ⑩ ① ① ① ① ①

❿ 17¢
⑩ ⑤ ① ①

⑤ ⑤ ⑤ ① ①

202 • Measurement and Geometry

NOTE TO HOME
Students use money to form amounts through 40¢.

Copyright © SRA/McGraw-Hill

---

② Teach

Demonstrate Provide a variety of problems in which students must form specific amounts of money through 40¢. For example, "A banana costs 36¢. How much money should I give the clerk?" Remind students to count dimes first, then nickels, and then pennies.

Introducing the "Store" Activity This activity provides practice forming and counting money. Divide the class into "Storekeepers" and "Shoppers" and give both groups **play money.*** Have the storekeepers put prices from 1¢–40¢ on various classroom objects. Then have the shoppers bargain with and purchase the various items from the storekeepers, who must give change when necessary.

Using the Student Pages Allow students to use play money to help them complete pages 201–202 on their own. Remind them to start with dimes, then nickels, and then pennies to help make each amount.

Using the Thinking Story Present three new problems from among those following "Ms. Eng's Fish Stories" on pages 76–77 of the Thinking Story Book or pages 196a–196b of this Guide.

③ Wrap-Up

In Closing Have volunteers demonstrate to the class how to count specified amounts of money through 40¢.

Performance Assessment Use students' answers to pages 201–202 as a performance assessment of their ability to count and make money amounts through 40¢.

Assessment Criteria

Did the student . . .

✓ make correct money amounts during the demonstration?

✓ give the correct amount of money and change during the "Store" activity?

✓ correctly answer eight of ten problems on pages 201–202?

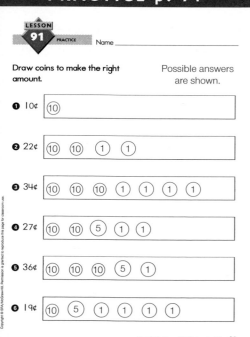
*available separately

LESSON 92

Using Numbers to 40

Student Edition pages 203–204

LESSON PLANNER

Objective

▶ to teach students to solve addition problems with numbers through 40 using concrete objects

Context of the Lesson In earlier lessons students solved addition problems in the 0–40 range using play money. Addition in the 0–40 range continues in the next lesson.

MANIPULATIVES

craft sticks (loose and four bundles of 10)

play coins*

rubber bands

Program Resources

Number Cubes

Practice Master 92

Enrichment Master 92

For extra practice: CD-ROM* Lesson 92

① Warn-Up ⏱ 5 MINUTES

Problem of the Day Present the following problem to the class. Every day Grant saves twice as much money as the day before. On Monday he saves $1.00. How much has he saved by Thursday? How do you know? ($15; $1 + $2 + $4 + $8 = $15)

Problem-Solving Strategies Ask students who have solved the Problem of the Day to share how they solved it and any strategies they used.

MENTAL MATH Have students add and subtract ten from various numbers from 0–40.

② Teach

Demonstrate Hold up two bundles of ten craft sticks and three single **craft sticks**. Tell students that each bundle contains ten sticks. Ask how many sticks there are. (23) Give a volunteer 14 sticks (one bundle and four loose sticks). Then give him or her four more sticks, one at a time, as the group counts on from 14. Confirm that there are now 18 sticks. Give the student four more sticks. Tell the student to make a new bundle when there are ten loose sticks. Ask students how many they have now. (2 bundles and 2 sticks = 22 sticks)

203 Measurement and Geometry

LESSON 92

Name _____

Using Numbers to 40

There are too many crayons.
Ring the right number of crayons.

1 30

2 20

3 10

4 5

5 0

6 15

GAME Play the "Add the Coins" game.

 NOTE TO HOME Students count fives and tens to form amounts through 40.

Unit 3   Lesson 92 • **203**

Copyright © SRA/McGraw-Hill

 Literature Connection To reinforce lesson concepts, read aloud to students *The Cat's Midsummer Jamboree* by David Kherdian and Nonny Hogrogian.

 Social Studies Connection Tell students that the tallest building in the United States is the Sears Tower in Chicago. Explain to them that it has 110 stories, or floors. Tell them that you can tell the number of stories a building has by counting its windows from the ground up. Have students draw buildings that have up to 40 stories.

RETEACHING

Extra teaching is not essential at this time because the topic is continued in the next lesson.

*available separately

◆ LESSON 92 Using Numbers to 40

There are too many crayons. Ring the
right number of crayons.

7 32

8 25

9 17

10 11

11 6

12 0

 Using the Number Cubes
Present addition problems as in the
demonstration. Tell the class the
starting amount. Then position the volunteer with his or her
back to the class so that other students cannot see how
many bundles and single sticks he or she has. Present
problems with sums as high as 40. Ask students to count
mentally as you give the volunteer more sticks. Students
should show the final amount with Number Cubes. After
each problem, have the students count the sticks to check.

 Introducing the "Add the Coins" Game
Demonstrate and then have pairs of students play
this game to practice adding coin values and
changing money. Give each player ten play **pennies,***
nickels,* and **dimes,*** which are placed in a "bank." One
player counts aloud as he or she takes from the bank coins
that total 30¢ or less. The player covers these coins with a
book and then takes from the bank additional coins whose
value is ten cents or less. These are placed so that the
second player can see them. The first player then asks how
much money there is all together. If the second player
guesses the correct amount, he or she wins the round. The
players take turns selecting the coins and determining their
total value. A copy of this can also be found on page 22 of
the Home Connections Blackline Masters.

Using the Student Pages Have students do the
exercises on pages 203–204 independently.

③ Wrap-Up

In Closing Present given numbers of play coins and ask
students to count on as you add other coins, to a total of
40¢ or less.

Performance Assessment Have students
count out a specified number of paper clips,
forming them into chains of ten as indicated.

Assessment Criteria

Did the students . . .

✓ complete the exercises on pages
203–204 with 80% accuracy?

✓ understand how to group objects
into bundles of ten?

✓ demonstrate how to use play money
for addition problems adding up to
40¢ or less?

PRACTICE p. 92

92 PRACTICE Name_____

There are too many sticks. Ring the
right number of sticks.

1 38
2 30
3 24
4 20
5 16
6 12
7 7

NOTE TO HOME
Students count fives, tens, and
units to form numbers through 40.

ENRICHMENT p. 92

92 ENRICHMENT Name_____

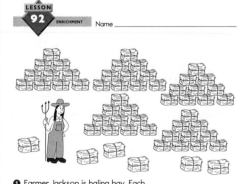

56

1 Farmer Jackson is baling hay. Each
haystack has ten bales. Color all
the bales of hay gold. How many
bales has she made today?

2 The cows will get 32 bales of hay.
Ring 32 bales of hay in green.
Students should ring 32 bales.

3 The sheep will get eight bales of
hay. Ring eight bales in brown.
Students should ring 8 bales.

4 The horses will get 15 bales of
hay. Ring 15 bales in red.
Students should ring 15 bales.

*available separately

Student Edition pages 205–206

LESSON 93
Adding with Numbers 0–40

LESSON PLANNER

Objectives

▶ to provide practice solving addition problems with numbers through 40 by using concrete objects

▶ to provide opportunities to explore the relationship between triangles and parallelograms

Context of the Lesson Subtraction with concrete objects is taught in Lesson 94.

MANIPULATIVES   **Program Resources**

counters*   Number Cubes

can   Practice Master 93

tracing paper   Enrichment Master 93

For extra practice:
CD-ROM* Lesson 93

1 Warm-Up

Problem of the Day Present the following riddle to the class. I am more than the number of legs on a dog. I am less than the number of sides on a box. What number am I? (5)

Problem-Solving Strategies Ask students who have solved the Problem of the Day to share how they solved it and any strategies they used.

MENTAL MATH Whisper instructions to four students as to how many fingers they must each show to the class in order to make the following sets. Have the class count finger sets and answer orally.

a.	36	**b.**	12
c.	39	**d.**	30
e.	32	**f.**	29
g.	11	**h.**	19

Meeting Individual Needs
Allow kinesthetic learners to use **counters*** to help them complete page 205.

205 Measurement and Geometry

LESSON 93

Name _____

Adding with Numbers 0–40

Use counters and a can.
How many now?

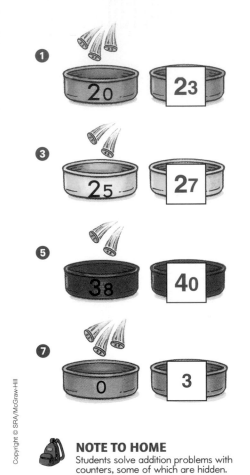

① 20 | 23

② 25 | 26

③ 25 | 27

④ 24 | 27

⑤ 38 | 40

⑥ 10 | 13

⑦ 0 | 3

⑧ 29 | 32

Copyright © SRA/McGraw-Hill

 NOTE TO HOME
Students solve addition problems with counters, some of which are hidden.

Unit 3   Lesson 93 • **205**

Literature Connection Read aloud to students *Moon To Sun* by Sheila Samton to reinforce number concepts. Each page of this book adds an object to the landscape and to the addition problem on the page.

RETEACHING

Provide counters-in-a-can addition problems with numbers through 10. When students have reviewed this, present problems with numbers through 20. Be sure students have mastered these levels before going on to adding with numbers through 40.

*available separately

◆ **LESSON 93** Adding with Numbers 0–40

Listen to the story.

Trace the park on a sheet of paper.

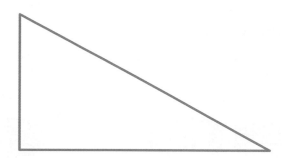

Move the tracing over the park to see
what new shapes the park can be.

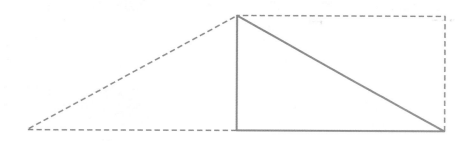

Write in your Math Journal what
shapes the larger park might be.

206 · Measurement and Geometry

NOTE TO HOME
Students explore the rotation of
triangular figures.

Copyright © SRA/McGraw-Hill

2 Teach

Demonstrate Have a student count out 24
counters* and put them into a **can** all at once.
Then have him or her put in four more, one at a
time, as you count on 25, 26, 27, 28. Count all the counters
in the can to confirm that there are 28. Repeat with other
numbers.

Using the Number Cubes Present
addition problems as in the demonstration. Have
students count on silently and then show their
answers with their Number Cubes.

Using the Student Pages Have students complete page
205 on their own. When finished, have them correct their
papers with you. Then work together to complete page 206.
Read the following story: "Triangle Park is shaped like a
triangle. The village council wants to make the park twice as
big." Provide each student with a sheet of **tracing paper** and
have students trace the triangle and then move their tracings
around the triangle to discover new shapes. Guide students
to see that they can create a rectangle, a diamond, and a larger
triangle from two triangles.

Using the "Add the Coins" Game After
students finish pages 205–206, have them play the
"Add the Coins" game introduced in Lesson 92.

3 Wrap-Up

In Closing Have students demonstrate how they would
use counters and a can to add 17 + 4.

Informal Assessment Observe students
during the demonstration and Number Cube
exercises as an informal assessment of their
ability to add with numbers through 40 using concrete objects.

Assessment Criteria

Did the student . . .

✓ find the correct sums during the
demonstration and Number Cube
activity?

✓ correctly answer six of eight
problems on page 205?

✓ correctly trace and identify the
shapes on page 206?

PRACTICE p. 93

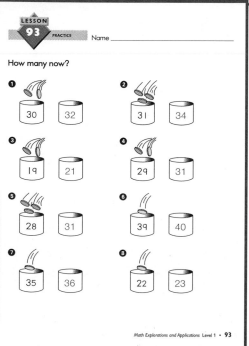

LESSON **93** PRACTICE   Name _____

How many now?

① 30 | 32   ② 31 | 34

③ 19 | 21   ④ 29 | 31

⑤ 28 | 31   ⑥ 39 | 40

⑦ 35 | 36   ⑧ 22 | 23

Math Explorations and Applications Level 1 · 93

ENRICHMENT p. 93

LESSON **93** ENRICHMENT   Name _____

Draw only five lines. Divide the
circle into 14 pieces.

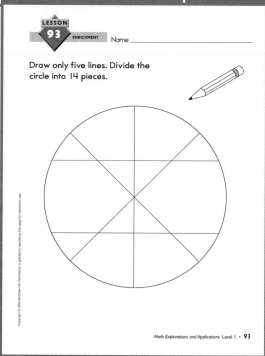

Math Explorations and Applications Level 1 · 93

*available separately

Keeping Sharp

Name _____

Keeping Sharp

How many now?

❶ 12 **15**

❷ 12 **9**

❸ 36 **34**

❹ 19 **21**

❺ 31 **29**

❻ 32 **30**

 Do the "Pencil Line" activity.

NOTE TO HOME
Students solve addition and subtraction problems
with counters, some of which are hidden.

Unit 3   Lesson 94 • **207**

LESSON PLANNER

Objectives

▶ to provide practice estimating and measuring length

✓ to assess students' ability to use concrete objects to
solve addition and subtraction problems with
numbers through 40

Context of the Lesson Practice in measurement is
presented throughout the year. This lesson includes
Mastery Checkpoint 15 for assessing students' ability to
use concrete objects or representations of them to solve
both addition and subtraction problems with numbers
through 40.

 MANIPULATIVES

centimeter
  rulers*

craft sticks

rubber bands

25–30 pencils of
  varying
  lengths

Program Resources

Number Cubes

Number Strips

Reteaching Master

Practice Master 94

Enrichment Master 94

Assessment Master

For extra practice:
  CD-ROM* Lesson 94

❶ Warm-Up 5 MINUTES

 Problem of the Day Present the following
problem to the class. There are 25 steps on a
staircase. Randy walked up ten steps, then back
four, up two more, then back down three more. How many
steps must he walk up now to get to the top? (20)

Problem-Solving Strategies Ask students who have
solved the Problem of the Day to share how they solved it
and any strategies they used.

 Have students count from one number to another.

a. 17 to 40   b. 26 to 40   c. 35 to 40
d. 14 to 0   e. 28 to 0   f. 28 to 40

❷ Teach

 Demonstrate Present subtraction problems
with **craft sticks**. Hold up two 10-bundles and
three single sticks. Have a student remove five

207 Measurement and Geometry

RETEACHING p. 22

LESSON
94 RETEACHING   Name _____

3 counters going in
14 + 3 = 17

2 counters taken out
21 − 2 = 19

How many now?

❶ 18 20   ❷ 14 17

❸ 22 19   ❹ 19 18

❺ 28 30   ❻ 26 29

22 • Math Explorations and Applications Level 1

PRACTICE p. 94

LESSON
94 PRACTICE   Name _____

How many now?

❶ 27 25   ❷ 39 36

❸ 20 19   ❹ 25 23

❺ 18 16   ❻ 40 38

❼ 32 29   ❽ 39 38

94 • Math Explorations and Applications Level 1

*available separately

◆ **LESSON 94** Keeping Sharp

❼ Which line is longer? Estimate.
Ring the line you think is longer.
Then measure to check.

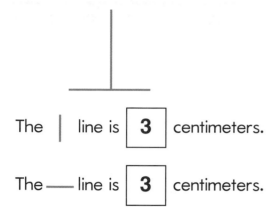

The ┃ line is [**3**] centimeters.

The —— line is [**3**] centimeters.

❽ Which line is longer? Estimate.
Ring the line you think is longer.
Then measure to check.

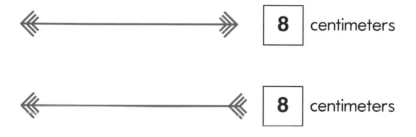

[**8**] centimeters

[**8**] centimeters

208 • Measurement and Geometry

NOTE TO HOME
Students practice estimating and
measuring in centimeters.

Copyright © SRA/McGraw-Hill

ENRICHMENT p. 94

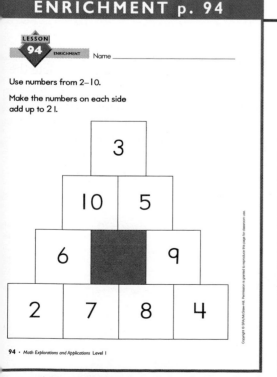

LESSON **94** ENRICHMENT   Name _____

Use numbers from 2–10.

Make the numbers on each side
add up to 21.

```
        3
    10     5
   6         9
  2    7   8    4
```

94 • Math Explorations and Applications Level 1

*available separately

ASSESSMENT p. 35

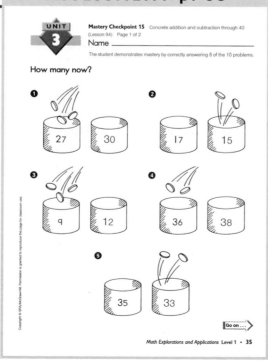

UNIT **3**   **Mastery Checkpoint 15** Concrete addition and subtraction through 40
(Lesson 94) Page 1 of 2
Name _____

The student demonstrates mastery by correctly answering 8 of the 10 problems.

How many now?

❶ 27 30   ❷ 17 15

❸ 9 12   ❹ 36 38

❺ 35 33

[Go on →]

Math Explorations and Applications Level 1 • 35

---

sticks, one at a time, as students count down from 23. When
the fourth stick is needed, have that student undo one
bundle of ten to get it. Have the class show the result (18)
with their Number Cubes. Then count the sticks to confirm
the answer. Continue to present similar problems with
numbers through 40.

 Introducing the "Pencil Line" Activity
Provide **pencils** of varying lengths and have
students measure them with Number Strips.
Discuss the range of lengths. Then have different groups of
students use their pencils to measure a desk top. Discuss
why the measurements differ. (They are all using different-
sized pencils.) Then discuss how to make a better
measurement such as using one pencil as a model and
making a piece of cardboard of that length.

Using the Student Pages Have students complete page
207 on their own. Then work together to complete page 208.
Have **centimeter rulers*** available.

❸ Wrap-Up

In Closing Have students explain how they would find the
total length of two sticks, if one was 32 centimeters and the
other was 3 centimeters. (Students can use either
measurement skills or addition to solve this problem.)

 **Mastery Checkpoint 15**

Most students will now be able to use concrete objects
to add and subtract with numbers through 40.
Proficiency can be demonstrated by correctly
answering four of six problems on page 207 or by
satisfactorily completing pages 35–36 in the
Assessment Blackline Masters. Results can be recorded
on the Mastery Checkpoint Chart.

Assessment Criteria

Did the student . . .

✓ demonstrate mastery of using
concrete objects to solve addition and
subtraction problems through 40?

✓ make sensible estimates of
measurement on page 208?

LESSON
95

LESSON 95 — Identifying the Operation

Student Edition pages 209–210

Identifying the Operation

LESSON PLANNER

Objectives

▶ to teach students to choose the appropriate operation (either addition or subtraction) for a problem

▶ to teach students how to estimate and measure lengths of up to 40 units

▶ to provide practice identifying function rules

Context of the Lesson This lesson continues practice in using function tables and measuring lengths.

MANIPULATIVES

counters* or craft sticks (optional)

string (about 5 ft long)

0–40 chalkboard number line (about 5 ft long)

Program Resources

Number Cubes

Thinking Story Book, pages 78–81

Practice Master 95

Enrichment Master 95

For career connections:
Careers and Math*

For extra practice:
CD-ROM* Lesson 95

---

① Warm-Up ⏱ 5 MINUTES

Problem of the Day Write the following pattern on the chalkboard: 40, 38, 36, 34, 32. Ask what number comes next in the pattern and why. (30, because the pattern is –2)

Problem-Solving Strategies Ask students who have solved the Problem of the Day to share how they solved it and any strategies they used.

Have students count from one number to another.

a. 9 to 17	**b.** 13 to 26
c. 22 to 31	**d.** 34 to 40
e. 7 to 37	**f.** 29 to 33

② Teach

Demonstrate To measure a certain length of **string**, have a volunteer hold one end at the 0 point of a chalkboard **number line** as you read the

---

Name _____

Identifying the Operation

```
0  1  2  3  4  5  6  7  8  9  10
```

Use the number line.
What is the missing sign? Draw + or –.

1 $4 \; \boxed{+} \; 1 = 5$ **2** $3 \; \boxed{-} \; 1 = 2$

3 $6 \; \boxed{-} \; 1 = 5$ **4** $7 \; \boxed{+} \; 1 = 8$

5 $5 \; \boxed{-} \; 2 = 3$ **6** $9 \; \boxed{-} \; 1 = 10$

7 $2 \; \boxed{+} \; 8 = 10$ **8** $4 \; \boxed{-} \; 4 = 0$

9 $40 \; \boxed{-} \; 10 = 30$ **10** $23 \; \boxed{+} \; 1 = 24$

**Talk about the Thinking Story
"Manolita's Magnificent Minus Machine."**

NOTE TO HOME
Students select a relation sign to make a true number sentence.

Unit 3　Lesson 95 • **209**

Literature Connection Read aloud *Is It Larger? Is It Smaller?* by Tana Hoban to provide practice in estimating size. In this book, photographs of animals and objects of different sizes are used to make comparisons between the two.

RETEACHING

Have students use **counters*** or **craft sticks** to complete the student pages. For example, to solve the first problem on page 209, have students lay out four counters. Ask: "Should you add or subtract one counter to get five?" Have students act out both operations to see which one is correct.

*available separately

◆ **LESSON 95** Identifying the Operation

Find the rule.

⑪
In	Out
2	1
4	3
7	6

Rule -1

⑫
In	Out
5	7
6	8
7	9

Rule $+2$

⑬
In	Out
8	10
10	12
15	17

Rule $+2$

⑭
In	Out
5	8
10	13
20	23

Rule $+3$

⑮
In	Out
27	25
19	17
10	8

Rule -2

⑯
In	Out
18	18
20	20
21	21

Rule $+0$ or -0

210 • Measurement and Geometry

 NOTE TO HOME
Students identify addition and subtraction function rules for numbers up to 40.

number measurement at the other end. Mark various points on the string and have students estimate, then measure, the length of each point on the string.

Using the Student Pages Do the first problem on page 209 with the class. Have a volunteer try each operation sign in the number sentence to see which makes the sentence true. Then have students complete the rest of page 209 and all of page 210 on their own.

 Using the Thinking Story Read aloud and then discuss "Manolita's Magnificent Minus Machine" on pages 78–81 of the Thinking Story Book.

❸ Wrap-Up ⏱ 5 MINUTES

In Closing Have students explain a strategy, such as guess and test or use of a physical model, that they used to identify the function rules on page 210.

 Informal Assessment Use page 209 to informally assess students' understanding of operation signs.

Assessment Criteria

Did the student . . .

✓ correctly solve 13 of 16 problems on pages 209–210?

✓ make sensible estimates of length during the demonstration activity?

✓ actively participate in the Thinking Story discussion?

 **Meeting Individual Needs**
Have auditory learners draw a plus sign on one index card and a minus sign on another. Give them problems like those on page 209. Have students show the operation sign that would make a true number sentence.

PRACTICE p. 95

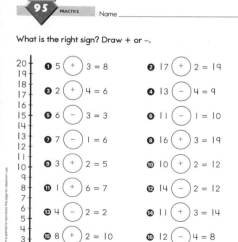

LESSON 95 PRACTICE   Name _____

What is the right sign? Draw + or −.

❶ 5 (+) 3 = 8   ❷ 17 (+) 2 = 19
❸ 2 (+) 4 = 6   ❹ 13 (−) 4 = 9
❺ 6 (−) 3 = 3   ❻ 11 (−) 1 = 10
❼ 7 (−) 1 = 6   ❽ 16 (+) 3 = 19
❾ 3 (+) 2 = 5   ❿ 10 (+) 2 = 12
⓫ 1 (+) 6 = 7   ⓬ 14 (−) 2 = 12
⓭ 4 (−) 2 = 2   ⓮ 11 (+) 3 = 14
⓯ 8 (+) 2 = 10   ⓰ 12 (−) 4 = 8
⓱ 9 (−) 1 = 8   ⓲ 20 (−) 2 = 18
⓳ 3 (−) 3 = 0   ⓴ 17 (+) 1 = 18

Math Explorations and Applications Level 1 • 95

ENRICHMENT p. 95

LESSON 95 ENRICHMENT   Name _____

One side of the Symbol Bank is for plus, and one side is for minus. The answers are filled in, but part of each problem is missing.

Find numbers at the Lost and Found. Fill in the blanks.

Symbol Bank

7	+	12	=	19
8	+	6	=	14
10	+	1	=	11
22	+	5	=	27
38	+	0	=	38
30	+	2	=	32

40	−	31	=	9
12	−	7	=	5
19	−	1	=	18
31	−	5	=	26
37	−	3	=	34
24	−	8	=	16

Lost and Found

| 7 | 10 | 22 | | 12 | 19 | 24 |
| 6 | 0 | 2 | | 31 | 5 | 3 |

+ | −

Math Explorations and Applications Level 1 • 95

Manolita's Magnificent Minus Machine

① Manolita dreamed about a different kind of machine. She put in three acorns and got back six. She put in two cards and got back four. She put in one card and got back two.
What was the machine doing? doubling the number
What will Manolita get back if she puts in four sticks? eight sticks

② All the children were eating pizza. Willy was the second one to finish. Manolita was the fourth.
Who ate faster — Manolita or Willy? You can't tell for sure. Willy might have had fewer pieces of pizza than Manolita.

③ Portia saves two pennies every day.
How long will it take her to save ten cents? five days
Ferdie saves one penny a day.
How long will it take him to save ten cents? ten days

④ Portia was learning to walk on stilts. The first day she could take two steps before falling. The next day she could take four steps. The next day she could take six steps.
How many steps would you guess she could take the day after that? Why do you think so?
[Any answer will do, although eight is the obvious one. What is of interest is the reason given.]

Manolita's Magnificent Minus Machine

Manolita was dreaming about a giant machine again. This machine was just like the ones she had dreamed about before, except that if you put in five things, it would give back four; if you put in six things, it would give back five; if you put in nine things, it would give back eight.
What was the machine doing? subtracting 1

When Manolita woke up, she decided that she could build a machine like that. She found a big, big box. On it she painted a sign that said "MAGNIFICENT MINUS MACHINE. Whatever you put in to the top, you get back one fewer at the bottom. FREE!"

Manolita put the machine out by the sidewalk and hid inside it. Soon children began flocking around the machine and reading the sign. "It's free!" Portia said.

Marcus was the first to try it. He put in seven sticks. The machine went "Glinka-Glinka" and out came six sticks at the bottom.
What do you think made the machine go "Glinka-Glinka"? Manolita
What do you think happened to the other stick that Marcus put into the machine? Manolita kept it.

Ferdie wanted to try the machine next. He put in nine marbles.
How many marbles will he get back? eight

"Hey," said Ferdie, "the machine kept one of my marbles!" Ferdie was angry and walked away.

Marcus tried the machine again. He put in four crayons.
How many crayons will he get back? three

The machine went "Glinka-Glinka" and out came three crayons at the bottom. Marcus didn't like that very much, but he said, "I'm going to put them back into the machine, and maybe this time more will come out." He put his three crayons into the machine.
Will he get back more than three? no

This time the machine gave him back only two crayons. That made Marcus angry, and he walked away.

Portia felt in her pocket and found five pumpkin seeds that she had been saving to plant. She dropped them into the Magnificent Minus Machine and waited eagerly to see what would happen.
What will happen? She will get back four seeds.

Story 13 • **79**

5. Willy got four strawberries. "I'm only going to eat two strawberries every day," said Willy, "so they'll last a long time."
How many days will they last? two

6. Portia walked one block by herself. Then she walked three times as far with her friend Taro.
How many blocks did Portia walk all together? four

7. Willy walked half a block to the library. Then he walked half a block to get home.
How many blocks did he walk all together? one

8. Ferdie decided he was going to be nice to five people today. He tried and tried, but so far he has managed to be nice to only two people — himself and Mr. Muddle.
How many more people does Ferdie need to be nice to? three

9. This is the fourth time I've been to the zoo," said Portia.
How many times had she been to the zoo before? three

10. Portia had four dolls. She gave a doll to Willy and a tennis ball to Manolita.
How many dolls does Portia have left? three

◆ **STORY 13** **Manolita's Magnificent Minus Machine**

The machine went "Glinka-Glinka," and out came four pumpkin seeds. "Nasty machine!" said Portia, and she walked away. Soon none of the children would have anything to do with Manolita's Magnificent Minus Machine. **Why not?** It kept subtracting one.

Then Willy the Wisher came along. He had just finished eating a banana. "I wish I had someplace to put this banana peel," said Willy. "I wish there were a wastebasket right here." Then he noticed the Magnificent Minus Machine. He put the banana peel into the top.

What do you think will come out the bottom? nothing

When you put in one banana peel, how many banana peels do you get back? zero

80 • Manolita's Magnificent Minus Machine

The machine went "Glinka-Glinka," but no banana peel came out at the bottom. After that, whenever people had some trash to get rid of, they put it into Manolita's Magnificent Minus Machine.

. . . the end

Story 13 • **81**

LESSON 96

Student Edition pages 211–212

Measuring Length in Feet and Yards

LESSON PLANNER

Objectives

▶ to demonstrate how to measure in yards

▶ to teach students there are three feet in a yard

▶ to provide practice using addition in a realistic situation

▶ to teach the concept of the greater the unit of measure, the fewer the number of units

Context of the Lesson This lesson continues practice in measurement from Lesson 95.

MANIPULATIVES **Program Resources**

foot rulers   Thinking Story Book, pages 82–83

yardsticks   Practice Master 96

   Enrichment Master 96

   For extra practice:
   CD-ROM* Lesson 96

1 Warm-Up

5 MINUTES

Problem of the Day Present the following problem to the class. If you take me away from the number 13, you will have 9 left. What number am I? (4)

Problem-Solving Strategies Ask students who have solved the Problem of the Day to share how they solved it and any strategies they used.

 MENTAL MATH Have students count up or down the following number of steps from the starting number:

a. 5 up from 15 (20) b. 3 up from 28 (31)

c. 7 up from 31 (38) d. 5 up from 29 (34)

e. 4 down from 17 (13) e. 4 down from 31 (27)

LESSON 96

Name _____

Measuring Length in Feet and Yards

about 3 feet long

about 1 yard long

Most doors are about 3 feet wide.

There are 3 feet in 1 yard.

Accept all reasonable estimates.

Estimate in yards.
Then measure to check.

	Estimate	Measure
	Yards	
length of classroom		
width of classroom		
width of window		

Copyright © SRA/McGraw-Hill

 NOTE TO HOME Students estimate and measure length in yards.

Unit 3   Lesson 96 • **211**

RETEACHING

Language Arts Connection Have students measure classroom objects and write letters to each other explaining what they measured. Have students include a labeled drawing of an object they measured.

Have students use **yardsticks** to draw lines of different lengths on the chalkboard. Guide students to see that they can connect lines one at a time to make lines that are greater than one yard. Then have them measure the lines with **foot rulers**.

*available separately

◆ **LESSON 96** Measuring Length in Feet and Yards

❶

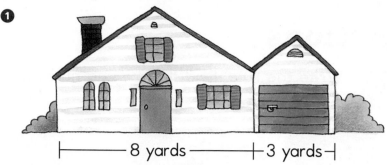

|— 8 yards —|— 3 yards —|

How many yards all together? __11__

❷

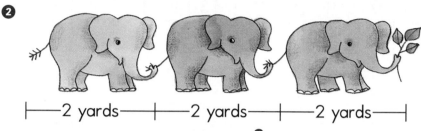

|— 2 yards —|— 2 yards —|— 2 yards —|

How many yards all together? __6__

❸

|— I yard —|— 2 feet —|

Ring the longer dog.
How many feet longer? __1__

212 • Measurement and Geometry

NOTE TO HOME
Students add and compare
measurements in yards and feet.

PRACTICE p. 96

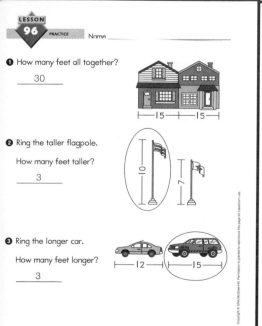

LESSON **96** PRACTICE Name _____

❶ How many feet all together?
30

❷ Ring the taller flagpole.
How many feet taller?
3

❸ Ring the longer car.
How many feet longer?
3

96 • Math Explorations and Applications Level 1

ENRICHMENT p. 96

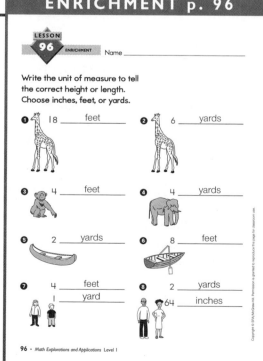

LESSON **96** ENRICHMENT Name _____

Write the unit of measure to tell
the correct height or length.
Choose inches, feet, or yards.

❶ 18 __feet__   ❷ 6 __yards__

❸ 4 __feet__   ❹ 4 __yards__

❺ 2 __yards__   ❻ 8 __feet__

❼ 4 __feet__   ❽ 2 __yards__
   I __yard__   64 __inches__

96 • Math Explorations and Applications Level 1

---

❷ Teach

Using the Student Pages Have students
work in small groups. Provide some groups with
foot rulers and others with **yardsticks** and have
each group measure the height of your desk. Discuss
students' measurements, emphasizing the fact that because
they used two different units of measure (feet and yards), it
is important to say which unit was used. Then have a
student measure the yardstick with the foot ruler to show
that there are three feet in one yard.

Then read page 211 to the class. Have students work in pairs
or individually to complete the table by first writing their
estimates and then measuring. Students' estimates should
get more accurate as more measurements are made. Have
students share their results. Then do page 212 together with
the class. Pause after reading each problem so that students
can record their answers.

Using the Thinking Story Present three
new problems from those following
"Manolita's Magnificent Minus Machine" on
pages 82–83 of the Thinking Story Book or pages
210a–210b of this Guide.

❸ Wrap-Up 5 MINUTES

In Closing Have students estimate the height of the
classroom door in yards. Write the estimates on the
chalkboard. Then have a volunteer measure.

Performance Assessment Observe which
students are able to use a yardstick to
accurately measure length as they complete
page 211.

Assessment Criteria

Did the student . . .

✓ make sensible estimates and
accurate measurements when
completing page 211?

✓ correctly answer all of the questions
on page 212?

LOOKING AHEAD You will need a large box like the one used
in Lesson 52 for the next lesson.

LESSON 97 Student Edition pages 213–214

Functions

LESSON PLANNER

Objectives

▶ to provide practice using inequality and equality signs in addition and subtraction sentences

▶ to provide practice solving addition and subtraction function problems

Context of the Lesson This lesson expands the "Amazing Number Machine" activity introduced in Lesson 52. Functions are continued in Lesson 98.

 MANIPULATIVES

large box (like the one from Lesson 52)

maps (optional)

Program Resources

Number Cubes

Thinking Story Book, pages 82–83

Reteaching Master

Practice Master 97

Enrichment Master 97

For extra practice:
CD-ROM* Lesson 97
Mixed Practice, page 369

① Warm-Up ⏱ 5 MINUTES

Problem of the Day Present the following problem to the class: Three students held up all of their fingers. Another student held up the fingers on only one hand. How many fingers were held up? (35)

Problem-Solving Strategies Ask students who have solved the Problem of the Day to share how they solved it and any strategies they used.

MENTAL MATH Present the following problems orally. Have students use Number Cubes to show each sum.

a. 21 + 3 = (24)   b. 26 + 2 = (28)

c. 39 + 1 = (40)   d. 21 + 4 = (25)

e. 25 + 3 = (28)   f. 23 + 2 = (25)

LESSON 97

Name _____

Functions

 ALGEBRA READINESS

Write the rule. Find the missing numbers.

①

In	Out
4	6
7	9
11	13
15	17

Rule **+2**

②

In	Out
14	13
13	12
10	9
9	8

Rule **−1**

③

In	Out
21	23
25	27
29	31
39	41

Rule **+2**

④

In	Out
3	6
4	7
5	8
6	9

Rule **+3**

⑤

In	Out
15	12
14	11
13	10
9	6

Rule **−3**

⑥

In	Out
15	14
19	18
20	19
21	20

Rule **−1**

 NOTE TO HOME Students complete function tables and identify function rules.

Unit 3   Lesson 97 • **213**

Copyright © SRA/McGraw-Hill

 **Literature Connection** To reinforce their understanding of the importance of symbols, read *I Read Symbols* by Tana Hoban to the class.

Social Studies Connection Have students look at different **maps** and map legends to see how symbols are used in other areas besides math.

LESSON 97 RETEACHING   Name _____

The arrow always points to the lesser number.

4 > 3
4 is greater than 3.

2 + 1 < 5
2 + 1 = 3
3 is less than 5.

What is the right sign?
Draw <, >, or =.

❶ 4 + 5 (>) 8   ❷ 4 + 4 (<) 9

❸ 2 + 3 (<) 7   ❹ 7 + 4 (>) 6

❺ 6 + 4 (=) 10   ❻ 8 + 4 (>) 11

Math Explorations and Applications Level 1 • **23**

*available separately

◆ LESSON 97 Functions

Make these signs with your hands.

Use the Mixed Practice on page 369 after this lesson.

 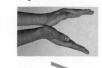

$<$ $>$ $=$

What is the right sign?
Draw <, >, or =.
Discuss the possible shortcuts.

❼ 4 + 3 ⟨>⟩ 5   **❽** 4 + 2 ⟨<⟩ 10

❾ 3 – 1 ⟨=⟩ 2   **❿** 4 + 2 ⟨>⟩ 3

⓫ 2 + 2 ⟨<⟩ 6   **⓬** 4 + 2 ⟨=⟩ 6

⓭ 3 + 3 ⟨=⟩ 6   **⓮** 10 + 5 ⟨>⟩ 12

⓯ 10 + 2 ⟨<⟩ 13   **⓰** 9 + 1 ⟨=⟩ 10

 Do the "Amazing Number Machine" activity.

214 • Measurement and Geometry

NOTE TO HOME
Students choose the signs that complete the number sentences.

---

2 Teach

Using the "Amazing Number Machine" Activity Have students use a **large box** as an "Amazing Number Machine." Let volunteers take turns being in the box. After other students pass in numbers, have the volunteer inside the box cross out and write a new number based on a secret subtraction rule (–0, –1, –2, –3) you have provided him or her. Have the class try to guess the rule. Record the input and output numbers on the chalkboard in a chart like those on page 213.

Using the Student Pages After doing the activity, students can work in pairs to complete page 213. Then have students look at the photographs at the top of page 214. Demonstrate for students how they can use their hands to make the signs. Do several demonstration problems with students before assigning page 214.

Using the Thinking Story Present three new problems from those following "Manolita's Magnificent Minus Machine" on pages 82–83 of the Thinking Story Book or pages 210a–210b of this Guide.

3 Wrap-Up

In Closing Have students explain how knowing 4 + 1 = 5 could help them determine which sign to put in 4 + 3 ○ 5. (Students should realize that because 4 + 1 = 5, 4 + 3 > 5.)

Informal Assessment Use student work on pages 213–214 to informally assess understanding of function machines and relation signs.

Assessment Criteria

Did the student . . .

✓ correctly identify function rules during the activity?

✓ participate during the Thinking Story problem solving?

✓ correctly answer 12 of 16 problems on pages 213–214?

LESSON 98 · Using Inequalities

Student Edition pages 215–216

LESSON PLANNER

Objectives

▶ to teach quick approximation of addition and subtraction problems in the 0–20 range

▶ to provide practice using inequality and equality signs

▶ to provide practice with addition and subtraction functions

▶ to provide practice using paper-folding techniques to test for squares

Context of the Lesson Paper-folding techniques were last practiced in Lesson 77. Work with approximating and with inequality and equality signs will be continued in future lessons.

 MANIPULATIVES

"Amazing Number Machine" (from Lesson 97)

scissors

Program Resources

Number Cubes

Thinking Story Book, pages 82–83

Practice Master 98

Enrichment Master 98

For extra practice:
CD-ROM* Lesson 98

❶ Warp-Up ⏱ 5 MINUTES

Problem of the Day Present the following problem to the class. Dominic gives Ariella 15 craft sticks. How many bundles of ten can she make? (1) How many more sticks does Ariella need to make another bundle of ten? (5)

Problem-Solving Strategies Ask students who have solved the Problem of the Day to share how they solved it and any strategies they used.

MENTAL MATH Present the following problems orally. Have students show the answers using Number Cubes.

a.	13 + 2 = (15)	**b.**	19 – 1 = (18)
c.	9 + 3 = (12)	**d.**	18 – 2 = (16)
e.	15 + 1 = (16)	**f.**	13 – 0 = (13)
g.	11 – 6 = (5)	**h.**	9 + 6 = (15)
i.	15 – 2 = (13)	**j.**	8 + 8 = (16)
k.	16 – 4 = (12)	**l.**	8 + 2 = (10)
m.	12 – 7 = (5)	**n.**	7 + 6 = (13)
o.	5 + 9 = (14)	**p.**	17 – 4 = (13)

215 Measurement and Geometry

LESSON 98

Name _____

Using Inequalities

 What is the right sign?
Draw >, <, or =.
Talk about shortcuts.

❶ 6 + 2 $<$ 10

❷ 8 + 7 $>$ 10

❸ 6 + 1 $=$ 7

❹ 5 + 10 $=$ 15

❺ 5 – 2 $<$ 5

❻ 14 + 6 $>$ 8

❼ 5 + 2 $>$ 6

❽ 16 – 5 $<$ 17

❾ 8 + 3 $>$ 5

❿ 12 – 3 $>$ 5

⓫ 7 – 2 $<$ 8

⓬ 7 – 6 $=$ 1

⓭ 2 + 7 $>$ 8

⓮ 8 + 2 $>$ 9

⓯ 7 + 3 $>$ 5

⓰ 13 – 4 $<$ 8

 NOTE TO HOME
Students choose the signs to complete number sentences.

Unit 3   Lesson 98 · **215**

 Science Connection Direct students' attention to the postage stamp on page 216. Ask them if they can identify the planet that is pictured on the stamp. (Saturn) Challenge groups of students to find out more about Saturn or other planets. Set up a reading center of books about planets. Have students list ten or more facts about their planet and present these to the class with visual aids such as illustrations from books or their own drawings.

RETEACHING

No extra teaching of the topics in this lesson is considered necessary at this time, although you may want to remind students who labored over page 215 to look for sums that are obviously greater or lesser so that no precise calculation is necessary.

*available separately

◆ LESSON 98 Using Inequalities

Is Ferdie's drawing a square?
Can you fold it to find out?
Cut it out and try.

32¢

216 · Measurement and Geometry

NOTE TO HOME
Students explore the properties of squares.

Copyright © SRA/McGraw-Hill

---

❷ Teach

Demonstrate Explain to students that it is possible to estimate the answers to addition and subtraction problems without having to figure them out. Put this problem on the chalkboard: $8 + 7 = \square$. Ask the class if they think 9 is a reasonable estimate. Ask them why or why not. (No, because $8 + 1 = 9$, so $8 + 7$ must be much more than 9.) Follow this line of thinking with other possible answers and for other addition and subtraction problems.

Using the Number Cubes Repeat the problems from the demonstration, but this time give students a choice of two answers, one that is correct, the other far from correct. Have students pick the reasonable answer and show it with Number Cubes.

Using the Student Pages Have students answer the exercises on page 215. Check their answers before having students do the paper-folding activity on page 216. They should see that the stamp is not a square.

Using the "Amazing Number Machine" Activity Continue the activity from Lesson 97 so that all students have a chance to be inside the **machine**.

Using the Thinking Story Present two problems from those following "Manolita's Magnificent Minus Machine" on pages 82–83 of the Thinking Story Book or pages 210a–210b of this Guide.

❸ Wrap-Up ⏱ 5 MINUTES

In Closing Provide a number sentence, such as $9 + 5 = 14$ or 6. Have students tell how they knew that 6 was not a reasonable answer.

Portfolio Assessment Have students make up their own problems using inequality and equality signs to add to their portfolios.

Assessment Criteria

Did the student . . .

✓ use paper-folding techniques to correctly test for squareness?

✓ understand how to approximate answers to addition and subtraction problems in the 0–20 range?

PRACTICE p. 98

LESSON 98 PRACTICE Name _____

What is the right sign? Draw <, >, or =.

❶ $7 - 3 \;\bigcirc< \; 7$ ❷ $11 - 3 \;\bigcirc> \; 6$

❸ $10 - 5 \;\bigcirc> \; 2$ ❹ $15 - 4 \;\bigcirc> \; 8$

❺ $3 - 2 \;\bigcirc= \; 1$ ❻ $9 - 2 \;\bigcirc< \; 11$

❼ $18 - 1 \;\bigcirc< \; 19$ ❽ $8 - 2 \;\bigcirc= \; 6$

❾ $20 - 5 \;\bigcirc> \; 10$ ❿ $16 - 3 \;\bigcirc> \; 7$

⓫ $14 - 2 \;\bigcirc> \; 7$ ⓬ $19 - 2 \;\bigcirc< \; 20$

⓭ $13 - 3 \;\bigcirc< \; 14$ ⓮ $17 - 5 \;\bigcirc< \; 15$

⓯ $8 - 3 \;\bigcirc= \; 5$ ⓰ $9 - 3 \;\bigcirc> \; 3$

98 · Math Explorations and Applications Level 1

ENRICHMENT p. 98

LESSON 98 ENRICHMENT Name _____

REAL-WORLD CONNECTION Find out how much postage you need to mail a letter.

_____ ¢
Answers will vary depending on current postage rates and the combination chosen.

In each row ring the stamps that make the right amount to mail a letter.

❶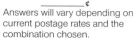

❷

❸

❹

98 · Math Explorations and Applications Level 1

Unit 3 Lesson 98 **216**

LESSON 99

Missing Addends

LESSON PLANNER

Objectives

▶ to teach students to solve missing-addend problems presented in numerical form

▶ to provide practice using relation signs

Context of the Lesson Students learned about missing addends in Lesson 65 using Number Strips and in Lesson 66 using counters-in-the-can.

MANIPULATIVES

counters*

overhead counters*

overhead projector

Program Resources

Number Cubes

Reteaching Master

Practice Master 99

Enrichment Master 99

For extra practice:
CD-ROM* Lesson 99

1 Warm-Up

 Problem of the Day Present the following problem to the class. Harry had seven cookies. He kept three for himself. He shared the rest evenly between his two younger brothers. How many cookies did he give to each of his brothers? (2)

Problem-Solving Strategies Ask students who have solved the Problem of the Day to share how they solved it and any strategies they used.

 Have students use Number Cubes to show each sum.

a. 9 + 3 = (12)   b. 29 + 3 = (32)

c. 17 + 4 = (21)   d. 23 + 3 = (26)

e. 28 + 3 = (31)   f. 15 + 3 = (18)

2 Teach

Demonstrate Write the following false statement on the chalkboard: $4 + \boxed{1} = 6$. Ask students if it is correct. Erase the 1 and ask what number would make the

---

LESSON 99

Name _____

Missing Addends

$$0 \quad 1 \quad 2 \quad 3 \quad 4 \quad 5 \quad 6 \quad 7 \quad 8 \quad 9 \quad 10$$

 ALGEBRA READINESS   Solve these problems.

1. $5 + \boxed{2} = 7$ 2. $1 + \boxed{4} = 5$

3. $8 + \boxed{2} = 10$ 4. $4 + \boxed{5} = 9$

5. $2 + \boxed{3} = 5$ 6. $4 + \boxed{2} = 6$

7. $6 + \boxed{4} = 10$ 8. $4 + \boxed{0} = 4$

9. $5 + \boxed{2} = 7$ 10. $3 + \boxed{3} = 6$

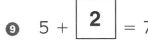 **GAME** Play the "Hidden Counters Puzzle" game.

NOTE TO HOME Students use a number line to find the missing addend.

Unit 3   Lesson 99 • **217**

Meeting Individual Needs
Some students may need further practice using concrete objects to find missing addends. Do the "Missing Addend Puzzle" activity or the missing addends-in-the-can activities from Lessons 65 and 66 with students before assigning them the pages in this lesson.

SPECIAL NEEDS   **MANIPULATIVES**

RETEACHING p. 24

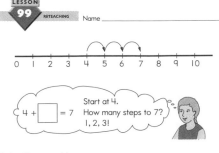

LESSON 99   **RETEACHING**   Name _____

$$0 \quad 1 \quad 2 \quad 3 \quad 4 \quad 5 \quad 6 \quad 7 \quad 8 \quad 9 \quad 10$$

$4 + \boxed{} = 7$ Start at 4. How many steps to 7? 1, 2, 3!

Solve these problems.

1. $4 + \boxed{1} = 5$ 2. $3 + \boxed{2} = 5$

3. $7 + \boxed{3} = 10$ 4. $6 + \boxed{1} = 7$

5. $9 + \boxed{0} = 9$ 6. $5 + \boxed{3} = 8$

7. $2 + \boxed{1} = 3$ 8. $5 + \boxed{1} = 6$

9. $6 + \boxed{3} = 9$ 10. $7 + \boxed{2} = 9$

24 • Math Explorations and Applications Level 1

*available separately

◆ **LESSON 99 Missing Addends**

Draw the right sign. Draw <, >, or =.
Most are easier than they look.

⑪ $9 - 3$ $<$ | o   ⑫ $8 - 5$ $<$ 9

⑬ $7 - 6$ $<$ 8   ⑭ | o $- 8$ $<$ | |

⑮ $5 + 5$ $>$ 4   ⑯ $5 + 1$ $>$ 3

⑰ $5 + 2$ $>$ 4   ⑱ $5 + 3$ $>$ 4

⑲ | $5 + 1$ $=$ | 6   ⑳ | $4 + 2$ $=$ | 6

㉑ | $3 + 3$ $=$ | 6   ㉒ | $2 + 4$ $=$ | 6

㉓ | $8 - 2$ $=$ | 6   ㉔ | $9 - 3$ $=$ | 6

㉕ $20 - 4$ $=$ | 6   ㉖ $21 - 5$ $=$ | 6

218 • Measurement and Geometry

NOTE TO HOME
Students identify inequalities and
equalities in number sentences.

PRACTICE p. 99

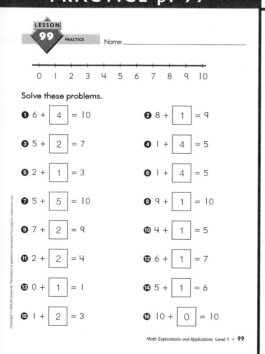

0 1 2 3 4 5 6 7 8 9 10

Solve these problems.

❶ $6 + \boxed{4} = 10$ ❷ $8 + \boxed{1} = 9$

❸ $5 + \boxed{2} = 7$ ❹ $1 + \boxed{4} = 5$

❺ $2 + \boxed{1} = 3$ ❻ $1 + \boxed{4} = 5$

❼ $5 + \boxed{5} = 10$ ❽ $9 + \boxed{1} = 10$

❾ $7 + \boxed{2} = 9$ ❿ $4 + \boxed{1} = 5$

⓫ $2 + \boxed{2} = 4$ ⓬ $6 + \boxed{1} = 7$

⓭ $0 + \boxed{1} = 1$ ⓮ $5 + \boxed{1} = 6$

⓯ $1 + \boxed{2} = 3$ ⓰ $10 + \boxed{0} = 10$

Math Explorations and Applications Level 1 • **99**

ENRICHMENT p. 99

Mr. Muddle has to put 32¢
postage on each letter.
Write how much more he
needs on each letter.

Mr. and Ms. Eng
1062 Apple Street
Storytown, IL 61301

Math Explorations and Applications Level 1 • **99**

---

statement true. (2) Repeat with several similar false
statements. Then present sentences in which the second
term is missing, such as: $4 + \boxed{\ } = 7$. Ask what number
should go in the space to make a true statement. (3)

Using the Number Cubes Present missing
addend problems such as $9 + \boxed{\ } = 10$; $4 + \boxed{\ } >$
6. Have students show answers on Number
Cubes. Test student answers by completing the number
sentences and determining if the statement is correct. Point
out that inequality statements may have more than one
correct answer. For example, $4 + \boxed{3} > 6$; $4 + \boxed{4} > 6$; and
$4 + \boxed{5} > 6$ are all true.

**Introducing the "Hidden Counters
Puzzle" Game** To provide practice in solving
missing-addend problems using concrete objects,
demonstrate and play this game. Separate students into
groups of three. Each group places ten **counters*** in a
central pile. Player 1 counts aloud and takes up to ten
counters from the pile. Then, as the other two players look
away, Player 1 hides these counters under the other players'
workbooks. Players 2 and 3 then look under their
workbooks to see how many counters are there. The first
one to guess the correct number of counters under the
other one's workbook leads the next round. You might want
to use overhead counters* to demonstrate this game on an
overhead projector. A copy of this game can also be found
on page 23 of the Home Connections Blackline Masters.

Using the Student Pages Do the first problem on each
page together with students. Then have them complete the
pages on their own.

❸ Wrap-Up ⏱ 5 MINUTES

In Closing Have students explain how they arrived at
their answers on the student pages.

Performance Assessment Observe to see
which students correctly guess the number of
counters as they play the "Hidden Counters
Puzzle" game.

Assessment Criteria

Did the student . . .

✓ correctly identify missing addends
during the demonstration?

✓ correctly complete 20 of 26
problems on pages 217–218?

---

*available separately

The Mid-Unit Review pinpoints troublesome skill areas for students, allowing plenty of time for additional practice and reteaching before the unit ends. If students did not do well on the Mid-Unit Review and have completed additional practice, you may want to use the Mid-Unit Review provided on pages 37–39 in the Assessment Blackline Masters.

Using the Student Pages Have students complete problems 1–20 on pages 219–220 on their own. You might treat this review as a formal assessment of students' skills, and have students complete this review as a timed test. See suggestions for administering timed tests on page 48. Have **counters*** available for students to use.

Name _____

Mid-Unit Review

Draw a ring around groups of ten.
Then write how many.

❶ How many? __27__

Draw coins to make the right amount. **Possible answers are shown.**

❷ 36¢ (10)(10)(10)(5)(1)

❸ 42¢ (10)(10)(10)(10)(1)(1)

❹ 29¢ (10)(10)(5)(1)(1)(1)(1)

How many now?

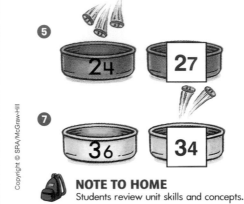

❺ 24 **27**

❼ 36 **34**

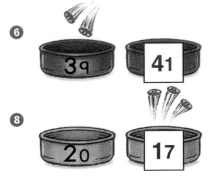

❻ 39 **41**

❽ 20 **17**

NOTE TO HOME
Students review unit skills and concepts.

Unit 3 Mid-Unit Review • 219

◆ UNIT 3 Mid-Unit Review

9 The line is [**5**] centimeters long. ——————

10 The line is [**4**] centimeters long. ——————

ALGEBRA READINESS

What is the missing sign?
Draw + or −.

11 $6 \langle + \rangle 3 = 9$ **12** $8 \langle - \rangle 3 = 5$

13 $7 \langle - \rangle 4 = 3$ **14** $5 \langle + \rangle 2 = 7$

What is the right sign?
Draw <, >, or =.

15 $4 + 2 \langle < \rangle 7$ **16** $3 + 5 \langle = \rangle 8$

17 $6 + 4 \langle > \rangle 9$ **18** $5 + 5 \langle > \rangle 6$

Solve these problems.

19 $4 + \boxed{3} = 7$

20 $5 + \boxed{4} = 9$

220 • Measurement and Geometry

NOTE TO HOME
Students review unit skills and concepts.

Copyright © SRA/McGraw-Hill

Literature Connection To provide practice with counting and addition, use the big book *Squeeze In* in the Literature Library*. As you read the book, students can count and add the number of friends who squeeze into the tent of two sisters camping out.

Home Connections You may want to send home the letter on pages 48–49 in the Home Connections Blackline Masters Book, which provides additional activities families can complete together. These activities apply the skills being presented in this unit.

Performance Assessment The Performance Assessment Tasks 1–3 provided on page 69 of the Assessment Blackline Masters can be used at this time to evaluate students' abilities to solve simple addition and subtraction problems through 40. You may want to administer this assessment with individual students or in small groups.

Portfolio Assessment If you have not already completed the Portfolio Assessment task provided on page 80 of the Assessment Blackline Masters, it can be used to evaluate students' skills in adding and subtracting 0, 1, or 2 to two-digit numbers.

Unit Project This would be a good time to assign the "Paper Folding" project on pages 258a–258b. Students can begin working on the project in cooperative groups in their free time as you work through the unit. The Unit Project is a good opportunity for students to apply the concepts of the properties of squares and the relationship between fractions and a whole in real-world problem solving.

ASSESSMENT p. 37

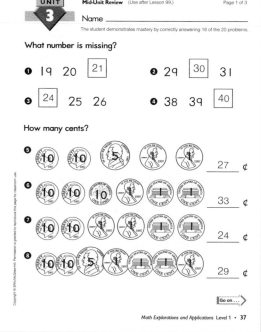

UNIT 3 Mid-Unit Review (Use after Lesson 99.) Page 1 of 3

Name _____

The student demonstrates mastery by correctly answering 16 of the 20 problems.

What number is missing?

1 19 20 [21]   **2** 29 [30] 31

3 [24] 25 26   **4** 38 39 [40]

How many cents?

5 10 10 5 ... ... ____ 27 ¢

6 10 10 10 ... ... ____ 33 ¢

7 10 10 ... ... ____ 24 ¢

8 10 10 5 ... ... ____ 29 ¢

Go on ...

Math Explorations and Applications Level 1 • 37

Student Edition pages 221–222

Dividing Sets into Halves

LESSON PLANNER

Objectives

▶ to teach students to divide an even number of objects through ten into two sets of equal numbers

▶ to teach students to recognize that an odd number of objects through nine cannot be divided into two equal sets of numbers

Context of the Lesson This is the first in a series of lessons in which students work with common fractions of number and length.

 MANIPULATIVES   **Program Resources**

flannel board and felt objects

Half a Slice of Bread and Butter* from the Literature Library

Number Cubes

Practice Master 100

Enrichment Master 100

For extra practice:
   CD-ROM* Lesson 100

① Warm-Up

 Problem of the Day Present the following problem to the class. I am thinking of a number. It is greater than 1. It is less than 10. When you double it, the sum is the same as the difference of 10 – 2. What is the number? (4)

Problem-Solving Strategies Ask students who have solved the Problem of the Day to share how they solved it and any strategies they used.

MENTAL MATH Have students show doubles of the following using Number Cubes:

a. 0 (0)	**b.** 9 (18)
c. 7 (14)	**d.** 10 (20)
e. 2 (4)	**f.** 4 (8)
g. 3 (6)	**h.** 5 (10)
i. 6 (12)	**j.** 9 (18)

Name _____

Dividing Sets into Halves

Draw a line between one half of each group and the other half. Then write how many in each half.

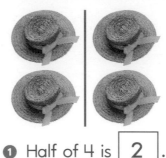   

① Half of 4 is ⬚**2** .   ② Half of 10 is ⬚**5** .

③ Half of 8 is ⬚**4** .   ④ Half of 2 is ⬚**1** .

⑤ Half of 6 is ⬚**3** .

 NOTE TO HOME
Students divide groups of objects into halves.

Unit 3   Lesson 100 • **221**

RETEACHING

Extra teaching on dividing sets is not considered essential at this time, although individual work on a **flannel board** may be helpful.

For those students who are having trouble with missing-addend problems, relate problems to sports scores. For example, a baseball team trailed an opposing team 5 to 3. How many runs does the team need to tie the score? (2)

Literature Connection
You may wish to read to students *Fraction Action* by Loreen Leedy to reinforce lesson concepts.

Read aloud *Half a Slice of Bread and Butter* from the Literature Library* to develop intuitive understanding of sharing and fractions.

◆ LESSON 100 Dividing Sets into Halves

Fill in the missing number.

⑥ 6 + **1** = 7   ⑦ 3 + **2** = 5

⑧ 6 + **0** = 6   ⑨ 6 + **2** = 8

⑩ 2 + **2** = 4   ⑪ 7 + **2** = 9

⑫ 5 + **2** = 7   ⑬ 4 + **3** = 7

What is the missing sign?
Draw + or −.

⑭ 5 ⟨ **−** ⟩ 1 = 4   ⑮ 5 ⟨ **+** ⟩ 1 = 6

⑯ 6 ⟨ **−** ⟩ 6 = 0   ⑰ 7 ⟨ **+** ⟩ 2 = 9

⑱ 7 ⟨ **−** ⟩ 2 = 5   ⑲ 5 ⟨ **+** ⟩ 2 = 7

⑳ 10 ⟨ **−** ⟩ 2 = 8   ㉑ 8 ⟨ **−** ⟩ 3 = 5

NOTE TO HOME
Students complete simple number sentences.

222 • Measurement and Geometry

Copyright © SRA/McGraw-Hill

---

② Teach

Demonstrate Draw six objects on the chalkboard in random order, or use **felt objects** on a **flannel board**. Ask a volunteer to draw a line between the objects so that there is the same number of objects on either side. Erase the line. Repeat the exercise using even numbers through ten. Allow students to experiment with separating objects in various ways. Ask students to predict how many objects will be in each set. Point out that students are dividing the set in *half*. Then follow the same procedure for a set of nine objects. Students should realize that this cannot be done. Continue giving problems using both odd- and even-number sets of objects.

Using the Student Pages Have students complete the exercises on pages 221–222 on their own.

Using the "Hidden Counters Puzzle" Game You may wish to continue this game from Lesson 99. A copy of this game can also be found on page 23 of the Home Connections Blackline Masters.

③ Wrap-Up

In Closing Invite volunteers to create problems like those in the demonstration for their classmates to solve, using concrete objects instead of drawings.

Informal Assessment Note students who are having difficulty separating sets into halves during the demonstration, and provide individual help before they begin work on page 221.

Assessment Criteria

Did the student . . .

✓ demonstrate understanding of how to divide sets of objects into halves?

✓ understand that odd numbers cannot be divided into two equal parts?

✓ use the correct arithmetic signs on page 222?

LOOKING AHEAD You will need string, glass containers, a pitcher of water, and food coloring for Lesson 101 and subsequent lessons.

PRACTICE p. 100

LESSON 100 PRACTICE Name_____

Draw a line between one half of each group and the other half. Then write how many in each half.

❶ Half of 8 is ___4___ .

❷ Half of 10 is ___5___ .

❸ Half of 6 is ___3___ .

❹ Half of 4 is ___2___ .

❺ Half of 2 is ___1___ .

❻ 1 + [1] = 2   ❼ 3 + [3] = 6

❽ 5 + [5] = 10   ❾ 4 + [4] = 8

100 • Math Explorations and Applications Level 1

ENRICHMENT p. 100

LESSON 100 ENRICHMENT Name_____

Use 12 sticks or strips of paper to form four squares.

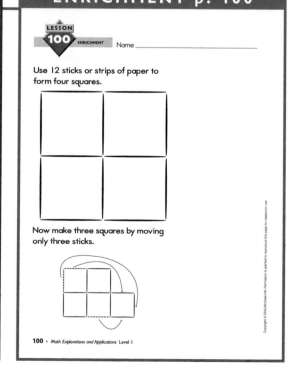

Now make three squares by moving only three sticks.

100 • Math Explorations and Applications Level 1

Estimating One Half

LESSON PLANNER

Objective

▶ to teach students to estimate half of a length or height

Context of the Lesson Other fractional lengths are presented in the next lesson.

 MANIPULATIVES   **Program Resources**

ball of string	Practice Master 101
food coloring	Enrichment Master 101
pitcher of water	For extra practice:
three identical jars or clear plastic cups	CD-ROM* Lesson 101
	Mixed practice, page 370

❶ Warm-Up ⏱ 5 MINUTES

 Problem of the Day Present the following problem to the class. Charlie had seven pencils when he went to school and returned home with five. What number sentence describes what happened to the pencils? (7 – 2 = 5)

Problem-Solving Strategies Ask students who have solved the Problem of the Day to share how they solved it and any strategies they used.

 Have students practice oral counting to 40 and addition facts with sums to 10.

❷ Teach

 Demonstrate Pour colored water into one **jar**. Then begin pouring **water** into another jar. Have students say "stop" when they think there is half as much water in the second jar as in the first. Pour water into a third jar so that it has the same amount as the second. Then pour the water from the second jar into the third. Compare to see if it is at the same level as the first jar. Repeat until students can identify halves of heights reasonably well.

 Introducing the "Estimating Halves" Activity Have students work in pairs. Have one partner hold up a length of **string** while the other tries to estimate half its length with another piece of string. Check for accuracy by folding the longer string in half and comparing the two strings. Change roles and repeat.

223 Measurement and Geometry

Name _____

Estimating One Half

Listen to the problems.

❶

❷

❸

 C❂❂PERATIVE LEARNING   Do the "Estimating Halves" activity.

 NOTE TO HOME Students estimate half of a given capacity or length.

Unit 3   Lesson 101 • **223**

 Real-World Connection Have students act out the first problem on page 223. Have students draw a line to where they think the juice will be after three students each drink a cup. Have students drink and then check to see how close the line is. Allow other students to guess and drink different amounts.

 Literature Connection Read *Give Me Half!* by Stuart J. Murphy to learn more about estimating halves. It is a simple rhyming story about a brother and sister who do not want to share.

RETEACHING

Because estimating measurement is continued in the next lesson, reteaching this topic is not considered essential at this time.

*available separately

◆ LESSON 101 Estimating One Half

Listen to the problems.

Use the Mixed Practice on page 370 after this lesson.

④

⑤

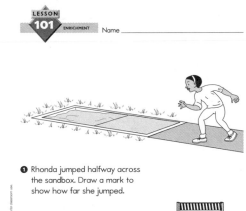
⑥

NOTE TO HOME
Students estimate time and distance.

Copyright © SRA/McGraw-Hill

Using the Student Pages Read each problem aloud.

Page 223 problems:

1. This jug has six cups of juice in it. What will it look like after Ferdie, Portia, and Marcus each drink a cup? Draw a line to show how much juice will be left.

2. Joe is filling a bucket with a hose. Ren is filling the same size bucket, but he is using a hose that lets more water come out. Both boys started at the same time. Put an X beside the boy who will take longer to fill the bucket.

3. Irene runs fast. Nina runs half as fast. A minute ago both girls started to race from one post to the other. Irene has just won the race. Draw a line to show where you think Nina was when Irene reached the post.

Page 224 problems:

1. It takes Mitch ten minutes to walk from his home to the library. He left five minutes ago. Place an X where Mitch is now.

2. Holly is making orange juice. So far she has squeezed 10 oranges. Draw a line on the jar to show how full the jar will be when she has squeezed 20 oranges.

3. It takes Raulito five minutes to ride his bicycle from his home to school. He left five minutes ago. Place an X where you think Raulito is now.

❸ Wrap-Up ⏱ 5 MINUTES

In Closing Have students explain how they would find half the length (or width) of the classroom.

ALTERNATIVE ASSESSMENT

Performance Assessment Observe which students make accurate estimates of length during the string activity.

PRACTICE p. 101

LESSON **101** PRACTICE   Name _____

Solve these problems.

❶ Jason swam across the pool in ten minutes. Put an X where Jason was after five minutes.

❷ The carton holds 4 cups. Draw a line to show how much milk will be left after the Johnson twins each drink 1 cup.

MILK

❸ Two bathtubs are filled the same. The bathtub on the left has a bigger drain. Put an X on the bathtub that will empty first.

ENRICHMENT p. 101

LESSON **101** ENRICHMENT   Name _____

❶ Rhonda jumped halfway across the sandbox. Draw a mark to show how far she jumped.

❷ Rhonda can jump over the hurdle, but the top bar must be half as high as it is now. Draw a mark to show how high it must be.

❸ Rhonda drank half a bottle of water. Draw a line to show how much is left.

Assessment Criteria

Did the student . . .

✓ correctly estimate half lengths of string during the activity?

✓ correctly answer five of six problems on pages 223–224?

LESSON 102

Fractional Length

Student Edition pages 225–226

LESSON PLANNER

Objectives

▶ to provide practice estimating one unit of length when given a length of two through six arbitrary units

▶ to provide practice solving missing-addend problems

Context of the Lesson The use of fractional terms and notation in reference to problems such as these will be formally introduced in Lesson 103. In this lesson students will continue working informally with fractions by estimating $\frac{1}{2}$ through $\frac{1}{6}$ of any given length.

 MANIPULATIVES

fraction tiles* (optional)

Program Resources

Thinking Story Book, pages 82–83

Practice Master 102

Enrichment Master 102

For extra practice: CD-ROM* Lesson 102

---

❶ Warm-Up

 Problem of the Day Write the following numbers on the chalkboard. Challenge the class to find the number that does not belong and to explain why. (5; It is an odd number—you cannot divide the set in half.)

    2   5   10   6   8   4

Problem-Solving Strategies Ask students who have solved the Problem of the Day to share how they solved it and any strategies they used.

 Provide oral-counting practice with numbers through 40:

a. Stop at 40. Count up from 19.

b. Stop at 0. Count down from 34.

c. Stop at 40. Count up from 27.

d. Stop at 0. Count down from 16.

e. Stop at 40. Count up from 5.

f. Count from 12 to 36.

g. Count from 32 to 40.

h. Count from 10 to 17.

i. Count from 19 to 31.

225 Measurement and Geometry

LESSON 102

Name _____

Fractional Length

Listen to the problems.
Mark your answer.

❶

❷

❸

 NOTE TO HOME
Students make an estimate based on a given length.

Unit 3 Lesson 102 • **225**

Literature Connection You may wish to read aloud to students *The Line Up Book* by Marisabina Russo to reinforce lesson concepts.

Real-World Connection Challenge students to brainstorm situations in real life in which estimating a fraction of a given length would be useful, such as dividing a loaf of bread into six equal parts to distribute to six family members.

RETEACHING

MANIPULATIVES Extra teaching on fractional lengths is not considered essential at this time, because mastery of this concept is not considered essential. However, students may benefit from using **fraction tiles*** to explore various fractional parts.

Students who are still having trouble with missing-addend problems might play the "Hidden Counters Puzzle" game introduced in Lesson 99.

*available separately

◆ **LESSON 102** Fractional Length

How many now?

 ④ 9 | 11

 ⑤ 40 | 39

 ⑥ 29 | 31

 ⑦ 29 | 27

 ⑧ 6 | 9

 ⑨ 12 | 10

 ⑩ 17 | 20

 ⑪ 18 | 15

226 • Measurement and Geometry

NOTE TO HOME
Students add and subtract to 40 with counters, some of which are hidden.

Copyright © SRA/McGraw-Hill

PRACTICE p. 102

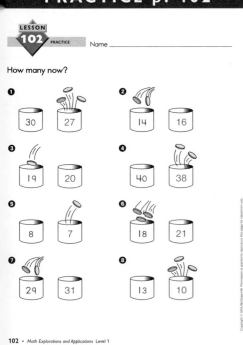

ENRICHMENT p. 102

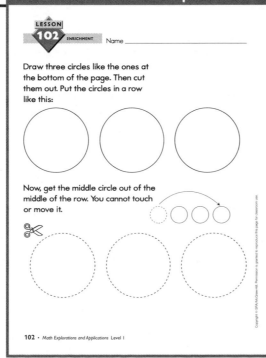

② Teach

Demonstrate Draw a line on the chalkboard one foot long and say: "This line stands for a road. The road is six miles long. I want to go three miles. Tell me when to stop." Move your chalk along the line until students tell you to stop. Make a mark. Work similar problems varying the length to four, five, or six units long.

Using the Student Pages Call attention to the illustration as you read each problem aloud. Problem 1: "The bench is 4 feet long. Mark an X on it 1 foot from where the child is sitting." Problem 2: "The front post is 2 meters high. Draw a bug on it 1 meter from the top." Problem 3: "The road is 5 miles long. Ferdie has walked 1 mile. Mark an X to show where Ferdie is." Then have students complete the exercises on page 226 on their own.

Using the Thinking Story Present two new problems from those following "Manolita's Magnificent Minus Machine" on pages 82–83 of the Thinking Story Book or pages 210a–210b of this Guide.

③ Wrap-Up ⏱ 5 MINUTES

In Closing To summarize the lesson, present problems such as those in the demonstration and on page 225. Ask students to explain how they estimated the distances.

SELF ASSESSMENT Have students write six missing-addend problems for a partner to solve. Have each student note how many he or she got wrong, if any. Students can add these problems to their Math Portfolios.

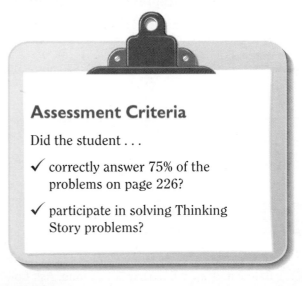

Assessment Criteria

Did the student . . .

✓ correctly answer 75% of the problems on page 226?

✓ participate in solving Thinking Story problems?

LOOKING AHEAD For Lessons 103, 104, and 107 you will need the string, the glass containers, and the pitcher of colored water used in Lesson 101. You will also need masking tape.

LESSON 103

Student Edition pages 227–228

Estimating Fractional Parts

LESSON PLANNER

Objective

▶ to introduce students to the use of fractional terms and notation

Context of the Lesson This lesson continues practice with fractional lengths from Lesson 102.

 MANIPULATIVES

food coloring

masking tape

string (about 5 ft long)

two identical jars

water

Program Resources

Number Cubes

Thinking Story Book, pages 84–87

Reteaching Master

Practice Master 103

Enrichment Master 103

For career connections:
   Careers and Math*

For extra practice:
   CD-ROM* Lesson 103

❶ Warm-Up

⏱ 5 MINUTES

 Problem of the Day Present the following problem to the class. Ozzie has more trading cards than Sandy, but fewer than Manuel. Sandy has 15 cards. Manuel has 20. How many cards could Ozzie have? (either 16, 17, 18, or 19)

Problem-Solving Strategies Ask students who have solved the Problem of the Day to share how they solved it and any strategies they used.

MENTAL MATH Have students use Number Cubes to show their answers.

a. 21 − 2 = (19)	**b.** 36 + 3 = (39)
c. 13 − 4 = (9)	**d.** 38 − 2 = (36)
e. 22 − 3 = (19)	**f.** 29 + 2 = (31)

❷ Teach

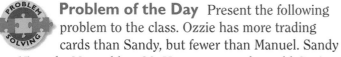 **Demonstrate 1.** Draw a line on the chalkboard. Below it, draw a line that is $\frac{1}{3}$ as long. Ask how many short lines it would take to make the long line. (3) Test answers using **string**. Explain that the short line is $\frac{1}{3}$ as long as the long line. Write $\frac{1}{3}$ on the chalkboard. Have students say it aloud. Repeat with $\frac{1}{4}$, $\frac{1}{5}$, and $\frac{1}{6}$.

227 Measurement and Geometry

Estimating Fractional Parts

Listen to the problems.
Write the missing number in the box.

❶

About 1 full

[3]

❷

About 1 as tall

[3]

❸

About 1 as tall

[2]

❹

About 1 as long

[4]

  THINKING STORY

Talk about the Thinking Story "Mr. Mudancia Makes Lunch."

🎒 **NOTE TO HOME**
Students estimate fractional parts.

Copyright © SRA/McGraw-Hill

Physical Education Connecton

Draw a chalk line on the ground outside or put a tape line on the gym floor. Have students try jumping various fractional amounts of the line. For example, have them jump three equal jumps of about two feet each to get from one end of a six-foot line to the other. Ask, "What part of the line did you jump each time?" ($\frac{1}{3}$) Repeat with other fractions and line lengths.

RETEACHING p. 25

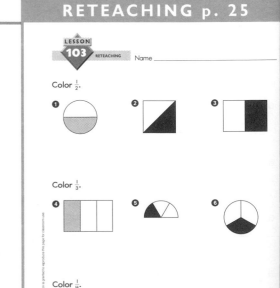

◆ LESSON 103 Estimating Fractional Parts

Listen to the problems.

❺ Morgan and Georgia ate some pizza. About how much of the pizza did they eat? Ring the right number.

$\frac{1}{2}$ $\frac{1}{3}$ $\frac{1}{4}$

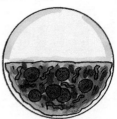

❻ Ron and Jen ate pizza too. About how much of the pizza did they eat?

$\frac{1}{2}$ $\frac{1}{3}$ $\frac{1}{4}$

❼ Abby said the glass is half full. Annie said the glass is half empty. Who is right? Tell why you think so.

Accept all reasonable answers. They are both right.

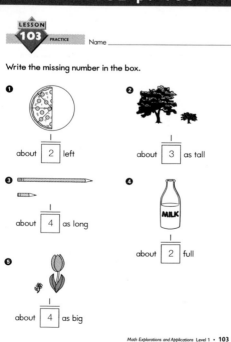

228 · Measurement and Geometry

 NOTE TO HOME
Students estimate fractional amounts.

Copyright © SRA/McGraw-Hill

---

2. Pour **water** into one **jar** about $\frac{1}{3}$ high. Mark the level with a piece of **tape**. Have students estimate how many times you would pour that amount of water to fill an identical jar. (3) Act out students' estimates as they count the number of times with you.

Using the Student Pages Read each problem aloud and have students mark their answers below on page 227 before going on to the next.

1. Say: "This jar holds one liter of juice when it is full. About how full is the jar now? Write the missing number in the box."

2. Say: "This rabbit is sitting in the shade of a plant. About how tall is the rabbit compared to the plant?"

3. Say: "About how tall is the little tree compared to the big one?"

4. Say: "This car has just driven up alongside the airplane. About how long is the car compared to the plane?"

For page 228, read aloud the problems from the page.

 **Using the Thinking Story** Read aloud and discuss "Mr. Mudancia Makes Lunch" on pages 84–87 of the Thinking Story Book.

❸ Wrap-Up

In Closing Have students name objects that are about half as tall as first graders are.

Informal Assessment Use the answers to pages 227–228 to informally assess students' understanding of fractional terms.

Assessment Criteria

Did the student . . .

✓ correctly answer five of seven problems on pages 227–228?

✓ make sensible estimates of the various fractional lengths given during the demonstration?

✓ actively participate in the Thinking Story discussion?

LOOKING AHEAD You will use this lesson's demonstration materials in Lesson 104.

PRACTICE p. 103

LESSON 103 PRACTICE   Name _____

Write the missing number in the box.

❶

about [2] left

❷

about [3] as tall

❸

about [4] as long

❹ MILK

about [2] full

❺

about [4] as big

Math Explorations and Applications Level 1 · **103**

ENRICHMENT p. 103

LESSON 103 ENRICHMENT   Name _____

❶ Color about $\frac{1}{2}$.

Answers shown are examples only.

❷ Color about $\frac{1}{3}$.

❸ Color about $\frac{1}{4}$.

❹ Color about $\frac{1}{5}$.

❺ Color about $\frac{1}{6}$.

Math Explorations and Applications Level 1 · **103**

STORY 14 — Mr. Mudancia Makes Lunch

① Mr. Muddle said, "I started out with three tickets to the circus, and then either I gave one away or somebody gave me one—I can't remember which."
How many tickets does Mr. Muddle have now? two or four; you can't tell for sure
What do you need to know to be sure? whether he gave one ticket away or someone gave him one

② When his father came into the house, Willy was standing in the middle of the stairs. Willy went up two steps. Then he went down three steps and stayed there.
Is Willy higher or lower now than when his father came in? lower
How much lower? one step

③ Mr. Muddle has three lamps in his living room. Each lamp has a lightbulb in it, but two of the bulbs have been burned out for a long time, so in the evening he always sits by the third lamp. Last night the bulb in that lamp burned out, too, so Mr. Muddle had to go to bed. This morning he went to the hardware store and bought four lightbulbs.
Will Mr. Muddle have enough bulbs for all the lamps in his living room? yes, and one extra

---

STORY 14

THINKING STORY

Mr. Mudancia Makes Lunch

One day it was Mr. Mudancia's turn to make lunch. But, of course, he wasn't happy making an ordinary lunch. Mr. Mudancia decided to change everything for lunch—just a little.

The first thing Mr. Mudancia did was take out three stalks of celery and put them on a plate. But that didn't look like very much, so he changed the celery a little. He cut each stalk of celery in half.
How many pieces of celery are there now? six
Is there more celery than before? no, just smaller pieces

Next Mr. Mudancia took out six muffins "These look like tasty muffins," said Mr. Mudancia, "but they're on the small side. I think I'll change them a little."

He took two muffins, put one on top of the other, and squeezed them until they were mashed together.
What did he make? one big, messy muffin

84 • Mr. Mudancia Makes Lunch

Then he did the same thing with two other muffins, and then with two other muffins after that.
Now how many muffins does Mr. Mudancia have all together?
three

"Three big muffins," said Mr. Mudancia. "That's just right: one for me, one for my dear wife, and one for my little Manolita."

Next Mr. Mudancia took two pitchers of juice out of the refrigerator. There were 3 cups of grape juice and 2 cups of tomato juice. He mixed them together.
How many cups of juice does he have now? 5

What do you think it tastes like?
not very good

❹ Ms. Eng bought two skirts and a sweater for her daughter Patty. Then she bought exactly the same things for her other daughter, Pitty.
How many skirts did she buy all together? four
How many sweaters did she buy all together? two

❺ Mr. Mudancia had a belt with eight holes in it, but he changed it a little. He filled in half of the holes.
How many holes are left in the belt? four

❻ Portia has an extra wheel fastened to the back of her wagon in case she has wheel trouble.
How many wheels are on the wagon? five

❼ Ping used to walk a block to school. Now she has to walk twice as far.
How far does she have to walk now? two blocks

❽ Chewies cost ten cents apiece. Ferdie bought one of them with money from his piggy bank. Marcus bought three of them with money his father gave him.
How much did Ferdie pay? 10¢

❾ "I'll give you ten cents, Marcus, if you mail this letter for me," said Mr. Breezy, "and I'll give you twice as much if you go very fast." Marcus ran like an antelope (that's very fast).
How much money did Marcus earn? 20¢

◆ STORY 14   Mr. Mudancia Makes Lunch

Finally Mr. Mudancia took out some vegetables. There were green peas and chickpeas all mixed together in a bowl. He measured them with a big spoon. There were ten spoonfuls. "We have ten tasty spoonfuls of vegetables," said Mr. Mudancia, "but I think I'll change them a little."

He carefully picked out all the green peas. When he was done, there were six spoonfuls of chickpeas left.

Can you figure out how many spoonfuls of green peas he took out? four

86 • Mr. Mudancia Makes Lunch

At lunchtime Manolita was amazed. "These muffins are much bigger than they used to be," Manolita said. "What did you do to them, Papa?"

"Just used a little squeeze-power," said Mr. Mudancia.

Then Manolita tasted the juice. She took a sip, made a face, and put it down. "I don't know what you did to this juice," said Manolita, "but I wish you could do something to change it back to the way it was!"

Could Mr. Mudancia change the juice back to the way it was? Why not?
No, the juice is already mixed together.

. . . the end

Story 14 • **87**

LESSON 104

Student Edition pages 229–230

Estimating Length

LESSON PLANNER

Objective

▶ to teach students to estimate the length of a line

Context of the Lesson This lesson teaches a related concept to that of Lesson 102 in which students estimated one unit when given the length of a longer line. In this lesson, they are given the unit and asked to estimate the length of the longer line.

 MANIPULATIVES   **Program Resources**

food coloring	Thinking Story Book, pages 88–89
masking tape	Practice Master 104
string	Enrichment Master 104
three identical jars	For extra practice: CD-ROM* Lesson 104
water	
interlocking cubes*	

❶ Warm-Up ⏱ 5 MINUTES

Problem of the Day Present the following problem to the class. Raoul has ten pennies. He keeps four. He shares the rest evenly between his friends Megan and Sal. How many pennies did Sal get? (3)

Problem-Solving Strategies Ask students who have solved the Problem of the Day to share how they solved it and any strategies they used.

 Draw lines of various length on the chalkboard. Have students mark the lines for various fractional amounts, such as $\frac{1}{2}$, $\frac{1}{4}$, $\frac{1}{3}$, or $\frac{1}{6}$.

❷ Teach

Demonstrate 1. Draw two lines on the chalkboard with one line four times the length of the other. Present story problems such as: A turtle walked one block (show the shorter line). How many blocks has the other turtle walked (show the longer line)? (4) Ask for estimates and check answers using a **string**. Point out that the long line equals four of the shorter lines. Repeat with other multiples of length.

LESSON 104

Name _____

Estimating Length

Listen to the problems.

❶

❷

❸

 **NOTE TO HOME** Students estimate one length compared to a second length.

Copyright © SRA/McGraw-Hill

Unit 3   Lesson 104 • **229**

 **Literature Connection** Read aloud *The Case of the Missing Zebra Stripes Zoo Math* by Time-Life, Inc., to reinforce logical thinking.

LEARNING STYLES **MANIPULATIVES**

Meeting Individual Needs Have kinesthetic learners work with **interlocking cubes*** to estimate units of length. For example, provide one cube and have them use more cubes to make twice the length, three times the length, and so on.

RETEACHING

Because work with multiples of length continues in Lesson 107, it is not necessary to reteach the concept at this time.

*available separately

◆ LESSON 104 Estimating Length

4 This is how far Mark got in one minute. Make an **X** to show where he will be after three minutes.

5 Steve collected old cans. He filled three bags. His sister got twice as many cans. How many bags will she fill? __6__

6 Sandy made this belt. Her dad wants one twice as long. Draw what it will look like. The drawing is started for you.

NOTE TO HOME
Students explore doubles and triples in quantity, distance, and length.

Copyright © SRA/McGraw-Hill

---

2. Pour about $\frac{1}{5}$ of a **jar** of **water** into one jar and mark its level with **tape**. Then fill a second jar with water. Have students estimate how many of the lesser amounts it will take to make the greater amount. Check estimates by repeatedly filling the first jar to the tape mark and pouring that amount into a third jar.

Using the Student Pages Read each problem below. Have students mark their answers on page 229.

1. Say: "This is how far Jonas gets with one step. Make an X to show how far he will get with three steps."

2. Say: "A big turtle and a little turtle left the rock at the same time. They crawled toward the stream. You can see how far the little turtle got. The big turtle crawls twice as fast. Draw an X to show where the big turtle should be."

3. Say: "This is Pinocchio. When he tells a lie, his nose becomes four times as long. Finish the second picture to show how long Pinocchio's nose gets when he tells a lie."

Read aloud page 230 to students.

Using the Thinking Story Present three new problems following "Mr. Mudancia Makes Lunch" on pages 88–89 of the Thinking Story Book or pages 228a–228b of this Guide.

❸ Wrap-Up 5 MINUTES

In Closing Have a student take one step toward the door. Then have him or her move twice as far. Repeat with other students and multiples of length up to six.

Performance Assessment Observe which students make accurate estimates of length during the wrap-up activity to informally assess students' ability to estimate multiples of length.

Assessment Criteria

Did the student . . .

✓ correctly answer five of six problems on pages 229–230?

✓ make sensible estimates of multiples of length in the wrap-up activity?

LOOKING AHEAD You will need a mask or handkerchief for the next lesson.

PRACTICE p. 104

LESSON 104 PRACTICE Name _____

Solve the problems.

1
Mark threw a ball three times as far as this one. Put an X where Mark's ball landed.

2 The tree is four years old. In four years it will be twice as tall. Draw a picture to show how tall the tree will be then.

3 A truck is twice as long as this car. Draw the truck.

ENRICHMENT p. 104

LESSON 104 ENRICHMENT Name _____

The fish are swimming in a circle.

Read the clues to find the names of the fish. Then, write the first letter of the name on each fish.

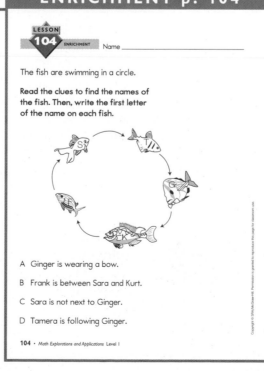

A Ginger is wearing a bow.

B Frank is between Sara and Kurt.

C Sara is not next to Ginger.

D Tamera is following Ginger.

LESSON 105

Student Edition pages 231–232

Fractional Parts

Name _____

Fractional Parts

Listen to the problems.

LESSON PLANNER

Objectives

▶ to provide practice dividing a circle into equal parts using a paper-folding technique

▶ to teach the concept of feedback to solve a location problem

▶ to teach expressions such as "three times as long"

Context of the Lesson The topic of multiples of length will be explored again in Lesson 107. Students were introduced to paper folding in Lesson 72 and last used it in Lesson 98.

 MANIPULATIVES **Program Resources**

handkerchief

scissors

string (optional)

Number Cubes

Thinking Story Book, pages 88–89

Practice Master 105

Enrichment Master 105

For extra practice:

   CD-ROM* Lesson 105

① Warm-Up

Problem of the Day Present the following problem to the class. A school band marched in a parade. The parade route was 3 miles long. The parade lasted three hours. After one hour, how far had the band marched? (assuming a constant speed, 1 mile)

Problem-Solving Strategies Ask students who have solved the Problem of the Day to share how they solved it and any strategies they used.

MENTAL MATH Call out a number from 0–40. Tell students to count up or down from there. Tell them at what number to stop counting.

② Teach

Demonstrate Draw a line representing 3 kilometers and mark one third of its length. Then draw a line underneath the first one that represents 1 kilometer. Tell students that the shorter line is one third as long as the longer line. Then teach the corresponding statement, "The big line is three times as long as the little line." Present other problems similar to this.

1 Ferdie had ten worms. He went fishing and used up half of them. Cross out the worms Ferdie used up.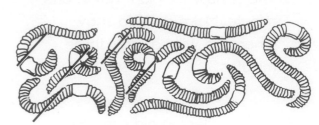

How many worms does Ferdie have? __5__

2 Marcus had three books. You can see them. He was given more for his birthday. Now he has twice as many. Draw the ones he was given.

How many books does Marcus have now? __6__

 NOTE TO HOME
Students solve word problems.

Unit 3 Lesson 105 • **231**

RETEACHING

 Science Connection Tell students that Orville and Wilbur Wright were the first people to successfully fly an airplane. Their aircraft was called "The Flyer" and the design was based on a box kite. Challenge volunteers to find some books on early aviation in the United States. Read one or more with the class.

Literature Connection Read aloud *How Big Is a Foot?* by Rolf Myller to reinforce lesson concepts.

Work at the chalkboard with students who are having trouble with multiples of length. Repeat problems like those in the Number Cube exercise. Allow students to do the **string** measurements themselves.

231 Measurement and Geometry

*available separately

◆ **LESSON 105 Fractional Parts**

Make a dot where you think the center of the circle is.

Cut out the circle. Then fold to check.

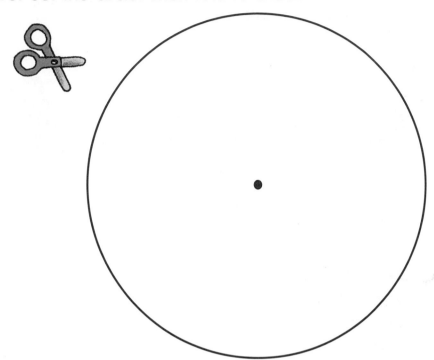

FANTASTIC FACT

Sharks come in all sizes. Some are as big as buses. The dwarf shark is the smallest of all. It is a little bigger than your hand.

REAL-WORLD CONNECTION

Do the "Control Tower" activity.

232 • Measurement and Geometry

NOTE TO HOME
Students divide a circle into parts.

Copyright © SRA/McGraw-Hill

Using the Number Cubes Draw a short line. Above it draw lines that are two, three, and four times as long. Ask how many times longer the top line is than the bottom line. Have students show the answers with Number Cubes. Reverse the procedure by drawing the long line first. Below it draw lines that are one half, one third, and one fifth as long, and so on.

Introducing the "Control Tower" Activity This activity illustrates the value of feedback, or information from others, that facilitates reaching the goal. Blindfold a volunteer with a **handkerchief**. Explain that he or she is a pilot who cannot see the airport due to fog and must receive signals from the control tower to help land the plane. Mark an X on the floor to indicate the airport. The class acts as a radar signal by saying "beep, beep," with the signals getting louder as the pilot gets closer to the X and softer as the pilot moves away. Give other students the chance to be the pilot, and vary the landing spot each time.

Using the Student Pages Read aloud each problem on page 231, allowing students time to write their answers. Then have students do the paper-folding activity on page 232.

Using the Thinking Story Present three new problems from among those following "Mr. Mudancia Makes Lunch" on pages 88–89 of the Thinking Story Book or pages 228a–228b of this Guide.

③ Wrap-Up ⏱ 5 MINUTES

In Closing Challenge students to list ways to find the center of a circle. Then have students test their methods on a paper plate.

Performance Assessment Present problems like those in the Number Cubes exercises.

Assessment Criteria

Did the student . . .

✓ understand how to divide the circle into four equal parts?

✓ correctly use expressions of relative length, such as "three times as long"?

LOOKING AHEAD Lesson 106 will require counters and two large cans. Four to six boxes filled with sand or foam particles are also needed.

PRACTICE p. 105

LESSON 105 PRACTICE Name _____

Solve these problems.

❶ Molly had eight pretzels. She ate half of them. Cross out the pretzels Molly ate.

❷ How many pretzels does Molly have left? _____ 4

❸ A parking lot had four cars. One hour later the parking lot had twice as many cars. Draw the cars that arrived one hour later.
Check students' drawings.

❹ How many cars are in the parking lot now? _____ 8

❺ Brad had six pennies. He gave half of them to his brother. Cross out the pennies Brad gave away.

Math Explorations and Applications Level 1 • **105**

ENRICHMENT p. 105

LESSON 105 ENRICHMENT Name _____

Color two triangles yellow in the pattern below. Color twice as many green.

Color two squares orange. Color three times as many blue.

Color half the circles red.

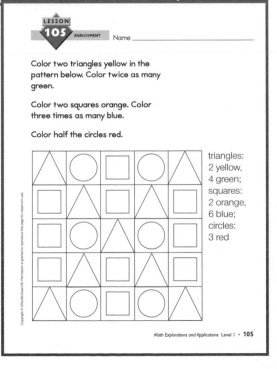

triangles: 2 yellow, 4 green;
squares: 2 orange, 6 blue;
circles: 3 red

Math Explorations and Applications Level 1 • **105**

LESSON 106

Student Edition pages 233–234

Using Doubles

LESSON PLANNER

Objectives

▶ to provide practice using doubles in the 0–5 range or halves of even numbers to solve concrete problems

▶ to provide practice with indirect measurement

▶ to teach the use of shortcuts to solve addition problems

Context of the Lesson Doubling numbers to solve story problems is introduced in this lesson.

 MANIPULATIVES

counters*

craft sticks

four numbered boxes

four objects (such as sandal, clock, candle)

sand or sawdust

two cans

Program Resources

Number Cubes

Practice Master 106

Enrichment Master 106

For extra practice:
CD-ROM* Lesson 106

① Warp-Up 5 MINUTES

 Problem of the Day Read and write the following on the chalkboard. If you rode your bike two miles each day on Monday through Friday, how many miles would you ride all together? (10)

Problem-Solving Strategies Ask students who have solved the Problem of the Day to share how they solved it and any strategies they used.

 Have students subtract using finger sets or a number line.

a.   17 − 5 = (12)   b.   29 − 2 = (27)

c.   31 − 3 = (28)   d.   27 − 1 = (26)

e.   30 − 4 = (26)   f.   22 − 3 = (19)

233 Measurement and Geometry

LESSON 106

Name _____

Using Doubles

How many buttons are on each coat all together?

❶ Brant

6

❷ Bob

8

❸ Brittany

10

❹ Brenna

2

❺ Baby

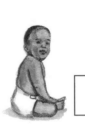

0

❻ Blair's coat has four buttons all together. How many buttons are in back? __2__

How many are in front? __2__

 NOTE TO HOME
Students double numbers 0–5.

Unit 3   Lesson 106 • **233**

 Science Connection
Draw simple pictures of various animals or insects on the chalkboard, with only half the appropriate number of legs. Have volunteers come up and complete the pictures. For example, draw an insect with three legs, an octopus with four legs, a bird with one leg, and a cat with two legs.

Literature Connection
Students can read *Look Twice* by Duncan Birmingham to reinforce math concepts.

RETEACHING

Have students work in small groups to find the sums of doubles. Present simple word problems as you did in the demonstration and have groups use **craft sticks** or **counters*** to solve them.

*available separately

Copyright © SRA/McGraw-Hill

◆ LESSON 106 Using Doubles

Solve these problems. Look for shortcuts.

7

$4 + 4 = \boxed{8}$

$4 + 5 = \boxed{9}$

$4 + 3 = \boxed{7}$

8

$5 + 5 = \boxed{10}$

$5 + 6 = \boxed{11}$

$5 + 4 = \boxed{9}$

9

$2 + 2 = \boxed{4}$

$2 + 3 = \boxed{5}$

$2 + 1 = \boxed{3}$

10

$3 + 3 = \boxed{6}$

$3 + 4 = \boxed{7}$

$3 + 2 = \boxed{5}$

11

$1 + 2 + 3 + 4 = \boxed{10}$

$4 + 3 + 2 + 1 = \boxed{10}$

12

$2 + 3 + 4 + 5 = \boxed{14}$

$5 + 4 + 3 + 2 = \boxed{14}$

SOCIAL STUDIES CONNECTION

Do the "Buried Treasure" activity.

234 • Measurement and Geometry

 NOTE TO HOME Students find shortcuts to solve addition problems.

Copyright © SRA/McGraw-Hill

PRACTICE p. 106

 LESSON **106** PRACTICE   Name _____

Both sides of each card have the same number of dots. How many dots are on each card all together?

1 [••• / •••] → 10   **2** [•••] → 6

3 [•] → 2   **4** [•• / ••] → 4

5 [blank] → 0   **6** [•••/•••] → 8

Two cards have 8 dots all together.

7 How many dots on each card? [4]   **8** How many dots on each side? [2]

Two cards have 4 dots all together.

9 How many dots on each card? [2]   **10** How many dots on each side? [1]

106 • Math Explorations and Applications Level 1

ENRICHMENT p. 106

 LESSON **106** ENRICHMENT   Name _____

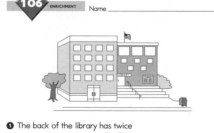

1 The back of the library has twice as many big windows as the front. How many are in back? ___6___

2 The back of the library has twice as many little windows as the front. How many are in back? ___10___

3 The back of the building has twice as many doors as the front. How many are in back? ___6___

On a separate sheet of paper draw a picture of the back of the library.
An acceptable drawing contains 6 large windows, 10 small windows, 32 medium-size windows, and 6 doors.

106 • Math Explorations and Applications Level 1

vailable separately

 # **2** Teach

 Demonstrate Have a student put up to five **counters*** or **craft sticks** into one **can** as you put the same number into the other can. Ask how many counters are in both cans all together. (10) Have students indicate their answers with Number Cubes. Combine counters and count to check. Next, present simple story problems involving doubling, such as: "I have two cats but you have twice as many. How many cats do you have?" Have students indicate their answers with Number Cubes and confirm these with finger sets.

 Introducing the "Buried Treasure" Activity Present four **boxes** with **sand** or **sawdust** and with buried **objects**. Have students work in teams to find out about each object without uncovering it or feeling it with their hands. They can probe with pencils to help identify the dimensions and shape. Have them write down what they find out about each object. When ready, have teams share their findings and then reveal the objects.

Using the Student Pages Have students do pages 233–234 independently. Remind them that the Button children (on page 233) always have the same number of buttons on the front and back of their coats.

Using the "Roll a Double" Game Have students play the "Roll a Double" game as introduced in the Take Home Activity in Lesson 58. A copy of this game can also be found on page 17 of the Home Connections Blackline Masters.

3 Wrap-Up ⏱ 5 MINUTES

In Closing Have students describe the shortcuts they used to add problems on page 234. Encourage students to say when they were able to use doubles.

Informal Assessment Use students' answers to pages 233–234 to informally assess their ability to find sums through 10.

Assessment Criteria

Did the student . . .

✓ make sensible observations during the "Buried Treasure" activity?

✓ correctly complete nine of 12 problems on pages 233–234?

LESSON 107

Estimating Length

Student Edition pages 235–236

LESSON PLANNER

Objective

▶ to teach students to produce lengths two to six times longer than a given unit of length

Context of the Lesson This is the third of three lessons on multiples of length.

 MANIPULATIVES

glass jars
masking tape
pitcher of water
string

Program Resources

Number Cubes
Thinking Story Book, pages 88–89
Reteaching Master
Practice Master 107
Enrichment Master 107
For extra practice:
CD-ROM* Lesson 107
Mixed practice, page 371

1 Warm-Up

 Problem of the Day Present the following problem. Jeremy has a red block, a blue block, and a yellow block. In what ways can he line them up? (red, blue, yellow; red, yellow, blue; blue, red, yellow; blue, yellow, red; yellow, red, blue; yellow, blue, red)

Problem-Solving Strategies Ask students who have solved the Problem of the Day to share how they solved it and any strategies they used.

MENTAL MATH Have students count up and down from the following numbers. Stop at 40 or 0:

a. up from 27   b. up from 19   c. up from 22
d. down from 34   e. down from 15   f. up from 36

2 Teach

 Demonstrate 1. Draw a short line on the chalkboard. Explain that you want to draw another line two times as long. Draw slowly and have students inform you when to stop. Measure the line using **string**. Repeat for lines from three to six times longer than the short one.

235 Measurement and Geometry

LESSON 107

Estimating Length

Name _____

① Make a nail three times as long as this.

② Make a nail five times as long as this.

③ Make a nail two times as long as this.

④ Make a nail four times as long as this.

⑤ Make a nail six times as long as this.

 **COOPERATIVE LEARNING** Do the "String Out the String" activity.

 **NOTE TO HOME** Students draw objects two to six times as long as a model.

 Literature Connection Read aloud *Much Bigger Than Martin* by Steven Kellogg to reinforce measurement concepts.

 **Meeting Individual Needs** Have groups of students make paper strips that are two or three times as long as a given strip to provide experience in making multiples of length.

Unit 3   Lesson 107 • **235**

RETEACHING p. 26

LESSON 107 RETEACHING   Name _____

...Two times as long.

① Color to make a row 3 times as long.

② Color to make a row 4 times as long.

③ Color to make a row 2 times as long.

④ Color to make a row 5 times as long.

26 • *Math Explorations and Applications Level 1*

*available separately

◆ **LESSON 107** Estimating Length

Use the Mixed Practice on page 371 after this lesson.

The small boats are $\frac{1}{3}$ as long.

6 Draw two cars. Make each $\frac{1}{2}$ as long as this one.

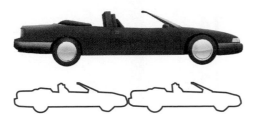

7 Draw four wagons. Make each $\frac{1}{4}$ as long as this one.

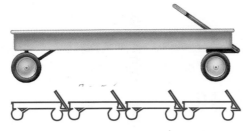

8 Draw three pencils. Make each $\frac{1}{3}$ as long as this one.

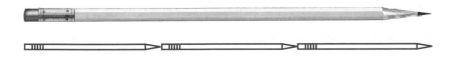

NOTE TO HOME
Students explore the relationship between whole numbers and fractions.

236 • Measurement and Geometry

---

2. Pour a small amount of **water** into a jar. Mark the level with **tape**. Say that you want to pour five times as much into a second jar. Pour slowly until students tell you to stop. Then refill the first jar to the tape mark and pour it into a third jar five times. Compare the amounts in the second and third jars. Repeat by pouring amounts from two to six times as much in the second container.

Using the Student Pages Do the first problem on each page together with the class. Then have students complete the remaining problems on their own.

Introducing the "String Out the String" Activity Have students work in pairs to practice estimating multiples of length. One student folds a string to a given length. The other student rolls a 0–5 Number Cube and tries to form a string that many times as long as the other student's. Students trade roles and repeat the activity.

Using the Thinking Story Present three new problems from those following "Mr. Mudancia Makes Lunch" on pages 88–89 of the Thinking Story Book or pages 228a–228b of this Guide.

❸ Wrap-Up

In Closing Have students demonstrate the methods they used to estimate multiples of lengths.

Performance Assessment Observe students during the activity to informally assess their ability to estimate multiples of lengths.

Assessment Criteria

Did the student . . .

✓ make sensible estimates during the demonstration and activity?

✓ correctly complete six of eight problems on pages 235–236?

PRACTICE p. 107

LESSON **107** PRACTICE   Name _____

1 Draw a piece of rope four times as long as this.
Check students' drawings.

2 Draw a piece of rope two times as long as this.

3 Draw a piece of rope five times as long as this.

4 Draw a piece of rope three times as long as this.

ENRICHMENT p. 107

LESSON **107** ENRICHMENT   Name _____

1 Make this pattern twice as long.
△○△○△○△○△○△○△○

2 Make the scarf three time as long.

3 Draw a pencil four times as long.

4 Make the tail five times as long.
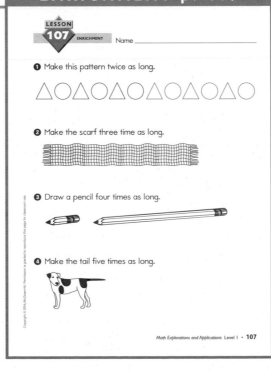

LOOKING AHEAD You will need about 50 pictures labeled and pasted onto cards for Lessons 108 and 109.

LESSON 108

Using Prices

Student Edition pages 237–238

Name _____

Using Prices

Find the answers to these problems.
Use your addition table.

❶ 3¢ + 7¢ = **10** ¢

❽ 7¢ + 7¢ = **14** ¢

❷ 9¢ + 5¢ = **14** ¢

❾ 7¢ + 6¢ = **13** ¢

❸ 9¢ + 4¢ = **13** ¢

❿ 5¢ + 6¢ = **11** ¢

❹ 6¢ + 6¢ = **12** ¢

⓫ 7¢ + 2¢ = **9** ¢

❺ 6¢ + 7¢ = **13** ¢

⓬ 8¢ + 4¢ = **12** ¢

❻ 8¢ + 2¢ = **10** ¢

⓭ 6¢ + 3¢ = **9** ¢

❼ 5¢ + 7¢ = **12** ¢

⓮ 8¢ + 8¢ = **16** ¢

 Do the "Play Money Auction" activity.

Copyright © SRA/McGraw-Hill

 NOTE TO HOME
Students solve addition problems using cents.

Unit 3   Lesson 108 • **237**

LESSON PLANNER

Objectives

▶ to teach students the relationship between money and the prices of real things

▶ to provide a review in the use of doubles to find sums

Context of the Lesson Students begin an auction activity in this lesson and continue to play it in Lesson 109.

 MANIPULATIVES

Program Resources

pictures of 50 objects (valued from $1 to $40) with the prices $1–$40 written on the back

play money*

Practice Master 108

Enrichment Master 108

For extra practice:
   CD-ROM* Lesson 108

❶ Warm-Up

Problem of the Day Write the following on the chalkboard: $1, $2, $4, $8. Have students identify the pattern and say what comes next.
(Each amount is followed by its double; $16.)

Problem-Solving Strategies Ask students who have solved the Problem of the Day to share how they solved it and any strategies they used.

MENTAL MATH Have students count from one given number to another:

a. 17 to 29   **b.** 21 to 36

c. 10 to 26   **d.** 1 to 16

e. 14 to 33   **f.** 19 to 28

 Real-World Connection Take a trip to a local variety store, supermarket, or toy store. Have students guess the prices of various items and then look at the price tags to see how close they came.

 Literature Connection Read *The Purse* by Kathy Caple to reinforce money concepts. In this story, Katie buys a purse, then finds that she has no money to put into it.

RETEACHING

Display **pictures of objects** on cards and ask students whether they think the price is more or less than a specific amount you state. For example, display a picture of a video game. Ask, "Do you think this game costs more than $1 or less than $1?" Make the choices closer to the real price as students become more proficient in estimating prices.

*available separately

◆ LESSON 108 Using Prices

These problems are easy if you remember your doubles.

15. 3¢ + 3¢ = **6** ¢

16. 3¢ + 4¢ = **7** ¢

17. 8¢ + 8¢ = **16** ¢

18. 8¢ + 7¢ = **15** ¢

19. 6¢ + 6¢ = **12** ¢

20. 6¢ + 7¢ = **13** ¢

21. 5¢ + 5¢ = **10** ¢

22. 5¢ + 6¢ = **11** ¢

23. 2¢ + 2¢ = **4** ¢

24. 2¢ + 1¢ = **3** ¢

25. 4¢ + 4¢ = **8** ¢

26. 4¢ + 5¢ = **9** ¢

If you spent $1.00 every minute, it would take you about 2,000 years to spend one billion dollars.

238 • Measurement and Geometry

NOTE TO HOME
Students practice doubling amounts up to 10¢.

Copyright © SRA/McGraw-Hill

---

❷ Teach

Introducing the "Play Money Auction" Activity To provide practice relating amounts of money and prices, conduct an auction. Each student starts with a specific amount of **play money***, such as $100. Students bid on merchandise as you show its **picture**. Sell the item to the highest bidder. Appoint a broker who has a supply of money. The broker buys pictures back from students for a price that you have earlier written on the back. Thus, if a student buys an object for less than the stated price, he or she makes money; a student who buys one for more loses money. At the end of the activity, students count to see if they have more or less money than when they started.

Using the Student Pages Review using the addition table, which was introduced in Lesson 63. Then have students complete pages 237–238 on their own.

❸ Wrap-Up ⏱ 5 MINUTES

In Closing Have students share which problems they solved on page 238 using doubles and how they did it.

Performance Assessment Evaluate students' bids during the auction to see who shows an understanding of the value of money.

Assessment Criteria

Did the student . . .

✓ make sensible bids during the auction?

✓ correctly solve 20 of 26 problems on pages 237–238?

The main purpose of teaching mathematics is to educate people to use mathematical thought to solve real problems.

–Stephen S. Willoughby,
Teaching Mathematics: What is Basic?

LESSON 109

Student Edition pages 239–240

Mental Math

Name _____

Mental Math

Can you solve these problems in your head? Write the answers.

❶ $10 + 1 =$ __11__

❷ $19 + 1 =$ __20__

❸ $40 - 1 =$ __39__   **❹** $10 + 2 =$ __12__

❺ $28 - 0 =$ __28__   **❻** $29 + 2 =$ __31__

❼	❽	❾	❿
$\begin{array}{r} 17 \\ +\ 0 \\ \hline 17 \end{array}$	$\begin{array}{r} 18 \\ +\ 2 \\ \hline 20 \end{array}$	$\begin{array}{r} 25 \\ -\ 2 \\ \hline 23 \end{array}$	$\begin{array}{r} 32 \\ -\ 2 \\ \hline 30 \end{array}$

⓫	⓬	⓭	⓮
$\begin{array}{r} 15 \\ +\ 1 \\ \hline 16 \end{array}$	$\begin{array}{r} 36 \\ +\ 2 \\ \hline 38 \end{array}$	$\begin{array}{r} 26 \\ +\ 2 \\ \hline 28 \end{array}$	$\begin{array}{r} 19 \\ -\ 1 \\ \hline 18 \end{array}$

Copyright © SRA/McGraw-Hill

 NOTE TO HOME
Students add or subtract
0, 1, or 2 from numbers 0–40.

Unit 3   Lesson 109 • **239**

LESSON PLANNER

Objective

✓ to teach and assess students' ability to add or subtract 0, 1, or 2 mentally, with numbers through 40

Context of the Lesson In previous lessons, students were expected to add and subtract 0, 1, and 2 with numbers through 40 by using concrete objects. Mental addition and subtraction is continued in subsequent lessons.

 MANIPULATIVES

pictures used in
Lesson 108

play money*

Program Resources

Number Cubes

Practice Master 109

Enrichment Master 109

Assessment Master

For extra practice:
   CD-ROM* Lesson 109

❶ Warm-Up ⏱

 Problem of the Day Present the following problem. Marvin's desk is in the first row. It is the fourth desk from the front and the second desk from the back. How many desks are in the first row? (5)

Problem-Solving Strategies Ask students who have solved the Problem of the Day to share how they solved it and any strategies they used.

MENTAL MATH Have students write <, >, or = for the following problems:

a. $5 + 4 \bigcirc 6$ (>)   b. $4 - 2 \bigcirc 3$ (<)

c. $3 + 3 \bigcirc 6$ (=)   d. $9 + 1 \bigcirc 8$ (>)

e. $6 + 1 \bigcirc 5$ (>)   f. $7 + 2 \bigcirc 9$ (=)

❷ Teach

Demonstrate Have students review oral counting up or down from given numbers. Then ask questions such as, "What is 1 more than 35? 2 more? 0 more? 1 less? 2 less? 0 less?" Have students explain how they figured out each answer. Students should realize that they are counting up and down mentally to solve these problems.

239 Measurement and Geometry

RETEACHING

Provide students who have difficulty mentally adding and subtracting 0, 1, and 2 with more practice in counting up and down from specific numbers. Start with a number, such as 24. Ask a student to count up by two more numbers. (25, 26) If correct, let that student pick a number between 0 and 40 and ask another student to count up or down 0, 1, or 2 numbers.

PRACTICE p. 109

LESSON 109 PRACTICE   Name _____

Can you solve these problems in your head? Write the answers.

❶	❷	❸	❹
$\begin{array}{r} 16 \\ +\ 2 \\ \hline 18 \end{array}$	$\begin{array}{r} 25 \\ -\ 2 \\ \hline 23 \end{array}$	$\begin{array}{r} 31 \\ +\ 1 \\ \hline 32 \end{array}$	$\begin{array}{r} 38 \\ +\ 2 \\ \hline 40 \end{array}$

❺	❻	❼	❽
$\begin{array}{r} 17 \\ -\ 2 \\ \hline 15 \end{array}$	$\begin{array}{r} 32 \\ -\ 2 \\ \hline 30 \end{array}$	$\begin{array}{r} 19 \\ +\ 2 \\ \hline 21 \end{array}$	$\begin{array}{r} 29 \\ -\ 1 \\ \hline 28 \end{array}$

❾ $13 + 2 =$ __15__   **❿** $24 - 2 =$ __22__

⓫ $21 - 2 =$ __19__   **⓬** $11 + 1 =$ __12__

⓭ $17 + 1 =$ __18__   **⓮** $18 - 2 =$ __16__

⓯ $29 - 0 =$ __29__   **⓰** $39 + 1 =$ __40__

Math Explorations and Applications Level 1 • **109**

*available separately

◆ **LESSON 109 Mental Math**

ALGEBRA READINESS

Write the rule. Find the missing numbers.

⑮

In	Out
2	5
15	18
20	23
36	39

Rule is $+3$

⑯

In	Out
20	20
7	**7**
6	6
5	5

Rule is $+0$
or -0

⑰

In	Out
8	10
10	12
12	14
14	**16**

Rule is $+2$

⑱

In	Out
5	6
25	26
35	36
40	41

Rule is $+1$

⑲

In	Out
6	5
26	25
36	**35**
41	40

Rule is -1

⑳

In	Out
2	4
3	6
4	8
5	**10**

Write the rule.
Double the number.

240 · Measurement and Geometry

NOTE TO HOME Students identify addition and subtraction function rules.

Copyright © SRA/McGraw-Hill

Using the Number Cubes
Write problems on the chalkboard (horizontally and vertically) in which 0, 1, or 2 is added to or subtracted from numbers in the 0–40 range. Have students indicate their answers with Number Cubes.

Using the "Play Money Auction" Activity
MANIPULATIVES Continue playing the auction activity started with students in Lesson 108. Guide students to see that their bids should be as realistic as possible. You will need **play money*** for this activity.

Using the Student Pages
Have students complete pages 239–240 on their own. Then have them share and compare their strategies and answers.

❸ Wrap-Up ⏱ 5 MINUTES

In Closing Have students make up an addition and a subtraction problem they can solve mentally and then share them with other classmates.

✓ Mastery Checkpoint 16
At about this time, you may want to formally assess students' ability to mentally add and subtract 0, 1, and 2 with numbers through 40. Mastery can be demonstrated during the Number Cube activity, by correctly answering 11 of 14 problems on page 239, or by correctly answering 80% of the problems on page 40 of the Assessment Blackline Masters. Results can be recorded on the Mastery Checkpoint Chart.

ENRICHMENT p. 109

LESSON 109 ENRICHMENT Name _____

Connect the dots. Start at 0 and count up.

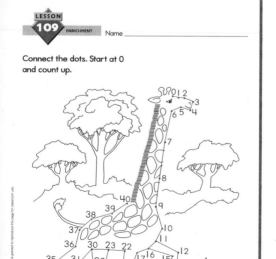

Math Explorations and Applications Level 1 · 109

ASSESSMENT p. 40

UNIT 3 Mastery Checkpoint 16 Mental addition and subtraction of 0, 1, or 2, with numbers through 40. (Lesson 109)
Name _____
The student demonstrates mastery by correctly answering 12 of the 15 problems.

Can you solve these problems in your head? Write the answers.

❶ 28 + 2 = ___30___   ❷ 20 + 1 = ___21___

❸ 31 − 2 = ___29___   ❹ 20 − 1 = ___19___

❺ 29 + 1 = ___30___   ❻ 10 − 2 = ___8___

❼ 38 − 0 = ___38___   ❽ 19 + 2 = ___21___

Solve these problems.

❾ 28
− 2
―――
26

❿ 30
− 1
―――
29

⓫ 15
+ 0
―――
15

⓬ 19
+ 1
―――
20

⓭ 31
− 1
―――
30

⓮ 16
+ 2
―――
18

⓯ 24
+ 1
―――
25

40 · Math Explorations and Applications Level 1

Assessment Criteria

Did the student . . .

✓ correctly answer 11 of the 14 problems on page 239?

✓ correctly answer 80% of the problems during the Number Cube activity?

✓ correctly complete five of six tables on page 240?

LESSON 110

Student Edition pages 241–242

Making Ten

Name _____

Making Ten

Ring the two numbers that add up to 10. Then use them to write an addition sentence.

❶ ⑦ ③ 8

$7 + 3 = 10$

❷ 7 ⑧ ②

$8 + 2 = 10$

❸ ② 6 ⑧

$2 + 8 = 10$

❹ ⓪ 9 ⑩

$0 + 10 = 10$

❺ ⑥ ④ 3

$6 + 4 = 10$

❻ 4 ⑨ ①

$9 + 1 = 10$

❼ ⑤ 4 ⑤

$5 + 5 = 10$

❽ ④ 7 ⑥

$4 + 6 = 10$

 NOTE TO HOME
Students identify numbers that sum to 10.

Unit 3 Lesson 110 • **241**

LESSON PLANNER

Objective

▶ to teach students to find pairs of numbers whose sum is 10 without using concrete objects

Context of the Lesson Students began finding complements that sum to 10 by using concrete objects and then went on to use finger sets. This lesson is the next step leading to mastery of addition facts.

 MANIPULATIVES

double-pan balance* (optional)

index cards (optional)

Program Resources

Number Cubes

Practice Master 110

Enrichment Master 110

For extra practice:
CD-ROM* Lesson 110

❶ Warm-Up ⏱

 Problem of the Day Present the following problem to the class: There are 21 students in Mr. Hart's first-grade class. Today two students are absent and a new student is introduced to the class. How many students are in Mr. Hart's classroom today? (20)

Problem-Solving Strategies Ask students who have solved the Problem of the Day to share how they solved it and any strategies they used.

MENTAL MATH Have students write <, >, or = for the following problems:

a. 3 – 1 ◯ 4 (<)

b. 4 + 0 ◯ 2 (>)

c. 2 – 1 ◯ 3 (<)

d. 10 + 5 ◯ 15 (=)

e. 9 + 1 ◯ 10 (=)

f. 11 – 2 ◯ 8 (>)

 Science Connection Place a ten-unit weight on one side of a **double-pan balance***. From a selection of three other weights, have students choose two that they think will balance the scale.

 Literature Connection Students can use *Richard Scarry's Best Counting Book Ever* by Richard Scarry to reinforce counting skills.

RETEACHING

 Write pairs of numbers on the chalkboard. Have students show "thumbs up" if their sum is 10 and "thumbs down" if it is not.

Then repeat the "Find Your Partner" activity introduced in Lesson 61, in which students found partners to make ten. Use **index cards** with numbers from 0–10.

241 Measurement and Geometry

*available separately

♦ **LESSON 110** Making Ten

Take-Home Activity

Roll a Ten

Players:	Two or more
Materials:	Two 0–5 cubes and two 5–10 cubes

RULES

Take turns. Roll all four cubes. Try to find two numbers that add up to 10. If you find one set, you win an extra turn. If you find two sets, take two extra turns. If you cannot find one, and another player can, that player wins an extra turn.

I win a turn. 3 and 7 make 10.

I played the game with _____.

Copyright: © SRA/McGraw-Hill

242 • Measurement and Geometry

---

② Teach

Demonstrate First, provide several addition problems with sums of 10. Then write three numbers on the chalkboard, such as: 6, 9, 1. Have students indicate with Number Cubes the two numbers that add up to 10. (9, 1) Finally, present problems in which you provide one number and students indicate with Number Cubes the number needed to make a sum of 10.

Using the Student Pages Discuss the sample problem on page 241 with students and have them complete the page on their own.

 Introducing the "Roll a Ten" Game Follow the rules on student page 242 to demonstrate the game. Then have students take page 242 home to practice identifying numbers that sum to 10. Students can play the game with a friend or family member. Or, have pairs of students play the game in class. A copy of this game can also be found on page 24 of the Home Connections Blackline Masters.

③ Wrap-Up

5 MINUTES

In Closing Have students share the answers to page 241 as they correct their papers. Ask which number sentence shows doubles. ($5 + 5 = 10$)

 Performance Assessment Observe which students indicate the appropriate Number Cubes during the demonstration to informally assess their knowledge of sums of 10.

PRACTICE p. 110

ENRICHMENT p. 110

Assessment Criteria

Did the student . . .

✓ indicate correct answers during the demonstration?

✓ play the "Roll a Ten" game?

✓ correctly solve six of eight problems on page 241?

LESSON 111
Student Edition pages 243–244
Counting by Tens

Name _____

Counting by Tens

How many pieces of macaroni?

1. **10**
2. **30**
3. **50**
4. **60**
5. **70**
6. **40**

LESSON PLANNER

Objectives
▶ to extend the range of numbers that students work with to 100
▶ to teach students to set off tally marks in groups of five by using the cancel mark

Context of the Lesson This is the first of three lessons on counting by tens with the use of concrete objects. In this lesson students are taught to count to 100 by tens using macaroni tens cards.

 MANIPULATIVES **Program Resources**

glue
index cards
macaroni
(2–2½ lbs) or
small pieces of
colored paper

magazine clippings
or collage materials
(optional)

Number Cubes
Practice Master 111
Enrichment Master 111

For extra practice:
CD-ROM* Lesson 111
Mixed practice, page 372

 ART CONNECTION
Do the "Making Macaroni Cards" activity.

 NOTE TO HOME
Students count to 100 by tens.

1 Warm-Up

 **Problem of the Day** Draw these coins on the chalkboard, then challenge students to solve the problem that follows.

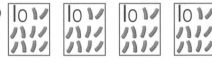

Which set does not belong? Explain. (3 dimes, 8 pennies does not belong, because its value is only 38¢ and all others are worth 40¢.)

Problem-Solving Strategies Ask students who have solved the Problem of the Day to share how they solved it and any strategies they used.

MENTAL MATH Read aloud the following problems and have students show their answers with Number Cubes:

a. 1 + 9 = (10)
b. 2 + 8 = (10)
c. 4 + 3 = (7)
d. 6 + 4 = (10)
e. 5 + 4 = (9)
f. 7 + 3 = (10)

243 Measurement and Geometry

 Literature Connection You may wish to read aloud *Blast Off! A Space Counting Book* by Norma Cole to reinforce lesson concepts.

 **Art Connection** Challenge students to make their own fanciful set of tens and units cards. Students might want to draw different objects on each card. For example, one card might have one castle, the second two princesses, and so on. Students can also use **magazine clippings** or **collage materials**.

RETEACHING

 Help students to understand the concept of tens cards. Have objects like pumpkin seeds, beans, and paper clips on hand so students can make other types of tens cards. Explain it is not the objects that are important but the amount glued onto the card.

*available separately

◆ **LESSON 111** Counting by Tens

Use the Mixed Practice on page 372 after this lesson.

How many tally marks? Ring sets of ten to help you count.

⑨ 60 　||||| ||||| ||||| ||||| ||||| ||||| ||||| ||||| ||||| ||||| ||||| |||||

⑩ 50 　||||| ||||| ||||| ||||| ||||| ||||| ||||| ||||| ||||| |||||

⑪ 40 　||||| ||||| ||||| ||||| ||||| ||||| ||||| |||||

⑫ 30 　||||| ||||| ||||| ||||| ||||| |||||

⑬ 20 　||||| ||||| ||||| |||||

⑭ Try to make 60 tally marks here.

||||| ||||| ||||| ||||| ||||| ||||| ||||| ||||| ||||| ||||| ||||| |||||

244 • Measurement and Geometry

 **NOTE TO HOME**
Students use tally marks to count by tens.

PRACTICE p. 111

LESSON **111** PRACTICE　Name _____

How many stars?

❶ ☆☆☆☆☆ ☆☆☆☆☆　　20

❷ ☆☆☆☆☆ ☆☆☆☆☆ ☆☆☆☆☆ ☆☆☆☆☆ ☆☆☆☆☆　　50

❸ ☆☆☆☆☆ ☆☆☆☆☆ ☆☆☆☆☆　　30

How many stars? Ring sets of ten to help you count.

❹ 30 ☆☆☆ ☆☆☆ ☆☆☆ ☆☆☆

❺ 50 ☆☆☆ ☆☆☆ ☆☆☆ ☆☆☆ ☆☆☆

❻ 20 ☆☆☆ ☆☆☆ ☆☆☆

Math Explorations and Applications Level 1 • **111**

ENRICHMENT p. 111

LESSON **111** ENRICHMENT　Name _____

Jenni, Mandy, Lee, and Radeel made pinwheels. Write how many paper cards each child used.

❶ Mandy made four pinwheels today and two pinwheels yesterday. How many paper cards did she use?　　60

❷ Radeel made three pinwheels today and five pinwheels yesterday. How many paper cards did he use?　　80

❸ Lee used 100 paper cards. How many pinwheels did she make?　　10

❹ Jenni made two pinwheels yesterday. She used 50 paper cards today. How many pinwheels did she make in all?　　7

Math Explorations and Applications Level 1 • **111**

---

② **Teach**

 Introducing the "Making Macaroni Cards" Activity Have each student **glue** ten pieces of **macaroni** or colored paper onto a 5" × 8" **index card** and label the card with the number 10. Then have nine volunteers each make a macaroni units card, one for each number from 0–9, labeling the cards with the correct numbers.

Demonstrate Stand three tens cards in a line on the chalk tray. As you put each card in place ask how many pieces of macaroni are on it. Then point to each card in turn and count 1 ten, 2 tens, 3 tens, and so on. Explain that this is called counting by tens and have students count in unison with you. Practice counting by tens through 100, or 10 tens. Guide students to see how counting by tens is faster than counting each individual piece of macaroni.

 Using the Number Cubes Display 10 tens cards. Ask students to use units Number Cubes to show how many cards are displayed. Then ask students to use both tens and units cubes to show how many pieces of macaroni there are all together. Count by tens in unison to confirm the answer.

Using the Student Pages Have students complete page 243. Before beginning student page 244, review how to use tally marks. Teach students how to use a diagonal line, or cancel mark, instead of the fifth tally mark.

③ **Wrap-Up** ⏱ 5 MINUTES

In Closing Remind students that using the diagonal tally mark every fifth mark and circling sets of ten is an easier way to count tallies.

 Informal Assessment Observe students as they count by tens using macaroni cards.

Assessment Criteria

Did the student . . .

✓ complete pages 243–244 with 75% accuracy?

✓ count by tens to 100 using the macaroni tens cards?

LOOKING AHEAD For Lesson 112 you will need macaroni tens cards, a supply of loose macaroni, and a can.

LESSON 112

Student Edition pages 245–246

Tens and Ones

LESSON PLANNER

Objectives

▶ to teach students to count up to 100 objects by counting groups of ten and then adding the extras

▶ to provide opportunities to estimate how long it will take to do an activity based on the time it takes to do a related activity

Context of the Lesson This is the second of three lessons on counting by tens. Students first estimated time intervals in Lesson 32.

👋 **MANIPULATIVES** | **Program Resources**

counters* | Number Cubes
macaroni cards | Practice Master 112
two pounds | Enrichment Master 112
of macaroni | For extra practice:
stopwatch* | CD-ROM* Lesson 112

❶ Warm-Up ⏱ 5 MINUTES

Problem of the Day Present this problem: Jenna lives with her parents, two brothers, and three sisters. How many people are in Jenna's family? (8)

Problem-Solving Strategies Ask students who have solved the Problem of the Day to share how they solved it and any strategies they used.

MENTAL MATH Write these problems on the chalkboard. Then have students use hand signals to show <, >, or = to make true number sentences.

a. 4 + 1 ◯ 6 (<) b. 5 + 2 ◯ 6 (>) c. 3 + 1 ◯ 10 (<)

d. 7 + 2 ◯ 5 (>) e. 3 + 4 ◯ 10 (<) f. 9 + 2 ◯ 11 (=)

❷ Teach

Demonstrate Show students how to count by tens and extras by using the **macaroni tens and units cards**. Put four tens cards and a 6-card on the chalk tray. Ask how many pieces of macaroni in all. Have them count: 1 ten, 2 tens, 3 tens, 4 tens, and 6 make 46. Repeat with similar problems. Have students show their answers with Number Cubes.

245 Measurement and Geometry

LESSON 112

Name _____

Tens and Ones

How many pieces of macaroni?

❶ **12**

❷ **24**

❸ **32**

❹ **44**

❺ **53**

 Do the "How Long Will It Take?" activity.

 GAME Play the "Macaroni Tens" game.

 NOTE TO HOME Students count by tens and then add ones for numbers 0–100.

Unit 3 Lesson 112 • **245**

RETEACHING

 Have students use the **macaroni tens and unit cards** to make specific amounts up to 100. For example, write the number 62 on the chalkboard. Have a volunteer show the tens and unit cards that make that amount. (six tens cards and one two-unit card) Have the class count in unison to confirm the answer.

LEARNING STYLES **Meeting Individual Needs**

Have kinesthetic learners work in groups to use their fingers to represent numbers. For example, have five students stand in the front of the room. Have four of them show 10 fingers and one show 5 fingers. Count: 1 ten, 2 tens, 3 tens, 4 tens, and 5 make 45.

*available separately

◆ **LESSON 112** Tens and Ones

How many apples? There are ten apples in each bag.

6 **33**

7 **60**

8 **44**

Fill in the missing numbers.

9 | 10 20 30 **40** 50 60 **70** 80

10 | 10 20 **30** 40 50 60 70 **80**

Be careful.

11 80 70 60 **50** 40 30 **20** | 10

246 · Measurement and Geometry

NOTE TO HOME
Students count by tens and add ones for numbers 0–100.

Copyright © SRA/McGraw-Hill

GAME **Introducing the "Macaroni Tens" Game**
To provide practice in estimating quantity and making groups of 10, demonstrate and play this game. Place about 2 pounds of **macaroni** in a central location. Player 1 rolls either of the tens cubes and takes one or two handfuls of macaroni. Both players sort it into as many piles of 10 as the number rolled. To win a **counter***, Player 1 must have the same number of ten sets of macaroni as rolled. (For example, if a 6 is rolled, the player can have between 60 and 69 pieces of macaroni.) Replace the macaroni and repeat. The player with the most counters at the end wins. A copy of this game can also be found on page 25 of the Home Connections Blackline Masters.

MANIPULATIVES **Introducing the "How Long Will It Take?" Activity** To provide practice estimating durations of time, use this activity. Use a **stopwatch*** to time how long it takes a volunteer to tie his or her shoes. Have the class estimate how long it would take to tie two shoes. Try it and check the estimate. Repeat with similar examples as well as with examples in which you time a longer activity and students estimate the time for a shorter version. Compare the times it takes three or more students to tie their shoes. Have students put the times in order from greatest to least and from least to greatest.

Using the Student Pages Discuss page 245 with the class and have volunteers model how to count each amount. Then have students complete page 246 on their own.

③ Wrap-Up

In Closing Have students count aloud to show how they arrived at their answers to page 246.

ALTERNATIVE ASSESSMENT **Informal Assessment** Use the students' work on page 246 to informally assess their ability to count objects through 100.

Assessment Criteria

Did the student . . .

✓ provide correct answers during the demonstration?

✓ correctly work 80% of the problems on pages 245–246?

PRACTICE p. 112

LESSON **112** PRACTICE Name_____

How many stars? There are ten stars in each box.

1 | 10 | 10 | ★★★★ ★★★★ ___ 28

2 | 10 | 10 | 10 | 10 | 10 | ★★ ___ 52

3 | 10 | ★★★★★ ___ 15

4 | 10 | 10 | 10 | 10 | 10 | ___ 50

5 | 10 | 10 | 10 | ★★★★ ___ 34

6 | 10 | 10 | 10 | 10 | 10 | 10 | ★★★ ★★★★ ___ 67

7 | 10 | 10 | 10 | 10 | ★★★★ ★★★★★ ___ 49

8 | 10 | 10 | ★★★ ___ 23

112 · Math Explorations and Applications Level 1

ENRICHMENT p. 112

LESSON **112** ENRICHMENT Name_____

Each row seats ten children. Write how many children there are all together.

1 ___ 43

2 ___ 61

3 ___ 35

4 ___ 54

112 · Math Explorations and Applications Level 1

available separately

Unit 3 Lesson 112 **246**

LESSON 113

Student Edition pages 247–248

Counting with Dimes

LESSON PLANNER

Objectives

▶ to provide practice counting to 100 by tens using dimes

✓ to teach and assess students' ability to form given amounts of money up to $1 using pennies, nickels, and dimes

Context of the Lesson This is the last lesson on counting by tens with concrete objects. It includes Mastery Checkpoint 17 to assess students' ability to work with money in denominations of pennies, nickels, dimes, and dollars.

 MANIPULATIVES

play money*

Program Resources

"School Bookstore" Game Mat

Number Cubes

Thinking Story Book, pages 90–93

Reteaching Master

Practice Master 113

Enrichment Master 113

Assessment Master

For career connections:
  Careers and Math*

For additional math integration:
  Math Throughout the Day*

For extra practice:
  CD-ROM* Lesson 113

① Warm-Up

Problem of the Day Present the following problem to the class. Katy is five years old. Next year she will be twice as old as her brother. About how old is Katy's brother now? (2 years old)

Problem-Solving Strategies Ask students who have solved the Problem of the Day to share how they solved it and any strategies they used.

MENTAL MATH Have students use Number Cubes to show their answers.

a. □ + 7 = 7 (0) b. 7 + □ = 9 (2) c. 5 + □ = 8 (3)

d. 8 + □ = 10 (2) e. □ + 2 = 4 (2) f. 6 + □ = 9 (3)

247 Measurement and Geometry

LESSON 113

Name _____

Counting with Dimes

How many cents?

1 **72** ¢

2 **63** ¢

Ring the two numbers that add up to 10. Then use them to write an addition sentence.

3 4 ⑤ ⑤

| 5 | + | 5 | = 10 |

4 ⑦ 8 ③

| 7 | + | 3 | = 10 |

5 ⑨ ① 2

| 9 | + | 1 | = 10 |

6 ④ 5 ⑥

| 4 | + | 6 | = 10 |

 THINKING STORY

Talk about the Thinking Story "How Ms. Eng Doubled Her Money."

 NOTE TO HOME
Students count by tens and identify numbers that sum to 10.

Unit 3 Lesson 113 • **247**

RETEACHING p. 27

LESSON 113 RETEACHING Name _____

Count . . .
10, 20, 30, 40,
50, 51, 52!

How many cents?

1 _____ 37 ¢

2 _____ 20 ¢

3 _____ 35 ¢

4 _____ 44 ¢

5 _____ 63 ¢

Math Explorations and Applications Level 1 • 27

PRACTICE p. 113

LESSON 113 PRACTICE Name _____

How many cents?

1 __43__ ¢

2 __60__ ¢

3 __54__ ¢

4 __31__ ¢

Ring the two numbers that add up to 10. Then use them to write an addition sentence.

5 ④ 5 ⑥

| 4 | + | 6 | = 10 |

6 ⑧ 3 ②

| 8 | + | 2 | = 10 |

7 ⑤ 6 ⑤

| 5 | + | 5 | = 10 |

8 ⑦ 4 ③

| 7 | + | 3 | = 10 |

Math Explorations and Applications Level 1 • **113**

*available separately

◆ **LESSON 113** Counting with Dimes

REAL-WORLD CONNECTION

How many cents?

(7) _____ 53 ¢

(8) _____ 34 ¢

(9) _____ 51 ¢

(10) _____ 80 ¢

(11) _____ 27 ¢

(12) _____ 10 ¢

(13) _____ 5 ¢

GAME

Play the "School Bookstore" game.

248 • Measurement and Geometry

NOTE TO HOME
Students add dimes and pennies for amounts up to $1.00.

Copyright © SRA/McGraw-Hill

---

❷ Teach

Demonstrate Use **play money*** and have students count by tens as you give a volunteer one dime at a time. After each dime ask students how much you have given so far. Then say that you want to give another student 60 cents. Ask how many dimes you will need. (16) Then present problems such as: "I have seven dimes and three pennies. How many cents is that?" (73) Mix in problems such as: "I have 87 cents. What is the greatest number of dimes I can have?" (8)

Using the Student Pages Have students complete pages 247–248 on their own.

Using the Thinking Story Read aloud and discuss "How Ms. Eng Doubled Her Money" on pages 90–93 of the Thinking Story Book.

Introducing the "School Bookstore" Game Mat To provide practice with place value and changing dimes for dollars, have students play this game. Use the Game Mat transparency to demonstrate and play a round of this game. A copy of this game can also be found on page 408 of this Guide.

❸ Wrap-Up

In Closing Have students think of two different ways they could make 46 cents. (for example, 4 dimes, 1 nickel, and 1 penny or 9 nickels and 1 penny)

Mastery Checkpoint 17

At about this time you may want to formally assess students' ability to form specific amounts of money up to $1 and their skills in trading pennies for nickels, nickels for dimes, and dimes for dollars. Mastery can be demonstrated during the demonstration, during game time, or by using page 41 in the Assessment Blackline Masters.

ENRICHMENT p. 113

LESSON **113** ENRICHMENT Name _____

Put each animal in its own cage.
Draw only three lines to do so.

Copyright © SRA/McGraw-Hill. Permission is granted to reproduce this page for classroom use.

Math Explorations and Applications Level 1 • **113**

ASSESSMENT p. 41

UNIT **3** Mastery Checkpoint 17 Familiarity with money (coins) (Lesson 113)

Name _____

The student demonstrates mastery by correctly answering 4 of the 5 problems.

How many cents?

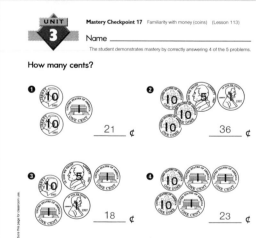

(1) _____ 21 ¢   **(2)** _____ 36 ¢

(3) _____ 18 ¢   **(4)** _____ 23 ¢

(5) _____ 45 ¢

Copyright © SRA/McGraw-Hill. Permission is granted to reproduce this page for classroom use.

Math Explorations and Applications Level 1 • **41**

Assessment Criteria

Did the student . . .

✓ correctly answer 10 of 13 problems on pages 247–248?

✓ demonstrate mastery in forming amounts of money to $1?

✓ actively participate in the Thinking Story discussion?

*available separately

STORY 15

How Ms. Eng Doubled Her Money

❶ If Mr. Breezy works all day, he can wash half the windows in his house.
How many days will it take him to wash all the windows? two

❷ Marcus had eight shells that he found on the beach. He showed two of them to his friend Willy.
How many shells did Marcus have then? eight

❸ "What a smart baby!" said Portia. "He spoke his first word when he was only ten months old, and he spoke his second word when he was only nine months old."
What's wrong with what Portia said? He spoke the second word before the first.

❹ A friendly baker gave a group of children two Danish rolls. "Break each one in half," he said.
How many pieces did the children have after they broke the rolls? four

There were eight children.
Did each of them get half a roll? no
What could they do? break each of the four pieces in half

❺ Ferdie had eight marbles and Marcus had four. Mr. Breezy gave two marbles to the boy who had fewer.
How many marbles does Ferdie have now? eight

❻ The Mudancias used to be able to bake enchiladas in 15 minutes, but Mr. Mudancia changed the oven a little. Now it takes ten minutes longer.
How many minutes does it take to bake enchiladas now? 25

STORY 15

THINKING STORY

How Ms. Eng Doubled Her Money

"You have two of everything, Ms. Eng," said Marcus. "You must be rich."

"That's right," said Ms. Eng.

"How did you get that way?"

"Simple," said Ms. Eng. "By getting lots of money."

"But how did you do that?" Portia asked.

"I'll tell you how it all started," said Ms. Eng. "One day when I was a young girl I found a quarter on the sidewalk. I used it to buy something."

"What?" Ferdie asked.

"A handkerchief, of course."

"Did you have a cold?"

"No," said Ms. Eng, "but I soon met a woman who did, and she gave me some money for the handkerchief. That's how I started to get rich."

"Wait a minute," said Marcus. "I have a question."

What question do you think Marcus will ask? How much did the handkerchief sell for?

"My question," said Marcus, "is how much did you sell the handkerchief for?"

"Twice as much as I paid for it," said Ms. Eng.

How much did Ms. Eng pay for the handkerchief? one quarter

So how many quarters did she get for the handkerchief? two

How much money is two quarters? 50¢

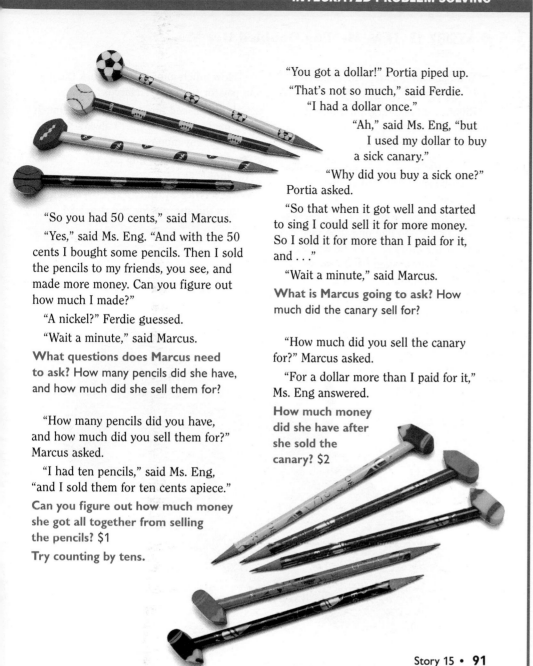

"So you had 50 cents," said Marcus.

"Yes," said Ms. Eng. "And with the 50 cents I bought some pencils. Then I sold the pencils to my friends, you see, and made more money. Can you figure out how much I made?"

"A nickel?" Ferdie guessed.

"Wait a minute," said Marcus.

What questions does Marcus need to ask? How many pencils did she have, and how much did she sell them for?

"How many pencils did you have, and how much did you sell them for?" Marcus asked.

"I had ten pencils," said Ms. Eng, "and I sold them for ten cents apiece."

Can you figure out how much money she got all together from selling the pencils? $1

Try counting by tens.

"You got a dollar!" Portia piped up.

"That's not so much," said Ferdie. "I had a dollar once."

"Ah," said Ms. Eng, "but I used my dollar to buy a sick canary."

"Why did you buy a sick one?" Portia asked.

"So that when it got well and started to sing I could sell it for more money. So I sold it for more than I paid for it, and . . ."

"Wait a minute," said Marcus.

What is Marcus going to ask? How much did the canary sell for?

"How much did you sell the canary for?" Marcus asked.

"For a dollar more than I paid for it," Ms. Eng answered.

How much money did she have after she sold the canary? $2

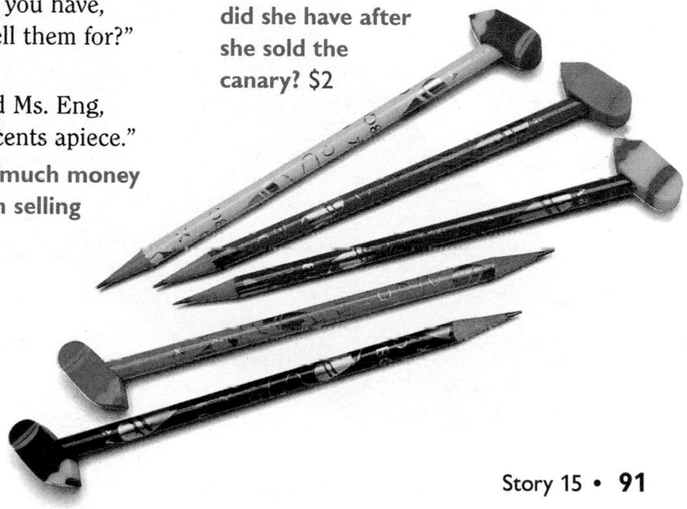

7. Once Mr. Eng grew a beard. It was 10 inches long, but Mr. Mudancia changed it a little. He cut off 8 inches.
How long was Mr Eng's beard after Mr. Mudancia changed it? 2 inches
How long is that? Show with your fingers. [Demonstrate]

8. Mr. Mudancia had a necktie that was 44 inches long. He cut an inch off one end and an inch off the other end.
How long is the piece of necktie now? 42 inches

9. There is a snail in Willy's fishbowl that is trying to crawl up the side. Every day it climbs up 3 inches and every night it slides down 3 inches.
How far up will the snail get after four days and four nights? 0 inches

10. There is another snail in Willy's fishbowl that does a little better. Every day it climbs up 3 inches, but at night it slides down only 1 inch.
How far up will the snail get after four days and four nights? 8 inches [Suggest that the children use a ruler or number line to work it out.]

11. Mr. Mudancia used to be able to seat five people around his dinner table. He made the table bigger, and now he can fit three more people.
How many people can sit around the dinner table now? eight

12. Manolita had seven colored markers. She sold some of them to Portia for 25¢ each.
How many colored markers does Manolita have left? can't tell
What do you need to know before you can tell? how many she sold

◆ STORY 15 How Ms. Eng Doubled Her Money

"You had two dollars!" the children said.

"Right," said Ms. Eng. "And I used the two dollars to buy a shoe."

"One shoe?" asked Ferdie.

"That's right."

"But one shoe isn't worth anything," Ferdie said.

"This one was," said Ms. Eng, "because I knew a man who had one shoe just like it for the other foot. So he was glad to pay me what I asked for the shoe, and with that money . . ."

"Wait a minute," said Marcus.

What question is Marcus going to ask? How much money did the man pay for the shoe?

"How much money did you ask the man to pay for the shoe?" Marcus asked.

"Why, I asked him to pay twice as much as I paid," said Ms. Eng. "I always like to double my money."

How much did Ms. Eng pay for the shoe? $2

What's twice as much? So how much money did she get for the shoe? $4

92 • How Ms. Eng Doubled Her Money

"Four dollars!" said Ferdie. "You really were getting rich!"

"But I didn't stop there," said Ms. Eng. "I used the four dollars to buy a clock with no hands."

"What good is a clock with no hands?" Portia asked.

"I don't know," said Ms. Eng. "In fact, I never could find anyone who wanted to buy the clock, so I still have it. If you happen to know anyone who wants a clock with no hands, I'll sell it for a good price."

"What price?" asked Marcus.

"Why, only twice as much as I paid for it," said Ms. Eng.

How much did she pay for the clock? $4

How much does she want to sell it for? $8

"But wait," said Manolita, who had been quiet until then. "You were going to tell us how you got rich. If you bought the clock for four dollars and you still have the clock, then you couldn't get rich that way."

Why not? How much money did Ms. Eng have left after she bought the clock with no hands? none

"Oh, I forgot to tell you one little thing," said Ms. Eng. "When I opened up that old clock with no hands, I found it had half a million dollars inside."

. . . the end

Story 15 • **93**

LESSON 114
Unit 3 Review

Student Edition pages 249–252

LESSON **114**

Name _____

Unit 3 Review

Using the Student Pages Use this Unit Review as a preliminary unit test to indicate areas in which each student is having difficulty or in which the entire class may need help. If students do well on the Unit Review, you may wish to skip directly to the next unit. If not, you may spend a day or so helping students overcome their individual difficulties before they take the Unit Test.

Next to each instruction line is a list of the lessons in the unit covered in that set of problems. Students can refer to the specific lesson for additional instruction if they need help. You can also use this information to make additional assignments based on the previous lesson concepts.

Have students complete pages 249, 250, 251, and 252. Read the directions to the students and explain what is being asked in each problem, if necessary.

Problems 1–3 For students having difficulty with numerical order, do Number Cube drill in which you say or write a number and the students show with cubes the number that comes just before or just after it in the counting order. Also, review counting by tens and problems such as "What's 10 more than 4 tens?" and "What's 10 less than 6 tens?"

 Problems 6–7, 22–25 Students who add when they should subtract, or vice versa, on these items quite possibly do not understand what operations the drawings are intended to represent. Help the students say aloud what each problem means.

Alternatively, you may draw counters-in-the-can problems on the board and have students work them out, using a real can and real **counters***

 Problems 4–5, 30–32 Students who are having difficulty with coin values could use **play money*** and play the "Add the Coins" game (Lesson 92) or a variation of the "School Bookstore" game (Lesson 113) for extra practice.

 Problems 8–11 Working through addition and subtraction problems with bundles of sticks or **base-10 blocks*** is probably the best way to help students who are having serious difficulty with addition and subtraction operations.

Fill in the missing numbers.

Lessons ❶ 84, 112   20   21   **22**   **23**   **24**   25   26

❷   17   18   **19**   **20**   21   **22**   23

❸   10   **20**   30   **40**   50   60

How many cents?

Lessons ❹ 88, 113   **36** ¢

❺   **23** ¢

Lessons 93, 94, **How many now?** 102, 113

❻  31   33

❼   14   11

NOTE TO HOME
Students review unit skills and concepts.

Unit 3   Review • **249**

Copyright © SRA/McGraw-Hill

249 Measurement and Geometry

*available separately

◆ **LESSON 114 Unit 3 Review**

Solve these problems.

Lesson 109

⑧ $19 + 1 =$ **20**   ⑨ $19 - 2 =$ **17**

⑩ $28 + 3 =$ **31**   ⑪ $31 - 2 =$ **29**

What is the right sign?
Draw + or −.

Lessons 95, 100

⑫ $4 \boxed{+} 1 = 5$ ⑬ $7 \boxed{-} 2 = 5$

⑭ $19 \boxed{+} 1 = 20$ ⑮ $29 \boxed{+} 2 = 31$

⑯ $16 \boxed{+} 2 = 18$ ⑰ $21 \boxed{-} 2 = 19$

What is the right sign?
Draw <, >, or =.

Lessons 97, 98, 99

⑱ $13 \boxed{<} 18$ ⑲ $27 \boxed{<} 37$

⑳ $9 + 2 \boxed{=} 11$ ㉑ $38 \boxed{>} 37$

NOTE TO HOME
Students review unit skills and concepts.

Copyright © SRA/McGraw-Hill

Problems 12–17 Spend a little time with a student who puts the wrong signs, or numbers instead of operation signs, in the hexagons. First, see if the student can write expressions like 4 + 3 = 7 and 8 − 4 = 4 when you dictate them. Then see if he or she can make up similar expressions independently and tell you what they mean.

 Problems 26–29 Play the "Hidden Counters Puzzle" game (Lesson 99) with students having difficulties with missing-addend problems, or have able students play with them.

Work through written problems with students who fail to understand the written problem form. Have them verbalize the problems. For example: "5 plus how many equals 8?"

Demonstrate missing-addend problems on a **math balance***. For instance, place a 10 on one side of the balance. Place a 6 on the opposite side. Then ask the student to find the number that when added to 6 will balance the 10 (4).

 Problems 18–21 Playing the "Hungry Alligator" game (Lesson 67) with an able partner may be helpful for students who have difficulty with relation signs, but students who are having a lot of trouble with this kind of problem need individual help in thinking through the problems and verbalizing the process of solution. For example: "7 plus 8 is 15. The other side has a 15 too, so they're equal. I put in an equal sign."

 Performance Assessment The Performance Assessment Tasks 4–6 provided on page 70 of the Assessment Blackline Masters can be used at this time to evaluate students' abilities to use coins to form amounts of money.

 Portfolio Assessment If you have not already completed the Portfolio Assessment task provided on page 81 of the Assessment Blackline Masters, it can be used at this time to evaluate students' abilities to use fractional lengths.

Unit Project If you have not already assigned the "Paper Folding" project on pages 258a–258b, you may want to do so at this time. The Unit Project is a good opportunity for students to apply the concepts of counting and writing numbers in real-world problem solving.

◆ **LESSON 114 Unit 3 Review**

Name _____

How many now?

Lessons
93, 94

㉒  16 18

㉓  38 38

㉔ 22 19

㉕  18 21

ALGEBRA READINESS

Solve these problems.

㉖ $8 + \boxed{2} = 10$ ㉗ $3 + \boxed{0} = 3$

Lessons
99, 100

㉘ $5 + \boxed{5} = 10$ ㉙ $2 + \boxed{1} = 3$

NOTE TO HOME
Students review unit skills and concepts.

Unit 3 Review • **251**

Students who have difficulty with this Unit Review should have further opportunity to review and to practice the skills before they proceed on with the next unit. For each set of problems there are specific suggestions for reteaching. These suggestions can be found in the margins.

◆ **LESSON 114** Unit 3 Review

Possible answers are shown.
Draw coins to make the right amount.

REAL-WORLD CONNECTION

Lessons 88, 91

③⓪ 23¢ (10) (10) (1) (1) (1)

③① 46¢ (10) (10) (10) (10) (5) (1)

③② 29¢ (10) (10) (5) (1) (1) (1) (1)

ALGEBRA READINESS

Fill in the missing numbers.
Write the rule.

Lessons 95, 97, 98, 109

③③
In	Out
8	7
33	32
27	26
18	**17**
6	5

③④
In	Out
4	6
6	8
11	13
18	20
24	26

③⑤
In	Out
2	4
5	7
8	10
6	**8**
10	12

Rule **−1**   Rule **+2**   Rule **+2**

Copyright © SRA/McGraw-Hill

252 • Measurement and Geometry

NOTE TO HOME
Students review unit skills and concepts.

PRACTICE p. 114

ENRICHMENT p. 114

Student Edition pages 253–256

Unit 3 Test

Using the Student Pages
This Unit Test on Student Edition pages 253–256 provides an opportunity to formally evaluate your students' proficiency with concepts developed in this unit. It is similar in content and format to the Unit Review. Students who did well on the Unit Review may not need to take this test. Students who did not do well on the Unit Review should be provided with additional practice opportunities, such as the Unit Practice pages, before taking the Unit Test. For further evaluation, you may wish to have these students take the Unit Test in standardized format, provided on pages 104–111 in the Assessment Blackline Masters or the Unit Test on pages 42–45 in the Assessment Blackline Masters.

Name _____

Unit 3 Test

Check your math skills.
Fill in the missing numbers.

1 19 | **20** | **21** | 22 | **23** | 24

2 10 | 20 | **30** | **40** | 50 | 60

3 25 | 26 | **27** | **28** | 29 | 30

4 20 | 19 | 18 | **17** | **16** | 15

How many now?

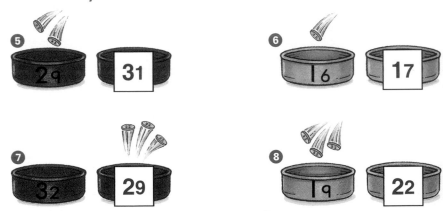

5 29 | **31**   **6** 16 | **17**

7 32 | **29**   **8** 19 | **22**

NOTE TO HOME
This test checks unit skills and concepts.

Unit 3 Test • 253

Copyright © SRA/McGraw-Hill

◆ **LESSON 115 Unit 3 Test**

How many cents?

⑨   **32** ¢

⑩   **27** ¢

Solve these problems.

⑪ $8 + 2 =$ __**10**__   ⑫ $18 + 2 =$ __**20**__

⑬ $29 + 2 =$ __**31**__   ⑭ $40 - 1 =$ __**39**__

What is the right sign?
Draw + or −.

⑮ $4 \; \langle + \rangle \; 4 = 8$ ⑯ $28 \; \langle - \rangle \; 3 = 25$

⑰ $6 \; \langle - \rangle \; 5 = 1$ ⑱ $28 \; \langle + \rangle \; 3 = 31$

⑲ $9 \; \langle - \rangle \; 2 = 7$ ⑳ $19 \; \langle + \rangle \; 2 = 21$

NOTE TO HOME
This test checks skills and concepts.

◆ **LESSON 115 Unit 3 Test**

Name _____

 Solve these problems.

㉑ 5 + **5** = 10   ㉒ 4 + **2** = 6

㉓ 6 + **1** = 7   ㉔ 3 + **1** = 4

㉕ 7 + **3** = 10   ㉖ 5 + **0** = 5

What is the right sign?
Draw >, <, or =.

㉗ 23 (<) 46   ㉘ 9 + 1 (>) 7

㉙ 7 + 1 (=) 8   ㉚ 12 (<) 21

㉛ 31 (>) 28   ㉜ 11 − 2 (<) 10

㉝ 18 + 7 (<) 30   ㉞ 5 + 5 (<) 15

㉟ 16 − 2 (<) 19   ㊱ 15 − 3 (=) 12

 NOTE TO HOME
This test checks unit skills and concepts.

Unit 3 Test • 255

RETEACHING

Students who have difficulty with this Unit Test should have further opportunity to review and to practice the skills before they proceed on with the next unit. After students have reviewed the skills, you may want to use the Unit Test on pages 42–45 in the Assessment Blackline Masters, which cover the Unit 3 concepts.

PRACTICE p. 115

LESSON **115** PRACTICE Name _____

What is the right sign? Draw <, >, or =.

❶ 32 (<) 35   ❷ 15 (<) 25

❸ 28 (>) 18   ❹ 34 (<) 40

❺ 40 (>) 20   ❻ 29 (=) 29

❼ 37 (>) 36   ❽ 12 (<) 21

❾ 22 (<) 31   ❿ 20 (>) 19

⓫ 17 (<) 25   ⓬ 33 (<) 39

⓭ 34 (=) 34   ⓮ 15 (>) 9

⓯ 27 (<) 30   ⓰ 31 (>) 13

Math Explorations and Applications Level 1 • **115**

◆ **LESSON 115 Unit 3 Test**

Draw coins to make the right amount.

37 36¢ ⓾ ⓾ ⓾ ⑤ ①

38 22¢ ⓾ ⓾ ① ①

Fill in the missing numbers.
Write the rule.

39

In	Out
3	6
8	11
15	18
30	33
24	27

Rule +3

40

In	Out
6	4
34	32
19	17
24	22
9	7

Rule −2

256 • Measurement and Geometry

NOTE TO HOME
This test checks unit skills and concepts.

ENRICHMENT p. 115

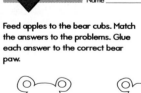
LESSON **115** ENRICHMENT   Name _____

Feed apples to the bear cubs. Match the answers to the problems. Glue each answer to the correct bear paw.

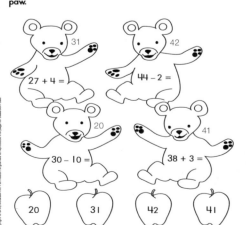

31   42

27 + 4 =   44 − 2 =

20   41

30 − 10 =   38 + 3 =

20   31   42   41

ASSESSMENT p. 42

UNIT **3**   Unit 3 Test (Use after Lesson 114.)   Page 1 of 4

Name _____

The student demonstrates mastery by correctly answering 32 of the 40 problems.

Fill in the missing numbers.

❶ 18 19 20 21 22 23

❷ 20 30 40 50 60 70

❸ 5 10 15 20 25 30

How many now?

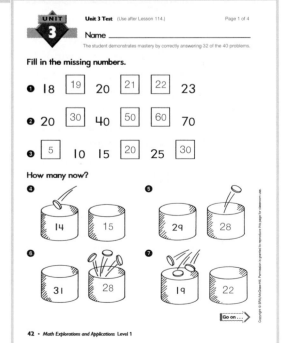

❹ 14 15

❺ 29 28

❻ 31 28

❼ 19 22

Go on ...

LESSON 116

Student Edition pages 257–258

Extending the Unit

Name _____

Extending the Unit

What is the answer in each space? **Check students' drawings carefully.**

Color 14 red.

Color 7 green.

Color 12 orange.

Color 8 purple.

5 + 2

8 + 4

7 + 7 ⊙

3 + 4

2 + 5

6 + 6

12 + 2

4 + 4

9 + 5

11 + 3

13 + 1

4 + 10

6 + 1

6 + 8

12 + 2

6 + 2

1 + 6

4 + 3

Copyright © SRA/McGraw-Hill

NOTE TO HOME
Students solve addition problems on a number puzzle.

Unit 3 Lesson 116 • **257**

LESSON PLANNER

Objective

▶ to provide practice in simple arithmetic using a fun activity

Context of the Lesson This is the third "Extending the Unit" lesson. The first was Lesson 41 and the second was Lesson 83.

Materials

crayons

Program Resources

"Addition Table" Game Mats

Practice Master 116

Enrichment Master 116

For extra practice:
  CD-ROM* Lesson 116
  Mixed Practice, page 373

---

❶ Warm-Up ⏱ 5 MINUTES

Problem of the Day Present the following problem to the class. You have two pennies and two nickels. Do you have enough money to buy a 22¢ bag of raisins? Why or why not? (No, because two pennies and two nickels are only twelve cents.)

Problem-Solving Strategies Ask students who have solved the Problem of the Day to share how they solved it and any strategies they used.

 Use mental math to add or subtract.

a. $24 + 3 = (27)$ b. $17 - 1 = (16)$

c. $30 - 2 = (28)$ d. $25 + 2 = (27)$

e. $19 - 2 = (17)$ f. $19 + 2 = (21)$

❷ Teach

Using the Student Pages Use page 257 for remediation and review of addition facts. Have students use **crayons** to complete the page on their own, then share the results and discuss the final picture.

Students can then work in pairs, using page 258 as enrichment. Have each pair create their own puzzle like the

---

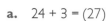

Art Connection Have students work in groups to make puzzles like those on page 258. Have them make rough copies of their puzzles on paper. Check that they are interesting and correct, then have each group copy the finished puzzle onto posterboard. Have them challenge other classes to complete the puzzles.

RETEACHING

Students who need reteaching with simple addition and subtraction facts can work with partners using flash cards to practice the facts.

---

257 Measurement and Geometry

*available separately

◆ **LESSON 116** Extending the Unit

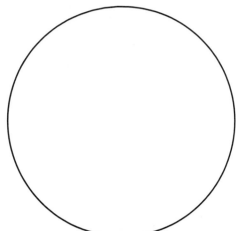
Make your own puzzle.
Write some problems.

Use the Mixed Practice on page 373 after this lesson.

Tell what to color.

Answers will depend on numbers chosen.

Color ☐ red.

Color ☐ green.

Color ☐ orange.

Color ☐ purple.

Trade puzzles with a classmate. Solve them.

258 • Measurement and Geometry

NOTE TO HOME
Students create their own number puzzles.

Copyright © SRA/McGraw-Hill

---

one on page 257. Explain that they can simply make a design as the ending picture. Have pairs exchange and solve each other's puzzles when finished.

 Using the "Addition Table" Game Mats Have students play the "Addition Table" or "Harder Addition Table" game to provide further practice with basic addition facts. These games were first introduced in Lesson 69. Complete directions for playing are on the Game Mats. A copy of this game can also be found on pages 392–393 of this Guide.

❸ Wrap-Up

In Closing Make copies of several student-made puzzles and have the rest of the class color them in.

 **Informal Assessment** Use students' answers to page 257 and puzzles on page 258 as an informal assessment of their knowledge of addition facts.

Assessment Criteria

Did the student . . .

✓ correctly fill in the puzzle on page 257 and make an interesting and accurate puzzle on page 258?

✓ correctly complete a classmate's puzzle?

PRACTICE p. 116

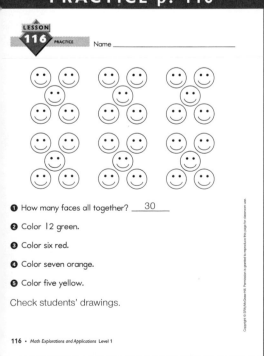

LESSON
116 PRACTICE Name _____

❶ How many faces all together? __30__

❷ Color 12 green.

❸ Color six red.

❹ Color seven orange.

❺ Color five yellow.

Check students' drawings.

116 • *Math Explorations and Applications* Level 1

ENRICHMENT p. 116

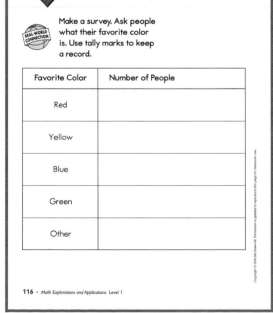

LESSON
116 ENRICHMENT Name _____

 REAL-WORLD CONNECTION
Make a survey. Ask people what their favorite color is. Use tally marks to keep a record.

Favorite Color	Number of People
Red	
Yellow	
Blue	
Green	
Other	

116 • *Math Explorations and Applications* Level 1

No matter how well children understand the basis for the addition facts, they will need lots of practice to make them automatic. Unless these facts are automatic, children will use their time and creativity to reconstruct the addition facts when they should have gone on to bigger and better things. Thus, practice is essential.

—Stephen S. Willoughby,
Mathematics Education for a Changing World

UNIT 3 Wrap-Up

PRESENTING THE PROJECT

Project Objectives

▶ to provide practice recognizing properties of a square

▶ to demonstrate the relationship between fractional parts and the whole

▶ to provide practice in counting

 MANIPULATIVES

two different-sized square sheets of paper, one of each size per student

Program Resources

Here Be Giants*
  from the Literature Library

SRA's *Minds on Math**

 In this project, students conduct a paper-folding exercise to explore properties of a square and the relationship between fractional parts and the whole. Start by giving each student a square sheet of **paper**, such as one trimmed to $8\frac{1}{2} \times 8\frac{1}{2}$ inches. Ask students to identify the shape of the paper. Have students fold the square in half, and in half again. Have students count the number of squares they have made as they unfold the paper. (4) Then have students refold the paper, and continue folding it in half until it is as small as they can make it. When students are finished folding, have them compare folded squares. Did each student fold the paper to the same size? Challenge students to estimate the number of squares they now have formed. Then have students count to check estimates. On the sheet of paper, have students record the number of small squares formed. Point out that each small square is the same size as each other small square. Each is one part or fraction of the whole square.

Provide a larger square sheet of paper to each student. Challenge students to predict how many squares they will form by folding this paper. Will there be more or fewer squares formed? (more) Have students repeat the folding, estimating, counting, and recording activities as they did with the first sheet of paper. Discuss the results.

What Is a Math Project? If this is the first time you have used math projects in your classroom, you may want to refer to pages 92a–92b in this Teacher's Guide for more detailed information about effectively implementing projects.

Wrapping Up the Project Ask volunteers to share the method they used to count the small squares. Remind students that marking items as they are counted is one way to help keep count. Then have students look through magazines to find food pictures that can be divided into equal parts. Have them cut the food pictures into equal parts and glue the parts onto a piece of paper.

*available separately

 **Minds on Math** SRA's *Minds on Math* is a series of units covering Problem Solving, Data Collection, Number Sense, Measurement, Money, and Geometry and Spatial Relations. Each unit provides a series of open-ended projects for individuals or small groups. These projects develop problem-solving and critical-thinking skills, utilize real-world materials, emphasize language, and integrate cross-curricular connections. Use projects from *Measurement* to focus on investigating a variety of nonstandard units.

 Assessing the Project Observe the students during the paper-folding activity. Did they identify the shape of the paper? Do they recognize that a fraction is a part of a whole?

 Performance Assessment Have students make several different shapes and divide them into equivalent parts.

 Literature Connection You may want to read aloud *Eating Fractions* by Bruce McMillan to extend the lesson by discussing foods that can be cut into pieces or fractions. You can also use the lap book *Here Be Giants* from the Literature Library* to follow a mapmaker's story as he uses statistics and measurement.

 Technology Connection The software *KidsMath* from Great Wave Software (Macintosh, for grades K–3) provides practice in identifying fractions, part-to-whole relationships, and counting.

UNIT 4
Numbers 1–100
USING NUMBERS

OVERVIEW

This unit begins with students expanding their ability to count numbers through 100. Students add and subtract multiples of 10 and, throughout the unit, learn to add or subtract 0, 1, 2, or 10 to a number less than 100. Students learn to estimate answers and expand their knowledge of basic facts through 10 + 10. In addition, students learn more about solid figures and identify open and closed figures and congruent figures. They record data, compare numbers, tell time, and do some multiplication readiness by exploring arrays and repeated addition. Students solve many problems about money and find the values of collections of coins that include quarters.

Integrated Topics in This Unit Include:

- ◆ counting through 100
- ◆ adding and subtracting multiples of 10
- ◆ approximating answers
- ◆ recording data
- ◆ twice as many and half as many
- ◆ comparing numbers
- ◆ finding missing addends
- ◆ using an addition table to find sums
- ◆ writing addition sentences for a given sum
- ◆ adding 0, 1, 2 or 10 to a number less than 100
- ◆ adding 8 or 9 to a number
- ◆ applying addition skills

- ◆ using calculators
- ◆ using arrays and repeated additions
- ◆ adding and subtracting money
- ◆ telling time
- ◆ using ordinal numbers
- ◆ counting by fives and using that skill with tallies and nickels

APPLYING ADDITION SKILLS
REPEATED ADDITION

> "*Intuition about number relationships helps children make judgments about the reasonableness of computational results and of proposed solutions to numerical problems. Such intuition requires good number sense. Children with good number sense (1) have well-understood number meanings, (2) have developed multiple relationships among numbers, (3) recognize the relative magnitudes of numbers, (4) know the relative effect of operating on numbers, and (5) develop referents for measures of common objects and situations in their environments.*"
>
> —*NCTM Curriculum and Evaluation Standards for School Mathematics*

GAMES

Motivating Mixed Practice

Games provide **basic math skills** practice in cooperative groups and develop **mathematical reasoning.**

THINKING STORY

Integrated Problem Solving

Thinking Stories provide opportunities for students to work in **cooperative groups** and develop **logical reasoning** while they integrate **reading skills** with mathematics.

Story Summaries "The Third House on Fungo Street" focuses on using the process of elimination to solve a problem.

"The Lemonade War" explores the uses of arithmetic facts in money transactions, pricing, and making change.

In "Mr. Mudancia Changes Houses" students will have an opportunity to use common sense and their arithmetic skills.

"Trouble in the Garden" focuses on using basic arithmetic facts in everyday situations.

In "How Deep Is the Water?" students get a chance to use common sense as well as their measuring and counting skills.

PROJECT

Making Connections

The Unit Project makes real-world connections. Students work in **cooperative groups** to problem-solve and to communicate their findings.

The project presented in the Unit Wrap-Up asks students to use calculators to form greatest and least numbers and patterns.

LESSON		PACING	PRIMARY OBJECTIVES	FEATURE	RESOURCES	NCTM STANDARDS
117	Numbers Through 100....261–262	1 day	to teach the ordinal position of numbers through 100		Practice Master 117 Enrichment Master 117	4, 6
118	Multiples of 10..........263–264	1 day	to teach students to add and subtract multiples of ten in which the answers are less than 100	Game	Practice Master 118 Enrichment Master 118	3, 7, 13
119	Adding and Subtracting Multiples of 10..........265–266	1 day	✓ to assess addition and subtraction of two numbers in the 0–100 range in which one or both of the numbers is a multiple of 10	Game	Reteaching Master Practice Master 119 Enrichment Master 119 Assessment Master	7, 8
120	Approximating Answers...................267–268	1 day	✓ to assess mastery of forming given amounts of money up to $100, using $1, $5, $10, $20, and $100 bills	Game	Practice Master 120 Enrichment Master 120 Assessment Master	1, 2, 3, 4, 5, 6, 7
121	Studying the Cube........269–270	1 day	to introduce the parts of a cube	Game	Practice Master 121 Enrichment Master 121	9
122	Mental Math.............271–272	1 day	✓ to assess mastery of mental addition and subtraction of 0, 1, or 2 with numbers through 100		Reteaching Master Practice Master 122 Enrichment Master 122 Assessment Master	1, 2, 3, 4, 7, 8
123	Counting and Recording Frequencies..............273–274	1 day	to practice using tally marks to count and record frequencies of events	Thinking Story	Practice Master 117 Enrichment Master 117	1, 2, 3, 4, 11
124	Using Doubles............274–276	1 day	to memorize doubles of numbers from 6 through 10		Practice Master 124 Enrichment Master 124	1, 2, 3, 4, 7, 8, 13
125	Twice or Half as Many 277–278	1 day	to teach students to solve problems that involve "twice as many" and "half as many"	Game	Reteaching Master Practice Master 125 Enrichment Master 125	1, 2, 3, 4, 7, 8, 12
126	Inequalities (0–100)......279–280	1 day	to teach students to use the correct relation sign between any two numbers in the 0–100 range	Game	Practice Master 126 Enrichment Master 126	6, 13
127	Comparing Numbers (0–100)..................281–282	1 day	✓ to assess mastery of inequalities and equalities in the 0-100 range		Reteaching Master Practicing Master 127 Enrichment Master 127 Assessment Master	6, 7, 8
128	Missing Addends..........283–284	1 day	to teach students to use concrete objects to solve problems that have the first term missing	Thinking Story Game	Practice Master 128 Enrichment Master 128	3, 7, 8
129	Number Sentences........285–286	1 day	to teach students to use an addition table to find the sums of numbers through 10 + 10	Game	Practice Master 129 Enrichment Master 129	7, 8
130	Adding 0, 1, 2, and 10 287–288	1 day	to teach students to give addition facts in which one or both addends are 0, 1, 2, or 10	Game	Practice Master 130 Enrichment Master 130	4, 7, 8
131	Adding 8 and 9 289–290	1 day	to teach students strategies for learning addition facts with 8 and 9		Reteaching Master Practice Master 131 Enrichment Master 131	7, 8
132	Open and Closed Figures 291–292	1 day	to teach students to distinguish between open and closed figures	Game	Reteaching Master Practice Master 132 Enrichment Master 132	9
133	Using Doubles 293–294	1 day	to practice addition facts for doubles		Reteaching Master Practice Master 133 Enrichment Master 133	1, 2, 3, 4, 7, 8
134	Make Ten.................295–296	1 day	to provide practice memorizing addition facts summing to 10	Thinking Story Game	Practice Master 134 Enrichment Master 134	1, 2, 3, 4, 8
135	Using a Known Fact.......297–298	1 day	✓ to assess mastery of addition facts through 10 + 10	Game	Practice Master 135 Enrichment Master 135 Assessment Master	7, 8

LESSON	PACING	PRIMARY OBJECTIVES	FEATURE	RESOURCES	NCTM STANDARDS
136 Reviewing Addition Facts 299–300	1 day	to provide practice using the addition facts through 10 + 10		Reteaching Master Practice Master 136 Enrichment Master 136	1, 2, 3, 4, 8
137 Two-Digit Addition 301–302	1 day	to prepare students to add two-digit numbers		Practice Master 137 Enrichment Master 137	3, 7, 8
138 Exploring Regrouping 303–304	2 days	to prepare students to subtract two-digit numbers		Reteaching Master Practice Master 138 Enrichment Master 138	7, 8
Mid-Unit Review 305–306	1 day		♦	Assessment Master	
139 Repeated Addition 307–308	1 day	to introduce the process of repeated addition	Game	Practice Master 139 Enrichment Master 139	7, 8, 10
140 Using Arrays and Repeated Addition 309–310	1 day	to introduce students to multiplication using arrays		Practice Master 140 Enrichment Master 140	1, 2, 3, 4, 7
141 Congruent Figures 311–312	1 day	to introduce the concept of congruency		Practice Master 141 Enrichment Master 141	9
142 What Comes Next? 313–314	1 day	to provide practice solving arithmetic problems that use conventional numbers	Thinking Story	Practice Master 142 Enrichment Master 142	1, 2, 3, 4, 6, 8
143 Adding and Subtracting Money 315–316	1 day	✓ to assess mastery of reading and writing conventional numbers	♦	Practice Master 143 Enrichment Master 143 Assessment Master	1, 2, 3, 4, 8, 11
144 Greatest and Least 317–318	1 day	to provide practice finding the greatest and least numbers in sets of up to five numbers	Game	Reteaching Master Practice Master 144 Enrichment Master 144	1, 2, 3, 4, 6
145 Telling Time—Hour and Half Hour 319–320	1 day	to introduce students to telling time to the hour and half hour	Game	Practice Master 145 Enrichment Master 145	10
146 Telling and Estimating Time 321–324	2 days	to provide experience in estimating and telling time of day	Game	Practice Master 146 Enrichment Master 146	10
147 Using a Calendar 325–328	1 day	to introduce the monthly calendar	Game	Reteaching Master Practice Master 147 Enrichment Master 147	6, 10
148 Symmetry 329–330	1 day	to introduce symmetry	Thinking Story	Practice Master 148 Enrichment Master 148	1, 2, 3, 4, 8, 9
149 Counting by Fives 331–332	1 day	to show students the relationship between fives and tens	Game	Practice Master 149 Enrichment Master 149	11, 13
150 Counting Nickels 333–334	1 day	to provide practice determining the value of a number of nickels	Thinking Story	Reteaching Master Practice Master 150 Enrichment Master 150	1, 2, 3, 4, 7, 8
151 Amounts of Money 335–336	1 day	to use quarters to make amounts of money		Practice Master 151 Enrichment Master 151	6, 7, 8, 13
152 Quarters, Dimes, and Nickels 337–338	1 day	to review forming amounts of money with combinations of coins	Thinking Story	Reteaching Master Practice Master 152 Enrichment Master 152	1, 2, 3, 4, 6, 13
153 Unit 4 Review 339–342		to review numbers 1–100		Practice Master 153 Enrichment Master 153	
154 Unit 4 Test 343–346		to review numbers 1–100	♦	Practice Master 154 Enrichment Master 154 Assessment Master	
155 Extending the Unit 347–348		to review numbers 1–100		Practice Master 155 Enrichment Master 155	
Unit 4 Wrap-Up 348a–348b		to review numbers 1–100	Project		

UNIT CONNECTIONS

INTERVENTION STRATEGIES

In this Teacher's Guide there will be specific strategies suggested for students with individual needs—ESL, Gifted and Talented, Special Needs, Learning Styles, and At Risk. These strategies will be given at the point of use. Here are the icons to look for and the types of strategies that will accompany them:

English as a Second Language
These strategies, designed for students who do not fluently speak the English language, will suggest meaningful ways to present the lesson concepts and vocabulary.

Gifted and Talented
Strategies to enrich and extend the lesson will offer further challenges to students who have easily mastered the concepts already presented.

Special Needs
Students who are physically challenged or who have learning disabilities may require alternative ways to complete activities, record answers, use manipulatives, and so on. The strategies labeled with this icon will offer appropriate methods of teaching lesson concepts to these students.

Learning Styles
Each student has his or her individual approach to learning. The strategies labeled with this icon suggest ways to present lesson concepts so that various learning modalities—such as tactile/kinesthetic, visual, and auditory—can be addressed.

At Risk
These strategies highlight the relevancy of the skills presented, making the connection between school and real life. They are directed toward students that appear to be at risk of dropping out of school before graduation.

TECHNOLOGY CONNECTIONS

The following materials, designed to reinforce and extend lesson concepts, will be referred to throughout this Teacher's Guide. It might be helpful to order this software, or check it out of the school media center or local community library.

 Look for this **Technology Connection** *icon.*

♦ *Home Grade Level Math Programs,* from Jostens Home Learning, Mac, IBM, for grade 1 (software)

♦ *Interactive Math Journey,* from The Learning Company, Mac, IBM, for grades 1–3 (software)

♦ *JumpStart First Grade,* from Knowledge Adventure, Mac, IBM, for grades K–1 (software)

♦ *The Math Majors,* from Nordic Software, Mac, IBM, for grades K–6 (software)

♦ *Math Shop Jr.,* from Scholastic, Mac, IBM, for grades 1–4 (software)

♦ *Peter's Growing Patterns,* from Strawberry Hill, Apple, for grades K and up (software)

♦ *Stickybear's Math Town,* from Optimum Resources, Mac, for grades K–4 (software)

♦ *Treasure Math Storm!,* from The Learning Company, Mac, IBM, for grades K–4 (software)

♦ *Treasure Galaxy!,* from The Learning Company, Mac, IBM, for grades K–9 (software)

CROSS-CURRICULAR CONNECTIONS

This Teacher's Guide offers specific suggestions on ways to connect the math concepts presented in this unit with other subjects students are studying. Students can connect math concepts with topics they already know about and can find examples of math in other subjects and in real-world situations. These strategies will be given at the point of use.

Look for these icons:

 Geography

 Social Studies

 Science

 Art

 Language Arts

 Health

 Music

 Math

 Physical Education

 Careers

LITERATURE CONNECTIONS

These books will be presented throughout the Teacher's Guide at the point where they could be used to introduce, reinforce, or extend specific lesson concepts. You may want to locate these books in your school or your local community library.

 Look for this **Literature Connection** *icon.*

◆ *Over in the Meadow: An Old Nursery Counting Rhyme,* adapted by Paul Galdone, Prentice-Hall, 1986

◆ *Anno's Math Games II* by Mitsumasa Anno, Philomel Books, 1989

◆ *Me First* by Helen Lester, Houghton Mifflin, 1992

◆ *Animal Orchestra* by Scott Gustafson, Contemporary Books, 1988

◆ *Domino Addition* by Lynette Long, Charlesbridge Publishing, 1996

◆ *The Doorbell Rang* by Pat Hutchins

◆ *Shapes* by Marion Smoothey, Marshall Cavendish, 1993

◆ *Time* by Henry Pluckrose, Childrens Press, 1995

◆ *The Boy Who Stopped Time* by Anthony Taber, Margaret K. McElderry Books, 1993

◆ *The Seasons of Arnold's Apple Tree* by Gail Gibbons, Greenwillow Books, 1983

◆ *Shapes in Nature* by Judy Feldman, Children's Books, 1991

◆ *Number Families* by Jane Jonas Srivastava, Crowell, 1979

◆ *Annabelle Swift, Kindergartner* by Amy Schwartz, Orchard Books, 1988

◆ *Arthur's Funny Money* by Lillian Hoban, HarperCollins, 1981

ASSESSMENT OPPORTUNITIES AT-A-GLANCE

LESSON	PORTFOLIO	PERFORMANCE	FORMAL	SELF	INFORMAL	MIXED PRACTICE	MULTIPLE CHOICE	MASTERY CHECKPOINTS	ANALYZING ANSWERS
117					✓				
118					✓	✓			
119			✓					✓	
120			✓					✓	
121		✓							
122			✓					✓	
123		✓				✓			
124					✓				
125				✓					
126					✓				
127			✓					✓	
128					✓				
129		✓				✓			
130				✓					
131				✓					
132	✓								
133					✓	✓			
134				✓					
135			✓					✓	
136					✓				
137		✓							
138		✓				✓			
Mid-Unit Review	✓	✓	✓						
139					✓				
140				✓		✓			
141		✓							
142		✓							✓
143			✓					✓	
144					✓	✓			
145		✓							
146					✓	✓			
147					✓	✓			
148	✓								
149					✓				
150					✓				
151		✓							
152				✓		✓			
Unit Review	✓	✓	✓						
Unit Test			✓				✓		
155		✓				✓			

✓ ASSESSMENT OPTIONS

PORTFOLIO ASSESSMENT

Throughout this Teacher's Guide are suggested activities in which students draw pictures, make graphs, write about mathematics, and so on. Keep students' work to assess growth of understanding as the year progresses.

Lessons 132, Mid-Unit Review, 148, 153, and Unit Review

PERFORMANCE ASSESSMENT

Performance assessment items focus on evaluating how students think and work as they solve problems. Opportunities for performance assessment can be found throughout the unit. Rubrics and guides for grading can be found in the front of the Assessment Blackline Masters.

Lessons 121, 123, 129, 137, 138, Mid-Unit Review, 141, 142, 145, 151, Unit Review, and 155

FORMAL ASSESSMENT

A Mid-Unit Review and Unit Test help assess students' understanding of concepts, skills, and problem solving. The *Math Explorations and Applications* CD-ROM Test Generator can create additional unit tests at three ability levels. Also, Mastery Checkpoints are provided periodically throughout the unit.

Lessons 119, 120, 122, 127, 135, Mid-Unit Review, 143, Unit Review, and Unit Test

SELF ASSESSMENT

Throughout the program students are given the opportunity to check their own math skills.

Lessons 125, 130, 131, 134, 140, and 152

INFORMAL ASSESSMENT

A variety of assessment suggestions is provided, including interviews, oral questions or presentation, debates, and so on. Also, each lesson includes Assessment Criteria—a list of questions about each student's progress, understanding, and participation.

Lessons 117, 118, 124, 126, 128, 133, 136, 139, 144, 146, 147, 149, and 150

MIXED PRACTICE

Mixed Practices, covering material presented thus far in the year, are provided in the unit for use as either assessment or practice.

Lessons 118, 123, 129, 133, 138, 140, 144, 146, 147, 152, 155

MULTIPLE-CHOICE TESTS (STANDARDIZED FORMAT)

Each unit provides a unit test in standardized format, presenting students with an opportunity to practice taking a test in this format.

MASTERY CHECKPOINT

Mastery Checkpoints are provided throughout the unit to assess student proficiency in specific skills. Checkpoints reference appropriate Assessment Blackline Masters and other assessment options. Results of these evaluations can be recorded on the Mastery Checkpoint Chart.

Lessons 119, 120, 122, 127, 135, and 143

ANALYZING ANSWERS

Analyzing Answers items suggest possible sources of student error and offer teaching strategies for addressing difficulties.

Lesson 142

Look for these icons:

> ❝*Although assessment is done for a variety of reasons, its main goal is to advance students' learning and inform teachers as they make instructional decisions.*❞
>
> —*NCTM Assessment Standards*

MASTERY CHECKPOINTS

WHAT TO EXPECT FROM STUDENTS AS THEY COMPLETE THIS UNIT

⑱ ADDING AND SUBTRACTING MULTIPLES OF 10—LESSON 119

Most students should be able to add and subtract multiples of ten (0–100) in problems that have both or only one of the numbers as a multiple of ten. Students should be able to correctly answer 80% of the problems on pages 265–266 or on pages 46–47 of the Assessment Blackline Masters. The results of this assessment may be recorded on the Mastery Checkpoint Chart.

⑲ FAMILIARITY WITH BILLS—LESSON 120

Students should now be able to form any amount of money through $100 by using $1, $5, $10, and $20 bills and to correctly trade bills of one denomination for those of a higher denomination. These skills may be assessed by using page 268 or by assigning page 48 of the Assessment Blackline Masters. The results of this assessment may be recorded on the Mastery Checkpoint Chart.

⑳ MENTAL ADDITION AND SUBTRACTION (0–100)—LESSON 122

Most students should now be able to add 0, 1, or 2 mentally with numbers through 100. This ability may be assessed during the demonstration, during work on page 271, or by assigning page 49 of the Assessment Blackline Masters. Results of this assessment may be recorded on the Mastery Checkpoint Chart.

㉑ INEQUALITIES AND EQUALITIES (0–100)—LESSON 127

At about this time students should be able to insert the correct sign between any two numbers or in addition and subtraction sentences in the 0–100 range. This ability may be assessed using page 281 or page 50 of the Assessment Blackline Masters. Results of this assessment may be recorded on the Mastery Checkpoint Chart.

㉒ ADDITION FACTS THROUGH 10 + 10—LESSON 135

At about this time students should demonstrate mastery of the addition facts through 10 + 10 by getting eight of the ten problems on page 298 correct in two to three minutes. You may also wish to assign pages 51–52 of the Assessment Blackline Masters to determine mastery. Results of this assessment may be recorded on the Mastery Checkpoint Chart.

㉓ CONVENTIONAL NUMBERS—LESSON 143

At about this time students should have made substantial progress in using conventional numbers. You can assess their progress through informal classroom observations or by assigning page 56 of the Assessment Blackline Masters. Results of this assessment may be recorded on the Mastery Checkpoint Chart.

UNIT 4

PROGRAM RESOURCES

THESE ADDITIONAL COMPONENTS OF *MATH EXPLORATIONS AND APPLICATIONS* CAN BE PURCHASED SEPARATELY FROM SRA/McGRAW-HILL.

LESSON	BASIC MANIPULATIVE KIT	GAME PACKAGE	TEACHER KIT	OPTIONAL MANIPULATIVE KIT	OVERHEAD MANIPULATIVE KIT	MATH EXPLORATIONS AND APPLICATIONS CD-ROM	LITERATURE LIBRARY
117	Number Cubes	School Bookstore Game				Lesson 117	
118	Number Cubes	10 Below 0 Game, play money			bills, coins	Lesson 118	
119	Number Cubes					Lesson 119	
120	Number Cubes	Yard Sale Game, play money			bills	Lesson 120	
121	Number Cubes	Space Game				Lesson 121	
122	Number Cubes					Lesson 122	
123	Number Cubes					Lesson 123	
124	Number Cubes					Lesson 124	
125	Number Cubes			counters	counters	Lesson 125	
126	Number Cubes					Lesson 126	*How Do You Measure Up?*
127	Number Cubes					Lesson 127	
128	Number Cubes					Lesson 128	
129	Number Cubes	Addition Table Game		counters	counters	Lesson 129	
130	Number Cubes	Harder Addition Table Game				Lesson 130	
131	Number Cubes	play money			coins	Lesson 131	
132	Number Cubes					Lesson 132	
133	Number Cubes					Lesson 133	
134	Number Cubes	Harder Pattern Game				Lesson 134	
135	Number Cubes	Frog Pond Game				Lesson 135	
136	Number Cubes, Number Strips		math balance, scale/balance			Lesson 136	
137		play money		base-10 blocks	coins	Lesson 137	
138	Number Cubes			base-10 blocks		Lesson 138	
Mid-Unit Review							*Two More*
139	Number Cubes, Number Strips			counters		Lesson 139	
140	Number Cubes	play money		counters	coins, counters	Lesson 140	
141	Number Cubes		beakers			Lesson 141	
142	Number Cubes					Lesson 142	
143		play money			bills, coins	Lesson 143	
144	Number Cubes					Lesson 144	
145	Number Cubes	Clock Game	learning clock	clock faces	clock faces	Lesson 145	
146		Harder Clock Game	stopwatch, learning clock			Lesson 146	
147	Number Cubes	Calendar Game	learning clock			Lesson 147	*The Three Billy Goats Gruff*
148	Number Cubes					Lesson 148	
149	Number Cubes	Harder Flea Market Game				Lesson 149	
150	Number Cubes	play money			coins	Lesson 150	
151	Number Cubes	play money			coins	Lesson 151	
152	Number Cubes	play money			coins	Lesson 152	
153	Number Cubes					Lesson 153	
154						Lesson 154	
155	Number Cubes					Lesson 155	
Unit Wrap-Up							*Half a Slice of Bread and Butter*

UNIT 4

Numbers 1–100

INTRODUCING THE UNIT

Using the Student Pages Begin your discussion of the opening unit photo by asking students, "How much does it cost to ride a bus in your city?" Then read aloud the paragraph on the student page that highlights a career as a bus driver. This helps make the connection between school and work and encourages students to explore how math is used in the real world.

ACTIVITY Help students determine how many passengers one bus can carry, then ask them to estimate how many people ride buses in their town in a single day. You may wish to call the local transit authority for information.

FYI Explain to students that public transit was developed when people began to live in big cities. The need to get large numbers of people from their homes to their places of work became vital as populations became denser. The first intracity transit line was a coach system set up in Paris in the 1660s. By the mid-nineteenth century London had come up with large horse-drawn vans known as "omnibuses," a term that would eventually be shortened to the familiar "bus." As heavy surface traffic in cities became a problem, mass transit moved underground. Again, London led the way in 1863 with an underground railway that became known as the Tube. By the first years of the twentieth century, Paris and New York also had large underground rail systems, or subways. But buses continued to serve, evolving little from the first motor coaches introduced around 1910. While buses create more pollution than the smooth-running electric trains of a subway, they are a more flexible system for getting people directly where they need to go. They also reduce the number of cars on the road, make it possible for more people to get by without cars, and reduce the amount of pollution from cars. Few modern cities could run smoothly without buses.

UNIT 4

Numbers 1–100

USING NUMBERS

- **two-digit addition**
- **two-digit subtraction**
- **time**
- **money**
- **graphing**

259

Junior Thinklab™

SRA's *Junior Thinklab*™* provides a series of creative and logical problem-solving opportunities for individual students. The problems are designed to appeal to different cognitive abilities.

▶ Use Activity Cards 61–65 with this unit to reinforce Ordering.

▶ Use Activity Cards 66–70 with this unit to reinforce Classifying.

▶ Use Activity Cards 71–75 with this unit to reinforce Perception and Spatial Relations.

▶ Use Activity Cards 76–80 with this unit to reinforce Reasoning and Deducing.

▶ Use Divergent Thinking Activity Sheets 16–20 with this unit to encourage creativity in art and in intellectual activity.

SCHOOL TO WORK CONNECTION

Bus drivers use math . . .

Bus drivers know a lot about numbers. They count the number of people on the bus and the money that passengers pay to ride. They also count the minutes it takes to drive from stop to stop to stay on schedule.

Point out how necessary it is for a bus driver to have the math skills required to take fares quickly and efficiently. Keeping track of the number of passengers is also important. A driver must make these transactions swiftly in his or her head without using a calculator. Passengers must often know whether they have the correct amount of money to ride the bus, and in the proper denominations, as many bus systems will not make change.

Home Connections You may want to send the letter on Home Connections Blackline Masters pages 50–51 to families to introduce this unit.

Unit Project This would be a good time to assign the "Greatest and Least" project on pages 348a–348b. Students can begin working on the project in cooperative groups in their free time as you work through the unit. The Unit Project is a good opportunity for students to apply the concepts of forming greatest and least numbers and identifying and creating patterns in real-world problem solving.

Numbers Through 100

Student Edition pages 261–262

LESSON PLANNER

Objectives

▶ to teach the ordinal position of numbers through 100

▶ to provide opportunities to complete and locate numbers in a 0–100 number table

Context of the Lesson In Lesson 84 students worked with the ordinal position of numbers through 40.

MANIPULATIVES

drum (optional)

Program Resources

"School Bookstore" Game Mat

Number Cubes

Thinking Story Book, pages 94–95

Practice Master 117

Enrichment Master 117

For extra practice:
CD-ROM* Lesson 117

❶ Warm-Up ⏱ 5 MINUTES

Problem of the Day Present the following problem to the class. I am thinking of a number that is greater than 70 but less than 100. The second digit is a 0. The sum of its digits equals 11 – 2. What is the number? (90)

Problem-Solving Strategies Ask students who have solved the Problem of the Day to share how they solved it and any strategies they used.

Have students count on or back in unison to solve these problems:

a. 54 + 2 = (56)   b. 88 + 2 = (90)

c. 21 + 2 = (23)   d. 32 – 2 = (30)

e. 40 + 2 = (42)   f. 19 – 2 = (17)

g. 25 + 2 = (27)   h. 79 – 2 = (77)

i. 84 – 2 = (82)   j. 89 + 2 = (91)

❷ Teach

Using the Student Pages Have students fill in the missing numbers in the table on page 261. Then use the table for the following exercises:

261 Numbers 1–100

Name _____

Numbers Through 100

Fill in the missing numbers.

0	1	2	3	4	5	6	7	8	9
10	11	12	13	14	15	16	17	18	19
20	21	22	23	24	25	26	27	28	29
30	31	32	33	34	35	36	37	38	39
40	41	42	43	44	45	46	47	48	49
50	51	52	53	54	55	56	57	58	59
60	61	62	63	64	65	66	67	68	69
70	71	72	73	74	75	76	77	78	79
80	81	82	83	84	85	86	87	88	89
90	91	92	93	94	95	96	97	98	99
100									

 NOTE TO HOME
Students practice writing numbers through 100.

Unit 4   Lesson 117 • **261**

 Literature Connection Read aloud *Over in The Meadow: An Old Nursery Counting Rhyme* adapted by Paul Galdone to reinforce counting skills.

 Music Connection Using a **drum,** tell students that each drum beat represents a group of ten and that each ringing of a bell represents a one. Beat the drum seven times and ring a bell four times. Ask students what the number is. (74) Repeat the exercise and then have volunteers present similar problems for the class to solve.

RETEACHING

 You may wish to have students who are having difficulty counting by tens use the "School Bookstore" Game Mat, which was introduced in Lesson 113.

*available separately

◆ **LESSON 117** Numbers Through 100

Connect the dots. Start at 100 and count down.

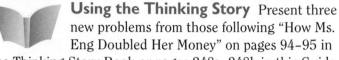

Start here.

262 • Numbers 1–100

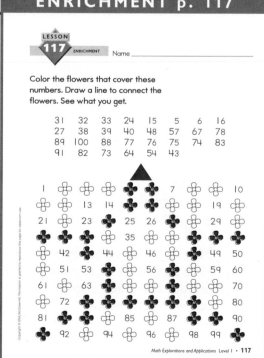

NOTE TO HOME
Students count backward from 100 to 75.

Copyright © SRA/McGraw-Hill

▶ Give further practice in unison counting. Have students point to the completed number table as they count

▶ Call out numbers. Have students quickly find and point to them.

▶ Ask students to find the number that is one more than 70, two less than 60, or 2 more than 55. Use differences of three or less.

▶ To prepare students to learn to add and subtract multiples of 10, give similar problems but specify 10 less, two tens more, and so on.

Then have students complete the connect-the-dots exercise on page 262.

Using the Thinking Story Present three new problems from those following "How Ms. Eng Doubled Her Money" on pages 94–95 in the Thinking Story Book or pages 248a–248b in this Guide.

③ Wrap-Up   5 MINUTES

In Closing Summarize the lesson by asking students to describe patterns they have noted on the number table.

Informal Assessment Observe students as they are completing the number table to identify those who need further practice with numbers through 100.

Assessment Criteria

Did the student . . .

✓ accurately count up and down from 100?

✓ complete the number table correctly?

✓ understand how to use the number table to locate numbers through 100?

LOOKING AHEAD You will need the macaroni tens cards for Lesson 118.

PRACTICE p. 117

LESSON **117** PRACTICE   Name _____

Fill in the missing numbers.

0	1	2	3	4	5	6	7	8	9
10	11	12	13	14	15	16	17	18	19
20	21	22	23	24	25	26	27	28	29
30	31	32	33	34	35	36	37	38	39
40	41	42	43	44	45	46	47	48	49
50	51	52	53	54	55	56	57	58	59
60	61	62	63	64	65	66	67	68	69
70	71	72	73	74	75	76	77	78	79
80	81	82	83	84	85	86	87	88	89
90	91	92	93	94	95	96	97	98	99
100									

Math Explorations and Applications Level 1 • 117

ENRICHMENT p. 117

LESSON **117** ENRICHMENT   Name _____

Color the flowers that cover these numbers. Draw a line to connect the flowers. See what you get.

31	32	33	24	15	5	6	16
27	38	39	40	48	57	67	78
89	100	88	77	76	75	74	83
91	82	73	64	54	43		

Math Explorations and Applications Level 1 • 117

Unit 4 Lesson 117 **262**

LESSON 118 — Multiples of Ten

Student Edition pages 263–264

Name _____

Multiples of Ten

0 10 20 30 40 50 60 70 80 90 100

Think: How many tens? Then add.

❶ $50 + 20 =$ **70**   ❹ $40 + 40 =$ **80**

❷ $30 + 30 =$ **60**   ❺ $20 + 20 =$ **40**

❸ $60 + 10 =$ **70**   ❻ $50 + 30 =$ **80**

Think: How many tens? Then subtract.

❼ $40 - 20 =$ **20**   ⓫ $50 - 30 =$ **20**

❽ $50 - 40 =$ **10**   ⓬ $80 - 40 =$ **40**

❾ $60 - 40 =$ **20**   ⓭ $70 - 10 =$ **60**

❿ $90 - 20 =$ **70**   ⓮ $80 - 30 =$ **50**

GAME

Play the "10 Below 0" game.

NOTE TO HOME
Students add and subtract multiples of tens.

Copyright © SRA/McGraw-Hill

Unit 4   Lesson 118 • **263**

LESSON PLANNER

Objectives

▶ to teach students to add and subtract multiples of 10 with sums and minuends up to 100

▶ to introduce students to the concept of numbers less than zero

▶ to provide practice identifying and creating patterns using function machines

Context of the Lesson Adding and subtracting multiples of 10 is continued in the next lesson. Practice with function machines occurs throughout the year.

 MANIPULATIVES

macaroni tens cards

play money* (optional)

Program Resources

"10 Below 0" Game Mat

Number Cubes

Thinking Story Book, pages 94–95

Practice Master 118

Enrichment Master 118

For additional math integration:
Math Thoughout the Day*

For extra practice:
CD-ROM* Lesson 118

Mixed Practice, page 374

❶ Warm-Up ⏱ 5 MINUTES

Problem of the Day Present the following problem to the class. Tim has three coins. Keisha has four coins. They each have 16 cents. What coins do Tim and Keisha have? (Tim has a dime, a nickel, and a penny; Keisha has three nickels and a penny.)

Problem-Solving Strategies Ask students who have solved the Problem of the Day to share how they solved it and any strategies they used.

 MENTAL MATH Write the following problems on the chalkboard. Then have students show their answers with Number Cubes.

a. $\square + 0 = 6$ (6)   b. $6 + \square = 8$ (2)   c. $3 + \square = 5$ (2)

d. $\square + 6 = 9$ (3)   e. $5 + \square = 9$ (4)   f. $\square + 8 = 10$ (2)

Literature Connection Use the puzzles, games, and activities in *Anno's Math Games II* by Mitsumasa Anno to reinforce math concepts.

SPECIAL NEEDS **MANIPULATIVES**

Meeting Individual Needs Have students work together to practice adding and subtracting tens with **play money***.

RETEACHING

Demonstrate for students how to use finger sets to keep track of tens. They can count each finger as ten. Thus, to subtract 90 – 20, they would hold up nine fingers for 9 tens, turn down two fingers, and observe the result as 7 tens.

*available separately

LESSON 118 Multiples of Ten

Use the Mixed Practice on page 374 after this lesson.

Complete the number machine charts.

Possible answers are shown.

⑮

In	Out
9	11
19	21
29	31
39	41

Rule +2

⑯

In	Out
0	3
3	6
6	9
9	**12**

Rule +3

⑰

In	Out
10	8
8	6
6	4
4	2

Rule −2

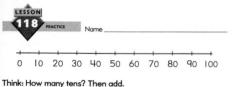 Make up your own problems. Have your friend solve them. **Answers will vary.**

⑱

In	Out

Rule _____

⑲

In	Out

Rule _____

⑳

In	Out

Rule _____

Copyright © SRA/McGraw-Hill

264 • Numbers 1–100

NOTE TO HOME
Students solve and make up function problems.

PRACTICE p. 118

ENRICHMENT p. 118

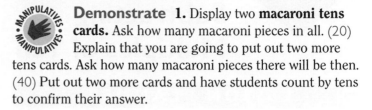 ## ② Teach

 Demonstrate 1. Display two **macaroni tens cards.** Ask how many macaroni pieces in all. (20) Explain that you are going to put out two more tens cards. Ask how many macaroni pieces there will be then. (40) Put out two more cards and have students count by tens to confirm their answer.

2. Demonstrate subtraction in the same way you demonstrated addition with the macaroni cards. Present more addition and subtraction problems using macaroni tens cards as well as written problems, such as: 30 + 30 = (60) and 90 – 20 = (70).

Using the Student Pages Have students complete page 263 on their own. For page 264, tell students that they should make a rule and fill in some numbers before having a partner complete each of the last three charts.

 Using the Thinking Story Present three new problems from those following "How Ms. Eng Doubled Her Money" on pages 94–95 of the Thinking Story Book or pages 248a–248b of this Guide.

Introducing the "10 Below 0" Game Mat To provide experience with numbers from –10 through 10 and intuitive addition and subtraction, use the Game Mat transparency to demonstrate and play this game. Complete directions are on the Game Mat and on page 412 of this Guide. While familiarity with thermometers and temperature is not required to play, you might want to point out that –10° is very cold, while 80° is very warm.

③ Wrap-Up

In Closing Have students share the function problems they made up on page 264.

Informal Assessment Use students' responses in the demonstration and their answers to page 263 to informally assess their ability to add and subtract multiples of 10.

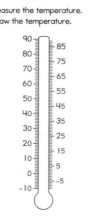

Assessment Criteria

Did the student . . .

✓ correctly answer 16 of 20 problems on pages 263–264?

✓ correctly respond to the problems during the demonstration?

LESSON 119

Adding and Subtracting Multiples of Ten

Student Edition pages 265–266

LESSON PLANNER

Objectives

✓ to assess addition and subtraction of two numbers in the 0–100 range in which one or both of the numbers are a multiple of 10

▶ to demonstrate the relationship between fives and tens

Context of the Lesson This lesson contains a Mastery Checkpoint for adding and subtracting multiples of 10.

MANIPULATIVES

macaroni cards (units and tens cards)

Program Resources

Number Cubes

Reteaching Master

Practice Master 119

Enrichment Master 119

Assessment Masters

For extra practice:
CD-ROM* Lesson 119

1 Warm-Up

Problem of the Day Ask the class. If you count by tens from 0 to 100, how many numbers do you say? (10)

Problem-Solving Strategies Ask students who have solved the Problem of the Day to share how they solved it and any strategies they used.

MENTAL MATH Present addition and subtraction problems, such as 50 + 20 or 60 – 10, where both numbers are multiples of 10. Have students show their answers with Number Cubes.

2 Teach

Demonstrate Introduce counting on by tens from any given number. For example, practice counting up and down by tens from 23. Stand three **macaroni tens cards** on the chalk tray. Have students say how many pieces of macaroni there are on the tray. (30) Then put a three card on the tray and ask how many pieces there are. (33) Demonstrate subtracting by removing two tens cards. Ask students how many pieces of macaroni are left on the tray. (13)

265 Numbers 1–100

LESSON 119

Adding and Subtracting Multiples of Ten

Name _____

How many tally marks? Ring sets of ten to help you count.

① ___23___

② ___31___

③ ___26___

Solve these problems in your head if you can. Use tally marks or macaroni cards if you need to.

④ 28 + 10 = __38__   ⑤ 32 + 20 = __52__

⑥ 29 + 10 = __39__   ⑦ 12 + 20 = __32__

NOTE TO HOME
Students add and subtract multiples of ten.

RETEACHING p. 28

LESSON 119 RETEACHING   Name _____

How many tally marks? Ring sets of 10 to help you count.

① [ ] 14

② [ ] 27

③ [ ] 32

④ [ ] 10

Add 10. Solve these problems in your head if you need to.

⑤ 14 + 10 = __24__   ⑥ 26 + 10 = __36__

⑦ 24 + 10 = __34__   ⑧ 15 + 10 = __25__

⑨ 34 + 10 = __44__   ⑩ 33 + 10 = __43__

28 • Math Explorations and Applications Level 1

PRACTICE p. 119

LESSON 119 PRACTICE   Name _____

Solve these problems in your head if you can. Use a number table if you need to.

① 45 + 10 = __55__   ② 33 + 10 = __43__

③ 56 – 10 = __46__   ④ 78 – 20 = __58__

⑤ 74 + 20 = __94__   ⑥ 13 + 20 = __33__

⑦ 91 – 20 = __71__   ⑧ 51 + 10 = __61__

⑨ 37 – 10 = __27__   ⑩ 39 + 10 = __49__

⑪ 68 + 20 = __88__   ⑫ 62 – 10 = __52__

⑬ 22 + 20 = __42__   ⑭ 99 – 20 = __79__

⑮ 83 – 10 = __73__   ⑯ 84 + 10 = __94__

Math Explorations and Applications Level 1 • **119**

*available separately

◆ **LESSON 119** Adding and Subtracting Multiples of Ten

Solve these problems in your head if
you can. Use a number table if you need to.

(8) 42
   + 10
   52

(9) 42
   + 20
   62

(10) 42
   + 30
   72

(11) 55
   − 10
   45

(12) 65
   − 10
   55

(13) 67
   + 20
   87

(14) 20
   − 20
   0

(15) 31
   + 30
   61

(16) 31
   + 40
   71

(17) 31
   − 10
   21

(18) 85
   + 10
   95

(19) 76
   − 10
   66

(20) 85
   − 10
   75

(21) 76
   − 20
   56

Play the "Get to 100 by Tens or
Ones" game.

NOTE TO HOME
Students add and subtract
multiples of ten.

Using the Number Cubes Continue with problems like those in the demonstration. Have students show their answers using Number Cubes. Then give written problems like the following: 47 + 30 = (77); 63 – 10 = (53); 50 + 16 = (66). If students are having difficulty, use the cards. Avoid subtraction problems in which the second number is not a multiple of 10.

Using the Student Pages Explain that the addition and subtraction problems on these pages are easier than they look. Challenge students to do them mentally.

GAME **Introducing the "Get to 100 by Tens or Ones" Game** Demonstrate and have pairs of students play this game to practice mental addition of numbers through 100. Give each player ten $10 bills and ten $1 bills. Players take turns placing one bill (either $10 or $1) in the middle of the playing area. The first player might put down a $10 bill. If the second player puts down $1, the total score is $11. A player who runs out of $1 bills must use $10 bills. Players should try to keep score mentally, if possible. The player who is first to reach $100 is the winner. A copy of this game can also be found on page 26 of the Home Connections Blackline Masters.

❸ Wrap-Up

In Closing Present more addition and subtraction problems with macaroni tens cards.

Mastery Checkpoint 18

Most students should be able to add and subtract multiples of ten (0–100) in problems that have both or only one of the numbers as a multiple of ten. Students should demonstrate mastery by correctly answering 80% of the problems on pages 265–266 or on Assessment Blackline Masters pages 46–47.

Assessment Criteria

Did the student . . .

✓ cooperatively play the math game?

✓ demonstrate mastery of adding and subtracting multiples of 10?

ENRICHMENT p. 119

LESSON 119 ENRICHMENT Name _____

The store sells ten cookies in each box. Tell how many cookies are left.

❶ Marnie wants to buy two boxes. How many cookies will be left?
__40__

❷ Cal wants to buy two boxes. How many cookies will be left?
__50__

❸ Shirley wants to buy two boxes. How many cookies will be left?
__20__

❹ Don wants to buy three boxes. How many cookies will be left?
__20__

Math Explorations and Applications Level 1 • 119

ASSESSMENT p. 46

UNIT 4 Mastery Checkpoint 18 Adding and subtracting multiples of 10 (Lesson 119)
Page 1 of 2
Name _____
The student demonstrates mastery by correctly answering 18 of the 20 problems.

Solve these problems in your head if you can. Use a number table if you need to.

❶ 15 + 10 = __25__   ❷ 38 – 10 = __28__

❸ 30 – 20 = __10__   ❹ 63 + 10 = __73__

❺ 30 + 30 = __60__   ❻ 51 + 20 = __71__

❼ 56 – 10 = __46__   ❽ 20 + 20 = __40__

❾ 34
  + 10
  __44__

❿ 52
  + 30
  __82__

46 • Math Explorations and Applications Level 1

Go on . . .

LESSON 120
Approximating Answers

Student Edition pages 267–268

LESSON PLANNER

Objectives

✓ to assess mastery of forming given amounts of money up to $100, using $1, $5, $10, $20, and $100 bills

▶ to teach students to approximate solutions to problems in which single-digit numbers are added to or subtracted from numbers through 100

▶ to teach students to trade bills of lower denominations for higher denominations

Context of the Lesson This lesson builds on Lesson 98 in which students were taught to make quick approximations of addition and subtraction problems in the 0–20 range. This lesson also contains a Mastery Checkpoint on familiarity with money (bills).

 MANIPULATIVES

play money*
(optional)

Program Resources

"Yard Sale" Game Mats

Number Cubes

Practice Master 120

Enrichment Master 120

Assessment Master

For additional math integration:
Math Throughout the Day*

For extra practice:
CD-ROM* Lesson 120

❶ Warm-Up ⏱ 5 MINUTES

 Problem of the Day Present the following problem. Mrs. Amos needs $65 to pay for groceries. Using $1, $5, $10, or $20 bills, what four bills could she use? (three $20s, one $5) What five bills? (two $20s, two $10s, one $5)

Problem-Solving Strategies Ask students who have solved the Problem of the Day to share how they solved it and any strategies they used.

MENTAL MATH Have students use Number Cubes to show which is the sensible answer to problems such as: 5 + 6 = 11 or 7? (11)

❷ Teach

Demonstrate Build on the Mental Math problems by presenting problems in which the first number has two digits. For example:

267 Numbers 1–100

LESSON 120

Name _____

Approximating Answers

Listen to the problems.

❶ ⬜ 50

❷ ⬜ 40

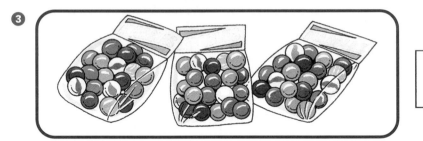
❸ ⬜ 60

Copyright © SRA/McGraw-Hill

🎒 **NOTE TO HOME**
Students solve word problems.

Unit 4   Lesson 120 • **267**

RETEACHING

GAME Reteaching of approximating the results of addition and subtraction problems is not essential at this time. Students who are still having difficulty working with money can practice by playing the "$1 and $5 Bills" game; the "Flea Market" game; the "Pennies, Nickels, and Dimes" game; and/or the "School Bookstore" game. Students can also practice working with money by playing "store." "Storekeepers" should set prices of items up to $100. Provide enough **play money*** for students to buy products and make change. Encourage group members to check that the proper amount of money is given to the cashier and that the correct amount of change is received in return.

PRACTICE p. 120

LESSON 120 PRACTICE

Name _____

How much money?

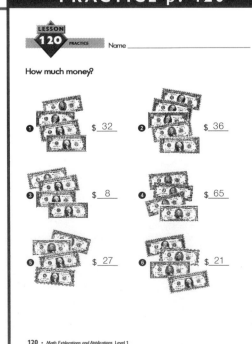

❶ $ 32   ❷ $ 36

❸ $ 8   ❹ $ 65

❺ $ 27   ❻ $ 21

120 • Math Explorations and Applications Level 1

*available separately

◆ **LESSON 120 Approximating Answers**

How much money?

 ❹ $ __35__

 ❺ $ __40__

 ❻ $ __36__

 ❼ $ __46__

 ❽ $ __22__

 ❾ $ __28__

 ❿ $ __21__

  ⓫ $ __27__

Play the "Yard Sale" game.

268 • Numbers 1–100

NOTE TO HOME
Students add amounts of money.

Copyright © SRA/McGraw-Hill

---

56 + 7 = 63 or 57, and 65 – 8 = 63 or 57. Discuss how you can tell when answers are not sensible. For instance, 56 + 7 does not equal 57, because 57 is only one more than 56. Present a variety of problems. Have students quickly show the correct answer with their Number Cubes.

Using the Student Pages Call students' attention to the illustrations on page 267 as you read each problem aloud. Problem 1: "Each child has ten sports cards. How many sports cards do the children have all together? Problem 2: "The lake is 80 meters long. Manolita is learning to swim from one end to the other. Her father rows beside her as she swims and picks her up when she becomes tired. The first day she swims 10 meters. The second day she swims 20 meters. The third day she swims 30 meters. If she swims 10 meters farther on the fourth day, how far will she swim? (40 meters) Write your answer in the box and draw a line across the lake to show how far she got on the fourth day." Problem 3: "Ferdie bought these bags of marbles. There are 20 marbles in each bag. How many marbles did he buy?" Discuss the answers and then have students do the exercise on page 268.

GAME Introducing the "Yard Sale" Game Mats
Use the "Yard Sale" transparency to demonstrate the game. Challenge students to play the harder version. Both versions provide practice with place value and changing money. Complete directions are on the Game Mats and on pages 413–414 of this Guide.

❸ Wrap-Up 5 MINUTES

In Closing Ask volunteers to explain how they selected sensible answers to this lesson's problems.

Mastery Checkpoint 19

Students should now be able to form any amount of money through $100 by using $1, $5, $10, and $20 bills and to correctly trade bills of one denomination for those of a higher denomination. These skills may be assessed by using student page 268 or by assigning Assessment Blackline Masters page 48.

Assessment Criteria

Did the student . . .

✓ quickly approximate to find the sensible answer?

✓ demonstrate mastery of forming given amounts of money using bills?

ENRICHMENT p. 120

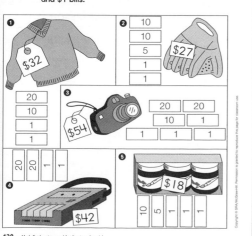

LESSON 120 ENRICHMENT Name _____

Show how much things cost. Draw bills by each item. Use a $20, $10, $5, and $1 bills.

Possible answers are shown. Other answers are likely.

❶ $32
❷ 10 / 10 / 5 / 1 / 1 $27
❸ 20 / 10 / 1 / 1 20 20 / 10 1 / 1 1 1 $54
❹ 20 20 1 1 $42
❺ $18 10 5 1 1

120 • *Math Explorations and Applications Level 1*

ASSESSMENT p. 48

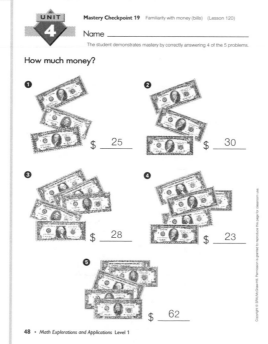

UNIT 4 Mastery Checkpoint 19 Familiarity with money (bills) (Lesson 120)

Name _____

The student demonstrates mastery by correctly answering 4 of the 5 problems.

How much money?

❶ $ __25__
❷ $ __30__
❸ $ __28__
❹ $ __23__
❺ $ __62__

48 • *Math Explorations and Applications Level 1*

Student Edition pages 269–270

Studying the Cube

LESSON
121

Name _____

Studying the Cube

How well do you know your Number Cubes?

This is a face.

❶ How many faces does each cube have? __6__

This is an edge.

❷ How many edges does each cube have? __12__

This is a corner.

❸ How many corners does each cube have? __8__

NOTE TO HOME
Students study the properties of a cube.

Copyright © SRA/McGraw-Hill

Unit 4   Lesson 121 • **269**

LESSON PLANNER

Objectives

▶ to provide practice solving mental word problems that involve adding or subtracting 0, 1, 2, or 3

▶ to introduce the parts of a cube: face, edge, and corner

▶ to provide experience estimating a volume of solid figures

▶ to provide practice solving mixed-addition and missing-addend problems with sums of 10 or less

Context of the Lesson   Mental arithmetic is continued in Lesson 122.

 MANIPULATIVES   **Program Resources**

photocopies of a cube net (optional)

tape (optional)

scissors (optional)

"Space" Game Mat

Number Cubes

Thinking Story Book, pages 94–95

Practice Master 121

Enrichment Master 121

For additional math integration:
   Math Throughout the Day*

For extra practice:
   CD-ROM* Lesson 121

❶ Warm-Up

 Problem of the Day   Write the following pattern on the chalkboard: 90, 80, □, □, 50, 40, 30. Have students copy the pattern and fill in the missing numbers. (70, 60)

Problem-Solving Strategies   Ask students who have solved the Problem of the Day to share how they solved it and any strategies they used.

MENTAL MATH   Have students determine how many dimes there are in each of the following amounts.

a.   65¢ (6)   b.   39¢ (3)

c.   42¢ (4)   d. $1 (10)

e.   90¢ (9)   e.   24¢ (2)

RETEACHING

Reteaching is not considered essential for this lesson as students will get more practice with word problems during the Thinking Story parts of most lessons. Mental arithmetic with numbers through 100 continues in the next lesson.

 **Art Connection**   Make copies of a **net** for a cube as shown below. Have students work in pairs to make a model of a cube using **tape** and the net.

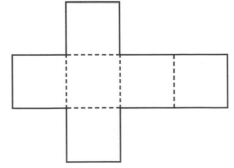

*available separately

◆ LESSON 121 Studying the Cube

Listen to the story.

❹

❺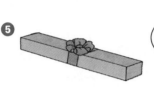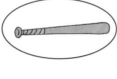

❻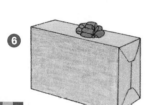

Play the "Space" game.

270 • Numbers 1–100

NOTE TO HOME
Students estimate the sizes of solid geometric figures.

---

2 Teach

Demonstrate Review the use of a number table. Then allow students to use the table, if needed, to solve word problems such as: "Pedro owns 19 fish and three dogs. How many pets does he own?" (22) and "Shiro had 60 marbles. He gave one to Teddy. How many does Shiro have now?" (59) Present similar word problems with addends and subtrahends of 0, 1, 2, or 3.

Using the Student Pages Work page 269 together. Allow students to use Number Cubes to help them answer the questions. Then read the following story to students and have them complete page 270: "Thomas received these presents for his birthday. Ring the item most likely to fit in each box."

Using the Thinking Story Present three new problems from those following "How Ms. Eng Doubled Her Money" on pages 94–95 of the Thinking Story Book or pages 248a–248b of this Guide.

Introducing the "Space" Game Mat Use the Game Mat transparency to demonstrate and play a round of this game, which involves solving mixed addition and missing-addend problems with sums of 10 or less. Complete directions are on the Game Mat. A copy of this game can also be found on page 410 of this Guide.

3 Wrap-Up

In Closing Have students name other objects they think are cubes.

Performance Assessment Observe students as they play the "Space" game to informally assess their understanding of addition and missing-addend problems.

Assessment Criteria

Did the student . . .

✓ correctly answer five of six problems on pages 269–270?

✓ correctly solve addition and missing-addend problems when playing the "Space" game?

PRACTICE p. 121

LESSON 121 PRACTICE   Name _____

This is a face of a box.

❶ How many faces does the box have? ____6____

❷ How many faces would two of these boxes have? ____12____

This is an edge.

❸ How many edges does the box have? ____12____

This is a corner.

❹ How many corners does the box have? ____8____

❺ How many corners would two of these boxes have? ____16____

Math Explorations and Applications Level 1 • 121

ENRICHMENT p. 121

LESSON 121 ENRICHMENT   Name _____

It takes one minute to paint each face.

❶ How long to paint ☐ ? ____6____ minutes

❷ How long to paint ☐ ? ____6____ minutes

❸ How long to paint △ ? ____5____ minutes

Math Explorations and Applications Level 1 • 121

LESSON 122

Student Edition pages 271–272

Mental Math

LESSON PLANNER

Objectives

✓ to assess mastery of mental addition and subtraction of 0, 1, or 2 with numbers through 100

▶ to provide practice mentally adding and subtracting 3 with numbers in the 0–100 range

▶ to review use of the calculator

Context of the Lesson This lesson contains a Mastery Checkpoint for mental addition and subtraction of 0, 1, or 2 with numbers through 100.

 MANIPULATIVES

calculators* or craft sticks, both loose and in bundles of ten

Program Resources

Number Cubes

Thinking Story Book, pages 94–95

Reteaching Master

Practice Master 122

Enrichment Master 122

Assessment Master

For extra practice:
CD-ROM* Lesson 122

❶ Warm-Up

Problem of the Day Present the following problem to the class. Elena has two more marbles than Andy. Together they have ten marbles. How many marbles does Andy have ? (4)

Problem-Solving Strategies Ask students who have solved the Problem of the Day to share how they solved it and any strategies they used.

 Have students show answers with Number Cubes as you review adding and subtracting 0, 1, or 2 in the 0–40 range.

a. 39 – 2 = (37)

b. 26 + 2 = (28)

c. 31 – 2 = (29)

d. 14 – 1 = (13)

e. 34 + 0 = (34)

f. 25 – 0 = (25)

g. 37 – 1 = (36)

h. 19 + 2 = (21)

271 Numbers 1–100

LESSON 122

Name _____

Mental Math

Solve these problems in your head if you can.

❶ 50 – 1 = __49__

❷ 29 + 1 = __30__

❸ 42 + 2 = __44__

❹ 62 – 2 = __60__

❺ 82 + 2 = __84__

❻ 42 – 0 = __42__

❼ 24 – 1 = __23__

❽ 39 + 2 = __41__

❾ 24 + 1 = __25__

❿ 28 + 2 = __30__

⓫ 70 + 0 = __70__

⓬ 27 + 2 = __29__

⓭
  40
– 2
__38__

⓮
  31
– 2
__29__

⓯
  94
+ 1
__95__

⓰
  38
+ 2
__40__

 **NOTE TO HOME**
Students add and subtract with numbers in the 0–100 range.

Unit 4 Lesson 122 • **271**

RETEACHING p. 29

LESSON 122 RETEACHING Name _____

Count on to add.

42 + 2 = 42…43, 44

Count back to subtract.

29 – 2 = 29…28, 27

Write the numbers you count.
Write the sum.

❶
  36
+ 1
__37__   37

❷
  42
+ 2
__44__   43 , 44

❸
  54
+ 2
__56__   55 , 56

❹
  47
+ 1
__48__   48

❺
  52
– 2
__50__   51 , 50

❻
  35
– 1
__34__   34

❼
  77
– 2
__75__   76 , 75

❽
  82
– 0
__82__   82

Math Explorations and Applications Level 1 • **29**

PRACTICE p. 122

LESSON 122 PRACTICE Name _____

Solve these problems in your head if you can.

❶ 59 + 1 = __60__

❷ 71 – 2 = __69__

❸ 63 – 2 = __61__

❹ 97 + 2 = __99__

❺ 29 – 2 = __27__

❻ 50 – 0 = __50__

❼ 65 + 2 = __67__

❽ 88 – 1 = __87__

❾ 44 – 2 = __42__

❿ 48 + 2 = __50__

⓫ 81 – 1 = __80__

⓬ 61 + 1 = __62__

⓭ 63 + 0 = __63__

⓮ 37 – 1 = __36__

⓯ 35 + 1 = __36__

⓰ 82 + 2 = __84__

⓱ 79 – 2 = __77__

⓲ 94 – 1 = __93__

⓳ 69 + 1 = __70__

⓴ 86 + 2 = __88__

122 • Math Explorations and Applications Level 1

*available separately

◆ **LESSON 122** Mental Math

Solve these problems. You may use a calculator if you need to.

⑰ 34 + 1 = **35**

⑱ 36 − 1 = **35**

⑲ 17 + 2 + 2 + 2 = **23**

⑳ 17 − 2 − 2 − 2 = **11**

㉑ 0 + 10 + 10 + 10 + 10 + 10 + 10 + 10 + 10 = **80**

Fill in the missing keys.

㉒ (7.) (+) (2) (=) (9.)

㉓ (17.) (+) (2) (=) (19.)

㉔ (7.) (+) (1 0) (=) (17.)

Do these differently.

㉕ (83.) (+) (0) (=) (83.)

㉖ (83.) (−) (0) (=) (83.)

NOTE TO HOME
Students use a calculator to do more difficult addition and subtraction.

272 • Numbers 1–100

Copyright © SRA/McGraw-Hill

② Teach

Demonstrate Build on the Mental Math problems by extending the range to 100. Then challenge students to solve problems mentally that involve adding or subtracting 3. Have students respond with Number Cubes.

Using the Student Pages Have students complete page 271 independently. Move on to page 272. Tell students that they may use their **calculators*** or **craft sticks** either before or after writing the answers.

Using the Thinking Story Present three new problems from among those following "How Ms. Eng Doubled Her Money" on pages 94–95 of the Thinking Story Book or pages 248a–248b of this Guide.

③ Wrap-Up

In Closing Ask students to tell how they solved the problems on page 272. Were there times when it was quicker to use a calculator? Discuss why this was so.

Mastery Checkpoint 20

Most students should now be able to add 0, 1, or 2 mentally with numbers through 100. This ability may be assessed during the demonstration, during work on page 271, or by assigning Assessment Blackline Masters page 49. Results may be recorded on the Mastery Checkpoint Chart.

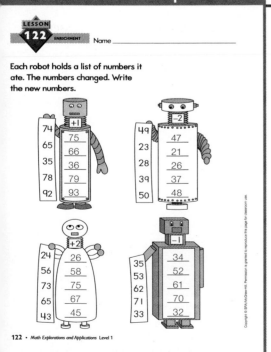

Assessment Criteria

Did the student . . .

✓ master mental addition and subtraction of 0, 1, and 2 with numbers through 100?

✓ demonstrate ability to add and subtract 3 from numbers in the 0–100 range?

LOOKING AHEAD Lesson 124 uses coded messages that you will need to make up in advance.

*available separately

LESSON 123

Counting and Recording Frequencies

LESSON PLANNER

Objective

▶ to provide practice using tally marks to count and record frequencies of events

Context of the Lesson Students were introduced to recording and comparing frequencies in Lesson 68. In Lesson 111, they learned to use a cancel mark to set off groups of five tally marks.

 MANIPULATIVES   **Program Resources**

Number Cubes

Thinking Story Book, pages 96–99

Practice Master 123

Enrichment Master 123

For career connections:
Careers and Math*

For extra practice:
CD-ROM* Lesson 123
Mixed Practice page 375

❶ Warm-Up ⏱

 Problem of the Day Present the following problem to the class. Mr. Ortiz looked out of his window and saw a man, a woman, and a dog. How many more legs did they have all together than Mr. Ortiz? (6)

Problem-Solving Strategies Ask students who have solved the Problem of the Day to share how they solved it and any strategies they used.

  Provide practice with mental addition and subtraction of numbers by 0, 1, 2, and 3. Have students indicate their answers with Number Cubes.

❷ Teach

Using the Student Pages Have students spend about five minutes counting and tallying the number of cars, trucks, adults, and children they see going each way on a nearby street. The empty box on the page can be used to keep track of another kind of vehicle, such as a bicycle or a bus. You may wish to have different groups keep count of each specific category.

273 Numbers 1–100

Name _____

Counting and Recording Frequencies

How many did you count?   **Answers will vary.**

Going this way.   Going this way.

❶  _____  _____

❷  _____  _____

❸  _____  _____

❹  _____  _____

❺ [_____]   [_____]

 THINKING STORY   **Talk about the Thinking Story "The Third House on Fungo Street."**

 NOTE TO HOME
Students use tally marks to record frequencies.

Unit 4   Lesson 123 • **273**

Copyright © SRA/McGraw-Hill

 **CULTURAL DIVERSITY** Have students work together to survey their classmates and record the names of different countries they have visited. List the countries on the chalkboard, then record the number of students who have been to each country by using tally marks. Students may enjoy doing the same survey with other classes or faculty members throughout the school. Combine and discuss results.

Literature Connection Read *Me First* by Helen Lester to reinforce lesson concepts.

RETEACHING

Reteaching is not considered essential for the material in this lesson.

*available separately

◆ **LESSON 123** Counting and Recording Frequencies

Listen to the story. Use tally marks to record how many times these words were said.

Use the Mixed Practice on page 375 after this lesson.

Students' tallies will vary.

Word	Tallies	Number Recorded	Correct Number
red			4
blue			5
green			2
yellow			2
the			10

Copyright © SRA/McGraw-Hill

274 • Numbers 1–100

 NOTE TO HOME
Students record and organize information.

PRACTICE p. 123

 LESSON **123** PRACTICE   Name_____

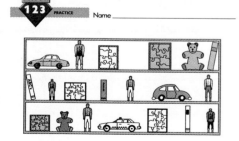

Use tally marks to show how many.

	Tallies	Total
🚗	|||	3
▬	||||	4
🧸	||	2
🧍	|||||	6
🖼	|||||	5

Math Explorations and Applications Level 1 • 123

ENRICHMENT p. 123

LESSON **123** ENRICHMENT   Name_____

❶ Roll one 0–5 cube many times. Use tally marks to show how many times each number is rolled.   Answers will vary.

Number	Tally Marks	Total
0		
1		
2		
3		
4		
5		

❷ Roll the cube again the same number of times. Compare results.

Number	Tally Marks	Total
0		
1		
2		
3		
4		
5		

Math Explorations and Applications Level 1 • 123

If this activity is impractical for the neighborhood surrounding your school, consider doing a similar survey of movements within the school building. For instance, direct your students to sit in a central location and count the number of students, teachers, or other adults headed one way or another in a hallway. After the results are counted, discuss what was observed most often and why. For example, why were most students headed one way while most adults were headed another?

For page 274, read the story that appears on page 274a. Have students use tally marks to record the frequency of words. Have different students keep count of specific words.

 Using the Thinking Story Read aloud and then discuss "The Third House on Fungo Street" on pages 96–99 of the Thinking Story Book.

❸ Wrap-Up

In Closing Have students name other events for which they might enjoy keeping tallies. Assign groups of students to record these events and share the results.

 **Performance Assessment** Observe students' accuracy as they count and record the frequency of events.

Assessment Criteria

Did the student . . .

✓ keep accurate counts of frequency as they completed page 273?

✓ actively participate in the Thinking Story discussion?

LOOKING AHEAD You will need to prepare coded messages for Lesson 124.

Counting and Recording Frequencies Read the following story slowly and clearly. It may be easier for your students to perform this tally activity if you emphasize the words to be tallied– *red, blue, green, yellow,* and *the*– as you read aloud. Remind students to record their tallies on page 274 as you read the story aloud.

Story: Students crowded into *the yellow* bus for a trip to *the* zoo. After a short ride, students saw *the red* and *blue* sign that told them they had arrived. In the parking lot, they followed *the green* arrow that pointed *the* way to *the* entrance. A zoo employee stamped each student's hand with a *red* monkey stamp and passed out *blue* name tags.

Students went inside a large *red* brick building. This was *the* aquarium, and *the* walls and ceiling were painted such a deep *blue* that students felt like they were underwater! They saw many kinds of fish. There were *red* fish, *yellow* fish, and fish with *blue* and *green* stripes. As students left *the* dark aquarium, *the* bright sun and *blue* sky made them squint.

After completing the read-aloud tally activity, you may want to give the students a print copy of the story and have them underline the specific words as you read aloud to them. Then have them count and record the number of appearances of each chosen word. Discuss whether it was easier to listen and tally or read along and tally.

LEARNING STYLES **Meeting Individual Needs**
Have students watch as you roll a 0-5 Number Cube. Ask questions such as: "Which number will come up?" "What number came up?" Ask students if they think one number will always come up more often or less often. Briefly discuss students' reasons. Then make a chart on the chalkboard. Inform students that you will keep track of the rolls and they are to help you find out which number will be the first to come up ten times. Have students take turns rolling the Number Cube. After each roll, record a tally on the chart. (Use single tallies instead of the traditional grouping of five.) After a few rolls, count to see how many of each number has come up. Remind students that the goal is to see which number is the first to come up ten times. Continue this way, checking the total more often as you get closer to the goal. Afterward, discuss the results. Do students think the number that "won" will always win? Help students to understand that each number on the Number Cube has an equal chance of "winning."

If a proper foundation that relies appropriately on physical manipulatives and other aspects of the learner's reality is built over a period of years, young children can learn important concepts that might escape their older brothers and sisters who have not had the necessary preparation. The fact that people without appropriate preparation fail to learn something does not, of course, suggest that younger people, with the appropriate foundation, should not be taught the concept...

—Stephen S. Willoughby,
Mathematics Education for a Changing World

STORY 16

The Third House on Fungo Street

❶ Ferdie sat in the first chair. Portia sat in the fourth chair.
How many chairs are between them? two
Which chairs are they? second and third

❷ Mr. Muddle decided to give a prize to the third person who came into this store that day. First came Marcus, then came Manolita, then Loretta the Letter Carrier brought in some mail; then came Portia; and then came Ferdie.
Who got the prize this? Loretta

The next time Mr. Muddle decided to give the prize to the fourth *child* who came in. First came Ferdie, then Marcus, then Portia, then Loretta the Letter Carrier, then Ms. Eng, then Willy, then Manolita, then Ferdie again.
Who got the prize this time? Willy

❸ Mr. Muddle drinks half a container of milk a day. He opened a container of milk just this morning.
When will he have to open another container? in two days, or the day after tomorrow

❹ "I'm trying to save up ten cereal box tops to get a free kite," said Marcus. "I've already saved two."
How many more box tops does he need? eight

❺ Ferdie had 15 cents. His mother gave him a quarter to go buy a newspaper for her.
How much money will Ferdie have after he buys the newspaper? 15¢, if the newspaper costs 25¢

❻ "How many years have you owned this store?"somebody asked Mr. Muddle. "I don't remember," said Mr. Muddle, "but I do know I was 40 years old when I got it, and now I'm 45 years old."
Can you figure out how long he's had the store? five years

STORY 16

THINKING STORY

The Third House on Fungo Street

One day Ferdie and Portia were walking along with their friend Loretta as she was delivering the mail. "Here's a hard one to figure out," said Loretta, looking at an envelope. "This is a letter for someone named Sandy Bright, and the only address on it is 'Third House on Fungo Street.'"

"That should be easy," said Ferdie. "Fungo Street is so short there aren't very many houses on it."

"Then perhaps you can tell me which house it is," said Loretta the Letter Carrier, as they started walking along Fungo Street.

There are just 13 houses on Fungo Street, and this map shows where they are. The numbers are house numbers.

[Show the illustration.]
"I know which house it is," said Ferdie. He counted off "One, two, three" and pointed to house number 1. "That's the third house on Fungo Street," he said.Ferdie marched up to the door of house number 6 and called, "We have a letter here for Sandy Bright!"

"Nobody named Sandy Bright lives here," said a gruff man who came to the door.
What could be wrong? What other house could be the third house on Fungo Street? number 5

"I know," said Ferdie. "It must be house number 5, across the street. That's the third house on Fungo Street too, only on the other side of the street!"

96 • The Third House on Fungo Street

Story 16 • **97**

7 Manolita's house is a block away from Portia and Ferdie's. Yesterday Manolita walked over to Portia and Ferdie's to play. When it was time for dinner, Manolita walked home. Then she walked back to Portia and Ferdie's house to spend the night.
How far did Manolita walk all together? three blocks

8 All the children are sitting in a row at the movie. Listen and figure out who is sitting next to Willy: Willy is sitting in the third seat. Ferdie in in the first seat. Marcus is in the fourth seat. Manoita in in the fifth seat, and Portia is in the second seat.
Who is sitting next to Willy? Portia and Marcus

9 Manolita found half a bagel in the cookie jar, half a bagel in the refrigerator, and half a bagel in a paper bag.
If she put them altogether, how many bagels would she have? three halves or $1\frac{1}{2}$

10 Marcus invited two boys for lunch. Each of the boys took his little brother along too.
How many boys went to Marcus's house for lunch? four

11 Mr. Mudancia had a candle that was 10 inches long. He let it burn until only 8 inches were left, and then he cut an inch off the bottom.
How long is the candle now? 7 inches

12 Six children had a race down to the beach. Manolita was the fourth child to get there.
How many children got there after she did? two

◆ STORY 16 The Third House on Fungo Street

They went across to house number 5, but no Sandy Bright lived there either. "I give up," said Ferdie. "Whoever wrote that letter didn't know where Sandy Bright lives."

Then Portia said, "I have an idea where the third house on Fungo Street might be."

Do you have an idea where it could be? It could be the third house from the other end.

"Maybe it's the third house from the *other* end," said Portia.

"We'll try your idea," said Loretta.

Which house is the third house from the other end? number 9

Which other house is also the third one from the other end? number 8

They started at the other end and counted house number 13, house number 11, and house number 9. "This must be it," said Ferdie. "House number 9 is the third house on Fungo Street."

So they knocked on the door. Mr. Muddle came to the door and said hello. Loretta the Letter Carrier said, "You don't have anyone named Sandy Bright living in your house, do you, Mr. Muddle?"

"Not that I can think of," said Mr. Muddle.

"There's only one other house it could be," said Portia.

What house is that? number 8

They went up to house number 8. A big man with reddish-brown hair was sitting on the front porch. "Is there anyone here named Sandy Bright?" asked Loretta the Letter Carrier.

"I'm Sandy Bright," said the man. "I wondered what you were doing, walking up and down the street that way."

They gave him the letter and walked away. "I'm afraid I have another hard letter to figure out," said Loretta. "This one is addressed to just 'Otto, The Fifth House on Fungo Street.'"

Which houses could be the fifth house on Fungo Street? Can you find four different ones? numbers 5, 4, 10, 9

First they tried house number 5, but no one named Otto lived there. Then they tried house number 4. No Otto. Then they started counting from the other end and tried house number 10. Still no Otto.

Which house haven't they tried yet? number 9

Who lives there? Mr. Muddle

It must be house number 9," said Portia. "But that's Mr. Muddle's house."

"Hey," said Ferdie, "something's wrong here. Mr. Muddle's house was the third house on Fungo Street. How can it be the fifth house on Fungo Street too?"

Can you figure out how it can be the third house and the fifth house at the same time? It depends on which end of the street you're starting from.

Ferdie thought for a minute and then said, "I get it. Mr. Muddle's house is the third house from one end and it's the fifth house from the other end."

They went up to Mr. Muddle's house again and knocked on the door. "Hello again, Mr. Muddle," said Loretta. "This time we're looking for somebody named Otto, who lives in the fifth house on Fungo Street."

Mr. Muddle was delighted. "That's me," he said, "Otto Muddle. Ah, I see you have my letter. I wrote it myself."

Portia asked, "Why did you write yourself a letter, Mr. Muddle?"

"I can't remember," said Mr. Muddle. "I'll have to read it and find out. Maybe it contains important news."

"If you write an answer to that letter," said Loretta, "I hope you'll put your whole name and your house number on it. Otherwise you may never get it."

"That would be dreadful," said Mr. Muddle. "Then I'd never know what happened, would I?"

. . . the end

Story 16 • **99**

LESSON 124

Using Doubles

Student Edition pages 275–276

LESSON PLANNER

Objectives

▶ to provide the opportunity to memorize doubles of numbers from 6 through 10

▶ to introduce the use of ordinal numbers

Context of the Lesson Students continue to memorize doubles to help them master all of the addition facts.

 MANIPULATIVES

five coded messages based on chosen reading material

reading material for each student

index cards (optional)

Program Resources

Number Cubes

Thinking Story Book, pages 100–101

Practice Master 124

Enrichment Master 124

For extra practice:
  CD-ROM* Lesson 124

❶ Warm-Up 🕐 5 MINUTES

Problem of the Day Present the following problem to the class. Name a two-digit number that follows both of these rules: 1. The sum of its digits is 12. The ones digit is double the tens digit. (48)

Problem-Solving Strategies Ask students who have solved the Problem of the Day to share how they solved it and any strategies they used.

 MENTAL MATH Have students use Number Cubes to show their answers.

a. $4 + 4 = (8)$ b. $3 + 3 = (6)$ c. $5 + 5 = (10)$

d. $2 + 2 = (4)$ e. $1 + 1 = (2)$ f. $6 + 6 = (12)$

❷ Teach

Demonstrate Write the addends for the doubles of 5 through 10 on the chalkboard, but leave the sums blank. Have students complete them, recite them, and then erase them one at a time as students recite the list from memory.

275 Numbers 1–100

LESSON 124

Using Doubles

 Listen to the problems.

❶  8 ❷  14

❸  16 ❹  12

Now solve these problems.

❺ $68 + 2 =$ __70__   ❻ $61 + 3 =$ __64__

❼ $61 - 1 =$ __60__   ❽ $59 - 2 =$ __57__

❾ $78 - 2 =$ __76__   ❿ $70 + 3 =$ __73__

⓫ $76 + 3 =$ __79__   ⓬ $44 - 3 =$ __41__

 COOPERATIVE LEARNING   Do the "Code Messages" activity.

 NOTE TO HOME Students solve word problems that use doubles.

Unit 4   Lesson 124 • 275

 LEARNING STYLES **Meeting Individual Needs**

Have kinesthetic and visual learners practice adding doubles. Have them close their eyes while one to ten students stand in the front of the class and the same number stand outside the classroom door. Have students open their eyes and guess how many students are outside. Have them say the addition sentence they used for their answer. Bring in the rest of the students and count to confirm answers.

RETEACHING

 Have students make **index cards** with doubles problems on the front (1 + 1 through 10 + 10). On the back, have them draw the correct number of dots and the number to show the answers. Students can work with partners to practice the doubles of numbers using their flash cards whenever they have spare time.

*available separately

◆ **LESSON 124 Using Doubles**

Complete the number machine charts.

⑬
In	Out
10	30
40	60
51	71
32	**52**

Rule **+20**

Possible answer:

⑭
In	Out
0	10
10	20
20	30
30	40

Rule + 10

Possible answer:

⑮
In	Out
50	40
40	30
30	20
20	10

Rule − 10

⑯ One marble costs 2¢. Fill in the chart so that it shows how much two, three, or more marbles will cost.

Number of Marbles	Cents
1	2
2	4
3	6
4	8
5	10
6	12

276 • Numbers 1–100

NOTE TO HOME
Students solve function problems.

Copyright © SRA/McGraw-Hill

Introducing the "Code Messages" Activity To provide practice with ordinal numbers, use this activity. Distribute copies of the relevant **reading material** to each student. Present **coded messages** using ordinal numbers such as, "The third word on page 9, the fifth word on page 2" . . . and so on. Have students find the indicated words and copy them in order. The words should form a short message such as "I like math."

Using the Student Pages For page 275, read the following problems, allowing time for students to write an answer. Then have students complete page 276 on their own.

1. You can see the wheels on only one side of this bus. How many wheels does it have all together?

2. Each of these fish has two eyes. How many eyes do the fish have all together?

3. You can see the wheels on only one side of these railroad cars. How many wheels do the two cars have all together?

4. Each of these horses has four legs. How many legs do the horses have all together?

Using the Thinking Story Present four new problems from those following "The Third House on Fungo Street" on pages 100–101 of the Thinking Story Book or pages 274c–274d of this Guide.

❸ Wrap-Up

In Closing Have students explain how they found the answers to problems 1–4 on page 275.

Informal Assessment Use students' responses during the demonstration to informally assess their knowledge of doubles of numbers.

Assessment Criteria

Did the student . . .

✓ correctly say the doubles of numbers during the demonstration?

✓ correctly answer 12 of 16 problems on pages 275–276?

PRACTICE p. 124

ENRICHMENT p. 124

LESSON
125 Student Edition pages 277–278

Twice or Half as Many

LESSON PLANNER

Objectives

▶ to teach students to solve problems that involve "twice as many" and "half as many"

▶ to provide practice in doubling numbers through 10

Context of the Lesson This lesson builds on Lesson 58 in which students doubled numbers through 5.

MANIPULATIVES   **Program Resources**

cans (2 large)   Number Cubes

counters*   Thinking Story Book,
              pages 100–101

              Reteaching Master

              Practice Master 125

              Enrichment Master 125

              For extra practice:
                CD-ROM* Lesson 125

❶ Warm-Up

Problem of the Day Present the following problem to the class. Willy has four marbles. Ferdie has one more than half as many as Willy. How many marbles does Ferdie have? (3)

Problem-Solving Strategies Ask students who have solved the Problem of the Day to share how they solved it and any strategies they used.

MENTAL MATH Review doubles through 10 with problems such as 3 + 3 and 6 + 6. Show your answers with Number Cubes.

❷ Teach

Using the Number Cubes Ask a volunteer to drop up to ten **counters*** into one **can**, counting aloud as he or she does so. At the same time, put the same number of counters into the other can. Ask how many counters are in both cans all together. Have students show their answers with Number Cubes. Continue with other numbers. Then

---

Name _____

Twice or Half as Many

How many now?

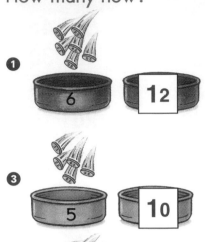

❶ 6 | 12   ❷ 8 | 16

❸ 5 | 10   ❹ 10 | 20

❺ 9 | 18   ❻ 7 | 14

❼ 10 | 5   ❽ 12 | 6

NOTE TO HOME Students solve problems that double or halve amounts.

Unit 4 Lesson 125 • **277**

GIFTED & TALENTED   **MANIPULATIVES**

Meeting Individual Needs

Have those students who quickly grasped the counters-in-the-cans problems repeat the exercise, but ask them to count by twos. For example, students would place one counter in the first can and the next in the second and say "two." They would then place the third counter in the first can and the fourth in the second and say "four." Ask students how many counters are in each can.

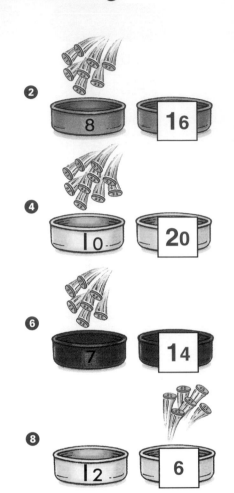

LESSON 125 RETEACHING Name _____

$$\begin{array}{r} 3 \\ + 3 \\ \hline 6 \end{array}$$

3 + 3...
That's a double!

Add these doubles.

❶ $\begin{array}{r} 2 \\ + 2 \\ \hline 4 \end{array}$ ❷ $\begin{array}{r} 5 \\ + 5 \\ \hline 10 \end{array}$ ❸ $\begin{array}{r} 4 \\ + 4 \\ \hline 8 \end{array}$ ❹ $\begin{array}{r} 6 \\ + 6 \\ \hline 12 \end{array}$ ❺ $\begin{array}{r} 7 \\ + 7 \\ \hline 14 \end{array}$

❻ 8 + 8 = __16__   ❼ 3 + 3 = __6__   ❽ 9 + 9 = __18__

Solve these problems. Remember your doubles.

❾ $\begin{array}{r} 2 \\ + 1 \\ \hline 3 \end{array}$ ❿ $\begin{array}{r} 5 \\ + 6 \\ \hline 11 \end{array}$ ⓫ $\begin{array}{r} 4 \\ + 3 \\ \hline 7 \end{array}$ ⓬ $\begin{array}{r} 6 \\ + 7 \\ \hline 13 \end{array}$ ⓭ $\begin{array}{r} 7 \\ + 8 \\ \hline 15 \end{array}$

30 • Math Explorations and Applications Level 1

*available separately

◆ **LESSON 125** Twice or Half as Many

Solve these problems.
Remember your doubles.

9 7 + 7 = __14__

10 7 + 8 = __15__

11 7 + 7 = __14__

12 7 + 6 = __13__

13 5 + 5 = __10__

14 5 + 4 = __9__

15 4 + 4 = __8__

16 4 + 3 = __7__

17 6 + 6 = __12__

18 6 + 7 = __13__

19 8 + 8 = __16__

20 9 + 8 = __17__

21 5 + 5 = __10__

22 5 + 6 = __11__

23 9 + 9 = __18__

24 9 + 10 = __19__

 Play the "Harder Roll a Double" game.

278 • Numbers 1–100

🎒 **NOTE TO HOME**
Students add doubles and related amounts.

PRACTICE p. 125

Solve these problems. Remember
your doubles.

1 1 + 1 = __2__   **2** 1 + 2 = __3__

3 5 + 5 = __10__   **4** 5 + 6 = __11__

5 6 + 6 = __12__   **6** 6 + 7 = __13__

7 7 + 7 = __14__   **8** 7 + 8 = __15__

9 8 + 8 = __16__   **10** 8 + 9 = __17__

11 9 + 9 = __18__   **12** 9 + 10 = __19__

13 3 + 3 = __6__   **14** 3 + 4 = __7__

15 2 + 2 = __4__   **16** 2 + 3 = __5__

ENRICHMENT p. 125

Look at the pet store animals.

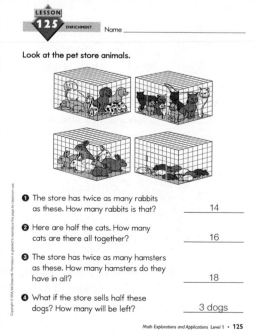

1 The store has twice as many rabbits
as these. How many rabbits is that? _____ 14

2 Here are half the cats. How many
cats are there all together? _____ 16

3 The store has twice as many hamsters
as these. How many hamsters do they
have in all? _____ 18

4 What if the store sells half these
dogs? How many will be left? _____ 3 dogs

---

present word problems using "twice as many" and "half as many." For example: It takes Willy 12 minutes to walk home from school. It takes Marcus half as long. How long does it take Marcus? (6 minutes)

Using the Student Pages Direct students' attention to page 277. Explain that some pictures show counters being added to a can, and the others show counters being taken out. Tell students that the number by the counters shows how many counters are added to or removed from the can. Work one or more problems on page 277 together. On page 278 call attention to the easy way to do the problems. After obtaining 7 + 7 = 14, it is easy to figure out 7 + 8 (15) because it is one more (like dropping one more counter in the can).

 Using the Thinking Story Present four new problems from those following "The Third House on Fungo Street" on pages 100–101 of the Thinking Story Book or pages 274c–274d of this Guide.

 **Introducing the "Harder Roll a Double" Game** Demonstrate the game and have students play to practice adding doubles through 10 + 10. This game follows the rules of the "Roll a Double" game introduced in Lesson 58, except that players roll two 0–5 Number Cubes and two 5–10 Number Cubes at once. For complete game directions see Lesson 58. A copy of this game can also be found on page 27 of the Home Connections Blackline Masters.

❸ Wrap-Up ⏱ 5 MINUTES

In Closing Present story problems using "twice as many" and "half as many." Have volunteers tell how they solved each problem.

 Have students make up their own problems using "twice as many" and "half as many." Ask them to exchange problems with a partner.

Assessment Criteria

Did the student . . .

✓ correctly answer 75% of the problems on pages 277–278?

✓ demonstrate understanding of the concepts of "twice as many" and "half as many"?

LESSON 126

Inequalities (0–100)

Student Edition pages 279–280

LESSON PLANNER

Objectives

▶ to provide practice in using relation signs between any two numbers in the 0–100 range

▶ to provide practice using ordinal numbers

Context of the Lesson Students continue to work with relation signs in Lesson 127. They used ordinal numbers to decode messages in Lesson 124.

 MANIPULATIVES **Program Resources**

bottle with an opening of about one to two inches

various objects for weighing (optional)

How Do You Measure Up?* from the Literature Library

Number Cubes

Thinking Story Book, pages 100–101

Practice Master 126

Enrichment Master 126

For extra practice: CD-ROM* Lesson 126

① Warm-Up

 Problem of the Day Present the following problem to the class. Bryan has more than 52 baseball cards, but not as many as his sister. His sister has 57 cards. How many cards could Bryan have? (53, 54, 55, or 56)

Problem-Solving Strategies Ask students who have solved the Problem of the Day to share how they solved it and any strategies they used.

MENTAL MATH Write pairs of numbers in the 0–100 range on the chalkboard. Have students show the lesser of the two numbers with their Number Cubes.

② Teach

 Introducing the "Make the Alligator Tell the Truth" Game Demonstrate and play a round of this game in which students must recognize true and false inequality statements with numbers through 100. Two players use the game form on page 279

279 Numbers 1–100

LESSON 126

Name _____

Inequalities (0–100)

What is the right sign?
Draw <, >, or =.

❶ 8 ⓐ> 7   ❷ 29 ⓐ< 33

❸ 20 ⓐ< 30   ❹ 65 ⓐ> 45

❺ 80 ⓐ< 90   ❻ 13 ⓐ< 31

❼ 70 ⓐ> 20   ❽ 15 ⓐ= 15

❾ 10 ⓐ< 100   ❿ 94 ⓐ> 49

 GAME Play the "Make the Alligator Tell the Truth" game.

Player 1   Player 2

 NOTE TO HOME
Students practice using relation signs.

Unit 4 Lesson 126 • **279**

 Science Connection Have students weigh and compare the weights of **various objects**. Have them write number sentences about the weights using relation signs.

Literature Connection Read *Animal Orchestra* by Scott Gustafson to reinforce math concepts.

To provide a review of measurement skills, read and discuss *How Do You Measure Up?* from the Literature Library*.

RETEACHING

Because inequalities are continued in the next lesson, reteaching may be postponed until after completing Lesson 127.

*available separately

◆ LESSON 126 Inequalities (0–100)

Fill in the missing numbers.

⑪　0　1　2　**3**　**4**　**5**　6　7

⑫　0　10　20　**30**　**40**　**50**　60　70

⑬　10　20　**30**　**40**　**50**　60　70　80

⑭　5　10　**15**　**20**　**25**　30　35　40

⑮　20　22　24　**26**　**28**　30　**32**　34

⑯　31　34　37　**40**　43　**46**　49　52

⑰　0　3　6　**9**　12　**15**　18　21

COOPERATIVE LEARNING　Do the "Pencil Drop" activity.

NOTE TO HOME
Students skip count to complete number patterns.

and two sets of units and tens Number Cubes. Each player uses the same side of the game form throughout the game. Player 1 rolls all four Number Cubes and selects one tens and one units Number Cube to make a number in either space on the game form. Player 2 rolls the other set of four Number Cubes and lays a number on his or her side of the game form. If the inequality statement is true, Player 2 wins the round; if not, Player 1 wins. Players switch roles and repeat. A copy of this game can also be found on page 28 of the Home Connections Blackline Masters.

Using the Student Pages Have students complete these pages independently.

MANIPULATIVES **Introducing the "Pencil Drop" Activity** To provide practice using ordinal numbers, use this activity. Have students try dropping a pencil into a **bottle**. Before each try, they should say: "This is my first try" or "This is my third try" and so forth.

Using the Thinking Story Present four new problems from those following "The Third House on Fungo Street" on pages 100–101 of the Thinking Story Book or pages 274c–274d of this Guide.

❸ Wrap-Up ⏱ 5 MINUTES

In Closing Have students explain a strategy they used to identify the missing numbers on page 280.

Informal Assessment Use students' answers to the inequality problems on page 279 to informally assess their understanding of relation signs with numbers from 0–100.

PRACTICE p. 126

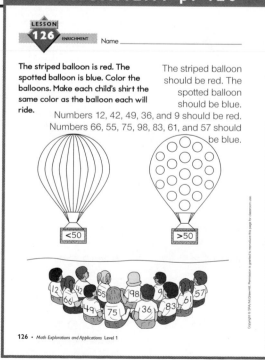

LESSON 126 PRACTICE Name _____

What is the right sign? Draw <, >, or =.

❶ 63 (<) 73　　❷ 26 (>) 20

❸ 98 (>) 89　　❹ 89 (<) 90

❺ 44 (<) 64　　❻ 55 (<) 59

❼ 70 (>) 50　　❽ 45 (>) 35

❾ 56 (=) 56　　❿ 76 (>) 69

⓫ 82 (<) 91　　⓬ 66 (<) 68

⓭ 97 (>) 87　　⓮ 99 (>) 90

⓯ 51 (>) 50　　⓰ 84 (<) 94

126 • Math Explorations and Applications Level 1

ENRICHMENT p. 126

LESSON 126 ENRICHMENT Name _____

The striped balloon is red. The spotted balloon is blue. Color the balloons. Make each child's shirt the same color as the balloon each will ride.

The striped balloon should be red. The spotted balloon should be blue.
Numbers 12, 42, 49, 36, and 9 should be red.
Numbers 66, 55, 75, 98, 83, 61, and 57 should be blue.

< 50　　> 50

126 • Math Explorations and Applications Level 1

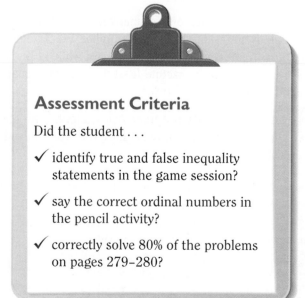

Assessment Criteria

Did the student . . .

✓ identify true and false inequality statements in the game session?

✓ say the correct ordinal numbers in the pencil activity?

✓ correctly solve 80% of the problems on pages 279–280?

LESSON 127

Student Edition pages 281–282

Comparing Numbers (0–100)

LESSON PLANNER

Objectives

✓ to assess mastery of inequalities and equalities in the 0–100 range

▶ to provide practice in repeated addition and skip counting by twos, threes, and tens

Context of the Lesson Inequalities and equalities with numbers through 20 were introduced in Lesson 67. This lesson contains a Mastery Checkpoint for this skill in the 0–100 range.

MANIPULATIVES

can
craft sticks

Program Resources

Number Cubes
Reteaching Master
Practice Master 127
Enrichment Master 127
Assessment Master

For extra practice:
CD-ROM* Lesson 127

1 Warm-Up

5 MINUTES

Problem of the Day Write these numbers on the chalkboard and present the following problem to the class:

12   19   6   26   11

Five students kept track of how many miles they walked each week. Kevin walked the least number. Stephanie walked the greatest number. Lana did not walk 11 or 12 miles. Tanya walked the second least number. How many miles did Jordan walk? (12 miles)

Problem-Solving Strategies Ask students who have solved the Problem of the Day to share how they solved it and any strategies they used.

Write the problems on the board. Have students use hand signals like those on p. 281 to tell whether the sum on the left is greater than, less than, or equal to the number on the right.

a. 17 + 0 ⟨<⟩ 20   b. 3 – 2 ⟨<⟩ 7

c. 5 + 10 ⟨>⟩ 13   d. 5 – 1 ⟨=⟩ 4

e. 15 + 1 ⟨<⟩ 19   f. 9 – 1 ⟨>⟩ 5

g. 13 + 2 ⟨<⟩ 18   h. 14 + 2 ⟨=⟩ 16

281 Numbers 1–100

LESSON 127

Name _____

Comparing Numbers (0–100)

Remember these signs?
Make them with your hands.

 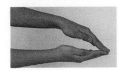 

<   >   =

What is the right sign?
Draw <, >, or =.

1. 43 ⟨<⟩ 48   2. 54 + 2 ⟨<⟩ 80

3. 100 ⟨>⟩ 98   4. 63 + 1 ⟨>⟩ 62

5. 70 ⟨<⟩ 80   6. 29 + 2 ⟨<⟩ 38

7. 98 ⟨>⟩ 89   8. 66 + 4 ⟨=⟩ 70

NOTE TO HOME
Students use <, >, or = to compare numbers.

Unit 4   Lesson 127 • **281**

RETEACHING p. 31

LESSON 127 RETEACHING   Name _____

< means less than.
> means greater than.
= means equal to.

 The arrow always points to the smaller number.

What is the right sign?
Draw <, >, or =.

1. 35 ⟨<⟩ 40   2. 50 + 2 ⟨=⟩ 52

3. 42 ⟨>⟩ 41   4. 46 + 1 ⟨<⟩ 48

5. 55 ⟨>⟩ 53   6. 38 + 2 ⟨>⟩ 36

7. 64 ⟨>⟩ 46   8. 26 + 1 ⟨<⟩ 29

9. 71 ⟨>⟩ 42   10. 29 + 2 ⟨=⟩ 31

*Math Explorations and Applications Level 1 • **31***

PRACTICE p. 127

LESSON 127 PRACTICE   Name _____

What is the right sign? Draw <, >, or =.

1. 84 + 2 ⟨>⟩ 62   2. 29 – 3 ⟨<⟩ 36

3. 65 + 5 ⟨<⟩ 90   4. 72 – 2 ⟨=⟩ 70

5. 83 + 1 ⟨>⟩ 79   6. 80 – 5 ⟨<⟩ 95

7. 76 + 4 ⟨>⟩ 38   8. 93 – 5 ⟨<⟩ 100

9. 89 + 2 ⟨>⟩ 89   10. 44 – 4 ⟨<⟩ 50

11. 57 + 1 ⟨=⟩ 58   12. 31 – 3 ⟨>⟩ 18

13. 60 + 10 ⟨=⟩ 70   14. 78 – 2 ⟨>⟩ 70

15. 71 + 4 ⟨>⟩ 71   16. 69 – 1 ⟨<⟩ 79

*Math Explorations and Applications Level 1 • **127***

*available separately

◆ LESSON 127 Comparing Numbers (0–100)

Solve each problem.

⑨ Each child has two hands.
How many hands are there in all? **14**

⑩ Each child has three pennies.
How many pennies are there in all? **21**

⑪ Each child has ten fingers.
How many fingers are there in all? **70**

⑫ Each child has one head.
How many heads are there in all? **7**

⑬ Each child has five crayons.
How many crayons are there in all? **35**

282 • Numbers 1–100

 NOTE TO HOME
Students use repeated addition or skip counting to solve problems.

Copyright © SRA/McGraw-Hill

---

② Teach

Demonstrate Review the hand signals for equality and inequality signs introduced in Lesson 97. On the chalkboard write pairs of numbers in the 0–100 range (such as 87 and 93) and in each case lead the students in forming the correct sign with their hands. Write the correct sign between the numbers to confirm students' responses. Then do the same with easy addition and subtraction sentences.

  Using the Student Pages Have students independently complete the exercises on page 281. Then to prepare students for page 282 and to introduce repeated addition, drop the **craft sticks** into a **can** one at a time while students count. Have students use their Number Cubes to show how many craft sticks are in the can. Now drop the same number of craft sticks in the can two at a time. Be sure the sticks make noise when they drop. Have students count and show with Number Cubes how many are in the can. Repeat the process with threes, then with tens.

③ Wrap-Up

In Closing Have students practice the use of relation signs with easy addition and subtraction problems.

Mastery Checkpoint 21

At about this time students should be able to insert the correct sign between any two numbers or in addition and subtraction sentences in the 0–100 range. This ability may be assessed using page 281 or Assessment Blackline Masters page 50. Results of this assessment may be recorded on the Mastery Checkpoint Chart.

Assessment Criteria

Did the student . . .

✓ master inequalities and equalities with numbers through 100?

✓ demonstrate understanding of counting by twos, threes, and tens?

LESSON
128

Student Edition pages 283–284

Missing Addends

LESSON PLANNER

Objectives

▶ to teach students to use concrete objects to solve problems that have the first term missing

▶ to provide practice using a calculator to find different solutions to the same problem

Context of the Lesson In Lesson 99 students worked with missing-addend problems that had the second term missing.

 MANIPULATIVES

calculators*
cardboard

Program Resources

Number Cubes
Thinking Story Book, pages 102–105
Practice Master 128
Enrichment Master 128
For career connections:
Careers and Math*
For extra practice:
CD-ROM* Lesson 128

❶ Warm-Up

5 MINUTES

Problem of the Day Present the following problem to the class. Kristen has four coins. One of them is a quarter. Each of the others is worth less. Does she have enough money to buy a card that costs $1.00? (No; for that she would need four quarters.)

Problem-Solving Strategies Ask students who have solved the Problem of the Day to share how they solved it and any strategies they used.

MENTAL MATH Quickly present addition fact problems with sums to 10.

❷ Teach

Demonstrate Draw seven objects on the chalkboard and hide them from view behind **cardboard**. Draw another object that students can see. Tell them there are eight objects all together. Challenge them to figure out how many are hidden. A satisfactory explanation is that 7 + 1 = 8 or 8 – 1 = 7. Work with more hidden objects. Draw ten pencils and then uncover three of them. Tell students that seven are still hidden. Students can then figure out that there are ten all together. Have them show their responses with Number Cubes.

283 Numbers 1–100

LESSON
128

Name _____

Missing Addends

 ALGEBRA READINESS

Solve these problems.

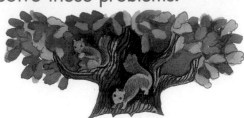

❶ There are ten squirrels in the tree. How many are hidden?

8

❷ There are seven kittens. How many are hidden in the box?

3

 Talk about the Thinking Story "The Lemonade War."

 GAME Play the "Stolen Treasure" game.

 NOTE TO HOME Students study pictures and solve missing addend problems.

Copyright © SRA/McGraw-Hill

Unit 4 Lesson 128 • **283**

 GIFTED & TALENTED

Meeting Individual Needs
Have students work in small groups of three to five to play the "Five Keys" game with a **calculator***. This game allows players to use ⓪, ①, ➕, and ➖ in addition to the chosen number key. A leader chooses a goal and the number key to be allowed. The others in the group determine the least number of keystrokes needed to reach the goal. Students take turns playing the leader.

RETEACHING

Extra teaching is not considered essential at this time, although students will gain practice playing any of the games introduced in this lesson.

*available separately

◆ LESSON 128 Missing Addends

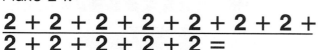

Use your calculator to find two solutions to each problem. Push as few keys as possible.

Write the keys you pushed.

Possible answers are given.
Number of keys pushed

3 Use only , , and . Make 24.

$2 + 2 + 2 + 2 + 2 + 2 + 2 +$
$2 + 2 + 2 + 2 + 2 =$

| 24 |

$22 + 2 =$

| 5 |

4 Use only , 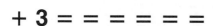, and . Make 18.

$3 + 3 + 3 + 3 + 3 + 3 =$

| 12 |

$+ 3 = = = = = = =$

| 8 |

Play the "Four Keys" game.

NOTE TO HOME
Students use calculators to find two solutions to a problem.

Copyright: © SRA/McGraw-Hill

Introducing the "Stolen Treasure" Game
To practice solving missing-subtrahend problems, have students play this game in pairs. The lead player places up to 20 counters in full view as his or her "treasure," and then looks away while the second player removes some of them. The lead player tries to figure out how many counters were removed and wins the round if correct. Play continues with all players taking turns. A copy of this game can also be found on page 29 of the Home Connections Blackline Masters.

Introducing the "Four Keys" Game
Play this game with the class to provide practice with **calculator*** and mental math skills and to develop mathematical reasoning skills. Players may use only the ＋, －, and ＝ keys and one other key to arrive at the designated number. For example, tell students to use the above keys plus the number 3 to arrive at 36. You can press ３ ＋ ３ ＋ ３ ＋ ３ ＋ ３ ＋ ３ ＋ ３ ＋ ３ ＋ ３ ＋ ３ ＋ ３ ＝ 36 or ＋ ３ ＝ ＝ ＝ ＝ ＝ ＝ ＝ ＝ ＝ ＝ ＝ ＝ ＝ 36, or you can press ３３ ＋ ３ ＝ 36. Challenge students to find the solution that involves the least possible keystrokes.

Using the Student Pages
Before doing the problems, have students draw a ring around all the squirrels and kittens on page 283. Then have students do the calculator activity on page 284, which is a continuation of the "Four Keys" game.

Using the Thinking Story
Read and discuss "The Lemonade War" on pages 102–105 of the Thinking Story Book.

③ Wrap-Up
5 MINUTES

In Closing Ask students to explain how they solved one of the problems on page 283.

Informal Assessment
Observe students as they work missing-addend problems. Interview them about the process they are using.

Assessment Criteria

Did the student . . .

✓ find different ways to solve problems in the calculator activity?

✓ correctly answer the problems on page 283?

LESSON **128** PRACTICE Name _____

Solve these problems.

❶ There are eight rabbits in the box. How many are hidden?
| 6 |

❷ There are 12 birds in the tree. How many are hidden?
| 8 |

❸ There are six bears in the cave. How many are hidden?
| 3 |

❹ There were eight doughnuts in the box. How many were eaten?
| 5 |

LESSON **128** ENRICHMENT Name _____

❶ Roll a 0–5 Number Cube five times. Write the numbers in column A.

❷ Roll a 5–10 Number Cube five times. Write the numbers in column C.

Answers will vary.

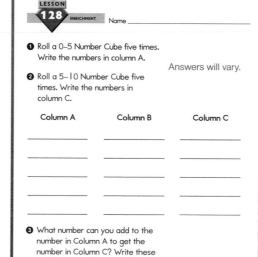

Column A	Column B	Column C
___	___	___
___	___	___
___	___	___
___	___	___
___	___	___

❸ What number can you add to the number in Column A to get the number in Column C? Write these numbers in Column B.

---

*available separately

The Lemonade War

① "Look at the nickel I found," said Willy.
"I could use a nickel like that," said his friend Ferdie.
"I'll give you four cents for it."
Should Willy sell it to him? Why not? No, a nickel is five cents, not four cents.

② Marcus brushes his teeth four minutes almost every day, but yesterday he was lazy and brushed them only half that long.
How many minutes did he brush his teeth yesterday? two

③ Manolita bought a toy airplane for two dollars and sold it for one dollar.
How much money did she make? none
How much money did she lose? $1

④ Marcus and Manolita were going fishing with Ms. Eng, but first they all had to dig worms. Ms. Eng dug three worms, Marcus dug one, and Manolita dug two.
How many worms did the children dig all together? three

⑤ One week Portia ate a peanut butter sandwich on Monday and another one on Tuesday. The next week she did the same thing.
How many did she eat in two weeks? four

⑥ Mr. Muddle is filling a barrel with water. He has already put in 10 gallons.
How many more gallons of water does he have to put in to fill up the barrel all the way? can't tell
What do you need to know? how many gallons the barrel holds

The Lemonade War

One day when Ferdie was walking along the sidewalk he saw Marcus standing behind a box. On the box were a pitcher and some glasses and a sign that said "Lemonade 5¢."

"What are you doing?" Ferdie asked.

"Selling lemonade," said Marcus.

"Do you get to keep the money?"

"Yes," said Marcus, "and I've already sold two glasses of lemonade."

How much money has Marcus made? 10¢

"That's a great idea," said Ferdie. "I think I'll do it too." So he got some lemonade and glasses and a box from his mother and set up a lemonade stand on the sidewalk, right next to Marcus's. But Ferdie was a little greedy. He wanted to make more money than Marcus, so he wrote on his sign "Lemonade 6¢."

Two children, Janet and Ken, came along. They read both signs and then they bought some lemonade from Marcus.

Why do you think they did that? Marcus's lemonade was cheaper.

"Hey!" said Ferdie. "Why didn't you buy from me?"

"You charge too much," Ken said. "Why should we pay you six cents when Marcus sells it for five cents?"

Ferdie thought about it and then he had an idea. He changed the sign so that now it said "Lemonade 4¢."

Why did he do that? so that people will buy his lemonade instead of Marcus's

Soon Manolita came along. She read both signs and went to Ferdie's stand. She held up a nickel and said, "One glass of lemonade, please."

How much is a nickel worth? 5¢

"My lemonade is four cents," said Ferdie. "Don't you have four cents?"

"No."

"Too bad," he said. "Come back when you do."

Instead, Manolita went to Marcus's stand and bought lemonade from him for a nickel.

What should Ferdie have done? given change

How much money should he have given Manolita? 1¢

"You should have taken the nickel," said Marcus, "and given Manolita a penny change."

"Oh," said Ferdie, "thanks. I'll remember to do that next time."

The next person to come along, Mr. Burns, had a dime. He handed it to Ferdie and asked for a glass of lemonade. Ferdie poured him a glass, took the dime, and gave him back one penny.

Was that right? How much should Ferdie have given him? 6¢

Why do you suppose Ferdie gave him just a penny? That's what he should have given Manolita.

Story 17 • **103**

⑦ "Be sure to bring back the change," said Portia's mother. Portia went to the checkout counter and bought a pack of gum. She gave the grocer five dimes and got back one penny.
How much did the gum cost? 49¢

⑧ Mr. Mudancia had a 12-string guitar, but he changed it a little. He put four more strings on it.
What kind of guitar does he have now? a 16-string guitar
How many strings does it have now? sixteen

⑨ Manolita had four crackers. She broke them all in two and ate them.
How many crackers does she have left? zero

⑩ Mr. Breezy is painting a shed. It has four sides. He can paint two sides in an hour.
How many hours will it take him to paint all four sides? two

⑪ Every time Portia dips her paintbrush, she can paint one side of a board. She wants to paint three boards on both sides.
How many times will she have to dip her brush? six

⑫ Willy was able to stand on one foot for eight minutes. "I'll bet I can stand on one foot for nine minutes," said Ferdie. If Ferdie can last three more minutes, he will make it.
How many minutes has Ferdie been standing on one foot so far? six

⑬ Ferdie and Manolita were arguing about whose jacket pocket was bigger. Ferdie put 15 acorns into his pocket. Manolita put 14 acorns into her pocket, and two of them fell out.
Whose pocket is bigger? Ferdie's
How do you know? He was able to put 15 acorns into his pocket without any falling out.

◆ STORY 17 The Lemonade War

Mr. Burns was angry. "That's not enough change," he said. "Here, keep your lemonade and give me back my dime." Then he took his dime to Marcus's stand and bought a glass of lemonade with it. Marcus gave him the right change.

How much change did Marcus give him?
5¢

"Next time I'll give the right change," said Ferdie.

Along came Mrs. Downey and Mrs. Kamato. They went to Ferdie's stand and each one asked for a glass of lemonade. Ferdie was delighted. "You came to the right place, ladies. Best lemonade. Best prices. And I always give the right change."

Mrs. Downey gave Ferdie a dime. Ferdie carefully counted out six cents change for her.

Why did he give her six cents? He thought she was paying for one glass of lemonade.

"Oh," said Mrs. Downey, "but I wanted to pay for *both* glasses of lemonade with my dime."

"Excuse me," said Ferdie, and he gave her six more cents change.

Was that the right thing to do? no

How much change did Ferdie give Mrs. Downey all together? 12¢

How can you tell that's too much? How much money did she give him? 10¢

Should you ever get more change than the amount you paid? no

104 • The Lemonade War

When Mrs. Downey and Mrs. Kamato left, Ferdie said, "At last I've sold some lemonade. I'm rich! I'm rich! I'm rich!" Then he counted out his money and found that he had less than when he started.

Why did he have less? He gave too much change.

"I've been robbed!" Ferdie screamed.

"No, you haven't," said a voice. It was Mrs. Downey, who had come back. "I just wanted to see if you would figure out that you made a mistake," she said. She gave Ferdie ten cents and told him to be more careful with his money next time.

"There isn't going to be a next time," said Ferdie. "I'm getting out of this business while I still have some money left."

Ferdie picked up his lemonade and glasses and box and sign, and left. As he was walking away he heard Marcus shouting, "Get your lemonade here, folks! Only six cents!"

What had Marcus done? raised his price

Why could Marcus charge six cents now? no competition

. . . the end

Story 17 • **105**

LESSON PLANNER

Objectives

▶ to teach students to use an addition table to find the sums of numbers through 10 + 10

▶ to provide practice using an addition table to find pairs of numbers that sum to specific numbers through 20

Context of the Lesson This is the first of seven lessons leading to mastery of the addition facts through 10 + 10.

 MANIPULATIVES

counters* or craft sticks (optional)

large addition table (chalkboard or transparency)

overhead projector

Program Resources

"Addition Table" Game Mats

Number Cubes

Thinking Story Book, pages 106–107

Practice Master page 195

Practice Master 129

Enrichment Master 129

For extra practice:
  CD-ROM* Lesson 129
  Mixed Practice, page 376

➊ Warm-Up

Problem of the Day Read the following riddle to the class. I am thinking of a number with two digits. The sum of both digits equals 9. The second digit is a double of the first digit. (36)

Problem-Solving Strategies Ask students who have solved the Problem of the Day to share how they solved it and any strategies they used.

 Have students use Number Cubes to indicate answers to addition fact problems.

a. 4 + 3 = (7)   **b.** 3 + 1 = (4)   **c.** 3 + 3 = (6)

d. 5 + 2 = (7)   **e.** 4 + 1 = (5)   **f.** 8 + 2 = (10)

➋ Teach

Demonstrate Display an **addition table** on the chalkboard or overhead transparency. Have students demonstrate how to use it to solve addition problems such

---

Name _____

Number Sentences

Solve these problems. Use an addition table to help you.

➊ 8 + 9 = __17__

➋ 6 + 6 = __12__

➌ 6 + 7 = __13__

➍ 8 + 5 = __13__

➎ 10 + 7 = __17__   ➏ 7 + 6 = __13__

➐ 7 + 7 = __14__   ➑ 7 + 5 = __12__

Copyright © SRA/McGraw-Hill

 NOTE TO HOME
Students review basic facts.

Unit 4   Lesson 129 • **285**

 Technology Connection You might want students to use the software *Stickybear's Math Town* from Optimum Resources (Mac, for grades K–4) for practice with basic addition facts. This software is available in English and Spanish.

RETEACHING

 Have students work with partners using **craft sticks** or **counters*** to practice finding pairs of numbers for various sums. Have one student display between 10 and 15 craft sticks or counters. The other student then tries to find as many ways as he or she can to divide the craft sticks or counters into two groups. Students write their findings into addition sentences, then trade turns and repeat the process.

*available separately

◆ **LESSON 129** Number Sentences

Use the Mixed Practice on page 376 after this lesson.

Write addition sentences to make each sum. Do each a different way.
Answers will vary. Possible answers:

⑨ | 7 | + | 8 | = 15   ⑯ | 7 | + | 7 | = 14

⑩ | 8 | + | 7 | = 15   ⑰ | 10 | + | 4 | = 14

⑪ | 9 | + | 6 | = 15   ⑱ | 4 | + | 10 | = 14

⑫ | 6 | + | 9 | = 15   ⑲ | 6 | + | 8 | = 14

⑬ | 8 | + | 8 | = 16   ⑳ | 9 | + | 4 | = 13

⑭ | 10 | + | 6 | = 16   ㉑ | 10 | + | 3 | = 13

⑮ | 6 | + | 10 | = 16   ㉒ | 3 | + | 10 | = 13

286 • Numbers 1–100

NOTE TO HOME
Students practice addition by writing number sentences.

as 10 + 4. Then help them use the addition table to answer questions, such as: "What are two numbers whose sum is 14?" Students must move their fingers from the number 14 to find the two numbers. Continue to present similar problems with sums from 5–15. Have students use the Practice Master, page 195, of the Addition Table to find the answers and then respond with their Number Cubes.

Using the Student Pages Have students complete these pages independently. Allow them to use their addition tables if they need to. When they have finished, correct the pages together with the class.

Using the "Addition Table" Game Mats To provide practice with addition facts through 10 + 10, have students play either version of this game introduced in Lesson 69. Complete directions for both games are on the Game Mats. A copy of the Game Mats can also be found on pages 392–393 of this Guide.

Using the Thinking Story Present four new problems from among those following "The Lemonade War" on pages 106–107 of the Thinking Story Book or pages 284a–284b of this Guide.

❸ Wrap-Up

In Closing Have students show how they used an addition table to work the problems on page 286.

Performance Assessment Observe students as they play the "Harder Addition Table" game to informally assess their ability to properly use an addition table to find sums.

Assessment Criteria

Did the student . . .

✓ correctly answer about 80% of the problems in the demonstration?

✓ find correct answers in the game?

✓ correctly answer 17 of 22 problems on pages 285–286?

LESSON 130

Student Edition pages 287–288

Adding 0, 1, 2, and 10

LESSON PLANNER

Objectives

▶ to teach students to quickly and accurately provide addition facts in which one or both addends are 0, 1, 2, or 10

▶ to provide practice in skip counting by fives

Context of the Lesson This is the second of seven lessons leading to mastery of the addition facts through 10 + 10.

 MANIPULATIVES

large addition table (chalkboard or transparency)

overhead projector

index cards (optional)

Program Resources

"Harder Addition Table" Game Mat

Thinking Story Book, pages 106–107

Practice Master page 195

Practice Master 130

Enrichment Master 130

For extra practice: CD-ROM* Lesson 130

---

① Warm-Up
5 MINUTES

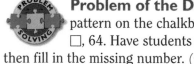 **Problem of the Day** Write the following pattern on the chalkboard: 54, 55, 57, 58, 60, 61, ☐, 64. Have students describe the pattern and then fill in the missing number. (+1, +2, +1, +2, and so on; 63)

Problem-Solving Strategies Ask students who have solved the Problem of the Day to share how they solved it and any strategies they used.

MENTAL MATH Have students answer the following problems aloud.

a. 2 + 0 = (2) b. 2 + 3 = (5)

c. 5 + 0 = (5) d. 3 + 5 = (8)

e. 5 + 1 = (6) f. 4 + 3 = (7)

g. 6 + 2 = (8) h. 7 + 1 = (8)

LESSON 130

Name _____

Adding 0, 1, 2, and 10

Solve these problems in your head.
Then write the answers.

❶ 6 + 1 = **7**   ❷ 1 + 8 = **9**

❸ 7 + 2 = **9**   ❹ 10 + 10 = **20**

❺ 2 + 10 = **12**   ❻ 0 + 0 = **0**

❼ 2
+ 8
10

❽ 8
+ 10
18

❾ 5
+ 0
5

❿ 9
+ 1
10

⓫ 9
+ 2
11

⓬ 2
+ 9
11

⓭ 10
+ 9
19

⓮ 2
+ 6
8

 NOTE TO HOME
Students practice addition.

Unit 4 Lesson 130 • **287**

RETEACHING

Use a number line to help students review +0, +1, and +2 addition facts. Then gradually have them see how many of these facts they can say without using the number line.

 COOPERATIVE LEARNING **MANIPULATIVES** Have students work in pairs or small groups to help each other learn addition facts. Have them make **index cards** with the addends on one side and answers on the other. Then have them sort the cards into piles of +0 problems, +1 problems, +2 problems, and +10 problems. Have students work together on specific groups of cards, one at a time, until they have mastered each type of problem.

◆ **LESSON 130** Adding 0, 1, 2, and 10

Solve these problems.

⑮ One eraser costs 10¢. Fill in the chart so that it shows how much two, three, or more erasers will cost.

Number of erasers	Cents
1	10
2	20
3	30
4	40
5	50
6	60
7	70

⑯ How many erasers could you buy with 35¢? __3__

How much would you have left over? __5__ ¢

⑰ How many erasers could you buy with 18¢? __1__

How much would you have left over? __8__ ¢

⑱ How much would nine erasers cost? __90__ ¢

 NOTE TO HOME Students do skip counting to complete a table.

Copyright © SRA/McGraw-Hill

288 • Numbers 1–100

PRACTICE p. 130

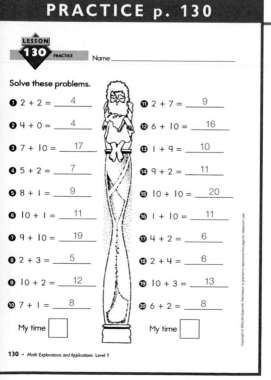

ENRICHMENT p. 130

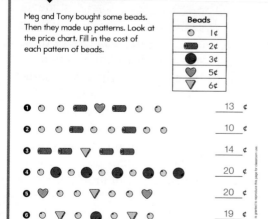

❷ Teach

Demonstrate Display an **addition table** on the chalkboard or overhead transparency. Work with the class to cross out those facts students have already memorized. Most students should already be familiar with facts using 0, 1, 2, and 10 as addends.

There are 121 addition facts in the table. Of these, 72 are included in the +0, +1, +2, and +10 facts and can be crossed out. That leaves 49 facts, 19 of which are doubles and +3 facts, which many students may already know. This leaves 30 facts to be learned, all of which are related pairs (8 + 7 and 7 + 8) . Therefore, there are really only 15 new facts that students need to learn.

GAME **Using the "Harder Addition Table" Game Mat** Have students play the "Harder Addition Table" game. Complete directions are on the Game Mat.

Using the Student Pages Have students complete page 287 on their own. Discuss page 288 with the class. Practice skip counting by tens. Then have students complete this page in pairs or independently. When finished, correct both pages with the class.

Using the Thinking Story Present three new problems from among those following "The Lemonade War" on pages 106–107 of the Thinking Story Book or pages 284a–284b of this Guide.

❸ Wrap-Up ⏱ 5 MINUTES

In Closing Have students share the charts they made on page 288. Encourage them to explain how they figured out the costs.

SELF ASSESSMENT Have students make a list of the addition facts that they already know.

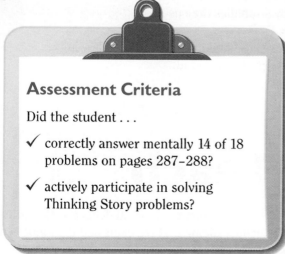

Assessment Criteria

Did the student . . .

✓ correctly answer mentally 14 of 18 problems on pages 287–288?

✓ actively participate in solving Thinking Story problems?

LESSON
131

Student Edition pages 289–290
Adding 8 and 9

LESSON 131

Name _____

Adding 8 and 9

Remember how to solve these problems?
Use one problem to help you
solve the next.

1 $4 + 10 = \underline{14}$

2 $4 + 9 = \underline{13}$

3 $4 + 8 = \underline{12}$

4 $7 + 10 = \underline{17}$

5 $7 + 9 = \underline{16}$

6 $7 + 8 = \underline{15}$

7 $6 + 10 = \underline{16}$

8 $6 + 9 = \underline{15}$

9 $6 + 8 = \underline{14}$

10 $5 + 10 = \underline{15}$

11 $5 + 9 = \underline{14}$

12 $5 + 8 = \underline{13}$

13
$$\begin{array}{r} 8 \\ + 4 \\ \hline 12 \end{array}$$

14
$$\begin{array}{r} 8 \\ + 3 \\ \hline 11 \end{array}$$

15
$$\begin{array}{r} 3 \\ + 9 \\ \hline 12 \end{array}$$

16
$$\begin{array}{r} 9 \\ + 3 \\ \hline 12 \end{array}$$

NOTE TO HOME
Students find relationships between
addition problems.

Unit 4   Lesson 131 • **289**

LESSON PLANNER

Objectives

▶ to teach students strategies for learning +8 and +9 facts

▶ to provide opportunities to memorize addition facts with 8 and 9

▶ to provide practice solving word problems

Context of the Lesson   This is the third of seven lessons leading to mastery of the addition facts through 10 + 10.

 MANIPULATIVES

large addition table (chalkboard or transparency)

overhead projector

index cards from Lesson 130 (optional)

play coins*

Program Resources

Number Cubes

Thinking Story Book, pages 106–107

Reteaching Master

Practice Master 131

Enrichment Master 131

For extra practice:
   CD-ROM* Lesson 131

1 Warm-Up

5 MINUTES

 Problem of the Day   Read aloud as you write the following on the chalkboard. Suppose you want to jog a total of 9 miles in two days. What are the different numbers of miles you can jog each day? (9, 0; 8, 1; 7, 2; 6, 3; 5, 4; 4, 5; 3, 6; 2, 7; 1, 8; 0, 9)

Problem-Solving Strategies   Ask students who have solved the Problem of the Day to share how they solved it and any strategies they used.

MENTAL MATH   Have students answer the following problems aloud.

a.   1 + 1 = (2)   b.   2 + 2 = (4)   c.   0 + 0 = (0)

d.   4 + 4 = (8)   e.   3 + 3 = (6)   f.   5 + 5 = (10)

2 Teach

Demonstrate   Have students use **play coins*** to model adding first ten cents and then nine cents to

  Have students continue to work in pairs or small groups to help each other learn the addition facts. Have them use the **index cards** made for the +0, +1, +2, and +10 problems. Have them make more cards with +8 and +9 problems and then work together on specific groups of cards, one at a time, until they have mastered each type of problem.

RETEACHING p. 32

LESSON 131   RETEACHING   Name _____

$7 + 10 = 17...$
$so\ 7 + 9 = 16$

Solve the first problem. Use it to solve the next.

1 $7 + 10 = \underline{17}$ **2** $7 + 9 = \underline{16}$

3 $2 + 8 = \underline{10}$ **4** $3 + 8 = \underline{11}$

5 $7 + 7 = \underline{14}$ **6** $7 + 8 = \underline{15}$

7 $6 + 6 = \underline{12}$ **8** $6 + 7 = \underline{13}$

9 $10 + 7 = \underline{17}$ **10** $9 + 7 = \underline{16}$

32 • Math Explorations and Applications Level I

*available separately

◆ **LESSON 131** Adding 8 and 9

Solve these problems.

⑰ 5 + 4 = __9__   ⑱ 8 + 8 = __16__

⑲ 10 − 5 = __5__   ⑳ 17 − 3 = __14__

㉑ 12 − 3 = __9__   ㉒ 16 + 3 = __19__

㉓ 21 + 2 = __23__   ㉔ 21 − 3 = __18__

㉕ 8 − 3 = __5__   ㉖ 6 + 4 = __10__

㉗ 72 − 2 = __70__   ㉘ 7 + 3 = __10__

㉙ 82 − 3 = __79__   ㉚ 8 + 2 = __10__

㉛ Whitney paid $6 for a hat. She has $9 left. How much did she have to start? $__15__

㉜ Susan and Maggie each have $8. They need $1 more to buy a ball. How much does the ball cost? $__17__

290 • Numbers 1–100

NOTE TO HOME
Students solve addition and subtraction problems.

---

numbers 0–10. Write the pairs of addition sentences on the chalkboard, for example:

0 + 10 = 10   1 + 10 = 11   2 + 10 = 12
0 + 9 = 9   1 + 9 = 10   2 + 9 = 11

Guide students to see that the pattern of adding 9 to a number is always one less than adding 10. Do the same procedure to help students discover that adding 8 to a number is always two less than adding 10.

Using the Number Cubes Provide practice in +8 and +9 addition problems. Have students indicate answers with their Number Cubes. If they have mastered these facts, cross off the appropriate rows and columns from your **addition table**.

Using the Student Pages Have students complete pages 289–290 on their own. They should be able to do most of the problems on page 289 from memory and use mental math strategies for the problems on page 290. When finished, correct answers with the class.

Using the Thinking Story Present three new problems from among those following "The Lemonade War" on pages 106–107 of the Thinking Story Book or pages 284a–284b of this Guide.

❸ Wrap-Up

In Closing Have students share their strategies for solving the +8 and +9 problems on page 289.

Have students add to their list of addition facts that they already know. Ask how many students were able to add the +8 and +9 addition facts to their list.

PRACTICE p. 131

LESSON **131** PRACTICE   Name _____

Use one problem to help you solve the next.

❶ 8 + 10 = __18__   ❿ 4 + 10 = __14__

❷ 8 + 9 = __17__   ⓫ 4 + 9 = __13__

❸ 8 + 8 = __16__   ⓬ 4 + 8 = __12__

❹ 3 + 10 = __13__   ⓭ 9 + 10 = __19__

❺ 3 + 9 = __12__   ⓮ 9 + 9 = __18__

❻ 3 + 8 = __11__   ⓯ 9 + 8 = __17__

❼ 7 + 10 = __17__   ⓰ 2 + 10 = __12__

❽ 7 + 9 = __16__   ⓱ 2 + 9 = __11__

❾ 7 + 8 = __15__   ⓲ 2 + 8 = __10__

Math Explorations and Applications Level 1 • 131

ENRICHMENT p. 131

LESSON **131** ENRICHMENT   Name _____

Answer these riddles.

❶ When you add 8 to me, you get 20. What number am I?
    __12__

❷ When I am added to 9, you get 18. What number am I?
    __9__

❸ I am greater than 4 but less than 7. If you add me to 9, you get 14. What number am I?   __5__

❹ When I am added to 8, the sum is 13. What number am I?   __5__

❺ If you add me to 9, you get 9. What number am I?   __0__

❻ When I am added to 8, the sum is 17. What number am I?   __9__

❼ If I am added to 9, the sum is 11. What number am I?   __2__

Math Explorations and Applications Level 1 • 131

Assessment Criteria

Did the student . . .

✓ correctly answer 25 of 32 problems on pages 289–290?

✓ actively participate in solving Thinking Story problems?

LESSON 132
Open and Closed Figures

Student Edition pages 291–292

LESSON PLANNER

Objectives

▶ to review previously learned addition facts

▶ to teach students to distinguish between open and closed figures

Context of the Lesson This is the fourth of seven lessons leading to mastery of the addition facts through 10 + 10.

MANIPULATIVES

blocks (optional)

string (optional)

Program Resources

Number Cubes

Thinking Story Book, pages 106–107

Reteaching Master

Practice Master 132

Enrichment Master 132

For extra practice: CD-ROM* Lesson 132

① Warm-Up ⏱ 5 MINUTES

Problem of the Day Present the following problem to the class. Miguel is not shorter than Paul. Ozzie is taller than Miguel. Order their names from shortest to tallest. (Paul, Miguel, Ozzie)

Problem-Solving Strategies Ask students who have solved the Problem of the Day to share how they solved it and any strategies they used.

 Provide students with practice with +0, +1, +2, +8, +9, and +10 addition problems. Have them indicate answers with their Number Cubes.

② Teach

Demonstrate Draw an open figure and a closed figure on the chalkboard. Explain and demonstrate that an open figure has ends, and a closed figure has an inside and an outside separated in all places by a line. Draw several other figures on the chalkboard for students to identify as open or closed.

291 Numbers 1–100

LESSON 132

Name _____

Open and Closed Figures

Make an X in each of the closed figures.

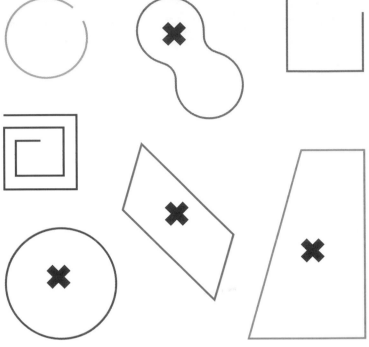

 Play the "Harder Roll and Add" game.

NOTE TO HOME
Students work with open and closed figures.

Unit 4   Lesson 132 • **291**

Carefully conceived educational games provide one of the most effective methods of practice.

—Stephen S. Willoughby, *Mathematics Education for a Changing World*

SPECIAL NEEDS   **MANIPULATIVES**

Meeting Individual Needs
Have students use **string** or **blocks** to build concrete examples of open and closed figures.

RETEACHING p. 33

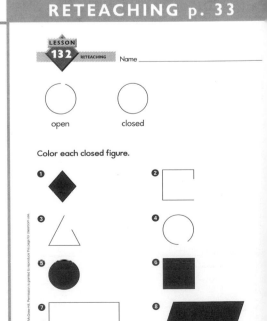

LESSON 132 RETEACHING   Name _____

open   closed

Color each closed figure.

Math Explorations and Applications Level I • 33

*available separately

◆ LESSON 132 Open and Closed Figures

If the rabbit can escape, mark the picture with an X.

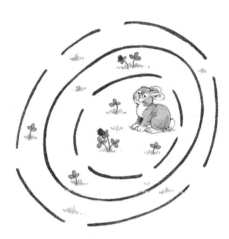

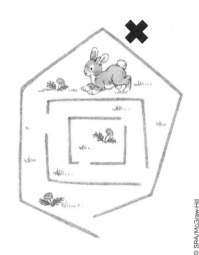

NOTE TO HOME
Students work with open and closed figures.

Introducing the "Harder Roll and Add" Game
Demonstrate and play this game in which students can explore probability and practice adding with two addends of 10 or less. Two or more players use two 5–10 units Number Cubes. Each player writes in a row of any five numbers in the 10–20 range. Player 1 then rolls both Number Cubes. Any player who has written a number that is the sum of the two numbers rolled can complete the number sentence. Players take turns rolling the Number Cubes as everyone tries to complete their sums. The first player to complete all five of his or her sums wins. A copy of this game can also be found on page 30 of the Home Connections Blackline Masters.

Using the Student Pages Read aloud the directions for pages 291–292. Then have students complete the pages. Correct them with the class.

Using the Thinking Story Present three new problems from among those following "The Lemonade War" on pages 106–107 of the Thinking Story Book or pages 284a–284b of this Guide.

❸ Wrap-Up

In Closing Have students draw examples of open and closed figures on the chalkboard.

Portfolio Assessment Have students draw and label examples of open and closed figures and save the pictures in their Math Portfolios.

Assessment Criteria
Did the student . . .
- ✓ draw an **X** in each of the closed figures on page 291?
- ✓ correctly mark each of the figures on page 292?

PRACTICE p. 132

LESSON 132 PRACTICE Name_____

Make an X in each of the closed figures.

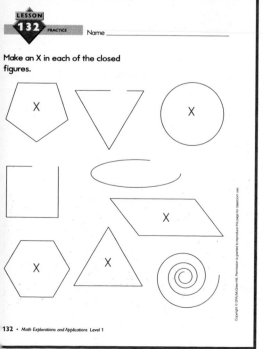

132 • Math Explorations and Applications Level 1

ENRICHMENT p. 132

LESSON 132 ENRICHMENT Name_____

Bart drew animals from Mars and Venus. The animals from Mars are open shapes. The animals from Venus are closed shapes.

Draw an M on the animals from Mars. Draw a V on the animals from Venus.

Help Bart finish the picture. Color the animals any way you want.

132 • Math Explorations and Applications Level 1

LESSON 133

Student Edition pages 293–294

Using Doubles

LESSON PLANNER

Objectives

- to provide practice with addition facts for doubles
- to teach a procedure for learning facts that differ from doubles by 1
- to provide opportunities to explore the relationship between doubles and "twice as much"
- to introduce the concept of measuring volume

Context of the Lesson This is the fifth of seven lessons leading to mastery of the addition facts through 10 + 10.

MANIPULATIVES

collection of absorbent materials such as newspaper, magazine pages, paper towels, tissues, rags, and sponges

large addition table (chalkboard or transparency)

measuring cup

water

index cards (optional)

overhead projector

Program Resources

Number Cubes

Reteaching Master

Practice Master 133

Enrichment Master 133

For extra practice:
CD-ROM* Lesson 133
Mixed Practice, page 377

1 Warm-Up (5 minutes)

Problem of the Day Present the following problem to the class. Emily had 12 grapes. She ate two and wants to save three. Can she share the remaining grapes evenly among her three brothers? Why or why not? (No, because she has 7 left and you cannot make three equal groups out of 7.)

Problem-Solving Strategies Ask students who have solved the Problem of the Day to share how they solved it and any strategies they used.

MENTAL MATH Have students use Number Cubes to answer the following word problems.

a. Ferdie had three balloons. Willy gave him five more. How many does Ferdie have now? (8)

b. Portia had six friends over on Monday and two on Tuesday. How many came over all together? (8)

LESSON 133

Name ____________

Using Doubles

Solve these problems. Remember your doubles.

1. 3 + 3 = 6
2. 3 + 4 = 7
3. 5 + 5 = 10
4. 5 + 4 = 9
5. 5 + 6 = 11
6. 7 + 7 = 14
7. 7 + 6 = 13
8. 7 + 8 = 15
9. 4 + 4 = 8
10. 4 + 5 = 9
11. 6 + 6 = 12
12. 6 + 5 = 11
13. 6 + 7 = 13
14. 8 + 8 = 16
15. 8 + 7 = 15
16. 8 + 9 = 17

SCIENCE CONNECTION Do the "Soak and Squeeze" activity.

NOTE TO HOME
Students practice adding doubles and related facts.

COOPERATIVE LEARNING · MANIPULATIVES Continue having students make **index cards** for the addition facts they have learned in this lesson. Have them work together with partners using the cards to practice their facts.

RETEACHING p. 34

LESSON 133 RETEACHING Name ____________

How many?

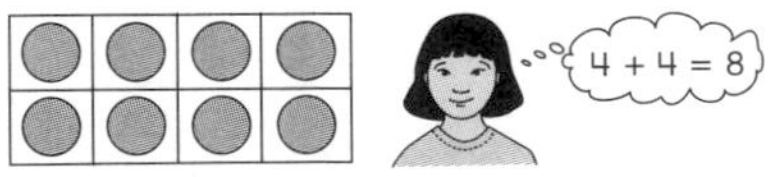

Solve these problems. Remember your doubles.

1. 3 + 3 = 6
2. 3 + 2 = 5
3. 3 + 4 = 7
4. 4 + 4 = 8
5. 4 + 5 = 9
6. 4 + 6 = 10
7. 9 + 9 = 18
8. 9 + 8 = 17
9. 9 + 10 = 19
10. 2 + 2 = 4
11. 2 + 1 = 3
12. 2 + 0 = 2
13. 8 + 8 = 16
14. 8 + 9 = 17
15. 5 + 5 = 10
16. 5 + 4 = 9

34 • Math Explorations and Applications Level 1

*available separately

◆ LESSON 133 Using Doubles

Listen to the problems.

Use the Mixed Practice on page 377 after this lesson.

⑰ William ran 2 miles. Sam wants to run twice as far. Draw an **X** on that spot. How many miles does Sam want to run? **4**

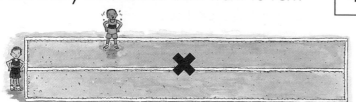

⑱ Anita has six apples. She'd like to have twice as many. Draw the number of extra apples Anita will need. How many apples will Anita have?

12

⑲ Patrick can throw a ball 10 meters. His older sister Kelsey can throw twice as far. Draw an **X** where you think Kelsey's ball will land. How many meters can Kelsey throw a ball?

20 meters

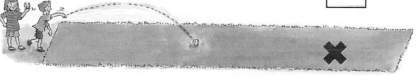

Copyright © SRA/M-Graw-Hill

294 • Numbers 1–100

---

c. Manolita bought three toys at a yard sale. Her mother gave her one more. Now how many toys does she have? (4)

❷ Teach

Demonstrate Review doubles of numbers through 10. Then ask: "If 7 + 7 is 14, how much is 7 + 8?" Guide students to see that it is one more than 7 + 7, which would be 15. Repeat with similar problems. Then provide problems, such as 7 + 6, which would be one less than 7 + 7. Repeat with similar problems.

Using the Number Cubes Provide problems like those in the demonstration and then practice with +0, +1, +2, +8, +9, and +10 addition problems. Have students indicate answers with their Number Cubes.

Introducing the "Soak and Squeeze" Activity Soak various **absorbent materials** in water; then, one at a time, squeeze out the water into a **measuring cup**. On the chalkboard, record the name of the material and the amount of water released. After a couple of trials with different materials, have students predict how much water will be squeezed out of the materials. Students should begin to acquire an intuitive sense of which materials are more absorbent.

Using the Student Pages Have students complete page 293 on their own. For page 294, read each word problem and have students complete it before going on to the next one. When students have finished both pages, correct them together with the class.

❸ Wrap-Up ⏱ 5 MINUTES

In Closing Have students make up examples of problems that they can solve using the doubles +1 or doubles –1 strategy.

Informal Assessment Use students' answers to pages 293–294 to informally assess their understanding of how to use doubles to solve similar addition problems. Cross off any mastered facts from the **addition table**.

Assessment Criteria

Did the student . . .

✓ make sensible predictions about how much water would be absorbed during the activity?

✓ correctly solve 15 of 19 problems on pages 293–294?

PRACTICE p. 133

LESSON 133 PRACTICE Name_____

Solve these problems. Remember your doubles.

❶ 9 + 9 = __18__   ❾ 8 + 8 = __16__

❷ 9 + 8 = __17__   ❿ 8 + 7 = __15__

❸ 9 + 7 = __16__   ⓫ 8 + 9 = __17__

❹ 9 + 6 = __15__   ⓬ 8 + 6 = __14__

❺ 6 + 6 = __12__   ⓭ 5 + 5 = __10__

❻ 6 + 5 = __11__   ⓮ 5 + 4 = __9__

❼ 6 + 7 = __13__   ⓯ 5 + 7 = __12__

❽ 6 + 4 = __10__   ⓰ 5 + 6 = __11__

Math Explorations and Applications Level 1 • 133

ENRICHMENT p. 133

LESSON 133 ENRICHMENT Name_____

How many legs? Look at the pictures. Write how many legs are hidden.

❶ _____ 6

❷ _____ 12

❸ _____ 8

❹ _____ 9

❺ _____ 4

Math Explorations and Applications Level 1 • 133

Student Edition pages 295–296

Make Ten

LESSON PLANNER

Objectives

▶ to provide practice memorizing addition facts summing to 10

▶ to show that for some calculations the mind is faster than the calculator

Context of the Lesson This is the fifth of six lessons leading to mastery of addition facts through 10 + 10. Students formally practiced this skill in Lesson 110.

 MANIPULATIVES

addition table transparency

calculators*

overhead projector

Program Resources

"Harder Pattern" Game Mat

Number Cubes

Thinking Story Book, pages 108–111

Practice Master 134

Enrichment Master 134

For career connections: Careers and Math*

For additional math integration: Math Throughout the Day*

For extra practice: CD-ROM* Lesson 134

❶ Warm-Up ⏱ 5 MINUTES

 Problem of the Day Present the following problem to the class. Mrs. Glenn asked ten students to arrange their desks in two rows. What are all the ways they could have arranged the desks? (1 left, 9 right; 9 left, 1 right; 2 left, 8 right; 8 left, 2 right; 3 left, 7 right; 7 left, 3 right; 6 left, 4 right; 4 left, 6 right; 5 left, 5 right)

Problem-Solving Strategies Ask students who have solved the Problem of the Day to share how they solved it and any strategies they used.

MENTAL MATH Ask students to find the number that added to the numbers below equals ten.

a. 4 (6)	**b.** 3 (7)
c. 0 (10)	**d.** 2 (8)
e. 1 (9)	**f.** 9 (1)
g. 6 (4)	**h.** 5 (5)
i. 9 (1)	**j.** 8 (2)

295 Numbers 1–100

Name _____

Make Ten

Which balloons have numbers that add up to ten? Color those balloons.

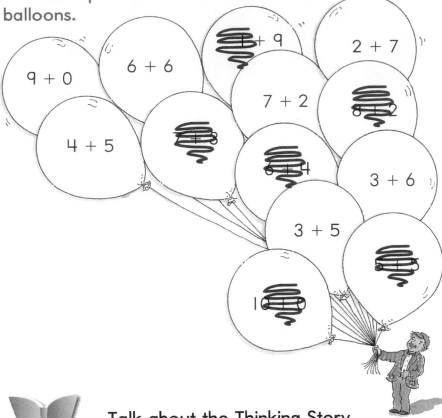

 THINKING STORY Talk about the Thinking Story "Mr. Mudancia Changes Houses."

Copyright © SRA/McGraw-Hill

 NOTE TO HOME Students identify numbers that sum to ten.

 Literature Connection You may wish to read aloud *Domino Addition* by Lynette Long to reinforce lesson concepts.

RETEACHING

 COOPERATIVE LEARNING Challenge pairs of students to quiz each other on addition facts. Have one student make up a problem and the other solve it. Remind students that as the class masters addition facts, more lines on the **addition table** can be crossed out. Encourage students to help one another meet this goal.

*available separately

◆ **LESSON 134** Make Ten

Solve these problems.
Use a calculator or your head. If you
use a calculator you must push all the
numbers and signs in each problem.
Which way is faster?

1 1 + 1 = __2__   **2** 10 + 10 = __20__

3 1 − 1 = __0__   **4** 40 − 10 = __30__

5 2 + 1 = __3__   **6** 30 + 10 = __40__

7 4 − 1 = __3__   **8** 30 − 10 = __20__

9 8 + 0 = __8__   **10** 40 + 1 = __41__

11 6 + 3 = __9__   **12** 50 + 10 = __60__

Play the "Harder Pattern" game.

296 • Numbers 1–100

NOTE TO HOME
Students learn that mental math can be
quicker than a calculator.

PRACTICE p. 134

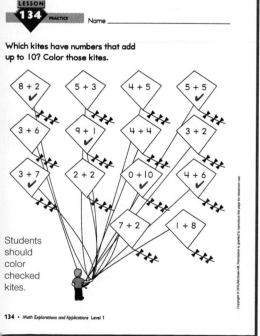

Which kites have numbers that add
up to 10? Color those kites.

Students should color checked kites.

134 • Math Explorations and Applications Level 1

ENRICHMENT p. 134

Each child got two throws. They
earned the scores shown below.
Write the numbers the children got
on each toss. The first one is done
for you.

Barb	8	7 and 1
Mike	4	4 and 0, 3 and 1, or 2 and 2
Shandra	5	4 and 1 or 3 and 2
Kiki	7	3 and 4 or 7 and 0
Julie	10	7 and 3
Scott	9	7 and 2
Emily	2	2 and 0 or 1 and 1

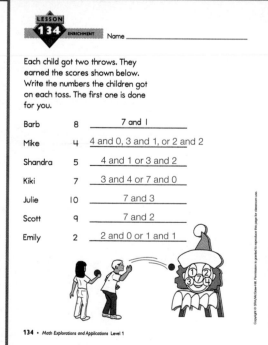

134 • Math Explorations and Applications Level 1

*available separately

---

2 Teach

Demonstrate Ask students to use their Number Cubes to show all possible combinations of two numbers that add up to 10. Write the **addition table** on the chalkboard or on a transparency. Then have students identify these combinations on the addition table. When students are able to quickly name pairs of numbers that sum to 10, a line may be drawn through the diagonal of tens on the addition table to indicate that the corresponding addition facts have been learned.

Using the Student Pages Have students complete the exercises on page 295. Then have students work on page 296, allowing half the class to use **calculators***. Have the class do the problems as quickly as possible. Discuss whether or not calculators made the exercises easier. Guide students to see that sometimes it is faster to solve the problems mentally and that mistakes can be made by pressing the wrong calculator key.

Using the Thinking Story Read aloud "Mr. Mudancia Changes Houses" on pages 108–111 of the Thinking Story Book.

Introducing the "Harder Pattern" Game Mat Have students use the "Harder Pattern" Game Mat to develop mathematic reasoning abilities in pattern recognition. Demonstrate the game by playing a round with a student. A copy of this game can also be found on page 407 of this Guide.

3 Wrap-Up

In Closing Give students more problems with addends that sum to 10.

Have students quiz one another on addition facts.

Assessment Criteria

Did the student . . .

✓ demonstrate fluency in solving addition problems that sum to 10?

✓ understand that mental math is sometimes more efficient than a calculator in solving problems?

Mr. Mudancia Changes Houses

❶ Do you know how a paper clip is shaped? [Show a paper clip or, if you're working with a large group, draw a paper clip on the chalkboard.]

Mrs. Mudancia had a paper clip that was 2 inches long. She straightened it so there was no more bend. **How long is the straightened paper clip?** about 5 inches; depends on the size of the paper clip

❷ Mr. Mudancia had a woolen scarf 40 inches long. He cut 10 inches off one end and sewed it onto the other end. **How long is the scarf now?** 40 inches

❸ Mr. Mudancia had a hose that was 6 yards long. He made it a yard shorter at one end, and then he made it 2 yards longer at the other end. **How long is the hose now?** 7 yards

❹ Mr. Muddle lives a block and a half from his store. He walks to the store in the morning and walks home in the afternoon. **How far does he walk all together?** three blocks

❺ Willy has ten marbles. Seven of them are little. **How many of them are round?** all ten

❻ Ferdie and Manolita wanted to buy some popcorn together, but it cost 50 cents. "I'll pay a quarter and you pay the rest," said Ferdie. **Is that fair?** yes **How much would Manolita have to pay?** 25¢

THINKING STORY

Mr. Mudancia Changes Houses

One day Mr. Mudancia made the mistake of changing his house into a bowling alley, and then his family had no place to live. "You can stay in our summer house," said Ms. Eng, who had two of everything, even houses. "Just make yourselves at home there and change anything into the way you want."

The Mudancias were very pleased with the Engs' summer house, but as soon as they moved in Mr. Mudancia started to change things a little. There was a clock on the wall that looked like this. [Show the illustration.]

How many points does the clock have? eight

Mr. Mudancia changed the clock a little by taking off all the long points.

How many points are left? four

"I hope the Engs like a four-pointed clock," said Manolita.

There was a poster on the wall that looked like this:

[Cover the illustration on the right and show the one on the left.]
How many corners does the poster have? Count them. four

Mr. Mudancia cut off one of the corners so that the poster looked like this.
[Show the second illustration.]
How many corners does the poster have now? Count them. five

Mr. Mudancia liked the way the poster looked so much that he clipped off the other three corners the same way.
How many corners does the poster have now? Picture it in your mind. eight

"I hope the Engs like an eight-cornered poster," said Mrs. Mudancia.

On the floor of the summer house was a very thick rug. It was 1 inch thick.
How thick is that? Show with your fingers. [Demonstrate.]

Story 18 • **109**

⑦ There are four doors in Mr. Mudancia's house, and each one had a doorknob. But Mr. Mudancia changed that. He put an extra doorknob on each door.
How many doorknobs are there now? eight

⑧ Ferdie was carrying three jars of pickles at the store, but he dropped two of them.
How many good jars are left? can't tell
What do you need to know? how many broke

⑨ Portia lives on the second floor.
How many floors down does she have to go to get to the basement? two

⑩ Mr. Tomkins drives a city bus. One day four people got on at his first stop. At the next stop one person got off. At the next stop two people got on.
How many passengers were on the bus then? five

⑪ Manolita belongs to a scout troop. There were ten scouts the first year. The next year five scouts moved away, but there was one new scout.
How many scouts were in the troop then? six

⑫ Mr. Eng used to weigh 10 pounds more than Mr. Muddle, but now Mr. Muddle weighs 15 pounds less than Mr. Eng.

This one is tricky. [Read it again.]

What could have happened? What else? Mr. Eng gained weight, or Mr. Muddle lost weight.

◆ **STORY 18 Mr. Mudancia Changes Houses**

Mr. Mudancia changed the rug a little. He cut it in half and put one half on top of the other.

How thick is it now? 2 inches

"I'm sure the Engs will be happy to have a rug 2 inches thick on the floor," said Mr. Mudancia.

"I'm not so sure," said Mrs. Mudancia. "The rug is twice as thick as it was before, but it isn't as long."

How long is it now? half as long

There was a fishbowl in the summer house. Mr. Mudancia changed the bowl by cutting it in half from top to bottom. **How many fishbowls do the Mudancias have now?** none

They don't have any fishbowl, because neither half holds water. So they put the fish in the bathtub. Now they have no fishbowl and no place to take a bath, either.

. . . the end

Story 18 • **111**

LESSON 135

Student Edition pages 297–298

Using a Known Fact

LESSON PLANNER

Objectives

✓ to assess mastery of addition facts through 10 + 10

▶ to provide opportunities for students to memorize the last four addition facts (3 + 5, 3 + 6, 4 + 7, 5 + 7)

Context of the Lesson As this is the last of several lessons on mastery of addition facts through 10 + 10, a checkpoint is provided to assess mastery.

 MANIPULATIVES

addition table from Lesson 134

Program Resources

"Frog Pond" Game Mat

Number Cubes

Practice Master 135

Enrichment Master 135

Assessment Masters

For additional math integration:
Math Throughout the Day*

For extra practice:
CD-ROM* Lesson 135

① Warm-Up ⏱ 5 MINUTES

 Problem of the Day Write the following problems on the chalkboard. Then tell students to change one addend in each problem to make each sum correct. (Responses will vary widely. Check to see that the sum of each problem is 10.)

```
   6          4          7
   2          5          4
  +3         +0         +1
  ――         ――         ――
  10         10         10
```

Problem-Solving Strategies Ask students who have solved the Problem of the Day to share how they solved it and any strategies they used.

MENTAL MATH Have students use their Number Cubes to show the answers to the following problems:

a. 3 + 4 = (7)	b. 10 + 10 = (20)
c. 6 + 10 = (16)	d. 5 + 5 = (10)
e. 9 + 6 = (15)	f. 2 + 2 = (4)
g. 10 + 5 = (15)	h. 5 + 3 = (8)

297 Numbers 1–100

Name _____

Using a Known Fact

Solve the easier problem first. Then let it help you solve the harder one.

Easier	Harder
❶ 7 + 10 = __17__	❷ 7 + 9 = __16__
❸ 5 + 5 = __10__	❹ 5 + 6 = __11__
❺ 7 + 7 = __14__	❻ 8 + 7 = __15__
❼ 10 + 4 = __14__	❽ 9 + 4 = __13__
❾ 6 + 6 = __12__	❿ 6 + 7 = __13__
⓫ 8 + 2 = __10__	⓬ 7 + 2 = __9__
⓭ 10 + 6 = __16__	⓮ 9 + 6 = __15__
⓯ 8 + 8 = __16__	⓰ 7 + 8 = __15__
⓱ 10 + 8 = __18__	⓲ 9 + 8 = __17__

 NOTE TO HOME
Students use an easier math fact to solve a more difficult one.

Unit 4   Lesson 135 • **297**

RETEACHING

 GAME Have students who still need practice with addition facts play the "Addition Table" game, the "Space" game, or one of the games previously introduced.

Subtraction facts are not systematically presented for memorization in Level 1. However, some students will see the relationship between them and the corresponding addition facts and will pick them up automatically. Memorization of subtraction facts is developed in Level 2.

PRACTICE p. 135

LESSON 135 PRACTICE Name _____

Solve these problems.
Remember your addition facts

❶ 3 + 7 ―― 10	❷ 6 + 8 ―― 14	❸ 7 + 4 ―― 11	❹ 8 + 5 ―― 13
❺ 9 + 9 ―― 18	❻ 10 + 6 ―― 16	❼ 4 + 8 ―― 12	❽ 9 + 4 ―― 13

❾ 8 + 6 = __14__	❿ 9 + 5 = __14__
⓫ 10 + 3 = __13__	⓬ 7 + 7 = __14__
⓭ 9 + 8 = __17__	⓮ 9 + 7 = __16__
⓯ 8 + 7 = __15__	⓰ 7 + 6 = __13__

Math Explorations and Applications Level 1 • **135**

---

*available separately

◆ **LESSON 135 Using a Known Fact**

Solve these problems.
Remember your addition facts.

⑲ 4 + 4 = **8**

⑳ 8 + 9 = **17**

㉑ 3 + 6 = **9**

㉒ 2 + 7 = **9**

㉓ 9 + 1 = **10**

㉔ 5 + 5 = **10**

㉕ 7 + 8 = **15**

㉖ 5 + 3 = **8**

㉗ 2 + 0 = **2**

㉘ 6 + 6 = **12**

Play the "Frog Pond" game.

298 • Numbers 1–100

 NOTE TO HOME
Students solve addition problems
from memory.

Copyright © SRA/McGraw-Hill

---

② Teach

 Demonstrate Review addition facts such as plus-1 facts. As soon as students have finished one kind of fact, erase or cross off the appropriate line on the **addition table** until all that remains are numbers that correspond to the sums of 3 + 5, 3 + 6, 4 + 7, and 5 + 7 and their inverses. Then present oral and written problems using these four addition facts.

Using the Student Pages Have students work independently to complete pages 297–298.

 Introducing the "Frog Pond" Game Mat Use the Game Mat transparency to demonstrate this game. Then have students play it to practice addition facts. A copy of this game can also be found on page 401 of this Guide.

③ Wrap-Up

In Closing Continue to drill students on addition facts through 10 + 10. Divide the class into two teams. Call out an addition sentence and ask for a quick answer. The team that answers first receives a point. The team with the most points wins.

 Mastery Checkpoint 22

At about this time students should demonstrate mastery of the addition facts through 10 + 10 by getting eight of ten problems on page 298 correct in two to three minutes. You may also wish to assign Assessment Blackline Masters pages 51–52 to determine mastery. Results of this assessment may be recorded on the Mastery Checkpoint Chart.

ENRICHMENT p. 135

 135 ENRICHMENT Name _____

Look at the square. You get the same answers when you add down as when you add across.

3	2	1
1	3	2
2	1	3

Fill in the numbers in the open squares so that you can add down and across to get the same answers.

❶
1	9	4
9	4	1
4	1	9

❷
8	5	7
7	8	5
5	7	8

❸
2	8	3
8	3	2
3	2	8

❹
4	9	7
7	4	9
9	7	4

❺
4	6	8
6	8	4
8	4	6

Math Explorations and Applications Level 1 • **135**

ASSESSMENT p. 51

UNIT 4 Mastery Checkpoint 22 Addition facts through 10 + 10 (Lesson 135)
Page 1 of 2
Name _____
The student demonstrates mastery by correctly answering 24 of the 30 problems.

Solve these problems.
Remember your addition facts.

❶ 5 + 5 = __10__ ❷ 3 + 7 = __10__

❸ 6 + 5 = __11__ ❹ 8 + 4 = __12__

❺ 1 + 9 = __10__ ❻ 4 + 5 = __9__

❼ 7 + 0 = __7__ ❽ 6 + 7 = __13__

❾ 3 + 8 = __11__ ❿ 4 + 9 = __13__

⓫ 9 + 3 = __12__ ⓬ 10 + 9 = __19__

⓭ 7 + 4 = __11__ ⓮ 2 + 8 = __10__

⓯ 8 + 8 = __16__ ⓰ 6 + 4 = __10__
Go on . . .

Math Explorations and Applications Level 1 • **51**

Assessment Criteria

Did the student . . .

✓ memorize the last four addition facts?

✓ demonstrate mastery of the addition facts through 10 + 10?

LOOKING AHEAD A math balance* or double-pan balance* will be useful for Lesson 136.

*available separately

LESSON
136
Student Edition pages 299–300
Reviewing Addition Facts

Name _____

Reviewing Addition Facts

ALGEBRA READINESS

What numbers are missing on some of these strips? Write them in.

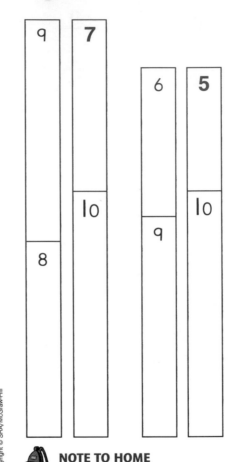
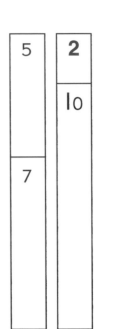
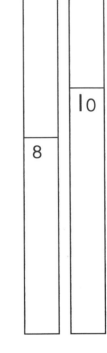

NOTE TO HOME
Students use Number Strips to solve missing addend problems.

Unit 4   Lesson 136 • **299**

LESSON PLANNER

Objective

▶ to provide practice using the addition facts through 10 + 10

Context of the Lesson Although Lesson 135 contained a Mastery Checkpoint for addition facts through 10 + 10, all students will need continued practice with the facts. During or after this lesson you may want to recheck those students who have not yet achieved this Mastery Checkpoint.

MANIPULATIVES
math balance* or double-pan balance*
colored paper discs (optional)
string (optional)

Program Resources
Number Cubes
Number Strips
Thinking Story Book, pages 112–113
Reteaching Master
Practice Master 136
Enrichment Master 136
For extra practice: CD-ROM* Lesson 136

① Warm-Up ⏱ 5 MINUTES

Problem of the Day Present the following problem to the class. I am thinking of a certain number. All the digits are different. There are three digits. The sum of the digits is 9. Each digit is 1 greater than the digit before it. What is the number? (234)

Problem-Solving Strategies Ask students who have solved the Problem of the Day to share how they solved it and any strategies they used.

MENTAL MATH Present the following problems to the students at a fast pace. Have them show their answers with the Number Cubes.

a. 7 + 2 = (9)	**b.** 3 + 5 = (8)
c. 10 + 3 = (13)	**d.** 3 + 6 = (9)
e. 9 + 4 = (13)	**f.** 3 + 0 = (3)
g. 4 + 7 = (11)	**h.** 10 + 4 = (14)
i. 5 + 7 = (12)	**j.** 8 + 2 = (10)
k. 3 + 6 = (9)	**l.** 5 + 2 = (7)
m. 5 + 7 = (12)	**n.** 8 + 3 = (11)

ART CONNECTION **MANIPULATIVES** **Art Connection** Have students make necklaces with different-**colored paper discs** threaded on **string.** The discs should represent numbers that sum to 10. For example, a student may choose to have three orange discs and seven blue discs, which equal 10, in addition to other combinations of tens on the necklace. Between each set of ten discs, string a black disc. Have students record the addition sentences represented by the discs.

RETEACHING p. 35

◆ **LESSON 136** Reviewing Addition Facts

What numbers are missing
on some of these strips?

Write them in.

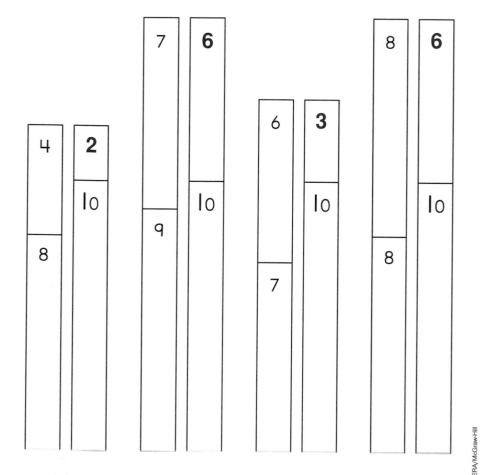

300 • Numbers 1–100

NOTE TO HOME
Students use Number Strips to solve missing
addend problems.

o. 9 + 3 = (12)   p. 3 + 3 = (6)
q. 7 + 3 = (10)   r. 2 + 1 = (3)

❷ Teach

COOPERATIVE LEARNING **MANIPULATIVES** **Demonstrate** Have students
pair off to give each other
practice with Number Strip
problems. One student combines two strips that sum to
more than 10. The other student tries to make the same
length by combining a 10-strip and one other strip. If there
is a **math balance*** or a **double-pan balance***, have one
student put two numbers or weights that sum to more than
10 on one side of the balance. The other student tries to
balance it by using a 10-unit weight and one other weight.

Using the Student Pages Have students complete the
exercises on pages 299–300. Remind them that they should
use their knowledge of addition facts to figure out the
missing numbers. They may use actual Number Strips if they
need to find or check their numbers.

Using the Thinking Story Present four
problems from those following "Mr. Mudancia
Changes Houses" on pages 112–113 of the
Thinking Story Book or page 296a–296b of this Guide.

❸ Wrap-Up ⏱ 5 MINUTES

In Closing Challenge students to share any strategies
they used to learn the four remaining addition facts.

Informal Assessment Note students who
seem to need more practice with the addition
facts. Establish a daily time period for them to
do so.

Assessment Criteria

Did the student . . .

✓ demonstrate understanding of the
Number Strip and/or weights
activity?

✓ complete pages 299–300 with 75%
accuracy?

PRACTICE p. 136

LESSON 136 PRACTICE Name _____

Solve these problems.
Remember the addition facts.

❶ 2 + 5 = ___7___   ❷ 1 + 6 = ___7___

❸ 9 + 6 = ___15___   ❹ 9 + 8 = ___17___

❺ 4 + 7 = ___11___   ❻ 4 + 10 = ___14___

❼ 0 + 8 = ___8___   ❽ 7 + 7 = ___14___

❾ 7 + 6 = ___13___   ❿ 4 + 0 = ___4___

⓫ 1 + 9 = ___10___   ⓬ 10 + 10 = ___20___

⓭ 4 + 4 = ___8___   ⓮ 9 + 2 = ___11___

⓯ 8 + 5 = ___13___   ⓰ 5 + 4 = ___9___

⓱ 3 + 7 = ___10___   ⓲ 6 + 6 = ___12___

⓳ 9 + 3 = ___12___   ⓴ 6 + 3 = ___9___

136 • Math Explorations and Applications Level 1

ENRICHMENT p. 136

LESSON 136 ENRICHMENT Name _____

Help the dogs find a seat. Draw lines
from the dogs to the cars they
should ride.

Who does not get a seat? ___8 + 4___

136 • Math Explorations and Applications Level 1

---

*available separately

Unit 4 Lesson 136 **300**

137
Two-Digit Addition

Student Edition pages 301–302

LESSON PLANNER

Objectives

▶ to prepare students to add two-digit numbers

▶ to teach students that in two-digit addition, the sum of the tens place depends on the sum of the ones place

Context of the Lesson This is the introductory lesson for two-digit addition. It includes addition problems with regrouping.

 MANIPULATIVES

base-10 blocks*
craft sticks
play money—
    dimes and
    pennies
    (optional)
rubber bands

Program Resources

Thinking Story Book,
    pages 112–113
Practice Master 137
Enrichment Master 137
For extra practice:
    CD-ROM* Lesson 137

❶ Warm-Up

 Problem of the Day Present the following problem to the class. Aaron said that there are six numbers greater than 38 but less than 43. Is he correct? Why or why not? (No, there are four numbers: 39, 40, 41, and 42. You cannot count 38 or 43 because 38 is not greater than 38, and 43 is not less than 43.)

Problem-Solving Strategies Ask students who have solved the Problem of the Day to share how they solved it and any strategies they used.

MENTAL MATH Read aloud the following problems and have students solve them mentally.

a. Mr. Breezy ate six crackers. Ferdie ate three. How many crackers did they eat in all? (nine)

b. Marcus found five shells. Manolita found two. How many did they find in all? (seven)

c. Willy saw three brown horses playing in a field. Mr. Muddle saw four white horses on another hillside. How many horses did they see all together? (seven)

d. Portia went fishing with Loretta the Letter Carrier. They each caught four fish. How many did they catch all together? (eight)

e. Ferdie had two pennies. Mr. Muddle gave him three more. How many did Ferdie have then? (five)

Two-Digit Addition

Name _____

Write how many. You may use manipulatives to help.

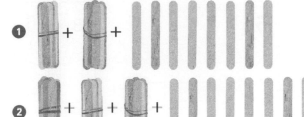

❶ 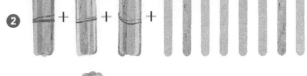 = **28**

❷ = **38**

❸ 38 + = **48**

❹ 38 + + = **51**

❺ 38 + 13 = **51**

❻ 38 + 14 = **52**

 NOTE TO HOME
Students use manipulatives to explore adding larger numbers.

Why teach it this way?

Although difficult, it is important to teach two-digit addition and subtraction with regrouping at the same time as two-digit addition without regrouping. Students who practice only two-digit addition without regrouping develop the concept that what happens in the tens place is independent of what happens in the ones place. This is a difficult concept to correct in later grades.

RETEACHING

 Use **pennies** and **dimes** to demonstrate how to add two-digit numbers. For example, have students add 18 + 27 by adding one dime + two dimes, and then eight pennies + seven pennies. Ask students if they can trade any pennies for a dime. (ten pennies for one dime) How many pennies are left? (five) Count the money to demonstrate that the result is four dimes and five pennies, or 45 cents.

*available separately

◆ **LESSON 137 Two-Digit Addition**

Solve each problem.
Watch how each problem builds on the one before it. You may use manipulatives to help.

7 $10 + 8 =$ <u>**18**</u>

8 $10 + 10 + 8 =$ <u>**28**</u>

9 $10 + 10 + 10 + 8 =$ <u>**38**</u>

10 $30 + 8 =$ <u>**38**</u>

11 $30 + 8 + 10 =$ <u>**48**</u>

12 $30 + 8 + 10 + 3 =$ <u>**51**</u>

13 $38 + 10 + 3 =$ <u>**51**</u>

14 $38 + 13 =$ <u>**51**</u>

302 • Numbers 1–100

NOTE TO HOME
Students use manipulatives to solve addition problems with two-digit numbers.

Copyright © SRA/McGraw-Hill

② Teach

Demonstrate Write 18 + 27 on the chalkboard. Have one student hold up ten fingers and another hold up eight fingers to show 18. Then have two students hold up ten fingers each and another student hold up seven fingers to show 27. Ask how many tens are up. (3) Have students count how many extra fingers are up. (15) Demonstrate how to make a group of ten from the extra fingers by having the one student with seven fingers put down two and the one student with eight fingers put up two. Ask: "Now how many tens are up?" (4) "How many extras?" (5) "So what is 18 + 27?" (four tens and 5, or 45) Repeat with similar problems. Demonstrate how to record what you are doing. For example, to record 18 + 27:

$$
\begin{array}{r}
18 \\
+27 \\
\hline
30 \\
15 \\
\hline
45
\end{array}
$$

30 ← First, add the tens, for 30
15 ← then add the ones, which is one ten and five.
45 ← Finally, add to find four tens and five, or 45.

You might want to point out that students could have started with the units digits and then added the tens.

Using the Student Pages Have students work in pairs or small groups using **craft sticks** to complete these pages.

Using the Thinking Story Present four new problems from among those following "Mr. Mudancia Changes Houses" on pages 112–113 of the Thinking Story Book or pages 296a–296b of this Guide.

③ Wrap-Up

In Closing Have students show how to add 17 + 14 using other students' fingers or **base-10 blocks***.

Performance Assessment Observe students' manipulative use to see if they regroup appropriately.

Assessment Criteria

Did the student . . .

✓ provide accurate responses during the demonstration?

✓ correctly answer at least 11 of 14 problems on pages 301–302?

PRACTICE p. 137

LESSON **137** PRACTICE Name _____

Solve each problem. Watch how each problem builds on the one before it. You may use manipulatives to help.

1 $10 + 6 =$ <u>16</u>

2 $10 + 10 + 6 =$ <u>26</u>

3 $10 + 10 + 10 + 6 =$ <u>36</u>

4 $30 + 6 =$ <u>36</u>

5 $30 + 6 + 10 =$ <u>46</u>

6 $30 + 6 + 10 + 2 =$ <u>48</u>

7 $36 + 10 + 2 =$ <u>48</u>

8 $36 + 12 =$ <u>48</u>

9 $10 + 3 =$ <u>13</u>

10 $10 + 20 + 3 =$ <u>33</u>

11 $10 + 20 + 3 + 30 =$ <u>63</u>

Math Explorations and Applications Level 1 • 137

ENRICHMENT p. 137

LESSON **137** ENRICHMENT Name _____

Each drawer below is filled with coins. Help put the coins in coin wrappers. Quarter wrappers hold $10. Dime wrappers hold $5. Nickel wrappers hold $2. Penny wrappers hold 50¢. Draw the wrappers you would need for each drawer.

Answers shown are examples only. Answers will vary.

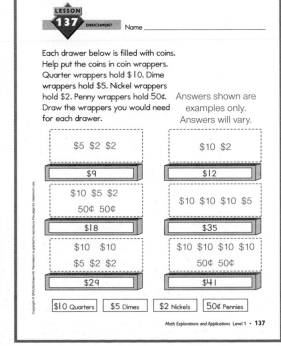

$5 $2 $2		$10 $2
$9		$12

$10 $5 $2 50¢ 50¢		$10 $10 $10 $5
$18		$35

$10 $10 $5 $2 $2		$10 $10 $10 $10 50¢ 50¢
$29		$41

$10 Quarters | $5 Dimes | $2 Nickels | 50¢ Pennies

Math Explorations and Applications Level 1 • 137

*available separately

Student Edition pages 303–304

Exploring Regrouping

LESSON PLANNER

Objectives

▶ to prepare students to subtract two-digit numbers

▶ to teach students that in two-digit subtraction, the difference of the tens place depends on the difference of the ones place

Context of the Lesson This is the introductory lesson for two-digit subtraction and is based on the same methods used in Lesson 137 for two-digit addition.

 MANIPULATIVES

base-10 blocks*

craft sticks

rubber bands

Program Resources

Number Cubes

Reteaching Master

Practice Master 138

Enrichment Master 138

For extra practice:
  CD-ROM* Lesson 138
  Mixed Practice, page 378

❶ Warm-Up

 Problem of the Day Write the following pattern on the chalkboard: 65, 63, 62, 60, 59, 57, ☐, ☐, 53, 51. Have students describe the pattern and then fill in the missing numbers. (–2, –1, –2, –1, etc.; 56, 54)

Problem-Solving Strategies Ask students who have solved the Problem of the Day to share how they solved it and any strategies they used.

 Have students use Number Cubes to indicate their answers.

a. 10 + 0 = (10)   b. 21 + 2 = (23)   c. 36 + 2 = (38)

d. 33 – 2 = (31)   e. 29 – 1 = (28)   f. 25 – 0 = (25)

❷ Teach

Demonstrate Have students use finger sets to demonstrate the following problem: 34 – 18. Have three students hold up ten fingers each and a last student hold up four fingers. Ask how many fingers. (34) Then ask students how to subtract 18 fingers. Take one bunch of ten away by having one student put down ten fingers. Ask: "How can we take eight more away?" Point out

---

Name _____

Exploring Regrouping

Make these amounts using your manipulatives. Then write how many.

❶ $10 + 10 =$ **20**

❷ $10 + 1 + 1 + 1 + 1 + 1 + 1 + 1 + 1 + 1 + 1 =$ **20**

❸ $10 + 10 + 10 + 1 + 1 + 1 =$ **33**

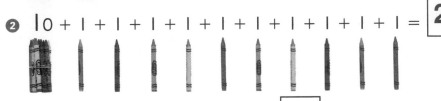

❹ $10 + 10 + 1 + 1 + 1 + 1 + 1 + 1$
$+ 1 + 1 + 1 + 1 + 1 + 1 + 1 =$ **33**

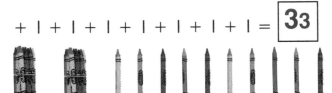

 NOTE TO HOME
Students solve two-digit addition problems with manipulatives.

Copyright © SRA/McGraw-Hill

Unit 4   Lesson 138 • **303**

 Real-World Connection Have students work in pairs or groups with **craft sticks** to solve addition and subtraction problems about their school. Ask, for example, "How many boys are in our class?" "How many girls?" "How many in all?" or "How many more boys than girls?"

RETEACHING p. 36

*available separately

◆ **LESSON 138** Exploring Regrouping

Work in small groups. Use manipulatives to solve these problems.

⑤ 30 = 20 + $\boxed{10}$ ⑥ 34 = 20 + $\boxed{14}$

⑦ 45 = 30 + $\boxed{15}$ ⑧ 62 = 50 + $\boxed{12}$

⑨ 87 = 70 + $\boxed{17}$ ⑩ 93 = 80 + $\boxed{13}$

⑪ 35 − 6 = $\boxed{29}$ Hint: 35 = 20 + 15

⑫ 42 − 16 = $\boxed{26}$ Hint: 42 = 30 + 12

⑬ 72 − 14 = $\boxed{58}$

⑭ 37 − 4 = $\boxed{33}$

 NOTE TO HOME
Students use manipulatives to solve addition and subtraction problems.

304 • Numbers 1–100

Copyright © SRA/McGraw-Hill

---

that they must come from one of the bunches of ten. Turn down eight fingers, leaving two fingers up for that student. This two plus the four fingers from the last student makes six. All together this makes six extra fingers and one bunch of ten, or 16, left over. Repeat with similar problems using fingers, **craft sticks,** or **base-10 blocks*** to model subtraction. Demonstrate for students how to record what they are doing. For example, to record 34 – 18 show:

$$\begin{array}{r} 34 \\ -\ 18 \\ \hline 24 \end{array}$$ ← First, subtract the tens, for 24
$$\begin{array}{r} -\ 8 \\ \hline 16 \end{array}$$ ← then subtract the ones from one of the tens.
16 ← This revealed that there was one ten left and six more, or 16.

You may wish to point out that students could start with the units digits and ungroup one of the tens to have two tens and 14. Then take away one ten and eight to find one ten and six, or 16, left.

 Using the Student Pages Have students work in pairs or small groups using base-10 blocks* or craft sticks to complete these pages. Check students' answers when finished.

❸ Wrap-Up ⏱

In Closing Have students demonstrate how to subtract 32 – 15 using other students' fingers.

Performance Assessment Observe students as they use manipulatives to add and subtract, checking to see if they recognize when they can make bunches of tens from ones in addition and when they can ungroup bunches of tens to subtract.

ALTERNATIVE ASSESSMENT

PRACTICE p. 138

ENRICHMENT p. 138

Assessment Criteria

Did the student . . .

✓ provide accurate responses during the demonstration?

✓ correctly answer 11 of 14 problems on pages 303–304?

*available separately

UNIT 4

Mid-Unit Review

Student Edition pages 305–306

The Mid-Unit Review pinpoints troublesome skill areas for students, allowing plenty of time for additional practice and reteaching before the unit ends. If students did not do well on the Mid-Unit Review and have completed additional practice, you may want to use the Mid-Unit Review provided on pages 53–55 in the Assessment Blackline Masters.

Using the Student Pages Have students complete problems 1–25 on pages 305 and 306 on their own. You might treat this review as a formal assessment of students' skills, and have students complete this review as a timed test. See suggestions for administering timed tests on page 48.

UNIT 4

Name _____

Mid-Unit Review

Solve these problems in your head if you can.

❶ $\begin{array}{r} 34 \\ +10 \\ \hline 44 \end{array}$ ❷ $\begin{array}{r} 34 \\ +20 \\ \hline 54 \end{array}$ ❸ $\begin{array}{r} 25 \\ +10 \\ \hline 35 \end{array}$ ❹ $\begin{array}{r} 25 \\ +30 \\ \hline 55 \end{array}$

How many tally marks? Ring sets of ten to help you count. Then write the number on the chart.

Flag	Tallies	Number
❺ 🚩	(卌 卌 卌)(卌 卌) 卌 卌 ‖	22
❻ 🚩	(卌 卌 卌) 卌 丨	16
❼ 🚩	(卌 卌)(卌 卌 卌) 卌 ⦀	28

🎒 **NOTE TO HOME**
Students review unit skills and concepts.

Unit 4 Mid-Unit Review • **305**

◆ UNIT 4 Mid-Unit Review

Solve these problems.
Remember your doubles.

(8) 8 + 8 = __16__   **(9)** 8 + 7 = __15__

(10) 7 + 7 = __14__   **(11)** 7 + 6 = __13__

(12) 5 + 5 = __10__   **(13)** 5 + 6 = __11__

(14) 9 + 9 = __18__   **(15)** 9 + 8 = __17__

What is the right sign?
Draw <, >, or =.

(16) 12 ⟨ < ⟩ 21   **(17)** 54 ⟨ > ⟩ 45

(18) 16 ⟨ = ⟩ 16   **(19)** 52 ⟨ > ⟩ 25

Write true number sentences.
Make them all different.

**Answers shown
are examples only.**

(20) | 7 | + | 6 | = 13   **(21)** | 9 | + | 4 | = 13

(22) | 10 | + | 3 | = 13   **(23)** | 8 | + | 5 | = 13

(24) | 6 | + | 7 | = 13

NOTE TO HOME
Students review unit skills and concepts.

Copyright © SRA/McGraw-Hill

Literature Connection To provide
practice in addition and intuitive
multiplication, read *Two More* from the
Literature Library*. As you read, students
can count, add, or multiply the number of animals that pile
into a boat.

Home Connections You may want to send home the
letter on pages 52–53 in the Home Connections Blackline
Masters, which provides additional activities families can
complete together. These activities apply the skills being
presented in this unit.

Performance Assessment The
Performance Assessment Tasks 1–6 provided
on pages 71–73 of the Assessment Blackline
Masters can be used at this time to evaluate students'
abilities to add multiples of 10 and count money up to $100.
You may want to administer this assessment with individual
students or in small groups.

Portfolio Assessment If you have not
already completed the Portfolio Assessment
task provided on page 82 of the Assessment
Blackline Masters, it can be used to evaluate students' skills
in solving function machine problems.

Unit Project This would be a good time to assign the
"Greatest and Least" project on pages 348a–348b. Students
can begin working on the project in cooperative groups in
their free time as you work through the unit. The Unit Project
is a good opportunity for students to apply the concepts of
forming greatest and least numbers and identifying and
creating patterns in real-world problem solving.

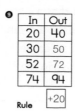

ASSESSMENT p. 53

UNIT 4 Mid-Unit Review (Use after Lesson 138.)   Page 1 of 3

Name _____

The student demonstrates mastery by correctly answering 24 of the 30 problems.

Solve these problems.
Watch the signs.

1 20 + 10 = __30__   **2** 50 – 20 = __30__

3 37 + 20 = __57__   **4** 47 – 10 = __37__

5 40   **6** 66   **7** 80   **8** 73
   + 20   + 10   – 20   – 10
   ────   ────   ────   ────
    60   76   60   63

Fill in the missing numbers.
Write the rule.

9
In	Out
20	40
30	50
52	72
74	94

Rule __+20__

10
In	Out
33	31
46	44
57	55
71	69

Rule __–2__   [Go on …→]

Math Explorations and Applications Level 1 · **53**

---

*available separately

LESSON 139

Repeated Addition

Student Edition pages 307–308

LESSON PLANNER

Objectives

▶ to introduce the process of repeated addition

▶ to provide practice with estimating length

Context of the Lesson This is the first of two lessons on repeated addition. Repeated addition prepares students for multiplication, which is formally introduced in Level 2.

 MANIPULATIVES

can

counters* (20)

Program Resources

Number Cubes

Number Strips

Thinking Story Book, pages 112–113

Practice Master 139

Enrichment Master 139

For extra practice:
CD-ROM* Lesson 139

❶ Warm-Up ⏱ 5 MINUTES

 Problem of the Day Present the following problem. There are 18 chairs to be set up in rows for the audience at a school play. Draw several ways you could arrange them into even rows. (one row of 18; two rows of 9; nine rows of 2; six rows of 3; three rows of 6)

Problem-Solving Strategies Ask students who have solved the Problem of the Day to share how they solved it and any strategies they used.

 Ask students to use their Number Cubes to show the answers to doubles problems up to 10 + 10.

❷ Teach

 Demonstrate Without counting aloud, drop **counters*** into a **can** one at a time. Have students show with Number Cubes the total number of counters in the can. Next drop counters into the can two at a time—then three, four, and five at a time. Have totals go up to 20. Have students count in unison with you as you take the counters out of the can. As you count, emphasize the numbers corresponding to the

---

LESSON 139

Name _____

Repeated Addition

Listen to the problems.

1  `9`

2  `12`

3  `8`

NOTE TO HOME
Students use repeated addition or skip counting to solve story problems.

GIFTED & TALENTED GAME

Meeting Individual Needs Challenge selected students to play the "Harder Add to Number Strip" game. Players are allowed to substitute combinations of Number Strips for a single strip. For example, assume that a 4-strip is needed to make a given length but was lost in an earlier play. A 3-strip and a 1-strip may be used instead.

RETEACHING

Work individually with students who find the Number Cube exercise in the demonstration difficult. Do not expect complete accuracy.

◆ **LESSON 139** Repeated Addition

Solve the easier problem first.
Then let it help you solve the
harder one.

Easier	Harder
❹ 5 + 10 = __15__	❺ 5 + 9 = __14__
❻ 6 + 10 = __16__	❼ 6 + 8 = __14__
❽ 4 + 4 = __8__	❾ 4 + 5 = __9__
❿ 7 + 3 = __10__	⓫ 7 + 4 = __11__
⓬ 9 + 1 = __10__	
⓭ 5 + 5 = __10__	
⓮ 4 + 10 = __14__	

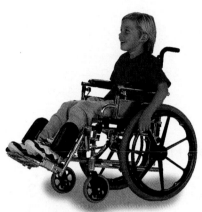

 GAME Play the "Add to the Number Strip" game.

308 • Numbers 1–100

 NOTE TO HOME Students use easier facts to solve harder ones.

Copyright © SRA/McGraw-Hill

---

grouping you used. For example, if you dropped the counters in three at a time, count: one, two, *three*, and four, five, *six*.

 Using the Student Pages Call attention to the illustrations on page 307 as you read aloud each problem. **Problem 1:** "Each of these cars has three flat tires. How many tires need to be fixed?" **Problem 2:** "Ms. Chou wants to put a horseshoe on each horse's hooves. Horses have four legs. How many horseshoes does she need all together?" **Problem 3:** "Each of these children has a penny in a front pocket and a penny in a back pocket. How many pennies do they have all together?" Have students solve the problems on page 308 on their own.

Introducing the "Add to Number Strip" Game To provide practice with estimating length, demonstrate and then have pairs of students play the following game. Give each player a complete set of Number Strips. The lead player lays out a Number Strip, face up, and places a shorter strip face down beside it. The second player selects another Number Strip that together with the face-down strip equals the same length as the face-up strip. If the answer is correct, he or she captures the lead player's face-down strip. If not, then the lead player captures the strip presented by the second player. Players take turns. The one who has the most strips at the end of the game is the winner.

Using the Thinking Story Present four new problems from those following "Mr. Mudancia Changes Houses" on pages 112–113 of the Thinking Story Book or pages 296a–296b of this Guide.

❸ Wrap-Up ⏱ 5 MINUTES

In Closing Summarize the lesson by asking volunteers to tell how they solved the story problems on page 307.

Informal Assessment Observe students during the demonstration to determine if anyone is having difficulty skip counting.

Assessment Criteria

Did the student . . .

✓ demonstrate understanding of the concept of repeated addition?

✓ make reasonable estimates of length?

PRACTICE p. 139

LESSON 139 PRACTICE Name _____

Solve the easier problem first. Then let it help you solve the harder one.

Easier	Harder
❶ 8 + 10 = __18__	❷ 8 + 9 = __17__
❸ 9 + 1 = __10__	❹ 9 + 2 = __11__
❺ 10 + 7 = __17__	❻ 9 + 7 = __16__
❼ 5 + 5 = __10__	❽ 5 + 6 = __11__
❾ 8 + 2 = __10__	❿ 8 + 3 = __11__
⓫ 6 + 6 = __12__	⓬ 6 + 7 = __13__
⓭ 5 + 10 = __15__	⓮ 5 + 9 = __14__

Math Explorations and Applications Level 1 • **139**

ENRICHMENT p. 139

LESSON 139 ENRICHMENT Name _____

SOCIAL STUDIES CONNECTION Some early Native Americans lived in tepees. To start the tepee people tied four poles together.

❶ How many poles would be needed to start three tepees? __12__

❷ After the four poles were tied at the top, 12 more poles were added. This made the tepee stronger. How many poles would there be in one tepee so far? __16__

❸ People covered tepees with animal hides. At the top, small flaps let out smoke. Two small poles held the flaps open. How many small poles would be needed for three tepees? __6__

Math Explorations and Applications Level 1 • **139**

LESSON 140

Using Arrays and Repeated Addition

Student Edition pages 309–310

Name _____

Using Arrays and Repeated Addition

Using Arrays and Repeated Addition

LESSON PLANNER

Objectives

▶ to introduce students to multiplication using arrays

▶ to informally demonstrate for students the commutative property of multiplication

Context of the Lesson This is the introductory lesson for intuitive multiplication. Mastery is not expected.

 MANIPULATIVES

counters* or play money* (optional)

Program Resources

Number Cubes

Practice Master 140

Enrichment Master 140

For extra practice:
CD-ROM* Lesson 140
Mixed Practice, page 379

① Warm-Up

 Problem of the Day Present the following problem to the class. Mr. Wise has 12 cousins. He has two more girl cousins than boy cousins. How many boy cousins does Mr. Wise have? (5)

Problem-Solving Strategies Ask students who have solved the Problem of the Day to share how they solved it and any strategies they used.

MENTAL MATH Have students use Number Cubes to indicate their answers to the following problems.

a. 1 + 9 = (10)   b. 2 + 8 = (10)   c. 3 + 7 = (10)

d. 4 + 6 = (10)   e. 5 + 5 = (10)   f. 6 + 2 = (8)

② Teach

Using the Student Pages Have students look at the top illustration on page 309. Ask: "How many bears are there in all?" (eight) Challenge students to name as many different ways as they can to arrive at that answer. (for example, count one by one; add 4 + 4; add 2 + 2 + 2 + 2) Have students complete the number sentences to answer the question. Follow the same procedure with the next two

309 Numbers 1–100

❶ How many bears?  __8__

❷ 4 + 4 = __8__

❸ 2 + 2 + 2 + 2 = __8__

❹ How many birds?  __15__

❺ 5 + 5 + 5 = __15__

❻ 3 + 3 + 3 + 3 + 3 = __15__

❼ How many flowers?  __15__

❽ 3 + 3 + 3 + 3 + 3 = __15__

❾ 5 + 5 + 5 = __15__

 NOTE TO HOME Students use arrays to solve addition problems.

RETEACHING

 Literature Connection To provide more practice with arrays, read aloud *The Doorbell Rang* by Pat Hutchins in which Ma's wonderful cookies must be shared with an ever-growing number of visitors.

MANIPULATIVES Provide groups of students with 12 **counters*** or **pennies***. Have them work together to make three rows of counters with 4 counters in each row. Ask: "How many in all?" (12) Challenge students to make a different array using the same number of counters. Remind them that each row must always have the same number of counters. Have students share and compare arrays. Repeat with 8 and 10 counters.

*available separately

◆ LESSON 140 Using Arrays and Repeated Addition

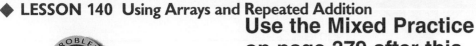

Listen to the problems.

Use the Mixed Practice on page 379 after this lesson.

⑩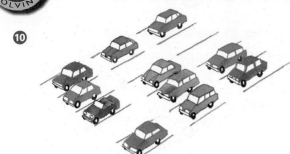

_____15_____

⑪

_____24_____

⑫

_____2_____

NOTE TO HOME
Students use arrays to solve word problems.

310 • Numbers 1–100

Copyright © SRA/McGraw-Hill

---

illustrations on this page. Next have students look at the top illustration on page 310. Ask: "How many cars can park there all together?" (15) Have students identify the different ways to arrive at that answer. Then read aloud the following problems one at a time. Allow enough time for students to write the answer and then correct it before going on to the next.

2. Ana planted flowers in her garden. Yesterday she picked three of them. How many were in her garden to begin with? Write your answer.

3. Twenty-three students will be in school today. How many seats will remain empty? Write your answer.

❸ Wrap-Up ⏱ 5 MINUTES

In Closing Explain that when objects are arranged in rows with each row having the same number of objects, they are arranged in an array. Have students describe three different methods for determining the total number of objects in an array. (for example: count one by one; add the number of objects in each row; add the number of objects in each column)

SELF ASSESSMENT Have students share which method they feel they have the most success with when determining the total number of objects in an array.

Assessment Criteria

Did the student . . .

✓ correctly solve at least 9 of 12 problems on pages 309–310?

✓ recognize that there are several different ways to solve these problems?

LEARNING STYLES Meeting Individual Needs
Have visual learners draw arrays using Xs on the chalkboard and then have them count the total number of Xs. For example, with an array of three rows of Xs with five in each row, ask: "How many in all? How can you tell?"

LOOKING AHEAD You will need tracing paper, clay, and measuring cups for Lesson 141.

PRACTICE p. 140

LESSON 140 PRACTICE Name_____

Solve these problems.

❶ How many fish? ___15___

5 + 5 + 5 = ___15___

3 + 3 + 3 + 3 + 3 = ___15___

❷ How many cookies? ___12___

6 + 6 = ___12___

2 + 2 + 2 + 2 + 2 + 2 = ___12___

❸ How many bugs? ___8___

4 + 4 = ___8___

2 + 2 + 2 + 2 = ___8___

140 • Math Explorations and Applications Level 1

ENRICHMENT p. 140

LESSON 140 ENRICHMENT Name_____

Rita put some flowers in a vase.

❶ How many flowers are in the vase? ___9___

❷ How many petals are on each flower? ___5___

❸ How many petals are in one vase? ___45___

Rita wants three vases of flowers exactly the same.

❹ How many flowers does Rita need for three vases? ___27___

140 • Math Explorations and Applications Level 1

LESSON 141 Congruent Figures

Student Edition pages 311–312

LESSON PLANNER

Objectives

▶ to teach students to count aloud to 100 in conventional form

▶ to provide a second experience involving measurement of volume

▶ to introduce the concept of congruency

Context of the Lesson This is the first lesson making the transfer from expanded to conventional numbers. This is the second lesson involving the concept of volume. Students did their first activity with volume in Lesson 133.

 MANIPULATIVES

glass or clear plastic measuring cup*

tracing paper

various objects that can be submerged in water

water

Program Resources

Number Cubes

Practice Master 141

Enrichment Master 141

For extra practice:
CD-ROM* Lesson 141

① Warm-Up ⏱ 5 MINUTES

 Problem of the Day Present the following problem to the class. Jake kicked a soccer ball nine times. He kicked the ball into the goal twice as often as he missed. How many times did he miss the goal? (three)

Problem-Solving Strategies Ask students who have solved the Problem of the Day to share how they solved it and any strategies they used.

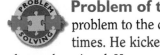 Write the following series of numbers on the chalkboard. Have students use their Number Cubes to indicate the two numbers in each group that add up to 10.

a.	2	8	6	(2 + 8)
b.	5	9	5	(5 + 5)
c.	4	7	6	(4 + 6)
d.	3	2	7	(3 + 7)
e.	9	0	1	(9 + 1)

② Teach

Demonstration Review counting aloud in the expanded

LESSON 141

Name _____

Congruent Figures

Mark the two figures in each row that are the same shape and the same size.

SCIENCE CONNECTION Do the "How High Will the Water Rise?" activity.

NOTE TO HOME Students match figures that are the same shape and size.

LITERATURE CONNECTION **Literature Connection** Read aloud *Shapes* by Marion Smoothey. This book explores the world of shapes and how they can be drawn, measured, and used in various activities, including congruency.

RETEACHING

Have a volunteer start to count aloud conventionally from 0, and then have that student stop at a random number and have another continue. Say "Stop" again and have another continue. Repeat until they have reached 100.

◆ **LESSON 141** Congruent Figures

Ring the figure in each row that
is different from the others.

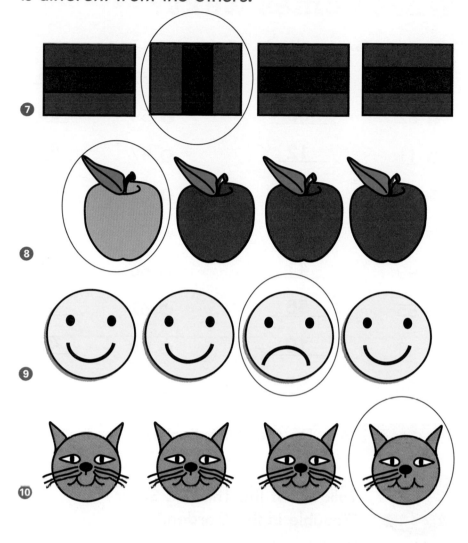

7

8

9

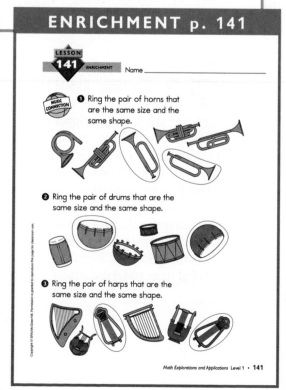

10

312 • Numbers 1–100

 **NOTE TO HOME**
Students identify figures that are
different from others.

---

form from 20–29: two tens and one, two tens and two, and
so on. Demonstrate how to count in the conventional form:
twenty, twenty-one, twenty-two, and so on. Encourage
students to join in as you pass 30. Emphasize the multiples
of 10: 20, 30, and so on. Introduce conventional numbers
from 11–19 last. Practice unison and individual counting of
given numbers in the 0–100 range. Also, say numbers in the
expanded form (four tens and seven) and have volunteers
say the conventional number. (47) Finally, say a number,
such as 36, and have students say the next number. (37)

 **Introducing the "How High Will the
Water Rise?" Activity** Fill a **measuring cup***
halfway with water. Mark the water level. Then
submerge various **objects** in the **water** and record on the
chalkboard the level to which the water rose for each object.
Discuss why the water rose to different levels. Encourage
students to predict how far the water will rise when
submerging different objects. Experiment with submerging
the same piece of modeling clay molded to different shapes
to see if the water level varies based on the clay's shape.

Using the Student Pages Read the directions and
work the first problem on page 311 with the class. Then
have students complete the page on their own. Have them
check their answers by tracing one of their marked figures
on **tracing paper** and then putting the tracing over the
second marked figure. Have students complete page 312 on
their own.

❸ Wrap-Up

In Closing Have students name numbers in expanded
form and then in conventional form.

Performance Assessment Observe which
students understand the relationship between
expanded and conventional form when
counting aloud during the demonstration.

PRACTICE p. 141

Fill in the missing numbers.

0	1	2	3	4	5	6	7	8	9
10	11	12	13	14	15	16	17	18	19
20	21	22	23	24	25	26	27	28	29
30	31	32	33	34	35	36	37	38	39
40	41	42	43	44	45	46	47	48	49
50	51	52	53	54	55	56	57	58	59
60	61	62	63	64	65	66	67	68	69
70	71	72	73	74	75	76	77	78	79
80	81	82	83	84	85	86	87	88	89
90	91	92	93	94	95	96	97	98	99
100									

Math Explorations and Applications Level 1 • 141

ENRICHMENT p. 141

❶ Ring the pair of horns that
are the same size and the
same shape.

❷ Ring the pair of drums that are the
same size and the same shape.

❸ Ring the pair of harps that are the
same size and the same shape.

Math Explorations and Applications Level 1 • 141

Assessment Criteria

Did the student . . .

✓ correctly count aloud using
conventional form during the
demonstration?

✓ make sensible predictions about the
water level during the activity?

✓ correctly complete at least eight of
ten problems on pages 311–312?

---

*available separately

LESSON 142

What Comes Next?

Student Edition pages 313–314

LESSON PLANNER

Objectives

▶ to introduce reading and writing numbers through 100 in conventional form

▶ to provide practice solving arithmetic problems that use conventional numbers

▶ to demonstrate the function of the ⊠ key on the calculator

Context of the Lesson This is the second of three lessons on the transfer from expanded to conventional numbers.

 MANIPULATIVES
calculators*

Program Resources
Number Cubes
Thinking Story Book, pages 114–117
Practice Master 142
Enrichment Master 142
For career connections: Careers and Math*
For extra practice: CD-ROM* Lesson 142

1 Warn-Up ⏱ 5 MINUTES

Problem of the Day Present the following problem to the class: Which fact does not belong? 8 + 2, 4 + 6, 9 + 2, or 3 + 7? (9 + 2)
Why? (because its sum is 11; all others sum to 10)

Problem-Solving Strategies Ask students who have solved the Problem of the Day to share how they solved it and any strategies they used.

MENTAL MATH Write the following numbers on the board and have students show the next greater number using Number Cubes.

a.	27 (28)	b.	85 (86)
c.	14 (15)	d.	81 (82)
e.	37 (38)	f.	44 (45)
g.	59 (60)	h.	74 (75)
i.	66 (67)	j.	50 (51)
k.	7 (8)	l.	92 (93)
m.	13 (14)	n.	38 (39)

313 Numbers 1–100

LESSON 142

Name _____

What Comes Next?

Write the next number.

❶	24	__25__	❷	37	__38__
❸	82	__83__	❹	59	__60__
❺	11	__12__	❻	47	__48__
❼	77	__78__	❽	23	__24__
❾	33	__34__	❿	99	__100__
⓫	40	__41__	⓬	66	__67__
⓭	55	__56__	⓮	62	__63__
⓯	9	__10__	⓰	46	__47__
⓱	98	__99__	⓲	55	__56__

 **COOPERATIVE LEARNING** Do the "Dictation" activity.

 THINKING STORY Talk about the Thinking Story "Trouble in the Garden."

 NOTE TO HOME Students write the next consecutive number.

Unit 4   Lesson 142 • **313**

RETEACHING

 Extra teaching on reading and writing numbers in conventional form is not necessary at this time because further practice is provided in subsequent lessons.

Go over the **calculator*** exercises step by step with students who had difficulty with them. Make sure they press the appropriate keys, and have them guess what the final display will show before pressing the ▬ key.

 Real-World Connection Explain to students that they can see numbers written in conventional form all around them. Point to the clock in your classroom. Show students that the digits are all the same size. You may wish to take students on a walk around the school. Have them note numbers they see that are written in conventional form, such as the numbers on classroom doors. Make a class list of their observations.

*available separately

◆ LESSON 142 What Comes Next?

 What do you think the × key does? Try these problems. Fill in the missing numbers.

19 (6) × (2) = (**12**) .

$2 + 2 + 2 + 2 + 2 + 2 =$ __**12**__

20 (3) × (8) = (**24**) .

$8 + 8 + 8 =$ __**24**__

Write problems like the ones above. Check with a calculator.

21 (3) × (5) = (**15**) .

__**5**__ + __**5**__ + __**5**__ = __**15**__

22 (5) × (2) = (**10**) .

__**2**__ + __**2**__ + __**2**__ + __**2**__ + __**2**__ = __**10**__

 NOTE TO HOME
Students relate the × key on the calculator to repeated addition.

314 • Numbers 1–100

Copyright © SRA/McGraw-Hill

---

② Teach

Demonstrate Practice unison counting in conventional form. Then tell students that they should begin writing numbers with all digits the same height. Write *35* on the chalkboard and say the number aloud in conventional form: "thirty-five." Then write *36* and ask students to say the number aloud in conventional form. Continue to present numbers in and out of sequence until students understand the concept.

 Using the Student Pages Have students complete page 313 on their own. Then ask them to try to figure out what the ▣ key on the **calculator*** does by using this key to do problems 19 and 20 on page 314. Then have them do problems 21 and 22 on their own.

Introducing the "Dictation" Activity Say a number in conventional form and have students write it in conventional form. You may also have them write the number that comes before or after. Have students exchange papers with a partner who circles any incorrectly written numbers. Students should then correct their own mistakes.

 Using the Thinking Story Read aloud and discuss "Trouble in the Garden" on pages 114–117 of the Thinking Story Book.

③ Wrap-Up

In Closing Have students work in pairs. Present each of the following problems: 36 – 0 = (36); 16 + 3 = (19); 39 + 3 = (42); 45 – 2 = (43). Have one student solve the answers mentally while the other uses the calculator. Discuss which way is faster.

ANALYZING ANSWERS Students who read numbers backwards or who reverse the tens and units cubes may be having difficulty making the transition to conventional form.

Assessment Criteria

Did the student . . .

✓ read and write numbers through 100 in conventional form?

✓ understand the function of the ▣ key on the calculator?

PRACTICE p. 142

LESSON 142 PRACTICE Name_____

Write the next number. Count up.

❶ 36 __37__   ❷ 10 __11__

❸ 19 __20__   ❹ 84 __85__

❺ 71 __72__   ❻ 75 __76__

❼ 30 __31__   ❽ 99 __100__

❾ 9 __10__   ❿ 28 __29__

⓫ 43 __44__   ⓬ 16 __17__

⓭ 66 __67__   ⓮ 49 __50__

⓯ 12 __13__   ⓰ 57 __58__

⓱ 90 __91__   ⓲ 6 __7__

142 • Math Explorations and Applications Level 1

ENRICHMENT p. 142

LESSON 142 ENRICHMENT Name_____

Count up. Fill in the missing numbers. Use the numbers to find the missing letters. Read the secret message.

I	C	A	N		C	O	U	N	T
50	51	52	53		54	55	56	57	58

T	O		O	N	E
59	60		61	62	63

H	U	N	D	R	E	D
64	65	66	67	68	69	70

52	62	68	65	60	58
A	N	R	U	O	T

142 • Math Explorations and Applications Level 1

*available separately

Trouble in the Garden

1 Ferdie is trying to help by pulling weeds in his grandpa's garden. Every time he pulls up three weeds, he pulls up a bean plant by mistake. Ferdie has pulled up 12 weeds. **Can you figure out how many bean plants he has pulled up?** four

2 "That's a tall pear tree, Grandpa," said Ferdie. "I know it is," said Grandpa. "I climbed up 6 yards in it and then I could just reach the top with a 2-yard pole." **Can you figure out how tall the pear tree is?** Not exactly, but it's more than 8 yards.

3 Mr. Mudancia had a picture that was 20 inches high and 30 inches wide. He cut an inch off one side of the picture and an inch off the other side. Then he cut an inch off the top and an inch off the bottom. **What size is the picture now? How high? How wide?** 18 inches high, 28 inches wide

4 "When will I ever get done planting these beans?" asked Ferdie. "It took me an hour to plant the first two rows and an hour to plant the next two." **He has four rows left to plant. How many more hours will it take him?** two hours, at the rate he is going

5 The Engs live two blocks from the post office. The Breezys live one block further away from the post office than the Engs do. **Can you tell how far the Engs live from the Breezys?** no **What are some possible answers?** one block, five blocks

Trouble in the Garden

In the springtime Ferdie went out to the country to help his grandfather plant his garden. The first thing that Grandpa wanted Ferdie to do was dig holes to plant some little trees in. "Please dig the holes exactly 8 inches deep," said Grandpa.

Ferdie grabbed a shovel and dug the holes in a hurry. "I'm done, Grandpa!" said Ferdie. "What's next?"

"We'll see," said Grandpa. He took a ruler and measured the holes. They were all 10 inches deep.

Is that what they should have been? no **Were they too deep or not deep enough?** too deep

"Rats," said Ferdie, "I made the holes too deep. Now I'll have to start over and dig new ones."

"I think there might be an easier way," said Grandpa.

Can you think of an easier way? put some dirt into the holes **How much dirt should Ferdie put into the holes to make them right?** enough to fill 2 inches

Grandpa showed Ferdie how to pack 2 inches of dirt into the holes so they would be just 8 inches deep. Then he gave Ferdie some onions to plant. "Please plant them 5 inches apart," said Grandpa.

Ferdie took the onions and quickly planted a row of them. "I'm done," he said. "What's next?"

"Take your time," said Grandpa. He took his ruler and measured how far apart the onions were. "These onions are 10 inches apart," said Grandpa. "I asked you to plant them 5 inches apart."

How far apart is 10 inches? Show with your hands. [Demonstrate.]

How far apart is 5 inches? Show with your hands. [Demonstrate.]

"Rats," said Ferdie. "I'll have to pull out the onions and start all over."

Does he really have to pull them out and start over? no

What else could he do? He could plant another onion between every two that he had planted.

Story 19 • **115**

❻ Mr. Mudancia had a square handkerchief. He cut the handkerchief in half, going from one corner to another corner.
How many pieces of handkerchief does he have now?
two
What shape are they? triangles

❼ The Mudancia's bathtub used to be 20 inches deep, but Mr. Mudancia filled in the bottom of it with cement 4 inches deep.
How deep is the tub now? 16 inches

❽ Mr. Eng bought a banana for 18¢. He got 2¢ back in change.
How much money had Mr. Eng given the grocer? 20¢

❾ Portia has a stack of books that is 8 inches high. Her friend Marcus has a stack of books that is 11 inches high.
Whose stack of books is shorter? Portia's
How much shorter? 3 inches

❿ Willy was growing a flower and a weed in his flowerpot. Last week they were both 10 inches high. This week the weed is 14 inches high and the flower is 8 inches high.
What could have happened? the weed grew; something made the flower shorter—the stem broke or the bloom was picked

⓫ Ferdie, Portia, Marcus, and Willy were drawing pictures. Portia was the second one to finish, Ferdie was the third one to finish, and Marcus was the fourth one to finish.
What can you figure out about Willy? He was first.

◆ STORY 19 Trouble in the Garden

Grandpa showed Ferdie how he could stick another onion between every two onions that he had planted. Then the onions would all be 5 inches apart.

For his next job Grandpa gave Ferdie a package of radish seeds. "Please spread this out so that the whole package makes one row," said Grandpa.

Ferdie tried to be careful this time. He spread out the radish seeds slowly with his fingers. But when he finished the row he still had half the package left. "I did it wrong," Ferdie moaned. "I was supposed to use up the whole package and I used up only half of it. Now what do I do?"

Can you think of any way he can make it turn out right? He could plant the other half over the same row.

"No problem," said Grandpa. "Just go over the row again and plant the other half of the seeds."

"Now for your last job today," said Grandpa, "I'd like you to plant four rows of beans–exactly four. I have to go back to the house, so I hope you can do this job all right by yourself."

"Don't worry," said Ferdie.

Do you think Ferdie will do it right? no **Keep track of what Ferdie does so you can tell.**

116 · Trouble in the Garden

Ferdie planted one row of beans, then another row and another row. "Oh, my!" said Ferdie. "I can't remember how many rows I've planted.

Do you know? How many? three

Ferdie didn't remember that he had planted three rows. "I just can't remember," said Ferdie. "I guess I'll have to start over."

Is there any way Ferdie could find out how many he'd planted? by going back and counting

But Ferdie didn't go back and count how many rows he'd planted. Instead, he went ahead and planted four *more* rows of beans. When Grandpa came back from the house, he said, "That looks like a lot of bean rows."

How many rows did Ferdie plant all together? seven

"I lost count," said Ferdie. "I planted some rows, and then I had to start over and plant four more."

"Well," said Grandpa, "it looks as if we're going to have seven rows of beans instead of four. I hope you like beans, Ferdie, because you're going to be eating a lot of them!"

. . . the end

Story 19 • **117**

LESSON 143
Adding and Subtracting Money

LESSON PLANNER

Objectives

✓ to assess mastery of reading and writing conventional numbers

▶ to provide practice using conventional numbers with addition, subtraction, and money

▶ to provide practice recording frequencies

Context of the Lesson This lesson, the third of three lessons on the transition to conventional numbers, contains a Mastery Checkpoint for this skill. Students last recorded and compared frequencies in Lesson 123.

 MANIPULATIVES

labels

overhead projector and transparency (optional)

play money*

Program Resources

Thinking Story Book, pages 118–119

Practice Master 143

Enrichment Master 143

Assessment Master

For extra practice: CD-ROM* Lesson 143

① Warm-Up ⏱ 5 MINUTES

 Problem of the Day Write *January, February, March, April,* and *May* on the chalkboard. Then present the following problem to the class. Each of these six-year-olds was born in a different month. Amber's birthday is not in January or March. Brad's birthday is in February. Marti's birthday is after Brad's and before Dan's. Odella's birthday is before Brad's. Amber's birthday is before Dan's. Tell when Amber, Marti, Odella, and Dan have birthdays. (Amber: April; Marti: March; Odella: January; Dan: May)

Problem-Solving Strategies Ask students who have solved the Problem of the Day to share how they solved it and any strategies they used.

 MENTAL MATH Write the following problems on the chalkboard. Have volunteers say the answers in conventional form:

a. 88 + 1 = (89)   b. 62 – 0 = (62)

c. 91 + 3 = (94)   d. 50 – 2 = (48)

LESSON 143

Adding and Subtracting Money

Name

 REAL-WORLD CONNECTION

Write the number of dollars Ms. Eng has for each thing. If that is not enough money, put an X on the picture.

① $ 60

② $ 12

③ $ 47

④ $ 9

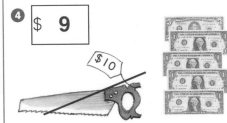

⑤ $ 25

⑥ $ 45

🎒 **NOTE TO HOME** Students add amounts of money.

Unit 4   Lesson 143 • **315**

RETEACHING

Extra teaching is not considered essential at this time, because students will practice using conventional numbers in all subsequent lessons.

PRACTICE p. 143

LESSON 143 PRACTICE   Name

Write the number of dollars Mrs. Garcia has for each thing. If that is not enough money, put an X on the picture.

① $31

② $31 / $10

③ $25 / $20

④ $23 / $40

Math Explorations and Applications Level 1 • 14

◆ **LESSON 143** Adding and Subtracting Money

Connect the dots. Start with 1 and count up.

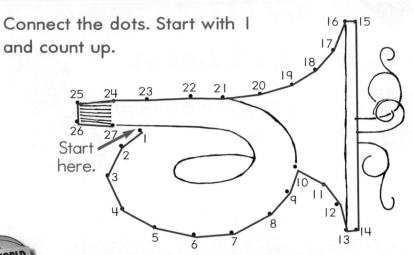

Do the "Birthday Survey" activity.

Month	Number of People	Month	Number of People
January		July	
February		August	
March		September	
April		October	
May		November	
June		December	

Answers will vary.

316 • Numbers 1–100

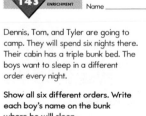

NOTE TO HOME
Students practice counting. They also complete and record the results of a birthday survey.

---

② Teach

Using the Student Pages Explain to students that the bills shown on page 315 show how much money Ms. Eng has with her on a shopping trip. The price tags tell how much each item costs. Work one or two problems with the class, as needed. Have **play money*** available. Then have students work the dot-to-dot puzzle on page 316.

To give students practice in counting and recording frequencies, ask students for their birth dates. Copy the chart on page 316 onto the chalkboard or onto a **transparency**. As a class, tabulate the birthdays in each month, having students work along with you by recording their results in conventional form on page 316. Ask them questions such as "In which month do most birthdays fall?" or "Do any months show more than four birthdays?"

Using the Thinking Story Present three problems from those following "Trouble in the Garden" on pages 118–119 of the Thinking Story Book or pages 314a–314b of this Guide.

③ Wrap-Up ⏱ 5 MINUTES

In Closing Put price **labels** on classroom objects. Tell students they have a specific amount of money. Challenge volunteers to tell you if they have enough money to buy each of the objects.

Mastery Checkpoint 23

At about this time students should have made substantial progress in using conventional numbers. You can assess their progress through informal classroom observations or by assigning Assessment Blackline Masters page 56. Results of this assessment may be recorded on the Mastery Checkpoint Chart.

Assessment Criteria

Did the student . . .

✓ demonstrate mastery of the use of conventional numbers?

✓ use play money correctly with conventional numbers?

✓ understand how to count and record frequencies?

ENRICHMENT p. 143

LESSON 143 ENRICHMENT   Name _____

Dennis, Tom, and Tyler are going to camp. They will spend six nights there. Their cabin has a triple bunk bed. The boys want to sleep in a different order every night.

Show all six different orders. Write each boy's name on the bunk where he will sleep.

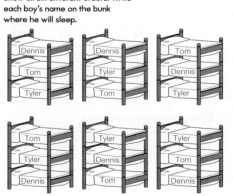

Math Explorations and Applications Level 1 • **143**

ASSESSMENT p. 56

UNIT 4   Mastery Checkpoint 23   Use of conventional numbers   (Lesson 143)

Name _____

The student demonstrates mastery by writing 15 well-formed numbers.

Write the next number. Count up.

❶ 36 __37__   ❷ 65 __66__

❸ 73 __74__   ❹ 19 __20__

❺ 10 __11__   ❻ 52 __53__

❼ 88 __89__   ❽ 89 __90__

❾ 64 __65__   ❿ 27 __28__

⓫ 39 __40__   ⓬ 32 __33__

⓭ 21 __22__   ⓮ 76 __77__

⓯ 42 __43__

56 • *Math Explorations and Applications Level 1*

*available separately

LESSON
144

LESSON
144 Student Edition pages 317–318
Greatest and Least

LESSON PLANNER

Objective
▶ to provide practice finding the greatest and least numbers in sets of up to five numbers

Context of the Lesson Students learned to identify the greater and the lesser of two numbers in Lesson 67.

 MANIPULATIVES
craft sticks (optional)
slips of paper (optional)

Program Resources
Number Cubes
Thinking Story Book, pages 118–119
Reteaching Master
Practice Master 144
Enrichment Master 144
For extra practice:
CD-ROM* Lesson 144
Mixed Practice, page 380

1 Warm-Up 5 MINUTES

Problem of the Day Present the following problem to the class. Sophie has two dimes. Dale has one more dime than Sophie. Niverka has three more dimes than Dale. How much money does Niverka have? (60¢)

Problem-Solving Strategies Ask students who have solved the Problem of the Day to share how they solved it and any strategies they used.

MENTAL MATH Write pairs of numbers on the chalkboard. Ask students to show the lesser number, using Number Cubes.

a. (33), 91   b. 72, (27)

c. 54, (45)   d. (17), 27

e. (13), 19   f. (57), 59

g. (6), 7   h. 21, (12)

2 Teach

Demonstrate Write three different numbers on the chalkboard. Ask students to show with their Number Cubes which number is the least and which is the greatest. Repeat this exercise with other numbers. Then challenge students to find the least and greatest of four numbers. Finally, extend the exercise to sets of five numbers.

317 Numbers 1–100

Greatest and Least

 GAME Play the "Greatest and Least Numbers" game.

Name _____

Name _____   Name _____

	Greatest Number	Least Number	Greatest Number	Least Number
1				
2				
3				
4				
5				
6				
7				
8				
9				
10				

Copyright © SRA/McGraw-Hill

NOTE TO HOME
Students play a game in which they try to make the greatest and least numbers.

Unit 4   Lesson 144 • **317**

 SPECIAL NEEDS **MANIPULATIVES**

Meeting Individual Needs
Help students who are having trouble finding the greatest and least number by writing consecutive numbers on separate **slips of paper**. The student can then arrange the numbers in order to see which number is the greatest and which is the least. You might also have them count out **craft sticks** or other manipulatives to verify their choices.

RETEACHING p. 37

LESSON
144 RETEACHING   Name _____

47 is greater than 33.

Ring the greater number in each box.

❶ 17   (21)   ❷ 36   (51)

Ring the lesser number in each box.

❸ 43   (32)   ❹ 72   (54)

❺ 26   (19)   ❻ (63)   71

❼ (49)   94   ❽ 33   (27)

Math Explorations and Applications Level I • **37**

*available separately

◆ **LESSON 144** Greatest and Least Use the Mixed Practice on page 380 after this lesson.

Ring the greater number in each box.

❶ 28 ⑧①
❷ 46 ⑦①
❸ ⑥② 38
❹ 22 ③①

Ring the greatest number in each box.

❺ 17 ㉖ 21
❻ 15 8 ㉛
❼ ㊃⑤ 23 76
❽ 23 ㊅⑥ 49

Ring the lesser number in each box.

❾ 33 ㉖
❿ ㊃⑧ 92
⓫ 87 ㊄④
⓬ ㊅② 71

Ring the least number in each box.

⓭ 17 ⑨ 52
⓮ 56 77 ㊃⑨
⓯ 83 ⑱ 21
⓰ ㉙ 35 54

318 • Numbers 1–100

NOTE TO HOME
Students identify the greater, greatest, lesser, and least numbers.

Copyright © SRA/McGraw-Hill

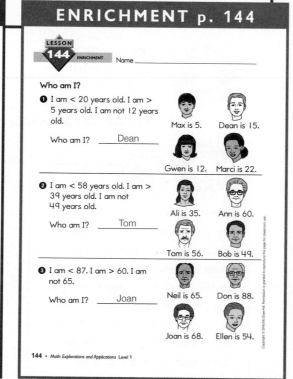
Using the Student Pages Using page 317, demonstrate and have students play the "Greatest and Least Numbers" game to practice work on place value. Divide students into pairs. Each pair uses only one Student Edition. The lead player's name is written on the left side of the game sheet, and the other player's name is written at the top right. The lead player rolls both units and both tens Number Cubes and arranges them in two pairs to make the greatest and least numbers possible. For example, if a player rolled 8 tens, 3 tens, 2, and 7, an 87 and a 32 could be made. The player then writes these numbers on line 1 in the appropriate column. The other player repeats this procedure, writing his or her numbers on line 1 in the appropriate column under his or her name. Players ring the greatest and least of the four numbers. At the end of ten rounds the rings are counted. The player with the most is the winner. Pairs can continue playing the game, using the other Student Edition to record rounds. A copy of this game can also be found on pages 31–33 of the Home Connections Blackline Masters.

As students finish, have them complete page 318 on their own.

Using the Thinking Story Present three new problems from those following "Trouble in the Garden" on pages 118–119 of the Thinking Story Book or pages 314a–314b of this Guide.

❸ **Wrap-Up** 5 MINUTES

In Closing Write sets of up to five numbers on the chalkboard. Have students find the greatest and the least numbers in each set.

Informal Assessment Observe students as they look for the least and the greatest numbers in a set. At this level, mastery of this concept with sets of three or four is sufficient.

Assessment Criteria
Did the student . . .
✓ identify the greatest and least numbers in a set of three or four?
✓ follow the rules of the "Greatest and Least Numbers" game?

LOOKING AHEAD For Lesson 145 you will need a television guide and a clock with movable hands.

LESSON
145

Student Edition pages 319–320

Telling Time— Hour and Half Hour

LESSON
145

Name _____

Telling Time—Hour and Half Hour

What time is it?

❶

3:00

❷

3:30

❸

8:00

❹

8:30

❺

5:00

❻

10:30

 GAME

Play the "Clock" game.

Copyright © SRA/McGraw-Hill

 NOTE TO HOME
Students tell time to the hour and half hour.

LESSON PLANNER

Objective

▶ to introduce students to telling time to the hour and half hour

Context of the Lesson This topic is continued in the next two lessons.

 MANIPULATIVES

clock faces for each student*

learning clock*

Program Resources

Number Cubes

"Clock" Game Mat

Thinking Story Book, pages 118–119

Practice Master 145

Enrichment Master 145

For additional math integration:
Math Throughout the Day*

For extra practice:
CD-ROM* Lesson 145

❶ Warm-Up

Problem of the Day Present the following problem to the class. Al is 47 inches tall. He is 3 inches taller than Ben. Carla is 2 inches shorter than Ben. How tall is Carla? (42 inches)

Problem-Solving Strategies Ask students who have solved the Problem of the Day to share how they solved it and any strategies they used.

MENTAL MATH Write the following series of numbers on the chalkboard. Have students use their Number Cubes to indicate the two numbers in each group that add up to 10.

a.	0	10	2	1	(10 + 0)
b.	6	3	4	1	(6 + 4)
c.	9	7	1	0	(9 + 1)
d.	0	5	5	7	(5 + 5)
e.	8	1	2	6	(8 + 2)

319 Numbers 1–100

Literature Connection
Read aloud *Time* by Henry Pluckrose to reinforce time concepts.

GIFTED & TALENTED **MANIPULATIVES**

Meeting Individual Needs
Have small groups of students make a schedule poster. Have them list daily events that start on the hour or half hour, such as Start School, Go to Lunch, Go to Recess, and Go Home. Next to each event, have them draw a clock with the starting time.

RETEACHING

Keep a real clock on display during the school day. Call attention to it at various times during the day when it is on the hour and half hour. Have volunteers determine what time it is.

*available separately

◆ **LESSON 145** Telling Time—Hour and Half Hour

Draw a line between the clocks that tell the same time.

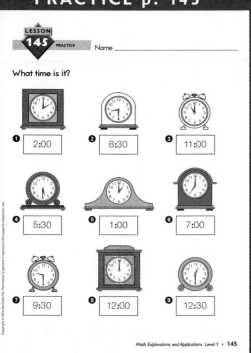

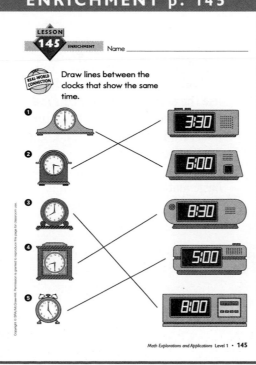

320 • Numbers 1–100

NOTE TO HOME
Students tell time on digital and analog clocks.

Copyright © SRA/McGraw-Hill

PRACTICE p. 145

LESSON **145** PRACTICE   Name _____

What time is it?

① 2:00   ② 8:30   ③ 11:00

④ 5:30   ⑤ 1:00   ⑥ 7:00

⑦ 9:30   ⑧ 12:00   ⑨ 12:30

Math Explorations and Applications Level 1 • **145**

ENRICHMENT p. 145

LESSON **145** ENRICHMENT   Name _____

Draw lines between the clocks that show the same time.

① 3:30
② 6:00
③ 8:30
④ 5:00
⑤ 8:00

Math Explorations and Applications Level 1 • **145**

*available separately

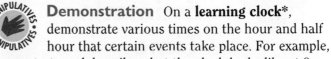

② Teach

Demonstration On a **learning clock***, demonstrate various times on the hour and half hour that certain events take place. For example, demonstrate and describe what the clock looks like at 9 o'clock when students start school or at 11: 30 when they eat lunch. Move the hands to demonstrate different times on the hour and half hour. Have students say where the hands are pointing to and what time the clock indicates. Include some times in which the hands are near the hour or half hour to show "about" what time it is. If **clock faces*** are available for each student, call out times to the hour and half hour and have students indicate them on their clocks.

Using the Student Pages Do page 319 with the class. Then have students complete page 320 on their own.

Introducing the "Clock" Game Mat To provide practice in telling time to the hour and half hour, use the Game Mat transparency to demonstrate and play a round of this game. Complete directions are on the Game Mat. A copy of this game can also be found on page 395 of this Guide.

Using the Thinking Story Present two new problems from among those following "Trouble in the Garden" on pages 118–119 of the Thinking Story Book or pages 314a–314b of this Guide.

③ Wrap-Up

In Closing Have students describe what a clock looks like when it is 11:00 and when it is 3:30.

Performance Assessment Observe students as they play the "Clock" game to see if students indicate the correct times.

Assessment Criteria

Did the student . . .

✓ indicate the correct times when playing the "Clock" game?

✓ correctly answer 9 of 12 problems on pages 319–320?

LESSON 146

Student Edition pages 321–324

Telling and Estimating Time

LESSON PLANNER

Objectives

▶ to provide experience in estimating and telling time of day

▶ to provide experience in estimating and telling elapsed time

Context of the Lesson This is the second lesson involving time.

 MANIPULATIVES   **Program Resources**

analog clock

clock or stopwatch* to show seconds

crayons (red and blue)

digital clock

learning clock*

Practice Master 146

Enrichment Master 146

For extra practice:
 CD-ROM* Lesson 146
  Mixed Practice, page 381

❶ Warm-Up

 Problem of the Day Present the following problem to the class. Ellen is five years old. Jeff is three years older than Craig. Craig is twice as old as Ellen. How old is Jeff? (13 years old)

Problem-Solving Strategies Ask students who have solved the Problem of the Day to share how they solved it and any strategies they used.

MENTAL MATH Have students answer each of the following problems aloud.

a.   80 – 20 = (60)

b.   30 + 60 = (90)

c.   40 + 20 = (60)

d.   70 – 50 = (20)

e.   40 – 40 = (0)

f.   50 + 10 = (60)

LESSON 146

Name _____

Telling and Estimating Time

Answers will vary. Check students' clocks.

Draw hands on the clock to show about the right time. Make the short hand red. Make the long hand blue.

❶

Arrive at school

❷

Lunch

❸

Go to bed

 NOTE TO HOME
Students draw the time on analog clocks.

Unit 4   Lesson 146   •   **321**

Technology Connection You might want students to use the software *JumpStart First Grade* from Knowledge Adventure (Mac, IBM, for grades K–1). Eight interactive storybooks provide practice with time telling, mapmaking, basic math skills, color mixing, reading, science, and geography.

Literature Connection Read aloud *The Boy Who Stopped Time* by Anthony Taber to explore time concepts. In this story, Julian stops a pendulum from swinging on the clock and has a remarkable adventure while the rest of the world is suspended in time.

*available separately

◆ **LESSON 146** Telling and Estimating Time

Write the numbers on the clock to show about the right time.

Use the Mixed Practice on page 381 after this lesson.

Possible answers are shown.

❹

Wake up

7:00

❺

School's out

3:00

❻

Eat dinner

6:00

322 • Numbers 1–100

 NOTE TO HOME
Students write the time on digital clocks.

 ❷ Teach

 Demonstrate Draw a clock or display a **learning clock***. Have students practice showing different times to the hour and half hour. Have them demonstrate these times both on an **analog clock** and the way it would look on a **digital clock**. For example, have a volunteer demonstrate or draw 3:00 on an analog clock face while another student writes the numerals 3:00 next to it. Do the same for half-hour times.

Using the Student Pages For page 321, discuss the time at which each event shown on this page takes place. As you agree on a time for each event, have students indicate the time by drawing in the hands on the clocks on page 321 and filling in the numerals on the clocks on page 322. Students will need **red** and **blue crayons**.

 Real-World Connection Work as a class to make a schedule of a typical student's day including the time at which each event begins. Start with wake-up time in the morning and end with bedtime. Be sure to write the time in digits as well as represent it with a clock face in each case.

Physical Education Connection
To further explore estimating elapsed time, have students hold a relay race from a starting line to an object and back again. Start with one student's time and ask the class how long they think it would take for three, seven, and ten students. Check the estimates by timing new races in each case.

◆ **LESSON 146** Telling and Estimating Time

Teach

Using the Student Pages Before students begin page 323, count aloud ten seconds to provide them an idea of how long a second is. Then have students work in small groups to complete the chart on this page. Each student should estimate how long it will take to do each task. Group members should time each other as they perform each task and then write down the actual time it took. Then have them compare the times for the four activities and put them in order from shortest to longest or vice versa. You will need to display a clock with a second hand, or provide watches or **stopwatches*** for each group. Estimates should improve as students do each task on the page.

At the top of page 324, students must determine what time it will be after a certain amount of time has elapsed. Consider doing this part of the page together with the class, demonstrating how to count the hours on a 12-hour analog clock. Point out that when you count 13 hours, you pass 12:00 again and go to 1:00. For extra practice, have volunteers come up and count numbers of hours greater than 1:00 on a learning clock.

Finally, have students estimate how long it will take them to complete the problems at the bottom of page 324. Have them write their estimates on the page. Then have partners time each other as they complete the page and then write their actual time next to their estimates. Correct the problems together with the class. Discuss how close their estimated times were to the actual time it took them to do the problems.

 Introducing the "Harder Clock" Game Mat To provide practice in telling time to hour, half hour, and quarter hour, use the Game Mat transparency to demonstrate and play a round of this game. Complete directions are on the Game Mat. A copy of this game can also be found on page 396 of this Guide.

◆ **LESSON 146** Telling and Estimating Time

Name _____

How many seconds does it take you to do each of these things?

First write your estimate. Then measure to check. **Answers will vary.**

Estimate   Check

7 Tie your shoelaces.   _____ _____

8 Write your name neatly ten times.   _____ _____

9 Correctly work the problems on the bottom of page 324.  _____ _____

10 Say the Pledge of Allegiance.  _____ _____

Copyright © SRA/McGraw-Hill

 NOTE TO HOME
Students estimate and measure durations of time.

Unit 4   Lesson 146 • **323**

Keep a real clock with a second hand on display during the school day. Call attention to it at various times during the day. Have students estimate and then check how long it takes them to complete various tasks during the day, such as taking out their books for reading, cleaning off their desks, standing in line, etc.

---

323 Numbers 1–100

*available separately

◆ **LESSON 146** Telling and Estimating Time

The time is

⑪ Complete the chart.
What time will it be in...

1 hour	**2:00**
2 hours	**3:00**
3 hours	**4:00**
10 hours	**11:00**
12 hours	**1:00**
13 hours	**2:00**

How fast can you solve these problems?

⑫ 5 + 5 = **10**   **⑬** 15 − 10 = **5**

⑭ 10 − 5 = **5**   **⑮** 9 − 2 = **7**

⑯ 8 + 7 = **15**   **⑰** 8 + 6 = **14**

 NOTE TO HOME
Students calculate the time it will be in
various numbers of hours.

 ③ Wrap-Up

In Closing Ask students to share experiences in which
they have needed a clock or a watch.

Informal Assessment Compare students'
estimates of duration with the measured
durations for various tasks to see if estimates
increased in accuracy as they did each task.

Assessment Criteria

Did the student . . .

✓ indicate the correct time on the
clocks on pages 321–322?

✓ make reasonable estimates of
duration for the tasks listed on
page 323?

✓ make better estimates as he or she
gained more experience?

✓ correctly complete in less than 30
seconds at least five of six problems
at the bottom of page 324?

PRACTICE p. 146

LESSON 146 PRACTICE Name _____

Draw hands on the clock to show
the right time. Make the short hand
red. Make the long hand blue.

❶ Joseph wakes up in the morning
at seven o'clock.

❷ School ends at three o'clock.

Write the numbers on the clock to
show the right time.

❸ School starts at eight o'clock.

8 | 0 0

❹ Dinner begins at six o'clock.

6 | 0 0

❺ The time is 2:00. Complete the
chart to show what time it will be in . . .

1 hour	3:00
2 hours	4:00
3 hours	5:00

146 • Math Explorations and Applications Level 1

ENRICHMENT p. 146

LESSON 146 ENRICHMENT Name _____

Write the correct time.

❶
3 o'clock   10:30   8:30

❷ Draw the hands on each clock for
the time shown.

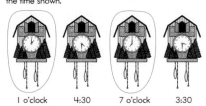
1 o'clock   4:30   7 o'clock   3:30

❸ The cuckoo comes out of the
clocks above "on the hour." Ring
the clocks where the time is on
the hour.

146 • Math Explorations and Applications Level 1

Unit 4 Lesson 146 **324**

LESSON 147

Student Edition pages 325–328

Using a Calendar

LESSON 147

Name _____

Using a Calendar

Fill in the missing numbers.

May

Sunday	Monday	Tuesday	Wednesday	Thursday	Friday	Saturday
		1	2	3	4	5
6	7	8	9	10	11	12
13	14	**15**	**16**	**17**	**18**	**19**
20	**21**	**22**	**23**	**24**	**25**	**26**
27	**28**	**29**	**30**	31		

❶ What day is May 15? — **Tuesday**

❷ What day is May 21? — **Monday**

❸ What is the last day of the month? — **Thursday or May 31**

NOTE TO HOME
Students learn about the monthly calendar.

Copyright © SRA/McGraw-Hill

LESSON PLANNER

Objectives

▶ to introduce the monthly calendar

▶ to provide practice telling time

▶ to provide practice with ordinal numbers

Context of the Lesson This is the third lesson involving time.

 MANIPULATIVES

chalkboard calendar for the present month

learning clock*

Program Resources

The Three Billy Goats Gruff* from the Literature Library

"Calendar" Game Mat

Number Cubes

Thinking Story Book, pages 118–119

Reteaching Master

Practice Master 147

Enrichment Master 147

For additional math integration:
Math Throughout the Day*

For extra practice:
CD-ROM* Lesson 147
Mixed Practice, page 382

❶ Warm-Up 5 MINUTES

 Problem of the Day Present the following problem to the class. Julie bought a balloon for 28¢. She used six coins. What were they? (two dimes, one nickel, three pennies)

Problem-Solving Strategies Ask students who have solved the Problem of the Day to share how they solved it and any strategies they used.

MENTAL MATH Have students add and subtract multiples of 10 mentally and give answers orally.

a. 70 + 20 = (90)

b. 30 + 30 = (60)

c. 90 + 10 = (100)

d. 70 – 60 = (10)

e. 80 + 10 = (90)

f. 50 – 20 = (30)

Technology Connection You might want students to use the software *Treasure Galaxy!* from The Learning Company (Mac, IBM, for grades K–9) for practice with calendar skills, analogies, number patterns, measurement, geometric shapes, and basic arithmetic (addition, subtraction, multiplication, and division).

*available separately

◆ **LESSON 147 Using a Calendar**

Color the right animal or thing.

❹ The <u>second</u> pumpkin

❺ The <u>third</u> bear

❻ The <u>tenth</u> chick

❼ The <u>first</u> car

❽ The <u>sixth</u> mug

❾ The <u>eighth</u> ant

❿ The <u>fourth</u> pencil

NOTE TO HOME
Students use ordinal numbers to identify
objects in a sequence.

326 • Numbers 1–100

Copyright © SRA/McGraw-Hill

❷ Teach

Demonstrate Point to the chalkboard **calendar**.
Demonstrate for students how to read today's day and date.
Read the days of the week at the top of the calendar
together with the class. Have students practice finding other
days on the calendar by asking questions such as: "What is
tomorrow's day and date? What was yesterday's? What date
is the first Wednesday of this month? the second Friday?"

Using the Number Cubes Students can
use Number Cubes to answer questions about
the calendar. For example, name a day, such as
the second Tuesday of the month, and have students
indicate the date with Number Cubes.

Using the Student Pages For page 325, point out that
May has only 31 days and that students must stop at number
31 when filling in the numbers.

Before beginning page 326, draw a row of ten stars on the
chalkboard. Point to each star as you identify the first,
second, third, and fourth star, and so on. Then read aloud
each problem, allowing enough time between problems for
students to respond.

**Literature
Connection** Read
*The Seasons of
Arnold's Apple Tree*
by Gail Gibbons to reinforce calendar
concepts. As the seasons pass, Arnold
enjoys a variety of activities as a result
of his apple tree.

To review the concept of sequence,
read aloud *The Three Billy Goats
Gruff* from the Literature Library*.

**Literature
Connection** Read
All Year Long by
Nancy Tafuri to
reinforce calendar concepts. This book
pictures a variety of activities that take
place on different days of the week
during various months of the year.

*available separately

◆ LESSON 147 Using a Calendar

Teach

Using the Student Pages Explain to students that the calendar on page 327 should have numbers up to only 30 because June has 30 days. Then have students complete these two pages on their own. When finished, discuss answers to each page together with the class. You may want to use a **learning clock*** to review page 328.

 Introducing the "Calendar" Game Mat
Use the Game Mat transparency to demonstrate and play a round of this game in which students practice using a monthly calendar. Complete directions are on the Game Mat, a copy of which appears on page 394 of this Teacher's Guide.

Using the Thinking Story Present three new problems from among those following "Trouble in the Garden" on pages 118–119 of the Thinking Story Book or pages 314a–314b of this Guide.

◆ LESSON 147 Using a Calendar

 Name _____

Fill in the missing numbers.

June

Sunday	Monday	Tuesday	Wednesday	Thursday	Friday	Saturday
				1	2	3
4	5	6	7	8	9	10
11	12	13	14	15	16	17
18	19	20	21	22	23	24
25	26	27	28	29	30	

⓫ What is the first Wednesday?   June __7__

⓬ What is the last Saturday?   June __24__

⓭ What is the third Tuesday?   June __20__

 Play the "Calendar" game.

 NOTE TO HOME
Students complete and read a calendar.

Unit 4   Lesson 147 • **327**

Art Connection
Explain to students that the names for the days of the week are based on the myths of ancient times. Sunday was the day of the sun. Monday was the day of the moon. Have students draw a picture about one day of the week and include images of some of their favorite things to do.

RETEACHING p. 38

LESSON 147 RETEACHING Name _____

July

Sunday	Monday	Tuesday	Wednesday	Thursday	Friday	Saturday
		1	2	3	4	5
6	7	8	9	10	11	12
13	14	15	16	17	18	19
20	21	22	23	24	25	26
27	28	29	30	31		

Ring the answer.

❶ What is the name of the month?
Tuesday   (July)

❷ On what day of the week is July 4th?
(Friday)   Saturday

❸ How many Thursdays are in this month?
4   (5)

❹ What day comes next after July 16?
Wednesday   (Thursday)

❺ How many days are in a week?
(7)   5

38 • Math Explorations and Applications Level 1

---

*available separately

◆ **LESSON 147** Using a Calendar

What time is it?

Use the Mixed Practice on page 382 after this lesson.

⑭

2:00

⑮

4:30

⑯

9:30

⑰

10:00

⑱

12:30

⑲

8:00

⑳

3:30

㉑

8:00

㉒

11:00

328 • Numbers 1–100

 NOTE TO HOME
Students practice telling time to the hour and half hour.

Copyright © SFA/McGraw-Hill

---

③ Wrap-Up 🕐 5 MINUTES

In Closing Ask students to say the days of the week in order, starting with Sunday.

 **Informal Assessment** Use students' answers to pages 325–328 as an informal assessment of their ability to read a calendar, tell time to the hour and half-hour, and to understand ordinal numbers.

Assessment Criteria

Did the student . . .

✓ correctly fill in the calendars and answer the related questions on pages 325 and 327?

✓ correctly answer six of seven problems on page 326?

✓ write the correct time on seven of nine clocks on page 328?

✓ say the correct days as he or she played the "Calendar" game?

ESL **Meeting Individual Needs**
Have second-language learners pair with fluent English-speaking students to review the names and pronunciations of the 12 months. Write the names of the months on the chalkboard if necessary and ask students to list them in categories according to the seasons.

PRACTICE p. 147

LESSON **147** PRACTICE   Name_____

October has 31 days.

Fill in the missing numbers.

 October

Sunday	Monday	Tuesday	Wednesday	Thursday	Friday	Saturday
					1	2 3
4	5	6	7	8	9	10
11	12	13	14	15	16	17
18	19	20	21	22	23	24
25	26	27	28	29	30	31

❶ What day is October 9?   Friday

❷ What day is October 12?   Monday

❸ How many Wednesdays are there in October?   4

❹ How many Thursdays are there in October?   5

Math Explorations and Applications Level 1 • **147**

ENRICHMENT p. 147

LESSON **147** ENRICHMENT   Name_____

 REAL-WORLD CONNECTION **Read the clues. Fill in the calendar.**

Clues
There are 30 days in June. The first day of the month is a Wednesday. The last day of the month is a Thursday. June 14th is Flag Day.

JUNE

SUNDAY	MONDAY	TUESDAY	WEDNESDAY	THURSDAY	FRIDAY	SATURDAY
			1	2	3	4
5	6	7	8	9	10	11
12	13	14	15	16	17	18
19	20	21	22	23	24	25
26	27	28	29	30		

On what day of the week is Flag Day?   Tuesday

Math Explorations and Applications Level 1 • **147**

LESSON PLANNER

Objectives

▶ to introduce symmetry

▶ to review addition and subtraction with numbers in the 0–100 range

Context of the Lesson This lesson provides an introduction to symmetry. At this level students are not expected to understand symmetry as a concept but only to get an idea of what some kinds of symmetry look like.

 MANIPULATIVES

scissors

magazines or books for cutting pictures (optional)

symmetric and non-symmetric objects

Program Resources

Number Cubes

Thinking Story Book, pages 120–123

Practice Master 148

Enrichment Master 148

For career connections: Careers and Math*

For extra practice: CD-ROM* Lesson 148

❶ Warm-Up ⏱ 5 MINUTES

 Problem of the Day Write the following problems on the chalkboard and present the question to the class:

$$\begin{array}{cccc} 18 & 15 & 16 & 12 \\ -\ 9 & -\ 7 & -\ 8 & -\ 6 \end{array}$$

Which problem does not belong? Explain. (15 − 7; all the others are doubles.)

Problem-Solving Strategies Ask students who have solved the Problem of the Day to share how they solved it and any strategies they used.

 MENTAL MATH Review addition and subtraction by having students show the answers to the following problems with their Number Cubes:

a. 32 − 2 = (30)

b. 9 + 0 = (9)

c. 43 − 1 = (42)

d. 13 + 2 = (15)

e. 29 − 3 = (26)

f. 54 + 10 = (64)

g. 35 + 1 = (36)

h. 48 + 3 = (51)

i. 65 − 0 = (65)

j. 28 − 10 = (18)

Name _____

Symmetry

 ART CONNECTION

Draw the other half of this face. Make both halves look the same.

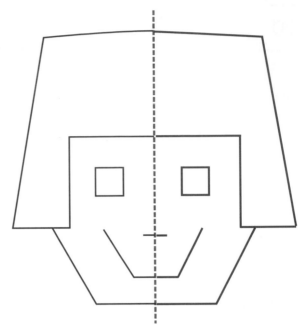

 THINKING STORY

Talk about the Thinking Story "How Deep is the Water?"

 **NOTE TO HOME**
Students are introduced to symmetry.

Unit 4 Lesson 148 • **329**

RETEACHING

Extra teaching is not considered essential at this time, because students are not expected to master the concept of symmetry.

 SCIENCE CONNECTION

Science Connection Arrange for students to gather examples of symmetry in nature such as different kinds of leaves or fruits. Or have students gather pictures of animals or plants. Have them organize their findings into a classroom display. You might also wish to create a contrasting display of objects that are not symmetrical.

 LITERATURE CONNECTION

Literature Connection You may want to read *Shapes in Nature* by Judy Feldman to reinforce lesson concepts.

*available separately

◆ **LESSON 148** Symmetry

Draw the other half of this figure.
Make both halves look the same.

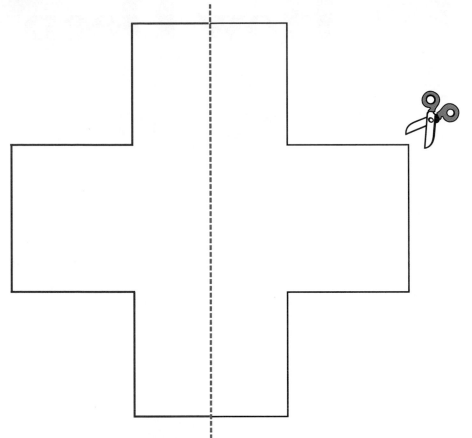

Now cut out the figure. Fold it to see
if both halves are the same.

330 • Numbers 1–100

NOTE TO HOME
Students explore symmetry by completing a
shape and folding to check.

Copyright © SRA/McGraw-Hill

② Teach

Demonstrate Draw a vertical line on the chalkboard.
Draw half of a face on one side of the vertical line. Finish
the face on the other side of the line, drawing features that
differ greatly from those in the first half. Ask students if one
side is the same as the other. As students point out
differences, make changes until both sides look the same.
Explain that when two sides of an object look the same we
say it is symmetrical. Show various **objects** to the class and
discuss whether or not they are symmetrical.

Using the Student Pages Have students work on pages
329–330 on their own.

 Using the Thinking Story Read aloud
"How Deep Is the Water?" from pages
120–123 of the Thinking Story Book.

③ Wrap-Up

In Closing Fold a piece of paper in half. Then have a
student draw half of a flower, a heart, or a face on one side.
Ask another student to draw the other half.

Portfolio Assessment Have students
create a symmetrical drawing, or find an
example of symmetry in a magazine clipping,
photograph, or piece of art to share with the class. Have
students place their work or clipping in their Math Portfolios.

PRACTICE p. 148

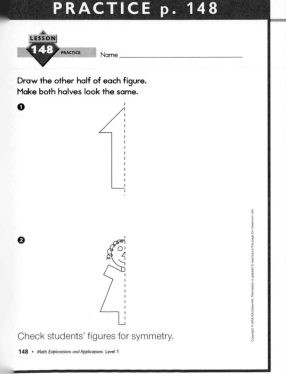

LESSON 148 PRACTICE Name _____

Draw the other half of each figure.
Make both halves look the same.

❶

❷

Check students' figures for symmetry.

148 • *Math Explorations and Applications Level 1*

ENRICHMENT p. 148

LESSON 148 ENRICHMENT Name _____

Draw a line through half of each
picture. Make both halves look the
same.

Either line is correct.

148 • *Math Explorations and Applications Level 1*

Assessment Criteria

Did the student . . .

✓ understand the concept of
symmetry?

✓ demonstrate proficiency with the
addition and subtraction practice?

✓ actively participate in the Thinking
Story discussion?

How Deep Is the Water?

1 The next time Ferdie and Mr. Muddle went fishing, they caught five fish all together. Ferdie caught five of them.
How many fish did Mr. Muddle catch? zero
But Mr. Muddle did catch four weeds, two tin cans, and an old bicycle tire.
So who caught the most living things? Ferdie

2 Do you know how Ms. Jones gets the toys she sells in her store? She has to buy them. So naturally, she has to sell them for more than she paid. That's how she earns her money. If she buys a toy for $2, she sells it for $3. If she buys a toy for $5, she sells it for $6. If she buys a toy for $1, she sells it for $2.
If Ms. Jones bought a toy for $4, how much would she sell it for? $5

3 "How much is that yo-yo?," asked Ferdie.
"Forty cents," said Ms. Jones. "But because you're such a good customer, I'll sell it to you for half that price."
How much will Ferdie have to pay for the yo-yo? 20¢
"If they're half-price, I'll take two of them," said greedy Ferdie.
How much will he pay for two yo-yos? 40¢

4 The cuckoo clock in the Engs' house goes "Cuckoo" once every hour. One day when the Breezys dropped in to visit, they heard the clock go "Cuckoo" just as they came in the door. The next time the clock went "Cuckoo" was when they were just leaving.
Be careful! Can you figure out how long the Breezys were there? one hour

How Deep Is the Water?

Mr. Muddle did not go fishing very often, because there were too many things to remember, and he was always forgetting something. But Ferdie had been begging Mr. Muddle to take him fishing for a long time. So one day they packed up Mr. Muddle's boat with everything they thought they would need. They remembered to take fishing poles and string and worms.
Did they forget anything? yes, hooks

Once they got into the boat, they rowed out onto the lake to a place where Mr. Muddle said there were sure to be some fish. But when they were ready to start fishing, they discovered that they had no fishhooks.

"I did it again," said Mr. Muddle. "I'm sorry. I'm afraid this fishing trip won't be much fun for you."

120 • How Deep Is the Water?

"That's all right," said Ferdie. "I like just being out here on the lake. I wonder if the water is too deep to stand in."

How could Ferdie find out? by testing the depth of the water with his fishing pole

Ferdie looked around the boat for something he could use to test the depth of the water. "My fishing pole!" Ferdie exclaimed. "This pole is longer than my height," Ferdie said. "Is it longer than your height?" he asked Mr. Muddle.

Mr. Muddle looked carefully at the pole. "It looks like it's exactly as long as my height," said Mr. Muddle.

"Good," said Ferdie. Then he pushed the pole straight down into the water until it touched bottom. There were still 10 inches of the pole sticking out of the water.

Is the water too deep for Mr. Muddle to stand in? no

"The water isn't too deep for the fishing pole, so it isn't too deep for me!" said Mr. Muddle. And he jumped into the water and stood on the bottom.

How much of Mr. Muddle was out of the water? 10 inches

What part of him? his head

Story 20 • **121**

⑤ Willy has 12¢, Portia has 9¢, and Ferdie has 14¢.
One of them has a dime. Who could it be?
Willy or Ferdie
Could it be Portia? no
Why not? She has less than 10¢.

⑥ Mr. Mudancia used to have 26 teeth in his mouth, but he changed that. He went to the dentist and had two false teeth put in.
How many teeth does he have in his mouth now? 28

⑦ Loretta the Letter Carrier bought a pound of peanuts. She gave 30 peanuts to Liz and 30 peanuts to Ivan.
How many peanuts does she have left? can't tell
What do you need to know? how many peanuts are in a pound

⑧ Marcus ran around the block in four minutes. Manolita ran around in six minutes, and Ferdie did it in five minutes.
Who is fastest? Marcus

⑨ It costs a quarter for a bag of pretzels. "Guess I can't buy any," said Mr. Muddle. "I have only 30 cents."
Is he right? no
Why not? 30¢ is worth more than a quarter.

⑩ Mr. Muddle was going to visit Willy, who lives three blocks away. Mr. Muddle forgot and walked one block past Willy's house. Then he remembered where he was going and walked back to Willy's house.
How far did Mr. Muddle walk all together? five blocks

◆ **STORY 20 How Deep Is the Water?**

Only Mr. Muddle's head was out of the water, so his clothes were all wet. "You'd better climb back into the boat," said Ferdie.

"If I do, it might tip over," said Mr. Muddle. "I think I'd better wade back to shore."

"But how will I get back?" asked Ferdie. "I don't know how to row."

"I'll push the boat," Mr. Muddle said, and he gave the boat a push. It glided through the water 3 yards.

"This is fun," said Ferdie, enjoying the ride. "I wonder how far it is back to shore."

122 • How Deep Is the Water?

Mr. Muddle kept shoving the boat. Every time he shoved the boat, it moved ahead 3 yards. Ferdie counted and discovered that Mr. Muddle had to shove the boat ten times before it got to shore.

Can you figure out how far they were from shore?
30 yards

How far did Mr. Muddle have to push the boat? 30 yards

When they were finally back on land, Mr. Muddle was dripping and shivering. "By the way," said Ferdie, "why did you jump into the water with all your clothes on, Mr. Muddle?"

"I remembered how deep the water is," said Mr. Muddle, "but I forgot how wet it is."

. . . the end

Story 20 • **123**

LESSON
149

Student Edition pages 331–332

Counting by Fives

LESSON PLANNER

Objectives
▶ to teach students to count aloud by fives to 100
▶ to demonstrate for students the relationship between fives and tens

Context of the Lesson Counting by fives is continued in the next lesson. Students have already learned to count by twos and tens.

 MANIPULATIVES

Program Resources

Number Cubes
"Harder Flea Market" Game Mat
Thinking Story Book, pages 124–125
Practice Master 149
Enrichment Master 149
For extra practice:
CD-ROM* Lesson 149

① Warm-Up

Problem of the Day Present the following problem to the class. Mark has seven coins. They are worth 25 cents all together. What coins does he have? (two dimes and five pennies)

Problem-Solving Strategies Ask students who have solved the Problem of the Day to share how they solved it and any strategies they used.

 Have students use Number Cubes to answer the following problems.

a. 89 − 0 = (89) **b.** 6 + 2 = (8) **c.** 72 − 3 = (69)
d. 13 + 3 = (16) **e.** 91 − 0 = (91) **f.** 68 + 3 = (71)

② Teach

Demonstrate Draw a set of five tally marks on the chalkboard. Ask how many there are. (5) Then draw two more sets. Demonstrate for students how to count by fives to find out how many there are now. Next draw six sets of tally marks. Ask how many tally marks there are (30) and how many sets of five. (6) Then circle sets of ten tally marks to demonstrate that there are half as many circles as sets of five tally marks and twice as many sets of five tally marks as circles.

331 Numbers 1–100

LESSON
149

Name _____

Counting by Fives

How many tally marks? Count by fives. Then ring tens to check.

❶ 55 〔卌 卌〕〔卌 卌〕〔卌 卌〕〔卌 卌〕〔卌 卌〕〔卌〕

❷ 40 〔卌 卌〕〔卌 卌〕〔卌 卌〕〔卌 卌〕

❸ 60 〔卌 卌〕〔卌 卌〕〔卌 卌〕〔卌 卌〕〔卌 卌〕〔卌 卌〕

❹ 57 〔卌 卌〕〔卌 卌〕〔卌 卌〕〔卌 卌〕〔卌 卌〕〔卌 卌〕 II

❺ 25 〔卌 卌〕〔卌 卌〕〔卌〕

❻ 53 〔卌 卌〕〔卌 卌〕〔卌 卌〕〔卌 卌〕〔卌 卌〕III

Make the right number of tally marks. Then ring tens to show that you have the right number.

❼ 20 〔卌 卌〕〔卌 卌〕

❽ 35 〔卌 卌〕〔卌 卌〕〔卌 卌〕〔卌〕

 NOTE TO HOME
Students use tally marks to count by fives and tens.

Unit 4 Lesson 149 • **331**

 Literature Connection Read aloud *Number Families* by Jane Jonas Srivastava to provide an explanation of how every number is part of a family and functions differently.

RETEACHING

You can postpone reteaching until the next lesson, as counting by fives is continued, using nickels.

*available separately

◆ LESSON 149 Counting by Fives

Fill in the missing numbers.

9   10   20   30   **40**   **50**   60   70   80

10   5   10   **15**   20   **25**   30   **35**   40

Find the pattern.

11 Color spaces with 20 red.
Color spaces with 15 green.

5	10	green 15	20 red	25

10	15 green	20 red	25	30

green 15	20 red	25	30	35

12 Color spaces with 45 orange.
Color spaces with 55 blue.

5	15	25	35	45 orange

15	25	35	45 orange	55 blue

Write your own pattern problem.
Give it to a friend to solve.

332 • Numbers 1–100

PRACTICE p. 149

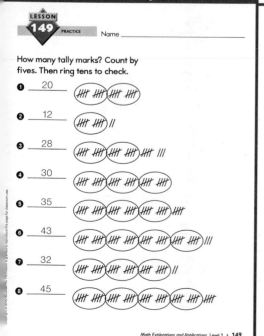

LESSON 149 PRACTICE   Name _____

How many tally marks? Count by fives. Then ring tens to check.

1 20
2 12
3 28
4 30
5 35
6 43
7 32
8 45

Math Explorations and Applications Level 1 • 149

ENRICHMENT p. 149

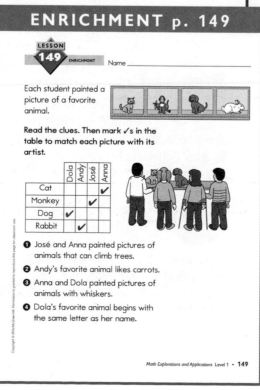

LESSON 149 ENRICHMENT   Name _____

Each student painted a picture of a favorite animal.

Read the clues. Then mark ✓s in the table to match each picture with its artist.

	Dola	Andy	José	Anna
Cat				✓
Monkey		✓		
Dog	✓			
Rabbit			✓	

1 José and Anna painted pictures of animals that can climb trees.
2 Andy's favorite animal likes carrots.
3 Anna and Dola painted pictures of animals with whiskers.
4 Dola's favorite animal begins with the same letter as her name.

Math Explorations and Applications Level 1 • 149

Using the Number Cubes Present more sets of tally marks on the chalkboard. Have students count silently by fives and indicate answers with their Number Cubes.

Using the Student Pages Have students complete these pages on their own and then check their answers with the class.

Using the "Harder Flea Market" Game Mat To provide practice with counting by fives and tens and with changing $1 bills for $5 bills and then for $10 bills, have students play this game, introduced in Lesson 49. A copy of this game can also be found on page 400 of this Guide.

Using the Thinking Story Present three new problems from among those following "How Deep Is the Water?" on pages 124–125 of the Thinking Story Book or pages 330a–330b of this Guide.

❸ Wrap-Up

In Closing Ask students to count aloud to 100 by fives.

Informal Assessment Use students' answers to pages 331–332 as an informal assessment of their ability to count by fives.

Assessment Criteria

Did the student . . .

✓ correctly trade bills when playing the "Harder Flea Market" game?

✓ correctly answer ten of 12 problems on pages 331–332?

GIFTED & TALENTED   **Meeting Individual Needs**
Ask students to figure out how much money their class would have if each student had $5. How many tens would that make? Compare answers when finished.

LESSON 150 Counting Nickels

Student Edition pages 333–334

LESSON PLANNER

Objectives

▶ to provide practice counting by fives through 100

▶ to provide practice determining the value of a number of nickels

▶ to demonstrate the relationship between fives and tens

Context of the Lesson The topic of counting by fives is continued from Lesson 149. Throughout the year students have used money as a concrete aid for addition and subtraction.

 MANIPULATIVES

bank or box with slot in it

play nickels*

items to play "store" with (optional)

Program Resources

Number Cubes

Thinking Story Book, pages 124–125

Reteaching Master

Practice Master 150

Enrichment Master 150

For extra practice: CD-ROM* Lesson 150

① Warm-Up ⏱ 5 MINUTES

Problem of the Day Present the following problem to the class. Casey has five nickels. Jackie has three dimes. Who has more money? (Jackie) How much more? (5¢)

MENTAL MATH Write the following problems on the chalkboard. Have students use their Number Cubes to show the missing numbers.

a. 5, □, 15, 20 (10)   b. 10, 15, □, 25 (20)

c. □, 20, 25, 30 (15)   d. 35, □, 45, 50 (40)

e. 50, 55, □, 65 (60)   f. 25, 20, □, 10 (15)

g. 80, □, 90, 95 (85)   h. 55, □, 65, 70 (60)

i. 75, □, 85, 90 (80)   j. 40, 45, □, 55 (50)

LESSON 150

Name _____

Counting Nickels

 REAL-WORLD CONNECTION

How many cents?
Ring tens to check.

❶ __35__ ¢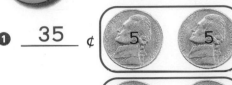

❷ __50__ ¢

❸ __55__ ¢

 **NOTE TO HOME**
Students count by fives and tens using nickels.

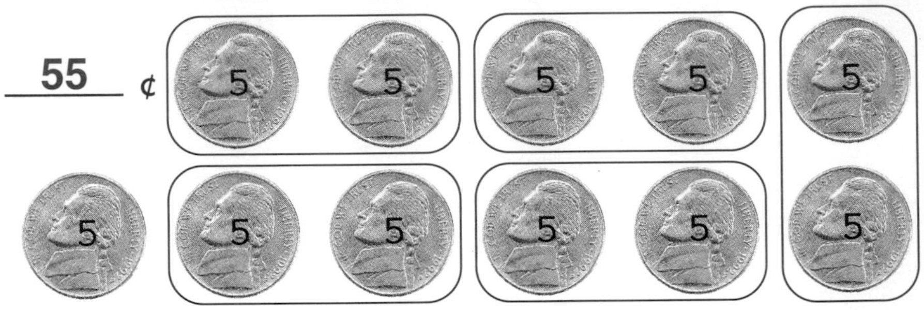

Unit 4   Lesson 150 • **333**

 LITERATURE CONNECTION

Literature Connection You may wish to read aloud to students *Annabelle Swift, Kindergartner* by Amy Schwartz to reinforce lesson concepts.

 REAL-WORLD CONNECTION **MANIPULATIVES**

Real-World Connection Set up a play store in which all of the **items** have prices that are multiples of 5. Have students "buy" items with their play **nickels***.

RETEACHING p. 39

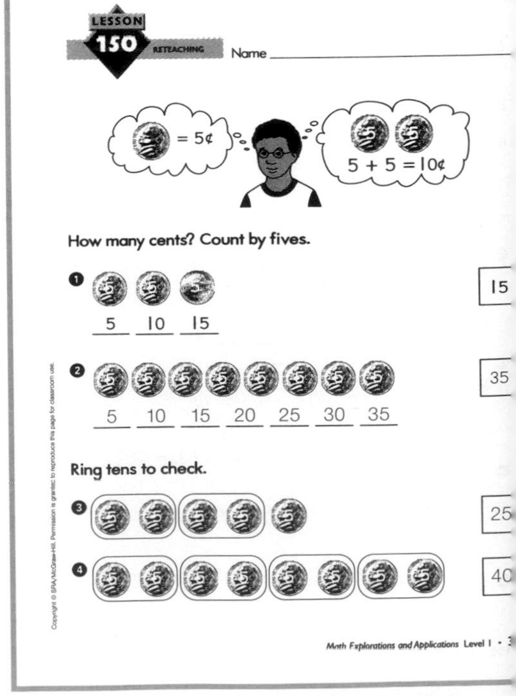

LESSON 150 RETEACHING   Name _____

How many cents? Count by fives.

❶  | 15 |
    5 10 15

❷  | 35 |
    5 10 15 20 25 30 35

Ring tens to check.

❸  | 25 |

❹  | 40 |

Math Explorations and Applications Level I • 3

*available separately

◆ **LESSON 150** Counting Nickels

Start at 0. Count by fives.
Connect the dots.

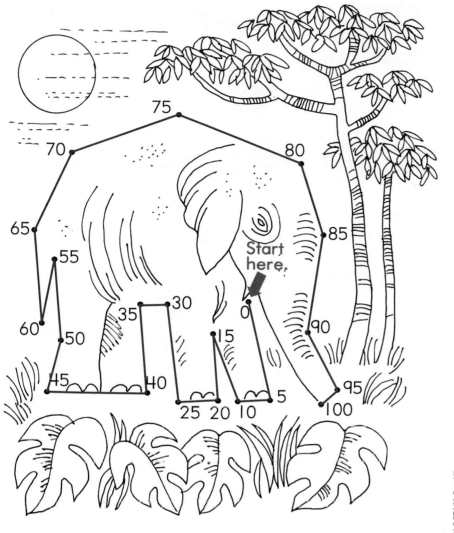

 NOTE TO HOME
Students count by fives to connect the dots.

Copyright © SRA/McGraw-Hill

② Teach

Demonstration Count by fives with the class through 100. Then hold up six **nickels*** and challenge students to figure out how many cents the nickels are worth. (30) Tell them they can figure the amount by counting by fives. Repeat, using different numbers. Have students use tally marks to keep track of the number of fives or nickels.

Using the Student Pages Have students complete the exercises on pages 333–334 on their own. Point out that they will need to count by fives in order to connect the dots on page 334.

Using the Thinking Story Present three new problems from those following "How Deep Is the Water?" on pages 124–125 in the Thinking Story Book or pages 330a–330b of this Guide.

③ Wrap-Up

In Closing Drop two nickels into a **bank** or small box with a slot in it. Ask students how much money you have put into the bank. (10¢) Continue dropping nickels into the bank. Students should count by fives to determine the total number of cents deposited.

Informal Assessment Note any students who are having difficulty counting by fives by observing their work throughout this lesson.

Assessment Criteria

Did the student . . .

✓ count by fives to 100?

✓ complete page 333 with 75% accuracy?

✓ use mental math to convert a given number of nickels to cents?

PRACTICE p. 150

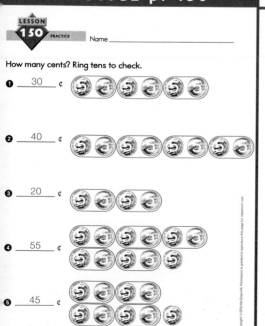

LESSON **150** PRACTICE   Name _____

How many cents? Ring tens to check.

❶ ___30___ ¢

❷ ___40___ ¢

❸ ___20___ ¢

❹ ___55___ ¢

❺ ___45___ ¢

150 • Math Explorations and Applications Level 1

ENRICHMENT p. 150

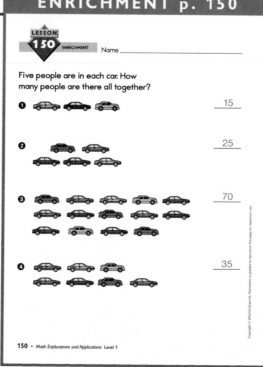

LESSON **150** ENRICHMENT   Name _____

Five people are in each car. How many people are there all together?

❶ ___15___

❷ ___25___

❸ ___70___

❹ ___35___

150 • Math Explorations and Applications Level 1

---

*available separately

LESSON 151

Amounts of Money

Student Edition pages 335–336

Name _____

Amounts of Money

 REAL-WORLD CONNECTION

How much money?

LESSON PLANNER

Objectives

▶ to teach students to identify the value of a set of coins that includes quarters

▶ to use quarters to make amounts of money

Context of the Lesson This is the first lesson involving quarters.

 MANIPULATIVES

four play quarters*

Program Resources

Number Cubes

Thinking Story Book, pages 124–125

Practice Master 151

Enrichment Master 151

For extra practice: CD-ROM* Lesson 151

❶ 25¢ + 5¢ = $\boxed{30¢}$

❷ 25¢ + 25¢ = $\boxed{50¢}$

Use coins to help.

❸ Make 35¢ with two coins. ⑩

❹ Make 40¢ with four coins.   ⑤ ⑤ ⑤

❺ Make 45¢ with three coins. ⑩ ⑩

❶ Warm-Up ⏱ 5 MINUTES

 PROBLEM SOLVING

Problem of the Day Present the following problem to the class. Kim has six bills worth $15 in all. What bills does she have? (a $10 bill and five $1 bills)

Problem-Solving Strategies Ask students who have solved the Problem of the Day to share how they solved it and any strategies they used.

MENTAL MATH Have students use Number Cubes to indicate their answers to the following problems.

a. 27 + 1 = (28) b. 35 − 2 = (33) c. 50 + 2 = (52)

d. 64 − 1 = (63) e. 48 + 0 = (48) f. 59 + 3 = (62)

❷ Teach

Demonstrate Have students suggest different ways to make 25 cents. Then display for students a **quarter***. Explain that it is worth 25 cents and that it takes four quarters to make one dollar. Draw different sets of coins on the chalkboard all involving a quarter and have students determine how much each set is worth. Draw sets, such as: a quarter and a dime and a quarter and two pennies. Then ask students to determine how to make 28 cents using a quarter. (one quarter and three pennies) Repeat with similar examples.

335 Numbers 1–100

🎒 **NOTE TO HOME**
Students use nickels, dimes, and quarters to make given amounts.

Copyright © SRA/McGraw-Hill

RETEACHING

Reteaching is not considered essential for the material in this lesson.

*available separately

◆ LESSON 151 Amounts of Money

Fill in the missing numbers. Then solve the addition problems.

6   3   6 $\boxed{9}$ $\boxed{12}$ 15

$3 + 3 + 3 = \boxed{9}$

$3 + 3 + 3 + 3 = \boxed{12}$

7   4   8   12 $\boxed{16}$ 20 $\boxed{24}$ 28

$4 + 4 + 4 + 4 = \boxed{16}$

$4 + 4 + 4 + 4 + 4 + 4 = \boxed{24}$

8   2   4 $\boxed{6}$ 8 $\boxed{10}$ 12

$2 + 2 + 2 = \boxed{6}$

$2 + 2 + 2 + 2 + 2 = \boxed{10}$

336 • Numbers 1–100

NOTE TO HOME
Students do skip counting to solve addition problems.

Using the Number Cubes Draw combinations of coins on the chalkboard and give simple word problems, such as: "I have one quarter and one nickel. How much do I have in all?" (30 cents) Have students give answers with Number Cubes. Finally, show addition problems in which one of the addends is 25, such as 25 + 10 and 25 + 13. Have students show answers with Number Cubes.

Using the Student Pages Have students complete these pages on their own and then check answers together with the class.

Using the Thinking Story Present two new problems from among those following "How Deep Is the Water?" on pages 124–125 of the Thinking Story Book or pages 330a–330b of this Guide.

❸ Wrap-Up ⏱

In Closing Ask students how many quarters are in $2. (eight) Have students explain how they found the answer.

Performance Assessment Observe which students can consistently determine the correct amounts in the Number Cube activity.

Assessment Criteria

Did the student . . .

✓ correctly determine amounts in the Number Cube activity?

✓ correctly answer five of eight problems on pages 335–336?

Meeting Individual Needs
Provide play money for students to use to complete page 335. Work on more examples with them in small groups using play coins.

PRACTICE p. 151

LESSON 151 PRACTICE   Name _____

How much money?

1 $25¢ + 10¢ + 10¢ = \boxed{45¢}$

2 $25¢ + 4¢ = \boxed{29¢}$

3 $25¢ + 5¢ + 5¢ + 5¢ = \boxed{40¢}$

Use coins to help.

4 Make 50¢ with four coins.   10 10 5

5 Make 30¢ with two coins.   5

6 Make 40¢ with three coins.   10 5

7 Make 75¢ with three coins.   25 25

Math Explorations and Applications Level 1 • 151

ENRICHMENT p. 151

LESSON 151 ENRICHMENT   Name _____

Spiders 25¢   Beetles 10¢   Ants 5¢

Each machine takes one coin.
Tell what bugs these coins will buy.

1
3 spiders, 1 beetle, 2 ants

2
2 spiders, 4 ants

3
1 spider, 5 beetles, 2 ants

Math Explorations and Applications Level 1 • 151

LESSON 152

Student Edition pages 337–338

Quarters, Dimes, and Nickels

LESSON PLANNER

Objectives

▶ to review forming amounts of money with combinations of coins

▶ to provide practice working with the sequence of numbers 1, 3, 5, . . .

Context of the Lesson Lesson 153 will include work with further sequences of numbers.

 MANIPULATIVES

play coins*

egg carton (optional)

Program Resources

Number Cubes

Thinking Story Book, pages 124–125

Reteaching Master

Practice Master 152

Enrichment Master 152

For extra practice:
  CD-ROM* Lesson 152
  Mixed Practice, page 383

---

① Warm-Up 5 MINUTES

Problem of the Day Present the following problem to the class. Elise buys some popcorn for 35¢. What is the greatest number of coins she could use? (35: pennies) What is the least number of coins? (2: 1 quarter, 1 dime)

Problem-Solving Strategies Ask students who have solved the Problem of the Day to share how they solved it and any strategies they used.

MENTAL MATH To provide practice in addition, write the following problems on the chalkboard. Have students show their answers with Number Cubes.

a. 27 + 1 = (28)   **b.** 60 + 0 = (60)

c. 58 + 2 = (60)   **d.** 30 + 30 = (60)

e 28 + 2 = (30)   **f.** 92 + 2 = (94)

Name _____

Quarters, Dimes, and Nickels

Put a coin in each circle to make the right amount. Write your answers.

❶ 25¢ (10) (10) (5)

❷ 15¢ (5) (5) (5)

❸ 15¢ (10) (5)

❹ 25¢ (10) (5) (5) (5)

❺ 35¢ (10) (10) (10) (5)

 REAL-WORLD CONNECTION Do the "Make It a Different Way" activity.

 NOTE TO HOME Students use coins to form given amounts of money.

Unit 4 Lesson 152 • **337**

 Real-World Connection Talk about cash registers students may have seen. Ask students how they think cashiers keep different kinds of coins and bills separate. Then have students use an **egg carton** or other divided box to make their own "cash register" to hold play money.

 Literature Connection You may wish to read to students *Arthur's Funny Money* by Lillian Hoban to enrich their understanding of monetary amounts.

RETEACHING p. 40

LESSON 152 RETEACHING Name _____

 = 1¢   = 5¢   = 10¢

Put a coin in each circle to make the right amount. Write your answers.

❶ 30¢ (10) (10) (10)

❷ 30¢ (5) (5) (5) (5) (5) (5)

❸ 35¢ (10) (10) (5) (5) (5)

❹ 10¢ (5) (5)

❺ 10¢ (5) (1) (1) (1) (1) (1)

❻ 15¢ (10) (5)

40 • Math Explorations and Applications Level 1

---

*available separately

◆ **LESSON 152 Quarters, Dimes, and Nickels**

Connect the dots. Start at 1 and count by twos. Draw a line to 3, then to 5, and so on.

Use the Mixed Practice on page 383 after this lesson.

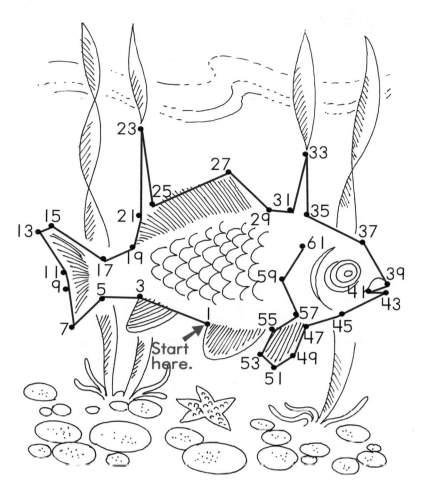

Start here.

338 • Numbers 1–100

NOTE TO HOME
Students skip count by twos using odd numbers to 61.

Copyright © SRA/McGraw-Hill

PRACTICE p. 152

LESSON 152 PRACTICE Name _____

Put a coin in each circle to make the right amount. Write your answers.

❶ 20¢ ⑤ ⑤ ⑤ ⑤

❷ 20¢ ⑩ ⑩

❸ 30¢ ⑩ ⑩ ⑩

❹ 30¢ ⑩ ⑤ ⑤ ⑤ ⑤

❺ 45¢ ㉕ ⑩ ⑩

❻ 45¢ ㉕ ⑤ ⑤ ⑤ ⑤

❼ 50¢ ㉕ ㉕

❽ 50¢ ㉕ ⑩ ⑤ ⑤ ⑤

152 • Math Explorations and Applications Level 1

ENRICHMENT p. 152

LESSON 152 ENRICHMENT Name _____

PROBLEM SOLVING

COOPERATIVE LEARNING

Myra has 27¢.

Chan has 55¢.

Paulo has 18¢.

Xandra has 64¢.

Make up problems to show how the children spent their money. Trade problems with another student.

Answers will vary.

_____
_____
_____
_____
_____

152 • Math Explorations and Applications Level 1

---

❷ Teach

Introducing the "Make It a Different Way" Activity Divide students into pairs. Give each student a set of **play coins***. Have students take turns rolling one tens and one units Number Cube to get a number, such as 36. Each partner must show that amount of cents in a different way. For example, the first partner might use three dimes, one nickel, and one penny while the other might use one quarter, one dime, and one penny. Continue the activity with another number.

Using the Student Pages You may wish to complete page 337 as a whole-group activity. Students can do page 338 on their own.

Using the Thinking Story Do two new problems from those following "How Deep Is the Water?" on pages 124–125 in the Thinking Story Book or pages 330a–330b of this Guide.

❸ Wrap-Up

5 MINUTES

In Closing Talk about instances when students might need to be able to form amounts of money in different ways, such as when a snack machine accepts only certain coins.

SELF ASSESSMENT Have students work in pairs using play coins. One student names an amount and the other shows that amount with play coins. Students then switch roles. Invite students to record any amounts with which they had difficulty.

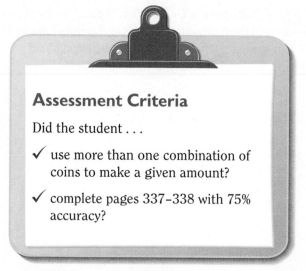

Assessment Criteria

Did the student . . .

✓ use more than one combination of coins to make a given amount?

✓ complete pages 337–338 with 75% accuracy?

*available separately

LESSON 153

Student Edition pages 339–342

Unit 4 Review

Using the Student Pages Use this Unit Review as a preliminary unit test to indicate areas in which each student is having difficulty or in which the entire class may need help. If students do not do well on the Unit Review, you may spend a day or so helping students overcome their individual difficulties before they take the Unit Test.

Next to each instruction line is a list of the lessons in the unit covered in that set of problems. Students can refer to the specific lesson for additional instruction if they need help. You can also use this information to make additional assignments based on the previous lesson concepts.

Have students complete page 339 and the top half of page 340 as a timed test.

For page 342 you might want to have a large clock at the front of the room. Have students complete these pages on their own.

Problems 21–40 Many students at the end of first grade cannot easily handle numbers from 10–100. Activities that continually involve the use of such numbers will help to increase the student's familiarity and sense of security in dealing with them. Useful games are "Macaroni Tens" (Lesson 112), "Get to 100 by Tens or Ones" (Lesson 119), "School Bookstore" (Lesson 113), and "Yard Sale" (Lesson 120). The "Harder Pattern" game (Lesson 134) and the "Add the Coins" game (Lesson 92) may also be played.

Problems 33–35 The "Space" game (Lesson 121) will provide practice and reinforcement for students who fail to grasp missing-addend problems. It should be played with able partners.

339 Numbers 1–100

LESSON 153

Name _____

Unit 4 Review

Add the numbers. Write the sums.

Lessons 125, 133, 135, 136, 139

1. $3 + 4 =$ __7__
2. $8 + 3 =$ __11__
3. $9 + 5 =$ __14__
4. $2 + 3 =$ __5__
5. $8 + 8 =$ __16__
6. $9 + 2 =$ __11__
7. $4 + 2 =$ __6__
8. $4 + 8 =$ __12__
9. $6 + 6 =$ __12__
10. $1 + 8 =$ __9__

11. $3 + 3 =$ __6__
12. $3 + 9 =$ __12__
13. $9 + 8 =$ __17__
14. $7 + 7 =$ __14__
15. $5 + 0 =$ __5__
16. $2 + 7 =$ __9__
17. $6 + 9 =$ __15__
18. $10 + 9 =$ __19__
19. $6 + 5 =$ __11__
20. $8 + 4 =$ __12__

My time

My time

Copyright © SRA/McGraw-Hill

NOTE TO HOME
Students review unit skills and concepts.

Unit 4 Review • **339**

*available separately

◆ **LESSON 153 Unit 4 Review**

Write the sums.

Lessons
125,
133,
135,
136,
139

㉑ 9 + 9 = __18__   ㉒ 10 + 4 = __14__

㉓ 0 + 6 = __6__   ㉔ 10 + 3 = __13__

㉕ 5 + 5 = __10__   ㉖ 7 + 4 = __11__

㉗ 8 + 1 = __9__   ㉘ 9 + 6 = __15__

㉙ 8 + 7 = __15__   ㉚ 5 + 7 = __12__

My time

Solve these problems too.

Lessons
118,
119
128,
129

㉛ 25 + 10 = __35__   ㉜ 29 + 20 = __49__

㉝ 3 + | 5 | = 8   ㉞ 6 + | 4 | = 10

㉟ 5 + | 3 | = 8

 NOTE TO HOME
Students review unit skills and concepts.

 Performance Assessment The Performance Assessment Tasks 7–8 provided on Assessment page 73 of the Assessment Blackline Masters can be used at this time to evaluate students' skill with basic facts. You may want to administer this assessment with individual students or in small groups.

Portfolio Assessment If you have not already completed the Portfolio Assessment task provided on page 83 of the Assessment Blackline Masters it can be used at this time to evaluate students' skill in writing number sentences.

Unit Project If you have not already assigned the "Greatest and Least" project on pages 348a-348b, you may want to do so at this time. The Unit Project is a good opportunity for students to apply the concepts of counting and writing numbers in real-world problem solving.

◆ **LESSON 153 Unit 4 Review**

Name _____

Lesson ㊱ One glass of lemonade costs 4¢.
124 How much will two, three, or more
glasses of lemonade cost?
Fill in the chart.

Number of glasses	Cents
1	4
2	8
3	12
4	16
5	20
6	24

Use manipulatives to help solve
these problems.

Lesson ㊲ 23 – 15 = __8__   ㊳ 44 – 9 = __35__
138

㊴ 34 – 5 = __29__   ㊵ 28 – 12 = __16__

NOTE TO HOME
Students review unit skills and concepts.

Unit 4   Review • **341**

RETEACHING

Students who have difficulty with this
Unit Review should have further
opportunity to review and to practice
the skills before they proceed. For each
set of problems there are specific
suggestions for reteaching. These
suggestions can be found in the margins.

◆ **LESSON 153** Unit 4 Review

Draw the hands on the clock to show about the right time.

41 Eat dinner

Answers will vary.

Lesson 146

The time is

Complete the chart to show what time it will be in . . .

0 I hour	3:00
42 2 hours	**4:00**
43 3 hours	**5:00**
44 10 hours	**12:00**
45 12 hours	**2:00**

Copyright: © SRA/McGraw-Hill

342 • Numbers 1–100

NOTE TO HOME
Students review unit skills and concepts.

PRACTICE p. 153

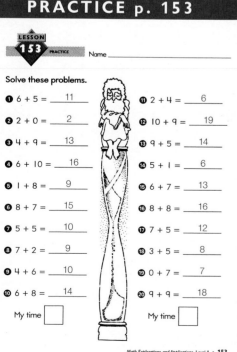

LESSON **153** PRACTICE Name _____

Solve these problems.

❶ 6 + 5 = ___11___

❷ 2 + 0 = ___2___

❸ 4 + 9 = ___13___

❹ 6 + 10 = ___16___

❺ 1 + 8 = ___9___

❻ 8 + 7 = ___15___

❼ 5 + 5 = ___10___

❽ 7 + 2 = ___9___

❾ 4 + 6 = ___10___

❿ 6 + 8 = ___14___

⓫ 2 + 4 = ___6___

⓬ 10 + 9 = ___19___

⓭ 9 + 5 = ___14___

⓮ 5 + 1 = ___6___

⓯ 6 + 7 = ___13___

⓰ 8 + 8 = ___16___

⓱ 7 + 5 = ___12___

⓲ 3 + 5 = ___8___

⓳ 0 + 7 = ___7___

⓴ 9 + 9 = ___18___

My time [ ]   My time [ ]

Math Explorations and Applications Level 1 • 153

ENRICHMENT p. 153

LESSON **153** ENRICHMENT Name _____

Finish writing these addition problems. Put one number in each spoke on the wheel. Then solve the problems you have made. The first one is done for you.

Answers will depend upon the problems students have written.

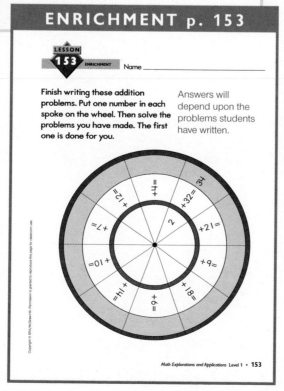

Math Explorations and Applications Level 1 • 153

Student Edition pages 343–346

Unit 4 Test

Name _____

Unit 4 Test

Using the Student Pages This Unit Test on Student Edition pages 343–346 provides an opportunity to formally evaluate your students' proficiency with concepts developed in this unit. It is similar in content and format to the Unit Review. Students who did well on the Unit Review may not need to take this test. Students who did not do well on the Unit Review should be provided with additional practice opportunities, such as the Unit Practice pages, before taking the Unit Test. For further evaluation, you may wish to have these students take the Unit Test in standardized format, provided on pages 112–120 in the Assessment Blackline Masters or the Unit Test on pages 57–60 of the Assessment Blackline Masters.

Check your math skills.

Solve these problems.

1 $73 + 10 =$ __**83**__

2 $46 + 30 =$ __**76**__

3 $48 + 2 =$ __**50**__

4 $87 - 20 =$ __**67**__

5 $61 - 2 =$ __**59**__

6 $7 + 7 =$ __**14**__

7 $9 + 9 =$ __**18**__

8 $6 + 6 =$ __**12**__

9 $8 + 8 =$ __**16**__

10 $4 + 4 =$ __**8**__

NOTE TO HOME
This test checks unit skills and concepts.

Unit 4 Test • 343

◆ **LESSON 154 Unit 4 Test**

Solve these problems.

⑪   59
    + 2
     61

⑫   32
    + 2
     34

⑬   81
    − 2
     79

⑭   73
    − 2
     71

⑮ $8 + 9 =$ __17__

⑯ $8 + 6 =$ __14__

⑰ $7 + 4 =$ __11__

⑱ $7 + 8 =$ __15__

⑲ $6 + 9 =$ __15__

⑳ $7 + 9 =$ __16__

㉑ $4 + 8 =$ __12__

㉒ $9 + 3 =$ __12__

NOTE TO HOME
This test checks unit skills and concepts.

◆ **LESSON 154 Unit 4 Test**

Name _____

What is the right sign?
Draw <, >, or =.

㉓ 4 $\boxed{<}$ 8   ㉔ 46 $\boxed{>}$ 39

㉕ 60 $\boxed{>}$ 30   ㉖ 63 $\boxed{>}$ 36

㉗ 38 $\boxed{<}$ 51   ㉘ 10 + 20 $\boxed{=}$ 30

㉙ 100 $\boxed{>}$ 98   ㉚ 30 + 20 $\boxed{>}$ 40

㉛ 49 + 2 $\boxed{=}$ 51

Solve these problems.

㉜ 8 + $\boxed{2}$ = 10   ㉝ 3 + $\boxed{7}$ = 10

㉞ 5 + $\boxed{2}$ = 7   ㉟ 3 + $\boxed{0}$ = 3

㊱ 7 + $\boxed{3}$ = 10   ㊲ 6 + $\boxed{1}$ = 7

 NOTE TO HOME
This test checks unit skills and concepts.

Unit 4 Test • **345**

RETEACHING

Students who have difficulty with this Unit Test should have further opportunity to review and to practice the skills before they proceed. After students have reviewed the skills you may want to use the Unit Test on pages 57–60 in the Assessment Blackline Masters, which covers the Unit 4 concepts.

PRACTICE p. 154

LESSON 154 PRACTICE Name _____

Solve these problems.

❶ 52 + 10 = ___62___   ❷ 37 + 20 = ___57___

❸ 4 + 4 = ___8___   ❹ 6 + 6 = ___12___

Solve these problems.

❺   39   ❻   51   ❼   27   ❽   62
   + 3   – 4   + 4   – 2
   ____   ____   ____   ____
    42   47   31   60

What is the right sign? Draw <, >, or =.

❾ 28 $\boxed{<}$ 32   ❿ 41 $\boxed{>}$ 14

Solve these problems.

⓫ 5 + $\boxed{5}$ = 10   ⓬ 4 + $\boxed{6}$ = 10

⓭ 6 + $\boxed{6}$ = 12   ⓮ 9 + $\boxed{9}$ = 18

154 • *Math Explorations and Applications Level 1*

◆ **LESSON 154 Unit 4 Test**

38 Sara is six years old. Her brother Mark is nine years old.

Who is older? ___**Mark**___

How much older? ___**3 years**___

39 There are four glasses in each box.

How many glasses in all? ___**16**___

40 Eight children will go to the circus. Each car will hold five children.

How many cars are needed? ___**2**___

346 • Numbers 1–100

NOTE TO HOME
This test checks unit skills and concepts.

ENRICHMENT p. 154

LESSON
154 ENRICHMENT Name _____

Joan is lost in space. Help her get back to Earth. Solve the problems. Follow the right answers on the sky path. Color the correct path.

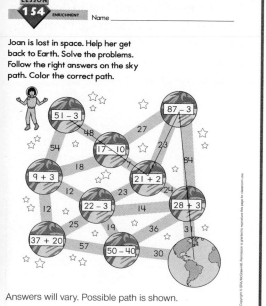

Answers will vary. Possible path is shown.

154 • Math Explorations and Applications Level 1

ASSESSMENT p. 57

UNIT **4** Unit 4 Test (Use after Lesson 153.) Page 1 of 4

Name _____

The student demonstrates mastery by correctly answering 36 of the 45 problems.

What is the right sign?
Draw <, >, or =.

❶ 5 (<) 10   ❷ 54 (>) 47

❸ 70 (>) 35   ❹ 23 (<) 32

❺ 48 (>) 39   ❻ 20 + 20 (=) 40

❼ 100 (>) 97   ❽ 10 + 30 (<) 55

Solve these problems.

❾ 9 + $\boxed{1}$ = 10   ❿ 2 + $\boxed{8}$ = 10

⓫ 6 + $\boxed{2}$ = 8   ⓬ 4 + $\boxed{3}$ = 7

⓭ 8 + $\boxed{2}$ = 10   ⓮ 5 + $\boxed{0}$ = 5

Go on ...

Math Explorations and Applications Level 1 • 57

LESSON
155

Student Edition pages 347–348

Extending the Unit

LESSON PLANNER

Objective

▶ to provide practice identifying number patterns

Context of the Lesson This is the fourth and last "Extending the Unit" lesson in this book.

 MANIPULATIVES

tracing paper (optional)

Program Resources

Practice Master 155

Number Cubes

Enrichment Master 155

For extra practice:
  CD-ROM* Lesson 155
  Mixed Practice, page 384

① Warm-Up

Problem of the Day Present the following problem to the class. How many different ways can you show 21 cents using at least one dime or one nickel, and at least one penny? What are they? (eight ways; two dimes, one penny; one dime, eleven pennies; one dime, two nickels, one penny; one dime, one nickel, six pennies; four nickels, one penny; three nickels, six pennies; two nickels, eleven pennies; one nickel, sixteen pennies)

Problem-Solving Strategies Ask students who have solved the Problem of the Day to share how they solved it and any strategies they used.

 Use mental math to add these multiples of 10. Show answers with Number Cubes.

a.	20 + 10 = (30)	b.	30 + 20 = (50)
c.	40 + 30 = (70)	d.	10 + 30 = (40)
e.	60 + 30 = (90)	f.	50 + 40 = (90)

② Teach

Using the Student Pages The number-pattern problems provided for enrichment on pages 347–348 are more challenging than those students have practiced throughout the book. Have students who do not need remediation complete these pages while remediation work is going on. When finished, have them help other students in the games or other remedial work they are doing.

347 Numbers 1–100

Name _____

Extending the Unit

Fill in the missing numbers. Then color a pattern on each chart.

❶

2	3	2	3	2	3
6	7	**6**	7	6	**7**
10	**11**	10	11	10	11

❷

9	12	15	18
5	8	11	**14**
1	**4**	7	10

❸

10	8	6	4	2
24	22	20	**18**	16
32	30	**28**	26	24

 NOTE TO HOME
Students fill in missing numbers by discovering patterns.

Unit 4   Lesson 155 • **347**

Copyright © SRA/McGraw-Hill

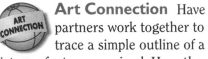 **Art Connection** Have partners work together to trace a simple outline of a picture of a tree or animal. Have them then draw dots along the outline and number them from 1 through 40. Have students then put **tracing paper** over the dots and trace only the dots and numbers. Have them exchange dotted drawings and complete each other's pictures.

Use results of the Unit Test to determine which skills need reteaching. Provide extra practice worksheets for small groups of students in each skill that needs reteaching.

*available separately

◆ **LESSON 155** Extending the Unit

Use the Mixed Practice on page 384 after this lesson.

Fill in the missing numbers.

4

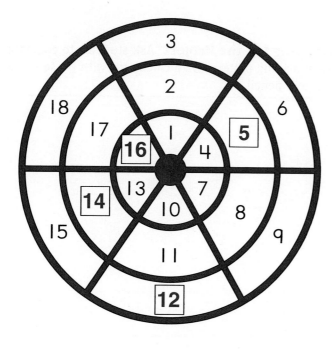

5

5	7	9
3	5	7
1	3	5

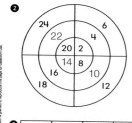 **NOTE TO HOME** Students solve number patterning and sequencing problems.

Students who need remediation in addition, subtraction, or money skills can play games to review specific skills. Have students play one of the following games, depending on their needs: the "Addition Table" game for practice with using an addition table, the "Yard Sale" or "Flea Market" game for practice with changing money, or the "Space" game for practice solving addition and missing-addend problems. You can use the Unit Test to determine which students need remediation in each skill area. A copy of each recommended game can be found on pages 392, 413, 399, and 410 respectively of this Guide.

❸ Wrap-Up

In Closing Have students explain how they identified missing numbers in any pattern on page 347 or 348.

Performance Assessment Observe which students can play the games accurately and without difficulty to informally determine if remediation is still needed.

Assessment Criterion

Did the student . . .

✓ correctly complete 80% of the problems on pages 347–348?

PRACTICE p. 155

LESSON 155 PRACTICE Name _____

Fill in the missing numbers.

1

9	8	9	8	9
8	7	8	7	8
7	6	7	6	7

2

3

6	9	12	15
2	5	8	11
10	13	16	19

Math Explorations and Applications Level 1 • 155

ENRICHMENT p. 155

LESSON 155 ENRICHMENT Name _____

All the bricks on the walkways in Numberland have numbers. Fill in the missing numbers.

Math Explorations and Applications Level 1 • 155

PRESENTING THE PROJECT

Project Objectives

▶ to develop calculator techniques to solve problems

▶ to create patterns

▶ to copy and continue established patterns

 MANIPULATIVES

calculators*

paper and pencil

Program Resources

*Half a Slice of Bread and Butter**
   from the Literature Library

SRA's *Minds on Math**

 In this project students use **calculators*** to form greatest and least numbers and to identify and create patterns. Students also learn that some calculator numbers, when viewed upside down, spell words. Begin by challenging students to form the greatest number possible on the calculator. Talk about whether they could use a paper and pencil to write an even greater number. (yes) Challenge students to form the least number on the calculator. Ask students whether they could write an even lesser number on paper. (Assuming that students show only whole numbers, the least number in both instances is 1.)

Then write a number pattern on the chalkboard, for instance, *34343*. Challenge students to continue the pattern on their calculators. Write another pattern, for instance, *48604860*. Ask students to see if they can continue this pattern on the calculator. (Most calculators will not allow more than eight digits in the display, so the pattern probably cannot be continued.) Have a student continue the pattern on the chalkboard. Invite students to write their own patterns to share with the class.

Then have students enter *335* on their calculators. Have students turn their calculators upside down and read the display. (It says SEE.) Challenge students to explore other letters than can be formed from numbers. Have them make a list of these number-letter relationships. (1 = I, 3 = E, 4 = h, 5 = S, 6=g, 7 = L, 8 = B, 9 = b, 0=O) Then challenge students to write words with their calculators. Have students record each word and the key sequence used to form it. As a final activity, have students make a letter pattern on their calculators and challenge a partner to continue the pattern. Invite students to share their work.

What Is a Math Project?

If this is the first time you have used math projects in your classroom, you may want to refer to pages 92a–92b in this Teacher's Guide for more detailed information about effectively implementing and assessing projects.

Wrapping Up the Project Ask students to compare the ease of making patterns on a calculator with those made with paper and pencil.

Minds on Math SRA's *Minds on Math* is a series of units covering Problem Solving, Data Collection, Number Sense, Measurement, Money, and Geometry and Spatial Relations. Each unit provides a series of open-ended projects for individuals or small groups. These projects develop problem-solving and critical-thinking skills, utilize real-world materials, emphasize language, and integrate cross-curricular connections. Use projects from *Money* to help students recognize coins, currency, and situations that involve money.

 Assessing the Project Observe students as they work with calculators. Watch to see that individuals identify and extend patterns. When spelling words on the calculator, students should discover that they should enter numbers in the opposite order of the letters in the word because they will be looking at the display upside down.

 Performance Assessment To assess students' calculator techniques, present addition and subtraction problems for students to enter and solve with calculators.

Literature Connection You may want to share *Anno's Math Games* by Mitsumasa Anno to explore other fun math concepts and puzzles. You can also use the Literature Library lap book *Half a Slice of Bread and Butter** to have students practice counting, addition, fractions, and prediction skills.

Technology Connection The software *Peter's Growing Patterns* from Strawberry Hill (Apple, for grades K–up) provides further practice in identifying and continuing patterns.

Name _____

Mixed Practice
Pages 1–10

Draw what comes next.

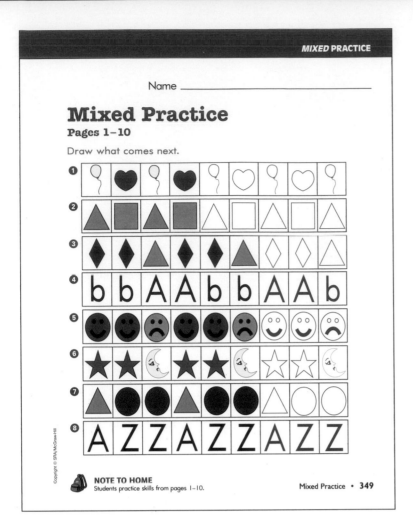

NOTE TO HOME
Students practice skills from pages 1–10.

Mixed Practice • **349**

Mixed Practice
Pages 1–20

0 1 2 3 4 5 6 7 8 9 10

Copy the correct number.

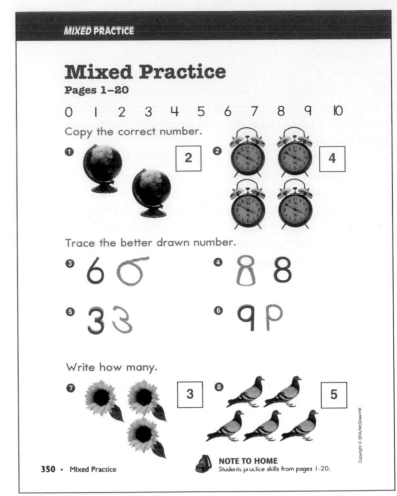

Trace the better drawn number.

Write how many.

350 • Mixed Practice

NOTE TO HOME
Students practice skills from pages 1–20.

Name _____

Mixed Practice
Pages 1–30

Write how many.

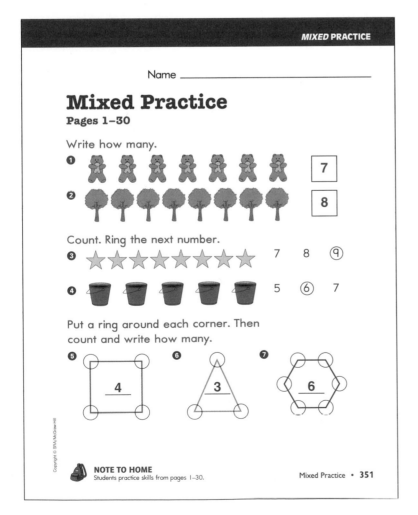

Count. Ring the next number.

Put a ring around each corner. Then count and write how many.

NOTE TO HOME
Students practice skills from pages 1–30.

Mixed Practice • **351**

Mixed Practice
Pages 1–40

Draw an X on the number, word, or picture that doesn't belong.

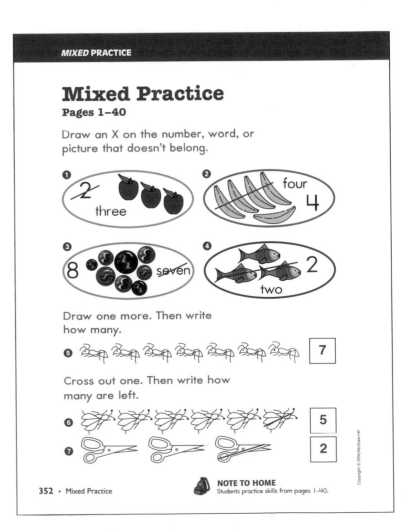

Draw one more. Then write how many.

Cross out one. Then write how many are left.

352 • Mixed Practice

NOTE TO HOME
Students practice skills from pages 1–40.

Name _____

Mixed Practice
Pages 1–50

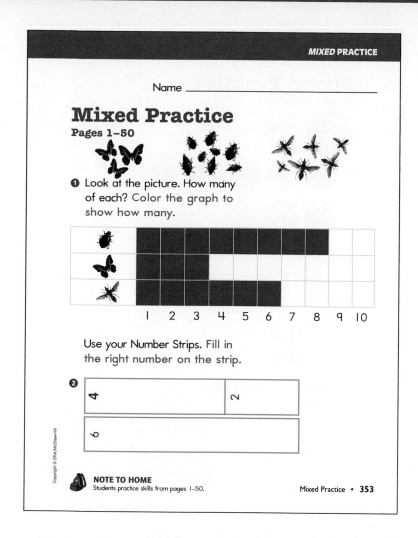

❶ Look at the picture. How many of each? Color the graph to show how many.

🪲										
🦋										
🐝										

|1|2|3|4|5|6|7|8|9|10|

Use your Number Strips. Fill in the right number on the strip.

❷

4		2

6		

NOTE TO HOME
Students practice skills from pages 1–50.

Mixed Practice
Pages 1–60

❶ Draw a straight line from the rabbit to the nearest hole. Use your Number Strips to measure.

How many all together?

❷ __5__ 2

❸ __10__ 7

❹ __8__ 5

❺ __9__ 6

Fill in the missing numbers. Look for patterns.

❻ 3 2 3 2 **3** 2 **3** **2** 3 2

NOTE TO HOME
Students practice skills from pages 1–60.

Name _____

Mixed Practice
Pages 1–70

How many now?

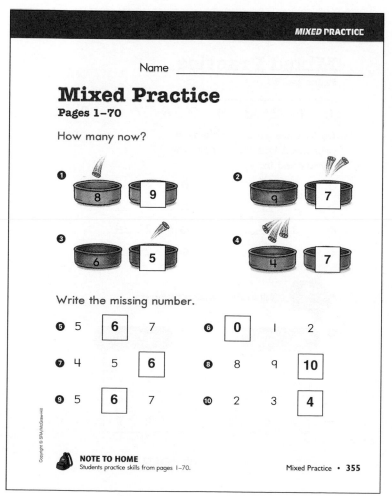

❶ 8 9

❷ 9 7

❸ 6 5

❹ 4 7

Write the missing number.

❺ 5 **6** 7

❻ **0** 1 2

❼ 4 5 **6**

❽ 8 9 **10**

❾ 5 **6** 7

❿ 2 3 **4**

NOTE TO HOME
Students practice skills from pages 1–70.

Mixed Practice
Pages 1–80

How many now?

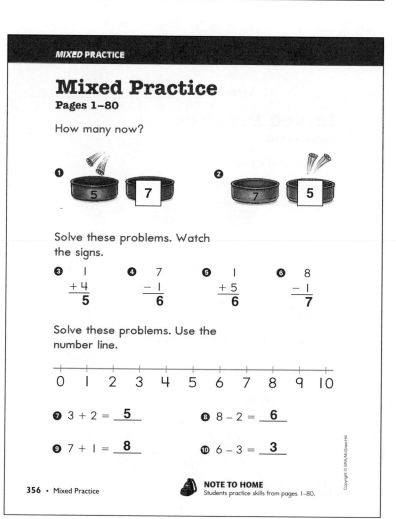

❶ 5 7

❷ 7 5

Solve these problems. Watch the signs.

❸ $\begin{array}{r} 1 \\ +4 \\ \hline 5 \end{array}$
❹ $\begin{array}{r} 7 \\ -1 \\ \hline 6 \end{array}$
❺ $\begin{array}{r} 1 \\ +5 \\ \hline 6 \end{array}$
❻ $\begin{array}{r} 8 \\ -1 \\ \hline 7 \end{array}$

Solve these problems. Use the number line.

|0|1|2|3|4|5|6|7|8|9|10|

❼ $3 + 2 = $ __5__

❽ $8 - 2 = $ __6__

❾ $7 + 1 = $ __8__

❿ $6 - 3 = $ __3__

NOTE TO HOME
Students practice skills from pages 1–80.

Name _____

Mixed Practice
Pages 1–92

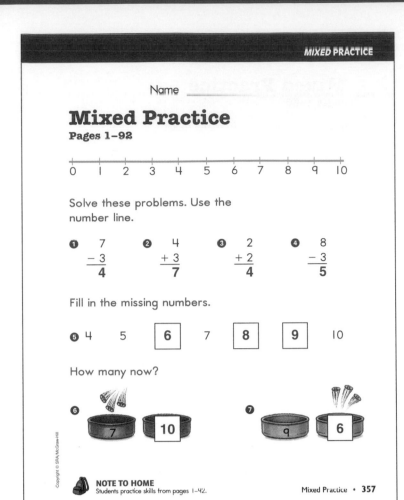

Solve these problems. Use the number line.

❶ 7
− 3
4

❷ 4
+ 3
7

❸ 2
+ 2
4

❹ 8
− 3
5

Fill in the missing numbers.

❺ 4 5 **6** 7 **8** **9** 10

How many now?

❻ **7** **10**

❼ **9** **6**

Mixed Practice
Pages 1–100

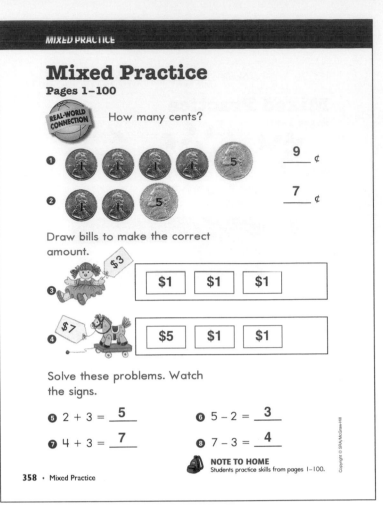

REAL-WORLD CONNECTION

How many cents?

❶ **9** ¢

❷ **7** ¢

Draw bills to make the correct amount.

❸ | $1 | $1 | $1 |

❹ | $5 | $1 | $1 |

Solve these problems. Watch the signs.

❺ 2 + 3 = **5**   ❻ 5 − 2 = **3**

❼ 4 + 3 = **7**   ❽ 7 − 3 = **4**

Name _____

Mixed Practice
Pages 1–110

Listen to these problems.

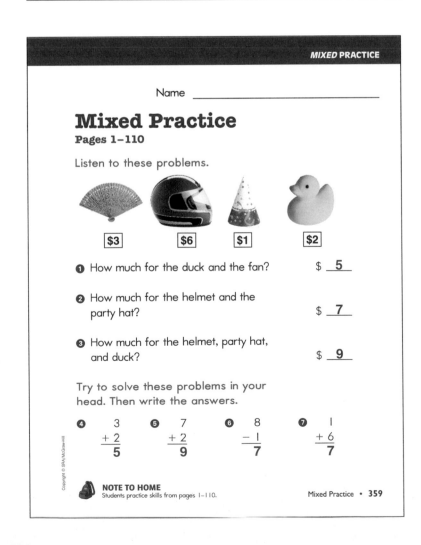

| $3 | $6 | $1 | $2 |

❶ How much for the duck and the fan? $ **5**

❷ How much for the helmet and the party hat? $ **7**

❸ How much for the helmet, party hat, and duck? $ **9**

Try to solve these problems in your head. Then write the answers.

❹ 3
+ 2
5

❺ 7
+ 2
9

❻ 8
− 1
7

❼ 1
+ 6
7

Mixed Practice
Pages 1–120

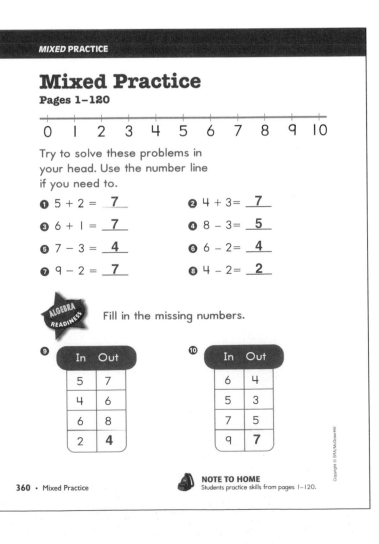

Try to solve these problems in your head. Use the number line if you need to.

❶ 5 + 2 = **7**   ❷ 4 + 3 = **7**

❸ 6 + 1 = **7**   ❹ 8 − 3 = **5**

❺ 7 − 3 = **4**   ❻ 6 − 2 = **4**

❼ 9 − 2 = **7**   ❽ 4 − 2 = **2**

ALGEBRA READINESS

Fill in the missing numbers.

❾
In	Out
5	7
4	6
6	8
2	**4**

❿
In	Out
6	4
5	3
7	5
9	**7**

357–360

Name _____

Mixed Practice
Pages 1–130

 What is the number machine doing?

Tell the rule.

1

In	Out
2	4
3	5
7	9
5	7

Rule **+2**

2

In	Out
4	2
6	4
8	6
10	8

Rule **−2**

Write the number sentence.

3    5 + **5** = **10**

4   5 + **0** = **5**

5   5 + **4** = **9**

NOTE TO HOME
Students practice skills from pages 1–130.

Mixed Practice • **361**

Mixed Practice
Pages 1–140

Fill in the missing numbers.

+	0	1	2	3	4	5
0	0	1	2	3	**4**	5
1	1	2	**3**	4	**5**	6
2	2	3	4	**5**	6	7
3	3	4	5	6	7	**8**
4	**4**	5	6	**7**	8	9
5	5	**6**	7	**8**	9	10

Now use the table to solve these problems.

1 2 + 2 = **4**   **2** 2 + 5 = **7**

3 4 + 3 = **7**   **4** 6 + 3 = **9**

5 7 + 2 = **9**   **6** 2 + 3 = **5**

7 2 + 4 = **6**   **8** 5 + 3 = **8**

362 • Mixed Practice

NOTE TO HOME
Students practice skills from pages 1–140.

Name _____

Mixed Practice
Pages 1–150

What is the right sign? Draw <, >, or =.

1 8 **<** 10   **2** 17 **<** 19

3 15 **>** 14   **4** 18 **=** 18

5 5 **<** 14   **6** 20 **>** 17

 Solve these problems.

7 8 + **0** = 8   **8** 7 + **1** = 8

9 5 + **0** = 5   **10** 4 + **1** = 5

11 Ring each number that is greater than 5.
⑦   4   ⑧   5   ⑥

12 Ring each number that is less than 5.
②   6   ④   7   9

NOTE TO HOME
Students practice skills from pages 1–150.

Mixed Practice • **363**

Mixed Practice
Pages 1–162

Solve these problems.

1 10 − 2 = **8**   **2** 7 − 2 = **5**

3 10 − 3 = **7**   **4** 5 − 1 = **4**

5 9 − 3 = **6**   **6** 9 − 2 = **7**

7 8 − 3 = **5**   **8** 6 − 2 = **4**

REAL-WORLD CONNECTION How many cents?

9   **9** ¢

10   **13** ¢

11   **12** ¢

Fill in the missing numbers.

12 3   5   7   **9**   11   13

13 8   10   **12**   14   16   **18**

364 • Mixed Practice

NOTE TO HOME
Students practice skills from pages 1–162.

Name _____

Mixed Practice
Pages 1–174

 Solve these problems. Use play money to help you.

❶   and

7 + 6 = **13**

❷   spend

12 – 9 = **3**

Solve these problems.

❸ 8 + 4 = **12** ❹ 6 + **1** = 7

❺ 6 + **2** = 8 ❻ 3 + 3 = **6**

❼ 6 + 4 = **10** ❽ 3 + **2** = 5

NOTE TO HOME
Students practice skills from pages 1–174.

Mixed Practice • **365**

Mixed Practice
Pages 1–184

Solve these problems. Use coins to help.

❶   10 + 4 = **14**

❷   15 + 2 = **17**

Fill in the missing numbers.

❸ 9 10 11 **12** 13 **14** **15**

❹ 12 **13** **14** 15 **16** **17** 18

What is the right sign? Draw <, >, or =.

❺ 14 **<** 15   ❻ 16 **>** 14

❼ 19 **>** 18   ❽ 20 **=** 20

Solve these problems.

❾ 4 + 4 = **8**   ❿ 6 + 4 = **10**

⓫ 5 + 5 = **10**   ⓬ 8 + 2 = **10**

366 • Mixed Practice

NOTE TO HOME
Students practice skills from pages 1–184.

Name _____

Mixed Practice
Pages 1–194

 Use coins to make the right amount. Draw the coins. **Answers are examples only.**

❶ 25¢ (10)(10)(5)

❷ 36¢ (10)(10)(10)(5)(1)

How many cents?

❸ **26** ¢

❹ **33** ¢

Solve these problems.

❺ 13 + 2 = **15**   ❻ 12 – 3 = **9**

❼ 7 + 7 = **14**   ❽ 17 – 3 = **14**

❾ 8 + 5 = **13**   ❿ 6 + 7 = **13**

NOTE TO HOME
Students practice skills from pages 1–194.

Mixed Practice • **367**

Mixed Practice
Pages 1–202

 ALGEBRA READINESS Fill in the missing numbers. Write the rule.

❶
In	Out
6	8
7	**9**
13	**15**

Rule **+2**

❷
In	Out
10	5
15	**10**
5	**0**

Rule **–5**

Solve these problems.

❸ 6 + **2** = 8   ❹ 8 + **2** = 10

❺ 10 + **2** = 12   ❻ 7 + **2** = 9

Count how many fingers.

❼   How many? **20**

❽  How many? **40**

368 • Mixed Practice

NOTE TO HOME
Students practice skills from pages 1–202.

Name _____

Mixed Practice
Pages 1–214

 ALGEBRA READINESS

Draw the missing sign.
Draw + or −.

❶ 5 〈 − 〉 2 = 3   ❷ 24 〈 + 〉 1 = 25

❸ 40 〈 − 〉 10 = 30   ❹ 4 〈 + 〉 4 = 8

Draw the right sign.
Draw <, >, or =.

❺ 2 + 2 〈 < 〉 6   ❻ 10 + 2 〈 < 〉 13

❼ 5 + 9 〈 > 〉 12   ❽ 7 + 7 〈 = 〉 14

Solve these problems.

❾ $\begin{array}{r} 13 \\ -\ 3 \\ \hline 10 \end{array}$ ❿ $\begin{array}{r} 12 \\ -10 \\ \hline 2 \end{array}$ ⓫ $\begin{array}{r} 10 \\ -\ 3 \\ \hline 7 \end{array}$ ⓬ $\begin{array}{r} 14 \\ +\ 2 \\ \hline 16 \end{array}$

 NOTE TO HOME
Students practice skills from pages 1–214.

Mixed Practice • **369**

Mixed Practice
Pages 1–224

Ring one half of each group. Then write how many in each half.

❶ △△△△△△   Half of 6 is **3**.

❷ ♡♡♡♡♡♡♡♡♡♡   Half of 10 is **5**.

How many now?

❸ [2 8] [**26**]   ❹ [1 9] [**15**]

 ALGEBRA READINESS

What is the missing sign?
Draw + or −.

❺ 5 〈 − 〉 5 = 0   ❻ 7 〈 − 〉 2 = 5

❼ 5 〈 + 〉 5 = 10   ❽ 8 〈 − 〉 3 = 5

❾ 8 〈 + 〉 2 = 10   ❿ 9 〈 − 〉 1 = 8

⓫ 16 〈 − 〉 2 = 14   ⓬ 7 〈 + 〉 2 = 9

370 • Mixed Practice

NOTE TO HOME
Students practice skills from pages 1–224.

Name _____

Mixed Practice
Pages 1–236

PROBLEM SOLVING

❶ There were ten candles on a cake. Elena blew out half. Cross out the candles Elena blew out.

How many are out? **5**

❷ Ferdie cut a pizza into eight slices. He ate half of them. Cross out the slices Ferdie ate.

How many are left? **4**

❸ Draw a Number Strip three times as long as this one.

NOTE TO HOME
Students practice skills from pages 1–236.

Mixed Practice • **371**

Mixed Practice
Pages 1–244

Count by tens. Fill in the missing number.

❶ 50 [**60**] 70 [**80**] 90 100

How many tally marks? Ring sets of ten to help you count.

❷ 𝍩𝍩𝍩𝍩𝍩𝍩𝍩𝍩𝍩𝍩𝍩𝍩   **60**

❸ 𝍩𝍩𝍩𝍩𝍩𝍩𝍩𝍩𝍩   **45**

Circle the two numbers that add up to 10. Then use them to write an addition sentence.

❹ 4 (9) (1)
[**9**] + [**1**] = 10

❺ (5) 4 (5)
[**5**] + [**5**] = 10

❻ (6) 2 (4)
[**6**] + [**4**] = 10

❼ (7) 2 (3)
[**7**] + [**3**] = 10

372 • Mixed Practice

NOTE TO HOME
Students practice skills from pages 1–244.

369–372

Name _____

Mixed Practice
Pages 1–258

Write the rule.

❶
In	Out
14	16
9	11
15	17

Rule __+2__

❷
In	Out
1	4
2	5
12	15

Rule __+3__

What is the right sign? Draw <, >, or =.

❸ 27 (<) 37   ❹ 48 + 2 (>) 46

❺ 10 (<) 11   ❻ 9 (<) 10

Fill in the missing numbers.

❼ 30   31   **32**   **33**   **34**   35   36

❽ 32   34   **36**   38   **40**   **42**   44

 NOTE TO HOME
Students practice skills from pages 1–258.

Mixed Practice • **373**

Mixed Practice
Pages 1–264

❶ Fill in the missing numbers.

20   **30**   40   **50**   **60**   70   80

Think: How many tens? Then add.

❷ 30 + 20 = **50**   ❸ 40 + 30 = **70**

❹ 20 + 20 = **40**   ❺ 10 + 10 = **20**

❻ 20 + 10 = **30**   ❼ 50 + 20 = **70**

 What is the right sign? Draw + or –.

❽ 28 (+) 3 = 31   ❾ 5 (+) 5 = 10

❿ 8 (–) 2 = 6   ⓫ 28 (–) 3 = 25

What is the right sign? Draw <, >, or =.

⓬ 29 + 10 (=) 39   ⓭ 38 + 10 (<) 87

374 • Mixed Practice

 NOTE TO HOME
Students practice skills from pages 1–264.

Name _____

Mixed Practice
Pages 1–274

Write the rule.

❶
In	Out
10	20
40	50
90	100

Rule __+10__

❷
In	Out
30	20
20	10
70	60

Rule __–10__

Fill in the missing numbers.

❸ 38   39   **40**   **41**   42   **43**   44

❹ 60   62   **64**   **66**   **68**   70   72

Solve these problems.

❺ 6 + 6 = **12**   ❻ 7 + 6 = **13**

❼ 8 + 8 = **16**   ❽ 8 + 7 = **15**

NOTE TO HOME
Students practice skills from pages 1–274.

Mixed Practice • **375**

Mixed Practice
Pages 1–286

 Write addition sentences to make each sum. **Answers are examples only.**

❶ **7** + **5** = 12   ❷ **7** + **6** = 13

❸ **9** + **2** = 11   ❹ **2** + **8** = 10

❺ One postcard costs 4¢. Fill in the chart so that it shows how much two, three, or more postcards will cost.

Number of postcards	Cents
1	4
2	8
3	**12**
4	**16**
5	**20**

❻ Ring each amount that makes more than 40.

20 + 2   (41)

(30 + 20)   4 + 32

376 • Mixed Practice

NOTE TO HOME
Students practice skills from pages 1–286.

Name _____

Mixed Practice
Pages 1–294

 Solve these problems.

① 7
+ 9
16

② 8
+ 3
11

③ 5
+ 4
9

④ 4
+ 6
10

⑤ 7
+ 8
15

⑥ 7
+ 3
10

⑦ 4
+ 5
9

⑧ 6
+ 7
13

⑨ 9 + 9 = **18**

⑩ 9 + 8 = **17**

⑪ 6 + 6 = **12**

⑫ 6 + 5 = **11**

⑬  There are ten pears. How many are in the basket?

8

 NOTE TO HOME
Students practice skills from pages 1–294.

Mixed Practice • 377

Mixed Practice
Pages 1–304

① How many children?

 **6**

Solve these problems.

② 6 + 10 = **16**

③ 10 + 10 = **20**

④ 7 + 10 = **17**

⑤ 9 + 10 = **19**

0 10 20 30 40 50 60 70 80 90 100

Solve these problems. Use the number line to help you.

⑥ 10
+ 30
40

⑦ 50
− 30
20

⑧ 40
+ 20
60

⑨ 30
+ 30
60

⑩ 80
− 20
60

⑪ 70
+ 20
90

⑫ 70 − 20 = **50**

⑬ 20 − 20 = **0**

378 • Mixed Practice

 NOTE TO HOME
Students practice skills from pages 1–304.

Name _____

Mixed Practice
Pages 1–310

What is the right sign? Draw <, >, or =.

① 57 < 75

② 23 > 21

③ 64 > 47 + 3

④ 82 = 82

Draw the right sign. Draw + or −.

⑤ 20 + 20 = 40

⑥ 37 − 3 = 34

⑦ 6 + 40 = 46

⑧ 45 − 5 = 40

How many tally marks?

⑨ ‖‖‖ ‖‖‖ ‖‖‖ ‖‖‖ ‖‖‖ ‖‖‖ ‖‖‖ ‖‖‖ ‖‖‖ ‖‖‖ ‖‖‖ ‖‖‖   **60**

⑩ ‖‖‖ ‖‖‖ ‖‖‖ ‖‖‖ ‖‖‖ ‖‖‖ ‖‖‖ ‖‖‖ ‖‖‖   **45**

Fill in the missing numbers.

⑪ 2 **4** 6 8 **10** **12** 14

⑫ 22 **24** **26** 28 30 **32** 34

NOTE TO HOME
Students practice skills from pages 1–310.

Mixed Practice • 379

Mixed Practice
Pages 1–318

 Draw the correct amount.

① $42 | 20 | 20 | 1 | 1 |

② $16 | 10 | 5 | 1 |

Write the next number. Count on.

③ 57 **58**

④ 72 **73**

⑤ 49 **50**

Ring the greatest number in each box.

⑥ 46 64 (96)

⑦ 12 (26) 19

⑧ 57 (87) 75

⑨ (89) 65 42

Ring the least number in each box.

⑩ 96 (47) 89

⑪ (29) 82 61

⑫ (26) 30 41

⑬ 47 52 (46)

380 • Mixed Practice

 NOTE TO HOME
Students practice skills from pages 1–318.

Name _____

Mixed Practice
Pages 1–322

What time is it?

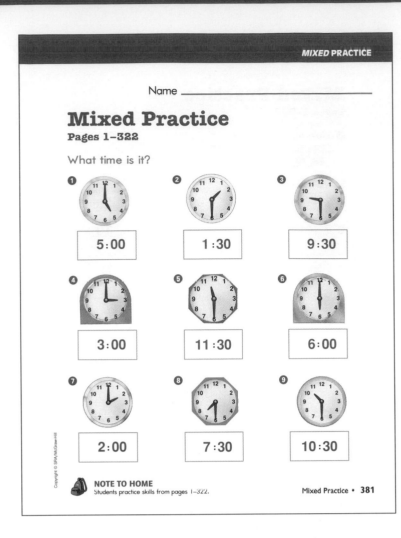

① 5:00 ② 1:30 ③ 9:30

④ 3:00 ⑤ 11:30 ⑥ 6:00

⑦ 2:00 ⑧ 7:30 ⑨ 10:30

NOTE TO HOME
Students practice skills from pages 1–322.

Mixed Practice
Pages 1–328

Solve these problems.

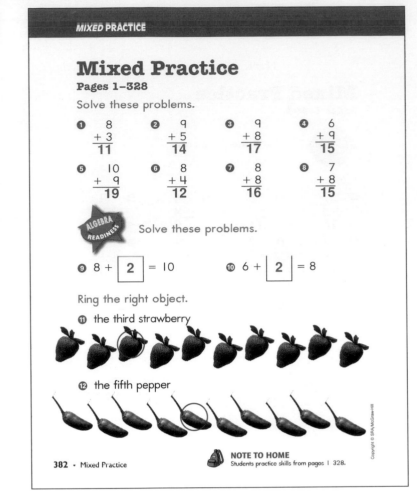

① 8
  + 3

  11

② 9
  + 5

  14

③ 9
  + 8

  17

④ 6
  + 9

  15

⑤ 10
  + 9

  19

⑥ 8
  + 4

  12

⑦ 8
  + 8

  16

⑧ 7
  + 8

  15

ALGEBRA READINESS Solve these problems.

⑨ 8 + 2 = 10   ⑩ 6 + 2 = 8

Ring the right object.

⑪ the third strawberry

⑫ the fifth pepper

NOTE TO HOME
Students practice skills from pages 1–328.

Name _____

Mixed Practice
Pages 1–338

Solve these problems.

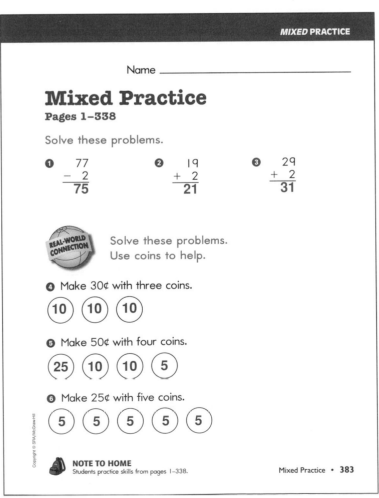

① 77
  − 2

  75

② 19
  + 2

  21

③ 29
  + 2

  31

REAL-WORLD CONNECTION Solve these problems. Use coins to help.

④ Make 30¢ with three coins.
  ⑩ ⑩ ⑩

⑤ Make 50¢ with four coins.
  ㉕ ⑩ ⑩ ⑤

⑥ Make 25¢ with five coins.
  ⑤ ⑤ ⑤ ⑤ ⑤

NOTE TO HOME
Students practice skills from pages 1–338.

Mixed Practice
Pages 1–348

① One sticker costs 3¢. Fill in the chart so that it shows how much two, three, or more stickers cost.

Number of stickers	Cents
1	3
2	6
3	9
4	12
5	15
6	18

Make the right number of tally marks. Then ring the tens to show that you have the right number.

② 25

③ 40

NOTE TO HOME
Students practice skills from pages 1–348.

381–384

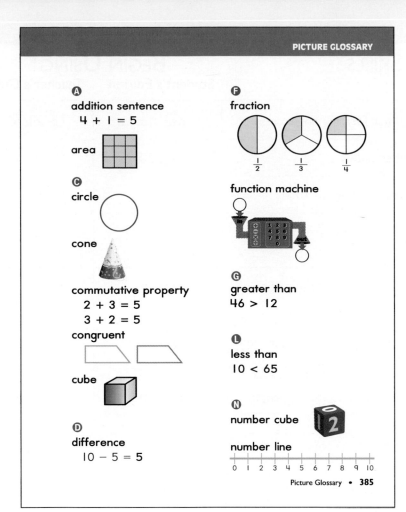

A

addition sentence
$4 + 1 = 5$

area

C

circle

cone

commutative property
$2 + 3 = 5$
$3 + 2 = 5$

congruent

cube

D

difference
$10 - 5 = 5$

F

fraction

$\frac{1}{2}$ $\frac{1}{3}$ $\frac{1}{4}$

function machine

G

greater than
$46 > 12$

L

less than
$10 < 65$

N

number cube

number line

0 1 2 3 4 5 6 7 8 9 10

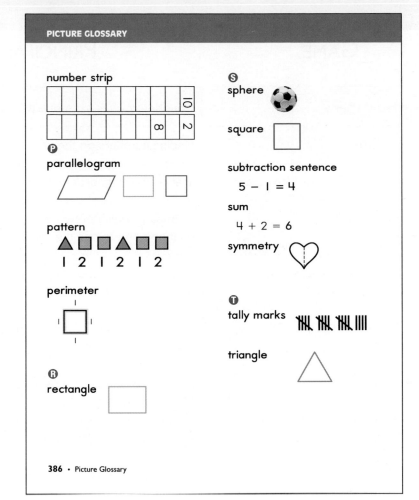

number strip

10   2

8   2

P

parallelogram

pattern

1   2   1   2   1   2

perimeter

R

rectangle

S

sphere

square

subtraction sentence
$5 - 1 = 4$

sum
$4 + 2 = 6$

symmetry

T

tally marks

triangle

GAME DIRECTORY

GAME	PRINCIPAL SKILLS	BEGIN USING* Student's Edition	Teacher's Guide
Guess How Many	Counting objects from one through ten; forming finger sets	page 13	Lesson 6
Find the Cube	Finding numbers on the units Number Cubes	page 20	Lesson 9
Tracing and Writing Numbers	Tracing, writing, ordering, and finding numbers 0–10	page 24	Lesson 11
Which Has More?	Estimating which of two groups of objects has a greater quantity; one-to-one correspondence	page 27	Lesson 13
What Number Comes Next?	Determining the next-higher number in the 0–10 range; finding numbers on the units Number Cubes	page 29	Lesson 14
What Number Comes Before?	Determining the next-lower number in the 0–10 range; finding numbers on the units Number Cubes	page 31	Lesson 15
Number Strip	Identifying Number Strips by length (1–10); estimating length (1–10 units)	page 50	Lesson 22
How Long Is It?	Estimating length (1–10 units)	page 52	Lesson 23
Add the Counters	Adding with concrete objects (sums through ten)	page 57	Lesson 26
Don't Take Them All	Subtracting 1 or 2 from numbers through 10 by using concrete objects	page 64	Lesson 29
Harder Don't Take Them All	Subtracting 1, 2, or 3 from numbers through 10 by using concrete objects	page 64	Lesson 29
Take Away the Counters	Subtracting concrete objects (minuends of 0–10, remainders of 0–10)	page 67	Lesson 31
Add or Take Away the Counters	Adding and subtracting with concrete objects (0–10), with either an addend or the minuend hidden; solving addition and subtraction problems	page 71	Lesson 33
Duck Pond**	Adding two numbers with a sum of ten or less	page 79	Lesson 37
Harder Duck Pond	Adding and subtracting in the 0–10 range	page 79	Lesson 37
Pennies and Nickels	Changing money (pennies for nickels)	page 95	Lesson 42
$1 and $5 Bills	Changing money ($1 bills for $5 bills)	page 98	Lesson 43
Flea Market	Changing money ($1 bills for $10 bills)	page 109	Lesson 49
Harder Flea Market	Changing money ($1 bills for $5 bills; $5 bills for $10 bills)	page 109	Lesson 49
Roll a Double	Adding doubles (0–5)	page 128	Lesson 58

GAME DIRECTORY

GAME	PRINCIPAL SKILLS	BEGIN USING* Student's Edition	Teacher's Guide
Roll and Add	Adding with two addends of 5 or less	page 142	Lesson 64
Hungry Alligator	Using the relation sign >, <, and =; determining the equality or inequality relationship between two numbers in the 0–10 range	page 147	Lesson 67
Addition Table	Using an addition table with two addends of 5 or less	page 152	Lesson 69
Harder Addition Table	Using an addition table with two addends of 10 or less	page 152	Lesson 69
Map	Using numbers to represent magnitude and direction; using compass directions	page 153	Lesson 70
Pattern	Detecting number patterns in which the numbers increase or decrease by 0, 1, or 2	page 155	Lesson 71
Pennies, Nickels, and Dimes	Changing money (pennies for nickels, nickels for dimes)	page 161	Lesson 74
Count to 20 by Ones or Twos	Counting on with numbers through 20	page 167	Lesson 77
Guess the Rule	Finding simple function rules; using a calculator	page 184	Lesson 83
Measurement	Choosing the appropriate standard unit of measure	page 192	Lesson 86
Add the Coins	Adding coin values summing to 40¢ when one of the addends is 10¢ or less; changing money (pennies for nickels, nickels for dimes)	page 203	Lesson 92
Hidden Counters Puzzle	Solving missing-addend problems in which the sum of both addends is ten or less (using concrete objects)	page 217	Lesson 99
Roll a 10	Finding, from a group of four numbers, two numbers that add up to ten	page 242	Lesson 110
Macaroni Tens	Estimating numbers of objects totaling 100 or less; grouping objects in bunches of 10	page 245	Lesson 112
School Bookstore	Changing money (dimes for dollars)	page 248	Lesson 113
Harder School Bookstore	Changing money (pennies for nickels, nickels for dimes, dimes for dollars)	page 248	Lesson 113
10 Below 0	Counting with numbers between 10 above and 10 below zero	page 263	Lesson 118
Get to 100 by Tens or Ones	Adding mentally with numbers through 100	page 266	Lesson 119
Yard Sale	Changing money ($1 bills for $10 bills, $10 bills for $100 bills)	page 268	Lesson 120

GAME DIRECTORY

Game	Principal Skills	Begin Using* Student's Edition	Teacher's Guide
Harder Yard Sale	Changing money ($100 and $10 bills for smaller denominations); regrouping for multidigit subtraction	page 268	Lesson 120
Space	Solving addition and missing-addend problems with sums of ten or less	page 270	Lesson 121
Harder Space	Solving addition, subtraction, missing-addend, missing-minuend, and missing-subtrahend problems with numbers of 10 or less	page 270	Lesson 121
Harder Roll a Double	Adding doubles (0–10)	page 278	Lesson 125
Make the Alligator Tell the Truth	Recognizing true and false inequality statements, with numbers through 100; using the relation signs > and <	page 279	Lesson 126
Stolen Treasure	Solving missing-subtrahend problems in which the minuend is 20 or less (using concrete objects)	page 283	Lesson 128
Four Keys	Using a calculator; mental math; finding multiple solutions to a problem	page 284	Lesson 128
Harder Roll and Add	Adding with two addends of ten or less	page 291	Lesson 132
Harder Pattern	Detecting number patterns in which the numbers increase or decrease by 0, 1, 2, 3, 4, 5, or 10	page 296	Lesson 134
Frog Pond	Adding with two addends of ten or less	page 298	Lesson 135
Harder Frog Pond	Adding with two addends of ten or less	page 298	Lesson 135
Add to the Number Strip	Estimating lengths (1–10 units)	page 308	Lesson 139
Harder Add to the Number Strip	Estimating lengths (1–10 units)	page 308	Lesson 139
Greatest and Least Numbers	Using knowledge of place value to make the largest and smallest numbers	page 317	Lesson 144
Clock	Telling time to the hour and half hour	page 319	Lesson 145
Harder Clock	Telling time to the hour, half hour, and quarter hour	page 319	Lesson 145
Calendar	Using a monthly calendar	page 327	Lesson 147

*These games and their variations should be used many times throughout the year. Feel free to use them again anytime after they are introduced.
**Games in red are from the Game Mat set.

ADDITION TABLE GAME

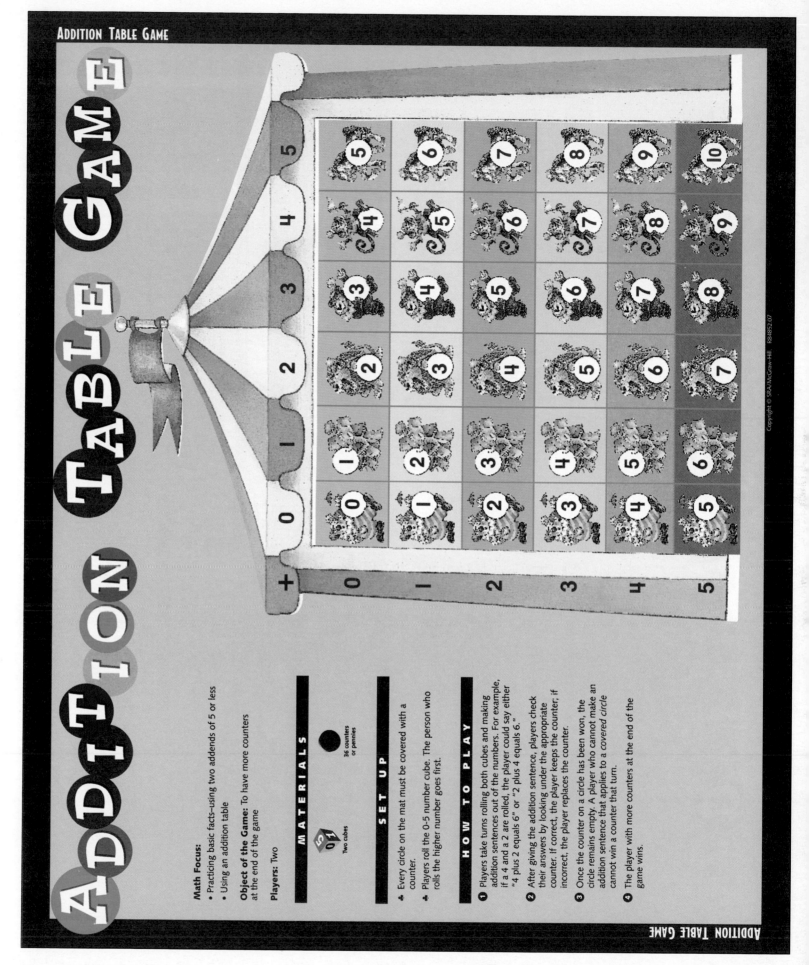

Math Focus:
- Practicing basic facts—using two addends of 5 or less
- Using an addition table

Object of the Game: To have more counters at the end of the game

Players: Two

MATERIALS

Two cubes

36 counters or pennies

SET UP

- Every circle on the mat must be covered with a counter.
- Players roll the 0–5 number cube. The person who rolls the higher number goes first.

HOW TO PLAY

1. Players take turns rolling both cubes and making addition sentences out of the numbers. For example, if a 4 and a 2 are rolled, the player could say either "4 plus 2 equals 6" or "2 plus 4 equals 6."

2. After giving the addition sentence, players check their answers by looking under the appropriate counter. If correct, the player keeps the counter; if incorrect, the player replaces the counter.

3. Once the counter on a circle has been won, the circle remains empty. A player who cannot make an addition sentence that applies to a covered *circle* cannot win a counter that turn.

4. The player with more counters at the end of the game wins.

R84852.07

HARDER ADDITION TABLE GAME

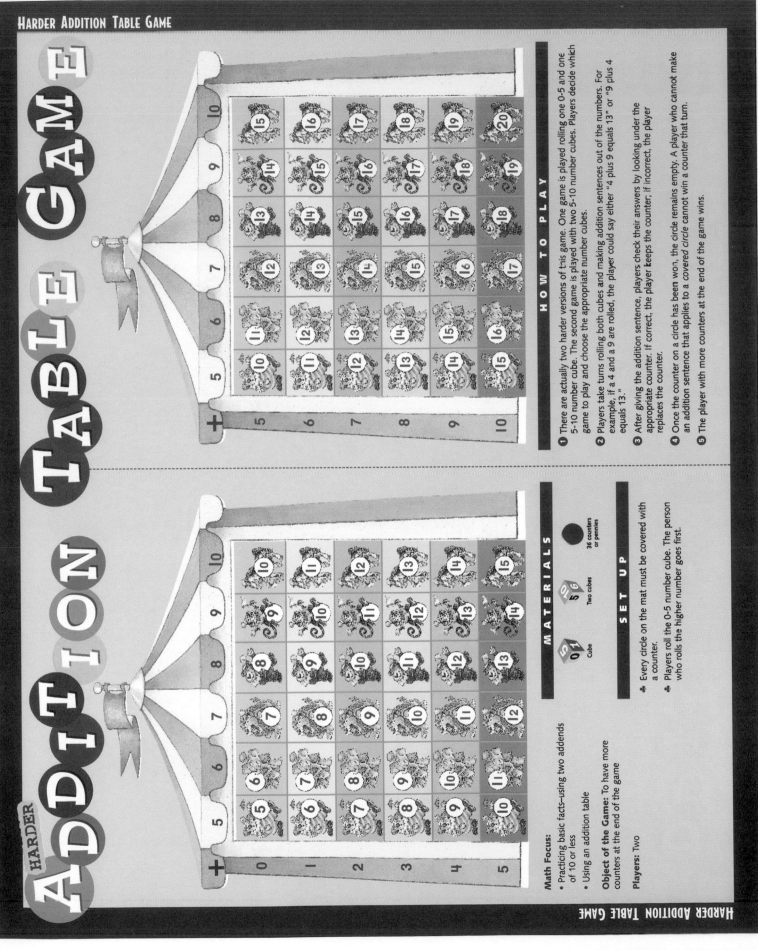

Math Focus:
- Practicing basic facts—using two addends of 10 or less
- Using an addition table

Object of the Game: To have more counters at the end of the game

Players: Two

MATERIALS

Cube

Two cubes

36 counters or pennies

SET UP

♣ Every circle on the mat must be covered with a counter.

♣ Players roll the 0-5 number cube. The person who rolls the higher number goes first.

HOW TO PLAY

1. There are actually two harder versions of this game. One game is played rolling one 0-5 and one 5-10 number cube. The second game is played with two 5-10 number cubes. Players decide which game to play and choose the appropriate number cubes.

2. Players take turns rolling both cubes and making addition sentences out of the numbers. For example, if a 4 and a 9 are rolled, the player could say either "4 plus 9 equals 13" or "9 plus 4 equals 13."

3. After giving the addition sentence, players check their answers by looking under the appropriate counter. If correct, the player keeps the counter; if incorrect, the player replaces the counter.

4. Once the counter on a circle has been won, the circle remains empty. A player who cannot make an addition sentence that applies to a covered circle cannot win a counter that turn.

5. The player with more counters at the end of the game wins.

CALENDAR GAME

SUNDAY MONDAY TUESDAY WEDNESDAY THURSDAY FRIDAY SATURDAY

START ➡ 1 2 3
4 5 6 7 8 9 10
11 12 13 14 15 16 17
18 19 20 21 22 23 24
25 26 27 28 29 30 31

FINISH

Math Focus: Using a monthly calendar

Object of the Game: To be the first to reach FINISH

Players: Two or three

MATERIALS

Cube

Place marker and counter of the same color per player

SET UP

♣ Players place their counters on one of the days of the week. Players must choose different days.

♣ The players then put their place markers on START.

♣ Players roll the 0-5 number cube. The person who rolls the highest number goes first.

HOW TO PLAY

1. Players take turns rolling the cube and advancing through the 31 days of the month. Players must say aloud the day of the week where they land.

2. A player who lands on an opponent's chosen day must either return to START if still within the first seven days of the month or go back seven days. The player remains on this space until the next roll.

3. If a player is already on an opponent's chosen day and rolls a 0, he or she must move back another seven days.

4. The first player to reach FINISH wins.

Copyright © SRA/McGraw-Hill.   R84852.03

CALENDAR GAME

CLOCK GAME

Math Focus: Telling time to the hour and half hour

Object of the Game: To have the most counters at the end of the game

Players: Two or three

MATERIALS

Place markers

Cube

16 counters or pennies

SET UP

- The small answer circles must be covered with counters.
- Players put their place markers on GO.
- Players roll the 0–5 number cube. The person who rolls the highest number goes first.

HOW TO PLAY

1. Players take turns rolling the cube and moving their place markers the number of spaces indicated.

2. After landing on a space, a player may win the counter there by correctly saying the time shown on the clock.

3. Players check their answers by lifting the counters. If correct, the player keeps the counter. If incorrect, the player replaces the counter.

4. A player cannot win a counter if there is none in a space. A player who gives an incorrect answer and rolls a 0 on the next turn can try to win the counter again.

5. Players who land on STOP must, if possible, place one of their own counters on an empty answer circle.

6. Players who land on GO may move to any unoccupied space on the mat and try to win a counter there if one is present.

7. The game ends when all counters have been won. The player with the most counters wins.

395

HARDER CLOCK GAME

Math Focus: Telling time to the hour, half hour, and quarter hour

Object of the Game: To have the most counters at the end of the game

Players: Two or three

MATERIALS

Place markers

Cube

16 counters or pennies

SET UP

- The small answer circles must be covered with counters.
- Players put their place markers on GO.
- Players roll the 0–5 number cube. The person who rolls the highest number goes first.

HOW TO PLAY

1. Players take turns rolling the cube and moving their place markers the number of spaces indicated.
2. After landing on a space, a player may win the counter there by correctly saying the time shown on the clock.
3. Players check their answers by lifting the counters. If correct, the player keeps the counter. If incorrect, the player replaces the counter.
4. A player cannot win a counter if there is none in a space. A player who gives an incorrect answer and rolls a 0 on the next turn can try to win the counter again.
5. Players who land on STOP must, if possible, place one of their own counters on an empty answer circle.
6. Players who land on GO may move to any unoccupied space on the mat and try to win a counter there if one is present.
7. The game ends when all counters have been won. The player with the most counters wins.

7:45

6:30

STOP

COVER AN ANSWER

5:15

12:30

3:00

9:30

2:30

1:00

5:30

10:30

8:00

9:15

6:00

1:30

START

GO

4:15

11:45

396

BANK

GO!

1 + 1 = 2
1 + 8 = 9
3 + 3 = 6
7 + 3 = 10
5 + 2 = 7
1 + 4 = 5
1 + 3 = 4
1 + 0 = 1
2 + 6 = 8
1 + 7 = 8
2 + 3 = 5
3 + 0 = 3
2 + 7 = 9
1 + 6 = 7
5 + 1 = 6
2 + 2 = 4

Math Focus: Adding two numbers that equal 10 or less

Object of the Game: To have the most counters at the end of the game

Players: Two or three

MATERIALS

Place markers

Cube

20 counters or pennies per player

SET UP

✦ Every circle on the mat must be covered with a counter.

✦ Extra counters are placed on the space marked BANK.

✦ Players put their place markers on GO.

✦ Players roll the 0-5 number cube. The person who rolls the highest number goes first.

HOW TO PLAY

① Players take turns rolling the cube and moving their place markers the number of spaces indicated.

② On each space where they land, players must correctly say aloud both the problem and the answer.

③ Players check their answers by lifting the counters. If correct, the player keeps the counter. If incorrect, the player replaces the counter and remains on that space.

④ Players collect two counters from the BANK each time they pass or land on GO.

⑤ A player cannot win a counter if there is none in the space. A player who rolls a 0 cannot move or win a counter.

⑥ The player with the most counters at the end of the game is the winner.

DUCK POND GAME

DUCK POND GAME

397

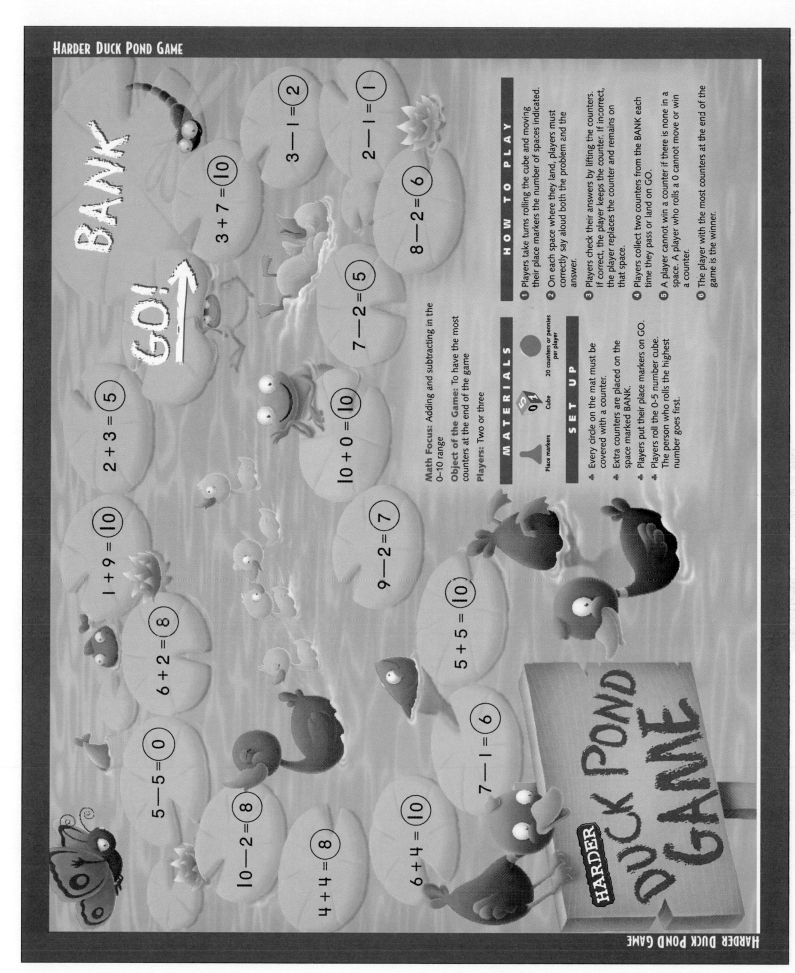

BANK

GO!

3 + 7 = (10)

3 — 1 = (2)

2 — 1 = (1)

8 — 2 = (6)

7 — 2 = (5)

2 + 3 = (5)

10 + 0 = (10)

1 + 9 = (10)

9 — 2 = (7)

6 + 2 = (8)

5 + 5 = (10)

5 — 5 = (0)

10 — 2 = (8)

4 + 4 = (8)

6 + 4 = (10)

7 — 1 = (6)

HARDER DUCK POND GAME

Math Focus: Adding and subtracting in the 0–10 range

Object of the Game: To have the most counters at the end of the game

Players: Two or three

MATERIALS

Place markers   Cube   20 counters or pennies per player

SET UP

♣ Every circle on the mat must be covered with a counter.

♣ Extra counters are placed on the space marked BANK.

♣ Players put their place markers on GO.

♣ Players roll the 0–5 number cube. The person who rolls the highest number goes first.

HOW TO PLAY

① Players take turns rolling the cube and moving their place markers the number of spaces indicated.

② On each space where they land, players must correctly say aloud both the problem and the answer.

③ Players check their answers by lifting the counters. If correct, the player keeps the counter. If incorrect, the player replaces the counter and remains on that space.

④ Players collect two counters from the BANK each time they pass or land on GO.

⑤ A player cannot win a counter if there is none in a space. A player who rolls a 0 cannot move or win a counter.

⑥ The player with the most counters at the end of the game is the winner.

398

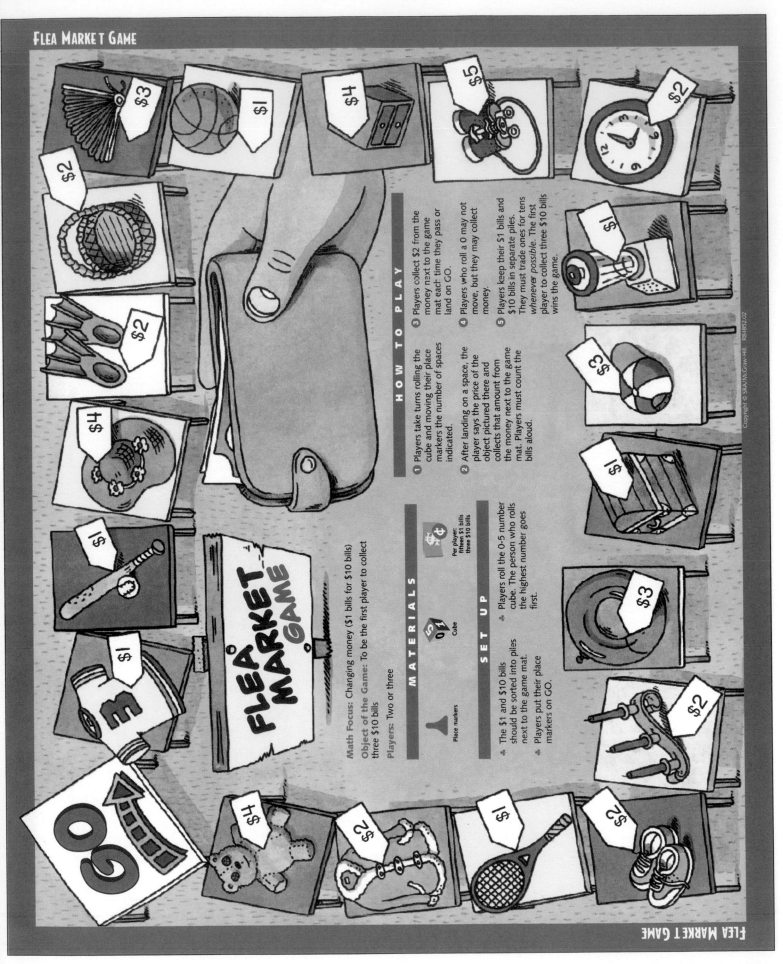

FLEA MARKET GAME

Math Focus: Changing money ($1 bills for $10 bills)

Object of the Game: To be the first player to collect three $10 bills

Players: Two or three

MATERIALS

Place markers

Cube

Per player:
fifteen $1 bills
three $10 bills

SET UP

- The $1 and $10 bills should be sorted into piles next to the game mat.
- Players put their place markers on GO.
- Players roll the 0–5 number cube. The person who rolls the highest number goes first.

HOW TO PLAY

1. Players take turns rolling the cube and moving their place markers the number of spaces indicated.

2. After landing on a space, the player says the price of the object pictured there and collects that amount from the money next to the game mat. Players must count the bills aloud.

3. Players collect $2 from the money next to the game mat each time they pass or land on GO.

4. Players who roll a 0 may not move, but they may collect money.

5. Players keep their $1 bills and $10 bills in separate piles. They must trade ones for tens *whenever possible.* The first player to collect three $10 bills wins the game.

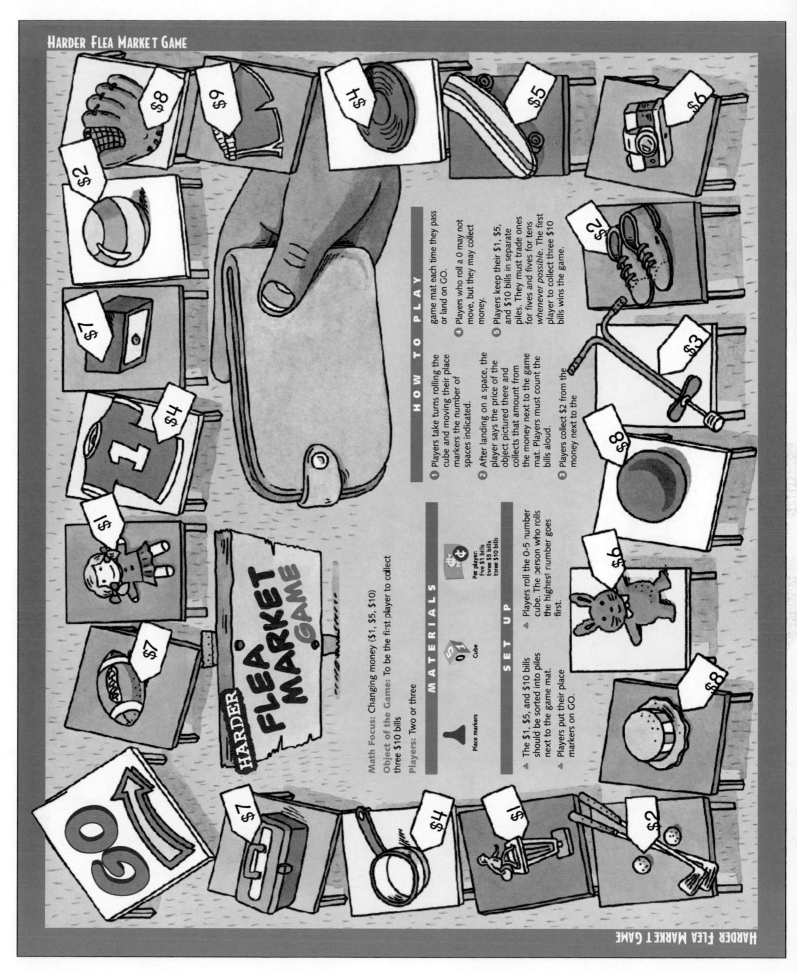

400

FROG POND GAME

Go

0 + 9 = 9

8 + 8 = 16

1 + 8 = 9

8 + 7 = 15

10 + 4 = 14

7 + 2 = 9

6 + 9 = 15

4 + 4 = 8

9 + 3 = 12

10 + 10 = 20

5 + 6 = 11

3 + 2 = 5

5 + 1 = 6

7 + 6 = 13

2 + 9 = 11

3 + 6 = 9

bank

Math Focus: Practicing basic math–using two addends of 10 or less

Object of the Game: To have the most counters at the end of the game

Players: Two or three

MATERIALS

Place markers

Cube

20 counters or pennies per player

SET UP

❖ Every circle on the mat must be covered with a counter.

❖ Extra counters are placed on the space marked BANK.

❖ Players put their place markers on GO.

❖ Players roll the 0–5 number cube. The person who rolls the highest number goes first.

HOW TO PLAY

❶ Players take turns rolling the cube and moving their markers the number of spaces indicated.

❷ After landing on a space, a player may win the counter there by correctly completing the addition sentence.

❸ Players check their answers by lifting the counters. If correct, the player keeps the counter. If incorrect, the player replaces the counter and remains on that space.

❹ A player cannot win a counter if there is none in a space. A player who gives an incorrect answer and rolls a 0 on the next turn can try again to win the counter.

❺ Players collect two counters from the bank each time they pass or land on GO.

❻ The player with the most counters at the end of the game wins.

401

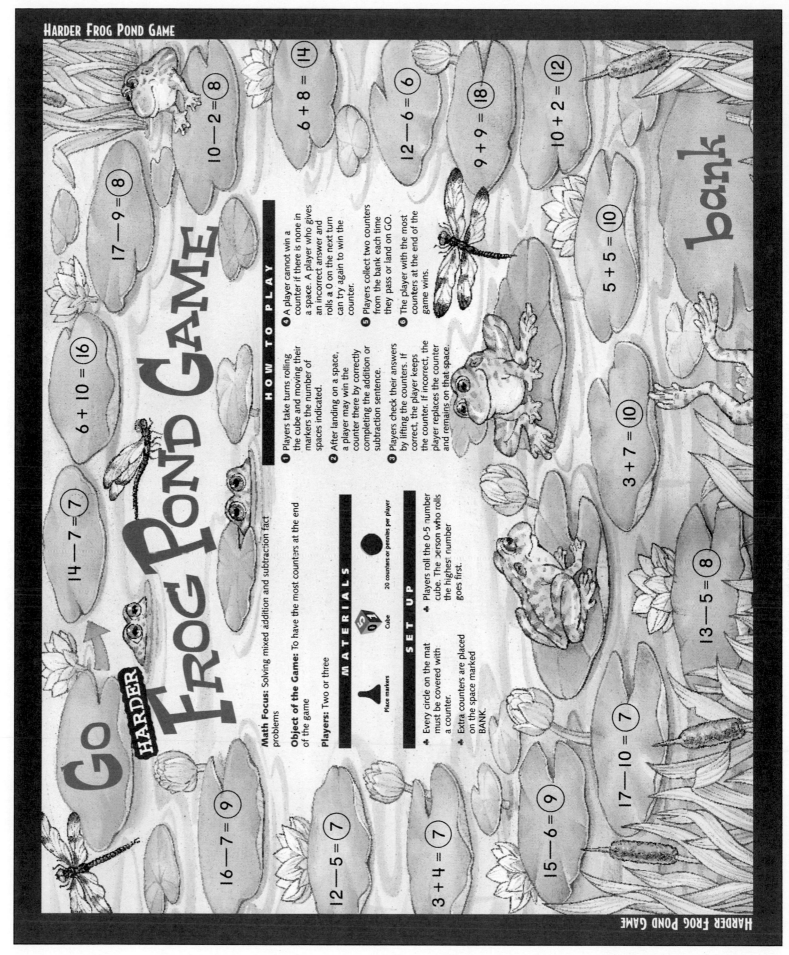

HARDER FROG POND GAME

Go

Math Focus: Solving mixed addition and subtraction fact problems

Object of the Game: To have the most counters at the end of the game

Players: Two or three

MATERIALS

Place markers

Cube

20 counters or pennies per player

SET UP

* Every circle on the mat must be covered with a counter.

* Extra counters are placed on the space marked BANK.

* Players roll the 0-5 number cube. The person who rolls the highest number goes first.

HOW TO PLAY

1. Players take turns rolling the cube and moving their markers the number of spaces indicated.

2. After landing on a space, a player may win the counter there by correctly completing the addition or subtraction sentence.

3. Players check their answers by lifting the counters. If correct, the player keeps the counter. If incorrect, the player replaces the counter and remains on that space.

4. A player cannot win a counter if there is none in a space. A player who gives an incorrect answer and rolls a 0 on the next turn can try again to win the counter.

5. Players collect two counters from the bank each time they pass or land on GO.

6. The player with the most counters at the end of the game wins.

Spaces on the board:

$16 - 7 = 9$

$12 - 5 = 7$

$3 + 4 = 7$

$15 - 6 = 9$

$17 - 10 = 7$

$13 - 5 = 8$

$3 + 7 = 10$

$5 + 5 = 10$

$10 + 2 = 12$

$9 + 9 = 18$

$12 - 6 = 6$

$6 + 8 = 14$

$10 - 2 = 8$

$17 - 9 = 8$

$6 + 10 = 16$

$14 - 7 = 7$

bank

402

MAP GAME

Math Focus: Using compass directions and mathematical reasoning

Object of the Game: To be the first to cover six pictures

Players: Two or three

Place markers

Ten counters of the same color for each player, or ten pennies, nickels, and dimes

Cube

S E T U P

♣ Players roll the 0–5 number cube. The person who rolls the highest number chooses which counters to use and is followed by the other players.

♣ Players put their place markers on START.

♣ The person who rolled the highest number also goes first.

H O W T O P L A Y

1. Before rolling, players must announce in which direction they intend to move that turn. Players who forget to announce their direction before rolling cannot move that turn.

2. Players roll the number cube and move their markers the number of spaces indicated. If they land on a picture, they cover it with a counter.

3. Players cannot move if they roll a number that would land them on a picture that is already covered. Also, players who roll a number that would take them off the board cannot move that turn.

4. During the game, players can move freely back and forth across the START square.

5. The first player to cover six pictures wins the game.

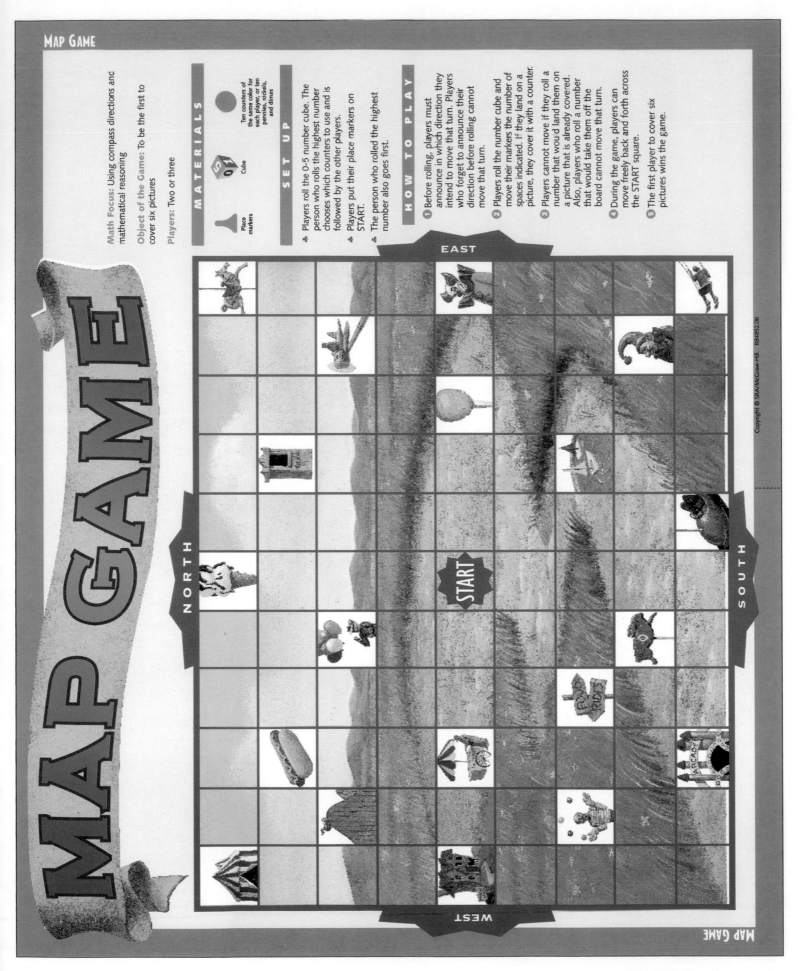

EAST

NORTH

SOUTH

WEST

START

MAP GAME

Measurement Game

START

FINISH

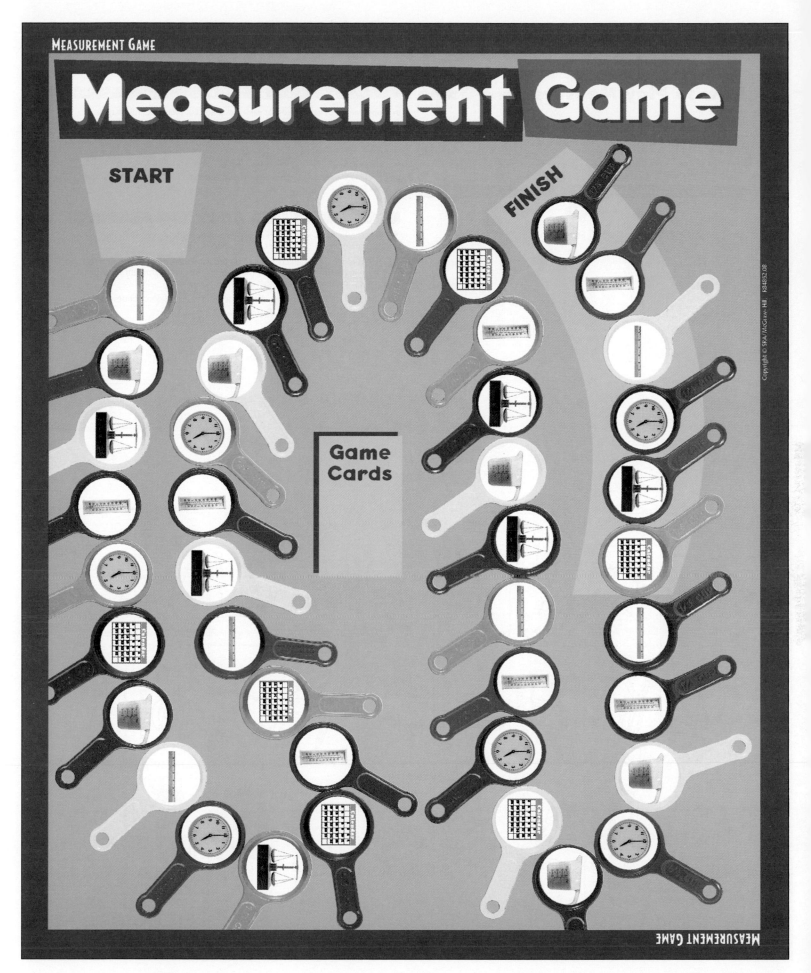

Game Cards

How to Play Measurement Game

Math Focus: Choosing the appropriate measuring instrument

Object of the Game: To be the first to reach FINISH

Players: Two or three

MATERIALS

Place markers

Cube

24 game cards

SET UP

▶ Copy one set of game cards for each group and cut them out. You may want to mount each card on half of an index card and laminate them for durability.

▶ The game cards are placed face down on the rectangle marked GAME CARDS.

▶ Players put their place markers on START.

▶ Each player rolls the number cube. The person who rolls the highest number goes first.

HOW TO PLAY

❶ Players take turns selecting the top card and deciding which measuring instrument would best answer the question.

❷ Players move their markers forward on the game mat to the nearest correct measuring instrument. If players move to an incorrect instrument, they must go back to the space where they started.

❸ If the card cards are used up, they are reshuffled and play continues.

❹ The first player to enter the FINISH area wins the game.

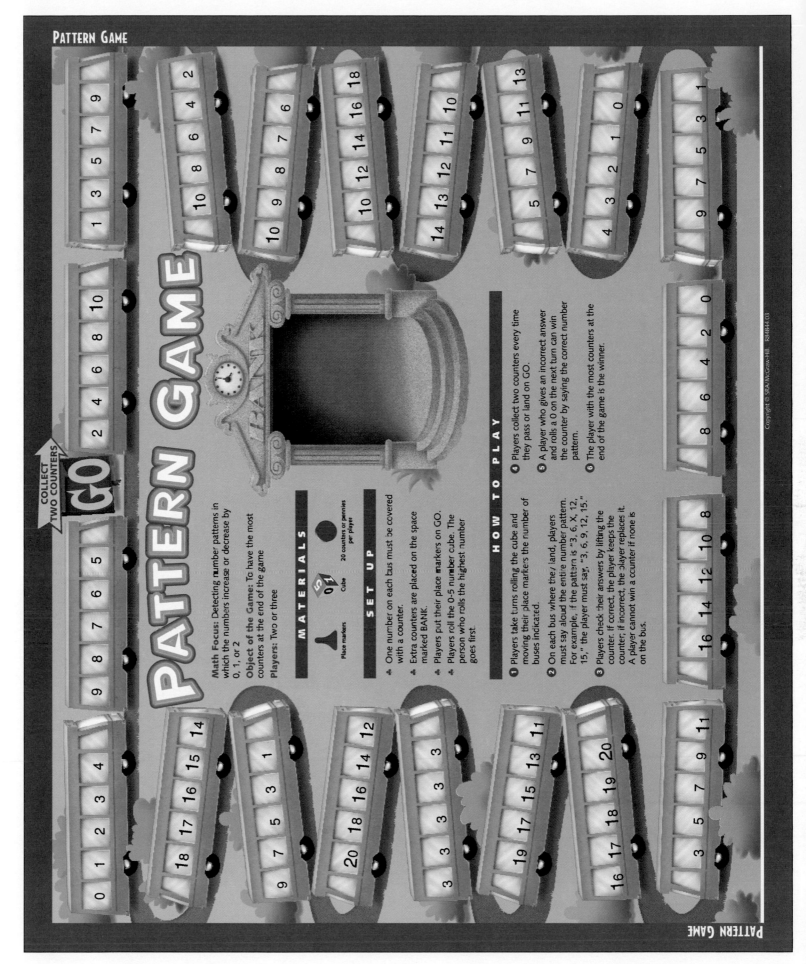

PATTERN GAME

Math Focus: Detecting number patterns in which the numbers increase or decrease by 0, 1, or 2.

Object of the Game: To have the most counters at the end of the game

Players: Two or three

MATERIALS

Place markers

Cube

20 counters or pennies per player

SET UP

- One number on each bus must be covered with a counter.
- Extra counters are placed on the space marked BANK.
- Players put their place markers on GO.
- Players roll the 0-5 number cube. The person who rolls the highest number goes first.

HOW TO PLAY

1. Players take turns rolling the cube and moving their place markers the number of buses indicated.
2. On each bus where they land, players must say aloud the entire number pattern. For example, if the pattern is "3, 6, X, 12, 15," the player must say, "3, 6, 9, 12, 15."
3. Players check their answers by lifting the counter. If correct, the player keeps the counter; if incorrect, the player replaces it. A player cannot win a counter if none is on the bus.
4. Players collect two counters every time they pass or land on GO.
5. A player who gives an incorrect answer and rolls a 0 on the next turn can win the counter by saying the correct number pattern.
6. The player with the most counters at the end of the game is the winner.

COLLECT TWO COUNTERS

GO

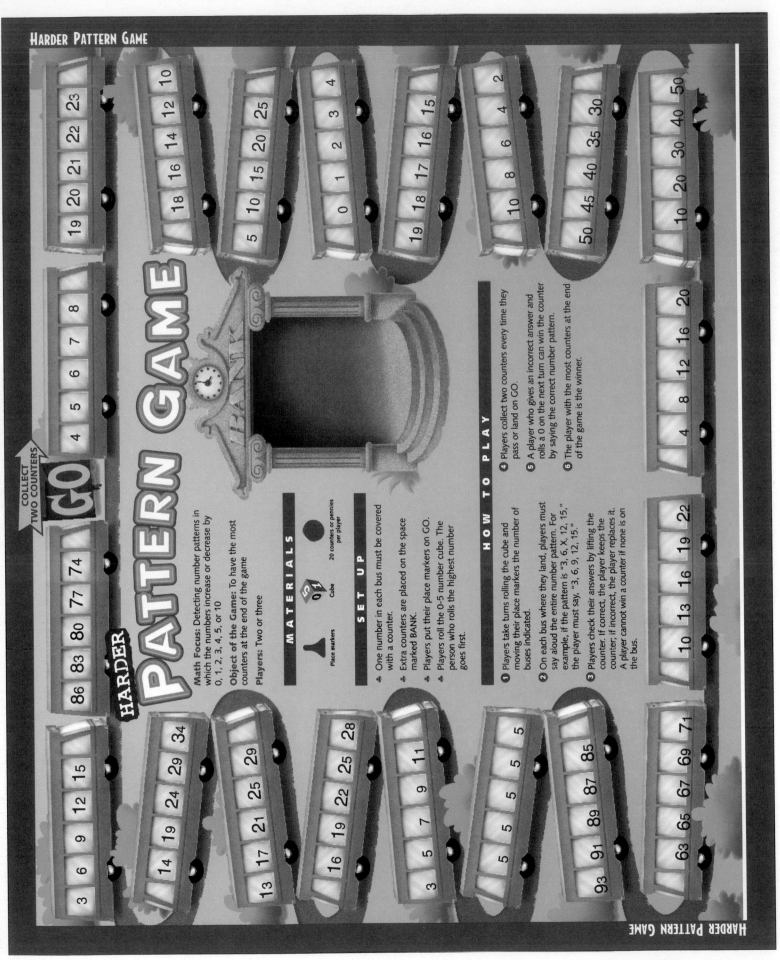

HARDER PATTERN GAME

Math Focus: Detecting number patterns in which the numbers increase or decrease by 0, 1, 2, 3, 4, 5, or 10

Object of the Game: To have the most counters at the end of the game

Players: Two or three

MATERIALS

Place markers

Cube

20 counters or pennies per player

SET UP

* One number in each bus must be covered with a counter.
* Extra counters are placed on the space marked BANK.
* Players put their place markers on GO.
* Players roll the 0–5 number cube. The person who rolls the highest number goes first.

HOW TO PLAY

1. Players take turns rolling the cube and moving their place markers the number of buses indicated.
2. On each bus where they land, players must say aloud the entire number pattern. For example, if the pattern is "3, 6, X, 12, 15," the player must say, "3, 6, 9, 12, 15."
3. Players check their answers by lifting the counter. If correct, the player keeps the counter; if incorrect, the player replaces it. A player cannot win a counter if none is on the bus.
4. Players collect two counters every time they pass or land on GO.
5. A player who gives an incorrect answer and rolls a 0 on the next turn can win the counter by saying the correct number pattern.
6. The player with the most counters at the end of the game is the winner.

COLLECT TWO COUNTERS

GO

20¢

90¢

30¢

50¢

30¢

60¢

10¢

10¢

Math Focus: Changing money (dimes for dollars)
Object of the Game: To be the first to collect three $1 bills
Players: Two or three

M A T E R I A L S

Per player:
three $1 bills
ten dimes

Place markers

Cube

S E T U P

♣ The money is sorted into piles next to the game mat.

♣ Players put their place markers on GO.

H O W   T O   P L A Y

① Players take turns rolling the cube and moving their place markers the number of spaces indicated.

② After landing on a space, the player says the price of the object pictured there. The player collects that amount from the money next to the game mat, counting tens aloud ("one ten, two tens . . .").

③ Players who roll a 0 cannot move and do not collect any money.

④ Players collect two dimes from the money next to the game mat each time they pass or land on GO.

⑤ Players must trade in dimes for dollar bills whenever they can, counting aloud as they do so.

⑥ The first player to have three $1 bills wins the game.

20¢

10¢

30¢

10¢

40¢

20¢

GO

Collect two dimes

20¢

30¢

80¢

60¢

30¢

408

25¢

99¢

48¢

21¢

34¢

55¢

12¢

10¢

20¢

35¢

11¢

13¢

43¢

20¢

Math Focus: Changing money (pennies, nickels, dimes, dollars)

Object of the Game: To be the first to collect three $1 bills

Players: Two or three

MATERIALS

Place markers

Cube

Per player:
three $1 bills
ten dimes

ten pennies
five nickels

SET UP

* The money is sorted into piles next to the game mat.
* Players put their place markers on GO.

* Each player rolls the 0–5 cube. The person who rolls the highest number goes first.

HOW TO PLAY

1 Players take turns rolling the cube and moving their place markers the number of spaces indicated.

2 After landing on a space, the player says the price of the object pictured there. The player collects that amount from the money next to the game mat, counting aloud ("two tens, three tens and five ones. . .").

3 Players who roll a 0 cannot move and do not collect any money.

4 Players collect two dimes from the money next to the game mat each time they pass or land on GO.

5 Players keep their money in separate piles, by denomination. Whenever possible, they must trade pennies for nickels, nickels for dimes, and dimes for dollars, counting aloud as they do so.

6 The first player to collect three $1 bills wins the game.

GO

Collect two dimes

20¢

25¢

18¢

65¢

21¢

HARDER SCHOOL BOOKSTORE GAME

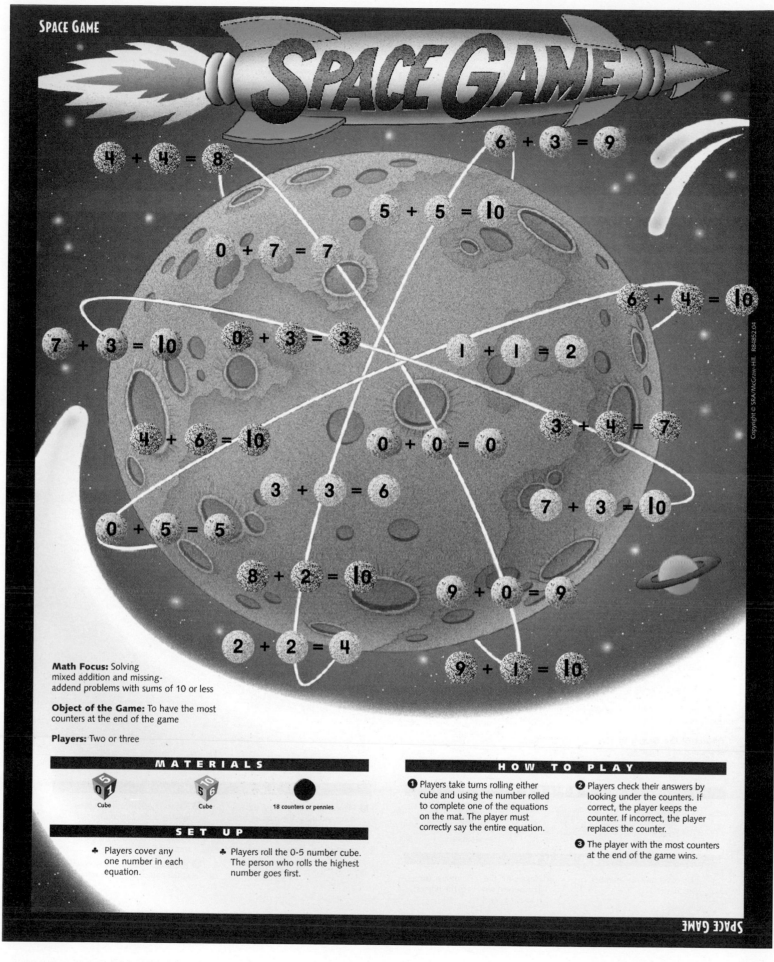

SPACE GAME

$4 + 4 = 8$

$6 + 3 = 9$

$5 + 5 = 10$

$0 + 7 = 7$

$6 + 4 = 10$

$7 + 3 = 10$

$0 + 3 = 3$

$1 + 1 = 2$

$3 + 4 = 7$

$4 + 6 = 10$

$0 + 0 = 0$

$3 + 3 = 6$

$7 + 3 = 10$

$0 + 5 = 5$

$8 + 2 = 10$

$9 + 0 = 9$

$2 + 2 = 4$

$9 + 1 = 10$

Math Focus: Solving mixed addition and missing-addend problems with sums of 10 or less

Object of the Game: To have the most counters at the end of the game

Players: Two or three

MATERIALS

Cube

Cube

18 counters or pennies

SET UP

♣ Players cover any one number in each equation.

♣ Players roll the 0-5 number cube. The person who rolls the highest number goes first.

HOW TO PLAY

❶ Players take turns rolling either cube and using the number rolled to complete one of the equations on the mat. The player must correctly say the entire equation.

❷ Players check their answers by looking under the counters. If correct, the player keeps the counter. If incorrect, the player replaces the counter.

❸ The player with the most counters at the end of the game wins.

410

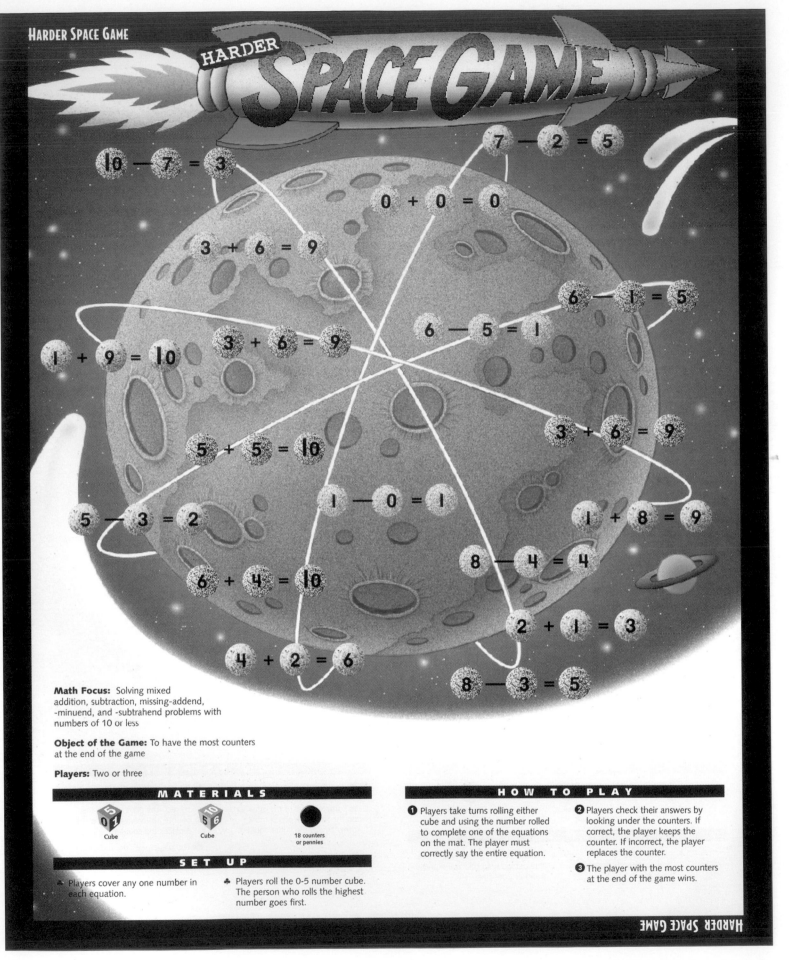

Math Focus: Solving mixed addition, subtraction, missing-addend, -minuend, and -subtrahend problems with numbers of 10 or less

Object of the Game: To have the most counters at the end of the game

Players: Two or three

MATERIALS

Cube

Cube

18 counters or pennies

SET UP

♣ Players cover any one number in each equation.

♣ Players roll the 0-5 number cube. The person who rolls the highest number goes first.

HOW TO PLAY

❶ Players take turns rolling either cube and using the number rolled to complete one of the equations on the mat. The player must correctly say the entire equation.

❷ Players check their answers by looking under the counters. If correct, the player keeps the counter. If incorrect, the player replaces the counter.

❸ The player with the most counters at the end of the game wins.

HARDER SPACE GAME

10 BELOW 0 Game

Math Focus: Familiarity with numbers above and below 0

Object of the Game: To have more counters at the end of the game

Players: Two

MATERIALS

Cube

Five counters or pennies

SET UP

♣ One counter is put at 0 on the game mat. The rest of the counters are placed on the space marked BANK.

♣ Each player rolls the number cube. The person who rolls the higher number goes first.

HOW TO PLAY

❶ The first player chooses to be either the Happy Weather Forecaster or the Gloomy Weather Forecaster.

❷ The Happy Weather Forecaster rolls the cube and moves the temperature counter *up* the number indicated. The Gloomy Weather Forecaster rolls the cube and moves the temperature *down* the number indicated.

❸ If the temperature reaches 10 above 0, the Happy Weather Forecaster wins the counter. If it reaches 10 below 0, the Gloomy Weather Forecaster wins the counter. A new counter is put on the 0, the players switch roles, and they play again.

❹ The player with more counters at the end of the game wins.

WIN A COUNTER!

HAPPY WEATHER FORECASTER

GLOOMY WEATHER FORECASTER

WIN A COUNTER!

START

10
9
8
7
6
5
4
3
2
1
0
1
2
3
4
5
6
7
8
9
10

BANK

412

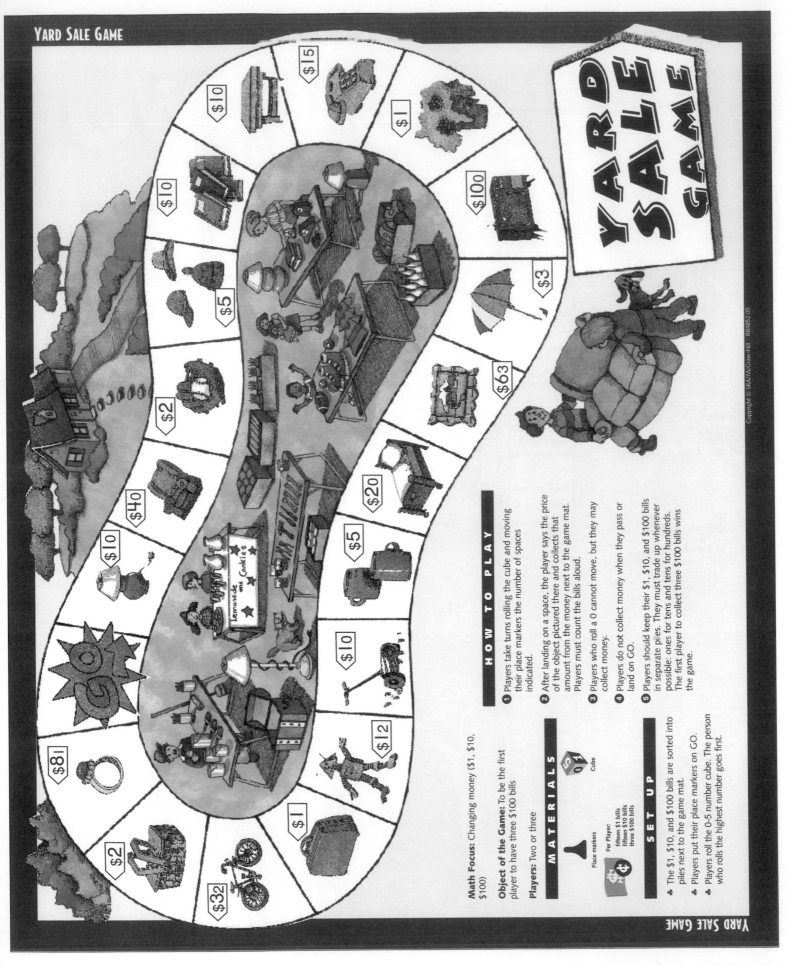

Math Focus: Changing money ($1, $10, $100)

Object of the Game: To be the first player to have three $100 bills

Players: Two or three

M A T E R I A L S

Place markers   Cube

Per Player:
fifteen $1 bills
fifteen $10 bills
three $100 bills

S E T   U P

+ The $1, $10, and $100 bills are sorted into piles next to the game mat.
+ Players put their place markers on GO.
+ Players roll the 0-5 number cube. The person who rolls the highest number goes first.

H O W   T O   P L A Y

1. Players take turns rolling the cube and moving their place markers the number of spaces indicated.

2. After landing on a space, the player says the price of the object pictured there and collects that amount from the money next to the game mat. Players must count the bills aloud.

3. Players who roll a 0 cannot move, but they may collect money.

4. Players do not collect money when they pass or land on GO.

5. Players should keep their $1, $10, and $100 bills in separate piles. They must trade up whenever possible: ones for tens and tens for hundreds. The first player to collect three $100 bills wins the game.

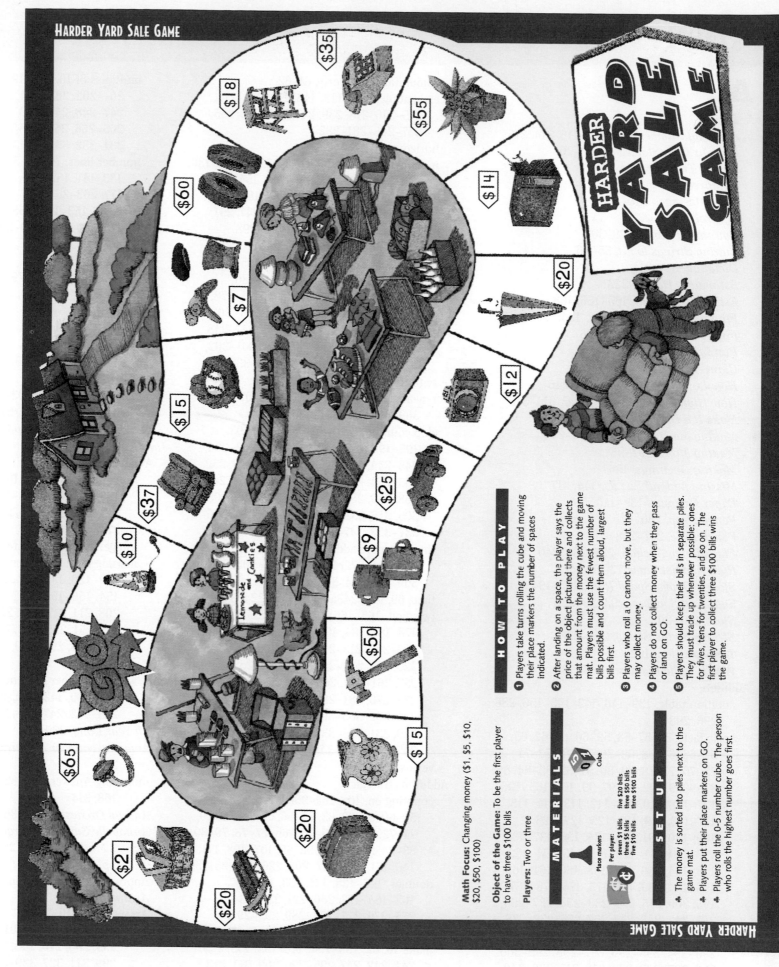

Math Focus: Changing money ($1, $5, $10, $20, $50, $100)

Object of the Game: To be the first player to have three $100 bills

Players: Two or three

MATERIALS

Place markers

Cube

Per player:
seven $1 bills
three $5 bills
five $10 bills
five $20 bills
three $50 bills
three $100 bills

HOW TO PLAY

1. Players take turns rolling the cube and moving their place markers the number of spaces indicated.

2. After landing on a space, the player says the price of the object pictured there and collects that amount from the money next to the game mat. Players must use the fewest number of bills possible and count them aloud, largest bills first.

3. Players who roll a 0 cannot move, but they may collect money.

4. Players do not collect money when they pass or land on GO.

5. Players should keep their bills in separate piles. They must trade up whenever possible: ones for fives, tens for twenties, and so on. The first player to collect three $100 bills wins the game.

SET UP

- The money is sorted into piles next to the game mat.

- Players put their place markers on GO.

- Players roll the 0–5 number cube. The person who rolls the highest number goes first.

INDEX

draw a picture or diagram, 21, 27, 39, 41, 55, 64, 71, 96, 101, 107, 117, 139, 165, 184a, 206, 231, 236, 239, 243, 248, 291, 295, 316

eliminate possibilities, 25, 57, 65, 91, 96a, 103, 127, 138, 281, 291, 318, 337

interpret data, 43–44, 73–74, 99, 112, 116a, 125, 132, 144a–144b, 147, 150, 152, 157, 164a, 168, 183, 192, 196a–196b, 210a, 228a, 245, 264, 274, 274d, 314

too much information, 10a–10b, 26b, 52a, 64a–64b, 76a, 96a–96d, 196a, 210b, 296a

use estimation, 59, 74, 144c, 148, 156, 246, 283, 296a, 314a, 323

use guess and check, 55, 75, 138, 145–146, 148, 150, 155, 156, 197, 201, 208, 221, 232, 246, 257, 261, 267, 271, 275, 284, 285, 297–298, 299, 309, 311, 323

use manipulatives, 37, 111, 121, 130a, 171, 183, 195, 197, 215, 226, 235, 263, 267, 293, 314a, 325, 331, 335, 347

use/find a pattern, 5, 7, 9, 15, 23, 63, 115, 131, 133, 165, 169, 184a, 189, 209, 210a, 225, 237, 243, 269, 287, 303, 313, 329

use/make a table, 96, 115–116, 132, 136, 178, 182, 183–184, 210, 213–214, 240, 252, 256, 264, 272, 276, 288, 306, 332, 341

Projects, *See also* Activities and Games.
Unit 1 Wrap-Up, Counting Charts, 92a–92b
Unit 2 Wrap-Up, Place Setting, 184a–184b
Unit 3 Wrap-Up, Paper Folding, 258a–258b
Unit 4 Wrap-Up, Greatest and Least, 348a–348b

The Purse, 237
Puzzles, 144, 257–258

R

Race Against Time Activity, 73–74
Ready, Set, Hop, 73
Real-World Connection, 5, 27, 43, 53, 63, 97–98, 108, 110, 112, 118, 125, 161, 164, 169–173, 189, 191–192, 195–197, 201–202, 207, 223, 225, 232, 237, 245, 248, 252, 254, 268, 270, 303, 313, 315–316, 321–323, 325, 327, 333, 335, 337, 342, 358, 364–365, 367, 380, 383
Rectangles, 5–6, 7–8, 28, 99–100, 101–102, 135, 165, 177
Regrouping, 301–302, 303–304
Renaming, 304, 341
Repeated addition, 78, 272, 284, 307–308, 309–310, 313–314, 336

Richard Scarry's Best Counting Book Ever, 241
Right in Your Own Backyard: Nature Math, 199
Roll a Double Game, 128, 234
Roll and Add Game, 142
Roll a Ten Game, 242

S

School Bookstore Game Mat, 248, 249, 267, 339, 408
Science Connection, 45, 69, 188, 193, 215, 231, 233, 241, 279, 293, 329
The Seasons of Arnold's Apple Tree, 326
Seconds, 194, 245–246, 323–324
The Seesaw, 189
Self Assessment, 38, 50, 58, 76, 128, 130, 138, 160, 194, 226, 278, 288, 290, 296, 310, 338
Shapes, *See* Geometry.
Shapes, 103, 311
Shapes in Nature, 329
Silly Dreamer Thinking Story, 129–130, 130a–130d, 132, 134, 138, 142
Skip counting, 141–142, 147, 155, 193, 195–196, 197–198, 201–202, 203–204, 243–244, 245–246, 247–248, 249, 252, 253–254, 256, 258, 263–264, 265–266, 268, 280, 282, 288, 294, 301–302, 303, 305, 315, 331–332, 333–334, 335–336, 337–338, 347–348
Six Sleepy Sheep, 137
Slow It Down, Speed It Up Activity, 193–194
Soak and Squeeze Activity, 293–294
Social Studies Connection, 153, 195, 203, 213, 234
Software, 32, 41, 105, 121, 133, 201, 285, 321, 325
   Dancing Dinos, 133
   The Graph Club of Fizz and Martina, 41
   James Discovers Math, 32
   JumpStart First Grade, 321
   Mathosaurus, 121
   Money Town, 105, 201
   Stickybear's Math Town, 285
   Treasure Galaxy!, 325
Solid figures, *See also* Geometry.
   cone, 103–104, 135
   corner, 269–270
   cube, 103–104, 135, 269–270
   cylinder, 103–104, 135
   edge, 269–270
   face, 269–270
   identifying, 103–104, 135, 269–270, 312
   net, 269

spatial visualization, 269
sphere, 103–104, 135
Space Game Mat, 270, 297, 339, 348, 410
Special Needs, 41, 97, 103, 139, 165, 201, 217, 235, 263, 291, 317
Sphere, 103–104, 135
Square, 3, 5–6, 9, 23, 32, 41, 90, 99–100, 101–102, 128, 157, 165, 168, 174, 177, 182, 216, 232, 258a–258b
Squeeze In, 107, 220
Statistics
   bar graphs, 42, 44, 45–46, 192
   charts/tables, 40, 43–44, 106, 150, 169–170, 188, 189, 191–192, 211, 274, 274a, 276, 288, 305, 316, 317–318, 324, 332, 341–342
   collecting data, 37–38, 39, 41–42, 43–44, 45–46, 106, 150, 169–170, 172, 189, 191–192, 211, 273–274, 274a, 316, 317–318
   picture graphs, 40, 41–42, 45, 48, 86
   real graphs, 39
   tallying, 37–38, 43–44, 45–46, 273–274, 274a, 305
Stickybear's Math Town, 285
Stolen Treasure Game, 283–284
Store Activity, 201–202
String Out the String Activity, 235–236
Subtraction,
   basic facts, 63–64, 65–66, 67–68, 69–70, 71–72, 73–74, 75–76, 77–78, 79–80, 81–82, 83–84, 86, 87, 90, 92, 95, 99, 101, 105–106, 109–110, 111, 113–114, 117–118, 121, 125, 127, 134, 145, 156, 162, 168, 169, 171, 176, 180, 183, 209–210, 222, 254
   estimating differences, 215–216, 218, 241, 255, 267–268, 281
   horizontal, 73–74
   missing term problems, 162, 184, 211, 276
   money, 76a, 106, 110, 113, 144, 164, 164a–164d, 173–174, 178, 284a–284d, 288, 296a, 304, 333
   renaming, 304, 341
   time, 144b, 224, 284a
   two-digit numbers, 165–166, 167–168, 173–174, 176, 178, 181, 184, 189, 191, 193, 195, 207–208, 209–210, 215–218, 219, 226, 227, 233, 239–240, 249–252, 253, 256, 261, 271–272, 275, 290, 303–304, 315, 329, 344–346
   vertical, 75–76
Subtraction strategies
   counting back, 62, 63–64, 65–66, 67–68, 69–70, 71–72, 73–74, 75–76, 77–78,

SCOPE & SEQUENCE

	K		Level 1				Level 2				Level 3				Level 4						Level 5						Level 6						Glencoe*		
Units	1	2	1	2	3	4	1	2	3	4	1	2	3	4	1	2	3	4	5	6	1	2	3	4	5	6	1	2	3	4	5	6	6	7	8

Addition (whole numbers)

	K1	K2	L1-1	L1-2	L1-3	L1-4	L2-1	L2-2	L2-3	L2-4	L3-1	L3-2	L3-3	L3-4	L4-1	L4-2	L4-3	L4-4	L4-5	L4-6	L5-1	L5-2	L5-3	L5-4	L5-5	L5-6	L6-1	L6-2	L6-3	L6-4	L6-5	L6-6	G6	G7	G8
Meaning of addition	•	•	•																																
Basic facts		✓	✓	✓	•	✓	✓	•	•	•	✓	•	•	•	✓	•	✓	•	•	•	•	•	•		•	•	•	•	•						
Missing addend problems	•	•	•	✓	•	•	•	•	•	•	•	•	•	•	•	•	•	•	•	•	•	•					•	•							
Three or more addends		•	•		•	•	•	✓	•	✓	•	•	•	•	•	•	•	•	•	•	•	•					•	•				•	•	•	
Two-digit numbers			•	✓	✓	•	✓	✓	•	✓	•	•	•	•	✓	•	•	•	•	•	✓	•					•	•				•	•	•	
Three-digit numbers					✓	•	•	•	•	✓	•	•	•	•	✓	•	•	•	•	•	✓	•					•	✓				•	•	•	
Greater numbers							•	✓	•	✓	•	•	•	•	✓	•	•	•	•	•	✓	•					•	✓				•	•	•	
Adding money	•	✓	•	✓	✓	•	•	•	•	✓	•	•	•	•	•	•	•	•	•	•	•	•					•	•				•	•	•	
Estimating sums			•	•	•		•	•	•	✓		•	✓	•	•	•	•	•	✓	•	•	•					•	•				•	•	•	

Algebra

	K1	K2	L1-1	L1-2	L1-3	L1-4	L2-1	L2-2	L2-3	L2-4	L3-1	L3-2	L3-3	L3-4	L4-1	L4-2	L4-3	L4-4	L4-5	L4-6	L5-1	L5-2	L5-3	L5-4	L5-5	L5-6	L6-1	L6-2	L6-3	L6-4	L6-5	L6-6	G6	G7	G8
Properties of whole numbers			•	•		•	•	•			•		•		•						•	•		•		•					•	•	•	•	•
Integers (negative numbers)	•			•		•		•			•	•		•	•		•	•			•			•		•			•		•	•	•	•	•
Operations with integers											•				•	•					•			•		•			•		•	•	•	•	•
Missing term problems	•	•	•	✓	•	•	•	•	•	•	•	•	•	•	•	•	•	•	•	•	•	•		•		•	•	•			•	•	•	•	•
Make and solve number sentences and equations		•	•	•	•	•	•	•	•	•	•	•	•	•	•	•	•	•	•	•	•	•		•		•	•	•			•	•	•	•	•
Variables							•	•	•	•	•	•	•		•	•	•	•			•	•					•	•			•	•	•	•	•
Parentheses and order of operations							•	•	•		•	•		•	•	•	•		•	•	•	•		•			•	•			•	•	•	•	•
Inverse operations						•				✓		•	✓		•	•	•		•	•	•	•					•	•	•					•	•
Function machines/tables	•	•		•	•	•	•	•	•	•		•			•	•	•		•		✓	•					•	✓				•	•	•	•
Function rules	•	•		•	•	•		•			•		•		•	•	•		•	•	✓	•	•				•	✓				•	•	•	•
Inverse functions								•			•		•			✓			•		✓	•					•	•					•	•	•
Composite functions								•			•		•			✓			•		✓						•							•	•
Coordinate graphing																																			
One quadrant								•	•			•	•	•		•			✓		•						✓					•	•	•	•
Four quadrants																					✓	•	•				✓					•	•	•	•
Graphing linear functions																✓	•		•	•	✓						✓					•	•	•	•
Graphing nonlinear functions																											•								•
Using formulas											•		•			•	•		•	•	•						•	•	•			•	•	•	•
Square numbers											•				•	•	•		•		•			•		•					•	•	•	•	•
Square roots																																	•	•	•

Decimals and money

	K1	K2	L1-1	L1-2	L1-3	L1-4	L2-1	L2-2	L2-3	L2-4	L3-1	L3-2	L3-3	L3-4	L4-1	L4-2	L4-3	L4-4	L4-5	L4-6	L5-1	L5-2	L5-3	L5-4	L5-5	L5-6	L6-1	L6-2	L6-3	L6-4	L6-5	L6-6	G6	G7	G8
Place value											•		•	•	•	•	•	•	•		•	✓	•				•	•	•	•			•	•	•
Comparing and ordering											•	•	•	✓	•	•	•		•		•	✓	•	•	✓	•	•	•	•		•		•	•	•
Rounding													•	•	•	•	•	•	•		•	•					•	•	•		•		•	•	•
Relating decimals and fractions											•			•		•			✓		•	•					•	•				•	•	•	•
Relating decimals and percents																•							✓				•	•				•	•	•	•
Adding											✓	•	•	•	•	•	•	•	✓	✓	•	•	•		•	•	✓	•	•				•	•	•
Estimating sums													•	•	•	•	•	•	•	✓	•	•					•	•	•				•	•	•
Subtracting											✓	•	•	•	•	•	•	•	✓	•	•	•					✓	•	•				•	•	•
Estimating differences													•	•	•	•	•	✓	•		•	•					•	•	•				•	•	•
Multiplying by powers of 10																	✓	✓	•	•	•	•					•	•	•	•			•	•	•
Multiplying by a whole number											•		•		•	•	•	✓	•	•	•	✓	•		•	•	•	•	•				•	•	•
Multiplying by a decimal															•						•	✓	•	✓	•	•	•	•	•				•	•	•
Estimating products														•		•	•	✓	•	•	•	•	•			•	•	•	•				•	•	•
Dividing by powers of 10																✓	✓	•	•	•	•	•					•	•	•				•	•	•
Dividing by a whole number															•	•	•	•	✓	•	✓	✓	•		•	•	•	✓	•				•	•	•
Dividing by a decimal															•						•				•	•	✓	•	•				•	•	•
Estimating quotients															•	•		•		•	•				•	•	•	•	•				•	•	•
Identifying and counting currency	•	✓	•	•	✓	✓	•		•	•	•	✓		•	•		•	•			•						•	•	•						
Exchanging money	•	•		•	✓	✓	•	•	•	✓	•	•	•	✓	•	•	•	•			•			•			•	•	•						
Making change				•	•	•	✓	•	•	•	•	•	•	•	•	•	•	•			✓	•					•		•						
Computing with money			•	✓	✓	✓	•	•	•	•	•	•	•	•	•	•	•	•	•	•	•	•					•	•	•			•	•	•	•

Division (whole numbers)

	K1	K2	L1-1	L1-2	L1-3	L1-4	L2-1	L2-2	L2-3	L2-4	L3-1	L3-2	L3-3	L3-4	L4-1	L4-2	L4-3	L4-4	L4-5	L4-6	L5-1	L5-2	L5-3	L5-4	L5-5	L5-6	L6-1	L6-2	L6-3	L6-4	L6-5	L6-6	G6	G7	G8
Meaning of division	•	•		•	•		•	•	•												•						•	•	•						
Basic facts								•	•	✓	•	•	•	✓	✓	•	•	•	•		•	•	•		•	•									
Remainders								•	•				•	✓	✓	•	✓	•	✓	✓	✓				•	•	•								
Missing term problems								•	•				•	•	•	•	•	•	•	•	•	•					•	•							
One-digit divisors								•	•				•	•	•	•	•	✓	•	✓	•	•		✓	•	•	•					•	•	•	•
Two-digit divisors															•	•	•	•	•		✓	•			•	•	•					•	•	•	•
Greater divisors															•	•	•	•	•			•			•	•	•					•	•	•	•
Dividing by multiples of 10													•	•	•	•	•	•	•		•	•			•	•	•					•	•	•	•
Dividing money													•	•	•	•	•	•	•		✓	•			•	•	•							•	
Estimating quotients															•	•	•	•	•	•		✓	•	•	✓	•	•					•	•	•	•

Fractions

	K1	K2	L1-1	L1-2	L1-3	L1-4	L2-1	L2-2	L2-3	L2-4	L3-1	L3-2	L3-3	L3-4	L4-1	L4-2	L4-3	L4-4	L4-5	L4-6	L5-1	L5-2	L5-3	L5-4	L5-5	L5-6	L6-1	L6-2	L6-3	L6-4	L6-5	L6-6	G6	G7	G8
Fractions of a whole	•	✓		•	•			✓	•		•	✓	•	•		•	•		•	✓							•				•	•			
Fractions of a set					•				•		•	✓	•	•					✓		•	✓					•								
Fractions of a number				•	•	•		•			•		•			•	•	•			•						•	•	•						
Comparing/ordering					•			•			•		•					•	•		•						•	•							
Equivalent fractions					•			•			•								•		•						•	•	•		•	•	•	•	•
Reduced form																					•			•			•	•	•		•	•	•	•	•
Mixed numbers and improper fractions											•	•	•						•							✓	•	•	•		•	•	•	•	•
Adding—like denominators																•					✓			•	✓	•	•	•	•		•	•	•	•	•

✓ indicates Mastery Checkpoints   • *Mathematics: Applications and Connections Courses 1–3, Levels 6–8* © 1999

Scope & Sequence (Page 424)

Column headers (Units):

Section / Skill	K‑1	K‑2	L1‑1	L1‑2	L1‑3	L1‑4	L2‑1	L2‑2	L2‑3	L2‑4	L3‑1	L3‑2	L3‑3	L3‑4	L4‑1	L4‑2	L4‑3	L4‑4	L4‑5	L4‑6	L5‑1	L5‑2	L5‑3	L5‑4	L5‑5	L5‑6	L6‑1	L6‑2	L6‑3	L6‑4	L6‑5	L6‑6	G‑6	G‑7	G‑8

Fractions (continued)

Skill	K‑1	K‑2	L1‑1	L1‑2	L1‑3	L1‑4	L2‑1	L2‑2	L2‑3	L2‑4	L3‑1	L3‑2	L3‑3	L3‑4	L4‑1	L4‑2	L4‑3	L4‑4	L4‑5	L4‑6	L5‑1	L5‑2	L5‑3	L5‑4	L5‑5	L5‑6	L6‑1	L6‑2	L6‑3	L6‑4	L6‑5	L6‑6	G‑6	G‑7	G‑8
Adding–unlike denominators														•							✓	•	•				✓	•	•	•	•	•			
Adding mixed numbers																✓					✓	•	•				✓	•	•	•	•	•			
Subtracting–like denominators																•					✓	•	•				✓	•		•	•	•			
Subtracting–unlike denominators																✓					✓	•	•				✓	•	•	•	•	•			
Subtracting mixed numbers																•					✓	•	•				✓	•	•	•	•	•			
Multiplying by a whole number																						•	•					•	•	•	•	•			
Multiplying by a fraction or mixed number														•							•	✓					•	•	•	•	•	•			
Reciprocals																					•	✓					✓	•	•	•	•	•			
Dividing a fraction by a whole number																												•	•	•	•	•			
Dividing by a fraction or mixed number																											✓	•	•	•	•	•			

Geometry

Skill	K‑1	K‑2	L1‑1	L1‑2	L1‑3	L1‑4	L2‑1	L2‑2	L2‑3	L2‑4	L3‑1	L3‑2	L3‑3	L3‑4	L4‑1	L4‑2	L4‑3	L4‑4	L4‑5	L4‑6	L5‑1	L5‑2	L5‑3	L5‑4	L5‑5	L5‑6	L6‑1	L6‑2	L6‑3	L6‑4	L6‑5	L6‑6	G‑6	G‑7	G‑8
Identifying/drawing figures	•	•	•	•	•	•	•	•	•	•	•	•	•	•	•	•	•	•	•	•	•	•	•		•					•	•	•	•	•	•
Classifying figures	•	•	•	•	•	•		•					•			•	•		•			•								•	•	•	•	•	•
Classifying triangles												•					•	•					•							•	•	•	•	•	•
Classifying quadrilaterals				•				•					•			•	•	•												•	•	•	•	•	•
Solid figures		•		•		•		•				•				•	•		•		•				•		•	•		•	•	•	•	•	•
Spatial visualization																•	•		•	•	•	•		•	•					•	•	•	•	•	•
Congruence	•	•			•	•	•	✓				•				•						•					•	•	•	•	•	•	•	•	•
Similarity												•				•						•	•							•	•	•	•	•	•
Symmetry	•	•		•	•	•		•				•				•						•				•		•	•	•	•	•	•	•	•
Translation/reflection/rotation											•					•	•					•					•	•	•	•	•	•	•	•	•
Measuring and classifying angles												•				•	•	•			•		•							•	•	•	•	•	•
Parallel and perpendicular lines												•				•	•	•				•								✓	•	•	•	•	•
Relationships with parallel lines																														✓	•	•	•	•	•
Perimeter		•			•		•		•			•			•	•	•	•	•		•		•		•					•	•	•	•	•	•
Radius and diameter															•	•		•	•											•	•	•	•	•	•
Circumference																•	•			•		•								•	•	•	•	•	•
Areas of triangles																														•	•	•	•	•	•
Areas of quadrilaterals											•		•		•		•		•	•	•	•	•	•	•	•	•	•		•	•	•	•	•	•
Surface area																														•	•	•	•	•	•
Volume															•		•			•										•	•	•	•	•	•
Pythagorean Theorem																														•	•	•	•	•	•

Manipulatives

Skill	K‑1	K‑2	L1‑1	L1‑2	L1‑3	L1‑4	L2‑1	L2‑2	L2‑3	L2‑4	L3‑1	L3‑2	L3‑3	L3‑4	L4‑1	L4‑2	L4‑3	L4‑4	L4‑5	L4‑6	L5‑1	L5‑2	L5‑3	L5‑4	L5‑5	L5‑6	L6‑1	L6‑2	L6‑3	L6‑4	L6‑5	L6‑6	G‑6	G‑7	G‑8
Used in concept development	•	•	•	•	•	•	•	•	•	•	•	•	•	•	•	•	•	•	•	•	•	•	•	•	•	•	•	•	•	•	•	•	•	•	•
Used in reteaching and individualized instruction	•	•	•	•	•	•	•	•	•	•	•	•	•	•	•	•	•	•	•	•	•	•	•	•	•	•	•	•	•	•	•	•	•	•	•

Measurement

Length

Skill	K‑1	K‑2	L1‑1	L1‑2	L1‑3	L1‑4	L2‑1	L2‑2	L2‑3	L2‑4	L3‑1	L3‑2	L3‑3	L3‑4	L4‑1	L4‑2	L4‑3	L4‑4	L4‑5	L4‑6	L5‑1	L5‑2	L5‑3	L5‑4	L5‑5	L5‑6	L6‑1	L6‑2	L6‑3	L6‑4	L6‑5	L6‑6	G‑6	G‑7	G‑8
Estimate	✓		•	•	•	•	•				•	•	✓	•	•	•	•	•	•	•	✓	•	•	•	•	✓	•		•	•	•	•	•	•	•
Compare	✓		•	•	•	•	•	•			•	•	✓	•	•	•	•	•	•	•	•	•	•	•	•		•	•		•		•	•	•	•
Use nonstandard units	✓		•	•	•	•		•			•	•	•			•	•		•		•	•					•					•	•	•	•
Use customary units			•	•	•	•	✓	•	•		•	•	•				•	•		•	•	•	•								•		•	•	•
Use metric units			•	•	•	•	✓	•	•		•	•	✓	•	•	•	•	•	•	✓	•	•	•	✓	•	•	•	•		•		•	•	•	•

Mass/Weight

Skill	K‑1	K‑2	L1‑1	L1‑2	L1‑3	L1‑4	L2‑1	L2‑2	L2‑3	L2‑4	L3‑1	L3‑2	L3‑3	L3‑4	L4‑1	L4‑2	L4‑3	L4‑4	L4‑5	L4‑6	L5‑1	L5‑2	L5‑3	L5‑4	L5‑5	L5‑6	L6‑1	L6‑2	L6‑3	L6‑4	L6‑5	L6‑6	G‑6	G‑7	G‑8
Estimate	✓	•	•		•	•	•						•	•	•		•	•			•	•		•	•	•		•					•		
Compare	✓	•	•		•	•		•				✓	•		•	•	•	•			•	•		•						•					
Use nonstandard units	✓	•		•	•						•																								
Use customary units			•	•					•	•		•		✓	•	•	•												•	•			•	•	•
Use metric units			•	•	•	•		•			•	✓		•	•	•	•				•		•						•	•			•	•	•

Capacity

Skill	K‑1	K‑2	L1‑1	L1‑2	L1‑3	L1‑4	L2‑1	L2‑2	L2‑3	L2‑4	L3‑1	L3‑2	L3‑3	L3‑4	L4‑1	L4‑2	L4‑3	L4‑4	L4‑5	L4‑6	L5‑1	L5‑2	L5‑3	L5‑4	L5‑5	L5‑6	L6‑1	L6‑2	L6‑3	L6‑4	L6‑5	L6‑6	G‑6	G‑7	G‑8
Estimate	•	•		•	•	•		•				•		•		•			•		•	•	•		•										
Compare				•	•	•		•				•		•			•				•														
Use nonstandard units			•	•	•									•																					
Use customary units			•	•				•		•		•		•	•	•	•	•	•		•							•	•				•	•	•
Use metric units				•				•				•		•	•	•	•	•	•		•		•					•	•				•	•	•

Temperature

Skill	K‑1	K‑2	L1‑1	L1‑2	L1‑3	L1‑4	L2‑1	L2‑2	L2‑3	L2‑4	L3‑1	L3‑2	L3‑3	L3‑4	L4‑1	L4‑2	L4‑3	L4‑4	L4‑5	L4‑6	L5‑1	L5‑2	L5‑3	L5‑4	L5‑5	L5‑6	L6‑1	L6‑2	L6‑3	L6‑4	L6‑5	L6‑6	G‑6	G‑7	G‑8
Estimate	•		•		•																										•	•			
Use degrees Fahrenheit					•			•			•		•			•		•			•	•						•	•	•		•			
Use degrees Celsius																•	•				•	•		•				•	•	•		•			
Converting within customary system							•	•	•	•		•		•		•	•	•		•		•						•	•			•	•	•
Converting within metric system							•	•	•			•		•	•	•	•	•		•		•						•	•			•	•	•

Telling time

Skill	K‑1	K‑2	L1‑1	L1‑2	L1‑3	L1‑4	L2‑1	L2‑2	L2‑3	L2‑4	L3‑1	L3‑2	L3‑3	L3‑4	L4‑1	L4‑2	L4‑3	L4‑4	L4‑5	L4‑6	L5‑1	L5‑2	L5‑3	L5‑4	L5‑5	L5‑6	L6‑1	L6‑2	L6‑3	L6‑4	L6‑5	L6‑6	G‑6	G‑7	G‑8
To the hour		✓			•			•	✓	•	•				•	•		•																	
To the half hour		•			•			•	✓	•	•				•	•																			
To the quarter hour		•			•			•	✓	•	•				•	•																			
To the minute								✓	•	✓					•	•		•																	
Adding and subtracting time			•	•	•	•	•	•	•	•	•	•	•	•	•	•	•	•			•	•		•								•			
A.M. and P.M.												•	•		•	•	•	•	•	•	•	•													
Estimating time	•	•	•	•		•	•		•			•																							
Calculating elapsed time			•	•	•	•	•	•			•	•			•	•	•	•	•	•	•			•	•	•	•			•	•	•	•		
Reading a calendar	•	•			•	•	•	•	•	•	•	•	•	•	•	•	•	•																	
Reading a map		•		•			•	•	•	•	•	•	•	•	•	•	•	•			•	•	•				•			•		•	•	•	•

Scope & Sequence

	K		Level 1				Level 2				Level 3				Level 4						Level 5						Level 6						Glencoe*		
Units	1	2	1	2	3	4	1	2	3	4	1	2	3	4	1	2	3	4	5	6	1	2	3	4	5	6	1	2	3	4	5	6	6	7	8

Mental Arithmetic

Basic fact strategies—addition and subtraction

	K1	K2	L1-1	L1-2	L1-3	L1-4	L2-1	L2-2	L2-3	L2-4	L3-1	L3-2	L3-3	L3-4	L4-1	L4-2	L4-3	L4-4	L4-5	L4-6	L5-1	L5-2	L5-3	L5-4	L5-5	L5-6	L6-1	L6-2	L6-3	L6-4	L6-5	L6-6	G6	G7	G8
Use patterns		•	•	•	•	✓	•																										•	•	•
Count on	•	•	✓	✓	✓	✓	•																												
Count up or back		•	✓	✓	✓	✓	•																												
Use doubles				✓	•	✓	•		•	•																									
Use doubles plus 1				✓	•	✓	•			•																									
Make 10	•		•	•	•	•	•		•																										
Use properties			•	•		•	•																												
Use related facts			•	•		•	•						•																						

Basic fact strategies—multiplication and division

	K1	K2	L1-1	L1-2	L1-3	L1-4	L2-1	L2-2	L2-3	L2-4	L3-1	L3-2	L3-3	L3-4	L4-1	L4-2	L4-3	L4-4	L4-5	L4-6	L5-1	L5-2	L5-3	L5-4	L5-5	L5-6	L6-1	L6-2	L6-3	L6-4	L6-5	L6-6	G6	G7	G8
Use patterns								•			•	•			•																		•	•	•
Use skip-counting			•	•	•			•			•	•			•	•																			
Use properties											•																								
Use related facts											✓				•	•			•		•														
Chain calculations			•	•	•	•	•	•	•	•	•	•	•	•	•	•	•	•		•	•	•	•		•		•	•		•	•		•	•	•
Multidigit addition and subtraction							•	•	•	•	•	•	•	•	•	•	•	•	•	•	•	•	•	•	•	•	•	•	•	•	•	•	•	•	•
Multidigit multiplication and division											•	•	•	•	•	•	•	•	•	•	•	•	•	•	•	•	•	•	•	•	•	•	•	•	•
Multiples and powers of 10					•	✓			•			✓	•		•		•				•	•					•		•				•	•	•
Using computational patterns			•	•	•	✓	•		•	•	•	•	•	•	•	•	•	•	•	•	•	•		•	•		•	•	•	•			•	•	•
Approximation			•	•	•	•			•	✓	•	•	•	✓	•	•	•	•										•					•	•	•
Find a fraction of a number				•	•	•		•				•		•							•						•						•	•	•
Find a percent of a number																					•			•	•	•		•					•	•	•
Use divisibility rules																							•				•						•	•	•
Find equivalent fractions, decimals, and percents											•	•						•				•	•	•			•						•	•	•

Multiplication (whole numbers)

	K1	K2	L1-1	L1-2	L1-3	L1-4	L2-1	L2-2	L2-3	L2-4	L3-1	L3-2	L3-3	L3-4	L4-1	L4-2	L4-3	L4-4	L4-5	L4-6	L5-1	L5-2	L5-3	L5-4	L5-5	L5-6	L6-1	L6-2	L6-3	L6-4	L6-5	L6-6	G6	G7	G8
Meaning of multiplication		•		•	•	•		•			•				•				•																
Basic facts					•					✓		✓	•	•	•	✓	•	•	•	•	•	•	•		•	•		•	•	•					
Missing factor problems								•			•	•			•	•	•				•														
One-digit multipliers								•				✓			•	•	✓	•	•	✓	•	•		•	•	✓	•	•		•			•	•	•
Two-digit multipliers															•	•	•	✓	•	•	•	✓	•	•	•	✓	•	•		•			•	•	•
Greater multipliers															•	•	•	✓	•	•	•	✓	•	•	•	✓	•	•		•			•	•	•
Multiplying by multiples of 10											✓	•	•	•	•	•	•	•	•	•	•	•	•	•		✓	•	•		•		•	•	•	•
Multiplying money								•			•					•			•	✓					•		•	•		•			•	•	•
Estimating products								•			•				•	•	•	•	•	✓				•	•	✓	•	•		•			•	•	•

Number and numeration

	K1	K2	L1-1	L1-2	L1-3	L1-4	L2-1	L2-2	L2-3	L2-4	L3-1	L3-2	L3-3	L3-4	L4-1	L4-2	L4-3	L4-4	L4-5	L4-6	L5-1	L5-2	L5-3	L5-4	L5-5	L5-6	L6-1	L6-2	L6-3	L6-4	L6-5	L6-6	G6	G7	G8
Reading and writing numbers	✓	•	✓	✓	•	✓	✓		✓	✓			•	✓			•	✓				•	✓				✓								
Number lines		•	✓	•	•	•	•	•			•	•		•			•			•		•				•	•								
Counting	✓	•	✓	•	•	✓	✓		•	✓			•	✓	•		•	✓	•				✓												
Skip counting		•		•	•	•	•		•			•	•	•			•	•																	
Ordinal numbers	•	•	•	•	•	•																													
Place value		•		•	•	•	•	•	•		•	•	•	•	•	•	•			•	✓		•			•		✓	•	•		•			
Roman numerals								•				•						•	•			•													
Comparing and ordering numbers	✓	•		•	•	✓	•	•		•	•	•	•	•	•	•			•	•	✓		•	•		✓	•		•	•		•		•	•
Rounding									•			•				•			•	•	•	•				•	•	•				•		•	•
Estimation/Approximation			•	•	•	•	•	•				•			•	•	✓	•	•	•	•	•	•	•		✓	•	•	•	•		✓	•	•	•
Integers (negative numbers)				•	•			•		•	•		•	•		•	•						•	•	•	•	•				•		•	•	•
Even/odd numbers				•	•		•		•	✓	•	•			•	•	•	•			•														
Prime and composite numbers																	•				•		•								•		•	•	•
Factors and prime factorization															•	•	•	•			•		•				•	•	•				•	•	•
Common factors																•					•						•	•	•	•			•	•	•
Common multiples																•						•	•	•			•	•	•				•	•	•
Checking divisibility																						•					•	•	•				•	•	•
Exponents												•					•							•				•					•	•	•
Exponential notation and scientific notation																		•				•						•					•	•	•
Square roots																																•	•	•	•

Patterns, Relations, and Functions

	K1	K2	L1-1	L1-2	L1-3	L1-4	L2-1	L2-2	L2-3	L2-4	L3-1	L3-2	L3-3	L3-4	L4-1	L4-2	L4-3	L4-4	L4-5	L4-6	L5-1	L5-2	L5-3	L5-4	L5-5	L5-6	L6-1	L6-2	L6-3	L6-4	L6-5	L6-6	G6	G7	G8
Classifying objects	✓	•	•	•																															
Number patterns	•	•	✓	•	•	•	•	•	•	•	•	•	•	•	•	•		•	•	•	•		•				•						•	•	•
Picture patterns	✓		•	•	•	•																													
Geometric patterns	✓	•	•	•	•			•	✓		•	•	•																				•	•	•
Ordered pairs															•	•	•	•		✓	•	•										✓	•	•	•
Graphing ordered pairs															•		•	•		✓	•	•										✓	•	•	•
Inequalities	✓	•		•	•	✓	•	•	✓	•	✓		•	•		•	•		✓	•	•		•	•			•						•	•	•
Function machines/tables	•	•		•	•	•	•		•		•			•	•	•	•	•			•	✓	•					•	✓				•	•	•
Function rules	•	•		•	•	•	•		•			•	•		•	•	•	•			•	✓	•					•	✓				•	•	•
Graphing functions																•				•		✓	•						✓				•	•	•

Probability

	K1	K2	L1-1	L1-2	L1-3	L1-4	L2-1	L2-2	L2-3	L2-4	L3-1	L3-2	L3-3	L3-4	L4-1	L4-2	L4-3	L4-4	L4-5	L4-6	L5-1	L5-2	L5-3	L5-4	L5-5	L5-6	L6-1	L6-2	L6-3	L6-4	L6-5	L6-6	G6	G7	G8
Determining possible outcomes		•				•			•			•			•	•					•			•		•		•		•		•		•	•
Predicting outcomes		•	•	•		•			•			•			•	•		•	•		•			•		•		•		•		•		•	•
Conducting experiments		•				•			•			•			•						•			•		•		•		•		•		•	•
Experimental probability																					•			•		•				•		•		•	•
Theoretical probability																					•			•		•				•		•		•	•
Using probability to plan strategies			•	•	•	•			•		•	•	•	•	•	•	•	•	•	•	•	•		•									•	•	•

✓ indicates Mastery Checkpoints • *Mathematics: Applications and Connections* Courses 1–3, Levels 6–8 © 1999

Scope & Sequence

Problem Solving

	K1	K2	L1·1	L1·2	L1·3	L1·4	L2·1	L2·2	L2·3	L2·4	L3·1	L3·2	L3·3	L3·4	L4·1	L4·2	L4·3	L4·4	L4·5	L4·6	L5·1	L5·2	L5·3	L5·4	L5·5	L5·6	L6·1	L6·2	L6·3	L6·4	L6·5	L6·6	G6	G7	G8
Work with various problem types	•	•	✓	•	•	•	•	•	•	•	•	✓	•	•	✓	•	•	•	•	•	•	•	•	•	•	•	•	•	•	•	•	•	•	•	•
• Multi-step problems																																			
• Multiple solutions																																			
• No solutions																																			
Use logical reasoning, including:	•	•	✓	•	•	•	•	✓	•	•	✓	✓	•	•	✓	✓	•	•	•	•	•	•	•	•	•	•	✓	•	•	•	•	•	•	•	•
• Interpreting data																																			
• Checking reasonableness																																			
• Solving problems with too much information																																			
• Interpreting the quotient and remainder																																			
• Choosing the appropriate operation																																			
• Using estimation																																			
• Using guess and check																																			
Choose an appropriate strategy, including:	•	•	✓	•	•	•	•	•	•	•	•	✓	•	•	✓	•	•	•	•	•	•	•	•	•	•	•	•	•	•	•	•	•	•	•	•
• Solving a simpler problem																																			
• Eliminating possibilities																																			
• Acting it out																																			
• Using/finding a pattern																																			
• Using/making a table																																			
• Using/drawing a picture or diagram																																			
• Using manipulatives																																			
• Conducting an experiment																																			

Ratio and Proportion

	K1	K2	L1·1	L1·2	L1·3	L1·4	L2·1	L2·2	L2·3	L2·4	L3·1	L3·2	L3·3	L3·4	L4·1	L4·2	L4·3	L4·4	L4·5	L4·6	L5·1	L5·2	L5·3	L5·4	L5·5	L5·6	L6·1	L6·2	L6·3	L6·4	L6·5	L6·6	G6	G7	G8
Meaning/use of ratio and proportion															•						•	✓	•	•			•	•					•	•	•
Rates															•	•	•	•	•	•	•	✓		•	•		✓	•	•	•			•	•	•
Similar figures															•								•					•					•	•	•
Map scales													•	•									•	•		•			•				•	•	•
Meaning of percent																								•				•					•	•	•
Percent of a number																	•						✓				✓	•	•	•			•	•	•
Percent discounts																							✓				✓		•				•		•
Sales tax															•			•	•				✓				✓		•				•		•
Simple/compound interest																	•						•					•	•				•	•	•

Statistics and graphing

	K1	K2	L1·1	L1·2	L1·3	L1·4	L2·1	L2·2	L2·3	L2·4	L3·1	L3·2	L3·3	L3·4	L4·1	L4·2	L4·3	L4·4	L4·5	L4·6	L5·1	L5·2	L5·3	L5·4	L5·5	L5·6	L6·1	L6·2	L6·3	L6·4	L6·5	L6·6	G6	G7	G8
Surveying	•	•	•			•		•			•		•		•			•					•	•				•					•	•	•
Tallying	•		•		•		•	•			•		•	•	•			•					•					•					•	•	•
Making tables with data	•	•	•	•	•	•	•	•			•	•	•	•	•	•	•	•	•	•	•	✓		•	•			•	•				•	•	•
Real and picture graphs	•	•	•			•		•			•				•	•												•	•				•	•	•
Bar graphs	•	•	•		•		•		•		•	•		•	•	•	•											•	•				•	•	•
Line graphs											•	•			•	•	•	•	•	•	•		•					•	•				•	•	•
Circle graphs											•										•						•	•		•	•	•	•	•	•
Finding the mean															•	•					•	✓	•	•				✓	•				•	•	•
Finding the median															•						•	•						•					•	•	•
Finding the mode															•						•	•						•					•	•	•

Subtraction (whole numbers)

	K1	K2	L1·1	L1·2	L1·3	L1·4	L2·1	L2·2	L2·3	L2·4	L3·1	L3·2	L3·3	L3·4	L4·1	L4·2	L4·3	L4·4	L4·5	L4·6	L5·1	L5·2	L5·3	L5·4	L5·5	L5·6	L6·1	L6·2	L6·3	L6·4	L6·5	L6·6	G6	G7	G8
Meaning of subtraction		•	•				•																												
...ic facts		•	✓	✓	•	•	✓	•	•	•	✓	•	•	•	✓	•	•	•		•	•	•	•		•	•	•	•	•	•					
...ng term problems				•	•	•	•	•			•				•		•				•	•	•		•	•	•	•		•					
...it numbers			✓	✓	✓	•	•	✓	•		•	✓	•	•	•	✓	•	•									•	•							
...git numbers							✓	✓	•	•	•	✓	•	•	•	✓	•	•	•		✓	•	•		•	✓	•	•	•	•					
...umbers							•	✓	•	•	•	✓	•	•	•					✓	•	•			•	✓	•	•	•						
...g money		•	✓		•	•	•	•	•	•	•	•	•	•	•	•	✓	•			✓	•	•												
...ifferences				•	•			•	✓		•	✓	•	•	•	•	✓	•			✓	•	•												

...logy

	K1	K2	L1·1	L1·2	L1·3	L1·4	L2·1	L2·2	L2·3	L2·4	L3·1	L3·2	L3·3	L3·4	L4·1	L4·2	L4·3	L4·4	L4·5	L4·6	L5·1	L5·2	L5·3	L5·4	L5·5	L5·6	L6·1	L6·2	L6·3	L6·4	L6·5	L6·6	G6	G7	G8
		•	•			•				•			•																						
...ng		•				•			•		•			•	•						✓														
...on with whole numbers		•	•	•		•	•		•	•	•	•		•	•	•					✓	•	•		•		•	•				•	•		•
...on with decimals											•				•						•	•	•	•	•	•	•	•		•		•	•	•	•
...on with fractions																					•	•		•	•			•				•	•	•	•
...with integers (negative numbers)											•				•	•					•	•		•				•				•	•	•	•
...rules			•				•				•				•	•		•	•		•								•	•		•	•	•	•
...ons											•				•	•			•			•											•	•	•	•
											•	•	•	•	•	•	•					•		•	•								•	•	•
															•						•	•	•	•	•	•	•	•				•	•	•	•
																•	•		•	•	•	•	•	•	•		•						•	•	•
											•	•			•	•	•	•	•	•	•	•					•	•	•	•			•	•	•
											•	•	•	•	•	•	•	•	•	•	•	•					•	•	•	•